László Kontler
A History of Hungary

László Kontler

A History of Hungary

Millennium in Central Europe

Published 2002 by
PALGRAVE MACMILLAN
Houndmills, Basingstoke, Hampshire RG21 6XS and
175 Fifth Avenue, New York, N.Y. 10010
Companies and representatives throughout the world

PALGRAVE MACMILLAN is the global academic imprint of the Palgrave Macmillan division of St. Martin's Press, LLC and of Palgrave Macmillan Ltd. Macmillan® is a registered trademark in the United States, United Kingdom and other countries. Palgrave is a registered trademark in the European Union and other countries.

Originally published in English under the title *Millennium in Central Europe: A History of Hungary* © Atlantisz Könyvkiadó, Budapest, 1999

ISBN 1–4039–0316–6 hardback
ISBN 1–4039–0317–4 paperback

This book is printed on paper suitable for recycling and made from fully managed and sustained forest sources.

A catalogue record for this book is available from the British Library.

Library of Congress Cataloging-in-Publication Data
Kontler, László.
  [Millennium in Central Europe]
  A history of Hungary: millennium, in Central Europe / László Kontler.
    p. cm.
  Published in 1999 in Budapest by Atlantisz under the title:
  Millennium in Central Europe.
  Includes bibliographical references (p.) and index.
  ISBN 0-40390-316-6 (cloth)
  1. Hungary–History. I. Title

DB25.1 .K57 2002
943.9–dc21   2002075298

10 9 8 7 6 5 4 3 2 1
11 10 09 08 07 06 05 04 03 02

Printed and bound in Great Britain by
Create Print & Design (Wales), Ebbw Vale

CONTENTS

PREFACE

This book was originally written at the request of Atlantisz Publishing House (Budapest) to answer the interest of non-Hungarian readers in Hungarian history. It is not primarily intended for a professional audience, but for the general educated reader of average knowledge in the humanities, though keen on maintaining high intellectual standards: present, past or future visitors to the country who wish to explore its peculiar identity in greater depth than found in guide-books, foreign students of diverse disciplines studying in Hungary, or undergraduates anywhere who follow a course in Hungarian or Central European history.

Most of this audience contemplates the history of Hungary in terms of convenient stereotypes. Even if the crudest associations of Hungarianness (csikós, gulyás, puszta, gypsy music etc.) are discounted, schematic simplifications – partly inspired from Hungary itself – dominate the Western European and North American picture drawn of Hungary's place in the world. In Central and Eastern Europe, Hungary's one-time status as a medium range power, her subsequent reduction in size as well as international importance, and the resulting impulses have evoked equally simplistic and emotionally coloured assessments of her role in the region's history. The models of 'a nation making ceaseless (and perhaps laudable) efforts at emerging from (half-) barbarity to the fold of Europe', or 'a small nation struggling and surviving against the odds', or 'a nation of oppressors turned troublemakers' and their likes offer stereotypes which the book intends to dispel or – since some of them, as most distortions, contain a grain of reality – fill with sound content.

In order to succeed, I have attempted to combine narrative and analysis, in the conviction that while telling a story (and telling it well) is indispensable to have an appeal to any readership, the audience described above is best served if it is provided with an occasion to examine that story against the background of the growth of historical 'structures' (social hierarchy, solidarity groups, religious and political ideas, material and spiritual culture, legal and political relations and institutions, systems of production and habits of consumption etc.) in a comparative framework. I have proceeded from the (supposedly better) known to the unknown, and recalled, whenever relevant, some aspects of the development of the Occident from Charlemagne to the European Union. At the same time, for the most part I endeavoured to avoid the quite general practice of chopping such comprehensive histories into chapters or sections on politics, economic development, culture etc., and tried to integrate these topics or to switch from one to the other within the same breath at the points which seemed suitable. I hope that what emerges is not an incomprehensible chaos, but an idea of the wholeness of a national history despite the ruptures and discontinuities that have marked it. For the sake of those who look for specific subjects, rather than want to read a continuous story, I have included references to such subjects under the section headings in the contents, and attempted to compile a sufficiently detailed index.

This is the first book of this kind to have been written in Hungary since the changes of 1989. Most of its predecessors, whose distinction it can only hope to approach, are long out of print or were conceived with priorities different from it, or both. I started working on the manuscript in August 1998 and finished it (with the exception of the Epilogue and the Bibliography, which I updated and extended at the request of Palgrave Macmillan in the autumnn of 2001) in July 1999. However, the backbone of the structure of the book stems from the courses I had the privilege of teaching to North American and Western European students in Budapest and in the United States on Hungarian and Central European history between 1985 and 1995. I started that activity as a teaching assistant of the late Péter Hanák, and I am thoroughly indebted to him for the initiation into the art of presenting an 'outline' of the subject to persons without a background in it. I hope this book did justice to the inspiration I have drawn from him, as well as from Éva H. Balázs, who has been the most affectionate critic of my works throughout my education as a historian. I am grateful to her as well as to András Gerõ, József Laszlovszky, László Péter, János Poór and Benedek Varga for having read the manuscript, correcting errors or lapses, and suggesting useful revisions. Stefan Halikowski Smith took meticulous care to polish my English manuscript. For the remaining weaknesses, as a matter of fact, only the author himself is to blame.

I owe a somewhat different debt to Tamás Miklós, the director of Atlantisz Publishing House, for the prompt to write this book, and for never losing faith that it would be completed. I am now delighted that the Palgrave Macmillan edition will provide a chance for the book to reach a broader audience. If a proper distance to my subject material has been achieved at all, it is to a great extent owing to the multicultural environment at Central European University where I have worked over the past ten years. During the final stages of the work, I was an Andrew W. Mellon Fellow at the Institute for Advanced Studies in the Humanities at the University of Edinburgh. Although I was focusing on a different project, this book also greatly benefited from the tranquillity and collegial atmosphere I enjoyed there. As always, my greatest thanks are due to my family, for the patience and support rendered to an author not infrequently in doubt, even despair.

Budapest, November 2001

László Kontler

INTRODUCTION

REFLECTIONS ON SYMBOLIC GEOGRAPHY

As the title of this book indicates, one of its chief underlying assumptions is that a contemplation of Hungary's location on the real and symbolic map of the European continent is quite crucial for a proper understanding of its history. Before my history is written, this assumption needs to be first vindicated.

As far as 'real' geography is concerned, matters at first glance seem fairly straightforward. Every place must have a middle somewhere, and Hungary lies indeed at the geometrical centre of Europe, at roughly equal distance from the Ural Mountains and the Atlantic, from Scandinavia and the Aegean islands; separated from the great plains of the East by the ring of the Carpathian mountains, from the Mediterranean by the mountainous areas of the Balkan peninsula, and from the Occident by the Alps. The basin marked off by these mountain ranges – the Carpathian Basin – looks on the map like a self-contained unit, displaying transitional features from the point of view of natural history and geology as well. True, this unit is further divided into sub-regions: hilly Transdanubia (western Hungary) is separated by the Danube from the Great Plain of eastern Hungary, which is cut asunder by the River Tisza; the mountainous area of the north, the Transylvanian Basin and the area south of the rivers Drava and Maros (which had all belonged to Hungary up to the end of the First World War). Still, no wonder the Hungarian cultural geographer Jenő Cholnoky thought in the interwar period that if Central Europe truly exists at all, it could only be the territory of the historic Kingdom of Hungary.

But for geography to become meaningful for the historian, the relatively static image of the land and the waters must be seen as wrought upon by the dynamics of human agency. Without this element, the notion of Hungary as Central European would be as empty as the idea of the ancient Chinese – one could surely add many others – of their own homeland being the centre of the universe. The momentum of such dynamics might confirm or rearrange boundaries marked out by orographic characters, and create a 'symbolic' geography constituted by subjective or emotional as well as objective or structural factors, and shaped by scholarly inquiry as well as political considerations, both of those within and outside the different units of such symbolic maps.

Discussion over the controversial notion of Central Europe – referring to the lands between the Baltic and the Balkans, and between the German- and Russian-inhabited territories of the continent – in its present shape is a relatively recent product of symbolic geography, not the least because its atlases were drawn, and the places of countries, peoples and cultures determined in them largely by those from outside this area. As Larry Wolff has pointed out, it was in the period of the Enlightenment, when Europe's centres of finance and culture had shifted from Rome, Florence and Venice to London, Paris and Amsterdam, that the old conceptual division of the continent into a refined South and a barbaric North was revised, and Western Europe invented Eastern Europe as its complementary other half. In terms of this 'philosophic geography' – as it was described, appropriately enough in the language of the age, by the American traveller John Ledyard – the lands of the Orient were undifferentiated. Prague, just north-west of Vienna, Warsaw, Cracow, Pressburg/Bratislava/Pozsony and Buda were often considered to be as oriental as St Petersburg, Moscow or Odessa; Bohemia, Poland and Hungary to be as non-western as Siberia. This model became intellectually convincing and politically convenient enough to start a tradition which has proved, and might also continue to prove ineradicable: witness the case of Hitler's concept of *Ostraum* before and during the Second World War, or Stalin's Eastern Bloc after it.

But the Enlightenment was also the period when serious reflection on the social and the historical in the modern sense began, and its impact in the region from the late eighteenth century on involved a national awakening which, after and besides sentiments of national consciousness and modernising endeavours, also generated implicit assertions of a regional identity as distinct both from the West and the East. At that time, the political map of Europe exhibited a threefold division. In the West and the North, the powerful monarchies of England, Spain, France and Sweden had, in the early modern period, more or less successfully completed the work of territorial unification, creating the 'historical accident' of the large nation-state, even if regional or ethnic separatism has never ceased to exist, and survives into the present-day of continental integration. The part of the middle zone adjacent to the West belonged to multi-state nations: Italians and Germans, dispersed (in the case of the former) in dozens or (in the case of the latter) in hundreds of sovereign political units, whose unification became the agenda of the nineteenth century. Next to it lay an area of multi-national states, where foreign dynasties and composite elites ruled over a great number of more or less populous ethnic groups among conditions of socio-economic backwardness which increased as one proceeded east and south-east: the Habsburg, the Russian and the Ottoman Empires.

In ethnic terms, this area could be identified as the region of relatively small nations wedged between Germany and Russia. In their case as well, the era of national awakening put political emancipation, besides industrialisation and civil and bourgeois development, on the agenda. Greek independence, the Hungarian and Polish freedom fights, the reorganisation of the Habsburg Empire into the dual monarchy of Austria-Hungary, and the creation of nation states in the Balkans resulted from these endeavours. But there has also been an alternative language of emancipation. Recognising the patchwork-like intertwining of ethnic groups and the resulting impossibility (or unacceptably high human cost) of sound territorial sovereignty, public figures, theorists and socio-political analysts have argued that the predicament of the nations concerned, especially in the Habsburg Monarchy, doomed them, despite long-standing rivalry and animosity, to the development of mutual understanding and co-operation, even a confederate state. This has hardly ever proved more than utopianism, an imaginary or 'relative truth' that ought according to reason to prevail despite the odds; but for many, a pleasing and convincing one.

The Czech historian František Palacký, the Slovenian Matija Kaučić, the Polish émigré aristocrat Adam Czartoryski, the Hungarian politicians Lajos Kossuth and József Eötvös, the Romanian revolutionary Nicolae Bălçescu and his countryman Aurel Popoviçi (to mention but a few) were important nineteenth-century advocates of this idea, which continued to be influential even after the watershed of the 1919-20 Paris peace settlement and its reissue after 1945. Most of the projects of Central European brotherhood and federation were originally conceived in terms of political expediency or contemporary *raison d'état:* on the grounds that by themselves the small nations of the region did not constitute viable political units in the face of the neighbouring great powers. But the past practice of supra-ethnic entities had also discredited the idea of any sort of federation, which in the wake of the Great War sealing the fate of the former empires lost out to the principle of national self-determination. By the time the new sovereign units might have overcome the ferment inevitably accompanying the effort to establish their separate identities, powerful initiatives to reshape their collective identity in terms of political spheres of interests were addressed to them from the outside – this time already keenly employing the whole paraphernalia of socio-economic and historical as well as geopolitical reasoning. Friedrich Naumann's concept of a German-dominated Mitteleuropa, developed according to nineteenth-century Austrian precedents during the First World War, added – however unwittingly – intellectual fuel to the fire of Nazi expansionism into the region. Because of these associations the concept became anathema after 1945. What replaced it was the 'Eastern Europe' of Cold War vocabulary, which translated the Soviet domination of the Eastern Bloc into a view whereby the lands east of the Elbe and which expanded from the Baltic to the Balkans were not merely geographically contiguous, but also structurally homogeneous with the former possessions of Big Brother.

This projection of the post-war political status quo into the past was cautiously questioned from the 1960s, and more boldly from the 1970s onward, by writers and other intellectuals in the region. By the 1980s the discourse on Central Europe became quite standard; it now originated not from Berlin and Vienna, but from Prague, Warsaw and Budapest. Nor was it completely confined to the underground; especially in Hungary, it also surfaced in the semi-public sphere. The Czech writer Milan Kundera wrote of 'The Tragedy of Central Europe' – western in terms of culture, though eastern in terms of politics, and thus 'kidnapped' from the West. Similarly, the Hungarian György Konrád emphasised the 'historical misfortune' of the area having been prevented from 'exercising the Western option taken out a thousand years ago'. The Hungarian historian Jenő Szűcs wrote a still influential historical essay on 'The Three Historical Regions of Europe', in which he analysed the distinctive 'historical structures' of especially Poland, the Czech lands and Hungary in greater depth and detail, but along lines similar to those on which Kundera explored cultural traditions, sensibilities and forms of expression. Szűcs arrived at the conclusion that ever since these countries established themselves on the eastern periphery of the West, they have exhibited structural features which – due to the fact of a relatively late migration into the Occident and the resulting permanent imperative of catching up in order to survive – are more or less incomplete when judged by western standards, but qualitatively akin to their western and different from their eastern (and south-eastern) neighbours. The list of authorities could be continued endlessly, and there would be certainly no exaggeration in the claim that the discussion over Central Europe significantly contributed to the growth of an intellectual atmosphere in which the changes of 1989 in the region became feasible.

Out of political imperative, Central Europe thus emerged as an object of literary and academic pursuits which have had important political consequences. It is not by chance that Central Europe became such a salient topic in the discourse on symbolic geography. Due to historical circumstances, out of some borderland groups in the West, the Walloon and the Flemish became Belgians, while Alsatians and Savoyards became French, to this very day jealously preserving their peculiar identity, even in some form of regionalism, but to my knowledge they never arrived at developing the notion of a larger coalescent unit at the boundary of French and German Europe – 'Central Western Europe', for instance (as there have been precedents of an idea of 'Central Eastern Europe'). Whereas through most of their history, their homelands too have been objects of ambition and rivalry beween their powerful neighbours, their identity in terms of symbolic geography seems never to have been problematic. As a result, there has been no need to create one out of a perceived 'historical community of fate' forged by a peculiar love-hate relationship, frequently referred to in the texts of the prophets of 'Central Europe'.

By and large, I think the historian might endorse the notion of Central Europe in two ways which, for the sake of brevity, I should label 'minimal' and 'maximal'. Minimally, the notion is like a self-fulfilling prophecy: it is the expression, at the immediate eastern periphery of the West, of the *consciousness* – at some times merely the *potential*, at others the *aspiration* – to be 'Western' in terms of values and structures: social hierarchy, solidarity groups, religious and political ideas, material and spiritual culture, legal and political institutions and relations, habits and patterns of sociability and so on which was sporadic before the nineteenth century but has been more frequent since then. Depending on historical conjuncture, this has been couched in optimism or bitterness, irony or resentment. There is certainly a great deal of truth in the claim that there is an ultimate identification in terms of fundamental historical structures between the Occident proper and this central zone of the European continent. At the same time it is also quite true that in many aspects this is mere wishful thinking, and the sharp distinction between this region and the ones east and south-east of it is over-emphasised: an outcome of prejudice, suspicion and contempt. As such, it fits into the general habit of each European nation considering its eastern neighbour in some sense inferior or 'less European': 'Asia begins at the gates of Vienna', Chancellor Metternich is alleged to have said in the 1830s. Moreover, in many cases the advocates of Central Europe have had a political axe to grind, however subtle, erudite and scholarly their argument was.

However, I also wish to argue that this does not really matter. The notion of Central Europe and the view of the nations and lands usually associated with it as Central European remains useful if we regard it, instead of a statement of fact, a heuristic device, as part of the modern self-reflection of the peoples concerned. Even the historian needs to reckon with collective memory as a force that to some extent shapes the very history he or she is claiming to investigate professionally. It is meaningful to distinguish between cultures where the belated catching up or integration with Western European civilisation has been reflected upon, accepted and affirmed or urged, while at the same time the fact of belatedness was acknowledged by introducing the idea of 'Central Europe', and such cultures where the repudiation of the Occident has a powerful tradition. This latter tendency is visible in Russia, for instance, where nineteenth-century Slavophile thinkers passed a devastating criticism over the commitments of their 'Westerner' rivals (their main target being the individualism associated with England and, interestingly, Austria-Hungary), and philosophers of history from the same period left behind the legacy of Eurasianism, the still-influential idea whereby Russia represents a distinctly non-western civilisation.

This does not warrant the undoubted exclusionist overtones of, say, Kundera's use of the idea of Central Europe, which some commentators have described as absurd – quite rightly, if we remind ourselves that Russia means, among many other things, Dostoevsky (to be sure, one of Kundera's non-European *bêtes noires*), Kandinsky, Stravinsky and so forth. But again, the distinction between the 'historical regions' of Europe, precisely according to the terms suggested earlier in this paragraph, seems justified in the light of a recent international sociological survey on identity. Across Europe, 'continental consciousness' is shown to be the most emphatic in the countries of Central Europe; it is far more languid in the West, and next to nothing in Russia. Part of the dismay with which the partisans of the Central European idea have watched the nations of the region scrambling for adoption into the European organisations since 1989 instead of first coming to an understanding with each other and creating institutions for the assertion of their regional identity, has been caused by the fact that they fell into their own trap. Central Europe in their discourse has mostly been a euphemism used to emphasise their affinity with the West. Now, it is not only the case that on the agenda of the West, the countries termed 'Central European' by the participants of the debate enjoy priority status from the point of view of integration, but also that this is reflected on the lists of the priorities of those concerned. These lines are written a few days after Hungarian MPs cast their votes on the country's joining NATO, 330 for and 13 against. Though by far not as overwhelmingly as these figures show, according to opinion polls the idea and prospect of entering NATO and the European Union is more popular and seen as less problematic in Poland, the Czech Republic and Hungary than in the countries behind them on the waiting list.

It is also true that the 'Western option' emphasised by Konrád has rarely been without indigenous competitors and has rarely gone unchallenged from the inside since it was 'taken out a thousand years ago' by the peoples of the region – an additional characteristic of 'Central Europeanness'. The image of the simple and valiant Hungarian horseman, his eyes resting on the infinity of the steppe and defying the effeminating effect of western luxury, was indeed a staple of nineteenth-century Hungarian national characterology; it was rooted ancient ancient tradition and has disturbing repercussions in the most atavistic manifestations of nationalism to this day. But what matters here is that nearly from the very beginning of the recorded history of these nations, it has been possible to interpret it, without the danger of distortion or anachronism, in similar terms to that of their western neighbours, as the history of their eastern and even south-eastern neighbours has not.

This is the reasoning which supports the endorsement of the notion of 'Central Europe' which I labelled 'maximal' above: the reasoning that suggests that besides seeing Central Europe as a utopia or a sort of virtual reality, a Central Europe does exist in terms that could be analysed objectively. Latin Christianity, sovereignty divided between the crown and the privileged estates or orders, a legally established feudal hierarchy, chartered towns and a division of labour between them and their rural environment, the culture of chivalry, Renaissance humanism and the Reformation: these are undoubtedly ideal types, but they are on the whole quite workable; they are also some of the most important, typically 'western' phenomena whose growth was facilitated by the first, medieval expansion of the Occident within the boundaries of this region, but not beyond them. The abundant and extremely valuable admixture of features associated with Orthodox and Muslim civilisation to these has provided a peculiar flavour to the lands 'in between'. But the history of substratum and superstratum is markedly different in the countries of Central Europe from those of Eastern and South-Eastern Europe. Only capitalist entrepreneurialship, the Enlightenment, modern political ideologies – the motive forces of the next great period of expansion – were structures sufficiently virulent for the Occident to be able to 'swallow up' to some extent, in civilisational terms, Eastern and South-Eastern Europe. This stadial aspect of the penetration of western structures into the East introduces a crucially important temporal dimension into the 'Central Europe problem' which in this form has quite often escaped its students.

Even in Central Europe, this growth was rather belated, occasionally incomplete, and never irreversible. Belatedness and the resulting imperatives pushed Hungary as well as other countries of the region in several periods on a fixed course, with a rather limited scope of action. It was out of the tensions and contradictions thus caused that some of the most exciting, challenging and puzzling features of Hungarian history have arisen. The historian of Hungary, for most of the time, faces the multiple paradox that, out of the unalterable fact of belatedness, that is, of having, as a 'latecomer' found herself at the periphery of Europe's western half, Hungary was able to forge merits and advantages in strictly adverse circumstances, while sometimes her backwardness increased under relatively favourable auspices. Alternatively, the semblance of success, a mistaken assessment of the nation's true standing and the resulting conceitedness has frequently put her to tests that, especially in view of her delicate geo-historical situation, proved too hard to stand.

Belatedness has been, for geographical and historical reasons, a permanent, nearly natural endowment for Hungary, which has occasionally pushed her into lethargy and exasperation, but also quite often stimulated flexibility, adaptability and a peculiar ability to respond to challenges – not infrequently at the expense of considerable opportunism. As a result, two sets of attitudes have in some shape coexisted in the country, especially in modern times as reflection on national identity and its embeddedness in more comprehensive structures became a self-contained intellectual pursuit. First, there arose a spirit of defiant reclusiveness and introversion, a kind of true-to-stock Magyarness taking satisfaction in the robustness of national character which rather oddly compounded a pagan sentiment with the Christian spirituality of Hungary as the 'Kingdom of the Virgin Mary'; second, a Europeanness, which was more intensively reflected upon, and therefore perhaps even more refined and deeply – maybe somewhat desperately – felt than in the countries often referred to as the 'centre'. To be sure, even optimistic representations of the history of Hungary could, I think, hardly allege more than that the latter set of attitudes has more often than not achieved an ascendancy, though never a full triumph over the former.

Finally, another conspicuous feature of Hungarian history arose out of the phenomenon mentioned last. Ever since the first attempt to close the gap between Hungary and the West – permanent settlement and the founding of the state by King Saint Stephen – it did not lag behind in terms of learning and spiritual culture, to the extent it did in terms of its socio-economic conditions. Even at times of calamity, the country preserved her ability to cultivate relations with her immediate and more remote western neighbours as their intellectual contemporary. Besides the great heroes of state and nation building, Hungary has had a great number of minor heroes who ensured, in one way or another, the maintenance of this peculiar dialogue: figures like Nicholas of Hungary, one of the first recorded students of Oxford University; sixteenth-century Calvinist pastors educated in one of the western (maybe even Catholic) universities, tending their parishes in the territory under Ottoman rule while at the same time corresponding with leading lights of Humanist and Reformation culture; eighteenth-century petty noblemen reading Latin novels at the fireplace in their country houses in evenings and citing Montesquieu at county assemblies or national diets; and so forth. The persistence of this last feature of Hungarian history lends cautiously optimistic overtones to the attempt that follows – a history of Hungary proposed to be written with a mixture of historical scepticism, irony and empathy.

CHAPTER I

THE LAND, THE PEOPLES, THE MIGRATIONS

1. Before the Magyars: ancient cultures and nomadic invaders

The history of lands and the history of peoples that currently inhabit them is usually not the same history. This is markedly the case in the history of European countries, especially the ones in the transitory zone identified in the Introduction as Central Europe, where even the remotest ancestors of the present occupants can only be considered as relative latecomers among the nations of the continent. Still, just as the features of the natural landscape are integrated into the realm of historical memory, so is the heritage of those who reshaped that landscape by creating and destroying, by producing and consuming, by thinking and inventing, by trying and succeeding or failing, by loving and hating within the territory defined by it. I do not think it is absurd to illustrate this point with the following example. At the threshold of the twenty-first century, the citizen of the United States travelling in Colorado, feels a certain sense of satisfaction and identification looking at the dwellings of the twelfth-century Anasazi Indians, carved ingeniously into the cliffs of the plateaux of Mesa Verde National Park, and contemplating the achievement of that long extinct, fully alien race. For the same reason, it will be useful briefly to glance at the pre-Hungarian legacy in the history of Hungary.

The pedigree is respectable indeed. The first evidence of human settlement in the Carpathian Basin dates back to nearly half a million years ago, when a peculiar type of prehistoric man – a transitory species called *Homo erectus seu sapiens paleohungaricus* – lived, as finds near Vértesszöllős have shown, in the hills of Transdanubia. A long interval seems to have followed, but from the mid-Palaeolithic (c. 80,000 to 30,000 BC) there is a great wealth of material to demonstrate that in this period the Neanderthal type of man coexisted here with an anthropologically more advanced species for quite a long while. They seem to have migrated into the area both from the West and the East; scholars describe a phenomenon of 'parallel-evolution', anthropological and cultural types not stratified upon or developing from one another, but existing side by side.

Although most of the finds are from the mountains of north-eastern Hungary, the Danube-bend and Transdanubia, man in this period was not a mere cave-dweller, but also lived in settlements consisting of huts dug into the earth. Their inhabitants were hunters who used refined chipped flint implements and weapons, and the appearance of specialised hunting in this period – concentration on one or two species providing prey in large quantities, instead of the whole range of animals – also implied some break away from the physical environment. The migrant groups of hunters, usually rather small in number and isolated from each other, despite the varieties of the fauna from place to place, mainly searched for those large animals which, though fast and more difficult to hunt, gathered in numerous herds, most characteristically reindeer in our region.

Climatic changes, the end of the last ice age and the resulting stabilisation of the natural environment in the Carpathian Basin around 10,000 BC meant that the boundary within which this lifestyle was feasible moved northwards. Accordingly, Palaeolithic hunting communities seem to have almost altogether left the area, although the relative scarcity of finds from the subsequent transitory age the Mesolithic, might have been caused by the same environmental changes which make it very difficult for archaeologists to trace the vestiges of the period. Neolithic culture certainly made its appearance in the area rather abruptly, at a highly developed stage and with a great population. In all probability, this was due to immigration from the Balkan Peninsula – a pattern that would repeat itself in the subsequent Copper and Bronze Ages – around 5000 BC.

The period thus inaugurated was identified by the nineteenth-century pioneers of archaeology according to technological criteria, that is, the manufacturing of tools by grinding, instead of chipping flint, but the real change was that out of being a mere creature of prey, man became a producer. By domesticating animals, cultivating crops and storing their yield in pots manufactured by newly developed technology (ceramics), by protecting his body with spun and woven clothing, he made a huge step towards becoming a master, instead of a slave of nature; the sustaining capacity of the soil became multiplied, and the thin communities of migrating hunters were replaced by populous villages. This process, described as the 'Neolithic revolution' despite its actually staggering pace, was imported into Europe, a peripheral area at the time of the dawn of civilisation, from the Near East, where it took place in the ninth and eighth millennia BC. In fact, by the time its impact was in full swing in this continent, the first urban centres were already emerging in Mesopotamia and Egypt.

For the first time in history, the peculiar geographic location of the Carpathian Basin became a factor that ambiguously influenced its civilising potential. Its proximity to the eastern Mediterranean, through which 'the light from the East' (*ex oriente lux*) would penetrate the European continent, and its fertile plains where the new technology could be applied with benefit, were favourable auspices, and according to the testimony of archaeology at least some of its territory was, throughout the Neolithic and the succeeding Copper, Bronze and Iron Ages, indeed the farthest fringe area of the eastern Mediterranean agrarian cultures. The settlements of the newcomers were mainly concentrated in the valley of the River Körös (hence the name of the 'Körös culture') where they introduced the cultivation of wheat and barley and the breeding of sheep and goat, weaving and spinning, making pottery and building houses during the fifth millennium BC. In addition, they grew other types of cereals found in the area and domesticated cattle and pigs from indigenous species, and it was through the Danube Basin that, by 4000 BC, Neolithic culture spread to the more northerly and westerly parts of Europe.

The Great Plain is the westernmost geographic area where a peculiar feature of the contemporary near-East and Balkans, the *tell* (multi-layered settlement), made its appearance and is still part of the landscape. The relatively high level of development is reflected in the belief system and community life of the Neolithic population in the territory of what is Hungary today. The cult of the goddess of female fertility, 'Magna Mater', still prevalent in most of the adjacent areas, was here during the late-Neolithic (the middle of the fourth millennium BC) replaced by that of gods associated, like the primeval ancient Greek supreme deity Kronos, with the fertility of the soil; and whereas the inhabitants of most of Europe north and west of the Carpathian Basin lived in matrilineal great families, small, patriarchal families living in their separate dwelling and thus constituting to some extent self-contained economic units, already appeared during the same period in the greater part of our region. However, precisely because of the nature of the neighbourhood and the conflict-ridden relationship between the primitive agriculturists of the Carpathian Basin, who had ties with the Mediterranean, and the half-barbarian population that continually harassed them, progress was not unilinear: higher and lower stages of development existed side by side or followed one another.

Shortly after the beginning of the third millennium BC, socio-economic transformations in the area and the introduction of another seminal technological innovation combined to shape the history of the Carpathian Basin. A drier climate, and possibly the exhaustion of the land and internecine warfare, resulted in a growing preference for stock-breeding to land cultivation; and the power of the emerging shepherd aristocracies over their dependants was firmly based on the use of copper – too soft to turn to cutting forests or breaking the fallow, but an excellent material from which formidable weapons could be manufactured. Similarly to the ones that preceded and followed it, the new technology originated in the Near East, where metallurgy goes back at least to the fifth millennium BC, and even bronze was cast shortly after around 4000 BC; and the settlers from the South, who introduced it, were also remarkable for having used for transport a further revolutionary invention from the cradle of civilisation: the four-wheel cart. The first known representation of the cart in Europe is a small Copper Age drinking vessel or object of religious cult, found at a site near Budapest (Budakalász). The carts were drawn by oxen, even though the domestication of the horse also took place during this period. It has also been established that ethnically the Copper Age inhabitants of the region belonged to the Indo-European family of peoples – the dominant race of the region and the whole Eurasian expanse of land between the Atlantic and India until the advent of the Huns and other Altaic nomads three millennia later.

By the end of the Copper Age around 2000 BC the population of the Carpathian Basin probably exceeded several times that of the early stages of the same period, and settled in most of the areas suitable for human habitation. This mass of population remained largely unmoved by the influx of further Indo-European elements into the area during the early Bronze Age, mainly from the South again. Social differentiation became more pronounced during the high Bronze Age, from around 1700 to 1300 BC, when about a dozen tribes of somewhat different origin, cultural and economic habits, were ruled by a military-pastoral aristocracy of horsemen living in earthwork fortresses. Their affluence is testified by the products of sophisticated craftsmanship they left behind. Bronze casting as well as pottery flourished greatly in this period across the continent, and burial grounds of several hundred graves have supplied Hungarian archaeologists with an immense wealth of richly ornamented weapons and implements, glazed pottery and golden jewellery.

This prosperity was brought to a temporary halt in the thirteenth century BC by the disastrous impact of a new conquest whose origins continue to puzzle archaeologists, but which may have been linked with the other profound changes that shocked the whole central and eastern Mediterranean at that time: the influx of Italic tribes into Italy, of Illyrians into the West of the Balkans, and the onslaughts of the so-called 'marine peoples' on Egypt and the Hittite Empire in Asia Minor. Bronze culture was revived in the Carpathian Basin during the eleventh to the eighth century BC. From around 800 BC on, however, bronze was supplemented and its dominance, though rather slowly, replaced by another new technology: the casting and use of iron.

Iron weapons and jewellery were first introduced into the area by tribes of horsemen which conquered the Great Plain from the East and probably spoke an Iranian language. Around 500 BC, another tribe of similar ethnicity arrived in the same territory: the famous Scythians, the model of Herodotus' somewhat later description of the 'barbarous' peoples of the East European steppe. The movement of the Scythians and other tribes allied with them might have been linked with the great campaign of the Persian King Darius across the Lower Danube and into the steppe of the present-day Ukraine in 513 BC. They maintained commercial relations with the Greek cities, from which they also learned the use of the potter's wheel, and left behind sumptuous specimens of bronze and golden craftsmanship, the finest being the numerous golden deer, the insignia of the Scythian chieftains.

During this period, the lands west of the Danube were divided between the possibly Celtic population belonging to the Hallstatt culture (so called after a site in Austria) that occupied the North, and the Illyrians living in the South of Transdanubia. The swarming of the Celtic tribes out of their original settlement area along the Rhine and the Upper Danube towards the Atlantic and Central Europe that had started in the sixth century BC, reached by the beginning of the fourth century not only Italy, where they conquered the valley of the River Po and sacked Rome according to tradition in 390 BC, but also the whole of the Carpathian Basin, leaving only the south-east to the Dacians (the northern branch of the Thracians who lived in the Balkans and who, besides the Celts and the Illyrians, constituted the third large Indo-European group of Central and South-Eastern Europe). Celtic power rested on the manufacturing of iron, which reached quasi-industrial dimensions in their hands, but they also produced glass, and following Roman and Greek examples, they coined silver money. The common people of the various tribes of the Celts mainly lived in small villages and cultivated the land with iron headed wooden ploughs and iron scythes and sickles. By the end of the first century BC there were already a few urbanised settlements (*oppida*) in the Carpathian Basin as well as in the whole, continent-wide, Celtic world: fortified places at some elevation that served as centres of power, exchange and artisanship, like the chief town of the Eravisci, Ak-inko ('Abundant Water') on the top of present-day Budapest's Gellért Hill.

True urban culture, however, had not been established in the area before the Romans; arguably, the prehistoric age had not come to an end in the Carpathian Basin until the arrival of the Roman legions in the first century BC. By the end of antiquity, the known world was sharply divided into civilised and barbarian peoples, both objectively and in the perception of contemporaries, and the notion and phenomenon of urbanity was crucial to that distinction. After all, the very word civilisation stems from Latin *civitas*, the urban community which symbolised a certain level of material culture – relatively sophisticated patterns of production, exchange and consumption – and organisational standards of human coexistence ('political' stemming from the Greek *polis*), both of which necessitated the use of written records. Also, the city, with its walls, streets and stone buildings, was the quintessential form of permanent settlement, in sharp contrast not only with the temporary tent camps of nomads taken down whenever they needed new pasture for their cattle, but also with the wooden villages of primitive agriculturists, easily erected at a different site if expelled by enemy forces. The tendency of urban civilisations was to defy conquerors, and the city became a place of refuge as well as a source of control for its immediate environment. As a result of all of this, the fundamental principle upon which civilised peoples organised themselves was remarkably different from those of barbarians. For the latter, identity and community was based on blood relationship and personal dependence, that is, the assumption that they constituted a *nation* because the were the offspring ('*natives*') of a common ancestor and relations of subordination replicated family hierarchies. By contrast, for the former, society was organised upon the territorial principle: allegiances were formed on the basis of living in the same province, and obedience was due to whoever, and in whatever fashion, exercised power from the urban centres where it was concentrated.

Though the walls of Jericho were erected as early as in the eighth millennium BC, civilisation in this sense became first fully developed between cca. 3500 and 1500 BC in the valleys of the great rivers of the Near East and Asia: the Nile, the Tigris, the Euphrates, the Indus and the Yellow River. The Roman conquest drew the Carpathian Basin into the orbit of the Hellenic and Roman civilisation that arose and spread in the Mediterranean areas between the eighth and third centuries BC. After the advances of the late republic into the area, it was under the first two emperors, Augustus and Tiberius, that Rome finally incorporated a substantial part of the region. The invasion of 156 BC failed, but of the two main Illyrian tribes, the Dalmatians were forced to surrender to Rome in 119 BC and the Pannons in 35 BC; by 11 BC the border of the empire had been established along the Danube. The last revolt of the Pannons was suppressed by 9 AD, and a new province, Pannonia, was organised in the western half of the Carpathian Basin. Rome was greatly annoyed by the creation of a powerful Dacian kingdom under the legendary Bure-bista around 60 BC, which motivated a further expansion into the Car-pathian area by the last great conqueror, Emperor Traianus. After the defeat and death of King Decebal in 106 AD, the province of Dacia was established in Transylvania.

Pannonia and Dacia became parts of the Roman Empire for four and one and a half centuries, respectively. They had a great strategic impor-tance, demonstrated by the mere fact that three or four out of the tewnty-five to thirty legions of the empire were permanently garrisoned in Pannonia; together with the auxiliaries recruited from the natives, Roman military force in the province might have been at least 40,000 strong. The new provinces were to constitute a hinterland to the *limes*, the tightly knit network of fortifications of different size along the border of the empire, a defence against as well as a medium across which to communicate and negotiate alliances with the peoples of the *Barbari-cum* that lay across it: the Germanic Marcomanni and Quadi, and the Iranian Sarmats. In the decades before and after the wars of Marcus Aurelius against a powerful alliance of Germanic peoples led by the Marcomanni (165–180 AD) the Danubian provinces enjoyed all the benefits of the Pax Romana, and under the reigns of Hadrian, Antoninus Pius in the middle of the second and under Septimius Severus (a pro-consul of Pannonia proclaimed emperor by the Pannonian legions) and his successors in the early third century the civilising influence of Ro-man rule also became visible.

Urban culture arose in a peculiar way. Instead of developing the ex-isting Celtic and Illyrian settlements into cities, the Romans, according to their wont, established entirely new centres displaying the same char-acteristic features as elsewhere in the Empire: streets laid out in a grid plan, stone architecture (monumental public buildings – forums, aque-ducts, baths, theatres and amphitheatres, temples and basilicas – as well as sumptuous private villas), settlement first by veterans of the legions and other settlers from Italy and gradually also by natives, especially the high-born who acquired Roman citizenship. Aquincum (the adminis-trative centre of the province, now in the north-western part of Buda-pest – recalling its Celtic predecessor only in name), Savaria (now Szombathely), Scarabantia (Sopron), Arrabona (Győr), Gorsium (Tác) and Sopianae (Pécs) were the most thriving towns in Pannonia Provin-cia that are in Hungary today. The rise of urban culture also implied the appearance of written records, as well as paved roads to ensure easy communication between them and with the centre of the empire (com-plementing the so-called 'amber road' along which, among other things, this popular product of the Baltic area had been imported into Italy since very ancient times across what was now Western Pannonia). Even after Roman power was swept away from the region, the roads and stone bridges as well as other constructions remained. Evidence suggests that they even supplied a 'passive basis' to medieval Hungarian urbanisation and communication, larger Roman buildings remaining in more or less continuous use after the fifth century and still standing at the end of the eighteenth century.

They became as lasting features of the physical landscape of the country as viticulture was for the cultural and Christianity for the spiritual one. Roman settlers planted the first vine-stocks near Sopianae (now the Villány region, famous for its red wine produced on volcanic soil under unique micro-climatic conditions) and in the hills north of Lake Balaton. Orchard-keeping and a few fruit species cultivated by the Romans in the area of Hungary also seem to constitute a continuous legacy of those times. Christianity came relatively late to Pannonia: no communities are known before the rule of Emperor Gallienus in the middle of the third century, and the new creed had to compete with pagan cults for a considerable time thereafter. After Emperor Constantine (314–337) had consolidated the positions of Christianity, it seems to have struck firm roots in Pannonia as well. Large Christian necropolises have been unearthed in Sopianae and Savaria, and there were some diocesan seats in the province, too; Saint Martin, who eventually became the patron saint of France, was born in Savaria and lived in Pannonia before moving to Gaul. The Christian experience of Dacia had been too short-lived to survive the Roman withdrawal which took place as early as 271 AD, and parishes in Pannonia started to dissolve at the beginning of the fifth century, too; however, since most of the conquering Germanic peoples had been Arian Christians, places of worship continued to be used, rebuilt and renovated, even if there was no continuity in church organisation. Continuity in ethnic and linguistic terms is an even more complex issue. The withdrawal of the Roman Empire from the region under the attacks of the barbarians meant the evacuation of the Romanised elite to the more central areas of the empire, in the case of Dacia in 271 and in that of Pannonia from the end of the fourth century onwards. As a result, Latinity decayed among the indigenous population in proportion with the dissolution of their ties with the Roman administration. Whereas there is evidence for the survival of Celtic, Illyrian and Dacian (Thracian) languages in the area from the late Roman period, their disappearance and the absorption of their speakers into the conquerors was accelerated by the fact that they possessed no framework of independent public authority. As groups with a common identity they ceased to exist, even if as individuals they physically survived the calamities inflicted by the Great Migration of Germanic and nomadic peoples from across the *limes*.

As already hinted at, nomadism goes back to the second millennium BC when the peoples of the vast Eurasian steppe, in adaptation to an increasingly dry climate, took to livestock breeding – mainly horse and sheep, since they are of stronger constitution than cattle or pigs –, grazing them in ever newer pastures after their former habitat had become exhausted.

This migratory lifestyle also helped them to emerge as fearful warriors, armed with bows and arrows used by them with artistic perfection, clad in leather armour and employing military tactics that proved unpredictable for their settled neighbours for a long time to come.

From the late republican and early imperial era on, Rome had to learn how to live with the repeated raids of the Germanic tribes from across the Rhine and the Danube into its territory: campaigns to retaliate for the losses thus caused were conducted, and the *limes* was ceaselessly strengthened, repaired and reorganised. In the Carpathian Basin the above-mentioned wars against the Marcomanni, the attack of the Vandals on Aquincum in 270, the withdrawal of the Romans from Dacia, now occupied by the Visigoths, were the most important episodes of this encounter before a fundamental change occurred in the last decades of the fourth century. The Germanic peoples who had been, with increasing difficulty, so far contained by the Roman legions, now became irresistible, and the several waves of their influx threw the various provinces of the empire into disarray. Some of them were appeased and settled as 'allies' (*foederati*) in the provinces, contributing to their 'barbarisation'. But the trend was for dissolution. Visigoths penetrated the Balkans, and, having sacked Rome in 410, settled in southern Gaul and Iberia; the Vandals proceeded similarly along a north-south axis, from the Rhineland, through Rome again, to North-Africa by 439; Angles, Saxons and Jutes conquered Britain, abandoned by Rome in order better to defend its remaining possessions, around 450. All of this was the result of a kind of 'domino effect': an attack of unprecedented ferocity causing panic among the Germanic peoples, most immediately the Goths, levelled from the East by the Huns.

The Huns were the first and most destructive of several nomadic peoples of Altaic origin from Central Asia to appear in Europe. Their ethnicity is still controversial. They might have been identical with the Hsiung-nu against whom the Chinese Great Wall was built from about 300 BC on. While most of the Huns that assaulted European territories – the 'Black Huns', to be distinguished from the 'White Huns' who destroyed the Gupta Empire in India and harassed the Persian Sassanids in the fifth century AD – spoke a Turkish language, anthropologically they certainly looked Mongoloid. Despite exaggerations in the sources of their defeated enemies, the bands of Hun warriors in individual raids were rarely stronger than a few hundred, and their aggregate fighting force might not have exceeded 30,000; nor did they invent and introduce into Europe, as sometimes alleged, the stirrup. Riding was made safe for them by the high pommel of their saddles, and their military success was largely due to their extraordinary discipline, the skill of their commanders in moving their troops fast in extensive areas, and thus the ability always to attack by surprise.

The Huns, having crossed the River Volga by 375, caused the half-nomadic Alans, an Iranian people, to flee west, conquered the 'empire' of the Ostrogoths north of the Black Sea, and soon expelled the Visigoths from Dacia. In the next few decades they consolidated their hold over the Germanic peoples compelled into 'alliance' with them: the Goths, Gepids and Quadi. It was only in the 420s that their princes – 'dual kingship' was a peculiar custom of nomadic peoples – set up their headquarters in the Great Plain within the Carpathians, from whence the Huns conducted lethal campaigns into the Balkan provinces of the East-Roman Empire and to the West as far as the Rhineland. The vivid memories of their bloody campaign against the Burgundians in 437 have been handed down in the *Nibelungenlied*, and the Etzel of this great German epic is of course the legendary Attila who ruled the Huns together with his brother Bleda in this period.

They were still joint princes in 441 when the Huns put an end to Roman rule in the whole of Pannonia whose once thriving settlements were now heaps of ruins. In 445, however, Attila killed his brother and became the sole ruler of the empire of the Huns. Breaking with tradition, he wielded a quasi-despotic power over his people, taking advantage of certain legends, such as the mysterious appearance of the sword of Mars to him, symbolising both his rule over the world and its divine origin. No wonder that his personality – probably faithfully described by the imperial envoy Priscus, who visited him in his wooden palace near the river Tisza, as oppressive as well as charismatic – continued to be awesome and commanding for posterity, with Bulgarian khans and other chieftains of the steppe, even medieval Hungarian kings claiming direct descent from him. 'The Scourge of God' also made an attempt to conquer the western half of the Roman Empire, but the great battle of Catalaunum (or Mauriacum, near today's Troyes), fought in 451 between him and Aetius, the last of the great Roman warlords, aided by a dozen peoples, remained undecided. The Huns still pillaged northern Italy the following spring, but, focused as their empire became during Attila's short reign on his own personality, it did not long survive his sudden death in 453. He was buried somewhere in the Tisza region, though the legend that his remains rest in triple (golden-, silver and iron) coffin under the river, diverted from its bed and then restored to its natural course by a host of slaves summarily killed thereafter in order to preserve the secret, is nineteenth-century literary fiction. When the subjugated Germanic tribes revolted against his sons, even Attila's closest adherents and counsellors turned against them – to become aristocrats of the Roman Empire during its swan-song, while the remaining Huns withdrew to the area between the Don and the Volga.

The fall of the Huns did not mark the end of the Great Migration. True, shortly after the deposition of the last western emperor in 476, the kingdoms of the Visigoths, the Vandals, the Franks, the Burgundians and the Ostrogoths seemed to have been quite firmly established in what had been the West Roman Empire. But most of them proved to be unstable by their very nature, exposed to conquest from among their own ranks – the rise of the Frankish Empire is a case in point –, to assaults of further barbarian peoples, and to reconquest by the still relatively well-organised, unshaken and defiant East Roman Empire. While Emperor Justinian's generals led ultimately successful campaigns against the kingdoms of the Vandals and the Ostrogoths between 534 and 553, Lombards who had left their original home along the River Elbe because of overpopulation, harassed the latter in Transdanubia and decimated the Gepids in the eastern half of the Carpathian Basin.

Shortly after the death of Justinian, however, a new situation arose in the area as a result of the appearance of another nomadic people of Altaic origin, the Avars. Having crossed the Carpathians from the east in 567, they assisted the Lombards in defeating the Gepids; in 568, the Lombards also chose to flee from them to northern Italy where they established a short-lived kingdom and left a distinctly Pannonian imprint on early medieval western art. The Avars, led by their bellicose king *(kagan)* Bayan, thus occupied Transdanubia as well. A multi-ethnic state was established under Avar rule in which Germanic and Romanised elements were supplemented by Asians as well as Slavic groups that started to migrate south as well as north-east from their original home in the present-day Ukraine and eastern Poland at the turn of the fifth and sixth centuries. It was a kind of historical precursor of the Hungarian state also in the sense that in it the three major geographical regions of the Carpathian Basin: Transdanubia, the Great Plain and Transylvania, were unified in a single political entity for the first time in history.

For several decades after their settlement, the Avars continued to combine nomadising with plundering campaigns, especially against the East-Roman Empire which purchased peace by paying an annual ransom to them. Their Central Asian type of armoured heavy cavalry used iron stirrups which made equestrian warfare much easier and more efficient, and later became the technical basis of medieval chivalry. The unsuccessful siege of Constantinople by the alliance of the Avars and the Persians in 626 marked the end of Avar military predominance, and in the 630s the subordinated Slavs revolted, carving out independent territories in the Balkans – that is, in the area laid open precisely by the earlier blows of the Avars on the East-Roman *limes* along the Lower Danube. The Avars then started to develop a more settled lifestyle, combining stockbreeding and the cultivation of crops; a few artisans, too, lived in their villages, and their houses dug into the earth were equipped with stone fireplaces. Their hegemony in the Carpathian Basin survived till the end of the eighth century, and was indeed reinforced by the influx between 670 and 700 of a populous group usually referred to as 'late Avars'. Byzantine sources identify them as a group of the tribal alliance of the Onogurs, being in a state of dissolution in the steppe at that time; they seem to have spoken a Turkish language, similarly to the Bulgars heading simultaneously towards the Lower Danube where they soon became absorbed into the group of Slavs to which they gave their name. There is, however, an alternative theory, according to which the newcomers consisted of some of the Magyars, who had also lived in the Onogur alliance. I shall return to this theory of the 'double (Hungarian) conquest', which has neither been substantiated, nor refuted beyond doubt.

To be sure, the Avars did not abandon harassing their wealthier neighbours – now that the Slavs were wedged between them and Byzantium in the south, mainly in the west, which was, however, coming increasingly under Frankish sway. In 692, a peace treaty between the Avars and the Franks fixed the boundary of Avar settlement area along the River Enns. During the following century of relative tranquillity the Carolingian rulers of the Frankish Empire consolidated their hold over its different provinces, and Charlemagne, after having conquered Lombardy, Friuli, Bavaria and Carinthia between 774 and 788, wanted to secure the new possessions by a campaign against their new neighbours in the east. The attack caused internal strife among the Avars, and by 796 they had to surrender. In vain did they rebel in 799 against taxation by the Franks and forced Christianisation. The remnants of Avar statehood were swept away in 804 by a Bulgarian offensive into the region east of the Tisza. Avars still continued to live in the power vacuum emerging east of the Danube, while those that remained west of it became vassals of the Franks in Pannonia, now a military frontier region.

After the death of Charlemagne, as his empire started to dissolve and was ultimately divided in the treaty of Verdun in 843, Pannonia became a part of the East-Frankish kingdom of 'German' Lewis, now as an ordinary province with a unified administration divided into counties. With these developments, the system of vassalage and western Church organisation appeared, too. Slavs also came to play an increasingly important role in the history of the area during this period, not only as a peasant population settled in villages and providing fundamental services, but both as influential vassals of the Franks in Pannonia – hence their distinctive name 'Pannonian Slavs' – and as their rivals who jealously protected their independence in the Moravian Principality that arose north of the Danube, in the north-western region of the Carpathian Basin in the early ninth century. Due to Moravian initiatives to create a Church organisation independent of the Franks, the Byzantine missionaries Cyril and Methodius also brought the Slavic alphabet and started to spread Slavic liturgy in the region, an attempt that ultimately failed.

Pannon Slav princes governing the province of Regio Pannonia for Arnulph, king of the East Frankish domains; the Principality of Moravia at the peak of its importance under Prince Svatopluk; Avars still nomadising in the Great Plain; Transylvania controlled by the Bulgarian Tsar Simeon. This was the status quo in the Carpathian Basin when the conquering Hungarians appeared at the eastern passes of the Carpathians in 894.

2. Ancient homelands: Magyars from the heart of Asia to the fringes of the Occident

The origin and ethnic identity of the Hungarians, as that of any people, has been an object of profound interest, and given rise to wild speculations as well as sound inquiry both among outsiders and themselves ever since they appeared on the stage of recorded history. Medieval western chroniclers usually derived their own nations from one of the sons of Noah – the only survivor of the flood –, Kham or Jephtah (Shem being considered the ancestor of the Jews and the Arabs, that is, the semitic peoples). Both views had a Hungarian variant. According to one of them, a son of Kham's, the great hunter Nimrod, had two twin sons who once chased a 'miraculous hind' as far as the shores of the Sea of Azov, where they lost track of the hind, but found a group of beautiful maidens. The twins, Hunor and Magor, married, and created their own nations, thus becoming the forefathers of the Huns and the Magyars. The idea of the kinship of the two nations – with the greatness of Attila thus radiating onto the Hungarians, and his one-time rule over the Carpathian area establishing a 'historical' title to it as well – remained influential into the period of the Enlightenment and the national awakening, as did the alternative hypothesis of Biblical derivation. According to this, the son of Jephtah, Magog, was the remotest ancestor of all Eurasian peoples of horsemen.

The scientific study of origins, however, is not older than historical linguistics. Anthropologically and even culturally 'Hungarian' is an extremely mixed phenomenon, so that no such a thing as 'pure stock Hungarian' in this sense has existed since time immemorial. As a result, the only criterion to establish the continuity of a Hungarian people is language; the history of Hungarian origins is the history of a community whose genetic composition and cultural character has been changing, but which has assuredly spoken Hungarian or its predecessor language for the last few thousand years. The question of the kindred nature of certain languages is, of course, crucial to this exercise – based not on superficial similarity but, for example, on regularities of alternating sounds (like in the case of the famous Germanic *Lautverschiebung* or vowel shift pointed out by the Grimm brothers) and the comparison of essential words: basic verbs, parts of the body, numbers, kinship relations, animals and plants, etc. Upon such criteria, Hungarian linguists postulated the Finno-Ugrian origin of the Hungarian language as early as two centuries ago. To many, this has seemed a less than fully prestigious pedigree; in their search for more venerable ancestry for the small Hungarian nation to boast of, some have insisted on the Biblical tradition, while others have been led to the Etruscans, the Sumers, recently even – believe it or not – the Incas. In serious scholarship, however, the Finno-Ugrian origin of the Hungarian language and people has long been the well established view, even though the story that unfolds from it is still full of question marks up to at least the seventh century AD when the linguistic, archaeological and geobotanical data are supplemented by written records – if not about the Hungarians themselves, at least about peoples of the steppe with whom they lived in a quasi-symbiosis at that time.

The search for the earliest of the original homes of the population to which the ancestors of the Hungarians once belonged leads us to the borderland between Europe and Asia, the so-called Uralian homeland – according to linguists, in western Siberia and in the northern part of the Ural Mountains, though some archaeologists believe that there was a 'large original home' of these peoples extending from the Baltic to western Siberia. The Uralian peoples spoke a common language there until in the fourth millennium BC they started to be diversified into smaller ethno-cultural and linguistic units. As is also depicted on drawings on rocks of the Urals, in this period they were still Palaeolithic hunters, mainly of the reindeer and the moose, and gatherers – Hungarian words referring to hunting and fishing belong to the most ancient, Uralian sub-

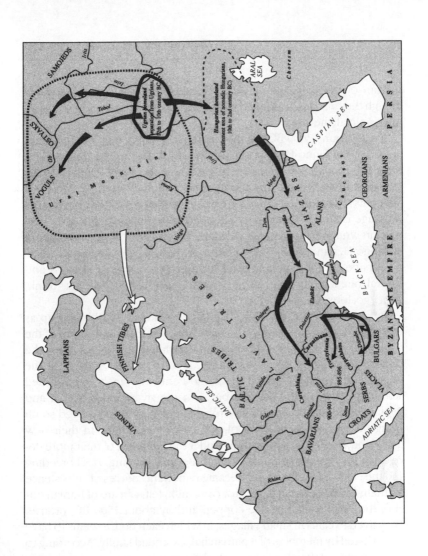

1. The homelands and the migration of the Hungarians

▪▪▪▪▪▪ boundary of the common Uralian (Finno-Ugric-Samojed) homeland

⇦ the migration of Finnish tribes

◀ the migration of Ugric tribes (Voguls and Ostyaks)

◀ the migration of Hungarian tribes

stratum of the language –, using chipped flint tools and weapons, though they also made skis and sledges and pottery, and had a domesticated animal: the dog.

It was around 3000 BC that the Uralian languages split into two main branches, the Finno-Ugrians and the Samojeds. During the third millennium BC, though still hunters and gatherers, the Finno-Ugrians – the ancestors of the Hungarians among them – already used Neolithic implements. The most important substratum in the present-day Hungarian language is Finno-Ugrian: only about 1000 basic words, but sixty percent (in written texts as much as eighty percent) of complex words are of Finno-Ugrian origin. They comprise, besides the examples mentioned above, the terminology of kinship, the names of seasons and natural phenomena (sky, snow, cloud), basic verbs (live, eat, drink, stand, go, look, give) etc.

By about 2000 BC the Finno-Ugrian community had broken up as well. Population growth seems to have been the main motivation of the migrations that commenced at that time. Earlier it was believed that the Ugrians – including the ancestors of Magyars as well as those of the Voguls and Ostyaks – joined the Finno-Permian branch and travelled across the Urals to the triangle between the rivers Volga, Kama and Byelaya, but now it seems more probable that they rather moved south along the rivers Isim and Tobol, still east of the Urals. In their new homeland, they came increasingly under the influence of their more developed neighbours of Iranian origin. Besides hunting, stockbreeding and the cultivation of the land became important sources of subsistence for them (the Hungarian words for cow, milk, felt, cart are of Iranian origin); they also started to use copper, and by about 1500 BC, bronze. They lived in clans in small villages, in which each house seems to have been shared by members of a patriarchal, extended family. According to the testimony of their burial sites, the horse occupied an ever more central role in their life, and indeed in their death: a status symbol as well as a near sacred animal, the horse was buried together with the deceased if he was well-to-do, and even in the graves of the poor, relatives placed the skull, the skin or the harness of the horse eaten at the funeral feast.

The Ugrian peoples were thus quite well prepared to switch to nomadism by the time it arose in the steppe by the end of the second millennium BC. This was also the period, between c. 1250 and 1000 BC, when the Ugrian community split. To escape the drought caused by rising temperatures, the Voguls and the Ostyaks moved back to the forests of the North, settled along the River Ob and returned to a hunting-gathering mode of subsistence (though the horse, rarely ever again seen by them after the climate turned cold and wet again around 800 BC, retained its cultic significance among them), while the proto-Magyars, adopting to the circumstances, remained in the steppe. The Finno-Ugrian relationship thus came to an end, although besides the linguistic tie some elements of a common belief system have – considering the circumstances, miraculously indeed – also survived. Comparative ethnography has revealed a few traditions among peasant communities within the Carpathians that are identical with or very similar to ones only found among other Finno-Ugrian peoples: the idea of the 'sky-high tree' connecting the earthly with the subterranean as well as the celestial world, the notion of the 'dual soul', or the specific nature of shamanism.

Nearly all that can be established about the following millennium of the history of the ancestors of the Magyars is conjecture, rather than certainty. Having turned to nomadism in the territory between the River Ural and the Aral Sea, during the first millennium BC they must have continued to be strongly influenced by the neighbouring Iranian nomadic peoples, the Sarmatians and the Scythians. The use of iron by the Magyars probably owes itself to them, and it is also somewhat symbolic of the source of nomadic bellicosity that the Hungarian word for sword is of Iranian origin. The above-mentioned myth of the miraculous hind can also be attributed to these influences. But we do not even know with any certainty when the proto-Magyars left their southern Siberian settlement area for their first European home east of the great bend of the Volga: Bashkiria, or Magna Hungaria as thirteenth-century travelling monks – like the Hungarian Dominican friar, Julian – called the territory where they found Magyar speakers left behind. It might have been as early as in the centuries directly preceding Christ, that they drifted there along with Iranian peoples; but it could also well be that this migration took place only between 350 and 400 AD, as a result of the great commotion in the area caused by the Huns, or even later, around 550, in response to the wave of Turkic peoples.

Even thereafter, hypotheses abound, and apparently well-established facts are to be treated with caution. It is beyond doubt, though, that since the dominant ethnicity and culture of the steppe during the centuries after the appearance of the Huns was Turkish, non-Turkish peoples like the Iranian Alans or the Magyars became greatly influenced by them as a result of long-term coexistence and interaction. The economic and cultural changes that occurred in this period of coexistence can be demonstrated by about 300 words of ancient Turkish origin that made their way into Hungarian – such as the ones signifying plough and sickle, wheat and barley; ox, calf, pig and hen; reason, number, write and law; sin, merit, confess and forgive –, and also the political institution of dual rulership they adopted (a nominal or sacral prince plus a military commander), even though not uniquely, was rather typically Turkish. The organisation of the clans into military units, that is, tribes, too, was a Turkish (Bulgarian) influence among the Magyars, as was the use of armour and the stirrup. These developments reflect that during the centuries of coexistence with the Turkish peoples of the steppe Magyars started to constitute a stratified community in which a fundamentally nomadic existence was supplemented with increasingly advanced knowledge of farming practices; legal and religious habits became somewhat sophisticated; and regular institutions of political and military command had arisen, mainly to co-ordinate campaigns whose goal was to capture war booty and slaves.

The framework in which the Turkish influences penetrated Magyar culture was initially the tribal alliance of the Onogurs (meaning 'ten peoples') along the Lower Don, which the Magyars joined some time in the sixth century, only to be incorporated, together with the Onogurs, in the Turkic Empire established in 552 with its core in Central Asia. After a short-lived independence of an Onogur-Bulgar 'empire' in the first decades of the seventh century, they all became subjects of the Khazar Khanate that emerged in 630 from the western parts of the Turkic Empire, between the Caspian Sea and the Black Sea. After 670, a group of Onogur-Bulgars escaped from Khazar rule and moved into the area along the Lower Danube.

As mentioned above, it has been suggested that a simultaneous influx of people into the Carpathian Basin consisted, in a similar fashion, of Magyar tribes seceding from the Onogur alliance. The theory of the 'double conquest' would provide attractive explanations to questions otherwise more difficult to account for, such as the origin of early Slav loan words in the Hungarian language whose acquisition seems to have been most feasible in the eighth and ninth centuries. Also, the campaigns of Charlemagne and the Bulgarians could not have fully extirpated the numerous Avar people, so there must have been Avars remaining in the Great Plain. However, there is no trace that a group of alien ethnicity joined the Magyars settling there after 895, so the Avars that we know for sure continued to live there after the Frankish conquest might have in fact been Hungarians. But today as many archaeologists and historians are against these assumptions as there are for them.

The Magyars only threw off Khazar rule around 830, and the centuries of their association with the Turkish peoples left a lasting imprint on the perception of them by others. They might have referred to themselves as *Magyar*, that is, 'speakers' (from the Finno-Ugrian *mon*, meaning 'speak' and *er*, meaning 'man'), which was adopted in early Islamic sources about them as *madzhgir*, but they are mentioned in the earliest written records in the West as *turci* or *ungri* – Turks and Onogurs, the latter giving rise to their name in the main European languages. This is how they are mentioned in a Byzantine account from 839, the first written record specifically and without doubt referring to the Magyars. In this period, they already lived in the vast territory called Etelköz in Hungarian tradition, the area between the River Don (Etil) and the Lower Danube. Since there were no great nomadic migrations in the steppe north of the Black Sea in the eighth and ninth centuries, it was not as a result of external pressure but internal recovery of strength that the Magyars, now a significant political power on the steppe, separated from the Khazar Khanate and obtained hegemony over this territory, where they had anyway been nomadising under Khazar suzerainty for several decades. It was from here that they launched their first raid against the East Frankish Empire in 862, which they later repeated several times on their own or allied with others, such as the Turkish Kabars and the Moravian Prince Svatopluk. In 894, they were the allies of the Byzantine Emperor Leo the Wise – to whom we owe the first detailed description of their peculiar customs, especially theose relating to warfare – in a successful campaign against the Bulgarian Tsar Simeon.

In the same year, however, the relative tranquillity of the steppe came to an end, with profound consequences for the Magyars. A massive influx of further Turkish peoples from the east compelled the Pechenegs, who had lived between the Urals and the Volga and are supposed to have already waged two 'wars' against the Magyars after the 850s, to cross the Don – a welcome development for Tsar Simeon who concluded an alliance with them against the Magyars. Urged by a double motivation now, the Pechenegs fell upon the Magyars who, wedged between two hostile forces, immediately looked for a new home further west.

CHAPTER II

THE MAKING OF A MEDIEVAL MONARCHY
(895–1301)

'From the arrows of Hungarians save us, Lord' – thus prayed, allegedly, horror-stricken tenth-century western Europeans to whom the last nomadic invasions were at that time already far beyond the compass of living memory, and whose chronicles recorded the similarly inspired expeditions of their own Goth, Frankish or Lombard ancestors as series of heroic feats. The most conspicuous feature of the latest newcomers to the periphery of the Occident was indeed their ferocious bellicosity, displayed both in the rapidity of the conquest of their new settlement area and the devastation caused by their raids, which was not the best of auspices for their accommodation to the order that was emerging in the continent. However, had the Magyars been only the next in a line of nomadic invaders, whose strength merely consisted of the ability to take their civilised neighbours by surprise and to tap their wealth, they might have hardly avoided the fate of their predecessors in the area and other peoples of the steppe who became absorbed in others or disappeared without trace. We have seen how the Avars, despite their numerical strength and efforts to adapt themselves to the increasing impossibility of continuing their ancient habits, failed in the end. True, a few historical contingencies favoured Hungarian survival – the different international status quo and the stature of dominant personalities, to mention but two important factors. Still, the image arising from the desperate prayer is, though not mistaken, a somewhat superficial one; and the first century of Magyar presence in the Carpathian Basin is essentially the history of the unfolding of tendencies already inherent in Hungarian society before the conquest, which made their adaptation to their new circumstances if not a smooth, at least a feasible process.

1. The arrows and the ploughs of Hungarians: conquest, raids, settlement

The broader context of the Hungarian conquest of the Carpathian Basin was a late or 'small' migration of peoples in the steppe, where the old rules of motion still whirled nomadic communities large distances within a short time. The state of the Persian Samanids, established as a vassal of the Abbasids of Baghdad south of the Aral Sea with Bukhara as its capital in 874, soon emerged as an independent power in Central Asia. Under pressure from its Emir Ismail ibn Ahmed, who launched a vast campaign against the nomadic 'Turks' in 893, the Uz people rushed west and compensated for the loss of its cattle by decimating those of the Pechenegs, who were at this time nomadising east of the Volga and were famous for their fine herds. The Pechenegs now crossed the Volga, to the annoyance of the Hungarians in Etelköz, whose forces were kept increasingly busy in alliance with the Byzantine Empire against the Bulgars.

Having first beaten the armies of Tsar Simeon in 894, the Magyar leaders received another offer, this time from Svatopluk, Prince of Moravia, whose status as an independent force in the Carpathian Basin was threatened by Frankish-Bulgarian collaboration against him in the region. According to legend, the Magyars actually purchased the country from him in a symbolic act of exchange: a white horse with saddlery sent to Svatopluk in return for some earth, water and grass, supposed to represent the country itself. The Moravian Prince allegedly disavowed this 'contract' and then drowned in the Danube in flight from the Magyars. In fact, the circumstances of his death in 894 are unknown, and the legend merely describes a common pagan rite of concluding alliances; and the Hungarian raiders of Pannonia in the same year were actually encouraged to plunder the area by Svatopluk himself. However, the main forces of the Hungarians only crossed the Carpathians at the Pass of Verecke in the spring of 895, after their initial successes compelled the powers of the Danube Basin to stop hostilities. The Franks and the Moravians quickly made peace, whereas Simeon temporised by suing for peace in Byzantium while concluding an alliance with the Pechenegs.

In all probability, the Hungarian campaign of 895 was intended not as a mere plundering raid but was a seriously considered act of conquest, aimed at preparing for permanent settlement. This is shown by the fact that the Magyar warriors were now, unlike in the earlier and later raids, led by their supreme military leader or *gyula*, Árpád. Árpád, as the bearer of one of the two main titles in what was probably a system of dual kingship, was also one of the first figures in Hungarian history whose name has been passed down to us, largely in works by two Byzantine emperors – the *Military Tactics* (c. 904–912) of Leo the Wise and *Of the Governance of the Empire* (c. 948–952) by Constantine Porphyrogennetus –, the *World Chronicle* (c. 908) of Regino, Abbot of Prüm, and various Muslim sources. Other figures include Kurszán, the *kende* (or *kündü*) or nominal ruler of the alliance of seven Hungarian tribes; different bearers of the third title, the *harka*, that is, another commander; Árpád's son Levente who led the Hungarian forces against the Bulgars; and Álmos, Árpád's father, who seems to have earlier borne either of the two titles mentioned above and died shortly before the settlement in Pannonia. He was either sacrificed after having served his tenure, which was the fate of the nominal king according to Khazar tradition, or died a voluntary death because unable to protect the people left behind by the warriors in Etelköz at the mercy of the Pechenegs. For the first singularly ironic fact about recorded Hungarian history is that the glory of the conquest of the historic homeland by the warriors of Árpád is inseparably linked with the disastrous flight of the common people from Etelköz into Transylvania.

The highly ideological *Gesta Hungarorum* of the unknown cleric Anonymus three-hundred years after the events recorded splendid victories over fictitious chiefs of the peoples 'found here' by the Magyars, actually projecting the twelfth-century status quo onto the ninth: Greeks, Vlachs (that is, Romanians), Khazars, Cumans and others. In fact, resistance was fairly scarce, most of the Carpathian Basin being a kind of march between the Frankish and the Bulgarian empires, where neither of these powers exercised very tight control. Transylvania and the Maros valley, a frontier region of the Bulgarian Empire, seems to have been the first portion of land within the Carpathians where Magyars gained a foothold, each of their seven chieftains having erected, according to legend, an earthen 'castle' (hence the German name of the province: *Siebenbürgen*, 'seven castles'). During the next few years, there might have been internal strife between the chieftains, caused as much by military failure against the Pechenegs, the loss of cattle to them and the conquest of new lands. Consequently, Hungarian control did not extend beyond the Danube until 899, when Arnulph, now Emperor, invited the Magyars to assist him against his rival, Berengar, King of Lombardy, who also raised a claim to the imperial crown. This was the origin of the first western raid of the Magyars. An approximately 5000 strong army, probably led by one of Árpád's sons, was repulsed from Venice, but spectacularly defeated Berengar along the River Brenta. Besides the booty, they also gained experience about the political relations of, as well as the shortest ways into the territories that were to become the targets of their raids in the following half century. Exploiting the turmoil occasioned in the Frankish Empire by the death of Arnulph in late 899, on their return the Magyars quite easily brought Pannonia (Transdanubia, including the eastern strip of what is Austria today) under their control in the course of the year 900, and the same lot fell to the Moravian Principality in 902. By the time Kurszán died, as a result of Bavarian intrigue, in 904 and Árpád in 907, the new geographic framework of Hungarian settlement had been established and was protected on all sides by a broad uninhabited pale, the *gyepü*.

Regarding the internal developments, a few things can be established with some certainty about this thinly documented period. Hungarian society was still based on blood kinship and the clan, a number of clans comprising the military organisation of the tribe, distinguished on the basis of its customs, its dialect and other features peculiar to it and also suggesting a kind of kinship tie. The medieval nobility later originated its authority and claimed direct descent from the supposedly 108 clans, the military aristocracy which had conquered the country. The process whereby the new territory was occupied and divided is little known and hotly debate. It seems to have been a gradual one, each of the seven tribes carving out an area of settlement in Transylvania, the Great Plain as well as Transdanubia during the seven or eight years of the conquest. This is shown by the fact that the names of the tribes (Nyék, Megyer, Kürt-Gyarmat – initially probably two separate tribes –, Tarján, Jenő, Kér, Keszi) are scattered across the Carpathian Basin in subsequent place names.

After the whole of the country had been occupied, the two rulers took the central region along the Danube; later, the princely title and authority as well as the whole of this central area came to be inherited within the family of Árpád. The chief ruler, however, was far from being in full control, even though Árpád did a lot to establish the predominance of his family by the sheer size of princely possessions. Still, each tribal chieftain or *úr* reigned as a prince in his own settlement area, the *úrság* (cf. *ország*, the Hungarian word for 'country'). Second in rank only to the chief prince, the *gyula* ruled quite independently over Transylvania, as did the *harka* over Western Transdanubia. Below the tribal chieftains, the clan heads (*fő*) and 'the abundant' (*bőség*) belonged to the military aristocracy, who were assisted in campaigns by a middling order of warriors who would somewhat later be referred to as 'serfs' (*jobbágy*). Taken together, these groups comprised only about one-fifth of the Hungarians who settled in the Carpathian Basin. The rest belonged either to the class of servants or 'the indigent' (*ínség*), to slaves or to the craftsmen rendering services, as their common name 'men of the court' (*udvarnok*) shows, chiefly for the elite but living in self-contained communities and enjoying some independence: carpenters, potters, blacksmiths, coopers, furriers etc. Parallels of such artisans' villages were common in neighbouring Slav countries, such as Poland and Bohemia, and in the Carpathian Basin, too, many of them seem to have been of Slavic origin. There were also quite a few Moslems in the country, settled by chieftains at ferries as toll collectors, or as long distance merchants who supplied the elite with luxury articles. It was only this narrow elite that lived, with their families and slaves, in separate residences in quite luxurious circumstances. The common warriors already lived in villages, as did the rest of the population. As to the size of this population, estimates range between 300,000 and 600,000 as to the whole, and between 100,000 and 400,000 as to the number of the Magyars, the higher figures usually considered more probable today.

Although geographic, and especially hydrographic conditions in the Carpathian Basin were markedly different from today, substantial areas along the lowland rivers becoming swamps or flooded throughout most of the year, it was suitable for continuing the semi-nomadic lifestyle developed by the Magyars in Etelköz. As described in late ninth century Moslem sources, for the winter they withdrew to dwellings in river valleys, especially at river mouths: these were the sites of permanent settlements or villages. They then sowed their vast arable lands adjacent to these winter dwellings, before setting out towards the pastures, which usually lay along the upper course of the rivers. Having grazed their cattle throughout the summer, they returned to the winter dwellings to reap their corn in the autumn.

This movement along the rivers might have covered, at least in the case of the chieftains and clan heads with their retinue, considerable distances even after settlement in the new homeland. Nevertheless, the common people were well accustomed to the requirements and habits of a settled mode of existence by the time of the conquest. Their favourite crops were wheat and rye, although they cultivated barley and millet as well; they were familiar with viticulture, but they also produced hops to brew beer, and their main industrial plant was hemp. Some artisans practised crafts, especially metal- and leather-work, which were well suited to nomadic circumstances, at a level of artistic perfection. Familiarity with the usages of the local Slav population – the cultivation of vegetables and flax and in general such crops that depended on human, rather than animal labour etc. –, which were in fact partly western (Frankish) structures passed on by them to the newcomers, and the fairly swift assimilation of the Slavs into Hungarian society, accentuated these tendencies. As a result, when the traditional plundering raids against neighbouring and more remote lands in the South and the West became impossible, the military aristocracy in particular and Hungarian society in general could increasingly rely, instead of war booty, on internal resources, which ultimately proved to be a matter of survival. To be sure, this was a gradual process which lasted several decades. For the time being, the horrified prayer quoted at the beginning of this chapter conveyed more than a grain of historical truth. The plundering raids – euphemistically, and with some vainglory, described as 'adventures' in common Hungarian discourse ever since the nineteenth-century romantic nationalist historiography –, with all the burning, rape, bestiality and carnage, were not conducted according to any consistent plan of 'foreign policy' but with the simple goal of pillage. Nevertheless, they were parts of a system in the sense that they were inseparable from the nature of this kind of society: Goth, Vandal and Frankish in the fourth and fifth, Lombard and Avar in the sixth and seventh, Norman and Hungarian in the ninth and tenth, Mongol in the thirteenth century. At the same time it might be pointed out that the supposedly more civilised contemporary Franks, Moravians and later the German princes ravaged each other's country in similar fashion, and they were keen on employing the efficient Hungarian light cavalry in these expeditions to the detriment of their rival (as was the practice of Byzantium with her Scythian neighbours throughout her thousand year history). Finally, the Magyar plunderers were not representative of the same society in another sense, namely that it was a small minority of aristocrats and warriors that took part in the campaigns. The aggregate number of these strata (adult males, without family members) might not have exceeded 20,000; in addition, it was usually not the whole of the tribal alliance, but just one or two of the tribes that set out on the raids, with an annual regularity, sometimes simultaneously in two directions. Their success was due to a combination of factors. Their fine horsemanship and their unique ability with their bows and arrows as well as their peculiar strategy was described in detail by the Byzantine Emperor Leo the Wise: a lightning attack, followed by feigned withdrawal to pull the enemy into encirclement, where it would be destroyed by a shower of arrows and in hand-to-hand combat. Even so, the effects would not have been so disastrous, were it not for the temporary internal anarchy of the Carolingian successor-states and the simultaneous difficulties of Byzantium caused by nomadic and Bulgarian attacks.

As it was, Magyar raiders burnt and pillaged cities and villages in lands as far away as Castile and the Omayyad Caliphate in Spain, Burgundy in France and Apulia in South-Italy, though their most common targets were Germany, northern Italy and Byzantium. According to well-established practice among the Turkish nomads, the Hungarians regularly pillaged a territory until its rulers felt compelled to purchase temporary tranquillity by paying an annual levy. The only significant counter-offensive of western rulers in the initial period, led in 907 by the Prince of Bavaria, collapsed in disaster. The first difficulties arose after the accession of the former Prince of Saxony, Henry I 'the Fowler', to the throne of Germany. In 924, Henry bought a nine year peace from the Magyars, which he used for strengthening and reorganising the German cavalry. Refusing to renew payment in 933, Henry's army met the spiteful Hungarians near Merseburg and inflicted the first serious defeat on them, although the main loss was not the military failure itself but the consequent termination of levies, which put an end to the most flourishing period in the history of the Hungarian Principality. From then on, the Magyar raiders concentrated their western efforts on southern Germany, but after Henry's son, Otto I 'the Great', had consolidated royal authority throughout Germany, they suffered repeated setbacks. In 951, Henry, Prince of Bavaria plundered Pannonia and beat Magyar troops in northern Italy; and the disastrous defeat of the forces led by Bulcsú, the *harka* and two other chieftains, Lél (Lehel) and Súr, in the battle of Augsburg in 955 put an end to the raids in the West. In fact, since Merseburg the main targets of Magyar raids had been the Balkans and Byzantium, from which they also received a regular tribute after the campaign of 934. As a result, however, the campaigns to the South were less ferocious and less regular than into Germany, and were mainly concerned with ensuring the continuation of the levies. They came to an end in 970, when Hungarian forces allied with Svyatoslav, Prince of Kiev, who was trying to gain a foothold in the Balkans, were defeated in the battle of Arkadiopolis near Byzantium.

Augsburg, 955, is usually regarded as a turning point in European and Hungarian history: it is supposed to have put an end to the barbarian threat to the civilised Occident and to have compelled Hungarian society to be converted from nomadism to a settled life-style, and from pagan worship to Christianity as a condition of accommodation into the community of Christian peoples. It should be obvious by now that the significance of the date and the event is symbolic rather than actual in more than one ways. The 'turning-point' was not a radical change, but it rather helped earlier tendencies to prevail; it was not the matter of a single year but the whole of the second half of the tenth century, while it was not confined to the Carpathian Basin and its relations with the Occident, but rather involved the whole of its periphery north and east of the Elbe and the Danube.

It was along those rivers that, after the conquests of Charlemagne, the boundary of the western world became stabilised, with the outlines of medieval society already emerging behind it in full strength. The most striking feature of this society was that, whereas it was ultimately established on the barbarian principle of hereditary inequality, the fundamental distinction was no longer merely between the free and the un-free, but – with property in land (*feudum*) and the relationship to it be-coming the criteria to define the place of each member in the new soci-ety – between noble and peasant, those who owned and those who cultivated the land. The organisation of the retinue of tribal chieftains, and from the eighth century on, the system of vassalage provided a ve-hicle for the common free warrior to retain his independence, maybe climb into the higher echelons, or sink into the order of serfs. In return for an oath of fealty to serve his overlord by arms and counsel, the vassal obtained an estate to cover the underlying necessuities of the new style of warfare; that is to say, the notion of nobility became associated with knighthood, whereby a fine horse, heavy weapons and armour and a few shieldbearers became *de rigeur*. Vassalage constituted a clearly hi-erarchical political organisation, with the king and the 'great vassals' – dukes and counts, bishops and archbishops – on top, in which, how-ever, only the immediately adjacent layers were in a relation of direct subordination.

As vassalage governed relationships within the elite, the manorial system ruled those between the landlords and their subjects, largely peasants who fell under the landlord's jurisdiction, owed dues and services in return for using his land, but retained some of the crop for themselves. Though in principle the nobility consisted of the descen-dants of the military aristocracy that had conquered the land and the peasantry of those of their subjects, and kinship ties remained im-mensely important as a principle upon which society was organised, the blood relationship was replaced by an ever more sophisticated system of territorial rule, in which the secular and monastic versions of Latin Christianity were both integrated.

By the time the semi-nomadic Magyars arrived at the borderland of the area where these structures had developed, they had not only fully emerged, but were already undergoing their first serious crisis as a result of the weakening of royal authority in the face of powerful vassals, the rivalry between the Pope in Rome or Latin and the Patriarch of Constan-tinople or Byzantine Christianity, and the proliferation of different sys-tems of regulation in monasticism. By the middle of the tenth century, however, the Occident and the structures briefly described above were emerging from chaos. The conflict between Rome and Byzantium was only solved definitively with the schism of 1054, but the reform of Benedictine monasticism, also assisted by the achievements of the re-vival of learning known as the 'Carolingian Renaissance', and the Otto-nian reforms which resulted in the revival of empire in the West in 962, meant that feudal society was at its apex once again and constituted a challenge to the northern and eastern neighbours.

Some, though not all of the neighbours were fairly quick to respond. Those which did not either perished altogether or came under foreign rule for a long period of time. It was in the case of peoples amongst whom the soil was to some extent ripe to accommodate to the new structures that the organisation of state hierarchies and the adoption of some version of Christianity by one of the pagan chieftains, having eliminated his rivals, and finally the consolidation of the newly created sovereignty against foreign threat, was a relatively easy process. In the Balkans in the ninth century and in Kievan Rus at the end of the tenth, this took place under Byzantine influence, relying on the foundations of strong princely rule organised by the Bulgarian khans in the former and the princes of Novgorod, who were of Vareg (Norman) origin, in the latter case. The same process took place under the banner of Latin Christianity among the Normans, or in the Bohemia of Saint Venceslas and the first Přemyslids, or in the Poland of Mieszko I and the first Piasts during the second half of the tenth century. For geographical as well as political reasons, both options were initially open to the Magyars.

It seems that the first serious steps towards the stabilisation of internal rule by laying the foundations of a secure territorial organisation as well as peaceful adaptation to the Christian environment were taken around 950, during the princely rule of Fajsz (Falicsi), Árpád's grandson. The fortification of princely dwellings in that period must have been directed against internal rival chieftains as well as external foes. As regards Christianity, since Hungarian-German (which was, to all intents and purposes, identical with Hungarian-Western) relations were at their nadir in the mid-tenth century, Rome was at that time no viable alternative of Byzantium, with which relations were less strained. Diplomatic contacts were as old as Hungarian presence in the region; the campaign of 934 was followed by a peace of nine years, and the demonstration of force in 943 by a peace of five years; indeed, during the legation that ensued in 948, Bulcsú converted to Greek Christianity, as did the *gyula* shortly afterwards, also receiving Greek missionaries in his domains along the Tisza.

However, in 957 the Byzantine Emperor Constantine cancelled the payment of the annual levy to the Hungarians, possibly as a result of Ottonian diplomacy. The German king, soon to be Holy Roman Emperor, did not pursue the policy of his great predecessor Charlemagne towards the Avars, and instead of aiming to extirpate his semi-nomadic neighbours, he wanted to subject them to vassalage, which could be achieved if he brought them to the fold of the Church himself. He seems to have persuaded the legates sent to him in 956 by Constantine about the ungodliness of the Magyars, which might have been one of the reasons for the disaffection between them and Byzantium. Campaigns against Constantinople became more frequent in the second half of the rule of Prince Taksony, another grandson of Árpád, who succeeded Fajsz in 955. True, he was reluctant to go the way Otto wanted him to pursue, and solicited Rome directly to send a bishop – an initiative thwarted by the new emperor.

All the same, by the time of his death and the accession of Prince Géza around 970 the conditions were ripe for laying the foundations of the future Kingdom of Hungary: the total failure of plundering raids, the traditions of farming and settled life brought from Etelköz and accentuated in the Carpathian Basin, and the replacement of the Greek with the Roman orientation all helped to pave the way. Incentives as well as opportunities thus presented themselves to rulers who had strength and vision but no scruples, for accomplishing a threefold task. The nominal rule of the prince over the *gyula* and a number of other chieftains, who acknowledged his supremacy and obliged themselves to assist him against foreign aggression, but maintained an independent court and retinue out of taxes and duties levied in their provinces, was to be turned into real territorial rule. Second, in order to ensure the resources for the military force thus required, a regular country-wide system of delivery and customs was to be established. Third, Christianity was to be propagated and established *en masse*, both as an end in itself and as a means to achieve the aforementioned goals: to encourage submissiveness ('yield unto Caesar what belongeth to Caesar') and to serve as a pretext to suppress old usages by which pagan beliefs were strongly intertwined with the clan organisation. Fortunately for Hungary, a succession of more than one figure of royal blood who possessed the necessary qualities, ensured – with iron and blood as well as authority and charisma – the achievement of these goals.

2. Dynasticism and Christianity, saints and lawgivers

As Taksony was buried, still according to pagan rite, and his son – Árpád's great-grandson – Géza was raised on the shield as ruler, again according to ancient custom, changes in the international status quo constituted new imperatives for the peoples of Central Europe, especially Hungarians, wedged as they were between the two expansionist powers of the Christian world. As long as they had been divided by buffer states from these empires, the pressures on them had been rather indirect. In 971, however, Byzantium annexed Bulgaria, and there was a slow but steady German advance in the Bavarian-Hungarian frontier region as well. The potential danger became really threatening when in 972 the two emperors concluded an alliance, sealed with a dynastic marriage between Otto's son and a Greek princess. In this critical situation, conversion to Christianity could have been the only security of a lasting peace for Hungary.

Considering the now over a decade long tension between Hungary and Byzantium in comparison with the relatively good terms Hungary entertained with the Holy Roman Empire, it was only logical that Géza turned to Otto, who duly ordained a Benedictine monk, Bruno of Sankt Gallen, as bishop and sent him to Hungary. It was already as a baptised prince that Géza sent his envoys to the assembly of Quedlinburg in 973 to express his friendly intentions to the Emperor. However, it is also of some significance that whereas the other new dynasties of Europe – Harald Blueteeth, King of the Danes, the Czech Prince Boleslav II and Bolesław the Brave, son of the Polish Mieszko – attended the event as vassals to take a personal oath of allegiance, Géza abstained, establishing the *Leitmotif* of medieval Hungarian foreign policy: Hungary was to be regarded as a member of the Christian community of nations, not subordinated to foreign powers. The Christian credentials of Géza himself are fairly doubtful. According to Thietmar, Bishop of Merseburg, he continued to worship pagan gods as well as the Almighty, and when reproached, he merely said: 'I am wealthy and powerful enough to afford to do so.'

Géza's wealth derived from the taxes and duties levied and collected across the whole country far more successfully than during the rule of his predecessors, which could not have been the case without the power he wielded by the ruthless suppression of unruly chieftains and other *úr* who were reluctant to recognise his supremacy. The first Christian prince of Hungary, who was also endowed with a great deal of political acumen, was at the same time a rude semi-barbarian, 'an immensely cruel man, who killed a great many persons in his sudden bursts of anger', the same Thietmar tells us. Little is known about the details of his struggles to establish a stable centralised rule in the country. Nevertheless, by the end of his reign supremacy had been established over the entire country, except that Gyula, the lord of Transylvania (the name of the office had become the name of the family that held it for generations) maintained his separate authority.

Géza's military success was due to a combination of factors. He managed to resettle and attract into his service in his fortresses and manors an increasing number of common *jobbágy* warriors who were leaving the tribal framework now that the era of plundering raids was over. At the same time, he could also rely on an elite of heavy cavalry, whose rank-and-file mainly consisted of foreign (Vareg, Croatian, Bulgarian) mercenaries, but whose commanders were almost certainly Swabian knights invited into Géza's escort along with the Christian missionaries. Last but not least, Géza carefully preserved peace and forged alliances with neighbouring princes, and apart from the conflict with Henry, Prince of Bavaria, he could concentrate on consolidating his rule internally.

Géza has been overshadowed by his successor King Stephen, though the achievement of father and son were complementary. Machiavelli and Rousseau agreed that what makes the work of a legislator difficult is not what must be established but what must be destroyed. Géza not only excelled in the latter, but also created a semi-barbarian state in which most of the economic resources and the military potential became centralised in the ruler's hands; at the same time, it was mainly that strong hand, stained with quite a lot of blood, that maintained unity, for the institutions of secular and ecclesiastical government as well as the order of manorial rights – which, impersonal as they were, were to lend continuity to the new system – were still in a rudimentary shape. Besides, adoption of the western model also implied that the christened prince was to be replaced by a crowned king: it was the act of coronation, a ceremony as sacred as the ordination of prelates, that symbolised the full conversion of the country into the fold of Christian Europe and ensured that its ruler was accepted as a counterpart of the sovereigns of the Occident.

Géza's son, born around 975 as Vajk and christened Stephen (István) at the new princely seat of Esztergom, received royal insignia from Pope Sylvester II, a fact that has usually been held to signify that the King of Hungary acknowledged no superior on earth, and in particular that he refused to recognise the overlordship of the German Emperor, considered in principle as the first in rank among the secular heads of western Christendom. The symbolic value of the crown as granted by the Pope rather than a secular ruler could hardly be overestimated from the point of view of the self-perception of Hungarian kings and posterity. However, viewed from a different angle, in the near-simultaneous creation of a Christian monarchy in Hungary and in Poland, the ambition of local rulers coincided with the project of the general expansion of the *respublica Christiana*, which both the Pope and Emperor Otto III sought to advance. Accordingly, the coronations took place with the blessing of both.

Besides the complicated international background, Stephen also needed to establish his title before being crowned. At a deeper level and in its long-term implications, this meant the assertion of the principle of primogeniture, also being established in Western Europe from that time on, against that of seniority, the a common tradition by which the oldest male member of the clan succeeded. At the time of Géza's death, this was his nephew, Koppány, the lord of the south-eastern region of Somogy, which he received as a compensation for his being neglected in the succession after Stephen had come of age.

Koppány revolted as soon as Géza died in 997, but the decisive battle he fought against the forces of Stephen was a replica of the last raids of the Magyars against Germany: Stephen's 'modern' heavy cavalry, trained and constituted as that of Otto at Augsburg, put the Somogy army to flight. Koppány himself died in the battle. His corpse was quartered and its parts were pinned to the gates of four castles: Veszprém, Győr, Fehérvár and Gyulafehérvár – the seat of Gyula, Stephen's uncle, the lord of Transylvania.

Gyula and his 'neighbour', Ajtony of the Maros valley, were surely among the nobles who refused to shout 'God save the King!' when Stephen was crowned at Christmas of the year 1000 (or on New Year's Day in 1001). Their domains remained a refuge for all adherents of the old order based on the kinship allegiance and paganism, to whom the retinue of Stephen and his Bavarian wife Gizella seemed slavish and alien, and the Latin muttering of the priests around him ungodly. Gyula and Ajtony did not take up arms against Stephen, but were content to pursue their own policies as independent territorial lords, which greatly prejudiced the creation of the new institutional order. Their separatism annoyed Stephen all the more because between them they controlled the production and transportation of an important commodity which was at the same time a monopoly of the princes of the House of Árpád: salt from the mines of Transylvania. In 1003, Stephen personally led his army against Gyula, who surrendered without a fight, and later (possibly as late as in 1018) assisted the king in suppressing Ajtony.

Simultaneous to these wars of unification and immediately after his coronation, Stephen set to creating the institutional framework of the Christian monarchy in Hungary. His Christian upbringing certainly played a central role in preparing Stephen to rule, and it imbued that rule itself; and his disposition in general was suitable for developing the intellectual scruple missing from his father, who was therefore unbridled in indulging his passions. Determination mollified by devotion made him a true *Rex christianissimus*, a champion of Christ. But there was even more than that to it. For the sovereign of a society in transition towards a settled mode of existence defined by property and security, Christianity was not a mere set of doctrines or a system of beliefs that provided metaphysical purpose to action. The ten commandments discourage arbitrariness, and prohibit murder and theft far more rigorously than nomadic customs. They protect property, the fruit of individual industry or lawful inheritance, while driving inheritance itself into a comprehensible, unambiguous channel by the regulation of sexual relationships. Finally, they exhort people to humility towards the community, and to obedience to the king. The Hungarian word for king (*király*) was adopted, like its immediate Slavic origin (*král*), from the name of Charlemagne, suggesting that he, like the emperor, had no superior on earth and was only accountable to God.

In addition, the advent of Christianity was largely due to the advent of monks accompanying the great missionaries (Saint Adalbert of Prague and his fellow Radla; Abbot Astrik, who is supposed to have fetched the crown for Stephen from Rome; Bruno of Querfurt, who proselytised among the 'Black Magyars' of Ajtony's lands), who were not only preachers of the new faith, but also the carriers of important 'knowhow'. Benedictine monasticism, reformed in the tenth century along lines indicated by the French monastery of Cluny, was influential in contemporary Europe not merely by effectively propagating a spirituality which helped to curb private wars, but also as laboratories of disciplined co-operation in which the old slogan *ora et labora* ('pray and work') was turned to implementing innovative agricultural technologies. The convents and monasteries, whether 'reformed' in the Cluny spirit or not, became models of the western frame of existence in the newly christianised lands, as well as the workshops of written culture. Besides tending the souls of their flocks, these clerics, truly devout as they were, provided for a wide variety of secular needs as well, from teaching common people how to till the soil with modern equipment to making out charters and other legal documents at ordinary places with notarial functions and at royal chanceries. Bishop Gellért of Csanád, who died a martyr and was later canonised, is the first known ecclesiastical writer in Hungary; Stephen himself also tried his talents at writing, addressing his famous *Admonitions* to his son Prince Imre. Written Latinity became soon imbued by elements of the oral culture of the vernacular, even though the first token of written Hungarian is the 'Funeral oration' from c. 1200.

The mission of Christ's champion was thus a civilising mission in the broadest sense of the word, and Stephen set to fulfilling it right after his coronation by proclaiming and submitting in writing to the Pope the creation of the archbishopric of Esztergom. The archbishop of Esztergom became the primate of the independent Hungarian ecclesiastical hierarchy organised thereafter, consisting of another archbishopric, that of Kalocsa, and eight bishoprics, with chapters set up besides the cathedral churches by the end of the eleventh century. The chapter house of Székesfehérvár, which became the royal seat of Stephen and the coronation city of subsequent Hungarian kings, became especially prestigious, being also commissioned throughout most of the Middle Ages for the keeping of the Hungarian crown. (In its present shape the Holy

Crown, held to represent the countinuity of Hungarian statehood, derives from the eleventh and twelfth centuries: in the opinion of most art historians, the top part or the 'Latin' crown was assembled with the bottom part or the 'Greek' crown, sent to King Géza I by the Byzantine Emperor in 1074, under the reign of Béla III at the end of the twelfth century.) At the same time, Stephen took care that the church organisation pervaded the capillaries of society, too, by issuing orders early in his reign for every ten villages to build a parish church. Monasteries were founded at Pannonhalma, Pécsvárad, Zalavár and other places. The annals of Pannonhalma, started in 998, just two years after the foundation of the monastery itself, are the first written records of Hungarian ecclesiastical culture. By the end of the eleventh century, the library there held about eighty valuable codices. Cathedral schools were organised as well: in all probability it was for educational purposes that Fulbert, Bishop of Chartres, sent, upon request by Bonifert, the first bishop of Pécs, the *Grammar* of Priscianus, the most common medieval handbook of Latin, around 1020.

To maintain and support the Church, Stephen ordained the collection of tithes, but the true bases of ecclesiastical power, as elsewhere in Europe, were the immense landed estates which he and his successors donated to bishoprics, chapters and monasteries. The significance of this phenomenon also surpasses the confines of ecclesiastical politics, since it was to a large extent on the model of church property that manorial organisation and manorial rights appeared in the country. The idea of immovable, indivisible and inalienable property was novel to Hungarian society to such an extent that secular landlords did not insist on the recording of the boundaries of their estates in writing until well into the thirteenth century, and the rights they claimed were preserved by custom and memory. To be sure, in consequence of the process known as the founding of the Hungarian state, which involved the confiscation of two-thirds of the clans' territories together with their inhabitants, the king, or rather the royal House of Árpád, became the greatest landlord in the country. Contiguous areas of the size of entire counties came in royal possession, their inhabitants settled in manors, with a manor-house erected in each of them to lodge the court, which travelled from manor to manor to consume the dues delivered. The preponderance of royal landholding throughout much of the Árpád period served as a basis for a patrimonial-despotic type of monarchy. The secular latifundia, whose significance was at this time far from what it later became, replicated this system on a smaller scale. Their owners were some of those clan heads who took sides with the Árpáds early enough, or appeased opponents, like Aba, the lord of the Kabar tribes who married a sister of

Stephen's, but at there were least as many immigrant knights richly rewarded for their help in putting down resistance to the king.

The castles (Hung. *vár*) – in fact, as most *civitas* of the contemporary
world, settlements fortified with stone walls or, more frequently,
earthen mounds – now taken into royal possession and the surrounding territories, the counties, became the centres of military control and
the units of secular administration respectively, which together formed
the backbone of the new political organisation of the country. Stephen
brought to an end the resettlement of the *jobbágy* warrior element of the
tribes into the royal fortresses. They now became the 'castle serfs' responsible for the military upkeep of the castles, while tillage of the dispersed 'castle lands' was the task of the 'castle people': common freemen who retained their legal status but were permanently obliged to
service around the castle. Organised into units by the hundred, they
were all subordinated to and commanded by the *comes* of the castle (the
rough equivalent of the count of the Carolingians and their successor
states, Hung. *várispán*) who administered the county (*vármegye*), that
is, the territory within the competence of the castle: representing the
king in his principal capacities, he was supreme judge, collected taxes
and led the warriors of the county to battle under his own banner. Forty-
five or so counties might have been organised during Stephen's reign,
the *ispáns* recruited from the staunchest supporters of the king and
some of them lending their names to their counties – Szabolcs, one of
the influential clan chiefs, the Swabian knight Hont, or Csanád, the de-
feater of Ajtony, being cases in point.

The *ispáns*, besides the prelates, were also members of the royal
council, the supreme organ of national government. The primate of
Esztergom and the *nádor* or palatine (*comes palatinus*, the supreme
judge over the people of the royal household like the *maiordomus* of
the Carolingians) were the two most outstanding figures of this body. It
was fully compatible with the king's extensive prerogative, as well as
proper and prudent, to request the counsel – thus, ultimately, the consent – of his most influential subjects in matters of great importance. It
was as a result of this collaboration that Stephen issued, in the first phase
of his reign, two statute books to consolidate his achievement. The issues addressed in the statutes, quite naturally, concerned ecclesiastical
and property relations: they provided for Christian worship and the
condition of the clergy in general, including the levying of tithes; they
sanctioned violence and perjury; they secured manorial rights, individual property holding and the landlord's jurisdiction over his subjects;
they protected the rights of widows and orphans; they enjoined the
punishment of witches and sorcerers.

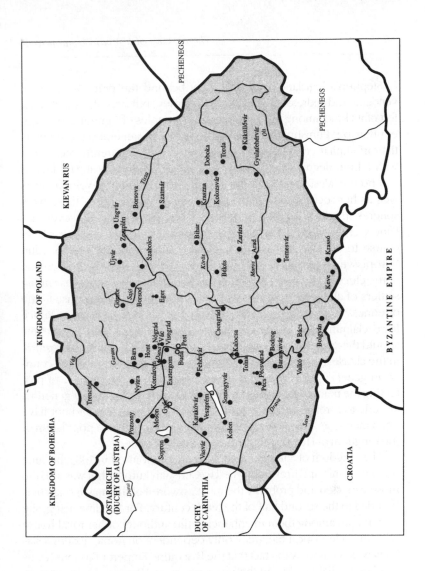

2. Hungary and her neighbours under Saint Stephen

● castles of *ispáns*

○ other important castle

⚓ important Benedictine abbey

⚓ archbishoprics

Stephen's legislation not only went beyond the practices of tribal vendetta and redressing grievances by parley, but was also the first effort of its kind among the 'new barbarian' peoples of Central and Northern Europe. Punishments were rigorous, but in general more humane than in similar contemporary penal codes, and apparently meted out with a high degree of efficiency. As a result, whereas Hungary lagged behind the West in terms of her wealth and economic development as well as her social stratification and system of institutions – these were spheres in which political decisions of one generation, however brilliant, were unlikely to bridge a gap of several centuries – as regards recourse to the law, she was at least on a level with the core of Latin Europe whose periphery she had now joined. This must have been one of the clues to Hungary's popularity in the subsequent centuries among settlers of all trades, religions and ethnicities, in part a response to the openness Stephen supposedly professed in his *Admonitions* to Prince Imre claiming that single language *regni* are weak and immigrants should therefore be encouraged and protected. True, the word *regnum* in the clause in point should probably be taken to refer not to the country in general, but to the royal retinue, and thus to the practice of protecting the person of the king by foreign knights, rather than a generous attitude to foreign settlers in general. Be it as it may, it could not have been merely as a result of natural growth that by 1200 the population of the Kingdom of Hungary might have reached 2 million.

The kingdom of Saint Stephen, who was canonised in 1083, became not only firmly and irreversibly tied to Christian Europe, but was also the most respected and probably the most powerful of the new monarchies founded in the second half of the tenth century. For the time being, she was unique among them in enhancing the authority of her royal house with an ecclesiastical hierarchy only dependent on Rome. External stability was secured by the fact that the Byzantine Emperor Basileus II was Stephen's reliable ally and the other emperor, Henry II, his brother-in-law; the one assisted him in war against Tsar Samuel of Bulgaria, the other in recovering territories occupied by the Polish King Bolesław. When Henry's successor Konrad II invaded Hungary in 1030, the new kingdom was powerful enough to resist on her own.

Shortly later, however, a succession crisis occurred, putting these achievements at risk. In 1031, Stephen's only son and heir Prince Imre died in a hunting accident. Stephen then escaped an attempt on his life and had his cousin Vazul blinded and molten lead poured into his ears (a common method both of punishing treasonable offences as well as making someone unfit for office). The sequence of these events is uncertain, but they were probably linked with each other and surely with the succession. Vazul, as the oldest male of Stephen's kin, could raise a claim to the throne either on his own or on his three sons' behalf (who fled the country after his mutilation) according to the old principle of seniority – a principle rejected by Stephen and his father in neglecting and then defeating Koppány. What is more, Vazul is described in sources as an irresponsible man with pagan inclinations. Apparently, then, Stephen had ample reason to set him aside in favour of Peter Orseolo, the son of his sister and the Doge of Venice. But his preference for the female line was equally against all tradition. Even among those who gained from the historic transition, the poor felt heavily burdened and the great severely restricted; not to speak about the losers, such as impoverished clan heads or freemen thrown into bondage. They were now all provided a pretext either to voice their discontent or to challenge the new order as soon as the founder's commanding personality passed away in 1038.

Peter was a perfect knight and a devout Christian, but lacked the additional qualities of adaptability, tolerance etc. which, according to Stephen's *Admonitions* amounted to political prudence. He engaged in useless foreign policy adventures in Poland and the Balkans; while a benefactor of the Church, he also entered into conflict with it, dismissing bishops and taking advantage of ecclesiastical revenues; he imposed higher taxes; and while Stephen's retinue was also packed with foreigners, it was probably not by chance that it was Peter who was openly blamed for surrounding himself with 'jabbering Italians' and 'roaring Germans'. In 1041, rebellious lords expelled and replaced him by another nephew of Stephen, the enigmatic Sámuel Aba. Few rulers started their reigns under less favourable auspices: his predecessor fled to Emperor Henry III who had thus a golden opportunity to interfere with the affairs of the country and make good the failure of his father in 1030; in addition, Vazul's exiled sons, Béla, Andrew and Levente also waited in neighbouring countries for better times. In due course, the Emperor first invaded the country in 1042, and in 1044 he personally restored his protégé to his royal rights at Fehérvár, obtaining in return Peter's oath of fealty.

Peter's subsequent shameless subordination of himself and the resources of the country to his overlord, however, swung the pendulum again. It was the ancient pagan sentiment, which broke out in a rebellion of elemental force in 1046, that the discontented Hungarian noblemen exploited to get rid of Peter and his foreign entourage. However, out of the sons of Vazul now invited back to the country, it was not the eldest one, the pagan Levente, to whom they offered the crown, but Andrew, a firm Christian whose experience in the Kievan court also convinced him of the indispensability of ecclesiastical authority for the stability of the polity. This demonstrates that the real design of the lords was not the dismantling of Stephen's work, quite on the contrary: instead of destroying the Christian monarchy, they wanted to restore its integrity. Counterfeiting sympathy with the rebels, to whose rage a great many bishops and priests had fallen victim by the time of his arrival (Gellért, mentioned above, thrown from the hill which today bears his name in Buda, being one of them), Andrew first defeated Peter and had him blinded, then immediately crushed the rebels. As Andrew I (1046–1060), he considered it his main task to preserve the independent status of the Kingdom of Hungary, and – enjoying the diplomatic support of Kiev and Byzantium, ever jealous of German expansionism – in 1051 and 1052 repelled two formidable efforts by Henry III to assert his rights of overlordship.

Andrew then sought to consolidate his position by obtaining the hand of Henry's daughter for his son Solomon, still a child, who was also appointed his heir. Not for the first and not for the last time in early Hungarian history, this resulted in the emergence of the 'Koppány syndrome': rivalry for succession between the ruler's son and his eldest male relative, that is, the conflict between the principles of primogeniture and seniority, always an opportunity for internal strife and foreign interference. Until the late birth of Solomon, Andrew seemed content to have his popular brother Béla, with the title of duke created for him and endowed with the vast ducal estates in the north and east of the country, succeed him. Now, in a scene made famous by chroniclers, he offered Béla to choose between the crown and the sword, symbols of the royal and the ducal office, with the hidden design of having him killed at once, should he make the 'wrong' choice. Béla was warned and wisely took the sword, but soon fled to Poland, only to return with an army. Andrew – assisted, ironically, by the German Emperor Henry IV, who was now the brother of his daughter-in-law – was mortally wounded in the battle that ensued, and was buried in the famous Benedictine abbey of Tihany founded by him. The main event of the short, thousand-day reign of Béla I (1060–1063) was the second pagan rebellion of 1061.

The circumstances are eloquent. Just as fifteen years earlier the rebels had pinned their hopes on the new ruler, now too it was the king whom they solicited at the royal assizes at Fehérvár to expel priests and return to pagan rites. This demonstrates that by the mid-eleventh century the old system of clans and allegiances based on them were in disarray: the direct superiors of the commoners were no longer their more affluent kindred, whom they could naturally understand and ally themselves with, but alienated noblemen, from whose control they felt it necessary and proper to appeal to the 'good king'. On the other hand, the new social fabric and institutions in both cases proved strong enough for the 'good king' to put down the rebellion without great difficulty, despite the precariousness of his title.

When Béla suddenly died in an accident, Emperor Henry IV had already launched an offensive to restore Andrew's son Solomon, who in 1060 had fled to Germany, to his inheritance, and the series of succession conflicts continued within the Vazul branch of the House of Árpád. It was now the turn of Béla's sons to go into exile. In a short while, however, they made their peace with Solomon (1063–1074), the eldest, Géza, even obtaining the ducal province once held by his father and assisting the king in successful campaigns against the Pechenegs and Byzantium. Quarrels over the war booty and possibly intrigue brought them into conflict with each other, out of which the older and more experienced Géza emerged victorious. Solomon, at merely twenty-two, fled for the second time, taking the royal treasury with him and offering an oath of fealty to Henry IV in return for assistance. Dazzled by the prospect, the Emperor sent an army, but was beaten off; on the other hand, Géza I (1074–1077), though master of the country, could not get himself crowned and thus gain legitimacy. As the Investiture Controversy was at its inception, it was reasonable for him to hope that Pope Gregory VII, now in conflict with the Emperor, would help him out. Gregory's ultimate aspiration, however, was, to make the papacy a universal political power, and the only step compatible with this would have been to send a crown to Géza in return for accepting the status of a papal vassal. This the new King of Hungary refused, and accepted a crown presented to him by his new father-in-law, Emperor Michael VII of Byzantium, who imposed no conditions. This splendid work of art became a hundred years later the bottom part of the Holy Crown of Hungary as we know it today.

The premature death of Géza put an end to a period of over a generation of contested titles, short reigns and royal minorities. His sons, Coloman and Álmos, were under age, yet the succession of his brother Duke Ladislas took place peacefully. The reigns of Ladislas I (1077–1095), who died heirless, and Coloman (1095–1116), the elder son of Géza, marked the final consolidation of the social and institutional order created during Prince Géza and Stephen I, and the emergence of the Kingdom of Hungary as a state with the potential and appetite of a leading regional power.

In Ladislas, as in Stephen before him, the character of the knight and the saint were united with that of a statesman. The valour he showed fighting the Pechenegs back in 1068 made him a hero of legends; he procured the canonisation, besides Bishop Gellért, of King Stephen and Prince Imre – an act of remarkable open-handedness, considering the fact that he was the grandson of Vazul – in 1083, and displayed a kind of chivalric magnanimity towards Solomon, too, who was allowed to return to the country, and was only detained after plotting against the king. Ladislas himself was canonised in 1192. The canonisation of Stephen was, of course, a political act, the testimony of Ladislas's commitment to preserving and strengthening the edifice erected by his predecessor. His practical measures to this purpose included, besides lavish gifts to the Church, an extensive legislative activity and the reorganisation of the system of royal revenues.

Ladislas issued three statute books, and Coloman another one; besides, synods of Hungarian prelates issued ecclesiastical orders during their reigns on two occasions. The over 250 articles of these codes are the only body of laws extant from the period between the reign of Stephen I and the Golden Bull of 1222: clearly, this was a period of exceptional importance and efficiency for the consolidation of the new order in state and church. One of the foci of Ladislas's legislation was the security and indeed the very idea of private property, despite all efforts rather imperfectly established under Stephen I, and rendered especially precarious during the turmoil of the subsequent four decades. Over half of the laws of Ladislas were directly and many others indirectly concerned with the defence of property, by quite Draconian measures: thieves caught in the act were to be hanged, just as minor offenders against property risked losing their eyes or hands, or being sold off as slaves. The last statute book of Ladislas even abandoned the universal contemporary practice of church asylum, and inflicted capital punishment for thefts over the value of a hen. At the same time, Hungarian jurisdiction owes to him the introduction of practices like the issuing of proper writs of summons and sanctions for ignoring them, or the cross-questioning of sworn witnesses. Statutes regulated the payment of ecclesiastical tithes and protected church property in general. The Gregorian reforms made an impact, too, on the regulation of church discipline, even if celibacy and the prohibition of simony were less than strictly imposed: with a view to 'human frailty', bishops and priests were allowed to live with their wives (though not to remarry), and family owned monasteries continued to be bought and sold among the great. As regards royal revenues, Ladislas did not introduce new ones, but developed and harvested more efficiently the existing ones: the 'profit of the treasury' (*lucrum camarae*) derived from minting coinage and financial exchange; customs duties on long distance trade, and especially fairs and river tolls within the country; the royal monopoly on the export of horses and the trade of salt; the tax imposed on foreign merchants, etc.

The tranquillity which enabled Ladislas to perform this vast work of reorganisation partly resulted from the fact that he was left relatively undisturbed by his neighbours, engaged more or less simultaneously in trying to overcome internal crises. This circumstance also helped him to pursue an unusually active foreign policy in the second half of his reign, when he no longer needed to worry about Solomon being a permanent pretext for interference with Hungarian affairs, and led Ladislas to abandon the cautious ways of Prince Géza and Stephen I. The most important gain of this turn was the acquisition, in the face of the rivalry of the Papacy, of Croatia in 1091. Most of present-day Croatia, the parts known as Slavonia, north of the River Sava, had probably been under Hungarian sway since shortly after the conquest of the Carpathian Basin, and the Bishopric of Zagreb was set up there under the reign of Ladislas. The small Slav kingdom founded south of it in the 920s had been, unlike its Orthodox neighbours in the Balkans, under the influence of Latin Christianity since the eighth century, and indeed in 1074 became a vassal of 'Saint Peter'. It had been on friendly terms with Hungarian rulers, to whom the main importance of the fairly barren land lay in the access it provided to the Adriatic, and who generally protected it against its enemies. In 1090, as the Croat throne became vacant, chaos ensued and one of the baronial factions turned to Ladislas to occupy it. The annexation of Croatia took place in 1091 without substantial resistance, although a raid of nomadic Cumans in Eastern Hungary compelled him to return, leaving the occupation of Dalmatia (the 'Latin' towns of the shore and the islands) to his successor. For the time being, Ladislas appointed his younger nephew Prince Álmos as governor. Thus began the historic association of the Kingdom of Hungary and Croatia, which lasted until the end of the First World War.

If we may believe some chroniclers, Coloman, who succeeded Ladislas, was in many respects just the opposite of his uncle: unlike the reign of the 'knight-saint', his was spotted with 'many evil deeds' and he himself was 'artful ... half blind, humpbacked, lame, and a stammerer'. However, these chroniclers' credibility is seriously called into question by the fact that they wrote under rulers descended from Coloman's brother Álmos – warlike and imposing, superficially certainly more of an ideal prince by the standards of the age – who desperately schemed against the king until, after the sixth plot in 1113, the lot of Vazul fell on him and his son Béla: both of them were blinded. Whereas the physical description might to some extent correspond to reality, the 'evil deeds' were largely ones aimed to thwart the ambition of the pretender, and the 'artfulness' mentioned by the chroniclers was described by other, less impartial observers as uncommon erudition and intellectual powers, also indicated by Coloman's by-name 'the Book-Lover'. And even though his bodily frame did not destine him to be the mighty warlord Ladislas was, and his cool deliberation sometimes proved less success-

ful than the instinctive political talent of his predecessor, it was still under Coloman's reign that the medieval Hungarian state became con-
summate and acquired its final structure.

Ladislas died suddenly, and Coloman had not yet obtained the papal
dispensation to resign from his bishopric and get himself crowned,
when he found himself in the limelight of European politics. At the end
of 1095, Pope Urban II proclaimed the first Crusade, and before the 'official' forces led by Gottfried de Bouillon could gather, large crowds of
zealots and adventurers set off in the spring of 1096 towards the Holy
Sepulchre on the pilgrimage route opened up across Hungary by Stephen I in 1018. What many of them sought in fact was booty, whether
taken from the infidel or closer to home, and two troops of plundering
'Crusaders' had been beaten out of the country by Coloman by the time
the regulars of Gottfried arrived. They were politely received and escorted by the Hungarian army to the southern border of the country,
while Gottfried's brother, who became King of Jerusalem in 1099 after
the success of the enterprise, was detained as a hostage in Coloman's
court to ensure that no atrocities arose. The skill with which Coloman
managed this first critical situation of his reign contrasted markedly with
his conduct a few years later, when he rashly interfered in the feud of
Kievan princes in Galicia. It is noteworthy that in this episode of 1099,
the Cuman allies of the enemy defeated the Hungarian army with the
same nomadic tactics which the Hungarians employed so successfully
two centuries earlier.

The lesson was not lost on Coloman: his next, and indeed most important foreign policy initiative was far better prepared and accomplished. It concerned Dalmatia, an economic and cultural beacon in the
Eastern Adriatic, whose long-standing traditions of urban civilisation
(Zara/Zadar, Spalato/Split, Ragusa/Dubrovnik), navigation and long
distance trade, Latinate culture, habits of literacy and urban self-
government could not have been more different from its Slavic hinterland; a hinterland with which, as Coloman personally discovered on a
visit to Croatia in 1102 to get himself crowned there, the littoral nevertheless existed in an ever more intensive symbiosis ethnically, economically and socially. To assert this interdependence under Hungarian
sway, however, was itself dependent on the development of the rivalry
between the two powers that had been competing for hegemony over
Dalmatia: Byzantium, the nominal overlord of the cities, and its one-
time vassal, the Republic of Venice. The marriage of Ladislas's fabu-
lously beautiful daughter Piroska to the Byzantine Emperor in 1103
earned the goodwill of Constantinople and was a warning to Venice; in
1105, Coloman marched into Dalmatia, and after a short siege of Zara
the whole province surrendered and accepted Hungarian overlordship

quite willingly, despite the enormous cultural gap between it and the conquerors. The point, however, was that the latter acted with remarkable self-restraint, respecting local customs, demanding no ransom and imposing no governors, merely requiring the acknowledgement of suzerainty and a moderate levy. Venice, which had been watching the prosperity of the Dalmatian towns ever more jealously, undoubtedly would have acted far less torerantly.

The reigns of Ladislas I and Coloman, then, brought about a fundamental change in the international standing and foreign relations of the Kingdom of Hungary. Whereas through most of the eleventh century the country had to defend her integrity in the face of German expansionism, and from the early fifteenth century on it was challenged again by the Ottoman Turks, in the intervening period of three centuries, inaugurated by the conquest of Croatia and Dalmatia, she pursued expansionist policies *vis-à-vis* her neighbours, and it was only in exceptional cases (most conspicuously, the disastrous Mongol invasion of 1241) that she was pushed to the defensive. This was a remarkable change indeed, even if the main dividend of the conquests, most of which continued to be stakes in international conflicts were and by no means permanent, was the proliferation of the ruler's titles.

Coloman's economic policies and legislation also continued the work of Ladislas, though the further increase of royal revenues during his reign was largely due to his curtailing those of the church, which would have never occurred to his predecessor. He imposed higher taxes on commerce, which was refreshed by the influx of Jews, expelled from Bohemia by the Crusaders. The severity of Ladislas' laws was toned down, while procedural formalities were tightened. All this reflects orderly conditions, which not only made it possible for Coloman to reorganise the military, but served also as a background to the spread of cultural attainments: the more intensive use of (however irregularly conceived and formulated) written records in the royal administration, the beginnings of the writing of legends and chronicles, and the rise of Romanesque art in the European fashion.

At the same time, Coloman's quarrel with his brother cast a shadow on his rule from beginning to end. Upon his succession, Álmos was called back from Croatia to obtain the ducal province, which was far more lucrative, but could be more closely watched and controlled from the royal court. All in vain: Álmos rebelled as early as in 1098, and several times again later on, now soliciting the help of the German Emperor, then that of the Kievan and Polish relatives of his wife, constituting a permanent menace to Coloman himself and the succession of his son and heir Prince Stephen, as well as a permanent source of instability for the whole of the country. The punishment which Coloman, to all appearances a man of a strong moral sense and high integrity, meted out upon the advice of his council, was perfectly justified and unusually light by the standards of an age when similar situations often culminated in quite a lot of bloodshed. The Álmos branch was, of course, unappeasable; yet, a generation later they had their compensation. As the Koppány motif before, the Vazul motif now repeated itself in the history of the House of Árpád. As was the case with Vazul's sons after 1046, after 1131 all Hungarian monarchs up until the extinction of the dynasty came from the line of Coloman's blinded brother.

3. Feudalism: Europe and Hungary to the mid-thirteenth century

During the eleventh century, the Kingdom of Hungary, like the other new monarchies north of it, firmly established itself as a member of the Christian community of nations, and it started to develop social and institutional structures that bore a superficial resemblance to those territories that had been integrated in western Christendom several centuries earlier, while also preserving features that tied it to its nomadic past and eastern and south-eastern neighbours. Having emerged from the turmoil caused by several waves of the migration of peoples, it was in the same century and the following one that the medieval West conformed most closely to the idealised representation of society as divided into *oratores, bellatores, laboratores* – those who prayed, those who fought and those who worked. By the thirteenth century, this 'classic' model was already modified, especially in the political and intellectual sphere, by new developments. Before looking at the peculiarities of Hungarian society, polity and culture in this period, I shall briefly survey these structures.

By the eleventh century, the feudal ruling class in Western Europe was neatly stratified in an international hierarchy of vassalage: ethnic consciousness might survive in some form or other among the village folk, but the outlook and allegiances of knighthood were mainly shaped by a sense of solidarity and the ethos of chivalry that transcended the boundaries of state and province. Christianity became another factor that inspired supra-national loyalties, especially as the reformed papacy of the eleventh century threw off the tutelage of the emperors, claimed to represent the moral and spiritual unity of the whole of the western world, and the Church arose as an independent authority. The emerging duality of the temporal and spiritual 'swords' and the ambiguous relationship between them remained an essential feature of the civilisation of the Occident even after, in the thirteenth century, the efforts that symbolised the mutual dependence and common calling of the two swords, the Crusades, had met their ultimate failure in the Holy Land; and even after the original conflict between Emperors and Popes for the hegemony over Christendom gave way to the struggle of consolidated national monarchies, like France and England, to achieve firm rule within their confines from the same period onwards. On the vast estates of the two privileged orders, peasant serfs with more or less uniform legal status, dues and services, tilled the land with improved methods, producing yields that were sufficient to support the increasing urban communities that arose in the gaps of feudal jurisdiction and obtained rights of self-government.

The 'agricultural revolution' and the commercial network operated by the guilds of urban artisans and merchants provided the keys to the economic prosperity of the medieval West, which was paralleled in the intellectual sphere as well; this, in turn, had important repercussions on public affairs. The rediscovery of Roman law not only supplied a framework in which the complex realities of vassalage, the manorial system or urban liberties could be lucidly expressed, but also facilitated the modernisation of primitive early medieval monarchies by reintroducing the abstract notions of state and subject and of mutual rights and obligations between them. The jurisdictional, administrative and fiscal institutions (the *curiae*, the chancelleries, the chambers or treasuries) through which these relationships were governed, started to function more regularly and professionally by the end of the twelfth century; and in the thirteenth, the idea of the limited and conditional nature of royal authority became embodied in the growth of medieval constitutionalism, the representation of all privileged orders or estates – besides prelates and aristocrats, counties and provinces, cities and corporations as well – in parliaments, diets, *états généraux* etc. in order to express their opinion and influence policies in important matters of public concern. But the study of Roman law was just one aspect of the general resuscitation of reason, owing much to the rediscovery of Aristotle and other authors of classical antiquity, and critically applied by the central figures of the 'Renaissance of the twelfth century' to all branches of knowledge. Theology itself became imbued by scholasticism, the mode of reasoning introduced in the schools that were to become the first universities. These came to be dominated by the two orders of mendicant friars, the Dominicans and the Franciscans, established both in response to the growing wordliness of the official Church and as an alternative to the passive asceticism of the monastic orders (among whom there were also reform minded initiatives by the Cistercians, the

Premonstratensians and the Carthusians). Speculative rationalism and the beginnings of experimental science, respectively, were the Dominican and Franciscan contributions to the intellectual outlook of the age (while the former also became notorious for their role in crushing movements of heresy). Finally, from the mid-twelfth century on, the robust and gloomy Romanesque style was replaced by graceful Gothic art and architecture, which was far more homogeneous and quintessentially western.

Most of these phenomena appeared in some shape in contemporary Hungary as well. There was, however, a fundamental difference in the ways they arose in Western Europe and Hungary. In the West, they were the results of successive stages in a more or less *organic* development that lasted several centuries. In Hungary, these structures resulted to quite a large extent from an *organised* response to historical challenge, the need to resist pressure from a more highly developed environment by acquiring some of the techniques that constituted their strength; from legislative and political action which, thanks to the powerful figures of Stephen I, Ladislas I and Coloman, compelled an initially half-nomadic society to observe property relations and Christian values. No wonder that the achievements often lacked the firm roots which they had struck in the West, and were rudimentary and incomplete when compared to them. While, for instance, the dominant principle of the western polities became, by the ninth century, the system of vassalage, and by the thirteenth, a system based on the estates, in Hungary it was a peculiar version of the relations and institutions characteristic of these systems that arose between the eleventh and the thirteenth centuries in the course of an accelerated, contracted, and to some extent imitative development. Finally, it should not be forgotten that although the 'Western option' demonstrated itself in the Roman organisation of the Church and the Carolingian institutions of the state, due to geographical proximity and intensive relations, Byzantine influences were also quite profound, and the *jobbágy* type retinue that characterised the fabric of authority long after the foundation of the state and church had more in common with the proto-feudal Eastern Slav *druzhina* than with western vassalage. In the same fashion, Greek (Byzantine) orders played an important role in monasticism at least until the late twelfth century. It was only after 1200, in the same period as Byzantium fell into a profound decline as a result of the sack and conquest by the 'diverted' Crusaders of 1204, and Russia was torn apart by the Mongol invasion, that western systemic features became really preponderant in Hungarian development through the rise of the nobility and the notion of the *communitas regni*, the emergence of the peasantry from the servile status and the growth of free cities.

In the Hungarian society of the eleventh and twelfth centuries, the fundamental distinction was still not between titled nobleman and peasant serf, but between freeman (*liber*) and 'servant' (*servus*), neither these nor the amorphous group of the 'semi-free' between them having a clearly defined, hereditary legal status. The ruling class was undoubtedly the aristocracy of 'the great' (*maiores*): the king's retinue who comprised his council or 'senate' and were of very heterogeneous origin. Descendants of the conforming chieftains of Stephen as well as those of foreign courtiers arriving with the rulers' consorts – Bavarians under Stephen, Poles under Béla, Swabians under Ladislas, Sicilian Normans under Coloman – all belonged to this most prestigious, but still not necessarily hereditary caste. Below them there was a heterogeneous and numerous group of common freemen, that is, *jobbágy* warriors of the king's court or his castles, or in the retinue of ecclesiastical or secular lords, as well as civil *ministers* of the same authorities. However, while *liber* in the socio-economic sense, namely, free from dues and services, their freedom of movement was restricted: the requirement of loyalty bound them to the estate of the overlord. The peasant cultivators were relegated into a servile status, but their obligations varied greatly in different localities and on estates of different type (that is, ecclesiastical, secular and royal).

The growth of urban communities with self-government in Hungary was largely a matter of the second half of the thirteenth century. Before 1150, it was only a few communities of French and Walloon, and after that date Flemish and German ('Saxon') settlers or 'guests' (*hospites*), who moved into centres like Székesfehérvár or Estergom, or established their own 'towns' that were endowed with privileges and thus, becoming *libera villae*, constituted the first beginnings of western type urban development. In all probability, it was roughly simultaneous to the influx of German settlers into the northern, Szepes (Zips, Spiš) region and Transylvania, that Romanians started to infiltrate Transylvania from the south where Byzantine sources first mentioned them in the tenth century. The alternative theory of 'Daco-Romanian Continuity', namely, that they were indigenous inhabitants of Transylvania as descendants of Romanised Dacians, despite their predominantly Latin language, has a twofold weakness. First, there is no trace of them, unlike the Slavs, in early place names; second, they were Orthodox Christians, whereas there is no trace of a large Orthodox community in the written and archaeological evidences of the region from before the thirteenth century. The Romanians were largely shepherds and thus good warriors, employed as frontier guards by Hungarian kings, and contributed to the increasing ethno-cultural colourfulness of the kingdom.

Hungarian society, rather amorphous and ethnically mixed as it was, seems to have lived in relatively prosperous conditions, if we may believe a few contemporary accounts by foreign authors. Otto, Bishop of Freising as well as Abu-Hamíd, a Moslem traveller from Granada, visited the country around 1150, and in the same period Idrísí, the court geographer of King Roger II of Sicily, also reported on it in his famous description of the world on the basis of first-hand reports, probably of Italian merchants. Whether hostile or sympathetic towards the country and its inhabitants, the land is described by all of them as one of plenty and prosperity: cheap corn, rich gold mines, busy fairs, affluent inhabitants. While exaggerated and generalised, this image might not be entirely out of touch with reality. It was certainly a great advantage that Hungary, then as later, suffered relatively little from famine, which regularly inflicted the population of Western Europe. The reason was, besides a relatively sparse population and abundant natural resources, her far greater reliance on stockbreeding and fishing, which were less dependent on the whims of weather than the cultivation of the land.

By and large, the peculiarity of the social situation of the eleventh and twelfth centuries consisted in the fact that whereas the traditional distinction between freedom and serfhood depended on birth, now one's position in the emerging manorial system became the decisive criterion, without the relations that arose within this new framework again being consolidated into hereditary terms. Both in the temporal and the spatial aspect, as we have seen, this was a transitory state, to which the ambivalent nature of political institutions and techniques, and cultural trends corresponded. The majority of landed property in the kingdom still being in the possession of the king, royal authority was preponderant in twelfth-century Hungary. According to the (alas, somewhat doubtful) testimony of a Paris manuscript around 1185, the king's revenues – from the monopolies on precious metals, on coinage (lawful and 'debased') and on salt, from customs on fairs and river tolls and taxes from the counties – equalled and perhaps surpassed those of his French and English colleagues. To be sure, the patrimonial basis of the economic power of the latter was far from being the same as that of the King of Hungary, which undermines the basis of comparison. Nevertheless, even when considered in isolation, the report indicates the efficient functioning of the system of royal counties, the chief units of administration, of levying taxes and of raising troops in the country. The military force from the counties alone might in this period amount to 30,000; the troops of the King of Hungary were 'innumerable', wrote Abu-Hamíd. Major decisions were still made by the king upon consultation with the royal council consisting of prelates, court office holders and the *ispáns* of the counties, a body of considerable and indefinite size, which, however, hardly ever convened in full number because of the constant movement of the royal household from manor to manor.

At the same time, the use of written documents spread in governance and administration as slowly as in ordinary legal affairs. Verbal agreement and arrangements witnessed and administered by the bailiff in common lawsuits or in mere contracts, and political decisions sanctioned by the authority of courtly memory alone, rather than by officially sealed charters, survived well into the twelfth century. A few official documents were irregularly issued by the priests of the court chapel until, in the second half of the twelfth century – tradition attributes it to King Béla III who in a charter of 1181 emphasised the indispensability of the use of writing – the chancellery arose. Following this example, from about 1200 private individuals soon began to have their own transactions, agreements or arrangement recorded and preserved at the peculiar institution of the 'place of authentication' (*hiteleshely*): an office with notarial functions, usually at chapter houses, abbeys or provostships.

Even this modicum of the alphabetisation of political and legal culture would have been inconceivable without increasing familiarity with western learning through diplomatic and commercial ties as well as academic peregrination. Luke, Archbishop of Esztergom after 1158, attended *the studium generale* in Paris as early as 1150. In 1177, the Abbot of Saint-Geneviève in Paris reported to Béla III the death of a Hungarian student called Bethlehem, who studied at the university there in the company of three of his countrymen, Hadrian, Michael and James; we also know by name 'Nicholas of Hungary', an early student of remote Oxford in the early 1190s; and we know of many other clerics who also studied in Paris, or from a little later on in Bologna or Padova, which were especially popular among Hungarian students into the early modern period.

These clerics, as well as the knights arriving in the retinue of queens from western dynasties, were also instrumental in introducing courtly and chivalric culture in Hungary. The Provençal troubadour Peire Vidal and the German Tannhäuser were welcome visitors in the court of King Imre in the early thirteenth century. The virtues of the knights of the Holy Grail, the valour of the Nibelungs, the mixture of gallantry and devoutness displayed by the troubadours thus became models for young Hungarian nobles; indeed, several Hungarian aristocrats received in baptism the names of the celebrated Frankish heroes Roland and Oliver as well as Alexander or Philip of Macedon, who also became idolised in the chivalric ethos. They were also presented an account in their own vernacular of one of the favourite readings of contemporary knights, the Trojan War, and the names of Achilles, Priam or Hector survive to this day in place names like Ecsellő, Perjámos and Iktár. The author of the

Latin original of this account might have been no other than the enigmatic 'Magister P.', also referred to as Anonymus, who himself probably
studied in France, before becoming the notary of King Béla (probably
the third of this name) and rising to fame through his *Gesta Hungarorum* (c. 1210): a chivalric romance of the Hungarian conquest of the
Carpathian Basin in which the adoption of Christianity is an undercurrent when compared to the knightly exploits of the chiefs from whom
the contemporary noble houses were supposed to have descended. Of
the orders of knighthood, the Hospitallers and the Knights Templars
appeared in Hungary before the mid-twelfth century, while the Teutonic Order was invited by Andrew II in 1211 for purposes of defence
and to convert the pagan Cumans.

Despite the 'chivalric awakening', the outlook of literature and culture in general was predominantly ecclesiastic. Codices recording legends of saints, rites and monastery annuals of Benedictine abbeys constitute the bulk of this heritage. Besides the Benedictines, the representatives of the reform movement within traditional monasticism, the Cistercians and the Premonstratensians, first arrived in Hungary in the
1140s, and after 1220, the impact of Dominican friars was also added.
The conspicuously early appearance of the the latter as well as the Franciscans in Hungary was probably owing to the fact that it was a suitable
basis for proselytising missions, an important task of the mendicant orders. Education, as a matter of fact, was also a monopoly of the Church.
There were no seats of higher learning in the country, and even secondary education – restricted in principle to the 'seven liberal arts', in fact
even further to Latin grammar, prosody, rhetoric and 'arithmetic' (little
more than familiarity with the church calendar) – was only available in
schools maintained by the more important chapter houses and monasteries. It was only in the most prestigious school of Veszprém that law
was also taught besides the liberal arts. The late twelfth century was a
period of fermentation in architectural styles as well: though the high
Romanesque of late eleventh century Lombard examples, whose most
splendid accomplishments in Hungary were the Cathedral of Pécs and
the Basilica of Székesfehérvár, was still dominant, French master build-
ers arriving around 1190 at Esztergom launched the first workshop of
Gothic in Central Europe.

Besides the ecclesiastical and secular versions of Christian culture,
the heritage of the pagan period survived only in verbal tradition. Folk
tales have preserved a great many motifs, such as the sky-high tree or
shamans fighting in the guise of animals; legendary stories of the migrations and the 'adventures' (that is, the plundering raids) like that of the
mythical hind, or the horn of Lél with which the chief defeated at
Augsburg hit the German warlord to death, or the axe of the warrior

Botond that struck a hole on the gate of Costantinople, were passed down in minstrels' songs before they found their way into chronicles. It was in the minstrels' tunes, too, that the ancient pentatonic structure was preserved through folk music, to be rediscovered in the twentieth century by Bartók and Kodály.

After this general survey of the social and cultural condition of Hungary in the twelfth and the early thirteenth centuries, let us turn back to the political history of the same period, by the end of which the system created by Stephen I started to change. It was an era in which periods of powerful central government alternated with those of shaken royal authority, caused either by conflicts over succession or aristocratic factions. In the first decades of the period the country also quite frequently faced Byzantine and, to a lesser extent, German interference with its affairs, not so much because of internal weakness but because strife within the House of Árpád supplied the pretext and opportunity for two outstanding emperors, Manuel Komnenos and Frederick Barbarossa, to attempt to bring it within their spheres of influence.

Coloman's son, the restless Stephen II (1116–1131), fought a war in nearly each year of his reign. Dalmatia was lost to Venice, then recovered and lost again; unsuccessful wars against neighbours including Bohemia, Russia and Byzantium made a group of barons attempt to depose him, which he survived, but leaving no heir, he was succeeded by the blinded son of Prince Álmos, Béla II (1131–1141). The chief events of this reign were the ruthless showdown with those held responsible for his and his father's suffering, and the defeat of the pretender Boris, who was the son of Coloman's Russian wife expelled because of adultery, and invited to the country by the remnants of the opposition to Béla's rule. Although Boris tried to assert his claim with German and then Byzantine aid even under Géza II (1141–1162), these efforts failed, and the cleansing of the 1130s seems to have consolidated central power to such an extent that both Otto of Freising and Abu-Hamíd wrote very highly of the authority of the King of Hungary. Géza was certainly powerful enough to afford, in the early 1150s, pursuing an aggressive foreign policy and waging a two-front war against Byzantium and in Russia, while also being on hostile terms with the Holy Roman Empire and its vassals.

However, whereas these adventures brought no effective gains, they put the hard-won internal unity at risk. Opinions about the country's proper foreign policy orientation were divided, and the king's neglected brothers sought refuge and assistance as pretenders first at the court of Barbarossa, then in Byzantium. The reign of Géza's son, Stephen III (1162–1172), was in fact a decade of strife over the succession between him and his uncles, who were also crowned as Ladislas II (1162–1163) and Stephen IV (1163–1165) and, after both of them died, against Manuel, who had supported them. The title of Stephen III was finally acknowledged by the Byzantine Emperor in return for taking the king's young brother Béla, Duke of Dalmatia and Croatia, to Constantinople – rebaptised as Alexios, hostage, client and prospective heir to the childless Emperor, who might once unite Byzantium and Hungary under a single crown.

This never came true. In 1169, Manuel's son was born, and the Emperor immediately dropped the plan of marrying his daughter to Béla/Alexios and making him succeed in Constantinople; nevertheless, Manuel supported the Hungarian prince in obtaining the throne of Hungary when it became vacant in 1172. Having overcome the resistance of the Church – whose head, Archbishop Luke, a Hungarian counterpart of Thomas Becket, took a strongly papalist side in the renewed debate between secular and spiritual power, and was afraid of an Orthodox influence upon the accession of a prince brought up in Byzantium – Béla III (1172–1196) ruled over a Kingdom of Hungary at the height of its power during the Árpád period. He was certainly superbly qualified: in Constantinople, his natural talents were refined by education in the ancient craft and secrets of rulership. By 1180, when his one-time patron Manuel died, Béla suppressed all internal opposition, waylaid the schemes of his rival younger brother Géza to the throne and quelled the and resentment of ecclesiastical lords over the issue of investiture. In 1106, Coloman had formally relinquished the right of investing prelates, but in practice the kings' nominees were usually obediently elected by the cathedral chapters and confirmed in their offices by the popes; kings occasionally also deposed bishops. Nevertheless, the Church jealously preserved a considerable degree of autonomy, to the extent that it became one of the chief vehicles of the development towards the system of estates.

The consolidation under Béla's reign was largely due to the increase of royal revenues and the growth of the chancellery, which have already been referred to. I have also mentioned the rise of chivalric culture in this period in Hungary, which certainly owed a great deal to the facts that the knightly code of honour was adopted from the West in the court of the innovative Manuel where Béla had been educated, and that his second wife was the French Princess Margaret, daughter of King Louis VII. The Hungarian 'knights' of Béla recovered Dalmatia and Syrmia from Byzantium, and though his conquests in Galicia and Serbia were short-lived, the fact that he assumed the role of a mediator in the conflict of the German and Byzantine Emperors occasioned by the march of the crusaders of Frederick Barbarossa across the East Roman Empire in 1190, and the dynastic links established with Byzantium, France, Germany and Aragon during his reign, demonstrate the international importance of Hungary in this period.

Béla's successors continued a warlike foreign policy towards the east and the south, enjoying the encouragement and sometimes the support of the Popes against Orthodox Russia and Serbia, pagan 'Cumania' (the steppe between the lower Danube and the Volga) and Bosnia, the land of Bogumil heresy. The difficulties they had to face within the country, however, prevented them from achieving lasting results. For Imre (1196–1204) it was the three revolts of his brother, Andrew, that made the Hungarian hinterland insecure. Upon Imre's death, Andrew still became the guardian of his infant nephew, King Ladislas III (1204–1205), and was certainly not distressed when the latter died, too, and he inherited the throne as Andrew II (1205–1235). It was amidst the sociopolitical turmoil during his reign that the relations, arrangements, institutional framework and social categories that arose under Stephen I, started to disintegrate in the higher echelons of society.

It has been mentioned that until the age of Béla III the main characteristic of the political system was royal preponderance, and the country's elite was confined to ecclesiastical and secular office holders (prelates, court officials, governors of provinces like the *voevodes* of Transylvania or the *bans* of the southern provinces, and the *ispáns* of the counties). The only persons who had a say in policy-making as members of the royal council, they were, in western style, increasingly referred to as 'barons', even though neither their office nor the title was inheritable or even necessarily for life. At the same time, during their tenure they enjoyed special revenues and privileges in return for their services – a portion of the incomes from the territories administered by them and the right to lead troops to the field under their own banner. These traditions were subverted by the 'new arrangements' (*novae institutiones*) introduced in the relationship between the monarch and his barons under Andrew II, urged by his adherents who wanted to establish their power on a more permanent footing. Whereas earlier that power had been based on incomes for the services rendered and was thus revocable, the king now started to distribute the royal estates that belonged to the castles among his followers 'in perpetuity', for the enjoyment of themselves and their progeny.

The dimensions of the transformation were immense: the structure of noble estates in medieval and early modern Hungary came into existence within this short period. It must be noted that the new system had little to do with vassalage, since the lands thus allocated were not fiefs dependent on future service, but hereditary estates, the unconditional rewards of past loyalty. Similarly, the peculiar Hungarian type of late medieval retinue, the system of *familiaritas* that arose subsequent to these changes (in its fully fledged shape, by the fourteenth century) was a fairly distant relative of western vassalage. The *familiaris* who undertook to render civil and/or military service to a baron socially far superior to him was an independent landholder whose estate was not affected by his 'servile' (*serviens*) status. On the other hand, the western ritual of the act of enfeoffment that emphasised the 'equality of the unequal', of lord and vassal, were also missing from Hungarian practice, demonstrating that the *familiaris* was considered inferior both in principle and in fact.

The motives of Andrew II are still less than sufficiently clear, though the circumstances of his accession certainly dictated him the need to consolidate the loyalty of a group of influential subjects. In this he succeeded. At the same time, the new policy was not a mere matter of political tactics but a consciously designed reform programme; the growth of a self-conscious, hereditary secular aristocracy of magnates indeed made the outlook of Hungarian society more 'western', and the ambition to establish the royal treasury more firmly on the basis of incomes from emerging market relations than on manorial revenues was also 'modern'. The accumulation of private latifundia and the growth of a money economy and urbanisation were recognisable trends in the contemporary West.

However, the King set to the task with all the heedlessness that characterised him. As a result, royal power suffered in the long run, and Andrew II himself was permanently annoyed by protest from different corners of society. Even Hungarian beneficiaries of the system resented the favours rendered to the courtiers and relatives who swarmed into the country with Andrew's German wife Gertrude, who was assassinated in 1213 – the grand theme of József Katona's 'national drama' *Bánk bán* (Ban [here: Palatine] Bánk, 1818) and Ferenc Erkel's opera of the same title (1861). Frequent wars that brought little actual benefit to Hungary also undermined Andrew II's support: most notably, during his crusade of 1217–1218, a group of magnates rebelled against Archbishop John, whom the King appointed to rule the country during his absence.

From 1220 on, Andrew was repeatedly compelled to promise to abandon his policies and revise earlier donations. Of the many opposition movements the most important was that of the so-called royal *servientes*. 'Servants' by name, they were in fact the freest agents in a society where even the relatively independent *jobbágy* warriors were highplaced subjects within the manorial system; the *servientes* themselves were landlords, small or great, and possessed subjects, few or many, and called themselves 'servants of the king' because it was *only* to the king that they owed service and obedience – not as their landlord but as the ruler of the country. To put it in yet another way, they were the highly differentiated class of independent landholders who were not barons and felt their status threatened by the new developments. Many of them started to style themselves '*de genere*', that is to say, traced their families from an ancient chief or the acquirer of the family estates in early times, with the implication that they were entitled to participate in decision-making processes just as well as the barons.

In 1222, the country-wide movement of the *servientes* compelled Andrew II to issue the famous Golden Bull, sometimes mentioned as a counterpart of the English *Magna Carta* of 1215. Most of its thirty articles concerned the encroachment of the king and his barons and the unlawfulness of these as well as the alienation of large royal estates, but the ones most important for posterity decreed the uniform rights and privileges of the nobility: the exemption from taxes and from quartering troops, from the jurisdiction of others than the king and the palatine, the freedom of the *servientes* from harassment by the barons, the requirement of a legal warrant to detain them, etc. An additional clause invested the secular and ecclesiastical lords with a right of resistance in case the aforementioned were violated by the king; a clause rarely invoked during the rest of the Middle Ages, but all the more often during the long period of Hungary's association with the House of Habsburg. However much a mere plot the movement of the *servientes*, and however rudimentary the Golden Bull was, these were the beginnings of a process in which the idea of *communitas regni* became influential in Hungary and an estates based parliamentarism developed, and groups outside the royal council had access to policy-making (for the first time at the assembly of 1277).

The short term impact of the movement, however, was meagre, and a true revision of Andrew's policies did not occur before he was succeeded by his son, Béla IV (1235–1270). Rather impatiently, Béla set to stop the dissolution of the system based on castles and royal counties, and his authoritarian style made him many an enemy at the worst of all times, on the eve of the Mongol invasion of Hungary.

The first reports about the real dimensions of the threat of the Mongol expansion, started under Dzhingis Khan (1206–1227) from the heart of Asia, reached Hungary through the Dominican friar Julian who set out with three companions in 1235 in search for the relatives of Hungarians left behind east of the Volga in *Magna Hungaria*. They did find a group of Magyar speakers, and in 1237 set out on a second journey to convert them to Christianity. However, this expedition was halted, and the eastern Magyars annihilated by the armies of Batu Khan, which also conquered Kiev in 1240 and compelled the Cumans of the steppe to seek refuge in Hungary. The appearance of the nomadic Cumans caused suspicion and only increased the tensions in a country torn by internal strife; incompetent command in the face of the nomadic military tactics once employed by the Hungarian raiders in Western Europe but forgotten by their thirteenth-century descendants, only contributed to the disastrous defeat of the Hungarian army in the battle of Muhi in northeastern Hungary on April 11, 1241. Béla IV narrowly escaped and fled as far as Dalmatia while Frederick 'the Warlike', Duke of Austria, whom he solicited for help, occupied three western counties while the Mongols ravaged the rest of the kingdom.

The Mongol campaign was probably only meant to prepare the ground for the future conquest of Hungary, for the hordes left the country after twelve months. Even so, they caused immense devastation. At least fifteen to twenty per cent of the population fell victim to the Mongol invasion and the famine that followed it. If not completely destroyed, as laconically reported by Abbot Hermann in the annals of the German monastery of Niederalteich, Hungary had to be rebuilt literally from the ashes, and it never became the same as it had been before.

4. Hungary's second founding and the last of the House of Árpád

The shock of the Mongol invasion taught Béla IV a bitter lesson. As 'junior king' beside his father since 1220 (a tradition under the Árpád dynasty in Hungary) and in the first years of his reign, his opposition to the 'superfluous and useless donations' that helped the aristocracy to gain preponderance in the government of the country, turned to mere conservatism: the desire to restore the *status* of the kingdom to what it had been in the times of 'King Béla [III] of blessed memory'. However, the institutional basis of that *status*, the royal county, was archaic by the second third of the thirteenth century. The more dynamic elite of the *jobbágy* warriors who were its constitutive element from the social and military point of view, started to proclaim themselves as royal *servientes*; their claims unacknowledged and given no free rein, they were not yet an efficient military force, just as the remaining county warriors were no longer one. The Mongol experience dramatically demonstrated this. It was only the heavy cavalry of the court knights, the type of army that might have been expected to be raised by a strong and loyal aristocracy of magnates, that fought with any effect against the invaders. It was as a result of the contradictory policies of the decades before the Mongol invasion that Hungarian military potential was paralysed precisely at the time when it was most needed. Finally, part of the lesson was that prop-

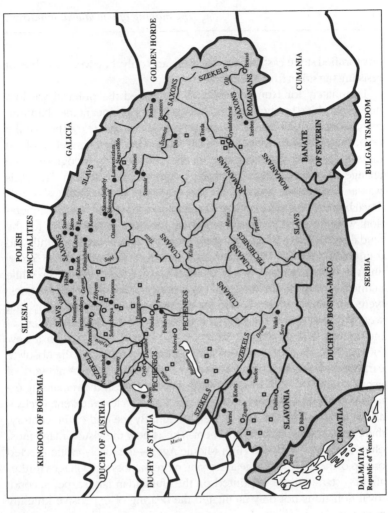

3. Hungary, her neighbours, dependencies and the network of privileged settlements in the late thirteenth century

- town with royal charter
○ jurisdictional self-government
□ privileged settlement of foreign settlers (*hospes*)

erly fortified stone castles were capable, and only they were capable, of resisting the storm from the steppe.

Fortunately for Hungary, Béla IV possessed the political wisdom needed to abide by such lessons, which in his case meant the abandonment, after 1242, of his earlier conservatism and the 'revocation of the revocations' of donations early in his reign. Also, the experience of the disaster lessened the arrogance of the nobles who, recognising the change in the king's attitudes, made a compromise with him. True, this was an ambiguous process, for the powerful descendants of Béla's 'loyal barons', 'the pillars of the kingdom' in the second or third generation, were the territorial lords who bore the main responsibility for the feudal anarchy into which Hungary fell at the turn of the thirteenth and fourteenth centuries. Up to the 1260s, however, the Csák, Aba, Kőszegi and the other baronial clans later notorious for their unruliness, while taking advantage of the renewed royal policy of lavish grants of estates, were not merely accumulating for themselves and their progeny, but were also partners of the king in reconstructing the defence system of the country and placing its structure of political authority on a new footing. First, they followed the royal example of replacing the obsolete earthworks from the times of Stephen I with stone castles. A network of nearly a hundred such modern fortifications arose in the remaining estates of the king and those of the secular and, to a lesser extent, ecclesiastical landlords by the end of Béla's reign. By the end of the century, there were several hundred of them. This is how the visual image most often associated with the High Middle Ages – the lordly castle erected on top of the hill, the village at its foot, more manors and villages further afield – started to be imprinted on the Hungarian landscape. Second, royal donations not only facilitated the bearing of expensive knightly armament for a far broader segment of society, but the grantees were also ready to place their arms as well as, in the case of the really mighty, those of the increasing number of their *familiares*, at the disposal of the king.

I have already mentioned a few differences between the system that prevailed in medieval Hungary and western vassalage. Let it be stressed here again that the charters conferring land on new lords merely stipulated the inalienability of the land and the 'loyalty' of the grantee in general, but no clearly defined obligations were involved. As often in Hungarian history, arrangements depended on uncodified consensus, rather than properly institutionalised forms. Specific military service depended on 'the pleasure' (in other words, the whim) of those concerned, but during most of Béla's reign it generally 'pleased' the barons to render it, and so the foundations of a new military system were laid. To supplement the regular army of the knights with efficient nomad style light cavalry, Béla IV re-invited the Cumans and settled them in the Great Plain. To seal the precarious friendship, the Cuman Princess Elisabeth was married to Béla's eldest son, Stephen. As part of the defence strategy, the King also married his other children to the offspring of neighbouring princes to ensure their assistance if needed.

After the depopulation caused by the Mongol invasion, the Cumans were not the only settlers arriving in the country. Indeed, Hungary became the target of an extensive movement of German *hospites* or guests', greatly encouraged by the king who settled them in the royal manors of the northern areas and endowed them with privileges, and an even greater influx of Slavs and Vlachs (Romanians) from the north and the south-east. Besides, Béla's reign is also remarkable because of the first attempt at a well-considered policy directed to the development of towns by conferring rights of self-government on them. As in the West, the procedure was to extend the privileges of a 'mother town' to the new community. The Hungarian model was the 'law of Fehérvár (that is, Székesfehévár)', a set of privileges very extensive by European Standards. Those settlements which enjoyed it became autonomous communities completely immune from the jurisdiction of the *ispán* or others, themselves collecting the taxes and duties they owed the king in an annual lump sum, even electing, besides the civil magistrate, their own parish priests. The twenty-odd towns thus 'emancipated' under Béla IV and the privileged *hospes* villages became increasingly important sources of income, making up for the revenue lost by the disintegration of the royal county system that resulted from the land donations, and supplementing the more traditional ones whose levying was reformed in a way that foreshadowed the great changes in economic policy under the Angevins in the following century.

The Kingdom of Hungary, thanks to the efforts of Béla, recovered its strength in a surprisingly short time, and though the 'Mongol terror' returned to haunt in the country nearly every other year for over a decade, a second invasion only came long after the death of Béla IV, in 1285, when it was easily repelled. As early as in 1269, as the Neapolitan legate reported from Hungary, the power of the king was 'incredible', and his neighbours did not dare to move in the face of his armies. In the south, Hungarian overlordship was consequently extended beyond the River Sava. However, Béla's ambition to acquire Austria was thwarted by Ottokar II, under whom Bohemian power in Central Europe rose and fell like a comet. A duchy since 1156, Austria was ruled along with Styria by the Babenberg family whose last member Frederick, Béla's old rival, died in 1246 in a battle fought between the two rulers. Béla was at war against Ottokar for four years before, in 1254, they divided the Babenberg possessions. A few years later, Prince Stephen was appointed as governor of Southern Styria, a region gained from the deal, but in 1260 the local lords rebelled, and appealed to Ottokar, who defeated the Hungarian army. In the peace of Vienna in 1261 Béla abandoned his claims to both provinces, and even married one of his granddaughters to Ottokar, who became the most powerful ruler of the region for a short while.

It was after this failure that the internal unity forged in the wake of the disaster of 1241–1242 started to dissolve. The pattern was the familiar one of family strife: Stephen, having been ousted from Styria, might have been dissatisfied with Transylvania being allocated to him, and after the ensuing war between father and son, the country was divided, Stephen acquiring the territories of the one-time ducal province as 'junior king' in 1262. This was fuel to baronial faction: two rulers meant two sets of offices, as well as bargains offered and desertions from both sides. Stephen pursued his own foreign policy as well, making war in the Balkans and forging an alliance in 1269 with Charles of Anjou, fresh on the throne of Naples, marrying his son to the latter's granddaughter and his daughter to the heir to the Neapolitan throne. Besides, and largely in response to, the increasing unruliness of the barons, the noble estate newly emerging out of the class of *servientes* also voiced their claims, namely, the confirmation of the privileges acquired in the Golden Bull and the consolidation of their property rights, which they were granted at the Esztergom assembly of 1267. With the demand that an annual meeting of deputies of the 'noble colleges' of each county should convene to discuss the affairs of the kingdom, the charter of 1267 is an important step in the development towards the rise of noble self-government, the 'noble county' as well as estates based parliamentariansm.

It was by the same period, the last third of the thirteenth century, that the stratification of society into freemen and servants, with a great variety of 'blurred' categories between them, became, through a process of polarisation, replaced by the dominant distinction between noble landholders and peasant serfs. The stages in the rise of a noble class with uniform legal status have been discussed. The condition of the peasantry was not yet regulated by uniform legal arrangements, yet the great number of individual contracts drawn between landlords and peasant communities at 'places of authentication' from the 1260s point in the same direction. Through the acquisition of liberties earlier restricted to *hospites*, the mere 'people' of the land started to emerge as 'free serfs' enjoying some degree of autonomy within the village, free to move and owing more or less uniform dues and services to the landlord.

The short reign of Stephen V (1270–1272) was already marked by the struggle of baronial parties that tore the country apart during the fol- .

lowing decades, an anarchy which the king's earlier conduct had done much to precipitate. The stability created under Béla IV became relative and then non-existent as one of the factions first invited Ottokar against the king, and then took his son and heir, still a child, as hostage. Stephen's premature death and the accession of the ten year old Ladislas IV (1272–1290) thwarted all hopes of the restoration of order. During the royal minority, civil war raged in the country between the parties led by the Csák and the Kőszegi clan.

In 1277, upon the initiative of the episcopacy, an assembly of prelates, a few barons, noblemen and Cumans was convened at the field of Rákos, near Pest, to seek a way out of the crisis. This meeting had a sequel in 1298 and the ensuing years, but in the decades of strong central power under the Anjous it declined, and only became indispensable in the fifteenth century. Yet, initiated by the ecclesiastical intelligentsia familiar with up-to-date legal scholarship from their studies at Bologna, it was the first beginning of parliamentariansm, of the idea that not merely the royal council but all 'members' of the *communitas regni* were entitled to take part in political decision-making. This was a rather early development by international standards, but with the significant difference from western counterparts that in Hungary the chartered towns were missing from the communities represented in the early diets.

The meeting also declared that the king had come of age and obliged him to set all his power against those guilty of the breach of peace. Ladislas did his best to do so. Having defeated the Geregye clan in the east, he allied himself with Rudolph of Habsburg, the new German king, against Ottokar, who supported the Kőszegis in West-Hungary. The defeat and death of the Czech king in the battle of Dürnkrut in 1278 put an end to the imperial pretensions of the Přemyslids and established those of the Habsburgs, who now became Hungary's neighbours.

Ironically, it was after these minor successes achieved against the forces of disintegration that, after so many appeals from Hungarian prelates, the Pope sent a legate, as much to help consolidation in the country as to interfere with its internal affairs. In the temporary abatement of tensions, the legate's attention turned (and probably *was* turned) towards the nomadic and pagan Cumans, from whom the king descended on the maternal line and who were his firm supporters, but represented an anomaly within a settled Christian society. The affair smacked of *Kulturkampf*, and the king, forced into a space with little room to manoeuvre, though twice compelled to disavow his Cumans, avoided humiliation by committing himself on the side of the only force still loyal to him. He came to be disparagingly referred to as 'Ladislas the Cuman', he was excommunicated in 1287, and even a crusade was contemplated against him. Before that could have taken place, he was assassinated.

In 1290, when this occurred, there was no longer a central government in Hungary, and it was doubted in many corners whether Andrew of Venice, allegedly a grandson of Andrew II, was a lawful heir. Yet he was prepared to take over from Ladislas even before the latter was killed. When 'the last golden bough' of the House of Árpád was crowned as Andrew III (1290–1301), the barons expected him to acknowledge the standing they had acquired, whereas the church and the nobility extorted a new type of document from him: the coronation diploma (*hitlevél*), obliging the ruler to observe the laws of the kingdom and the liberties of the nobility, which became a standard practice from the fifteenth century onwards. Andrew was also required by the nobles to commit himself to wiping out anarchy by destroying fortifications erected without permission, by recovering lands taken by force of arms and convening an annual assembly or diet to ensure stable government.

Relying on reforms designed to consolidate the structures of vassalage and the participation of the estates, Andrew managed, by the end of his reign, achieve some stability in his government and compel some of the barons to temporary compromises. On the whole, he was still unable to overcome the separatism of the oligarchs who ruled as kings in their provinces: members of the Kőszegi clan, who explicitly refused to acknowledge his title, in the West, László Kán in Transylvania, Amadé Aba and Kopasz ('the Bald') Borsa in the northeast, and – not to speak of their lesser fellows – the mightiest of all, Máté Csák, in fourteen counties with over fifty fortresses and five-hundred villages in the northwest of the country. Andrew was even handicapped in his struggle against the barons by his own contested title. An adventurer pretending to be the brother of Ladislas IV was easily expelled from the country, but in 1300 the Croatian barons invited the Neapolitan pretender, Charles Robert of Anjou. He was waiting for his turn in Dalmatia when Andrew died heirless nearly on the third centenary of the coronation of Saint Stephen, on January 14, 1301. A twelve year old boy at the time, it was to be this Italian prince who subdued the forces of anarchy let loose by the disappearance of the last semblance of central authority, after the wars against rival claimants had been fought during an interregnum of seven years.

CHAPTER III

GOLDEN AGES AND DECLINE (1301–1526)

As a result of the development that Hungary, along with her northern neighbours, had undergone by the late thirteenth century, the late Middle Ages and the Renaissance were periods in which her embeddedness in the civilisation of Western Christianity asserted itself in peculiar, ambiguous, often contradictory ways and processes. In terms of political and ecclesiastical organisation, and overwhelmingly in terms of cultural outlook as well, the country could be strictly distinguished from the Orthodox lands that lay east and southeast of it. Unlike the small kingdoms of the Balkans, which had been in a state of constant flux until their elimination by the Ottoman expansion in the fourteenth century, and even unlike the more powerful but still quite frequently disintegrating and reintegrating Kievan state, her permanence and integrity symbolised by the notion of the Holy Crown of Saint Stephen, the *regnum Hungariae* was a sound political unit with clearly definable and more or less stable boundaries, which helped her to survive the blows of the Mongol invasion, the extinction of the House of Árpád and the rage of baronial faction that went with it. The idea, if not the precise shape, of the organisation and the exercise of authority as a network of legally privileged bodies, the *communitas regni*, was also recognisably 'western'. The same could be said about ecclesiastical lords being mighty politicians and owners – though technically merely administrators – of great wealth in Hungary as in the whole of the Occident, while subject to the supreme authority of the Pope; unlike in Orthodoxy, where the patriarch of Constantinople was merely the first among equal heads of national Churches, but bishops remained integrated in monasticism, and even when at court, they rarely addressed questions associated with matters other than belief. Also, whereas charters and diplomas continued to be issued on rare and solemn occasions in the Balkans and the Russian states, the use of written documents by private individuals as well as the ever more sophisticated administrative and jurisdictional institutions proliferated in Hungary. Having been decimated by Tartar and Turkish pillages, only about 300,000 documents are extant from the period before 1526 – a figure relatively unimpressive in the light of the millions preserved in France or England, but one which suggest a difference in kind rather than number when compared to the mere hundreds from the Balkan countries.

The impression that by the late Middle Ages Hungary had made up for her disadvantage *vis-à-vis* the West might even be strengthened by the contemplation of the fact that whereas the fourteenth century is supposed to have been a period of profound 'crisis' in Western Europe, it was, by and large, one of economic prosperity and political stability in Hungary, again in tandem with Bohemia and Poland. Upon closer scrutiny, this image proves false: to put it simply, Hungary remained unaffected by the crisis precisely because it was also unaffected by important aspects of the development that occasioned it in the West. The crisis was one of hyperbolic growth, and is now considered as a series of birth pangs of the modernity that Europe's dynamism between the sixteenth and twentieth centuries rested upon. Its chief symptoms were overpopulation checked by the demographic disaster of famines and epidemics; horrible peasant *jacqueries* and devastating international wars; the relative impoverishment of nobles and the decline of ecclesiastical authority; liquidity crises and bankruptcies of commercial and banking enterprises. In general, it was associated with the disarray of the traditional division of society into knights, priests and peasants, secure and predictable as it was in its strictness; in one way or another, the symptoms all resulted from the growing circulation and importance of money, the cash relationship replacing relations of legal dependence.

In other words, the vehicle of the changes – the catalyst of the crisis as well as of the later recovery – was the rapid urbanisation of the continent. In German-speaking Europe, for instance, before 1200 and after 1300 the number of cities founded was usually under 50 per decade; between those years, that figure several times exceeded 100 and once even 250 per decade. Also, the urban centres of the late medieval West were of a new type: besides the long-distance trade of luxury articles, they became seats of capital formation to supply the needs of a growing industry, producing mainly textiles for a growing internal market.

Hungary lacked such catalysts, both of crisis and recovery. As we have seen, urbanisation started relatively late, and remained long confined, in the hands of largely foreign merchants, to luxury goods provided for the only groups that possessed the means of conspicuous consumption: the royal court and the aristocracy. As all generalisations, this is, of course, a simplified image: especially in western and northern Hungary as well as in Transylvania, there were quite a few urban settlements with prosperous local industry and patterns of production that resembled the western model of the putting-out system. Still, despite the policies of several kings who for one reason or another lent their favours to urban communities, the overall image is one of weak industrialisation and capital formation. The Kingdom of Hungary might be affluent, in a certain sense maybe the richest country of the continent, her gold mines supplying the mints and treasuries of all Europe. The wealth, and sometimes the centralised political command and military strength of Hungarian monarchs might also surpass that of many a western counterpart, as in the case of King Matthias in the fifteenth century, who also maintained a lavish renaissance court. But when, around 1500, the next period of ferment in European economic and social progress was inaugurated, Hungary's geographical location – her exposure to Ottoman expansion and her exclusion from direct overseas intercourse – was not the primary cause of her dramatic decline. It only aggravated the disadvantage stemming from a Janus-faced development, and the very incompleteness of structures that helped her to evade the worst difficulties experienced by her western neighbours before 1450, became accentuated and revealed its true character after 1500, with a lasting impact on the whole of modern Hungarian history.

1. The Angevin monarchy

Charles Robert of Anjou, supported by Pope Boniface VIII and the southern barons, was invited into Hungary even before the death of Andrew III, and swiftly crowned thereafter, some time before May 1301. However, for nearly a decade he had to compete with rival pretenders to the throne of Hungary, and for two decades with the separatism of the territorial oligarchs. Initially, the two difficulties were combined. Upon the pretext that Charles's coronation was 'irregular' (having taken place not with the Holy Crown, and at Esztergom instead of Székesfehérvár, as tradition by then required), and apprehensive of influence from Rome, the majority of the secular and ecclesiastical lords invited another adolescent, Prince Venceslas of Bohemia, grand-grandson of a daughter of Béla IV, grandson of Ottokar, and later the last Přemysl ruler of Bohemia. Crowned 'properly', but deprived of the means to exercise any authority, he, along with the Holy Crown, was withdrawn from the country by his father King Venceslas II in 1304. When in the next year he inherited the throne of Bohemia, he renounced his claim in favour of his relative and ally Otto Wittelsbach of Bavaria, himself a grandson of Béla IV. Without much support in the country, the attempt of Otto, crowned at the end of 1305, was doomed to failure. He was expelled from Hungary by László Kán, the Voevode of Transylvania, who also took the coronation insignia and refused to surrender them until as late as 1310 to

Charles, whose growing support in the country could earn him no more than a second 'improper' coronation in 1309. The third coronation in 1310, regarding the place as well as the paraphernalia, was fully legitimate. What was disturbing was the absence of some of the mightiest of the king's subjects, the most powerful of the territorial lords, Máté Csák among them, foreshadowing another decade of contest, this time between the king and the oligarchs. As we have seen, the power of the latter did not emerge as a result of the extinction of the Árpád dynasty, but originated in the last decades of the thirteenth century, when royal authority was weak. Its bases were personal wealth and high political office (palatine, voevode, ban, *ispán*) exercised nominally on behalf of the ruler, but in reality often in open opposition to him; it combined the features of an overgrown manor and a provincial state-within-the-state with a tendency to independence. The oligarchs maintained courts with fully fledged office hierarchies replicating that of the king; they had themselves addressed *princeps* or *dux*; they sought dynastic links with foreign houses, forged diplomatic ties and fought international wars.

It took courage to embark on the unification of the country in the face of oligarchy; to have fought it successfully is a sure mark of statesmanship as well as military ability. Having set up his headquarters in Temesvár (Timişoara) in the south, whose lord Ugrin Csák was one of his earliest and firmest supporters, Charles managed to defeat his adversaries, who rarely united against him, one by one. The king being much younger than his challengers helped as well: control over Transylvania and the northern areas was secured by a quick reaction to the deaths of László Kán and Máté Csák in 1315 and 1321, respectively. The victory in the battle of Rozgony (Rozhanovce) in 1312 against Csák and the Aba clan of the northeast did not decide, it rather began everything; it also took the defeat of the Kőszegi clan in 1316, that of Palatine Kopasz Borsa in 1317, and the south-western Šubić and Babonić clans by 1323 to create the preconditions of the peaceful work of state-building and economic reform that marked the second half of the reign of Charles Robert.

It was symbolic of consolidation that in 1323 the court of Charles moved to Visegrád, in the heart of the country. A hall erected at the feet of the citadel by the 1330s became the permanent royal residence, to be replaced by splendid new palaces under Louis I and especially Sigismund of Luxemburg later in the century. Out of two decades of struggle, Charles Robert forged for himself a figure of considerable authority, which he exercised with circumspection as well as efficiency. He was careful to emphasise his descent from the House of Árpád (among other things, by combining the motives of the Árpád coat-of-arms with those of the Angevins in the new insignia), as well as the 'restoration of the ancient good condition' of the kingdom as his main intention, while a number of important changes inevitably occurred because of the manner in which he established himself on the throne, and there were a few administrative innovations as well.

In the course of the wars, most castles and manors in the country were transferred to different hands. The king retained enough of them to secure, similarly to the early Árpáds, the preponderance of royal estates in the country: at the end of the reign of his successor Louis I, over half of the castles (nearly 150) and fifteen to twenty percent of all landed property belonged to the king. The rest was allocated among nobles who had been loyal to Charles from the very beginning. The very few influential families of the previous era who were able to retain their weight now joined this new court aristocracy, which was, surprisingly enough, overwhelmingly of native origin: besides Hungarian families as the Lackfi, the Szécsényi, the Újlaki, the Garai and others, the only foreign line that became illustrious was the one established by Fülöp (Filippo) Druget, born in a southern Italian family of French origin, who arrived in Hungary in the retinue of Charles when both were children. To symbolise the solidarity between the king and this new aristocracy, in 1326 Charles Robert established the Order of Saint George, the first secular order of knights in Central Europe (of whose later functioning, however, we possess no evidence).

The new barons were unquestionably loyal indeed; in addition, their estates were insufficient bases to constitute a challenge to royal authority, even when supplemented by the incomes of the royal castles they administered as *ispáns* of the counties – a practice introduced by Charles Robert precisely to re-establish the prestige and power of the old royal county system in a period when the county was increasingly an institution dominated by the nobility through the enhanced role of the justices elected by them. Loyal service of the crown thus became the route of upward mobility, just as the system of *familiaritas* provided the lesser nobility with a chance for advancement in the service of the king's most powerful subjects, the court barons.

This was important cement for the new monarchy of the Angevins. Once this system of 'office fiefs' (*honor*) – rather old-fashioned as it was, reflecting the relatively underdeveloped nature of market relations in Hungary – was in operation, Charles could neglect convening diets, which the budding ideology of the estates required since the last Árpáds, and which he reluctantly did until his position was firm enough. He as well as his successor frequently claimed to rule, as the Sicilian tradition going back to Emperor Frederick II suggested, with 'the plenitude of power' (*plenitudo potestatis*), a claim which became increasingly plausible as his reign advanced in the light of the developments described above, and also because of reforms in the administration of justice and the issuing of charters. Charles Robert secured his own firm control over the royal courts through the choice of loyal chief justices, and by the reign of Louis I the palatine was also compelled to abandon court sessions in the counties and adjudicate upon matters falling within his province at the royal court. In 1317, the head of the court clergy, the *ispán* of the royal chapel (later also called 'secret chancellor') was authorised to use a new royal seal, that is, the monopoly of the chancellery to issue royal charters ceased; at the same time, its vice chancellor was also a close royal confidant.

Angevin political consolidation mainly rested on the combination of a skilful treatment of subordinates and a well-proportioned exertion of authority, while structural reorganisation remained of secondary importance. The case is somewhat different with the royal revenues. Due to the system of 'office fiefs' described above, the preponderance of royal castles and estates was of relatively little economic significance, however profound its political impact was. To supplement his income, Charles Robert rationalised and reformed the system of *regalia* consisting of direct and indirect taxes, levies and monopolies. Newly explored salt mines in Transylvania in the Anjou period soon became the most important source of revenue for Hungarian kings, who had a monopoly in its trade. The 'thirtieth' tax, mentioned sporadically in earlier sources, was now imposed on all foreign trade and collected with much greater rigour. In that foreign trade, Hungary's main export commodities, besides cattle, were precious metals: the main attraction of the Hungarian market for Italian and South German merchants, who supplied it with luxury articles, was gold and silver, of which Hungary became the known world's greatest producer after the discovery of the gold mines near Körmöcbánya (Kremnica) and Nagybánya (Baia Mare) in the 1320s. According to estimates, until the discovery of the New World Hungary supplied one-third of the world's production of precious metals, c. 5,000 pounds of gold and over 20,000 pounds of silver per year. Formerly, local landlords were hardly interested in exploring new sites, the king possessing a monopoly in the income from mines. From 1327 on, landlords were entitled to retain one-third of this income, which greatly stimulated production, even though most of the mines were still on the estates of the king. At the same time, traffic in unminted gold and silver now became a royal monopoly. The delivery of all precious metals to the royal chambers was to be the precondition of Charles's monetary reform: the issue of the golden florin, modelled on the Florentine *fiorino*, in 1326, with a stable value and a relatively stable exchange rate between it and the silver *denarius*. The annual renewal of money – the compulsory delivery of coins for reminting, a means for medieval monarchs to 'corrupt' them and to benefit thereby – was abandoned; to make up for the resulting loss of the 'profit of the chamber' (*lucrum camarae*), a new tax of 1/5 florin per year was levied on all serf households. The net result of these reforms was a sound treasury, an end to economic anarchy, and enhanced strength and international weight.

These were spectacular achievements, though, ironically, partly based on and facilitated by Hungary's relative underdevelopment. Charles Robert recognised that among the very few assets of the country it was its resources of precious metals that might help it to figure prominently in the international economy, and exploited that opportunity admirably. Nevertheless, Hungary's rather unfavourable place within that international economy as a market of mainly western products of industry and luxury articles offering in return little else than gold, silver, cattle and wine, could not be altered. Similarly, the fact that Hungary was saved from the worst shocks that afflicted contemporary Western Europe, such as the Black Death of 1348, was due to it being an 'empty' land, as reported by a French Dominican friar who travelled around Eastern Europe in 1308. Despite the continuing settlement into the virgin areas of eastern and northern Hungary (now Slovakia) of Slavs from Moravia, Poland and the Russian principalities, of Germans and of Romanians – encouraged by the Angevin kings through privileges –, population density remained under 10 per square kilometre even as late as the early fifteenth century. There were broad gaps in the network of urban settlements, especially in the Great Plain in the east, but in the south-west, too, there were entire counties without a single chartered town. Most of the latter were concentrated in the estates of the kings, who were keen enough to draw carefully selected settlements from the authority of the *ispán*, to endow them with self-government and other privileges (the right to hold country-wide fairs, the right of 'staple', that is, to tap transit trade, etc.), and to place them directly under royal jurisdiction (more precisely, the court of the lord chief treasurer). There were other towns where commercial routes intersected, and were important as bishops' sees as well, but in the lack of urban privileges and self-government they did not belong to the urban estate proper, which remained weak and uninfluential both as a social model and as a political force.

To be sure, the taxes of towns contributed handsomely to the fiscal strength of the Angevin kings, much needed to maintain an increasingly frequently employed armed force. According to tradition, Charles Robert introduced the 'banderial' organisation of the military in Hungary, that is, the great led their troops to war under their own flags (*banerium*). In fact, this practice was known in Hungary a century earlier, and the group of barons entitled to a separate *banderium* was now limited. The new organisation was based on the system of *honor*: the court aristocrats, the *ispáns* went to war under the banner of the king, at the head of troops hired on money from the royal treasury. In addition, both Angevin kings relied on the device of noble insurrection, which, contrary to custom, was made compulsory even in the case of an offensive war.

Although the unification of the country baded well for an expansive foreign policy, and after 1323 Charles Robert's command over the country was unprecedented since the times of Béla III, he could not replicate his military success against the oligarchs in the international scene. The recovery of the Banate of Mačo from Serbia between 1317 and 1319, his first successful military expedition, also became his last. Though Bosnia was secured as a more or less reliable vassal, in vain did Charles bring the powerful Šubić clan of the south to obedience in 1322: his allies, the Croat barons divided the fortresses seized amongst themselves, while the towns of Dalmatia placed themselves under Venetian suzerainty. Charles's attempt to reduce Wallachia, the Romanian principality that had emerged across the Carpathians south-east of Hungary in the beginning of the fourteenth century, to vassal status, ended in a near-disaster. The king himself narrowly escaped from the decisive battle of a campaign against Voevode Basarab in 1330.

Charles fared far better in his peaceful foreign relations, which were largely directed towards Hungary's northern neighbours. Parallels in historical contingency also seemed to destine the three kingdoms of Central Europe to hold together. The dynasties of the Piasts and the Přemysls died out nearly at the same time in Poland and Bohemia, respectively, as that of the Árpáds in Hungary, and Charles Robert, Wladysław Łokietek and to some extent John of Luxemburg from the outset rendered each other mutual assistance in consolidating their rules in their new kingdoms. Charles later married Wladysław's daughter, Elisabeth, while the Polish king's successor, Casimir III (the Great), appointed the King of Hungary and the latter's successors as his own heirs, should he die without issue. The greatest success of Charles's diplomacy was in fact the reconciliation of John and Casimir: the former abandoned his claim to the throne of Poland, while the latter his claim to Silesia at a meeting in Trencsén (Trenčin) in 1335, followed shortly by the famous meeting of the three monarchs at Visegrád. There they concluded an alliance of mutual defence, and an important trade agreement. Just as the former was mainly directed against Austria, the purpose of the latter was to establish new trade routes to the German lands and thus to avoid the staple rights of Vienna.

These achievements redress the otherwise ambiguous foreign policy record of Charles Robert, whose resoluteness and persistence yielded results that might not seem spectacular, yet they were the foundations on which his successor, the splendid 'royal knight' Louis I (the Great) built a fame that overshadowed his father for a long time. Proud and ambitious as well as pious, Louis, who succeeded to the throne in 1342 at the age of sixteen, in many ways embodied the ideal medieval monarch, and against the solid background created by his judicious father it was safe for him to indulge in his passion for greatness and pageantry. Tradition and earlier historiography credited him with glorious conquests and the creation of an empire 'whose shores were washed by three seas'. In fact, his conquests proved rather ephemeral; Poland, which fell into a personal union with Hungary after the death of Casimir in 1370 for a short period, hardly extended to the Baltic Sea at this time (not to speak about the fact that the relationship was one of equal partners, so Poland was not ruled from Hungary); the loose vassal status of Moldavia and Wallachia, the two Romanian principalities that emerged in former 'Cumania' after the weakening and the collapse of the Tartar Golden Horde, hardly justifies the pretension that the Black Sea was 'Hungarian' under Louis I. Still, the overall impression of Louis is that of a talented and powerful figure under whose reign the status of the Kingdom of Hungary as a factor to reckon with on the international scene was preserved, even strengthened; also, it was a period when important processes in Hungarian society came to their culmination, and when relative economic prosperity and internal political stability visibly contributed to the flourishing of material and spiritual culture and the arts.

Early in his reign, Louis sought greatness in the limelight of European power politics. The occasion was the assassination of his brother Andrew in 1345 in Naples. Andrew had been married to Joan, who became Queen of Naples after the death of her father King Robert; it was her courtiers who murdered Andrew shortly after Louis and Queen Elisabeth had secured the Pope's consent to the coronation of Andrew as King of Naples. Dissatisfied with the half-hearted inquiry conducted by the Holy See, Louis decided to take vengeance himself. After an arduous march across Italy in the second half of 1347, his troops entered Naples in February 1348 without encountering resistance. Joan and her second husband having fled to France, Louis assumed the title of King of Naples and filled the castles with Hungarian knights and German mercenaries, while leaving his local Italian adherents in major offices. However, the coming of the Black Death compelled him to leave Italy. In his absence, Naples fell as early as in June 1348, and Joan – enjoying the support of the Pope, who was hardly enthusiastic to see the Hungarian Angevins gaining a foothold on the Italian side of the Adriatic as well – returned to Naples in the autumn. In vain did an army led in 1349 by the Voevode of

Transylvania, István Lackfi, and another one headed by the king himself in 1350, try to recover Naples. Though his troops remained in Italy for another two years, in the peace of 1352 Louis tacitly abandoned his claim. It was of some consolation that in 1381 Charles of Durazzo, a young Italian prince brought up in Louis's court, took the throne of Naples as Charles III after having had Joan suffocated.

Louis could reasonably expect more success in less remote Croatia and Dalmatia, the two provinces that had defied his father's efforts at the reunification of the lands of the Hungarian crown. In 1345, marching into the territory proved enough for him to extort the surrender of the Croatian barons, and even the Dalmatian port of Zara (Zadar), without fight. However, in the next year the Republic of Venice, jealously protecting her hegemony over the Adriatic, retook Zara, inflicting a grave defeat on the King of Hungary. Louis was only able to redress the situation a decade later. The campaign he led against Venice in 1356 was undecisive, but in 1357 the Dalmatian towns revolted against the Republic and acknowledged Louis as their suzerain, which the peace of 1358 with Venice confirmed.

At the same time, Louis pursued an expansionist policy towards the Balkans in order to exert traditional claims of overlordship as well as, ostensibly, to proselytise among the 'schismatics' (that is, the Orthodox) and to wipe out Bogomil heresy. He personally led several of over a dozen campaigns into Serbia, Bosnia and the two Romanian principalities. After the death of Tsar Dušan Stepan in 1355, the Serbian power he had created in the Balkans swiftly disintegrated, and Louis had little difficulty in extorting an oath of fealty from his successors after a series of campaigns between 1359 and 1361. A similar status for Bosnia was secured, not so much by the success of Hungarian arms, but because internal strife compelled Ban Tvrtko to give in to the claims of Louis in 1365. The attempts to reduce the 'disloyal vassals', the Voevodes of Wallachia and Moldavia, to obedience, met with alternating success, and the Vidin Banate, established by Louis on the ruins of the medieval Bulgarian Empire in 1369, was short-lived. While Hungarian military supremacy was quite evident throughout these Balkan encounters from the fact that none of the rivals were ever in the position of launching a counteroffensive, the political goals were either unachieved or secured only temporarily. And while Louis struggled to establish Hungarian overlordship over the nortehrn princes of the region, a new power from the south started to fill in the vacuum left behind by the weakening of Byzantium and the break-up of Serbia and Bulgaria: the Ottoman Turks, who first appeared in Hungarian territory in 1375 as allies of Vlajku, Voevode of Wallachia, who disavowed Louis's suzerainty. The terrible effect of the short Turkish raid was a foretaste of what was to become a

4. The Hungarian Angevins and their neighbours

more and more standard feature of the history of frontier areas in the subsequent decades.

Warlike in the south-west and the south-east, Louis maintained, even strengthened the peaceful ties his father had forged with Hungary's northern and western neighbours. His relations with the Habsburg princes of Austria were cordial, and apart from two short wars, he was on friendly terms with Charles IV of Luxemburg, King of Bohemia and Holy Roman Emperor (his father-in-law until the death of his first wife Margaret) as well. Louis's closest ally, however, was his maternal uncle, Casimir of Poland. Their friendship was sealed with a series of mutual visits, and wars fought jointly in the 1340s and 1350s against Lithuania, which emerged east of Poland as a power to reckon with. The union of the two sovereign kingdoms after the death of Casimir in 1370 brought Louis more trouble than glory. His Polish subjects resented that he stayed aloof of his new kingdom, leaving its governance to his mother Elisabeth, who, despite her origin – she was Casimir's sister – surrounded herself with Hungarian courtiers.

The mere fact that during the forty years of Louis's reign Hungarian armies fought in foreign campaigns thirty times, out of which the king personally commanded them sixteen times, shows that his rule at home was politically stable and social order was not threatened by any great vicissitudes. It was only in the 1370s, a period relatively uneventful in the battlefields when compared to the earlier decades, that some sweeping administrative reforms took place. First, the chancellery and the court system was reorganised. Jurisdiction became more uniform, thanks to the central *audientia* created under the *ispán* of the court chapel to record grievances, to appoint judges, and thus to help the king control the various courts. At the courts as well as in the chancelleries, the role of laymen increased. They might not have a university degree, but knew local customs thoroughly, which, similarly to England and her Common Law, was of greater importance than a formal education in the legal discipline. A new secret chancellery was organised and the secret seal, used since the times of Charles Robert, became the symbol of royal will, while the great seal was 'divided' between the king and his council, which suggested that the two were now in principle considered equal partners in government.

In documents issued from Louis's chancelleries it is frequently mentioned that his decisions were made after consultation with his prelates and barons, that is, the council. The barons, in turn, constituted merely the core of the court aristocracy, which, unlike the rather diffuse, unstable retinue of the Árpád kings, now became a well organised, near-institutionalised supplement for a yet non-existent proper bureaucratic state apparatus. Besides being the king's bodyguards in peace and the core of his army in war, the knights, squires and pages of the *aula regia*, as it came to be called, in fact administered the country through delivering orders from the council to the counties and provinces, conducting inquiries in the name of the king into matters at dispute, through foreign embassies and so forth. The lifestyle and attitudes these few hundred individuals acquired at court – a life of broad horizons and refinement, of opportunism as well as opportunities – set them worlds apart from the sedentary existence of the many thousand families of their kindred whose horizon was confined to the counties. County court sessions constituted all the excitement of public activity in the lives of the latter, who resented the 'renegade' courtiers for dropping their allegiance to the patriarchal clan and the value system associated with 'noble liberty' in favour of an autonomous career serving the authority of the monarchy.

Tensions and cleavages thus started to appear within the noble estate at a time when the long process of the growth of a ruling estate with more or less uniform legal status came to an end. Unusually numerous by western standards (three to five percent of the whole population) as a result of the amalgamation of the descendants of *ispáns* of the Árpád period, royal *servientes*, castle warriors, and different groups with local immunities and privileges, the nobility's status and landholding mutually defined each other. In other words, enfeoffed property in exchange for feudal service and a landless nobleman, a knight errant, were both phenomena unknown in Hungary (as well as in Poland). On the other hand, the caste-like nature of the nobility, its status protected by a network of specific privileges, was the same in Hungary as anywhere in Western Europe, and in this the laws of 1351 – issued by the only diet of Louis, convened in the critical situation caused by his military failure in Naples and the plague – were an episode of symbolic importance. It was emphasised that each of the 'true' nobles living in the country were entitled to the same liberty; the Golden Bull of 1222 was confirmed, except its stipulations relating to inheritance. The free disposition of the testator was abandoned in favour of the prevailing custom of entailment (*aviticitas* in Latin): the noble estate was considered to be the property of the ancestor of the line and his male descendants. This regulation remained in force up to 1848. The inalienability of noble property protected the lesser nobility from the tendency of the disintegration of the estate, but also served the interest of the crown, which remained the radix of property and to which the estate reverted upon the extinction of the male line.

Laws issued by the same diet also crowned the process of the growth of a uniform peasantry, which resembled its western counterpart more closely than was the case with the nobility. The great variety in the condition of peasants that characterised the Árpád period disappeared by the fourteenth century, by which time they overwhelmingly became non-landholding, that is, non-noble serfs (*jobbágy*), free in their persons and owing the landlord dues in cash and kind in return for using plots of his land as independent cultivators. The plot (Lat. *sessio*) was the basic unit of the medieval agrarian economy, consisting of an 'internal plot' adjacent to the house (Lat. *porta*, that is, 'gate', an alternative signification of the unit of production as well as taxation) allocated to the peasant within the village, and of an 'external plot' of arable land outside of it. The average size of the plot, varying according to local circumstances, was thirty to forty acres, but the 'full plots' became increasingly a legal fiction: the division of the *sessio* into halves, quarters and eighths began in the fourteenth century, and by the fifteenth there was already a sizeable community of cotters (Hung. *zsellér*) without a plot, even a house. As in the case of the nobility, the peasantry started to differentiate from the economic point of view, while its legal status became more standardised. Whatever proportion of the fields the serf cultivated, he was entitled to the hereditary use of it, and he also possessed the most precious token of personal independence, the right to free migration. At the same time, the laws of 1351 confirmed the landlord's right of jurisdiction over the serf (Hung. *úriszék*, that is, 'the lord's bench'), granted as a special privilege to noblemen with increasing frequency. On the obligation side, it must be emphasised that labour service (*corvée*), a mark of personal subservience, became minimal in this period, while the increasing dues to the royal treasury and the landlord clearly indicate the growing capacity of the peasant farm, despite the relatively primitive technology and the uneconomical nature of the two, even the three-field system. Besides the tithes owed to the Church, I have already mentioned the 'profit of the chamber', the standard tax levied on the peasant *portae* by Charles Robert from 1336; in addition, an irregular 'war tax' of one florin per year was sometimes imposed by the crown. As regards the landlord, he was entitled to receiving rent in cash and 'presents' in the form of produce. The laws of 1351 attempted, with relatively little success, to introduce uniform standards with regards to the delivery of the latter by extending the requirement of the *nona* (Hung. *kilenced*, that is, 'the ninth tenth' due after the delivery of ecclesiastical tithes) from vine-growers to all peasants. This was meant to protect lesser noblemen, whose serfs were frequently allured to the estates of magnates who could afford to offer more favourable terms, especially in the years after the Black Death when labour became more valuable. Even besides the growing burden of taxation to king, lord and Church, evidence shows that an ever more lively market of agrarian products developed in the country in the fourteenth and fifteenth centuries, based on the surplus produced by an increasingly affluent peasantry.

The economic prosperity and socio-political stability created under Charles Robert and preserved, despite frequent military engagements, under Louis I, could not but make an impact on culture, learning and the arts. Whether urban, ecclesiastical or courtly, the ideals and attitudes, the scenes and the institutions, as well as the physical and intellectual products of Hungarian culture in the fourteenth century could best be interpreted in terms of the contemporary western experience. But under the glaze that looked so familiar to the western observer, the substance of these phenomena was shaped by factors that introduced a strange distinctiveness into the picture as a whole.

The surface consists to a great extent of the few visible remains of, and the many conjectures about, Gothic architecture and art, whose products fell victim to massive destruction during the two centuries of Ottoman rule. The buildings include the earliest urban patrician homes and noble mansions unearthed in cities like Buda or Sopron, structures in which artistic grace is combined with functional expediency. Parish churches erected from the wealth of urban communities, like St. Mary's built for the German burghers of Buda, or the town churches of Kassa (Košice, Kaschau), Kolozsvár (Cluj, Klausenburg) or Brassó (Braşov) are also fine examples of Gothic architecture, following models provided by the monastic orders, traditional as well as mendicant. The latter arrived in Hungary at a fairly early date. The Dominicans, having established some twenty-five monasteries, fell from royal favour after having assisted Margaret, the daughter of Béla IV, in seeking recluse in a nunnery on Rabbit Island (now Margaret Island, between Buda and Pest) against the will of her father, who wanted her to conclude a politically important marriage. Yet, as late as 1304, the Dominicans launched a theological school at their most important centre, Buda. In the fourteenth century, they were ultimately surpassed in significance by the Franciscans, with over a hundred establishments around the country, built out of aristocratic patronage between the creation of the Hungarian province of the order in 1238 and the end of the Middle Ages. During the fourteenth century, a traditional order of indigenous origin, the Pauline, named after the hermit Saint Paul, approved by the papal legate in 1308, emerged to importance, too, with nearly a hundred monasteries erected in two centuries. Whereas ecclesiastical architecture was dominated by French and German influences, the most conspicuous features of the man-made landscape were new castles, such as the royal fortress-cum-palaces at Diósgyőr and Zólyom (Zvolen), which may have followed Italian models and were masterpieces of the highest European standards.

Apart from fine pieces of woodcarving from the northern Szepes area, which show German influence mediated through Bohemian and Polish schools, largely Italian models were followed in sculpture, painting and book illumination. Remnants of the well at the Visegrád palace of the Angevins and carvings in Louis I's funeral chapel at Székesfehérvár are impressive monuments of sculpture; the full figure, sculpted portraits unearthed in Buda, formerly dated to this period as well, are now considered to testify to the artistic achievement of the age of King Sigismund. Though the bronze statues of Saint Stephen, Saint Imre and Saint Ladislas cast by the famous brothers Martin and George of Kolozsvár, active between the 1360s and the 1390s, have been lost, their single surviving piece, Saint George and the Dragon (1373, today in Prague) shows that it was possible to become masters of European inspiration and quality in peripheral Transylvania. Similar is the case of the royal goldsmith's workshop, whose most splendid products adorned the chapel for pilgrims founded by Louis I in Aachen, with the frescoes of Esztergom, Nagyvárad (Oradea) or Zagreb, and especially with the miniature paintings that testify to a flourishing book culture. The codex known as the *Hungarian Angevin Legendary* (around 1330) was probably the work of Bolognese masters, but other fine illuminated manuscripts, such as the richly ornamented Bible of Demeter Nekcsei, Lord Chief Treasurer of Charles Robert, or the *Illuminated Chronicle* (cca. 1360) were masterpieces of Hungarian workshops.

Notwithstanding ecclesiastical predominance, features of secularisation were striking in fourteenth-century Hungarian culture. Although most officials in the royal chapel were clerics who graduated from one of the Italian universities, those of the chancellery were lay *literati* ('men of letters', Hung. *deák*), legal experts who had studied at schools in Hungary. The wave of founding universities in Central Europe also reached Hungary: after Prague (1348), Cracow (1364) and Vienna (1365), a university was launched in 1367 by Louis I at Pécs. The Pope refusing to authorise a faculty of theology, it only provided basic training in the arts, in law, and possibly in medicine. Its main purpose might have been to supply jurists for the royal chapel, but by the 1390s it seems to have ceased to function.

The two characteristic forms of medieval secular literature, chivalric poetry and historical writing, appeared in Hungary laden with interesting contradictions. The customs of knightly life – the wearing of armour, the use of coats-of-arms, tournaments – were to some extent adopted by the court, especially under Louis I. The cult of Saint Ladislas, considered his predecessor in the character of a 'royal knight' was cherished in Louis' reign; the twelfth-century Hungarian translation of the romance of Alexander was reshaped so as to make its protagonist resemble Louis himself; further, a history of the reign of Louis was written by János Küküllei in which the chivalric character and virtues of his endeavours and undertakings were emphasised. Apart from that, the only 'knightly legend' of any importance that survives from the Angevin period is that of Miklós Toldi. The real life Toldi served as a mercenary in Italy, but was portrayed as an honest hero who emerged as a knight of Louis in spite of the evil schemes of his courtier brother, and became immortalised in the nineteenth-century epic of János Arany. Lyrical poetry seems not to have existed. Instead of troubadours, Hungary had popular bards who praised the barons and their ancestors, but not their ladies. Despite promising twelfth-century beginnings, the ethos and mentality associated with chivalry in the West remained less than fully developed in Hungary. Contradictions abound in the compositions of historiography, too. While they were productions of clerics (with the partial exception of Küküllei, whose career started as a layman of the chancellery, but ended as an archdeacon), the Christian heritage of the country was almost eclipsed by that of the chieftains and the clans, that is, representations of the pagan past, also stressed by the supposed kinship link between the Huns of Attila and the Hungarians. First hinted at by Anonymus, the idea was given currency by the chronicle of Simon Kézai, who lived at the court of Ladislas IV, around 1285. Intertwined with an emphasis on the role of the nobility within the polity, the theory survived and became highly influential in the early modern period. Finally, whereas the vernacular was quintessentially the language of secular culture, since that culture was oral, the few written relics that have been passed down to us were also conceived within an ecclesiastical context. *The Lament of Mary*, the first known poem in Hungarian, was written around 1300 in refined verse, which suggests that poetry in the vernacular was not uncommon at that time.

2. Challenges and responses: unruly barons and faltering monarchs, conquering Ottomans and a charismatic warlord

Louis I died in 1382 without male issue, which made the succession anything but smooth in a patriarchal society, even though his daughters or their husbands could expect the support of his loyal aristocrats. His own dream to make his elder daughter Mary inherit both of his thrones was thwarted by the Polish barons, who disliked the idea of an absent ruler. The queen mother, Elisabeth, gave in: her younger daughter Hedwig was sent to Poland, crowned, and married to the still pagan Prince Jagiello of Lithuania, who received baptism and took the throne of Poland as Władysław II in 1386. In Hungary, however, though Mary had been betrothed to Sigismund of Luxemburg, Margrave of Brandenburg and the son of Emperor Charles IV, Palatine Miklós Garai and the queen mother herself first preferred to invite Louis of Orléans, brother of the King of France, to the throne; while the county nobility led by the Horváti clan, expressly finding inheritance in the female line an anomaly, favoured the succession of Charles of Durazzo, King of Naples, the last male member of the House of Anjou.

In the anarchy that followed, Sigismund was able to push through the wedding with his official fiancée at the end of 1385, and the two court parties were reconciled, only to face a hostile diet convened by the Horvátis. Sigismund fled to Bohemia, while the royal ladies were taken captive (Elisabeth later being strangled); but though Charles II was crowned on December 31, 1385, he reigned a mere thirty-nine days before he was assassinated. The nobles led by the Horvátis refused to surrender even after the return of Sigismund, escorted by his brother Venceslas, King of Bohemia and Germany. It was the assistance of the barons, now acting in a formal league that wielded power over the lordless country, that invested Sigismund with the title 'Captain of Hungary' and helped him get crowned in March 1387 and liberate his wife somewhat later.

The circumstances of his accession to the throne marked out a rather narrow scope of action for Sigismund during the first years of his reign, and also had far-reaching consequences for the balance of power in the country. Whereas Mary was co-regent in name only (that, too, ended with her untimely death in 1395), Sigismund had to accept the terms dictated by the barons who ruled the country during the interregnum of early 1386. He joined the league, authorising them to take coercive measures against him, should he refrain from keeping his promises. These included stipulations that members of his council would be picked from the circle of prelates and the barons or their successors – in other words, the league raised a hereditary claim to the government of the kingdom – and that no lands would be donated to foreigners. Indeed, the main offices, along with the *honor* lands belonging to them, were divided between the members of the league; and besides the distinctions and benefits, they also carved out immense private estates from the royal manors, the young king not being in a position to refuse remuneration for their services. Over half (around 80) of the castles of the Anjous were given away, about a half of the total (c. 150) now being concentrated in the hands of thirty baronial families; while the number of villages in royal possession fell to one-third of what it had been under the Angevins (c. 1100 or merely five percent of the total). The rule of the league was initially quite stable: the internal opposition still fuelled by the Horvátis was quelled, Sigismund's hold over the southern provinces was strengthened, and the area around Pozsony mortgaged by Sigismund at a time of hardship in 1386, was recovered a few years later. However, the years immediately before and after 1390 played a pivotal role in the long-term process by which the earlier preponderance of royal estates disappeared between the 1200s and the 1500s. The formidable family wealth accumulated by magnates transformed the socio-cultural outlook and the political power relations of the country, and made baronial faction ever a potential source of disintegration.

These were also the years when another force emerged across the southern borders of the Kingdom of Hungary and which similarly constituted a menace to its territorial integrity. Having gained a foothold this side of the Bosphorus by the conquest of Gallipoli in 1354, the Ottoman Turks – a few decades earlier an insignificant principality in Asia Minor – relentlessly moved into the power vacuum that arose in the Balkans as a result of the internal strife of Byzantium and the disintegration of Serbia and Bulgaria. Under Murad I and Bayezid I, they conquered most of

Anatolia, Rumelia and Bulgaria, subdued Serbia after the disastrous defeat of Lazar I at Kosovoploje (1389) and drew Wallachia into vassal status (1394). Even though the Kingdom of Hungary was a power of different order from the ailing Balkan states, and the Ottomans could not even contemplate its conquest for over a century to come, their repeated appearances and then permanent presence along the whole southern border seriously affected the country's foreign policy, economic resources and mood. First, whereas Hungarian kings had for centuries claimed rights of overlordship over the rulers of the northern Balkans and launched regular incursions against the region, such opportunities were now abruptly lost. Second, whereas no foreign armies had ravaged Hungarian territory since the Mongol invasion of 1241, Turkish raids now became a common experience in the southern counties, whose population fled or fell victim to the violence, and was started to be replaced by runaway Balkan Slavs already in the fifteenth century.

Shocked by the dramatically new situation, it is no wonder that the Hungarian elite found it difficult to adjust to its requirements. In the tradition of the quest for Hungarian glory, it demanded offensive retaliation, and then blamed the ruler or the government in power for the subsequent failure, which was quite inevitable: more powerful, stable and affluent European states than Hungary could have also found it difficult to resist Ottoman military might in this period.

Sigismund was the first to experience the internal tension thus caused, and he could not escape the consequences. Recognising, especially after the Serbian tragedy of 1389, the dimension of the danger, he led or sent armies to fight the Ottomans each year between 1390 and 1395, but could not manage to engage in a decisive battle, and the only result was the restoration of Sigismund's protégé, Voevode Mircea, on the throne of Wallachia in 1395. In 1396, he marched to the Balkans at the head of an international army of crusaders to expel the Ottomans from Europe 'once and for all', but the siege of the Bulgarian castle of Nicopolis (Nikopol) was a disastrous failure. Sultan Bayezid himself arrived to relieve the besieged, and the defective strategy adopted upon the insistence of the French knights resulted in a near-annihilation of the Christian army. Several Hungarian grandees fell or were take captive, and Sigismund himself could return home only after a narrow escape and a long circumnavigation of the Balkan peninsula.

The defeat gave occasion to a polarisation of political forces in the country. Sigismund could plausibly use the Ottoman threat as an argument to strengthen royal authority. In fact, he had been making efforts to rid himself of the tutelage of the barons since at least 1392, when he dismissed his first Palatine, István Lackfi, the most powerful of them. At the same time, Sigismund attempted to create a counterweight to the barons by raising a new elite out of the knights of the *aula* and foreign confidants. Their loyalty was bought, consolidated and rewarded by donations of vast estates as well as offices. Thus the Polish knight of Louis I, Stibor of Stiborc, became Voevode of Transylvania; Hermann Cillei from Styria became Count of Zagoria; the southern German Eberhard became Bishop of Zagreb and later chancellor; Miklós Garai became Ban of Croatia and Slavonia, later Palatine; Filippo Scolari (Pipo of Ozora), a former employee of a Florentine bank in Buda, became director of the salt chambers, then the *ispán* of Temes and finally a successful general. The Marcali, Perényi, Csáki, Rozgonyi, Pálóci and other families also established their weight and fortune under Sigismund.

The king first tested the strength of this new team at a diet convened in the autumn of 1397 in Temesvár. He confirmed the Golden Bull, but without the famous resistance clause, and suspending the clause limiting the nobility's military obligations to defensive war. The Ottoman threat, which obliterated the boundary between offensive and defensive war, indeed rendered that stipulation outdated, and Sigismund attempted to answer the requirements of the age by introducing a kind of militia: each landowner was to equip one light cavalryman for twenty (from 1435, thirty-three) peasant plots (hence the name, *militia portalis*). In addition, the Church was required to surrender half of its incomes for military purposes in times of war. All of this amounted to challenging the tax privileges of the first two estates.

It was in the atmosphere of the failure at Nicopolis that the disaffected barons first revolted against Sigismund's unmistakable assertions of his independence. The neglected Lackfi led this rebellion in early 1397, which was quite easily quelled because most of the barons still took sides with the king. From 1399 on, however, Sigismund was away on several occasions in Bohemia, also torn by baronial faction, where he hoped to succeed his heirless brother Venceslas. His long absence provoked a critical situation. Upon his return to Hungary, in April 1401 Sigismund was detained by Palatine Detre Bebek and Chancellor (also Archbishop of Esztergom) János Kanizsai in the castle of Buda. When refusing to remove his 'foreign' adherents from office, he was declared captive, and a council of barons and prelates assumed power and claimed to govern the kingdom under 'the Seal of the Holy Crown'. However, unable to agree on whom to replace Sigismund with (the candidates were Wladysław II of Poland, the Austrian prince William, and Ladislas, King of Naples and son of Charles of Durazzo), they negotiated a compromise with him: Sigismund retained his throne, in return for the promise to dismiss most of his foreign officials.

Soon, Sigismund was 'more powerful than ever', at least in the opinion of the King of Bohemia; indeed, the breaking of his promise of 1401

challenged the barons to a last major effort to depose him. When Sigismund concluded a mutual succession agreement with Albert IV, Duke
of Austria, also appointing the latter governor of Hungary in his absence, the opposition, led by Bebek and Kanizsai again, invited Ladislas
of Naples to the throne. Ladislas had already sent troops to Dalmatia,
and was crowned at Zara in August 1403; the country-wide movement,
involving most baronial houses that had arisen in the Anjou period and
the host of their *familiares*, seemed formidable indeed. But whereas this
many-headed hydra was unable to take concerted action, the king's
commanders acted swiftly and with great determination. Most of the
barons surrendered in time to take advantage of the general amnesty
offered by Sigismund; the few who persisted forfeited their property
and some were exiled, but none executed. Ladislas returned to Naples
as early as in November 1403, leaving behind his Bosnian vassal Hervoja to govern Dalmatia, the only province where Sigismund's power
was not restored. In 1408, most of the cities were recovered as a result of
a defeat over Hervoja, but Ladislas kept Zara and a few castles and islands, and then sold them along with his claim to Dalmatia to Venice. By
1420, in a series of wars Venice conquered all of the province, and although thereafter Sigismund's commanders triumphed several times
over the mercenaries of the Republic, in the peace of 1433 Dalmatia was
lost forever. The gains, however, were far more impressive: the struggle
for power ended, and Sigismund's adversaries, weakened and demoralised, were no longer able to constitute a threat to his hold over the
country for the rest of his long reign. Sigismund now set to realising his
plans of large-scale internal reform in a country that was to be the secure
hinterland for his equally large-scale foreign policy ambitions.

In laying the foundations of political stability, Sigismund could rely
on a group of firm supporters assembled in the struggles against the
barons. The new aristocracy, who, besides the vast estates and influential offices received for their services, also became attached to the king
via symbolic and dynastic links during the years after 1403. In 1405, Sigismund married Hermann Cillei's daughter Borbála, thereby also becoming the brother-in-law of his new Palatine Miklós Garai; and in 1408,
after a defeat over Bosnia, he founded the Order of the Dragon, a
knightly league of the king, the queen and twenty-two barons who had
rendered the ruler the most valuable services in suppressing the revolt
of 1403. At the same time, while the title of baron continued to refer to a
person of great wealth and high status, the main dignitaries no longer
received office fiefs (*honor*), and thus became mere councillors without
a territorial power base accruing to them from their titles. The royal castles were now administered by captains who did not take part in political decision-making. The barons' monopoly over state affairs also ceased

to exist, since the king often consulted 'special councillors' recruited from foreigners, the middle nobility and clerics, or legal, financial and military experts who might even be commoners. Since the latter were not donated estates but drew salaries for their services, Sigismund's reorganisation of the council foreshadowed elements of a future state bureaucracy. The simultaneous refinement of the functioning of the chancelleries was confined to a limited secularisation of the personnel, but did not make the chancelleries the executive organ of the central power; they merely put royal orders into writing, to be executed by the *aula*, whose character did not change much since the time of the Anjous. Jurisdiction was reformed to enhance its efficiency and professionalism. By the end of Sigismund's reign, the formerly several high courts within the *curia regis* were amalgamated into the court of 'the king's special presence' (in fact, the court of the chancellery), partly because Sigismund's long absences at the end of his reign obliged the delegation of 'the king's personal presence', too; and the court of the exchequer, which had started to adjudicate in the affairs of the free royal boroughs under the Anjous, was now exclusively authorised to do so, and became packed with commoners.

For a variety of reasons, the cities were also firm supporters of Sigismund's policies of consolidation. Their population consisted predominantly of foreigners, mainly Germans, who in a period of xenophobia could only expect protection from the king, himself a foreigner; furthermore, the weakening of central power threatened the loss of their privileged status. On the other hand, since the number of royal castles dropped dramatically after 1387, the significance of walled cities was greatly augmented in the eyes of the king, and the fact that the rebels were refused entry within city walls played some part in Sigismund's success against the barons. In recognition of this role, he made efforts thereafter to increase the number of fortified cities – around 1400, there was a mere twenty of them in the country – as well as their political role. It was under Sigismund that the walls of Kolozsvár, Késmárk (Kežmarok), Eperjes (Prešov) and Bártfa (Bardejov) were completed, although his plan to fortify a number of market towns or *oppida* (in fact, overgrown villages entitled to hold weekly markets and occasionally annual fairs) was thwarted by a lack of financial resources. In an unprecedented move, Sigismund summoned representatives from urban communities to a nation-wide assembly in 1405, which issued in important decrees. Free cities were exempted from internal customs duties; the staple rights of Buda were suspended *vis-à-vis* them; foreign merchants were only allowed to undertake wholesale trade. They acquired rights of jurisdiction; the supreme jurisdiction over them by the court of the exchequer has already been mentioned. After 1405, the Statute Book of

Buda was worked out, replacing the 'law of Székesfehérvár' as the model of urban statutes and becoming the basis of the 'law of the exchequer', the common law of free cities. All of this greatly contributed to the growing economic weight and prosperity of the cities, and especially of the rich merchant patriciate that had a firm grasp over the city magistrates in the face of rather meagre competition from the guilds. Nevertheless, Sigismund's reforms could not amend the anomalies of urban development in Hungary. Cities continued to be small, Buda with its roughly eight thousand inhabitants being the most populous of them; there was no proper network of 'genuine' (i. e., chartered) towns, all of them of any significance having been erected at the gateways of the trade routes leading to Austria, Poland and the Balkans, and thus leaving a vacuum in the central areas of the country. The few hundred market towns were more evenly spread. These second class settlements also provided exchange facilities for the peasant families who lived in and around them, and to some extent even a cultural infrastructure, some social privileges and personal liberty, too. At the same time, they contributed to the decentralisation of an internal market that was anyway limited, and they were ultimately still at the mercy of the local landlord, whether secular or ecclesiastical.

Besides the new aristocrats and the cities, the Church also became one of the foundations of Sigismundian consolidation. Unlike most European monarchs, the Hungarian Angevins in the fourteenth century exercised broad control over the investiture of prelates, but in the turbulent 1380s these ties became loosened, and in 1403 both archbishops and several bishops took sides with the rebels. In this, they were also encouraged by the fact that Pope Boniface IX, who had enjoyed Sigismund's goodwill against his rival Benedict XIII, supported the Neapolitan pretender. This was a pretext for the king, once the troubles were over, to curtail papal influence in Hungary very seriously: from 1404, no decree or verdict from Rome could take effect in Hungary unless it obtained royal assent (*placetum regium*), and the king specifically reserved for himself the right of investiture (confirmed by the Synod of Constance in 1417). Sigismund exercised this right vigorously, receiving considerable political support from the new incumbents of benefices. Nor did he scruple to put the wealth of the Church to the service of the monarchy: before replacing rebel prelates with ones whom he could expect to be loyal, he left their benefices vacant for several years, and the secular administrators to whom these were entrusted collected their incomes for the royal treasury. In the last years of his reign, Sigismund revived this method of raising revenue, this time in order to finance fortifications and anti-Turkish military preparations along the southern border.

The Church, or, to be precise, the restoration of the unity of the Latin Church, also became one of the main foci of Sigismund's foreign policy, besides and in close connection with his ambition to become Holy Roman Emperor, the highest in rank among Christian princes. Ever since the deterioration of the sanity of his brother Venceslas, Sigismund counted as a candidate to the German throne, and after the death of Venceslas's successor Ruprecht he was elected King of Germany in 1411. This development also affected his own status as King of Hungary as well as the history of Hungary itself. At the same time, the fact that the Kingdom of Hungary lay outside the Empire and was far more powerful than any of the German principalities, provided Sigismund with a solid political, economic and military background, enabling him to enjoy far greater independence than German kings usually did. But the title of emperor only accrued to the 'Kings of Rome' after being crowned by the Pope; and before Sigismund could undertake the risky and costly journey to Rome, the great schism of the western Church had to be repaired, the Papacy in Rome restored, and the general crisis of the Christian Church managed.

Since 1378, there had been two popes in the western Church, one in Avignon (where the papacy had been 'captive' of the kings of France since 1309), and one in Rome; in 1409, the Synod of Pisa even elected a third one. Sigismund set to putting an end to the schism with great determination. It was largely thanks to his diplomatic skill and personal charm, also exerted in the course of diplomatic visits ranging from Spain to England, that the greatest international congress of medieval and early modern Europe, the Synod of Constance (1414–1418), solved the most pressing issue: the three popes were forced to resign, and a new one was unanimously elected. Sigismund might now have himself crowned emperor. The fact that this was delayed until 1433 was partly due to the complications caused by the failure to resolve the second item on the Constance agenda: the reform of the Church, especially in regard of its growing worldliness and the preponderance of the papal hierarchy, which had been objects of criticism for several decades. Sigismund was committed to this goal as well, but was unable to persuade the conservative majority of the synod seriously to consider the internal renovation of the Church; on the contrary, they took a merciless stand against radical reform, and in 1415 sent John Hus to the stake. A theologian and preacher from Bohemia, where the ideas of the fourteenth-century English reformist theologian John Wycliffe were most influential, Hus's martyrdom fuelled a revolutionary atmosphere in his native land. Furthermore, the fact that he had arrived at Constance to discuss his tenets under Sigismund's safe-conduct certainly did not enhance the popularity of the King of Germany and Hungary in Bohemia, whose throne he also inherited in 1419. By that time, the country was in the hands of the Hussites, and although Sigismund, refusing to accept the demands of their 'Prague points', could get himself crowned in 1420, for over a decade thereafter he waged a defensive war against the Hussites along the north-western borders of Hungary. Only when he and the ecclesiastical potentates of the Synod of Basel – called, in vain, to proceed with ecclesiastical reform in 1431 – were ready for a compromise with the moderate wing of the movement, could the radicals of Hussitism be suppressed.

In military terms it was northern Hungary that suffered several devastating incursions at the hands of the Hussites (Pozsony/Bratislava, 1428; Nagyszombat/Trnava, 1430; Szepes county, 1433). However, the ideological impact of the Hussites can be detected primarily in the villages and market towns of the southern county Szerém (Srem), where the papal inquisitor Giacomo della Marca had many heretics burnt in 1436 and 1437, and where the first Hungarian translations of the Bible (extant in incomplete versions) were prepared by Hussite preachers. It seems, however, unlikely that Hussitism had any direct influence, as has been suggested, on the first major peasant revolt in Hungary. Its general background was the impact of Sigismund's financial difficulties on the demands of landlords from their tenants. Although the regular revenue of the crown was at least a very considerable 300,000 florins per annum (and quite possibly much more), politics was an increasingly expensive pursuit, especially for a ruler with great foreign policy ambitions, a court suitable to his rank, and the need to maintain a large defence force. Besides levying irregular taxes, particularly on the Church, and mortgaging royal estates (most notoriously, the Saxon towns of Szepes county, not recovered from Poland until 1772), he also renewed the old practice of debasing coinage.

The rebellion of 1437-38 was triggered off among Hungarian tenants, urban poor and petty freemen, and Romanian settlers in Transylvania by the demand of Bishop György Lépes that tithes be paid in new coins, including arrears of three years, during which he had refused to accept the old ones. In addition, petty noblemen and Romanian settlers, hitherto exempt from the tithe, were required to pay their due, and peasants were increasingly restricted in their freedom of migration. The rebel troops, led by Antal Budai Nagy, a poor nobleman, having scored a victory over the forces of Voevode László Csáki, extorted important concessions in the agreement of Kolozsmonostor (July 6, 1437): the 'community of the inhabitants of the realm' (*universitas regnicolarum*), as they were addressed, were promised diminished tithes, free migration and the abolition of the *nona* or seigneurial tithe; annual peasant meetings were to supervise compliance with the terms of the agreement, and culpable landlords were to be punished. The agreement held out the promise of corporate development for the hitherto unprivileged. However, in September the Hungarian nobles, the 'Saxon' (German) burghers and the Szekel free guards (the bodies that would be regarded as the established political estates or *nationes* of Transylvania from the sixteenth century onwards) concluded the Union of Kápolna, a pact of mutual assistance against the peasants. A month later this phalanx compelled the peasants to accept a less favourable agreement, sent for arbitration to Sigismund who had earlier repeatedly confirmed the right of free migration of peasants. As the news of Sigismund's death reached Transylvania in December 1437, the lords launched a counter-offensive, to which the peasants, disarmed by and tired of the protracted negotiations, became quite easy prey. The city of Kolozsvár, which took sides with the peasants, fell at the end of January 1438 and was punished by the temporary loss of its privileges. On February 2, 1438, the terms of Kápolna were confirmed in the Union of Torda, providing a framework for the Transylvanian estates' constitution for several centuries.

Sigismund's long reign was, as it were, framed by the years of baronial faction in the first and Hussite revolt in the last third of it. The third great challenge, the Ottoman menace, followed the same rhythm: the pressure on Hungary's southern border diminished after the defeat of Bayezid I in 1402 at the hands of the new conqueror from Central Asia, Tamerlane, thrust the Ottoman Empire into a temporary crisis, which lasted until Murad II (1421–1451) was able to launch a new wave of expansion in the 1420s. In the intervening period, Sigismund not only set his authority in Hungary on new foundations and arose as a ruler of European stature, but also attempted to strengthend his positions in the Balkans. His endeavour to create a zone of buffer states out of Bosnia, Serbia and Wallachia was apparently a renewal of the power policy of Louis I. But unlike his predecessor, who merely pursued glory and booty, what Sigismund expected of these states was reliable allies and sacrifices, and he did not expect it for nothing: he tried to make their rulers interested through donations of estates and distinctions. Thus, after the Ottoman failure at Ankara in 1402, the Serbian 'despot', Stepan Lazarević, accepted Sigismund's suzerainty, became a member of the Order of the Dragon and one of the greatest landowners of Hungary. His loyalty saved the southern counties adjacent to Serbia from Turkish raids until his death in 1427. Similar was the case with Wallachia, the difference being that Sigismund's loyal vassal Voevode Mircea died in 1418, and as a result of the erratic fortunes in the subsequent struggle between the pro-Hungarian and pro-Ottoman factions in the country, Transylvania was already exposed to several Turkish forays in the 1420s. Even more ephemeral was Sigismund's success in securing Bosnia where 'Great Voevode' Hervoja abandoned his loyalty, extorted by five campaigns and lavish favours, as early as in 1413.

It is much to the credit of Sigismund that as the system of buffer states started to crumble, he laid the foundations of an alternative defence network. In certain regions, he pushed direct Hungarian rule far to the south – for instance, as far as Jajca in Bosnia in whose southern part the Ottomans had been firmly entrenched by the 1430s. Simultaneously, he invested first Scolari as *ispán* of Temes, and then the Ragusan Tallóci brothers, whose career had also started as financial experts and who now controlled the Banates of Croatia, Slavonia and Szörény (Severin), with centralised command and substantial resources to build or modernise fortresses and organise and maintain mobile forces (consisting to a large extent of South Slav refugee noblemen with their retainers) to avert the Turks. Sigismund's last personal encounter with them, just as the first one, was rather inglorious. After an unsuccessful attempt in 1428 to seize, in terms of an agreement earlier made with Lazarević, the fortress of Galambóc (Golubac) from the Turks, to whom its captain surrendered it after the despot's death, Sigismund narrowly escaped the Turkish relief forces for a second time. Nevertheless, his achievement was remarkable: it was the system established in the last third of his reign – the combination of two lines of border fortresses from the Lower Danube to the Adriatic, and mobile troops which under favourable circumstances might even risk offensive action – that protected the Kingdom of Hungary for nearly a century, and provided a pattern for frontier warfare for decades after its eventual collapse.

These long term benefits, as well as Sigismund's achievement in general went unappreciated among the Hungarian elite. Peaceable and polished as he was, he could hardly have earned popularity among the warlike and robust Hungarian nobility. His spectacular failures in the battlefield against the Ottomans evoked contempt, his increasingly western political orientation (and the resulting long absences) impatience, and his list of priorities – such as the schism – incomprehension. Yet, his commanding personality could, after discouraging beginnings, bind the aristocracy to the crown, and master the corporate aspirations of the nobility. His death removed a major obstacle from the development of a polity based on the enhanced role of the estates in political decision-making.

As elsewhere, the 'estates' were groups of full property holders (*possessionati*) with identical status and privileges, or in other words, the 'proper' inhabitants of the realm (*regnicolae*). Besides the nobility, these included ecclesiastical bodies, the free cities and the Transylvanian Saxon communities, but in Hungary, unlike in most of Western Europe and similarly only to Poland, the nobility preponderated among them (corresponding to the fact that by the mid-fifteenth century two-thirds of the landed property in the kingdom were in the possession of the aristocracy and the nobility). In fact, the notion of the estates became nearly identical with that of the nobility. We have seen that the beginnings of corporate politics, along with its characteristic framework, the national assembly or diet (the *generalis congregatio*) in which the 'inhabitants' might appear personally (as was the case with the nobility) or were represented by estate, go back to the thirteenth century in Hungary. However, this tradition was abandoned under the Angevins and Sigismund, and the few diets they convened played the auxiliary role of providing the solemn trappings to the announcement of decisions already made by the king and his council. This situation changed dramatically after the death of Sigismund. Until the next ruler of stature, Matthias I, acceded to the throne in 1458, diets convened nearly each year, aiming to legislate rather than merely to consent. In two years, the nobility pulled down the edifice of Sigismund's reforms, inaugurating a reign of the estates which lasted two decades and laid the foundations of the corporate polity of the future.

Since Sigismund had no male heir, in terms of his 1402 agreement with Albert Habsburg he was to be succeeded by the latter's son (who was also his own son-in-law). Albert was indeed elected and crowned by the estates, which escaped the domination of the 'court party', but was forced to accept very serious demands: he promised to put an end to the influence of foreigners and to the taxation of the Church, to abandon all 'innovations and obnoxious usages' introduced by Sigismund, and to submit all important political issues and decisions to the prelates and barons. During an absence of the king in the following year, Sigismund's loyal barons increased their influence at court to such an extent that the estates compelled him to convene a diet immediately after his return and to 'restore the ancient customs of the realm' – in reality, to yield ultimate control over policy issues to the estates. In addition, the decay of the network of royal castles developed under Charles Robert now became complete, with a mere 35 remaining in royal possession by the time of the death of Albert. To make matters still worse, simultaneously with the weakening of the authority of the crown, Murad II smashed the last remnants of the southern buffer zone by overrunning the possessions of Djuradj Branković, who succeeded Lazarević as Despot of Serbia in 1439. Albert, who called the nobility to insurrection to relieve his ally, died of dysentery in his camp. From that time on, the Ottoman Empire constituted a direct menace to the integrity of Hungary: already in 1440, the Sultan made an abortive attempt to seize Belgrade, the keystone of the southern defence system.

Albert's death threw Hungary into a succession crisis, and the quarrel between the Habsburg or court party and the 'national' party – in effect, the county nobility – soon resulted in a civil war. The former, led by Ulrik Cillei, supported the widowed Queen Elisabeth, Sigismund's daughter who, a few months after the death of Albert, bore him a son and wanted to secure the throne to him. Ladislas V ('the Posthumous') was indeed crowned with the crown of Saint Stephen in May 1440. The estates, led by the 'soldier barons' of Sigismund such as the Rozgonyis, the Tallócis and others, refused to accept this *fait accompli.* They invited the young king of Poland, Władysław III (in Hungarian, Ulászló I), to the throne, expecting him to be able to lead the fight against the Ottoman Empire. Having signed election promises and sworn an oath to keeping the 'ancient privileges' of the country (that is, the nobility), Władysław, too, was crowned. This was a step of great symbolic significance. The claim that the coronation and the power of kings was dependent on the will of the inhabitants of the realm, rather than on the insignia, was an explicit declaration of the ascendancy of the estates over the crown, and a tacit challenge to the hereditary principle.

Ladislas enjoyed the support of his relative and ward Frederick, Duke of Austria and soon to be Frederick III, German Emperor, as well as the wealthiest barons; the talented Czech commander Jan Jiškra, a Habsburg supporter, employed Hussite strategy so successfully that he carved out and retained for several years large and rich territories in northern Hungary first on Ladislas', then on his own behalf. However, Władysław could strengthen his grasp over the rest of the country, largely owing to the services of two figures who dominated the following fifteen years: Miklós Újlaki, one of the most influential barons of his party, and János Hunyadi, who was propelled to prominence and an unparalleled career by his role in pacifying the eastern part of the kingdom in 1441.

Born in a Romanian noble family from Wallachia, Hunyadi was an infant when in 1409 his father Vojk obtained his first estate in Hungary, the manor of Hunyadvár (Vajdahunyad, Hunadoera). Brought up in the court of various magnates, he spent two years in the service of the Duke of Milan, then became a court knight of Sigismund and in 1439, Ban of Szörény. Władysław rewarded him for his services by raising him (with Újlaki) to Voevode of Transylvania, *ispán* of several counties, administrator of the salt monopoly; he was also in charge of Belgrade and the whole southern line of defence, and by the end of his life the proprietor of twenty-five castles, thirty towns and a thousand villages. Újlaki and Hunyadi, whose friendship was remarkably undisturbed by the joint commissions, shared full command over Hungary east of the Danube.

During the subsequent years, Hunyadi's own 'province' east of the Tisza became a haven of peace amidst the struggles that raged elsewhere in the country, and a solid hinterland for his campaigns against the Ottomans which added international fame to his domestic power.

Already in 1441, Hunyadi raided Serbian territory and beat the troops of the Bey of Szendrő (Smederevo); in 1442, he smashed a huge Turkish army pillaging southern Transylvania, and overwhelmed the soldiers of the Beglerbey of Rumelia, the commander-in-chief of the Ottoman forces stationed in Europe, at the River Jālomiţa in the eastern Carpathians. These feats made Hunyadi, the first in several decades to launch successful offensives, charismatic in the eyes of the Hungarian nobility, and the candidate of the Papal administration to lead an international anti-Ottoman crusade, solicited by the desperate Byzantine Emperor John VIII who was even willing to accept a reunion of the western and eastern Christian Churches under the leadership of the former. Cardinal Giuliano Cesarini was sent to Hungary to arrange for a truce between the adherents of the 'two Ladislases', and after it had taken effect, the first large scale military operation was launched.

In the 'long campaign' of the winter of 1443-44, a large Hungarian army commanded by Hunyadi and the king marched as far as Sofia, and while no territory was reconquered, they returned unbeaten after several battles, making an important psychological impact on both sides. A Christian coalition started preparations for the crusade to reconquer the Balkans, while the Sultan sued for peace. In the peace talks that followed, Murad II promised to evacuate Serbia and to pay a ransom, with Brankovič handing over several cities and estates to Hunyadi in return for his support and his role in the deal. However, Cesarini could not afford to let the cause of the crusade be lost. He persuaded the king and Hunyadi that oaths sworn to the infidel need not be kept. However, the news of the peace made the allies refrain from joining the campaign launched shortly thereafter, and in the battle of Varna on November 10, 1444, the superior Ottoman forces inflicted a defeat still more disastrous than Nicopolis on the Hungarian-Polish army. The king and the legate, as well as several Hungarian barons fell; Hunyadi himself barely escaped.

The debacle of Varna not only demonstrated the futility of crusading projects and weakened the determination among the Balkan peoples against the Ottomans, but also confused the situation in Hungary to an extent unknown since the times of the oligarchic challenge around 1300. Already amidst the anarchical conditions of the civil war, law courts ceased to operate and a great many castles were erected without authorisation; now the two factions fell on each other again, while Frederick III occupied fortresses along the western border, and Turkish retaliation for the breach of peace could also be expected. Among such

5. Hungary and her neighbours in the
age of the Hunyadis

The campaigns of János Hunyadi and Matthias I:

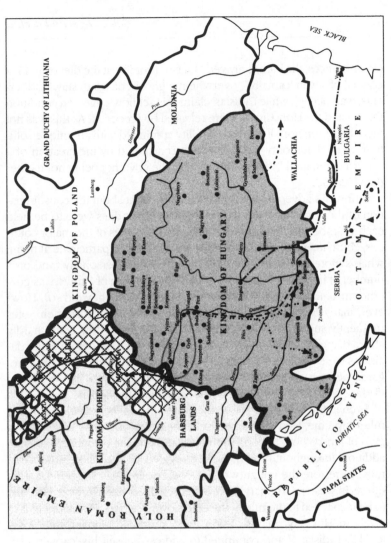

→ Hunyadi in 1443

→ Hunyadi and King Władysław in 1444

→ Hunyadi in 1447

→ Hunyadi in 1448

→ Matthias in 1463, 1464 and 1476

→ Matthias in 1468 and 1474

→ Matthias in 1485

circumstances, the barons arrived at a compromise at the diet of 1445: a council of seven 'captains', overwhelmingly out of Władysław's adherents, was elected, while Ladislas' claim was acknowledged on condition that he and the Holy Crown were released by Frederick. As this was not met, the restoration of political stability continued with an unique solution. Central authority was formally reconstituted by the creation of a governorship until Ladislas came of age, the governor being none other than Hunyadi.

Hunyadi's governorship (1446–1452) brought about the consummation of the corporate state. It was stipulated that diets were to be held each year; besides the upper nobility, the delegates of the major counties, churchmen and free cities were also entitled to participate at them; what is more, nobles retained the right to attend personally (and on a number of important occasions, such as the election of Hunyadi as governor in 1446 and his son Matthias as king in 1458, they did so). However, many of the nobles being retainers of the magnates, their votes frequently supported factional politics; in any case, they could hardly afford being long in attendance, so they often left diets before major decisions were taken by the forty-odd barons and high churchmen. As regards the cities, they soon realised that their votes carried little weight in the face of the preponderance of the barons and the nobles.

Even in the territories where the governor and the estates nominally ruled supreme, Hunyadi's exercise of the prerogative was limited in regard of jurisdiction, the donation of estates and the use of revenues. In addition, throughout his tenure, he struggled, on the whole unsuccessfully, to restore the integrity of the country. In 1447, Frederick's conquests in western Hungary were acknowledged, and Hunyadi also had to be reconciled to the rule of the Cilleis over Slavonia. His campaigns in northern Hungary against Jiškra, who remained uncompromisingly loyal to Ladislas V and continued to address himself his 'captain general', were a complete failure. Nor did fortune return to Hungarian arms against the Ottomans: a campaign to efface the memory of Varna led to a second disaster at Kosovopolje in 1448.

In spite of this series of fiascos, Hunyadi's authority among the nobility that had supported him from the outset remained unshaken, and his position was even strengthened by forging a league with his old friend Újlaki and Palatine László Garai, a leader of the Habsburg party. As a result, even Frederick III acknowledged his governorship, which came to an end in 1452 when the Austrian estates rebelled against Frederick (absent in Rome to get himself crowned emperor). One of their claims was the release of his ward Ladislas, who was confirmed by the diet as rightful inheritor of the throne of Hungary – without talk about a new election or coronation – in January 1453. For the first time since the death of Albert, the country had a crowned head acknowledged as legitimate by all factions. In the interest of reconciliation, an amnesty was proclaimed for all who fought against Ladislas on behalf of Władysław, and several of the still legally existing royal estates were sacrificed. The royal government, with the chancelleries and courts, was revived; Újlaki joined forces with Garai and Ulrik Cillei to restore the authority of the royal court; the new secret chancellor, János Vitéz, hitherto an ardent follower of the 'national' party and the tutor of Hunyadi's younger son Matthias, now devoted his exceptional talents and erudition to the same task. Hunyadi was compensated for resigning from the governorship in all possible ways: he was entrusted with the administration of royal revenues, nominated Captain General of Hungary and perpetual Count of Beszterce (the first precedent of the donation of an aristocratic title in Hungary), and remained in control of the country. Yet, among the circumstances he became increasingly isolated and his power ambition now seemed somewhat wanton.

Yet, he was the only person from whom successful resistance against the Turks could be expected, and this was a quality that looked indispensable after the Ottoman conquest of Constantinople in 1453. Soon it became evident that Sultan Mehmed II intended to come into the inheritance of the Byzantine Empire: in two campaigns in 1454 and 1455, he conquered nearly the whole of Serbia, and in 1456 he led a formidable army of some 100,000 men against Belgrade, the key fortress of Hungary's southern system of defence. The panic caused by the fall of Constantinople gave rise to rather ineffective counter-measures within and outside Hungary. The diet proclaimed a general noble insurrection, revived some of Sigismund's military reforms and decided to levy special taxes, as did the German imperial diets of 1454-55; all these yielded relatively little result. The Christian princes of Europe failed to respond to the call of the Pope for a crusade, and the masses gathered around Vienna by zealous Franciscan preachers in the summer of 1456 never marched against the infidel. As Mehmed's well-trained and well-equipped professional army started to besiege Belgrade in early July 1456, the defenders could only expect relief from the soldiers mobilised by Hunyadi from his estates and retinue, and insurrectionists from among the commoners of the south of Hungary, inflamed by the preaching of Giovanni da Capestrano, an old Franciscan monk from Italy. Combined, these forces equalled less than half of the besiegers, and yet, in the decisive battle of July 22 they inflicted such a serious defeat on the Ottomans that the Sultan decided to retreat. The opportunity of a counter-offensive was missed; indeed, it must be confessed that, as Varna and Kosovopolje had shown, such undertakings were not very promising. Hunyadi's achievement was to secure the southern system of defence, the most important heritage of Sigismund: no Turkish attempt of similar dimensions took place until sixty-five years later. The Pope proclaimed the day he received the news of the triumph a Christian holiday. Though Hunyadi fell victim to the plague that raged in his camp after the victory, his charisma and the belief in his mission became strengthened among his followers, and thus the road of his son to the throne was paved.

That road was not to be a smooth one: for the time being, Hunyadi's death signalled for his adversaries the moment to weaken his party, and unleashed another round of civil strife. Cillei was appointed captain general and demanded Hunyadi's sons to abandon royal castles and revenues. László Hunyadi, the new leader of the clan, pretended to give in, but his men murdered Cillei as the latter marched into Nándorfehérvár. Most of his supporters, alienated by this treachery, now took sides with the king, who temporised by investing László with the position of captain general and promising impunity to him, but in reality only waited for an opportunity to retaliate. That came in March 1457 as both Hunyadi brothers were in Buda, where they were arrested, and László court-martialled and put to death. Hunyadi's widow and brother-in-law, Mihály Szilágyi responded by rising up in arms, which caused Ladislas V to flee the country to Prague, taking his young captive, Matthias Hunyadi, also with him. As the king, not yet eighteen, died in Prague, the mightiest of the court party, such as Garai or Újlaki, could not but realise that they had no chance either to obtain the throne or to rule the country as oligarchs; nor was there any foreign pretender who could put down the powerful Hunyadi clan and undertake the expenses of defence against the Ottomans at the same time. Thus they were compelled to make a compromise with the Szilágyis in order to arrange for the retention of their own influence while having Matthias, the only suitable candidate, elected King of Hungary.

3. Hungary's renaissance king Matthias Corvinus

Born in 1443 (or in 1440), Matthias received a princely upbringing. His tutors, such as János Vitéz, introduced him not only into letters and languages, but also into the rudiments of new humanist learning. He acquired a fair expertise in statecraft, diplomacy and the art of war beside his father, and he also had the considerable prestige and economic, political and military resources of the Hunyadi party at his disposal. If the de facto interregnum of 1444–1452 and the subsequent pathetic performance of Ladislas V, amidst the Ottoman menace, risked the disintegration of the Kingdom of Hungary, the acclamation of the son of the hero of Belgrade as king by the nobility assembled on the frozen Danube near Pest on January 24, 1458, bode well to avert that risk.

The young monarch – released by his Bohemian counterpart George Poděbrady, elected governor by the Czech estates after the death of Ladislas and king in the following year, in return for a ransom and the promise that Matthias would marry his daughter Catherine – set to restoring order and central authority with surprising vigour. Breaking his family's deal, rejecting its patronising attitude and relying mainly on the advice of Vitéz (his chancellor, soon to become primate of Hungary as well), he thwarted Szilágyi's hopes of playing the role his own father had once played as regent, and replaced the barons with his well-to-do noble supporters at the head of the central law courts, the treasury and the court tribunal newly established to administer the royal estates. The laws of the diet of June 1458 also benefited the nobility. The disappointed barons, led by Garai and Újlaki, invited and elected Frederick III as king, and the emperor attacked Hungary to make good his claim in the spring of 1459. With skilful diplomacy, however, Matthias divided the enemy camp, and Frederick soon suffered a final setback. The protracted peace talks resulted in the compromise treaty of 1463. In return for 80,000 florins, the Holy Crown was surrendered to Matthias, whom Frederick adopted as his son; the latter could retain the title of king of Hungary, and he or his successors were entitled to inherit the throne should Matthias die heirless. The treaty thus became the foundation of the later Habsburg succession in Hungary (a rather unlikely prospect at the time, Matthias being the emperor's junior by twenty years). For the time being, however, it allowed Matthias to get himself crowned in 1464, and secured him against any serious challenge for the rest of his reign.

The coronation was also the first occasion for a reconciliation between Matthias and the barons, whose majority now rallied to his support. Matthias relied on the old Angevin and Sigismundian tactics of refreshing the ranks of the aristocracy with *novi homines*, and a few families that determined Hungarian politics in the half-century after his death and later, such as the Szapolyai or the Báthori, indeed started to rise during his reign. Nevertheless, half of the barons nominated by Matthias came from the old aristocracy; also, they were the ones who held their offices longest. On the other hand, only a few of the newcomers raised to office – such as his treasurer János Ernuszt or the commander Pál Kinizsi, both of them commoners by origin – managed to integrate among the magnates, who started to emerge as a distinct hereditary class in this period. The magnates or 'natural barons' (to be distinguished from the 'real barons', that is, the main office holders) were powerful lords personally invited to sessions of the broader royal council. It is also worth mentioning that Matthias displayed an extremely indulgent attitude towards the aristocracy: despite a rebellion and a conspiracy in which they were deeply implicated, he had no aristocrats executed. Furthermore – a final feature of his strategy towards the political elite of the country – whereas early in the reign Matthias enlisted the support of the nobility against the barons, later he often played off the barons against the nobles or one baronial faction against another, while ceaselessly extending his own authority and reducing the circle on whose support he depended. This is shown, among other things, by the conspicuously decreasing frequency of new appointments.

Matthias has often been credited with attempting to centralise the country's administration, even with laying the foundations of absolute monarchy. It is indeed tempting to draw a parallel between him and some near-contemporary western rulers who consolidated their realms after turbulent times by centralising measures, like Louis XI of France or Henry VII of England (however distorted and simplified this very image is in the case of the latter two monarchs). It is also true that especially in the latter half of his reign his new style of governing, the pretension that as king he had 'absolute power' and was 'unbound by the law', made him highly unpopular and earned him denunciations as a tyrant among his most powerful subjects. Finally, it is also true that the corporate structures that had operated so vigorously during the two decades preceding his election now lost some of their significance. diets were quite frequent, but some of their basic functions, like the voting of taxation, were often exercised by the royal council (that is, the first two estates only), while the role of the 'apparatus', the bureaucratic, judicial, fiscal and military bodies free from control by the estates, increased in the administration of affairs.

However, the character of these institutions suggests qualifications, to the extent that Matthias's centralisation must be acknowledged as arising from the personal abilities and aspirations of a singularly gifted ruler, rather than from the specific conditions of fifteenth-century Hungary. Most importantly, the royal council, far from becoming a group of officials trained in law, remained the same feudal body as it had been for centuries. The chancelleries were mere auxiliary offices to issue charters; Matthias's innovation here mainly consisted of preferring to rely on the minor or secret chancellery instead of the great chancellery, which was controlled by the council. He often left the latter office vacant, and filled the former with commoners who could be replaced with greater ease. It was in the administration of justice that professionalisation advanced most. The lesser nobles and commoners, a few of them trained at universities but most only through practising the customary and statute law of the realm in everyday business, who were raised to the central courts after an apprenticeship in the local administration or in lower courts, constituted the first significant stratum of secular intelligentsia in Hungary. Towards the end of Matthias's reign, important steps were taken towards the standardisation of law codes across the country. The comprehensive statute book of 1486, for instance, not only expanded the authority of the palatine as well as the counties, but also clarified procedural law. As a result of the judicial reforms, a rudimentary sense of the rule of law and security under the law emerged; for his personal efforts to suppress corruption and overbearing local potentates, the king was rewarded with the byname 'Matthias the Just' and became a popular hero of folk anecdote travelling in disguise among his subjects in order to detect and punish evildoers.

All of these changes are second in significance to the fiscal and military reforms of Matthias, which in turn served his ambitious foreign policy. On the accession of Matthias, the revenues of the crown were a rather miserable 250,000 florins per year, hardly enough to cover even the bare necessities of the defence of the country (not to speak about other expenses). To remedy this situation, Matthias embarked on a far-reaching reform of the financial administration. He levied an 'extraordinary' subsidy (usually one florin per *porta*) over forty times during the thirty-three years of his reign, and had it collected with increasing efficiency as his power became consolidated. Exemptions from the ordinary revenues (the salt monopoly, the *lucrum camarae* and the 'thirtieth' customs duty, renamed as *vectigal coronae*, duty of the Crown) were abolished in 1467, and they were magisterially administered by János Ernuszt, a Jewish merchant converted to Christianity and a brilliant financial expert (later Lord Chief Treasurer and Ban of Slavonia). Even more frequently than in the case of judicial system, the officials in the treasury were talented men of relatively humble – even of peasant – origin, thus fully the creatures of Matthias, who might therefore expect then to show unbending loyalty. As a result of these reforms, Matthias at least doubled the revenues of the crown; and in years when the irregular subsidy was levied twice, if the income from the provinces conquered by him in the second half of his reign were also added, the amount might approach the one million mark.

In absolute terms, this is indeed impressive. However, the proud comparisons in earlier historiography between Matthias's fiscal achievement and the incomes of western countries, France or England, for instance, are based on slightly earlier data from the latter, in which revenues also doubled in the course of the second half of the fifteenth century. Most importantly, the revenue of the Ottoman Empire in 1475 amounted to 1,800,000 florins, at least two, but rather three times as much as that of Hungary (and, to be sure, far more than of any European kingdom at the time). In light of this enormous imbalance, it is only understandable that nearly all the surplus raised by Matthias was immediately spent on his army. In other words, while he filled the treasury, he also left it empty at the end of his reign, and burdened the country's economy quite excessively. While he continued to rely on the royal and baronial *banderia*, the *militia portalis* introduced by Sigismund and the noble insurrection, Matthias was also able to maintain a mercenary army, which he started to build up by hiring Jiškra's ex-Hussites pacified in northern Hungary in 1462. The multi-ethnic 'Black Army' consisted of heavy cavalry and infantry, as well as Hussite type war-wagons and artillery, and, combined with the banderia and the light cavalry from the counties and banates, could be successfully employed to apply traditional Hungarian hit-and-run tactics. At the muster of 1487 at Wiener Neustadt, Matthias's Italian court historian Antonio Bonfini estimated that the king's standing army consisted of twenty thousand cavalry and eight thousand infantry, with nine thousand war-wagons – an impressive figure by the European standards of the time. There were another eight thousand soldiers permanently garrisoned in the fortresses of the superbly organised southern line of defence.

This formidable force needed an outlet (the more so because even the increased revenue was insufficient to pay for it regularly, so the soldiers had to supplement their income from booty), and throughout his reign Matthias was nearly constantly at war, struggling either in the south to avert the Ottoman menace, or in the north and the west to assert his hegemony in Central Europe. Towards the Turks, the basic principle of Matthias's policy was active defence, that is, a policy of more than merely beating off attacks, but from time to time to transfer the theatre of war into Ottoman territory and to achieve strategic objectives. After having completed the conquest of Serbia in 1459, Mehmed II also overran Bosnia in 1463. Matthias did not risk an immediate counteroffensive, which might have endangered Hungary itself. He concluded a treaty of mutual aid with Venice, which was also embarrassed by the Ottoman advance, and moved into the Balkans only after the Sultan's main forces had left. Having pillaged Western Serbia, he took Jajca, the most important castle in Bosnia, after an exhausting siege in late 1463. Three Hungarian banates were now set up in Bosnia, which became in effect divided between Hungary and the Ottoman Empire. Jajca was also defended against a Turkish attempt to recover it in the following year, and became the cornerstone of a 'second line of defence' extending from the border of Wallachia to the Adriatic 100–150 kilometres south of the one guarding the heart of Hungary. For most of the rest of

Matthias's reign, there were only minor skirmishes and occasional Turkish raids, such as the one culminating in the battle of Kenyérmező in 1479, in which the Turks were beaten by the legendary commander Pál Kinizsi. Such feats did little to obliterate the fact that the military balance perceptibly shifted to the advantage of the Ottoman Empire. Since one of the main hopes pinned on Matthias upon his election had been precisely his ability to defy the Turkish advance, this resulted in some impatience with what was considered as inaction on his part, especially among the nobility. Matthias placated this with a successful campaign, capturing the fortress of Sabać on the Lower Danube in 1476. Though this time a succession crisis in the Ottoman Empire made the prospect of a major campaign in the Balkans promising, Matthias turned back to the western projects which had been the main focus of his foreign policy interest since he had stabilised the situation on the southern border in 1463-64.

The treaties of 1463 with Venice and Frederick III put an end to Matthias' international isolation. In this new situation, once his wife Catherine had died in 1464, Matthias severed his ties with his father-in-law, Poděbrady, who was anyway more of an embarrassment than a source of support in his earlier conflict with the emperor. He volunteered to lead a crusade against the Hussite King George, excommunicated and proclaimed an usurper by the Pope in 1466. Since both Venice and the Pope rather expected him to fight the Ottomans, the crusade did not materialise, and Matthias only declared war on Bohemia in March 1468. After protracted logistical moves, but little actual fighting and even less diplomatic preparation, the Czech Catholic barons elected him King of Bohemia in May 1469. This step proved premature. The Habsburgs and the Polish Jagiellos as well as the German electors were jealous of Matthias' ambition to dominate the region, and Prince Wladysław, son of King Casimir IV of Poland, accepted the Bohemian crown offered to him according to the wish of George Poděbrady when the latter died in 1471.

The fiasco abroad accompanied difficulties at home. Matthias had already quelled a revolt among the Transylvanian estates caused by the rigorous fiscal measures in 1467. Now it was his former confidants, Vitéz and his nephew, the humanist poet and Bishop of Pécs, Janus Pannonius, who plotted against him – ostensibly because the king neglected the Ottoman front and wasted the country's resources on futile wars in the north, but in reality because they themselves felt neglected and were able to exploit the resentment caused by Matthias's pretensions to 'arbitrary rule'. They intended to replace him with Casimir, the youngest of the Jagiello princes, but by the time the latter invaded Hungary in the autumn of 1471, Matthias had stifled the movement, in effect merely by swiftly returning from Bohemia and appearing among his barons and nobles at the diet.

In the face of the nascent Austrian-Czech-Polish coalition, the goal of Matthias from the early 1470s was to make a respectable peace, which was facilitated for him by the repeated military blunders of Władysław and his father. In 1474, they missed a golden opportunity to break the ambition of the Hungarian king, surrounded by far superior forces in the Silesian city of Breslau (Wrocław). Matthias was saved by the miscalculation of the balance of forces by his enemies, as well as his commanders cutting off the supply routes of the Polish and Bohemian armies. In terms of the subsequent armistice, confirmed in the peace of Olmütz (Olomouc) in 1478, Matthias received Moravia, Lusatia and Silesia (the economically most highly developed area of Central Europe), while Władysław only retained Bohemia proper. Both of them were entitled to use the title of King of Bohemia. Though out of the two candidates, Frederick III at first only installed Władysław among the German electors, later he promised the same to Matthias as well, and indeed took steps to have him acknowledged among the princes of the empire. It seemed that these treaties of 1477 and 1478 settled the affairs of the region on a lasting basis.

In fact, however, the promise of the emperor was already an item in a peace treaty that concluded a short war fought in 1477 between him and Matthias, remarkably successful from the latter's point of view. Apart from a short period of détente after 1464, relations between the two rulers had been strained because of mutual (quite justified) suspicions of fomenting plots and revolts, and because Frederick did not, indeed could not, pay Matthias the sum stipulated in the 1463 agreement and lent no support against the Ottomans. Matthias' marriage in 1476 with Princess Beatrice, daughter of King Ferdinand I of Naples, provided him with influential new allies in Italy, his ultimate aim being no less than the imperial throne. Turkish forays into Hungarian territory reduced the conflict to strokes of diplomacy until 1482, when Matthias declared war, and by 1487 his forces, far superior to those of the emperor, occupied most of Styria and Lower Austria. He transferred his seat to Vienna, occupied in 1485, and assumed the title of Duke of Austria. Though the German electors, frightened by the military successes of Matthias, chose Frederick's son Archduke Maximilian as King of Rome (that is, heir to the imperial throne), at the end of his reign Matthias ruled a veritable empire of his own.

Ever since then, the reorientation of Hungarian foreign policy by Matthias has been an object of controversy. Even in his lifetime, he was accused by neglecting the Turkish menace for the sake of his quest of personal glory in the West. Others have suggested that since he practically received no external help against the Turks, he sought to offset the massive superiority of the Ottoman Empire in terms of territory and manpower by uniting the resources of East-Central Europe, where the trend had been anyway towards the confederation of the states of the region in personal unions.

Matthias indeed clearly recognised that power relations had been decisively modified to the advantage of the Ottomans, and until firm guarantees for the military and financial co-operation of Christian powers on a far larger scale than ever before could be had, the best policy was peaceful coexistence or 'active defence', instead of futile offensive undertakings. However, the different kingdoms of the region confederated in personal unions, retaining their independence in internal affairs, could hardly ever be regimented enough to take joint political and military action. Though Matthias undoubtedly endeavoured to secure a safe hinterland in Central Europe, in explaining his foreign policy the nature of his state and the place of the army in it are at least as important factors to consider. His army was raised in order to answer the needs of internal consolidation (later also, the maintenance of tranquillity) and defence against the Turks. As the southern campaigns of 1463-64 and 1476 show, against the Ottoman Empire even this most formidable of western armies of the time could only set itself the limited aims described above (it took over two months to capture Jajca, and nearly two to take Šabać, hastily erected a couple of years before!). Once the army was there, however, it needed to be occupied; and it was best to occupy it in the West, where, proverbially, 'war subsisted on war', rather than in the backward and ravaged Balkans which promised no booty to make up for the payment in arrears. Finally, as an explanation of Matthias's western ambition, we must contemplate his personal background. This archetypal founder of a dynasty, arrogant and power-thirsty as he certainly was, fumed at being considered an upstart among the established dynasties of the region. The success of arms could earn what legitimacy denied him.

To some extent at least, similar was the function of Matthias' lavish patronage of the arts and learning, the other conspicuous item in his expenditure besides his army. For the grandson of an immigrant knight from obscure Wallachia, his own erudition – he spoke several languages and not only collected but also read books – and the nearly one hundred thousand florins he spent ly on artistic patronage were excellent propaganda. Contemporary humanists ranked Matthias in this respect with the most famous patrons of the period: Giangaleazzo Maria Sforza of Milan, Federico da Montefeltro of Urbino, even Lorenzo de' Medici of Florence

The story of the reception of Renaissance humanism in Hungary is symptomatic of the ambivalence of the development of Hungarian culture in general. Whereas in most of Europe north of the Alps the new learning struck roots at the turn of the fifteenth and sixteenth centuries, the dynastic, political and economic ties forged between Italy and Hungary at the time of the Anjous brought its harbingers to Hungary considerably earlier. Still under Sigismund, in the 1420s, the painter Masolino and a disciple of the architect Brunelleschi worked for Filippo Scolari; the origins of the famous circle of literati in the Nagyvárad episcopal court of János Vitéz, 'the father of Renaissance humanism in Hungary', go back to the 1440s. It was from this group that Janus Pannonius, Vitéz's nephew, one of the most accomplished Latin lyricists of Europe at the time, emerged. It was also this group, mainly consisting of prelates educated at one of the Italian universities, that attracted leading humanists, such as the writer and philosopher Galeotto Marzio, Marsilio Ficino's neo-platonist friend Francesco Bandini, or the German astronomer Regiomontanus to visits in Hungary between the 1460s and the 1480s.

This early burgeoning was, however, not the tip of the iceberg of a generally flourishing culture, but the rather isolated initiative of an intellectual elite amidst circumstances of relative backwardness. The lack of places of higher learning was a distinct handicap. The university founded by Sigismund at Óbuda in 1395 (and refounded in 1410) soon met the fate of its predecessor in Pécs; nor did the university launched upon the initiative of Vitéz in Pozsony in 1467 (the *Academia Istropolitana*) much survive its founder who died in captivity soon after the plot of 1471. Towards the end of his reign Matthias tried, in vain, to develop the Dominican college in Buda as a university. Most of those who received an education in the country studied in village, town or chapter house schools, whose standards varied according to whether the schoolmaster had been trained at a foreign university or not. Future lawyers acquired the rudiments of customary law in the schools of the 'places of authentication' (*hiteleshely*). For a university education, a great many young nobles, and even more commoners, went abroad: to Vienna and Cracow, where Hungarian students had their own colleges, or to one of the Italian universities. Most of the were content with the curriculum in arts, and did not embark on the one in law or theology, still less in medicine. Still, mainly of course from Italy, they returned with changed visions. Characteristically, Janus Pannonius, having spent years studying in Ferrara and Padova, could never again feel comfortable with the conditions at home and complained bitterly about their rudeness and barbarity.

As his uncle, Janus died in the aftermath of the plot of 1471. Had he lived a decade longer, he might have been reconciled to a situation which, at least as regards the immediate courtly environment of Matthias, changed considerably. Italian masters such as Cimenti Camicia, sculptors from Dalmatia and Tuscany had by then transformed the palaces in Buda and Visegrád into splendid princely places of residence. Indeed, together with Sigismund, another great patron of secular and ecclesiastical building, the emergence of Buda as a worthy royal seat and capital city is largely owing to Matthias. Besides, he sponsored constructions in the Gothic and renaissance styles in about 110 localities around the country. Early renaissance architecture in Hungary mediated the new style towards the northern neighbours as well; the chapel built at Esztergom in the early 1500s and named after Tamás Bakócz, the prelate of commoner origin who started to rise to power under Matthias, was the first renaissance chapel built north of the Alps.

However, the Europe-wide fame of Matthias' court was primarily established by his library, the *Bibliotheca Corviniana*, a unique cultural monument of the time. The name derives from the byname first assigned to Matthias by Italian humanists: Corvinus, ostensibly an ancient Roman family, often associated with the raven (Lat. *corvus*) in the Hunyadi coat-of-arms, but possibly stemming from 'Corvino vico', the village Keve on the Lower Danube mentioned by Bonfini as the domicile of Matthias' father. The library, modelled after the ones of Vitéz and Janus, consisted of well over two-thousand volumes (a few hundred of which are extant, scattered around the world today), and thus in size it was only surpassed by that of the popes in the Vatican (as regards books in Greek, by none). Its composition was also fully up-to-date: comprising the full known corpus of all disciplines produced by the authors of antiquity and Hellenism, the Church fathers, Byzantine and scholastic literature as well as early humanism in bilingual (Greek-Latin) versions, the library provided the humanist scholars visiting Buda with excellent working conditions. Though from 1473 on, the German printer Andreas Hess issued printed texts in Buda, most of the items in Matthias' library were superbly illuminated manuscripts, initially ordered from Italy, and later increasingly from the workshops set up by Matthias in Buda.

Finally, it must be added that Matthias' patronage was not confined to the representatives of the new learning. He also invited into Hungary a remarkable thinker of late scholasticism, the Dominican Petrus Nigri, later appointed Regent of the Dominican college of Buda. The author of the first Hungarian chronicle to appear in print in 1488, János Thuróczy, was also hardly affected by humanism, and his historical thought focused on the idea of the kinship between the Hungarians and the Huns, who arrived to Hungary from Scythia, the 'great' among them electing the first rulers – an idea that became highly influential among the nobility.

Triumphant arms and cultural splendour might have earned fame and respect to Matthias, but he lacked one basic condition of establishing a dynasty: a legitimate heir. In vain did he try to secure the throne in the last years of his life by diplomatic manoeuvring for his natural son John Corvin, born in 1473. The issue of the succession was unsettled when he died, at the height of his victories, in Vienna on April 6, 1490. 'Dead is Matthias, lost is justice': this is how sixteenth-century tradition had the common man comment on the event. 'Dead is Matthias, books will be cheaper in Europe': this is how Lorenzo de' Medici reputedly exclaimed upon hearing the news of the death of Hungary's renaissance prince.

4. Socio-political crisis and Hungary's 'deviation' from the West

The near coincidence of Matthias's death with the discovery of America could be considered as symbolic of the fortunes of Hungary and indeed the whole of East-Central Europe (Matthias' Polish counterpart Casimir IV died in 1492). The period generally regarded as the commencement of the early modern era, when the progress of commerce, finance and industry, of armies, navies and administrative systems gradually raised Western Europe to the global ascendancy it enjoyed in the eighteenth and nineteenth centuries, marked the beginning of a trend towards little that was 'modern' by western standards in the region. An age of relative political strength had come to an end, and the long-term potential of economic prosperity and social progress was also seriously handicapped. Within a few decades, the estates dismantled the achievements of centralised monarchy, and although the Jagiello brothers seemed to have realised Matthias' dream of a Central European 'empire' by dividing the thrones of the region between themselves, their administrations and landed estates came increasingly under the control of the different baronial and noble factions.

Ironically enough, the power of the nobility in the area got reinforcement from the new European 'division of labour' arising from the geographical discoveries. As the resources of the New World were channelled into Western Europe, it now irrevocably became the centre of commerce, industry and finance in the old continent, while the role of the countries of Central and Eastern Europe as suppliers of raw material and agrarian products was also confirmed by the new developments. The 'price revolution' resulting from the influx of gold and silver from overseas in sixteenth-century Europe was primarily a steady and marked increase in the price of foodstuffs. The opportunities held out by this situation did not escape the attention of the landed nobility, which set out to maximise their agricultural output and export by strengthening their hold over the peasantry. Through the frequent diets dominated by them, they were able to push through the legislation required for this end. During the reigns of Władysław, John Albert and their successors in Bohemia, Hungary and Poland, the diets poured out edicts that tended to bind the peasants to the soil, to strengthen the nobility's jurisdictional powers over them, and to revive the duty of forced labour service *(corvée)* in the manor. All of this amounted to the rise of a system described as 'second serfdom': the earlier tendency towards the transformation of peasant obligations into cash and of the peasant himself into a freeholder was overturned, and he was relegated to a position more similar to the Russian semi-slave than to the independent farmer emerging in the West. The suppression of the resulting peasant unrest further increased the self-confidence of the nobility, which, in turn, further undermined centralised authority, creating favourable circumstances for conquest by external powers.

The structures Hungarian society had developed during the Middle Ages favoured such a turn of events under the stimulus of the new contingencies. Over sixty percent or even more of Matthias's fiscal revenues came from agriculture. It has already been mentioned that the main Hungarian export commodities were cattle – of which as many as an annual 100,000 could be driven out of the country in the fifteenth century –, wine and minerals. Besides gold and silver, with which Hungary supplied most of Europe prior to the appearance of precious metals from America and Africa on the market, copper became increasingly important by the end of the fifteenth century. Its mining was even mechanised by János Thurzó, a Cracow councillor of Hungarian noble origin, who operated a joint venture with the famous Fuggers of Augsburg to monopolise the industry. There was, therefore, nothing new in the absence of finished products among exports. On the other hand, the mere fact that the only substantial items on the list of imports were textiles and knives shows that home industries and the internal market functioned vigorously enough. Yet, the 'true' cities – the free royal boroughs with fortifications and rights of self-government – at the end of the fifteenth century (which seems to have been a period of decline or stagnation for them) numbered a mere thirty, with an aggregate population not exceeding ninety thousand. This was a figure unimpressive when compared to the mass of noblemen, most of whom possessed little more than the arrogance bred on their privileges amidst material and intellectual deprivation, but who could act as a formidable pressure group when fighting for their interests, real or imaginary. Among approximately three and a half million subjects of the Hungarian crown, one in twenty or twenty-five were noblemen (in France, the figure was one in a hundred), while only one in forty were free urban citizens (in France, one in ten) – provided that we accept the convincing suggestion that the dwellers of the *oppida* or market towns possessed a higher level of peasant 'liberties', rather than a lower level of urban freedom.

These circumstances were reflected in attitudes and political institutions and customs, which, in turn, affected social relations. While it occurred to no-one in England or France that the representatives of chartered town could be absent from parliaments or the estates general, respectively, it occurred to few and infrequently that they were as a matter of fact entitled to be represented at the diet. On the contrary, as the notion of an autonomous 'political society' started to take shape in Hungary in the late thirteenth century, and with greater intensity after 1400, it was believed axiomatically that the deputies of the nobility represented 'the whole body of the realm'. In the West, monarchs could rely on the strength of the urban economy in surmounting the crisis of the fourteenth and fifteenth centuries, the more so since they faced nobilities which had lost much of their prestige as well as the direct dependence of their peasants, and only expected offices and wars from the state. In the absence of such forces for constraint, the vigorous Hungarian nobility was able to shift the burden of the crisis to the segment of society which had become most 'westernised' during the preceding centuries: the peasantry, which now lost the struggle for the preservation of its limited rights and liberties acquired in that process. Thus the collapse of Matthias' state and the reorientation of the world economy consolidated the structures of Hungarian society that had even earlier diverged from their western counterparts, while it reversed trends that might have brought it closer to them.

After Matthias had died, a diet was summoned in order to elect his successor in May 1490. There was no shortage of claimants. Besides John Corvin, who enjoyed the support traditionally accorded to the Hunyadi clan among the nobility, and also possessed enormous family wealth, Maximilian of Habsburg claimed the throne on the basis of the treaty of 1463 between Matthias and Frederick III, as did both Jagiello brothers whose mother was a granddaughter of Sigismund and a sister of Lasdislas V. In addition, the widowed Queen Beatrice aspired to his husband's inheritance.

Corvin later proved to be a good soldier and organiser on the southern frontier, but was a much less able politician; he was anyway discarded by the most influential officials and generals of his father, probably on the consideration that the refusal of all foreign claimants might well have thrown Hungary into complications whose outcome was difficult to predict. While Maximilian's claim was the strongest, and it was also from him that efficient help against the Ottomans (who were expected to act soon once Matthias was dead) could be hoped, what the estates primarily wanted was a king 'whose braids they could hold in their hands', and found the ideal candidate in Władysław. He was crowned as Ulászló II on condition of signing election promises which included the abolition of the irregular subsidies and other 'harmful innovations' introduced by Matthias. Corvin was appeased by the title of Duke of Slavonia and by remaining by far the wealthiest magnate in the country, favours which he could even retain after having changed his mind, revolted, and having been defeated by Matthias' one-time commander Kinizsi. In 1491, invasions by Maximilian and Władysław's brother John Albert were beaten off, too. Matthias's mercenary army was used in these encounters, but when unpaid for several months it started to pillage the countryside and its remnants were finally dispersed by Kinizsi in 1492.

On the surface, most of the reign of Władysław was one of tranquillity, both at home and on the frontiers. The confusion that accompanied the succession raised the appetite of the Ottomans, who made unsuccessful attempts to capture important fortresses year after year until a peace was concluded in 1495. The peace was renewed several times, with a short interval in 1501 when Władysław joined the coalition of the Pope and Venice; however, his main objective was to obtain the lucrative subsidy offered by his allies, and he refrained from major battles or sieges. The situation changed in 1512, when the more warlike Selim I deposed his father, Bayezid II, and hostilities were resumed, with alternating success. On the whole, it was only the Bosnian Banate of Srebernik that was lost to the Turks. The balance was still far more unfavourable from the Hungarian point of view, since the skirmishes and raids that continued without a formal war devastated the lands around the fortresses erected by Matthias, and this cut their supply lines. It was increasingly difficult to defy Ottoman pressure.

The only significant conflict between Hungary and a Christian power was Maximilian's declaration of war in response to the decree of the Hungarian estates that no foreigner ought to be elected king of Hungary, should Władysław die heirless. The issue was resolved by the inheritance treaty of 1506: Maximilian's grandson Ferdinand was to marry the daughter of Władysław, whose son, yet to be born, was to marry Ferdinand's sister Mary. When the treaty was disclosed, it was the Hungarian estates that compelled the king to declare war on the emperor, but as Wladysław's son Louis was indeed born a few months later, the war seemed untimely.

Merely by the chronicle of events, Hungarian politics was more peaceful than at any time since the reign of Sigismund. Wladysław faced no attempt to depose him by the force of arms or art. However, the main reason for this was that the lords found 'legal' ways of asserting their interest *vis-à-vis* the ruler as well as other segments of society. They did not take steps to change Matthias' institutions and manner of government; rather, these were 'expropriated' by them. Control shifted into the hands of the royal council whose decisions Wladysław never contested (hence his nickname Wladysław Dobže: 'the Very Well'). The chancellor became an especially powerful figure. Throughout most of the reign, the office of great as well as secret chancellor was filled by Tamás Bakócz, whose spectacular career started as an official of commoner origin under Matthias, but when Wladysław came to the throne he was already Bishop of Győr, then Eger, and finally Archbishop of Esztergom and a cardinal besides the chancellorship. Even the levying of the extraordinary subsidy continued on a regular basis, with the difference that in the absence of the Black Army it was now collected partly by the barons to maintain their *banderia*, and partly by the counties to hire mercenaries – with the predictable result that while the country's defence strength shrank considerably, the royal revenue fell to 200,000 florins and even below, in other words, under the level from which once Matthias had raised it.

In order to clearly define military obligations (that is, the circle of those entitled to appropriate the subsidies), the diet of 1498 passed legislation which also confirmed the ongoing process of differentiation within the nobility. The laws spelled out the names of the 41 great landowners entitled and obliged to maintain banderial troops in a list that became the basis of a strict demarcation between the aristocracy and those noble families that had risen to power during the preceding decades, and the starting point of the development of the diet into the bicameral assembly it subsequently became. Besides the court, the aristocracy and the middle nobility became the poles of the complicated political contests fought with frequently changing positions and alliances at the tumultuous diets of the Jagiellonian period. Since the composition of especially the baronial interest groups was changing quite frequently, it is somewhat at the expense of historical accuracy that the aristocracy has been described as of 'pro-Habsburg', and the nobility as of a 'national' orientation. To be sure, debates at the diets resounded with the rhetoric of patriotism, Hungarian valour and the common good, couched in the language of Scythianism enshrined in the chronicle of Thuróczy – ironically enough at a time when the country's system of defence and its strategic position *vis-à-vis* the Ottoman Empire swiftly deteriorated. As earlier, the nobility, informed by sentiment as well as prudence, found its hero in a person arisen from their own rank, this time János Szapolyai, Voevode of Transylvania from 1510 on. It was with him in mind that the 1505 decree on foreign and 'national' kings, mentioned above, was passed.

The middle nobility, increasingly barred from upward mobility, tried to compensate themselves at the expense of the peasantry and the *oppida*, which earned most of the profits deriving from the circulation of agricultural commodities. Since these nobles had relatively few serfs, they were adversely affected by the free migration of peasants whose direction was always towards the greater estates where relations of dependence were more favourable and the exchange of goods more vigorous. Under the pressure of the masses of the middle nobility, from 1492 on diets first obliged all landlords (even urban citizens cultivating manors) to collect the *nona* in kind, then reduced the fine imposed for preventing peasants from transferring from one lord to another, and finally abolished the right of migration altogether. Landowners increasingly required their tenants to perform more *corvée* than earlier: whereas one day of *corvée* per week was considered as rather excessive under Matthias, three days a week became quite common as the Jagiellonian period advanced. The offensive of the nobility affected a highly stratified peasantry whose upper layer drew greater self-confidence and a broader vision from the affluence it had gained through the economic successes of the preceding half-century. These well-to-do, often also quite educated tenants and dwellers of the *oppida*, many of them involved in profitable business like the trade of cattle and viticulture, did not fail to respond to the challenge. Out of isolated local protests, an ill-advised move on the part of the elite provoked a concerted rural revolt, the greatest in the history of Hungary.

In 1513, Bakócz qualified as a candidate at the papal elections, and as a compensation for losing the contest, Leo X appointed him papal legate to organise a crusade against the Ottomans. Despite misgivings among the experts of Ottoman affairs in the royal council, the corresponding papal bull was proclaimed in Buda in April 1514, and soon some forty thousand peasant crusaders gathered in the camps, most of them in the central one near Pest, under the command of György Székely Dózsa, a cavalry officer from the southern frontier. The eagerness of the peasants may have been motivated by anti-Turkish sentiments and the remission of sins promised to the participants of the crusade, but it was mainly a symptom of general unrest and disaffection with their lot. This grew as the nobles, reluctant to let their scanty labour force leave their estates and worried of the inevitable offences of such an unruly mass, tended to prevent their peasants from joining the crusaders. In early May, this already led to bloody fights, in response to which Bakócz issued orders to cancel the campaign and to stop recruitment.

However, the peasants and Dózsa, who was still anxious to march against the Turks, refused to disperse. They defeated forces that attempted to stop them, and remained on the offensive for two months, burning manor houses, pillaging castles, and carefully destroying documents registering seigneurial rights. They were inflamed by the popular Observant Franciscan friars, originally entrusted with the preaching of the cross, who had long been impatient with the social injustice they witnessed in the villages and *oppida* they themselves came from, and developed a peculiar 'popular crusader' ideology. This was based on the idea that by sabotaging the defence of the realm and hindering the 'holy host of the Cross' from fulfilling their mission, the lords forfeited their rights, and that in the event of the success of the revolt the peasants should be invested with the same liberties as the Szekels of Transylvania. By the end of June, the king and the nobility awoke from the initial shock, and the lesser centres of the rebellion soon became pacified, whereas the main army of Dózsa surrendered to Szapolyai who came to rescue the castle of Temesvár, besieged by the peasants in vain for over a month, on July 15, 1514.

Dózsa was executed in a bestial way – burnt alive on a red-hot iron throne, his associates being forced to eat of his burning flesh before themselves being tortured to death –, but apart from occasions of similar brutality in the immediate aftermath of the revolt, most participants escaped serious punishment, obviously upon the recognition that their labour force was still needed. The peasants were of course required to pay for the damages caused. As a collective punishment, the diet of October 1514 passed legislation that subjected the peasants to 'eternal servitude' (*perpetua rusticitas*), that is, they were now uniformly forbidden to transfer from one landlord to another and to hold arms, and required to perform forced labour. Though not strictly and equally enforced at all times, this became the legal status quo down to 1848.

At the same diet, the famous *Tripartitum*, a vast collection of Hungarian customary law compiled on the order of the diet of 1498 by István Werbőczy, was presented to the deputies. Werbőczy was a jurist and a zealous partisan of Szapolyai and the dietal lesser nobility, so he insisted – not surprisingly, though in the face of realities – on the identical liberties of all noblemen and on the idea that it was the community of nobles that constituted the abstract 'crown'. The notion of a republic of nobles, like the one developed in Poland in the same century, was just one step further from this, so it is also hardly surprising that the text was neither promulgated, nor sent out to the counties by the royal council. Nevertheless, printed in Vienna in 1517, the work became widely known and was for three centuries the basis of the actual meting out of justice, which rested primarily with the local courts of the noble county.

The gravest consequence of the peasant war was the damage caused, which intensified the impact of the European economic slump that started in 1512, at a time when resources would have been needed more than ever. Even at the end of the fourteenth century, when the territory of the Ottoman Empire did not exceed that of the Kingdom of Hungary, it was far superior in military and strategic terms. The fifteenth-century conquests of especially Murad II and Mehmed II in the Balkans and Asia Minor changed the territorial balance to over two to one, and those of Selim I after 1512 in Syria, Egypt and Iraq, to three to one. Since other targets were either too remote or less attractive, Hungary could reasonably be expected to stand next in line as Wladysław's son Louis II acceded to the throne at the age of ten in 1516. As Selim, too, died and was succeeded by his son Suleyman I (later named 'the Magnificent'), the barons who governed in the name of the still under age king were so relieved that they failed to respond to the peace offer of the new Sultan (indeed, they imprisoned his envoy). It was a gross miscalculation: as early as the following year, Suleyman, ambitious and insulted, marched against Hungary. Sabać and Belgrade fell in the summer of 1521, leaving the country open to penetration from the south.

As the different projects hatched by the diets to organise defence became increasingly interwoven with factional politics, and thus neutralised each other or were mere declamation, in 1523 Louis II – persuaded by his wife Mary of Habsburg and following the example of his brother-in-law Ferdinand of Austria – attempted to take matters into his own hands. The changes in government, on the whole, did not work well, and only fuelled faction and instability, to the extent that the political atmosphere was that of a civil war until the diet of April 1526, when the king consolidated his position, ironically, by relying on a secret society created to protect the interests of the nobility in the previous year. Nor were otherwise well-advised initiatives, such as the revocation of the contract with the Fuggers regarding the northern mines, yield the desired result. The only decision of 1523 that proved successful was the appointment of Pál Tomori, Archbishop of Kalocsa, as captain general. Tomori as well as Szapolyai won a few victories against the Turks, who in turn broke the backbone of the first line of fortresses. Amidst the problems associated with the growing conflict between the Catholic and Protestant estates, the German peasant war and the contest with the France of Francis I, the imperial diets and Louis' other brother-in-law, Emperor Charles V, remained unmoved by the dozens of alarming pleas for assistance.

As the diet of 1526 convened, Suleyman's army, considerably larger than in 1521, was already on its way to the campaign that would mark the beginning of the dismemberment of the medieval Kingdom of Hungary. Serious preparations were not made in Hungary before June, when troops were finally mobilised and devotional objects sequestered for the purpose of coinage. The army that finally engaged the Turks at Mohács on August 29, 1526, consisted of the royal *banderia*, soldiers from the southern fortresses, and baronial *banderia* mainly from southern Hungary: some 25,000 men in the face of about three times as many Ottomans. The mercenaries from Louis' Bohemian kingdom, the troops from Croatia and those of Voevode Szapolyai failed to arrive in time for the battle, which was short and disastrous. As the initially promising Hungarian light cavalry attack collapsed, the outcome was decided, and within two hours the Hungarian army and administration suffered a mortal blow: at least ten thousand foot soldiers, virtually the whole cavalry, and thirty-five prelates and barons lay dead on the battlefield. While in flight, the king, clad in heavy armour, fell from his horse and drowned in a stream. Suleyman could now march to Buda at his pleasure, and as after the battle of Muhi in 1241, it seemed again that the Kingdom of Hungary was on the verge of being annihilated.

CHAPTER IV

WEDGED BETWEEN EMPIRES (1526–1711)

In the fifteenth century, Hungary figured as an important medium-ranking power of Europe. Its capital was a worthy residence of one of the greatest of Holy Roman Emperors in the first part of the century and the seat of the first of Renaissance princes north of the Alps in the second. The lament of Janus Pannonius in the 1460s concerning the barbarous conditions of the country, while certainly not fully unjustified, could still be interpreted as in the line of a literary tradition. By contrast, when in 1620 Márton Szepsi Csombor expressed his distress at the ever broadening gap between the conditions of the West and his native country in his travelogue, significantly entitled *Europica varietas*, it was a grievously objective assessment of the situation. While not generally shared by his contemporaries, it was from that time on that this sense of having fallen behind became a dominant element in the experience and attitudes of Hungarian thinkers for centuries to come. Indeed, by the end of the seventeenth century, Hungary had become devastated, impoverished and removed from the main thrust of European development. Contemplation of this predicament, the arduous resistance to full subjection by foreign powers and the mere survival helped Hungary to remain an integral part of European culture and system of values, though it was quite unpredictable how much the mainly moral and intellectual capital thus accumulated would be worth among the conditions of accelerated progress in the subsequent period.

Understandably enough, the causes of the decline have supplied one of the most often discussed and controversial topics of Hungarian historiography, in which the responsibility has been variously assigned to the rage of oligarchy under the Jagiellos, the subjection of the peasantry and its alienation from the cause of national defence after 1514, Hungary's remoteness from the stimuli of the Atlantic market, Ottoman conquest and Habsburg 'colonisation'. I have already stressed the structural weaknesses in the country's earlier development, which facilitated the adverse impact of some of these new factors. The ossification of the social structure was undoubtedly exacerbated by the consequences of Dózsa's revolt, and by the country's partitioning, especially the fact that its most fertile areas were conquered by the Ottoman Empire, a power whose whole outlook was completely alien from European standards.

At the same time, Poland, which experienced no major peasant war in the period and escaped Ottoman rule, became a classic example of 'second serfdom' as well as a 'democracy of nobles', where the vigour of corporate structures sapped the strength of the state and led to its fall at the end of the eighteenth century.

The trauma caused by the disintegration of the medieval Kingdom of Hungary and the fact that its territory became, for over a century and a half, a theatre of war in the struggle between two expansionist great powers, the Ottomans and the Habsburgs, was in some sense certainly a 'surplus' in comparison with Poland, accentuating the culturally and intellectually fertilising decadence and defiance which served as a background to the growth of and struggle between the Reformation and the Counter-Reformation. It only served to aggravate the perplexity apparent in the attitudes of the period that besides the disastrous demographic balance and the destruction of economic resources, the cycles of international prosperity did not fail to reach Hungary. However, the agrarian boom that continued to stimulate the Hungarian economy throughout most of the sixteenth century, failed to generate a structural transformation leading to the capitalisation of agriculture or the rise of industries linked with it. As regards the claim that such a development was impeded by Habsburg rule, it should be born in mind that the effects just mentioned were already apparent in the early seventeenth century, at a time when the Hungarian estates had just consolidated their positions *vis-à-vis* the Viennese court, well before the backlash of Habsburg absolutism later in the century. To be sure, the partial loss of independent statehood and the fact that its main repository, the Principality of Transylvania, emerged in the part of the medieval Kingdom of Hungary where western structures were the least advanced and which was compelled to a permanent diplomatic oscillation between the two neighbouring great powers, was not an advantage. Nevertheless, it must be realised that by the early sixteenth century Hungary was no longer able to arrest Turkish expansion. The inevitable outcome was that its remnants became a buffer zone between the Ottoman Empire dependent on the Habsburgs, whom the death of Louis II on the Mohács battlefield helped, along with the Hungarian crown, to the chance of fulfilling their main European mission: to contain, and at the end of the seventeenth century, to expel from Central Europe the most aggressive eastern conqueror since the rise of the Occident.

1. A bulwark of Christendom, or tripartite Hungary

Twelve days after the Battle of Mohács and little more than a generation after the death of Matthias, the triumphant Sultan and his army marched into Buda, evacuated by the court of the widowed Queen Mary, which had fled to Pozsony. The Sultan's retinue also left quite soon, having burnt the capital and much of the countryside in their way, and returned to the Balkans by mid-October with such an immense booty that even as late as 1528 it beat down the prices of slaves and items of precious metals at the market of Sarajevo. Apparently, Hungary was left to her own resources; in reality, from the garrisons left behind in the fortresses occupied in the southern Srem area, the Turks could challenge any development in the country unfavourable from their point of view.

In fact, the political situation of Hungary could hardly have been more favourable for them. Louis II having left no heir, two rival claims were raised to the Hungarian throne, one in terms of the 1505 decree of the diet requiring the election of a 'national king', and another one in terms of the 1506 Habsburg-Jagiello marriage treaty. Szapolyai, whose moment now came, had himself elected as King John I at the diet convened at Székesfehérvár by the vast majority of the nobility on November 11, 1526. By his quick action he hoped to deter the Habsburgs, whose adherents, a few magnates grouped around Queen Mary who had refused a marriage proposal by Szapolyai, nevertheless decided to follow the example of the Czech estates in recognising Ferdinand, Archduke of Austria, elected as Ferdinand I in Pozsony on December 17. For the Habsburgs, who repeatedly interfered with the affairs of Hungary during the reign of Louis II, it was imperative to seize his inheritance and to secure the western and northern parts of the country, even if they could not contemplate the suppression of the Turks. As the Habsburg forces, occupied in the Italian wars of Emperor Charles V, could be released after the sack of Rome in May 1527, well-trained German mercenaries started to drive Szapolyai's armies out of the central areas of Hungary. Recognising the status quo, most earlier supporters of Szapolyai rallied to Ferdinand at the diet of Székesfehérvár in November 1527, while King John was first pushed back to Transylvania, then sought refuge in Poland.

The Ottomans were now able to proceed to square two in their game of occupation by stages, well tried in the Balkans. They had already weakened the economic and military establishment of the region by a powerful first strike, and left behind garrisons in key fortresses. There was now also a political force in the country that could only continue in power with their support and would in return legalise their presence:

encouraged from the Porte, John sought the help of Suleyman against Ferdinand. In the treaty of Istanbul in January 1528, he was recognised as the only lawful ruler of the land conquered by the Sultan by the force of arms, and was promised the help solicited. The nobility that had brought Szapolyai to the throne could be lulled into believing that the Turks were in fact allies, which prepared the way for a final blow culminating in the incorporation of a part or the whole of the country into the Ottoman Empire, or at least reducing it to being a dependant buffer state, as was the case with the neighbouring Romanian principalities.

That third step would be taken in 1541, when Buda was finally captured and occupied for the next for 145 years by the Ottomans. Though in 1529 they took Buda and forced the court of Ferdinand to flee, the subsequent siege of Vienna was unsuccessful, and in 1532 a second attempt to march against the Habsburg seat was halted by the defenders of the tiny Transdanubian fortress of Kőszeg. During the 'years of peace' that followed – in fact a period of intermittent civil war, with frequent clashes between the partisans of the two kings – the Sultan was content to exercise increasing control over the country through the troops ostensibly assisting Szapolyai in his struggle against Ferdinand. While some of the estates, apprehensive of the dismemberment of the country, tried to take the initiative by holding 'kingless diets' in order to remove both monarchs, and the changing loyalties of others resulted in the continuous alteration of the boundaries between the domains of Ferdinand and John, most of the country was under the nominal jurisdiction of the latter. Besides Turkish military presence, John's authority was seriously curtailed by Lodovico Gritti, a Venetian banker (illegal son of the Doge), merchant and favourite of Suleyman, who was Szapolyai's treasurer, governor and finally commander-in-chief. When he was killed by Transylvanian nobles in 1534, Suleyman, occupied in a war in Persia, did not immediately take revenge, but in 1536 he expanded Ottoman sway by moving into eastern Slavonia.

After the experience of the Gritti episode and the collapse of Ferdinand's counter-offensive in Slavonia in the following year, Szapolyai started to realise that his insistence on the throne benefited the Turks, and began to be reconciled to the idea of leaving the country after his death to the Habsburgs, who possessed better means to defend it. Lengthy negotiations between representatives of the two kings resulted in the Peace Treaty of Várad on February 24, 1538, by the terms of which Ferdinand was to inherit the throne from Szapolyai, whose heirs would receive ample compensation. However, Szapolyai, childless until then, in the following year married Isabella, the daughter of King Sigismund I of Poland, who bore him a son in 1540. Already dying, King John took an oath from his barons to evade the Treaty of Várad, and his all-powerful

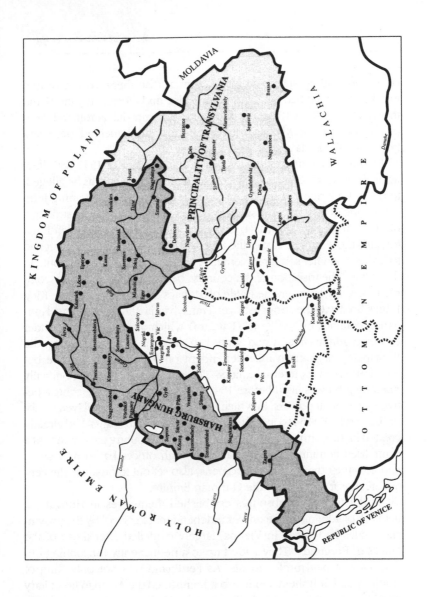

6. Tripartite Hungary at the
end of the sixteenth century

• important towns and fortifications

--- boundary of the survival of
Hungarian counties

······· boundaries of Turkish *vilayets*

counsellor and treasurer, György Martinuzzi ('Brother György', Bishop of Várad), indeed had the infant John Sigismund elected as John II and the election acknowledged at the Porte. In vain did Ferdinand send commissars to Transylvania to have the treaty implemented there, and troops to take Buda in both 1540 and 1541.

Ferdinand's army besieging Buda in the summer of 1541 withdrew upon the advance of that of Sultan Suleyman, determined, as he alleged, to protect the rights of the infant king. In fact, while entertaining John II's retinue in his camp, his soldiers occupied the city without striking a blow on August 29, 1541. Two days later, the royal household left Buda towards the territories east of the River Tisza and Transylvania, assigned to Isabella and her son for governance in return for an annual tribute to the sultan. The trisection of the country, begun in 1526, was now complete. Already between the Battle of Mohács and the fall of Buda, King John's hold was the strongest over Transylvania and the few east Hungarian counties or 'the Parts' (Partium) which after 1541 came under common administration and started to develop into a new state, the Principality of Transylvania, dependent on the Ottoman Empire but autonomous in its internal affairs. The rest of the country nominally ruled by John was even before 1541 a theatre of war in the contest between two great powers, in which the Hungarian military played a subordinate role. By 1541, one of these powers, the Habsburgs, had already created in the northern and western parts of the country the outlines of a centralised administration operated through offices based in Vienna, and now the other one, the Ottomans, also set out to organise the central areas as a province of the Ottoman Empire.

By the time the Habsburgs established themselves in Hungary, a network of administrative offices independent of control by the provincial estates had arisen in Vienna, largely modelled after those of the Dukes of Burgundy. They added up to a permanently functioning bureaucracy of paid professionals. As Ferdinand was not only King of Hungary and of Bohemia, but also administered the Austrian hereditary provinces and ruled, on behalf of Charles V, the Holy Roman Empire, the affairs of these lands were never clearly demarcated from each other. The chief policy-making body, the ruler's Privy Council, consisted of German and Austrian aristocrats and legal experts; decisions made by it as well as by the Court Treasury were issued by the Court Chancellery, which also had a share in conducting diplomacy. In 1556, a Military Court Council was also created. This was the only Viennese office whose competence officially extended to Hungary as well. Since he did not intend to reside in Hungary, immediately after he succeeded to the throne Ferdinand set up the governing council or Gubernium, whose chief was the Palatine, or if that position was vacant, one of the

Hungarian archbishops or bishops. Consequently, it never became a mere tool of the Habsburgs, and was not considered by the estates as an alien body, like the other office created in 1528 in Buda and reorganised in 1531 in Pozsony, the Hungarian Treasury. In principle, the new Hungarian offices were not dependent on their Viennese counterparts, but the Hungarian Treasury and the Hungarian Chancellery which functioned in the capital, were to some extent subordinated to them. The court residing outside Hungary, the king's Hungarian counsellors and other leading figures were moving awkwardly in a strange environment, and had little influence in shaping the ruler's policies.

Still, there were two important limits on the power of the Habsburg kings of Hungary, who could not but recognise that in the governance of Hungary her conditions and laws had to be taken into consideration. The first of these limits was the weight of the magnates, whose estates, partly as a result of the huge rewards obtained whenever changing their allegiance during the contest between Ferdinand and John, grew to the size of provinces. The authority of the centralised offices hardly penetrated beyond the boundaries of these estates. The Batthyány, the Báthori, the Erdődy, the Nádasdy, the Zrínyi and their likes held high offices at Pozsony or as *ispán*s of the counties, commanded the loyalty of the hosts of the local middle nobility, and maintained considerable private armies and princely courts that consciously endeavoured to play social and cultural roles that earlier belonged to that of the kings of Hungary. Second, the estates responded to the steps of the Habsburg administration which affected their rights as vigorously as if they had been its equal partners. The king could not neglect convening the diet because in principle he was not entitled to impose taxes unless voted by the estates, which usually refused to do so until they extorted a promise that their grievances would be redressed. While the sixteenth century was certainly not a period of 'anti-Habsburg struggles', as romantic historiography would have us believe, it was one of a constitutional division of power between Vienna and the Hungarian estates.

Nevertheless, the role of the estates was confined to a free scope of action in internal affairs. Although they claimed an influence over foreign and military affairs as well, the fact that these were managed directly from Vienna made this unrealistic. It was also undermined by the share Hungary was able to take in the expenses of maintaining system of defence. Upon the accession of the Habsburgs, the approximately one hundred fortifications within the country were not strong enough to resist artillery fire for more than a couple of days. Their modernisation and upkeep required enormous investments of capital, in addition to the pay of the fifteen to twenty thousand soldiers garrisoned in them even in peacetime, which rose in total from about 800,000 florins to one million annually between the middle and the end of the century. The income drawn by the treasury from Hungary was less than half of this figure, and was necessarily supplemented by considerable amounts of subsidy voted by the German imperial diet (the *Türkenhilfe*: 'Turkish aid') from 1530 on as well as by the estates of Austria (obviously allocated in the first place to the districts adjacent to their own borders). Diplomacy, especially towards the Popes, and the credit of the Habsburgs secured additional resources when, as often happened in years of war, even all this proved insufficient. Contemporaries could not but recognise that, were it not for the Habsburgs' access to these resources, Hungary might collapse in a matter of months.

Soon after the Szapolyai family and their entourage had left Buda, the Ottomans set to organising the territories occupied step by step between 1526 and 1541, as a province of the empire and as a base for further operations. As earlier in the Balkans, they disregarded the administrative divisions found in the country. Buda became the centre of the province or *vilayet* of Hungary, subdivided into *sandjaks*, and into further smaller units. The pasha or *beylerbey* of Buda was the military, administrative and jurisdictional governor of the *vilayet*, and he could also call troops from the *vilayet* established earlier in Bosnia, and the one created after the conquests later in the reign of Suleyman east of the Tisza, with its centre at Temesvár, into action. The pashas were assisted by numerous offices and were advised by the *divan*, a council consisting of the main dignitaries. They possessed extensive discretionary powers, and their scope of action comprised virtually anything that was in the political and military interest of the Porte. At the same time, whereas they could not select their own subordinates, who were also appointed directly from Istanbul, they themselves could be removed arbitrarily by the Porte: in 145 years, 99 pashas served in Buda. The military and civilian administration of the sandjaks was the responsibility of the beys, but the *kadis* or judges were independent of their authority and also exercised some control over them. In Hungary, unlike in the Balkans, institutions of local self-government also survived as long as they did not hazard Ottoman ascendancy and were able to perform their administrative functions. For instance, taxes were collected and justice was meted out by Hungarian authorities in the *oppida* of the Great Plain. Nor were the conquerors interested in making converts to Islam. As in the Balkans, where the Greek and South Slav Orthodox Churches were integrated in their system of authority, in Hungary they tolerated both the Catholic and the Protestant Churches, as long as this was compatible with their chief objectives: the stability of the Empire and the regularity of revenues.

In the footsteps of the Turkish soldiers, tax assessors soon arrived – the first extensive survey (*defter*) of the resources of the country was compiled as early as in 1545 – and developed a system of taxation with attention paid to earlier Hungarian practice. To be sure, the structure of landholding was fully adjusted to the Ottoman tradition: the most valuable sources of revenue (*oppida*, customs stations, ferries etc.) were retained by the imperial treasury (*haas* property), while the rest was either assigned to the main office holders as usufruct for the duration of their service, or distributed among soldiers and lesser officials as tenures (*ziamet* or *timar*). However, the basic units and amounts of taxation did not change considerably. The treasury demanded an annual poll tax (*haradzh* or *dzhizye*) levied by household whose value was 50 Ottoman *akches*, the equivalent of about one florin. In addition, a similar amount in cash was due to the new landlord, besides occasional dues, labour service and tithes on livestock, the production of wine (all of which some localities were entitled to transform into an annual lump sum payment).

In other words, the taxes did not differ markedly from those of pre-Ottoman times, either in kind or amount. Two factors still made the new situation far more oppressive from the point of view of the taxpayer. First, the frequent changing of landlords, who therefore wanted to benefit the most in the shortest time possible, and the arbitrary actions of the authorities made the actual burden unpredictable. Second, and even more grievously, besides the Turkish masters the Hungarian royal and church authorities, who considered the Ottoman occupation as a temporary anomaly, also expected the serfs of the area under Turkish rule to continue fulfilling their obligations. These claims were enforced by the soldiers of the fortresses, who effected this system of 'double taxation' far more successfully than their Ottoman counterparts in their forays beyond the frontier region.

This mainly resulted from the fact that there were gaps in the apparent dominance of the Ottomans in the triangular area carved out of the territory of Hungary. Unlike in the Balkans, where the consolidation of Turkish rule involved, among other things, a high rate of conversion to Islam and the emergence of many 'renegades' to high positions (even that of grand vizier) in the army or the local administration, in Hungary, especially after the disillusionment with Szapolyai's policies, co-operation with the Turkish authorities was minimal. Whereas a great many of the seventeen to nineteen thousand 'Turkish' soldiers in service in the Ottoman fortresses in Hungary were in fact Balkan Slavs (as indeed many of the frontier soldiers in Hungarian castles were), Hungarian peasants desirous of a military career preferred to flee across the border, as did the bulk of the nobility and many well-to-do dwellers of cities and *oppida*. In Hungary, the conquerors were in an overwhelmingly hostile environment, moving between their fortresses in carefully guarded convoys, their intercourse with the natives more or less confined to jousting with the warriors of the Hungarian fortresses across the frontier. These differences between the Balkans and Hungary where largely owing to the collapse of native rule in the case of the former and its partial preservation in the case of the latter, which itself was the result of the combination of two factors. First, in Hungary the Ottomans encountered a social and political structure organised, however incompletely, according to western standards, and the several centuries of stable development made these structures more capable of resistance than those of Hungary's more ephemeral Balkan neighbours. Second, when in the sixteenth century Hungary fell into a situation similar to that of the northern Balkans in the fifteenth, the hinterland of Habsburg power proved far stronger in the preservation of Hungary as a south-eastern buffer zone than the case was with the Hungary of the Jagiellos and the belt of defence created by Matthias in Bosnia.

Nevertheless, Suleyman did not abandon the endeavours to extend his domains even further, and led or ordered campaigns in Hungary at regular intervals throughout the rest of his reign. After the ignominious failure of Ferdinand's imperial forces to retake Buda in 1542, the Sultan wanted to secure the defence zone around the seat of the Hungarian province and the conquests along the Danube, which he did by capturing Esztergom, Székesfehérvár, Tata, Pécs and Siklós in the campaign of 1543. In the course of the following two years, local Turkish forces took further fortresses in southern Transdanubia and in the area between the Danube and the Tisza. Struggling with the task of fortifying the castles that fell within the frontier zone in the preceding years, Ferdinand could not even contemplate an attempt to recover the ones lost, in spite of the fact that Hungarian society adjusted to the conditions of constant warfare by rapid militarisation: nobles and commoners forced to flee from their lands, as well as the free heyducks (*hajdus*, originally drovers of cattle), volunteered to service in increasing numbers. In October 1547, however, Ferdinand concluded a five year armistice with the Sultan at Edirne, also obliging himself to pay an annual tribute of thirty-thousand florins to the Porte for the parts of the country controlled by him.

It was also amidst these struggles that the Principality of Transylvania started to emerge as a separate country, although its governor Martinuzzi, recognising the mistake committed by the sabotaging of the Treaty of Várad, at first also negotiated with Ferdinand for the reunification of the kingdom. Although Queen Isabella resisted these efforts, and the institutional framework of the earlier province started to take the shape of that of a separate polity, the 1549 agreement confirmed the earlier promise of Martinuzzi to surrender the domains of John Sigismund to Ferdinand in return for compensation in the form of ducal estates in Silesia. The imperial mercenaries sent to occupy Transylvania in 1551 were not numerous enough to deter Turkish retaliation. Although the fortresses taken in the short campaign of Mehmed Sokullu, the *beylerbey* of Rumelia, were soon recovered, in the situation that arose Martinuzzi felt forced to make gestures to convince the Porte of his loyalty, but his trimming was denounced as treasonable by the imperial general Giambattista Castaldo, who had him assassinated (with the knowledge of Ferdinand) in December 1551.

A major Ottoman campaign, commanded by Ali, Pasha of Buda, and Vice Vizier Ahmed Pasha, ensued in the following year, in the course of which Hungarian fortresses of great strategic importance were lost, but it was also shown that the combination of favourable circumstances and a great amount of determination might stop even the formidable Turks. While Ali captured Veszprém and a few smaller fortresses north of the Danube Bend, Ahmed took Temesvár, and the two armies were united under Szolnok, freshly erected on the Tisza. Having finished their job there, the approximately seventy thousand strong army marched to Eger, 'the gate of Upper Hungary', whose garrison could be augmented to a mere two thousand from the surrounding area. Though the relief force expected never came, the defenders, commanded by the legendary István Dobó, resisted all attempts of the ever more exhausted Turks during a siege of five weeks. As the armies of the pashas retreated at the end of the 1552 campaign season, the balance sheet was quite dismal from the Hungarian point of view, but the first example of successful resistance at Eger made a great psychological impact on the country.

Yet, partial successes like this one and others in the following years did not hold out the prospect of striking back. Although the great distance and the relatively short time available for major operations limited the efficiency of Ottoman campaigns, even the local forces could occasionally extend the occupied area, as in 1554 and 1555 in southern Transdanubia and Upper Hungary. On the other hand, Ferdinand could not afford attempting to recover places even in the absence of the Sultan's main army as long as the resources of the Holy Roman Empire were at the disposal of his brother Emperor Charles V, who was more interested in the religious strife within the Empire than in the general anti-Ottoman campaign long expected of him. But even after the religious peace of Augsburg in 1555 and the abdication of Charles V in favour of Philip II in Spain and Ferdinand in the Empire in 1556, the only important achievement was the growth of a uniform and expert administration of the fortress system by the newly created Military Court Council.

No major castles had been recovered from the Ottomans when the ageing Suleyman set out to his seventh and last campaign to Hungary in 1566. While the forces of Vice Vizier Pertav Pasha took the important fortress of Gyula in the Körös valley after a six week siege, the Sultan marched against Szigetvár, west of Pécs on the road to Vienna. The defenders, commanded by Miklós Zrínyi, a nobleman of Croatian origin whose grandfather, uncle and brother had died fighting against the Turks, held out for over a month, but when bombardment by the Ottoman artillery set the fortress on fire, they sallied forth from it and fell nearly to a man. In the meantime, the considerable relief force of Maximilian I (or II as Holy Roman Emperor), who had succeeded Ferdinand in 1564, recovered Veszprém and a few smaller castles in Transdanubia, but then encamped near Győr, to secure the foreground of Vienna. As Suleyman the Magnificent also died during the last days of the siege of Szigetvár, the Turks retreated well before the end of the campaign season, content with minor acquisitions.

The second peace of Edirne, concluded by Maximilian with Suleyman's successor Selim II on February 17, 1568, acknowledged the Turkish conquests of 1552 and 1566, and was preserved for a quarter of a century. The marauding expeditions, raids and local conflicts, sometimes resulting in the transfer of smaller strongholds from one master to another, were not considered as violations of the treaty and did not upset the balance of forces. Two years later another treaty finally settled the status quo among the former parts of the Kingdom of Hungary. In 1556, John Sigismund and his mother returned to Transylvania, where Ferdinand was unable to consolidate his rule. Unlike under Martinuzzi, when the Porte interfered with minor matters, Transylvania now started to obtain increasing independence in its internal affairs, although the Sultan expected its rulers to adjust their foreign policies to his own objectives; indeed, John Sigismund commanded the third wing of the Ottoman offensive of 1566, striking at northern Hungary from the east. In the Treaty of Speyer of August 16, 1570, John Sigismund acknowledged Maximilian I as the lawful ruler of Hungary and his claim to Transylvania after the extinction of the Szapolyai house. Though the latter point was not put into practice, this reissue of the Treaty of Várad of 1538 became the basis of the relationship between the two Hungarian states for over a century: in spite of their dependence on the Porte, the princes of Transylvania regarded their domain as an inalienable part of the lands of the Holy Crown, and themselves as subjects of the King of Hungary (against whom they never scrupled to rebel whenever it seemed to be in their interests).

Later referred to as 'Fairy Land' on account of its cultural glamour and international respect during its flourishing between the 1610s and 1640s,

Transylvania could also be called one because of its rather enigmatic character emerging from the ambivalence of its political, social and cultural conditions. Rich in resources and ethnically mixed, it had been a relatively poor region where western style structures and institutions were the weakest among the former territories of the Kingdom of Hungary. While the Saxon burghers and farmers, the Szekel freemen and the Hungarian nobles belonged to separate jurisdictions – unlike the fourth of the ethnic groups, the Romanians, who comprised nearly one-third of the population in the sixteenth century and a substantially greater proportion in the seventeenth, and were overwhelmingly serfs – which helped them to develop their distinct identities, corporate institutions were the least developed in all of Europe. This apparently contradicts the fact that John Sigismund and his successors held diets at frequent intervals, at least twice, and sometimes even five or eight times a year. However, the main reason for the frequency of diets was that they performed functions which in Hungary were fulfilled by lower level organs of self-government, such as the counties. In addition, their role largely consisted of the endorsement of the propositions of the prince. Princes chose and discarded the members of their council at will, often leaving seats vacant. Loyalty and reliability were more important qualities in the selection of advisors than either birth or expertise, and the same was true in the case of most other officials in the rather rudimentary bureaucracy. Instead of centralising, let alone absolutist endeavours, it is more appropriate to attribute to the princes of Transylvania a specific concentration of power, arising under the pressure of specific circumstances.

Princely power was in the first place based on the fact that the treasury was by far the greatest landowner in Transylvania, and since princes took special care to maintain this situation by avoiding the Hungarian practice of transferring revenues into private hands, no latifundia of the size of provinces and alternative power centres similar to the ones in Hungary ever emerged in Transylvania. In addition, whereas the princes after John Sigismund, who died childless in 1571, were all elected by the diet, their legitimacy to a large extent derived from the *atname*, the charter of appointment from the Porte, in which Ottoman support was promised against internal and external threat. As a result of the peculiar status of the prince, quite a lot depended on his personal abilities, and the fortunes of Transylvania rose and declined with the talents of its rulers.

Although Istanbul, regarding the Principality of Transylvania as a creature of Suleyman, insisted on its vassal status and on determining its foreign policies, the diplomatic horizon of its princes was increasingly broadened. Links were established with France in the sixteenth and the

Protestant powers, England, the United Provinces and Sweden in the seventeenth century; Transylvania sometimes evaded the call of the Porte to arms, and tried to reassert the claims of medieval Hungarian kings for overlordship over Wallachia and Moldavia, then the vassals of the Ottoman Empire. Transylvanians also maintained the hope that the unity of the kingdom would be re-established quite soon; initially they expected Habsburg arms to deliver them from the grasp of the Turks, whereas later the idea developed that Transylvania would be the basis of unification. The enchantment with this idea, rather illusory in the light of the fact that such a unification was contrary to the interest of the Ottomans who could easily thwart attempts merely by their local forces, stimulated them to achievements beyond their strength. The institutions and the court of royal Hungary being outside the country, those of Transylvania were cherished as the repositories of Hungarian statehood and culture.

That culture became increasingly imbued with Protestantism. John Sigismund, having been excommunicated by the Pope on account of his being an ally of the infidel, did not interfere with the spread of the new faith, and even adopted different versions of it himself. At a time when the Augsburg religious settlement of 1555 obliged Germans to follow the creed of their landlords, when Catholics and Puritans were subject to penal laws in England and the third religious war in a sequence of eight raged in France, Transylvania became remarkable as a home of religious tolerance, even if we consider that Orthodoxy, the religion of the Romanians, did not benefit from it.

2. Protestants and Catholics: a creative contest

Soon after Martin Luther is alleged to have nailed his tenets on the gate of the castle church of Wittenberg, they started to make an impact in Hungary. Their initial progress in the country can be implied mainly from counter-measures. In 1521, the papal bull excommunicating Luther was made public by the Archbishop of Esztergom; in the same year Werbőczy, who disputed with Luther personally at the imperial diet in Worms, urged anti-Lutheran legislation, which was first passed in 1523. The decrees of the diets of the 1520s, motivated to a great extent by fear of losing Papal support against the Ottomans, were severe, but although a few books and even preachers were initially burnt, the general spirit was that of persuasion rather than persecution.

This was favourable for the spread of the new creed, whose first followers were, for obvious linguistic reasons, German burghers of the free royal and Saxon cities and, remarkably enough, courtiers around Queen Mary. The first centres from which Lutheranism radiated to the countryside were manors of magnates like those of Péter Perényi, Voevode of Transylvania, at Siklós and Sárospatak, or Chief Justice Tamás Nádasdy at Sárvár, in the years after Mohács. They were persuaded to support the cause by graduates of foreign universities who recognised the value and the significance of the Lutheran demand of preaching in the vernacular, or by former Catholic priests and friars, some of whom, especially the Franciscans, had for some time been actively promoting the renewal of the Christian faith and Church. Afterwards, the rapid expansion and the immense popularity of Protestantism was largely owing to the fact that it could be construed to supply satisfactory answers to problems that disturbed Hungarian society. Needless to say, the most soaring of these issues were related to the Ottoman plight. According to the Catholic interpretation, it was brought to the Hungarians as a scourge of God in order to punish their idolatrous ways; by implication, the adoption of the true faith would regain God's grace for them and help them to expel the Turks. Alternatively, in the Protestant view, Hungarians could be seen as God's chosen people, which was always hit the hardest; but when showing firmness in their belief, they would be liberated from the Turkish yoke, as were the Jews from the Babylonian and Egyptian captivities.

Under such influences and considerations, and due to the devotion of fiery preachers mainly originating from the *oppida*, there was a watershed of Protestant feeling among the common folk in Hungary from the 1540s on. This timing was significant, for it meant that all of the important trends of the Reformation appeared nearly simultaneously with one another in Hungary and in a full blown fashion. Therefore, there was hardly enough time for a Lutheran church organisation to emerge before it lost quite a lot of its supporters to Calvinism, which was itself soon challenged by Anti-Trinitarianism (Unitarianism or Socinianism). Characteristically, the several waves of the reform movement were embodied in the individual careers of some of the pioneers of its propagation. A case in point is the humanist scholar Mátyás Dévai Bíró, who was credited with having first spread 'the plague of Luther' among the Hungarians, proceeded step by step, first from Catholicism to Lutheranism and then to Calvinism. Many of such innovators, like István Szegedi Kis, who traversed nearly the whole area under Ottoman occupation during his career as a preacher, were such magnetic personalities that their flocks immediately followed them in their conversions.

The chief mode of the contest between the creeds was the theological dispute of preachers before the audience of a parish, frequently resulting in the expulsion of the one deemed the 'loser'. Disputes in the frontier pale of Transylvania were especially heated. Disputants whose fame travelled far and wide, such as Péter Méliusz Juhász, the Calvinist Bishop of Debrecen, and Ferenc Dávid, the restless innovator of the faith who sought to pass even beyond Anti-Trinitarianism, were invited to measure the power of their erudition and convictions at the court of John Sigismund, himself an Anti-Trinitarian by the end of his life. Catholics tended to succumb in these debates to their Protestant rivals who were incomparably better versed in the Bible, and by the 1560s they practically disappeared from among the disputants. While the Catholic church hierarchy survived, its members held high offices, and tithes continued to be collected even from Protestants, only scattered islands of Catholicism remained in the country, and even Lutheranism was confined to the German and Slovak inhabited areas, while the most radical sects of the time (Anabaptists, Sabbatarians) also appeared. By about 1580, when the religious divisions in the country had become somewhat stabilised for half a century, at least 80 per cent of Hungary's inhabitants were Protestants, the Calvinists being more numerous than all other denominations taken together. The Habsburgs were supposedly ardent defenders of Catholicism, but even in their domains the changes were accompanied with remarkably little violence, largely directed against radicals. Whereas the official policy in royal Hungary was (rather lukewarm) persecution, and the Ottoman authorities were indifferent, the Transylvanian diet at Torda in 1568 decreed the free worship of the four 'received' denominations (recepta religio: Catholics, Lutherans, Calvinists and Anti-Trinitarians). Although further religious innovation was forbidden under John Sigismund's Catholic successor, Prince István Báthori, the status quo was preserved well into the seventeenth century.

The advent of the Reformation, its dialogue with other contemporary cultural trends amidst the late flourishing of some earlier ones and the rupture of the old organisation of culture as a result of the wars, make the sixteenth century a particularly exciting period in the history of Hungarian culture. The first decades of the century produced the finest achievements of late Gothic art and Catholic sermon literature. The splendidly carved triptych of Master Paul in the parish church of Lőcse (Levoča), made between 1508 and 1518, is the largest of its kind in Europe. Pelbárt Temesvári and Osvát Laskai, the two great innovators of Catholic preaching in the early sixteenth century, left behind homilies that continued to be used well into the century, and inspired important followers. One in four of the forty-six known Hungarian language codices were copied in monasteries during the decade after Mohács.

At the same time, Renaissance humanism did not die with King Matthias; on the contrary, whereas most of the nobility, whose tastes were rather rustic in those times, considered Matthias' generosity towards matters cultural as wasteful, now they started to be desirous of greater refinement, and to recognise the uses of humanistic culture for the analysis and the criticism of contemporary conditions. The cult of Matthias, whose strong hand seemed to be a blessing after 1526, slowly arose; Hungary's fortunes inspired statements of apprehension for and love of the *patria* whose maturity is striking in this early period; and the same fortunes were analysed in terms of the topoi of humanist historiography and political thought. Like the Protestants, the humanists blamed the sins of the Hungarians for their miserly lot, but they were all too mundane ones: for instance, Chancellor and Bishop István Brodarics, in his account of the disaster of Mohács, emphasised the ambition, faction and corruption which was rampant among the political class and undermined the vigour of the polity. Humanist historical writing tended to consolidate patriotic commitments and national self-awareness in various ways: the rhymed narrative songs of the scribe Sebestyén Tinódi, which recorded the heroic deeds of Hungarian fortress guardsmen between 1541 and 1552, were highly accessible to the lower classes, but at the same time there were also prose works following classical models and written in polished Latin, among others, by Bishop Ferenc Forgách and Vice Palatine Miklós Istvánffy.

As in the case of Janus Pannonius a century earlier, it was again in lyrical poetry that Hungarian letters rose to the highest standards with the achievement of Bálint Balassi, the first poet who wrote about non-religious subjects in Hungarian. Lacking all didacticism and very much art for its own sake, the images of love, gallantry and piety bequeathed by this soldier of aristocratic background, in whom a robust Renaissance personality was grafted upon the sensibilities of a troubadour, even today look fresher than those of many a modern poet. Balassi also tried his hand at drama, translating and adapting an Italian pastoral for the resultant *Fine Hungarian Comedy*. At the same time, since the genre in general was an efficient means of propaganda in the hands of the Protestants, it is no wonder that the only Hungarian drama from this period which can be successfully acted on the stage even today, is an adaptation of Sophocles' masterpiece, the *Hungarian Electra*, written by Balassi's master, the Lutheran preacher Péter Bornemisza.

As regards creative art and architecture, the circumstances of the age were hardly advantageous to their flowering; the role of the missing royal court could in this respect not be fulfilled by that of the princes of Transylvania until the period of prosperity beginning under the Báthoris later in the century. Besides aristocratic seats rebuilt according to recent western standards, such as the one of the Perényi family at Sárospatak or that of the Nádasdys at Sárvár, or urban buildings like the City Hall or the Thurzó house (both at Lőcse), it was mainly fortifications erected by Italian masters in the 1540s and 1550s that exemplify Renaissance architecture in the most striking manner.

Transylvanian magnates and princes were the patrons of the most sumptuous late Renaissance constructions in the early half of the seventeenth century, most importantly at the princely seat of Gyulafehérvár under Prince Gábor Bethlen.

The Protestant reformers had much in common with and also learnt a great deal from the preceding and contemporary generations of humanists. Above all, just like the humanists and later the members of the Enlightenment 'republic of letters', as a result of the conditions in which Protestantism and its propagation arose, they were imbued by a sense of belonging to a large continent-wide community of like-minded spirits who maintained permanent contacts with each other. This was of particular significance for those members of this community who served localities at best peripheral from the point of view of the nuclei of European intellectual development. Peregrination to one of the German or Swiss universities, such as Wittenberg, Heidelberg, Geneva or Zurich, and visits to the home of renowned figures of the Reformation not only supplied future pastors with intellectual rewards but also made them kept in mind in those centres. The resulting network of information helped them to keep track of European cultural and intellectual developments in extremely adverse conditions, and even to contribute to that progress: the Latin pamphlets and theological *summae* of István Szegedi Kis, composed in the 1560s in tiny Ráckeve (south of Pest, then in the Ottoman province) were found worthy of being printed in Basel in 1585 and used as educational material in the western centres of the Reformation.

Perhaps the greatest of the services rendered by the Reformation to Hungarian culture was the elevation of the vernacular to the status of a language of intellectual intercourse, which must be understood in conjunction with two other developments: the progress of schooling and the book culture based on the printed word. The Lutheran emphasis on native idioms evoked early responses. The author of the first Hungarian grammar, published in 1538, was none other than Mátyás Dévai Bíró, the 'Hungarian Luther'. Three years later, the first full Hungarian translation of the New Testament was published, and although the Hungarian rendering of the Bible as a whole by the Vizsoly minister Gáspár Károli was not completed until 1590, thereafter it supplied the standard of style and grammar in Protestant written culture and in the Hungarian literary language in general for a long while.

The Protestant denominations took great care to develop a well-functioning network of educational institutions at all levels. Excellent schoolmasters were not uncommon even in the elementary schools of tiny villages, while future ministers and teachers did not necessarily need to look abroad for higher training: there was a fine selection of Lutheran, Calvinist and Anti-Trinitarian colleges in the country, the most renowned ones to be found in Pápa, Sárospatak, Debrecen, Kolozsvár and Brassó (Braşov, Kronstadt). This network was well served by the numerous mobile or stationary printing presses established at the courts of magnates or at the colleges, and later as business ventures by preachers or burghers (like Johannes Honterus or Gáspár Heltai, who were themselves important Protestant authors). Between 1529, when after the ephemeral initiatives of the previous century the printing of books was re-launched in Hungary, and 1600, nearly nine hundred titles were printed, about sixty percent of them on religious subjects. They were intended to satisfy not only educational needs, but also the Renaissance curiosities of a growing and changing readership. The composition of public libraries like the ones maintained, to the great admiration of visitors, by the towns, for instance, of Bártfa (Bardejov) or Eperjes (Prešov), alongside many private ones, is evidence of the appearance of 'the reader' as we know him: one who consults books out of sheer interest, like a politician does a book on astronomy, a burgher one on artillery, a magnates one on theology, or anybody in sixteenth-century Hungary on newly discovered parts of the globe. Finally, it must be mentioned that the profound changes in the consumption of written culture also had important economic preconditions: whereas the characteristic format of a book of Matthias' time, the illuminated codex, cost a fortune, a century later a printed Homer could be bought at the marketplace for the price of two pounds of meat or a gallon of wine.

The growing prestige and polish of Hungarian did not mean the decline of Latin literacy, and indeed it seems that there was a widespread use of Latin as a spoken language in the country, even though – unlike before and after the Ottoman period – it was not the official language of the whole country: Hungarian became the language of diets and legislation in Transylvania, the language of communication between the authorities and the natives in the Ottoman province, and also that of the administration at the level of the county and below in the Habsburg domains. However, cultivated minds were supposed to be versed in Latin, and it also remained the main medium of intercourse with foreigners. It was with this Hungarian experience in mind that in 1620 Szepsi, mentioned at the beginning of this chapter, expressed his surprise at the difficulty of finding speakers of Latin among the men in the street of London. By contrast, a generation later the English traveller Edward Brown admired the Hungarians' proficiency in that language, finding that not only nobles and soldiers but also coach-drivers or ferrymen were quite fluent in it. Similar accounts are provided in the reports of the Jesuit missionaries, who were sent to Hungary in increasing numbers after Archbishop of Esztergom Miklós Oláh had first invited them in 1562 (even if it is quite plausible that they merely exaggerated in order to excuse their failure to learn Hungarian).

It took some time for Catholicism to recover from the shock caused by the torrent of the Reformation. It was not until the beginning of the seventeenth century that the tide began to turn, and whereas Calvinism remained the majority religion in Transylvania and in the Ottoman province, by the 1660s Catholic ascendancy was, by and large, restored in royal Hungary. In this initial phase this took place with little direct interference from Vienna, supposedly a champion of the Catholic cause, and with less violence than elsewhere (and unlike later in the century, when the centralising measures of Leopold I went hand in hand with much physical persecution of Protestants in Hungary). Rather, it was because the Hungarian estates, having reached a political compromise with the Habsburg government after the first anti-Habsburg movement led by István Bocskai between 1604 and 1606 (see below), became persuaded that the spirit of opposition in Protestantism was no longer indispensable for them, while it continued to encourage disobedience and resistance amongst the lower classes. 'Persuaded' was literally what they became: the promoters of the Counter-Reformation targeted primarily the magnates and the nobility with sermons, now in eloquent Hungarian, not failing to point out the general instability inherent in the tendency of Protestantism to fall into ever more numerous confessional divisions.

The conversion of a few magnates really seemed to work miracles, and what their example could not evoke was achieved by pressure put by them on the people living in their estates. But to bring about widespread conversion, personalities of uncommon ability and tactics suited to the particular conditions were needed on the Catholic side. These tactics included new attitudes, methods and styles in propagating the Gospel to the faithful. Fighting against Protestantism with its own weapons, the Catholics of the Counter-Reformation laid great emphasis on an intensive communication between the clergy and their flocks, but one based as much on the experience as on the truth of belief, facilitated by sermonising in the native tongue with a play of mystical allusions and yet accessible to the laity. At the same time, the new forms of artistic expression offered by the Baroque were made use of. Imposing and richly ornamented Catholic churches, well-orchestrated processions and saint's day festivities proved to be more efficient in capturing the imaginations of people than clinically purified Protestant churches and customs. All of these tendencies have been generally associated with the renewal of Catholicism brought about from the mid-sixteenth century onwards mainly by the Jesuits, whose convents soon constituted a dense network all over Hungary. Other orders, traditional ones like the Franciscans or the Paulines, as well as newer ones like the Piarists and the Capuchins, also drew encouragement from the advancement of the Jesuits.

The most outstanding exponent of the Catholic renewal in Hungary was Cardinal Péter Pázmány, Archbishop of Esztergom from 1616 to 1637. Born a Calvinist, he was converted by the Jesuits of Kolozsvár and studied in Cracow, Vienna, and finally in Rome, where his mentor was the great neo-scholastic theorist Roberto Bellarmino. Thereafter, he became a professor of philosophy at the Jesuit University of Graz, where he wrote influential polemical tracts and was largely responsible for developing the Hungarian variant of Counter-Reformation sermonising, described above. His vast erudition, comprising even Protestant theological literature, and the robust freshness of his style were the clues to his success. Just as the Protestants were the main promoters of vernacular culture in the sixteenth century, it is largely owing to Pázmány that in the seventeenth century the trend towards the standardisation and the modernisation of the Hungarian language continued, even though the important grammatical syntheses (accepted on both sides of the religious divide) were written by figures like the orthodox Calvinist Transylvanian bishop, István Geleji Katona, or the Puritan court chaplain Pál Megyesi, or the most influential, Miklós Misztótfalusi Kis. As regards persuasive power, Pázmány had his Protestant counterpart in the prolific and versatile Calvinist scholar Albert Szenci Molnár, who, besides his philological and linguistic achievement (he published the first Latin-Hungarian dictionary in 1604), endeavoured to counter Pázmány with a similar combination of theological vision, a style of sermon easy to comprehend and prayer of biblical inspiration. His translations of prayers by Calvin and Bullinger as well as the former's *Institutes of the Christian Religion* (1624) helped the Hungarian Reformed Church ultimately to take on its Calvinist character, while his book of translated psalms became an effective means of promoting Protestant practical piety.

Though early in the century aristocratic mansions and the castles of the princes of Transylvania were still rebuilt in late Renaissance style, the Baroque arrived along with the Catholic renewal, and soon became the dominant style in royal Hungary. This is all the more remarkable since, whereas the lavish structures demanded by the Baroque made it even more dependent on generous patronage than its predecessors, the royal court of Hungary completely withdrew from such involvement. Its role was supplemented by the aristocratic families of Transdanubia and Upper Hungary, which had stately mansions built for themselves and financed spectacular churches. The mansions of the Batthyánys at Borostyánkő (Bernstein), the Pálffys at Vöröskő (Rotenstein) and the Esterházys at Kismarton (Eisenstadt) are particularly worth mentioning here. The two Esterházy palatines, Miklós and Pál were also the greatest patrons of ecclesiastical buildings; the first of these, started in 1629 and modelled after the famous il Gesu of Rome at Nagyszombat (Trnava), owing to the former, is also one of the most splendid. Besides a few native architects, most of the masters active on these constructions were Italian and Austrian, some of whom were continuously employed in Hungary for several decades. Most of the painters of the images that decorated altarpieces of churches or the walls of aristocratic palaces – such as the fine murals in the Nádasdy mansion of Sárvár, depicting the valiant deeds of Ferenc Nádasdy against the Turks – were foreigners, too.

Nagyszombat is not only remarkable for the Jesuit church just mentioned, but also as the seat of the university founded by Pázmány in 1635, even though Hungarian students still needed to go abroad for a medical degree. Thereby the Jesuit educational inrastructure became complete, and the university as well as the academy launched in 1660 at Kassa and the network of Jesuit gymnasia all around the country offered very high-level training conforming to the uniform standards of the order. Educational facilities on the elementary level also proliferated: it seems that even the smallest villages in the country had a schoolmaster, most of them trained at institutions of higher learning, Catholic or Protestant. The renown of Protestant schools and colleges was less permanent, but most of them excelled for at least one or two decades in the century. Between 1650 and 1654, the College of Sárospatak hosted the most outstanding educational expert in the period, Comenius (Jan Amos Komenský). The College of Gyulafehárvár (Alba Iulia) was invigorated by the influx of German professors fleeing from the Thirty Years War. Germany continued to be one of the main sources of inspiration for the renewal of Protestantism, acutely needed in the contest with Catholicism: Pietism started to appear among the Lutherans of Hungary by midcentury. The other major influence on Protestantism in the seventeenth century was Puritanism, imported from England whose universities, similarly to those of the Netherlands, were visited by a fair number of young men from Protestant Hungary (while the chief destinations of academic peregrination, involving some five thousand Hungarians in the course of the century, were still German and Polish universities). Indeed, the seventeenth century has often been described as that of Jesuits and Puritans in Hungary where, given the lack of a strong secular intelligentsia, the highest standards of learning were represented by figures from these groups.

It was a Puritan, expelled from orthodox Calvinist Gyulafehérvár on account of his beliefs, the influential educator János Apáczai Csere, whose works reveal the first Hungarian repercussions of the dominant intellectual trend of the century, the rise of scientific thinking. Apáczai is sometimes mentioned as the first 'modern' Hungarian. His inaugural speech at Gyulafehérvár 'On the Study of Wisdom' (1653) was a finely reasoned espousal of the idea of progress based on a critical examination of sources and authorities; his *Hungarian Encyclopedia*, published in the same year, was Cartesian in its natural philosophy, while it followed natural law theorists like Johannes Althusius and flirted with ideas of popular sovereignty and tyrannicide in its social and political theory. There were few like-minded figures in the Hungary of the time. One of these was János Pósaházi of Sárospatak, who created an eclectic natural philosophy of his own along Baconian lines, and argued against the Hobbesian version of natural law in his dissertation defended in Utrecht in 1654. These rather isolated individuals worked in an environment where orthodox Protestant and Catholic schools (similarly, in fact, to most of their counterparts in Germany, and many still further west) stuck to Aristotelian scholasticism, and where the most characteristic themes and modes of political thinking – solidarity with Christian Europe, commitment to 'the nation' and 'the fatherland', reason of state or the art of political expediency – were determined by the grievous predicament of the tripartite division of the country.

3. Peace, war, and the century of Hungarian decay

The natural thrust of the political changes of the sixteenth century was to drift Hungary somewhat apart from the progress of the Occident, and to accentuate divisions within the former Kingdom of Hungary. In the last third of the century, there were two factors which still countered this tendency, and also ensured that when it became more intense in the next one, it was not irreversible. First, as we have seen, the Reformation helped Hungary to preserve its unitary cultural identity and to maintain, even strengthen and multiply its ties with western civilisation. Second, stimuli from the European economy affected Hungary in an ambivalent way in this period: whereas the potentials of long term modernisation were curtailed, the country could reap short term benefits as a result of which its economic unity and western trade relations were also maintained. This balance was upset by the blows suffered from the series of wars and epidemics that hit Hungary from the turn of the century on: it

was as a result of the losses of human lives and the devastation of resources beginning with the Fifteen Years War of 1591 to 1606 that by the
time the Ottomans were driven out of the country, Hungary reached a
nadir from which the realisation of even the limited potentials it possessed a century earlier seemed highly unlikely.

The Ottoman wars between 1526 and 1568 caused surprisingly little
damage to the medieval network of settlements in Hungary. While
many fields became desolate, evacuated villages were soon populated
again, and although Hungary did not partake of the general European
trend of population growth in this period, the immigration of Balkan
Slavs at least prevented decrease. The traditions of Hungary as an exporter of raw materials and foodstuffs, the new conditions of Western
Europe, the abandonment of previously worked lands and population
stagnation combined to shape the dominant patterns of the Hungarian
economy. Whereas the importance of Hungarian mines decreased as a
result of the influx of precious metals from the New World, demographic growth in the West generated unprecedented demand for
agrarian products, at a time when a stagnant population resulted in a
shrinking internal market in Hungary and the abandoned fields provided limitless opportunities for the grazing of cattle. As a result, Hungary was in an ideal position to supply the western demand, and became the world's greatest exporter of meat, driving an annual 200,000
cattle out of the country in the 1580s.

Hungary thus acquired a huge export surplus, but a substantial proportion of its profits remained in the hands of the foreign merchants at
the end of the commercial chain, and the successes of the Hungarian
agrarian sector in general favoured the conservation of the old structure
of production. The cheap textiles, pieces of metalwork and artefacts in
general that comprised the bulk of Hungarian imports suffocated craft-
work within the country, which was in an ailing condition anyway. The
number of crafts pursued in Hungarian towns, usually confined to supplying rather basic needs and remaining within the bounds of the increasingly obsolete guild system, was a quarter to a half of that of their
German counterparts, as was the proportion of artisans among the urban population. Industries that depended on a substantial concentration of capital, such as the textile or the building industry, were only
found, at a fairly rudimentary level, in a few important urban centres.

At the same time, among specific circumstances the primacy of open-
air stockbreeding was a relative advantage and a compensation for the
weakness of urban society and all that it implied for the prospects of a
capitalist and civic mentality. Being outside the feudal structure of production whose fundamental unit was the plot (*sessio*) of the serf, the
grazing of cattle was untaxed by landlords, who made futile efforts to

take this trade out of the hands of the peasants and the dwellers of the *oppida*, and had to remain content with the enormous profits from supplying grain to the armies in the country. Next, since the grazing and trade of cattle was to a great extent based on contracts and wage labour, it held out the promise of the capitalisation of the economy, and the participation of large numbers of peasants from formerly isolated localities in the long distance movements it implied, helped them to broaden their horizons, to develop independent habits of conduct and an openness to novelty. Similar were the effects of the trade of wine, whose centres shifted from the Srem area, where the thriving viticulture largely fell victim to Turkish conquest early in the century, to Tolna and Baranya in southern Transdanubia, and even more to Tokaj in the northern Tisza region. (Wine even started to replace cattle as Hungary's number one export item as, after the turn of the century, an economic slump in Italy and Germany, the principal markets for Hungarian cattle, caused the demand for beef to decline.) After the setback suffered in the wake of Dózsa's peasant war, the times seemed auspicious again for the emergence of a self-confident stratum of 'peasant bourgeoisie'. Finally, since the bulk of the cattle exported came from the Great Plain, occupied by the Ottomans and therefore a land where few western merchants risked to enter, and Turks and South Slavs were unwelcome guests in royal Hungary, the services of Hungarian merchants and their entourage from that area were indispensable for maintaining the trade. As, on the other hand, the latter rarely ventured beyond the borders of the country, the businessmen from royal Hungary played the important role of middlemen, and the net result was that Hungary, despite the political divisions and the customs posts erected along internal borders, remained an economic unit and a unitary market.

This precarious balance, which could still give rise to a cautious optimism regarding the conditions and the future of the country, was underpinned by the nearly quarter of a century of peace following the treaty of Edirne, and was overthrown by the fifteen years of war that followed it. To be sure, the official peace between the two great powers was often disturbed by skirmishes, marauding campaigns, and even surprise attacks which resulted in capturing minor fortresses. It was mainly the Turks who were responsible for the permanent instability in the frontier area. Although upon his accession to the throne Rudolph I (Rudolph II as head of the Empire) was ambitious to expel the Ottomans, the Military Council in 1577 accepted the proposal of Lazarus Schwendi, captain of the forces of Upper Hungary, who suggested refraining from provocations and preserving peace while strengthening the line of defence (the latter part of the proposal being carried out rather ineffectively). Similar was the attitude of István Báthori, who succeeded John Sigismund as Prince of Transylvania in 1571, and was also elected King of Poland in 1576. He (and in his absence after 1576, his governors) consolidated his position against challengers with the support of the Porte, and entertained the hope of bringing royal Hungary under his rule, though at the same time he also started to fortify the defence line between Transylvania and the Ottoman province. No 'war of liberation' was contemplated. Most important figures failed to recognise that with the death of Suleyman I Ottoman power had passed its zenith, and were reluctant, in the words of the Hungarian general Miklós Pálffy, to 'open a case' which they thought was full of 'poisonous snakes, vermin and scorpions'.

Even when in 1591, 1592 and 1593 Hassan, the Pasha of Bosnia, in open aggression against the peace treaty that had just been renewed, repeatedly attempted to capture the fortress of Sisek in Croatia, though his strong army was routed by much inferior Habsburg troops, it was the Emperor who hurried to appease the Sultan by a consignment of lavish presents. All in vain: Murad III declared war in August 1593 and sent the head of the war party in Istanbul, Grand Vizier Sinan Pasha, against Hungary. The Sisek episode was only the trigger that set off the war machine. A revolt of the janissaries, unoccupied and poorly paid since the conclusion of the long campaign in Persia in 1590, prompted the near-bankrupt Porte to compensate them with conquests and booty; and the recognition that the Habsburgs had consolidated their positions in Central Europe also urged it to strike back.

The war began with Ottoman successes, Sinan capturing not only Sisek but also important fortresses in Transdanubia, such as Veszprém and Várpalota. However, plans shelved in 1577 by the Military Council were now revived, and the new strategy became an offensive during the winter season, which the Ottomans traditionally deemed unsuitable for warfare, and holding on to acquisitions during the summer, when formidable Turkish armies were sent to Hungary for the campaign season. In other words, the Council wanted to exploit the circumstance that the Turkish military might have reached the limits of its 'range of action': Ottoman fighting force in great campaigns depended on the personal participation of the Sultan and the troops he marched up from the imperial residence, which, however, he never left for a period longer than from the spring to the autumn. For the first time since Mohács, the armies of royal Hungary were able to switch from defence to the offensive and reoccupied a relatively small but contiguous territorial unit from the Turks in the winter of 1593–1594: after a victory won in the battle of Romhány in November, Pálffy's troops forced Turkish garrisons to evacuate most fortresses in Nógrád county.

These unexpected successes greatly contributed to the revival of the idea of anti-Ottoman collaboration between Christian powers. This was all the more needed since the cost the of the war amounted to 6 million florins per year. From 1594 on, Pope Clement VIII secured subsidies (about 3 million florins over ten years), and later also Italian auxiliary troops for the purposes of the war in Hungary, and with clever diplomacy he also ensured the benevolent neutrality of France towards the Habsburgs. The imperial, Austrian and Bohemian estates also contributed more generous sums to the war effort, although less than half of the 13 million florins voted by the imperial diet in the course of the war actually reached Hungary. Most importantly, the Romanian principalities and Transylvania also defected from the Ottoman camp and joined the Holy League. In the absence of István Báthori, Transylvania was first ruled by his nephew Kristóf as Voevode, and then by a council, on behalf of Kristóf's son Zsigmond, who was elected prince when he was still under age upon the death of his father in 1581. A man of considerable talents but a muddled personality, Zsigmond Báthori, having been invested as prince in 1586, forged ties with Voevodes Mihai Viteazul of Wallachia and Aron of Moldavia to shake off Turkish tutelage and crushed the 'Ottoman party' among the Transylvanian estates. In January 1595 he also concluded an alliance treaty with Rudolph. Besides military co-operation, this involved the marriage of Báthori and the Habsburg Duchess Maria Christine, and his acknowledgement of the terms of the 1570 Treaty of Speyer.

Military events show that these developments equalised the earlier superiority of the Ottomans, but did not effect a complete turnabout in the relation of forces. Fortunes were erratic, and the war became a protracted one. In the summer of 1594, the attempt of Archduke Matthias to capture Buda collapsed already under the walls of Esztergom, while Győr, considered as the key to Vienna, fell to Sinan. In 1595, when the Porte was forced to fight a two-front war, the royal army of General Karl Mansfeld finally took Esztergom, Báthori captured fortifications in the Maros valley, and joined forces with Voevode Mihai to win a great victory at Djurdjevo on the Lower Danube. The campaign year of 1596, when the new Sultan Mehmed III led his army personally, belonged to the Turks again: they captured Eger and, reversing what at first seemed complete defeat, beat the forces of Báthori and Archduke Maximilian in the three-day battle of Mezőkeresztes, one of the greatest open field engagements of the century. 1597 saw futile efforts of the Holy League to take Temesvár and Győr, though the latter was captured by a surprise attack of Pálffy in the next year. The subsequent siege of Buda was unsuccessful, as were repeated efforts to reoccupy the Hungarian capital in 1602 and 1603. Apart from a few permanent acquisitions, such as the

Ottoman conquest of Eger and, in 1600, of Nagykanizsa, which was made the seat of the fourth *vilayet* in the territory of Hungary, the successes of both parties mainly consisted of recapturing fortresses lost earlier during the course of the war.

After the initial high hopes, this was disillusioning, especially in view of the immense human sacrifices and physical destruction caused by the war. In the territories most affected by the movement of troops, such as the Danube valley along which the Ottomans marched on their campaigns, the counties along the Transdanubian line of defence, the ones in Upper Hungary north of the Danube, or parts of Transylvania, tax assessments registered a decrease in excess of 60, even 70 per cent in the number of *portae* between the beginning and the end of the war. Frustration resulted in bitterness, which undermined the anti-Turkish co-operative efforts both within and outside the country. The whims of Báthori, whose troubled mind made him the weakest link in the chain, caused the first rupture. Having abdicated in favour of Rudolph in return for ducal estates in Silesia in 1598, he soon changed his mind and reoccupied his throne, only to leave it again in 1599. It was under Polish pressure that now he was replaced by his nephew, Cardinal András Báthori, who wished to lead Transylvania back to the fold of the Porte. To prevent this, Voevode Mihai of Wallachia, encouraged from Vienna, invaded Transylvania, defeated Báthori and was made Habsburg governor of the province. Zsigmond Báthori now reappeared on the scene for the last time in 1601. He was elected prince again, but the forces of Mihai and the Habsburg General Giorgio Basta expelled him. The latter's Walloon mercenaries having killed Voevode Mihai in the aftermath of the battle, the general now became the master of troubled Transylvania. His was a reign of terror, aggravating the famine raging in the country with mass persecution of Protestants, reckless depredation amongst the villagefolk by the mercenaries, and impossible ransoms imposed on towns still exhibiting marks of prosperity.

The temporary consensus forged between the estates and the court by the war effort in royal Hungary also fell victim to the increasing desperation caused by its futility. Even before the outbreak of the war, their relations were ridden with tensions, mainly because the Hungarian Council became increasingly neglected and more and more foreigners were appointed to influential posts in the Hungarian administration. Now, as the foreign subsidies were procured with ever greater difficulty, the Court Treasury decided to compensate for the deficit at the expense of the Hungarian nobility, whose contribution to the war effort it deemed insufficient. It instituted legal proceedings against several magnates in order to recover fiscal revenues mortgaged to them, and those who resisted were condemned to loss of life and property as guilty of high treason. Especially offensive was the trial of Chief Justice István Illésházy, an elderly magnate, who had been (similarly to several others affected) a firm supporter of the court. Alongside the clause added by the court to the laws passed by the diet of 1604, which prohibited any future discussion of religious issues by the legislature, it seemed that concerted action was being taken against the balance of power between the court and the estates that had evolved after Mohács.

The situation erupted when in October 1604 Giacomo Belgiojoso, Captain General of Upper Hungary, attacked the fortresses of the Calvinist magnate István Bocskai in Bihar county. Bocskai had been one of the staunchest supporters of the Habsburg orientation in Transylvania, but recently he also got into trouble with the court on account of revenues mortgaged to him, and now he found himself also accused of flirting with the Ottomans. Under pressure, Bocskai decided to resist. At first, he found support among the heyducks: the irregular reserve units of the imperial forces, originally drovers of cattle (hence the name) or peasants marginalised by the devastation of the war itself. Bocskai having scored a minor victory, people rallied to his support; towns and fortresses opened their gates to him, and although his poorly organised troops suffered defeat after defeat, amidst a generally hostile environment the forces of Basta, who was commanded to march against him, could not but withdraw ever further west. On February 21, 1605, Bocskai was elected Prince of Transylvania; two months later the estates of Upper Hungary acclaimed him as Prince of Hungary, and even though the magnates of Transdanubia persevered in their loyalty to the Habsburgs, he even started to consider the reunification of the two domains under his own sceptre. He solicited the Porte for a crown.

It was probably the Ottoman occupation of Esztergom in the autumn of 1605, which signalled the dangers of the Ottoman alliance, and the sober advice of Illésházy and others, who recognised that the Habsburgs were still indispensable for maintaining the line of defence and therefore suggested a compromise arrangement, that made Bocskai change his mind. He accepted the crown which he received in November merely as a personal present, not as insignia, and initiated negotiations with the court – namely, with Archduke Matthias, much in need of the help of the Hungarian estates to depose his mentally disturbed brother Rudolph, who had by then been living for many years in seclusion in his legendary Prague court, largely indulging in his passion for the occult, alchemy, the arts and sciences. The Peace Treaty of Vienna, signed on June 23, 1606, required the Habsburgs to observe the rights of Protestants, to fill the office of the Palatine which had been vacant for decades, to refrain from appointing foreigners to posts in the Hungarian administration and from taking legal action that violated the law. Bocskai, who in the meantime returned the support he received from the heyducks by settling nearly ten thousand of them in localities endowed with extensive privileges, was confirmed as Prince of Transylvania.

The peace that concluded the first anti-Habsburg movement of the Hungarian estates with a compromise arrangement highly favourable from their point of view also stipulated that the Ottoman war had to be brought to an end. The Porte, under pressure from revolt in Anatolia and attacks in Persia, had repeatedly aired its willingness to make peace from 1599 on, and now that the revolt of Bocskai also sapped the remnants of the strength of the Habsburgs, the situation was ripe. The Peace of Zsitvatorok, signed on November 11, 1606, was made on the basis of the status quo (that is, the Habsburgs retained the minor acquisitions made early in the war, and the Ottomans kept Eger and Nagykanizsa); instead of the annual ransom, the Emperor only paid a lump sum of 200,000 florins, and was to all intents and purposes acknowledged as an equal of the Sultan. Whereas the Porte acknowledged the tax exempt status of Hungarian landlords at the periphery of the occupied zone, it could not extort the prohibition of Hungarian taxation in their province. The Sultan seemed to have abandoned his absolute claim to the whole of Hungary.

In many respects, then, the peace treaties effected a settlement that looked permanent at the end of a war whose disastrous effect on material culture and demographic relations are difficult to exaggerate. Until the end of the sixteenth century, most of the damage suffered from the Ottoman occupation seemed reparable; at the end of the long war it was evident that Hungary would never become what its, albeit limited, potential a century earlier destined it to be. Unlike earlier, large parts of the Turkish army, including the Tartar auxiliaries which had particularly ferocious habits, remained permanently in the country during the war, transforming much of it into a wasteland by the time peace was made. The old settlement pattern was now thrown into disarray; villages destroyed were never rebuilt. The country's population was decimated; and what the war did not effect was wrought by repeated epidemics of plague, which remained endemic in Hungary after its outbreak in 1620 for half a century.

Together with the end of the agrarian boom and the consequent drastic fall of profit rates in the major Hungarian exports, which would have caused serious difficulties even among normal conditions, the effects of the war brought about economic decline and the eclipse of the mercantile groups, which arose vigorously in the preceding decades. They tended to lose the competition not only to the great, state financed monopolistic companies launched in the middle of the seventeenth century, but also against the 'Greek' merchants arriving from the Ottoman Empire with more modest capital. An important, or rather the most promising channel of the modernisation of Hungary's social structure became to a great extent blocked. The main route of upward mobility from the peasantry now became ascending into the privileged estate by obtaining patents of nobility, either in return for a modest payment, or for military service as fortress soldiers, or as heyducks. The earlier tendency towards a numerous nobility and the weakness of 'the middling sort' was thus reinforced in the seventeenth century, with far reaching consequences for the prevailing system of values.

In demographic terms, the effect was penetrating, not only as regards the figures of population number and density, but ethnic composition as well. The medieval Kingdom of Hungary had been a multi-ethnic country, with at least twenty per cent of its population being non-Hungarian. Most of these ethnic minorities lived in outlying areas, while the vast central regions were nearly exclusively Hungarian-speaking. It was the latter that were the main theatres of war; consequently, the ethnic balance now started to change in favour of other nationalities: Slovaks in the north, Romanians in the east, Serbs in the south. The resulting cultural colourfulness was a distinct gain. The admixture of Orthodox characteristics to the Roman Catholic and Reformed substratum had a far greater impact on the outlook of civilisation in Hungary than the few Turkish loan-words that infiltrated the Hungarian language, some dishes borrowed from Turkish cuisine, or the baths and religious structures left behind by the Ottomans. However, such gains were achieved at the expense of tensions that proved insoluble after the advent of modernity. The preconditions of Hungary's nationality problem in the shape it emerged in the era of national awakening arose in the century of Hungarian decay inaugurated by the Fifteen Years War.

At the same time, while the treaties consolidated the political division of the country, with sober detachment it was now possible to perceive of it as a more than temporary arrangement, and to attempt to forge merit out of necessity. The experience of the political history of the war showed that there was a path, however narrow, opened for the Hungarian elites of the different provinces to balance successfully between the two great powers. Through the Habsburgs, royal Hungary could secure the indispensable external support to contain Ottoman advance. At the same time, Transylvania could prevent – if necessary, by relying on the assistance of the Porte – the Habsburgs from squeezing the nobility out of its positions in royal Hungary. This division of labour was rarely consciously espoused and was often hindered by the multiple cleavages of political opinion, suspicions and hostilities on both sides of the internal border. As a result, Hungarian politicians sometimes strayed away from that narrow path, which was never without grievous consequences.

The settlement of 1606 at first seemed precarious. Emperor Rudolph was still dreaming of the expulsion of the Turks and of punishing the leaders of the Bocskai revolt in his Prague seclusion. However, when after more than a year of procrastination and growing unrest among the heyducks – who refused to be hired by Rudolph against the Hungarian estates – the diet convened in early 1608, the Peace of Vienna was ratified and religious differences were settled under the presiding of Archduke Matthias. The Archduke obtained the support of the Hungarian estates to extort the abdication of his brother, and Rudolph, facing the confederation of the Austrian, Moravian and Hungarian estates, indeed yielded sovereignty over these lands to Matthias (retaining the throne of Bohemia until 1611 and the title of emperor until his death in 1612). The price Matthias paid for the crown was the restoration of corporate government, nearly as fully as it had existed under the Jagiellos a century earlier. The 'pre-coronation laws' of 1608 deprived the monarch of the right to make war and peace without consulting the estates, and the Palatine was empowered to act with full authority on behalf of the absent ruler. One of the laws sealed an important development of the previous century: a separate chamber within the diet was established for the group of perpetual barons that emerged under Ferdinand I (a group in which a distinct stratum of magnates raised to the ranks of imperial count, even duke, was further distinguished). The same diet obliged the king to provide for the soldiers garrisoned in the fortresses, while it required him to remove foreign mercenaries and to appoint only Hungarians as officers. He was not allowed to issue further charters granting self-government to towns, and the regulation of the free migration of peasants was referred to the authority of the counties. In practice, however, the estates were neither powerful enough, nor did they have a sufficiently clear vision of their own goals to limit the authority of the government offices.

The situation in Transylvania remained highly unstable for several years after the peace treaties were signed. Bocskai died before the end of 1606, and his one-time governor and successor, Zsigmond Rákóczi, was removed by Gábor Báthori with the support of the *hajdus* in March 1608. An attractive and eccentric libertine, his character being remarkably similar to the previous prince of the same family, Báthori's five-year rule was a series of ill-advised initiatives that alienated most of his early supporters within and outside Transylvania. He started his reign by offending the autonomy of the proud Saxon towns, Nagyszeben (Sibiu, Hermannstadt) and Brassó; in 1611, he attacked Wallachia to restore Transylvanian hegemony over the Romanian principalities, evoking the anger of the Porte as well as Poland. Báthori survived several plots, some of them engineered from royal Hungary, until his earlier advisor Gábor Bethlen replaced him with Ottoman support in 1613.

It took some time for Bethlen to make the circumstances of his accession pass into oblivion, the more so since in 1616 he even besieged his own soldiers at Lippa, to surrender that fortress, as promised, to the Ottomans for the initial help he received from them. Although he had been reluctantly recognised in Vienna in the pervious year, now he was denounced as a traitor, and even a pretender was encouraged in an unsuccessful effort to replace him. In the meantime, however, Bethlen's extraordinary organisational abilities and political genius started to make an impact in Transylvania. His character and achievement has often been likened to that of Matthias Corvinus, and he certainly bears comparison with the first of Renaissance princes in Hungary. In Bethlen's case it is not only appropriate, but also no longer anachronistic to speak about a 'Hungarian Machiavelli'. The scion of a noble family of moderate wealth expelled from Temes county by the Turks, Bethlen's attitudes were not those of the magnate, but those of the counsellor of princes, and finally the prince himself. For this *par excellence* Hungarian practitioner of reason of state, virtue truly consisted of taking the opportunity offered by fortune, thus fulfilling historical necessity – notions of Machiavellian political wisdom finely tuned by Bethlen to his Calvinist belief in predestination.

Bethlen did relatively little to change the existing structure of institutions, and was content to exploit to the full the traditionally extensive authority of Transylvanian princes. He put an end to bloody showdowns, and replaced the unruly heyducks with a regularly paid army (in fact, largely recruited from among the heyducks and the Szekels). Relying on a group of immediate aids chosen with great skill, he was relentless in recovering princely revenues; as a result, the income of the treasury soared to an unprecedented million florins per year by the end of his reign. Although Transylvania may have lost as much as half of its population during the Fifteen Years War, economically it suffered less than the other parts of Hungary, and Bethlen's mercantilist policies consolidated the internal market and Transylvania's place in the international economy. The country's self-sufficiency was preserved, while the fact that the neighbouring Romanian principalities served as a bread-basket of the Ottoman Empire, stimulated its industries; and it also remained an important line of passage on the trade route between Europe and the Ottoman Empire.

On the basis of such economic achievement, Bethlen placed high priority on developing Transylvania, and especially the single remaining princely court in Hungary at Gyulafehérvár, an unique cultural island. 'There is nothing barbarian here', exclaimed a western envoy in

1621, hardly concealing his astonishment. The princely palace, destroyed during the wars, was renovated in a stately manner by Italian architects and sculptors, and lavishly decorated by frescoes, coffered ceilings, Flemish and Italian tapestries. The balls, the theatrical and musical performances and other forms of entertainment within its walls, the sundry exotic possessions, as well as courtly manners, reflected the highest contemporary standards of refinement. While Bethlen supported academic peregrination, he raised the Calvinist school of Gyulafehérvár to the rank of college in 1622, and hosted several renowned German professors who sought refuge from the Thirty Years War. Under Bethlen, Transylvania became home to a flourishing tradition of historiography, emerging as a fully secular discipline in the hands of István Szamosközy, Gáspár Bojti Veres, János Szalárdi and others.

It was also mainly during Bethlen's rule, through his participation in the Thirty Years War that the international strategic importance of tiny and peripheral Transylvania asserted itself in the most conspicuous manner. Transylvania's predominantly Hungarian elite took a profound and mutual interest in the affairs of their counterparts in royal Hungary, who, through the Habsburg link, in turn became an important factor to consider in European power games; while, conversely, the Habsburgs were also reluctant to abandon their claim to sovereignty over Transylvania. When it is added that even its Catholic princes, like István Báthori, were in favour of religious liberty, it is not surprising that Transylvania was potentially an ideal, well-placed ally in the back of the Habsburgs for Protestant and anti-Habsburg forces on the international scene. Bethlen clearly recognised all these relations, and once law, order and economic stability in the country had been restored, he only needed the opportunity to set to realising his political dream: the reunification of Hungary and maybe even the restoration of Matthias' 'empire'.

The opportunity was presented by the revolt of the estates of Bohemia against Ferdinand, raised to the throne to replace the ailing Matthias in 1617, who, disavowing his oath to keep the laws of the land, instituted a violent Counter-Reformation. When the revolt broke out on May 23, 1618, Ferdinand II had already become King of Hungary as well, and after some temporisation it was the Hungarian Protestant estates that established a common cause between the Bohemian insurrectionists and Bethlen. Whereas the Bohemian estates ultimately preferred the initial candidate, Frederick V, Elector of the Palatinate and leader of the German Protestant Union, to Ferdinand, Bethlen was the first European prince to move against the Habsburgs: his offensive in the autumn of 1619 was so powerful that, having conquered Upper Hungary, he could join forces with the Bohemian and Moravian armies to besiege Vienna.

Though he was forced to retreat, the subsequent armistice was highly favourable to Bethlen. He also remained in control of the territories occupied in the campaign; what is more, the Hungarian diet deposed the Habsburgs and acclaimed Bethlen as King of Hungary on August 25, 1620. Bethlen considered this step premature. The Porte would only have agreed to his accession to the throne of Hungary if at the same time he would have abandoned Transylvania: but to exchange his firm hold over the latter to the unpredictable wrangling with the Hungarian estates would have been a poor deal. Also, by the autumn of 1620 the Bohemian revolt had become an all-European war, with most powers of any significance taking sides with the Habsburgs. Bethlen's diversions were insufficient, and the relief forces he sent arrived too late to prevent the crushing defeat of the Bohemian estates in the Battle of the White Mountain on November 8, 1620, which put an end to the first phase of the war as well as to any semblance of autonomy in the Emperor's Bohemian domains.

This dramatic outcome caused some panic among the Hungarian estates, who hurried to assure Ferdinand of their loyalty. On the other hand, Bethlen, remaining alone on the battlefield, was able to persevere. He beat off a counter-offensive, gaining time for Protestant forces elsewhere in Europe to reorganise, and for Transylvania the Peace of Nikolsburg (December 31, 1621). Bethlen gave up the royal title and insignia as well as most of the territories occupied, but obtained ducal domains in Silesia and seven counties in Upper Hungary. It is of significance that the treaty, for the first time, failed to mention the Habsburg claim to Transylvania. A week later, Ferdinand assured the Hungarian estates that their privileges, including the Peace of Vienna, would be observed, and the diet elected a Lutheran Palatine.

Though the main theatre of war was thereafter removed to Germany, Bethlen continued to be involved in it diplomatically, and entered it militarily on two further occasions. In 1623, the pretext was the refusal of his offer to marry Ferdinand's daughter; in 1626, Bethlen answered the invitation of the English-Danish-Dutch alliance. In both cases, the outcome of actual fighting was inconclusive, and the peace treaties of Vienna and Pozsony merely confirmed the clauses of Nikolsburg. Especially in the case of the latter campaign, Bethlen's policy was no longer popular in Hungary: the estates considered them as mere assertions of power ambition, thinly veiled by the rhetoric of Protestant liberties, and also feared that an eventual failure would place their own privileges at risk, at a time when they were not directly threatened by Vienna. Still, Bethlen's achievement was considerable. He was the only member of the anti-Habsburg coalition who could boast of military successes – two of the best imperial commanders, Buquoi and Dampierre, died in battle against him in 1621, and a third, Wallenstein, retreated from him in 1623 –, and the maintenance of the integrity of Transylvania did strengthen the position of the Hungarian estates, whether they sympathised with Bethlen's policies or not.

Bethlen's untimely death in 1629 was followed by a minor succession crisis in Transylvania. The terms of his marriage treaty with Catherine of Brandenburg required that his unpopular and politically inexperienced wife should succeed Bethlen; a stipulation which the diet fulfilled, but at the same time appointed Bethlen's very mediocre brother István as governor. The squabble of the two only favoured the schemes of the Catholic estates in royal Hungary, led by Palatine Miklós Esterházy, to annex Transylvania to the Habsburg domains. The Transylvanian diet prevented this by removing Bethlen's widow and brother, and elected a wealthy magnate from Upper Hungary and a confidant of Bethlen, György Rákóczi, as prince. He proved to be an ideal successor to Bethlen: what his predecessor achieved with political imagination and resourcefulness, György I Rákóczi secured with cautiousness and reliability. His talents were inferior to those of his predecessor, but luckily he knew it; and it was largely owing to his self-discipline that the golden which age started under Bethlen continued until the end of György I's reign. He preserved the main thrust of Bethlen's domestic policies as regards absolutism and mercantilism, although the more liberal religious policies of Bethlen – who supported the Jesuit Bible translation of György Káldi, permitted the Orthodox Romanians to have their own bishop and sheltered Anabaptists – increasingly turned into Calvinist orthodoxy: the civil liberties of Unitarians were curtailed, while the more radical Sabbatarians were tried and sentenced to imprisonment and loss of property.

Nearly as soon as he had succeeded to the throne, Rákóczi was urged by the Protestant powers to attack the Habsburgs, which he did not hasten to do, even after he had beaten off pretenders like István Bethlen, who claimed the throne of Transylvania with Ottoman support in 1636. Finally, he joined the Swedish-French alliance in 1644, and at the end of a campaign fought with alternating success his troops occupied Upper Hungary and penetrated into Moravia to join forces with the Swedish commander Lennart Torstensson. In the subsequent Peace of Linz in late 1645, he regained the seven counties in Upper Hungary that had reverted to the Habsburgs upon Bethlen's death. In acknowledgement of the international prestige won by Bethlen and preserved by György I Rákóczi, Transylvania became one of the signatories of the peace treaties of Westphalia (Münster and Osnabrück) that concluded the Thirty Years War in 1648.

In the same year Rákóczi died, leaving behind a Transylvania at the height of its prosperity and in the forefront of the political vision of both major parties within the elite of royal Hungary. One of these could be described as 'pro-Habsburg', without imputing that they were traitors corrupted by donations and offices. From the course of the Fifteen Years War they concluded – or rather, they became confirmed in the conviction – that the major task of expelling the Turks was only feasible by relying on the Habsburgs, and all efforts against them, like the Bocskai revolt, played into the hands of the Porte as well as the forces outside corporate structures (such as the heyducks) and were thus antithetical to the interests of the nation (which they identified with their own interests). After 1608, when rulers, with short intervals, seemed willing to respect corporate privileges, the Hungarian estates had little to complain of, and the more or less harmonious co-operation between them and Ferdinand II (and after 1637, Ferdinand III) was reinforced by the advance of the Counter-Reformation within their ranks. They urged reforms in the military establishment and the tax system, and self-restraint *vis-à-vis* the Ottomans until the Habsburgs were relieved from the pressure of the Protestant estates in their western lands and – so it was believed – would turn south again. Accordingly, they were impatient with the attacks launched during the Thirty Years War against the Habsburgs by Transylvania, which they also saw as an outpost of the Ottoman Empire as well as a polity unattractive on account of its over-centralisation of princely power. Hence the repeated actions of Palatine Esterházy against the principality. The other party simply thought that foreign rule ought to be ended first, and looked to Bethlen's, and then Rákóczi's Transylvania to emerge as a cradle for a reunited Hungary. But though many became sufficiently dazzled by the hopes raised by the Bohemian revolt and Bethlen's early successes to allow themselves to be carried away by the idea of the re-establishment of the national kingdom, throughout most of the period it remained a minority opinion.

Hic Rhodus, hic salta–the Hungarian estates might have said to the Habsburgs after the Peace of Westphalia had released their forces in the west in 1648. But Ferdinand III had no inclination to jump, or even walk, into war against the Porte. The Habsburg Empire indeed became exhausted by the Thirty Years War, but nothing could have convinced a powerful group of predominantly Catholic and until then thoroughly pro-Habsburg magnates rallying around Pál Pálffy that it was not the time to fulfil the expectations of half a century. In 1649, Pálffy was elected Palatine by the diet, with much support from Zsigmond Rákóczi, the younger son of the deceased Prince of Transylvania. As the husband of Henrietta of the Palatinate, the daughter of the fallen King of Bohemia, Zsigmond Rákóczi was linked by marriage to several Protestant powers, and his family seat at Sárospatak in Upper Hungary became a rival political centre for Vienna; even a new anti-Habsburg movement was contemplated. As, however, both Pálffy and Rákóczi soon died, hopes were focused upon the latter's brother, György II Rákóczi, the new Prince of Transylvania – among others, by Miklós Zrínyi, Ban of Croatia and a leading supporter of Pálffy. Zrínyi, to whom I owe the last phrase in the title of this chapter, was not only a talented politician and a superb military commander, but at the same time a first-rate lyrical poet who also wrote the epic *The Peril of Sziget* (1651) about the valiant defence of Szigetvár by his great-grandfather in 1566; as well as important texts of military and political theory conceived in a Machiavellian fashion on the creation of a national army (*The Brave Lieutenant*, 1653) and a national monarchy (*Reflections on the Life of King Matthias*, 1656).

At first, György II Rákóczi seemed to warrant the expectations placed on him: interference on behalf of claimants, supported by popular uprisings, to the voevodships of Moldavia and Wallachia in 1653 and 1655, respectively, earned him the recognition of his overlordship over the two Romanian principalities. It was in his next undertaking that his weaknesses – lack of experience and political judgement, rashness and obstinacy, combined with immense personal ambition – ruined him and his country. His father had contemplated obtaining the throne of Poland for his brother Zsigmond when Władysław IV died in 1648, but the Polish estates elected the deceased king's son John Casimir. György II renewed the claim when Charles X, King of Sweden, had overrun Poland in 1655, but facing a coalition of the Habsburgs, Russia, the Netherlands and Denmark, called the Prince of Transylvania to his support, even offering the Polish crown to him.

Dazzled by the prospect, Rákóczi set out with his Romanian and Cossack allies for the campaign in a season completely unsuitable for it, in January 1657. He not only failed to recognise that the Catholic Poles would hardly welcome his zealous Protestant proselytising plans; the profound changes that were taking place in the Ottoman Empire as a result of the reforms of Grand Vizier Köprülü Mehmed from 1656 on also escaped his attention. He did not take heed of the order of the Porte to refrain from the campaign, and initially his advance seemed irresistible: in June 1657, he even occupied Warsaw. By this time, however, a Danish attack had forced the King of Sweden to withdraw his army, while a Polish counter-offensive penetrated into Transylvania. Rákóczi bought peace at an immense ransom of 1.2 million florins and rushed home, leaving behind the bulk of his army, which was then routed by Tartars on Ottoman orders. As also required by the Porte, the diet of Transylvania deposed Rákóczi, whose ill-advised adventure demonstrated that the remote King of Sweden and Transylvania's unstable eastern neighbours could lend but insufficient support to the principality in a conflict which was against the interests of the Ottomans and the Habsburgs at the same time.

The golden age of Transylvania had come to an end, but in the autumn of 1657 Rákóczi himself received a final chance from a group of Hungarian magnates including Zrínyi, Palatine Ferenc Wesselényi, Chief Justice Ferenc Nádasdy and Archbishop of Esztergom György Lippay. They had prevented a Habsburg attack against Rákóczi at the time of the Polish campaign, and now promised him armed assistance to consolidate his position domestically and *vis-à-vis* the Turks, while pressing for the same at the Viennese court. In return, they as well as Rákóczi would support young Leopold I, who had just succeeded to the throne of Hungary, at the upcoming imperial elections. Since French diplomacy, lead by Mazarin, schemed to thwart the Habsburg succession in the Holy Roman Empire, Leopold needed arguments to persuade the imperial estates of his superior merits, and taking an anti-Ottoman stance seemed a good one. The international atmosphere indeed looked auspicious for the rise of a new anti-Turkish league. A few thousand Habsburg troops were promised, while Rákóczi regained the principality in early 1658, and won a few battles.

Yet, the comeback was ephemeral. Soon after Leopold had been elected emperor in July, he assured the Porte that he did not intend to break the peace on behalf of Rákóczi. Within a month, 120,000 Turks and Tartars fell on Transylvania, and the systematic destruction that followed surpassed that of the Fifteen Years War. A fifth Ottoman *vilayet* in Hungarian territory, carved out of Transylvania, was soon organised with its centre at Várad. Rákóczi fought on for another two years until he died of wounds received in the Battle of Szászfenes. By that time he had been replaced as prince on the order of Köprülü by Ákos Barcsay, who in turn was ousted in 1661 by János Kemény, Rákóczi's one-time commander. Kemény took encouragement from the presence of the Habsburg troops commanded by General Raimondo Montecuccoli that finally arrived in Transylvania in the previous year. However, Montecuccoli also left as soon as the Porte made it clear that it did not want to incorporate Transylvania into the Ottoman Empire, by appointing Mihály Apafi, a learned and not very politically minded counsellor, as its newest puppet. Kemény having died in battle in June 1662, Apafi remained alone on the scene after years of turmoil from which Bethlen's one-time fairyland never recovered.

In view of the role that Transylvania had played during the past few decades and that it was expected to fulfil in the future, its demise, and especially what was generally regarded as the complicity of the Emperor in it, at first caused great perplexity and disappointment in Hungary. The Catholic estates were the first to react. Recognising and exploiting the willingness of the Holy See to renew its projects of an anti-Ottoman league, at the national synod of 1658 they urged the restoration of religious uniformity, represented as a precondition of national strength, in the interest of national defence. The violent Counter-Reformation thrust thus inaugurated was also 'national' in the sense that the lords participating in the resulting appropriation of churches, schools, printing presses and the property of those who fled, did so partly in order to anticipate the foreign Jesuits. This offensive determined the atmosphere of the diets of 1659 and 1662. At the former, in an atmosphere of general dissension, it was the authority of Zrínyi that reverted attention to the vital issue of military reform. In 1662, not even this could prevent the disaffected Protestant deputies from leaving the diet after their religious grievances were brushed aside. Nevertheless, the decrees of the diet revealed the growing influence of Zrínyi's vision as to how to put the country's defences on a new footing.

Although in 1649 the peace between the Habsburgs and the Porte had been renewed for another twenty-two years, the habitual frontier raids never ceased, and the young Zrínyi took a major role in them. At the same time, the Hungarian 'Phoenix of the century' (a description he used for King Matthias) devoted his energies to theory and propaganda: while he censured the indolence, the discord, the selfishness and the indifference to things public which he found rampant especially among the Hungarian nobility, he called for a revival of their martial spirit and the raising of a standing army from the ranks of the nobility as well as the heyducks, free frontier soldiers and even peasants, to be paid out of an income tax. Much of this programme was actually voted by the diet of 1662, and Zrínyi was composing his most influential pamphlet on the subject, *Remedy Against the Turkish Opium*, in 1663, when the new Grand Vizier, Köprülü Ahmed, commanded another campaign against Hungary.

The Habsburg high command under Montecuccoli, who early in 1662 effectively occupied Hungary at the head of a thirty-thousand strong army made notorious for its atrocities, did not make preparations to face the imminent offensive, and the Ottoman conquests of the autumn of 1663 resulted in the creation of a sixth *vilayet*, north of the Danube. Instead of the reluctant Emperor, it was Palatine Wesselényi who solicited and received assistance from the Rhenish Alliance of the imperial estates; upon pressure from the Hungarian estates, Zrínyi was appointed commander of the Hungarian forces. In that capacity, with the support of imperial troops led by Julius Wolfgang Hohenlohe, Zrínyi directed a spectacular campaign in the winter of 1664, penetrating deep into the area long occupied by the Ottomans in southern Transdanubia, liberating a number of fortresses and cutting Turkish supply lines by burning the bridge of Eszék (Osijek) on the River Drava. Amidst the applause of Europe, which also implied enthusiastic offers of support from France and Apafi, Zrínyi now started to besiege the huge fortress of Kanizsa, but Köprülü mobilised for the campaign season earlier than usual. The siege had to be abandoned, and Montecuccoli's army, upon orders that it should only intervene if the Turks actually threatened Vienna, watched idly as Zrínyi's newly erected fortress ('New Zrínyi Castle') was captured and demolished by the Turks. The Ottoman advance was finally halted on August 1, 1664: the united Christian forces won a great victory in the Battle of Szentgotthárd.

Both inside and outside the country it was generally believed that the strategic advantage thus gained would be used to launch the long-awaited anti-Turkish war of liberation. It caused great astonishment that Leopold I rather seized the chance to conclude the Peace of Vasvár. The Emperor thus became free to concentrate on the war against France, while Köprülü could turn against Venice for the possession of the Island of Crete. The Porte could keep the conquests of the previous year, and the treaty obliged both parties to refrain from giving aid to Hungary and mutually to inform each other about the hostile moves of the Hungarians. Zrínyi, in spite of his profound disillusionment and anger, recognised that the outrage caused by the peace in Hungary could only be turned into an anti-Habsburg uprising with Ottoman support, which the same treaty rendered impossible. He set to continuing the Hungarian political movement based on a systematic push towards a step-by-step recovery of strength and independence that had been unfolding since the Peace of Westphalia and that survived the demise of Rákóczi, the military rule of Montecuccoli and the campaign of Köprülü. He envisaged a modernised Hungarian polity with taxed noblemen and a peasantry protected by the state, with a standing army, in confederate union with Croatia and Transylvania and with prospects of liberation from Ottoman rule within two decades. Bethlen apart, the most far-sighted and robust political personage of the century, Zrínyi was left a far shorter time than the timetable he devised allowed for: three months after Vasvár, he died in a hunting accident.

His associates, led by Palatine Wesselényi, Archbishop Lippay, Chief Justice Nádasdy, Zrínyi's brother and successor as Ban of Croatia, Péter, and Ferenc Rákóczi (the son of György II and the son-in-law of Péter Zrínyi), unwilling to become reconciled to the status quo but frustrated by the narrowness of their scope of action, turned the movement into a conspiracy. Having sought the support of Louis XIV and Venice in vain, they approached the Porte with an offer to acknowledge Ottoman suzerainty if the Hungarian constitution and the right of free election were guaranteed, and no Hungarian troops were required to participate in the campaigns of the Sultan. This involved distinct risks: it could have thrown the country into a situation as hopeless as the much criticised Peace of Vasvár, while it also failed to warrant its security in the face of the rapidly militarising Habsburg power. For it must have been clear to the conspirators that Szentgotthárd was not a mere accident, but the outcome and symptom of the decline of Ottoman power. Authorities in the Turkish-occupied province were helpless in the face of the raids of the Hungarian frontier soldiers. Much of the administration of the occupied territories shifted into the hands of the 'refugee counties', and even the 'peasant counties', erected spontaneously by the commoners of these areas for their defence and self-government. The trend was towards the development of a Turkish-Hungarian condominium, which bade fair for the envisaged dependence being merely formal, but raised the question of the usefulness of depending on a power unable to defend the country against the Habsburgs.

The conspirators were saved from the dilemma by the lukewarm response of the Porte, and they decided to launch an uprising on their own. The fact that the ablest of the remaining leaders, Lippay and Wesselényi, died in 1666 and 1667, respectively, was not conducive to success, and the first attempt in 1668 was abortive: the plans were revealed to Vienna by some of the plotters themselves. In the spring of 1670, Rákóczi did launch the uprising in Upper Hungary, but as it failed to spread nation-wide and neither the Turks nor the western allies (alienated precisely by the overtures made to the Porte) interfered, the plotters hurried to seek the mercy of the Viennese court again. This time it was not granted: in April 1671, Zrínyi, his brother-in-law, Ferenc Frangepán, and Nádasdy were executed, a fate which Rákóczi escaped by paying a huge ransom (he was the wealthiest magnate of the country) and by showing extraordinary zeal in disavowing and disclosing his 'evil counsellors'. Some two hundred others were also tried for complicity in the plot.

The retaliation was far from replicating the procedure adopted against the Bohemian estates fifty years earlier (in Prague, twenty-seven heads fell and over six hundred nobles were sentenced to forfeiture of property after the Battle of the White Mountain): the incomparably more confined dimensions of the event and its international isolation would not have warranted it, and the country's military and political situation (the existence of Transylvania, the presence of the Turks and the strengthening of corporate structures in the preceding decades) would have rendered the complete destruction of the independence of the estates impracticable. Nevertheless, as Ferdinand in the case of the Bohemians, Leopold now said of the Hungarians that by their repeated acts of disloyalty they had forfeited their rights to governing themselves, deserved the suspension of their constitution, and to be ruled by imperial decrees through the centralised bureaucracy. A seven-member Gubernium was to govern the country, which was overflown with German mercenaries. In order to supply them, impossibly high taxes were levied. Failing to collect them, the mercenaries compensated themselves by pillaging the land, and the court (with enthusiastic support from the Hungarian Catholic high clergy) by initiating a violent persecution of Protestants. In 1674, over seven hundred preachers were summoned to a summary court, charged, among other things, with dealing with the Turks, and the most 'obstinate' forty-two (that is, those who refused to convert to Catholicism or at least to abandon their flocks) were sold as galley-slaves in Naples (where they were freed by the Dutch fleet two years later).

However, the resistance of the population made the confiscation of churches and schools a difficult process, and the Protestant denominations could not be outlawed either. Nor were the main corporate functions abolished, it was merely the office of the Palatine that was left vacant. What is more, by disbanding two-thirds of the Hungarian fortress soldiers upon the confiscation of the garrisons for the German military, the court in fact created a disgruntled and able fighting force that kept the spirit of revolt awake. Withdrawing to Transylvania or into the frontier zone where they drew support from the Ottomans, they called themselves initially 'outlaws' (*bujdosó*, literally: 'hiding') and later *kuruc* (supposedly referring to Dózsa's crusaders, in fact an expression of doubtful etymology) and continued to cause headaches to the Habsburg administration from the autumn of 1672 on.

The *kuruc* movement dragged on with alternating success and with much internal discord until it was reinforced by the Treaty of Warsaw between France, Poland and Transylvania in 1677. Louis XIV, who had suffered setbacks against the Emperor in the western front, offered Apafi a lucrative annual subsidy in return for lending support to the 'outlaws'. Apafi, relying on a group of able advisors, had been balancing surprisingly well on the tightrope between the Porte and Vienna, put the country's finances into order and consolidated his own position (indeed, the last of the princes of Transylvania ruled longer than any of his predecessors). However, the main beneficiary of the Treaty of Warsaw was the new and highly talented commander of the *kuruc*, Imre Thököly, the young and ambitious scion of a relatively new magnate family. He introduced some orderliness into the military and civil conduct of what had been a rather unruly mass of refugee irregulars, while being ready to devote some of his private income to this purpose as well as to share their lot. In the summer of 1678, the movement became the Thököly uprising. During the campaign of that year as well as in 1680, the *kuruc* cavalry raided lands as remote as Moravia, capturing several fortresses and towns in Upper Hungary, and although in light of the lack of a powerful infantry they could not hold occupied territory long, Thököly acquired international renown and an ever greater number of 'new *kuruc*' followers among established families in royal Hungary. Both in Vienna and at the Porte it was recognised that the main factor to reckon with in Hungary was Thököly, rather than Apafi, who watched the former's independent initiatives with increasing jealousy.

The lesson drawn at the Habsburg court from the impossibility of suppressing the Hungarian 'rebellion' was a revision of the absolutist policies launched a decade earlier. The Gubernium and the tax reform were abolished, the right to free worship of Protestants was acknowledged, and a Palatine was elected at the diet convened in 1681; thus, the division of power between the estates and the crown was restored. The *kuruc*, though invited, refused to attend the diet. Thököly rather looked to the Turks, whose interest in him was motivated by the fact that while having concluded a war against Russia, they were preparing for a final showdown with Vienna. Apafi seemed reluctant to abide by the orders of the Porte to launch attacks against royal Hungary in 1681 as well as in 1682. Thököly, on the other hand, while continuing the fight, not only married Ferenc Rákóczi's widow, Ilona Zrínyi, thereby extending his personal power base thanks to the immense Rákóczi estates, but also accepted the appointment by the Porte as Prince of Upper Hungary, a fourth unit in the territory of the one-time Kingdom of Hungary, after the capture of Kassa in the autumn of 1682.

With characteristic vigour and a fine organising ability, Thököly set to creating the framework of a polity which he believed would replace decrepit Transylvania as the repository of Hungarian statehood until full sovereignty could be restored. However, the mediocre Apafi proved to be a better *Realpolitiker* than the brilliant Thököly. Where they differed was the assessment of the relation of forces between the Habsburgs and the Porte, and that difference was crucial. Apafi, who cautiously refused to accept dominion over a united Transylvania and Hungary under Ottoman sway, was, in the short run at least, vindicated; while Thököly and all those numerous contemporaries who believed that the Turkish campaign, launched in 1683 partly encouraged by his own successes, would break Habsburg power, proved wrong. The third Ottoman siege of Vienna failed, and became the starting point for the war that expelled the Turks from Hungary while sweeping away first Thököly's ephemeral state, and a few years later the Principality of Transylvania as well.

4. *Hungaria eliberata?* *The expulsion of the Ottomans and Rákóczi's War of Independence*

By September 12, 1683, Grand Vizier Kara Mustafa and his 150,000 strong army had been besieging the Habsburg capital for nearly two months. However, the recently modernised fortifications and the desperate defenders defied the bombardment and the charges; and on that day, Leopold's alliance policy of the previous months bore fruit. While the diplomacy of Pope Innocent XI kept the French from attacking Austria from the rear, the imperial forces led by Charles, Duke of Lorraine, united with the troops of John III Sobieski, King of Poland, who came to the relief, as did the Electors of Bavaria and Saxony, and inflicted a crushing defeat on the besiegers. The Grand Vizier, retreating, refused the immediate peace offer; as a result, the Christian forces chased up their rear, winning further battles and capturing Esztergom, just outside of Buda. It became clear that what had long seemed desirable at best was now also feasible, and the Emperor reluctantly decided to embark on the expulsion of the Turks from Hungary.

This decision coincided with the expectations and the atmosphere across Europe, which the Pope responded to by organising in March 1684 the Holy League of the Emperor, Poland and Venice. Leopold was to launch an offensive against the Ottomans in Hungary, Sobieski in the Ukraine, and Doge Marcantonio Giustiniani in the Mediterranean. The main event of 1684 was the unsuccessful attempt to recover Buda. Drawing the lesson, in the following year Charles of Lorraine turned against the Turkish flanks, including Thököly's Upper Hungarian Principality, and by the end of 1685 most *kuruc* fortresses were in Habsburg hands (with a single one, Munkács, holding out under Thököly's valiant wife, Ilona Zrínyi, until the beginning of 1688). Thököly himself, who carefully avoided involvement in the siege of Vienna and exploited the turmoil to extend his domains, was now represented at the Porte as the cause of all mischief, and was arrested by the Pasha of Várad in October 1685. Although he was soon released, he was eventually compelled to leave Hungary along with the Turkish troops. His superior talent, which had made the Porte prefer him to Apafi, also accelerated the pace of his fall when the Ottoman card became a losing one. His horizon of European politics was insufficient to demonstrate the vanity of his endeavour to shake off Habsburg rule in Hungary; but, ironically, it was his tragically mistaken Ottoman commitment in 1683 that catalysed the speedy realisation of what he envisaged as the next step: the liberation of the country from Turkish rule.

It was also to a great extent the collapse of Thököly's power that made a significant Hungarian contribution to the military efforts of the Christian allies possible. At the outbreak of the war most of the potential Hungarian fighting force lined up on the Turkish side – a situation once feared by Zrínyi, who had urged the creation of a national army precisely in order to avoid the predictable consequences of being freed from the Ottoman yoke entirely by foreign arms. About fifteen thousand Hungarian soldiers would take part in the liberation of Buda in 1686, and up to thirty thousand in the subsequent operations of the war, most of them Thököly's former supporters. Besides the forces of the allied powers, which utilised the achievement of the European military revolution to the fullest, they largely played the role of auxiliaries: the regular Hungarian heyduck and hussar regiments in the imperial army did not exceed one tenth of the full number.

The material sacrifices the country made for the sake of its liberation, especially in view of its meagre capacity after the tribulations of the preceding one and a half centuries, were proportionately far more considerable. In each year of the war fifty to seventy percent of the subsidies of the Habsburg countries were collected in Hungary, in addition to the supply of the garrisons of the fortresses, the private donations of magnates and the labour force dispatched to transporting ammunition, erecting ramparts, digging trenches; not to speak of the arbitrary exactions of the armies whose needs even exceeded the upscaled impositions. The seventeenth century was one in which the bestiality of destitute privates and greedy officers was a commonplace. Hungary's case was special because the measures usually taken by the authorities to protect the civilian population and their resources were here wholly ineffective. The *oppidum* of Debrecen alone, where the troops of the notorious General Antonio Caraffa were quartered in the winter of 1686, paid merely as a ransom nearly one million florins, more than the *Türkenhilfe* of the three wealthiest districts of the German Empire combined. A year later, Caraffa fell on the town of Eperjes, where he set up a martial court and, upon trumped-up charges of plotting on behalf of Thököly, he had twenty-four nobles and burghers (all of them Protestant and wealthy) sentenced to loss of life and property. Europe was resounding with the news of the pillage of Hungary (while, paradoxically, the propaganda of Leopold that represented him as the heir of Hungary's status as 'a bulwark of Christendom' and Thököly's Hungary as 'the enemy of Christendom', also made an impact). In Hungary, it was generally held that the country paid more to the Germans than it had to the Ottomans in a century and a half. Undoubtedly, this is grossly exaggerated; nevertheless it is also indicative, and goes a fair way towards explaining the bitterness of the anti-Habsburg sentiment that emerged in the country by the end of the war of liberation.

That war was in full swing by 1686, when the allied armies under the command of Charles of Lorraine laid a two and a half month siege to Buda. This time their effort was crowned by success: on September 2, 1686, the Hungarian capital – now a heap of ashes, with its few hundred miserable inhabitants exposed to three days of free looting at the hands of the exhausted soldiers, sanctioned by the high command – was delivered from the Turks after 145 years. From Rome to Amsterdam and from Venice to Madrid, fireworks, festivals and thanksgiving processions celebrated the triumph of the European achievement of the age: of papal diplomacy, of international banking, of Polish and German military genius, of French and Italian military technology, of Venetian, Styrian and Silesian industry, of soldiers of dozens of nationalities and of Hungarian human and material sacrifices.

The offensive went on to recover, before the end of the year, Pécs and Szeged, and the acquisitions of 1686 were secured in the spectacular triumph of the forces of the Holy League in the Battle of Nagyharsány in August 1687. This victory paved the way to the capture of Belgrade, a feat of the Bavarian Elector, Maximilian Emmanuel, in September 1688; in the following year, the imperial forces, already commanded by Louis, Margrave of Baden, fought successfully along the Lower Danube. Many fortresses still held by the Turks amidst this vigorous offensive became isolated from their hinterland, and were more or less peacefully abandoned (like Eger in 1687, Székesfehérvár in 1688, Szigetvár in 1689 or Nagykanizsa in 1690).

Transylvania also came under Habsburg control in the course of the war. Still too cautious to accept the invitation to join the Holy League in 1684, in the autumn of 1687 Apafi could not but accept, despite the apparent maintenance of Transylvania's independence, the protection of the Emperor. This implied a yearly tribute to Vienna which was heavier than the one earlier exacted by the Porte, while the country was virtually occupied by the forces of Charles of Lorraine. The logical conclusion came in 1690, when Apafi died and Vienna refused to recognise the succession of his son. For the last time, Thököly attempted to intervene, had himself appointed prince by the Sultan and elected by the Transylvanian diet, and even won a great victory over the Habsburg troops, which, however, ultimately gained the upper hand and forced him to leave for ever. He died in exile at Nicomedia in 1705. On October 16, 1690, the Emperor issued the *Diploma Leopoldinum*, which settled the constitutional status of Transylvania until 1848: it was to be administered (initially by a new Gubernium, later by the Transylvanian Chancellery) as a separate province of the Kingdom of Hungary, according to its own laws.

After four years of steady advance, the Christian allies were temporarily halted by a combination of factors. At the end of 1688, Louis XIV denounced the peace treaty made four years earlier, and the best Habsburg regiments and generals were deployed on the western front, while the new grand vizier, Köprülü Mustafa, made desperate efforts at a counter-attack. In 1690, he managed to recover not only the fortresses lost in the northern Balkans during the previous year, but also Belgrade. Although the joining of England to the anti-French Grand Alliance of the Emperor, the imperial estates and the United Provinces relieved the Habsburgs in the west, which soon resulted in a great victory at Szalánkemén in September 1691, the imperial forces were largely on the defensive until the end of the war against France in 1697. On September 11 that year, the decisive blow was delivered on the Ottoman fighting force exhausted of fifteen years of warfare. In the battle of Zenta (Senta) – in many ways, the reversal of Mohács – the army sent by the Sultan to reconquer Transylvania or Upper Hungary was nearly annihilated. The victor was no other than Eugene of Savoy, whose spectacular career started after having fled the court of Louis XIV to fight the Turks besieging Vienna in 1683; he fought in the Ottoman wars until 1688 and then in northern Italy against the French, to be returned to the eastern front as supreme commander. In recognition of his services, Eugene was rewarded with a huge estate at Ráckeve (south of Pest), where he erected one of the most sumptuous baroque palaces in Hungary. Peace was signed between the powers of the Holy League and the Porte on January 26, 1699, at Karlóca (Karlowitz). The Habsburgs gained most: all of Hungary except for parts of the Temes and the Srem area.

After the theatre of war had been transferred to the southern frontier region, the situation within the country became normalised, while by that time Leopold's government had also set to realising its plans systematically. At the diet of 1687, still in the shadow of Caraffa's gallows at Eperjes, the Hungarian estates were quite willing to yield to the Emperor's demand to modify the constitution and to express their gratitude for his interference on their behalf against the Turks by recognising the Habsburgs' hereditary right to the throne of Hungary and giving up the right of resistance granted to them in the Golden Bull of 1222.

The docility of the Hungarian estates could have been conceived as a gesture, and as a basis of co-operation in the administration of the new Habsburg domains between the court and the local elite, which had retained much of its jurisdiction over the lands occupied by the Ottomans. Not for Leopold, who bears much of the personal responsibility for the deterioration of the relationship between the Habsburgs and Hungary.

Of the numerous projects submitted to him, those which were selected aimed at breaking the backbone of the estates without adopting the reform proposals they also put forward. What the court primarily expected of the new acquisitions was money to defray the deficit that soared to thirty million florins as a result of the debt incurred in wartime. The new territories were delegated to the competence of the Imperial Chamber, where a commission (the *Neoacquistica Commissio*) was set up and demanded the holders of estates in the recovered areas to produce legal documents of ownership; and even if they could do so, they were required to pay reparations for the damages of the war. Many estates were thus rented by auction to foreign generals, aristocrats and army contractors. The Hungarian regiments were disbanded, as well as the soldiers of the fortresses, which were to be demolished; the new southern line of defence was to be entrusted to the approximately 200,000 Serbs who fled the returning Turks in 1689 under Patriarch Arsenije Černojević. It was also generally felt at the time that the edge of Leopold's policy to resettle the depopulated areas of the Great Plain and Transdanubia was directed against the Hungarians whom he considered restless and rebellious. Catholic German ('Swabians', as they came to be known in Hungary) were settled in Transdanubia, the Teutonic Order obtained extensive areas between the Danube and the Tisza as mortgage, and the Serbs of Černojević received extensive civil and ecclesiastical autonomy – at a time when the same was flatly denied to Hungarian Protestants whose folk songs spoke of a 'reign of (Catholic) priests'.

The discontent first erupted in the spring of 1697, when Thököly's former officers, after over a year's preparation, gathered sufficient support to unleash a revolt among the peasantry of the Tokaj wine region, which had until recently preserved a semblance of prosperity, but was now ruined by heavy taxes. The uprising was suppressed after its organisers failed to secure the involvement of men of substance, in particular, the young Ferenc Rákóczi, whom they invited to lead them. The grandson of György II of Transylvania and the stepson of Thököly was separated from his mother, Ilona Zrínyi, after the castle of Munkács was captured, and received an education designed for future court aristocrats from Jesuits in southern Bohemia and at the University of Prague. Himself a duke of the Holy Roman Empire, he married a German duchess, and felt rather awkwardly in his native land when he returned to his vast estates in Upper Hungary in 1694. Declining the invitation of the *kuruc*, he hurried to Vienna to clear himself of suspicion, and even wanted to exchange his domains to ones in Germany. This being refused, he returned to restore and modernise his estates.

The regular intercourse with the neighbouring, predominantly Protestant magnates who fell outside the small circle of Hungarian aristocrats allowed to hold government office and who especially felt the edge of the economic, constitutional and religious restrictions imposed by the Habsburg court, completely changed his attitudes within two years. Miklós Bercsényi in particular made an impact on Rákóczi, awakening his sense of princely calling and responsibility for his country. As in 1700, Louis XIV raised a Bourbon claim to the throne of Spain which had become vacant upon the heirless death of its last Habsburg ruler, Charles II, and Europe was on the verge of a new war, the international situation being favourable for seeking support against the Habsburgs. Within weeks of the death of the King of Spain, Rákóczi sent a letter of the Hungarian malcontents to Louis XIV, which, however, his courier presented in Vienna. In April 1701, Rákóczi was arrested along with many of his fellow plotters, and was detained at Wiener Neustadt, while Bercsényi managed to escape to Poland. It was in Warsaw that the two were reunited a few months later, after Rákóczi had escaped from his captivity under romantic circumstances. But the King of France, although the War of Spanish Succession did break out in the spring of 1701, was reluctant to undertake specific commitments, Poland was torn apart by the northern war against Charles XII of Sweden, and the links established between Rákóczi and the exiled Thököly in 1702 did not hold out distinct promises either: in short, the situation seemed hopeless.

In Hungary, however, the situation was turbulent. The pressure of taxation, now aggravated through monopolies and excessive excises, gave rise to a burgeoning contraband trade that served to link up the whole country and harmonise the isolated actions of the hiding *kuruc*. Also, Habsburg military presence was considerably reduced in Hungary by the early successes of the French in the western war; in 1703, as they penetrated into Tyrol, it even seemed that if the *kuruc* could take concerted action, they might unite forces with the French to lay siege on Vienna. From the end of 1702 on, the main co-ordinator of the movement, Tamás Esze, a peasant entrepreneur *par excellence*, engaged in the trade of salt, looked for a new leader once again. Now that his arrest, fabulous escape and exile added some charisma to his background and status, Rákóczi looked ideal. Visited by Esze in the small castle of Brzeżany in the southeast of Poland, he agreed and on May 6, 1703, issued a manifesto calling to liberate Hungary from the 'illegal and intolerable yoke'. A month later he arrived in Hungary, under banners adorned with the slogan *Cum Deo pro Patria et Libertate* (With God, for the Fatherland and Liberty).

The common folk flocked to his initially rather small camp, especially after the patent of August 28, 1703, promising exemption from taxes and manorial obligation to those serfs who joined Rákóczi's army. This amounted to interference with lord-serf relations by appealing to reason of state. The nobility, which at first adopted a position of wait and see, was reassured about Rákóczi's intention to maintain discipline in the army and law and order in the country by the issuing of military statutes, and followed their serfs under Rákóczi's banner. Numerical strength was thus combined with hierarchy and authority in a temporary union of interests, with the result that the devastated country was able and willing to maintain a national army of about 70,000 soldiers for several years (the subsidies received from Louis XIV being sufficient for the supply of a mere fraction of this number). The successes of *kuruc* arms in the autumn of 1703, when the Habsburg forces were expelled from the richest, north-western areas of the country, earned further support for Rákóczi, and although the 1704 campaign of General Sándor Károlyi in Transdanubia swiftly collapsed, Rákóczi was elected first Prince of Transylvania, then, at the diet of Szécsény in September 1705, Commanding Prince of Hungary.

Rákóczi, who displayed a remarkable talent for organisation, governed the *kuruc* state with a senate consisting of prelates, aristocrats and noblemen, while the important tasks of diplomacy were assigned to the chancellery directed by Pál Ráday, and the economic council was responsible for raising revenue. The latter was a crucial, and finally insoluble problem in a country exhausted by the tribulations of the preceding decades. Ironically, the taxes imposed under Rákóczi were higher than the ones that had provoked the war led by him. At the same time, pioneering in Central Europe, his system of taxation was designed to reach the whole of society and to encompass all national resources, including those of the nobility. No wonder that there was no way of collecting revenue properly, and the prince experimented with the unpopular, and equally ineffective, method of debasing the currency. While economic difficulties multiplied, the initial social solidarity declined. The original leaders of modest social background felt irritated as the officers' posts were taken over by the aristocrats after their joining the movement; whereas the latter were less than enthusiastic of the prospect of peasant emancipation, which was the hope that drove serfs to fight 'for the Fatherland and for Liberty'. Rákóczi kept balancing between the two forces by trying to find a form of compromising his initial promises to the peasant soldiers. Finally, although to emphasise the endeavour of reconciling the interests of the various social strata, the nature of the state was defined as 'confederate', it did not escape the attention of his jealous magnates that what Rákóczi really meant was growing centralisation, relying largely on lesser nobles close to him. Despite all these tensions, the momentum of the struggle and the unifying force of the goal of independence were sufficient to bring about at the height of the war, at the diet of Ónod on June 13, 1707, the deposition of the Habsburgs.

By that time, changes on the international scene and in the military relationships had long made it evident that the separation of the country from the Habsburg Monarchy by force of arms was not feasible, and the realistic goal of the struggle was political compromise. After the great defeat of the French and Bavarian armies in the Battle of Höchstädt (Blenheim) at the hands of the Duke of Marlborough and Eugene of Savoy on August 13, 1704, no external military support could be expected, and the *kuruc* forces, apart from their enthusiasm and morale, were much inferior to the Habsburg troops. Though Rákóczi made strenuous efforts to adjust his Hungarian troops, accustomed to irregular warfare, to the requirements of modern, organised operations, he could not help realising that, besides the poor equipment of his soldiers, it was because of the salient ineptitude of the commanding officer corps that in eight years, not a single important battle was won by them. The feats of the few exceptions, like the renowned János Bottyán ('the Blind'), who conquered Transdanubia in a brilliant campaign in the autumn of 1705, did a lot to keep spirits high. Yet, in general, the initially large numerical superiority of the *kuruc* could chiefly be exploited against relatively small imperial units in surprise attacks, but in open battle a few thousand *labanc* (the nickname of loyalists, probably on account of the dishevelled, that is, *loboncos* German wigs they wore) could beat twice, or three or more times as many *kuruc*. Even so, until 1708 most of Hungary was under Rákóczi's control: Upper Hungary and the Great Plain quite firmly, and Transdanubia and Transylvania alternating in *kuruc* and Habsburg hands. By 1708, under the impact of discouraging news about the fortunes of the western coalition fighting the Habsburgs, the *kuruc* army started to ebb, and the humiliating defeat in the Battle of Trencsén on August 3, 1708, already foreshadowed the outcome of the fight for independence.

The fact that it only came nearly three years later was owing to the continuing western commitment of Emperor Joseph I, who succeeded his father Leopold in 1705 and had somewhat different attitudes to Hungary as well. Over-cautious to secure his new acquisitions in Italy, he was temporarily content to maintain a balance of forces in Hungary, where he made concessions to the small representation of estates that gathered at the diet of Pozsony in 1708. All of this created an opportunity for Rákóczi to attempt to shape a favourable international background for his endeavours. After the deposition of the Habsburgs, the Hungarian crown was offered to Maximilian Emmanuel, the Elector of

Bavaria, while Rákóczi himself entertained hopes of being elected King of Poland. The first of these plans was abortive, while the second needed careful preparation and depended on support from Peter I of Russia. Rákóczi clearly realised that in the given situation it was vital to win time and to persevere until the Hungarian settlement could be embedded in an all-European treaty system: his envoys attended the peace talks that started in Gertruydenberg in 1710, and were willing to accept the Habsburgs, but insisted on an act of succession, religious toleration, a Hungarian army and international guarantees. When the military balance of forces turned hopeless from the *kuruc* point of view, Rákóczi authorised General Sándor Károlyi to temporise by negotiations with the new Habsburg commander, János Pálffy, Ban of Croatia. At a personal meeting with Pálffy, Rákóczi stressed that only a settlement that took place between the Habsburgs and Hungary as a confederate state was acceptable to him, but not the arrangement based on private pardon and concessions, however generous, by the ruler. He then left for Poland and to conduct talks with Peter the Great. By the time the two met, Károlyi, authorised by the majority of the confederated estates, had signed the Peace of Szatmár on April 30, 1711, and on the following day the *kuruc* army surrendered.

The terms of the peace looked so mild to disappointed loyalist magnates that they bitterly complained about the arrogance of the *kuruc* leaders afterwards, 'as if they had triumphed over the Emperor'. Indeed, the amnesty involved not only impunity but also the restoration of estates for those who returned to the Emperor's allegiance (including even Rákóczi and Bercsényi, should they return); the ruler promised to observe the rights and liberties of the country, to co-operate with the diet in ruling Hungary in accordance with her own laws and customs, to secure free worship, and to abolish offices like the *Neoacquistica Commissio*. Thus the Peace of Szatmár reverted, with a somewhat stronger position of the crown, to the constitutional status quo before 1670: the division of power between the Habsburgs and the Hungarian estates, which temporarily shifted to the advantage of the former in consequence of the anti-Ottoman liberation war. For those of the *kuruc* whose primary objective was the restoration of corporate privileges and found independence increasingly illusory, this was nothing less than victory, especially because they knew only too well that crushing defeat was imminent. To that extent, Károlyi, often repudiated as a traitor, was a *Realpolitiker*.

At the same time, without international guarantees, the settlement rested upon the reliability of Charles III, the successor of Joseph I who died two weeks before the Peace of Szatmár: the new monarch stressed that the 'tranquillity of the Hungarians was a vital interest of Austria', and therefore that that nation 'ought to be treated with greater sympathy' and 'convinced that I trust and honour them as I do the others'. In addition, the settlement was a far cry from the objectives of a great many other *kuruc*, including the very first insurrectionists who belonged to the early, predominantly popular wing of the movement, of Rákóczi himself and his closest associates. It was not out of an obstinate, Quixotic perseverance against the odds that he never returned to Hungary and sought opportunities to revive the struggle – from Poland he went to France and finally to Turkey, where he died in 1735 –, even if his conviction that there was still hope of success was out of touch with reality. It was not the trappings of independence that attracted and animated him, but the potentials, inherent in the very fight for independence and its attainment, with a view to catalysing socio-economic progress and to raising the country to western standards. His experience of the union of interest early in the war, however short it lasted, was crucial from this point of view. He thought that a Hungary where the tendency was towards the abolition of tax privileges, the emancipation of serfs, professional administration and a national army would be more competitive than one in which corporate structures and perpetual serfdom became ossified.

Whether this was *Realpolitik* or not in the given circumstances has been and will be subject to debate among historians. Rákóczi's achievement is to have demonstrated that even in times of adversity, there was in Hungary, at least on the level of valiant if unsuccessful effort, an alternative to what followed: testing the limits of the possible in an often frustrating process of the slow recovery of strength amidst conditions of relative socio-economic backwardness and partial political sovereignty. As these conditions determined most of the history of Hungary in modern times, the period and the outcome of Rákóczi's War of Independence is also remarkable because it introduced one of the constant themes of that history: the dilemmas caused by the precarious relationship between constitutional independence, national survival and political, socio-economic and cultural modernisation.

CHAPTER V

ENLIGHTENMENT, REFORM AND REVOLUTION
(1711–1849)

The eighteenth century is distinguished in European history by the recovery of the self-confidence of the old continent. After two centuries in
which it had been inflicted with devastating religious, civil and international wars, the birth pangs of a new socio-economic order and hyperbolic doubt concerning the ethical foundations upon which its whole
civilisation was erected, Europe seemed to have climbed to a stage
where it could take satisfaction in its achievement when compared to all
alternatives, past or present. The sophisticated network of division of
labour and the wheels of commerce that tied European societies increasingly firmly together not only raised the satisfaction of needs to a
level which was far from ideal but still incomparably superior to anything experienced earlier or elsewhere; it also bred refinement in material, social and intellectual pleasures. The understanding of toleration
made religious diversity feasible without the evils of persecution; the
understanding of checks and balances in the polity adjusted the bureaucratic machineries that had emerged in the preceding centuries to the
requirements of the rule of law, while preserving their ability to perform
the functions of a modern state; and the understanding of the balance of
power, while it did not eliminate international conflicts, offset the
threats of 'universal monarchy' associated with figures like Emperor
Charles V or Louis XIV; it supplied a framework in which the destructive
potential of the huge armies also created in the preceding era was
brought under control, and a system of international law could transform the anarchy of competing powers into a 'commonwealth of Europe'.

Or so it seemed. To be sure, the enlightened minds who devoted
much profound thinking to create this interpretation of contemporary
civilisation – for these were ideas which most men of the Enlightenment
shared – never pretended that all this was reality, but they were convinced that it represented the general tendency, as it were, the meaning
of European history. The Enlightenment was not a mere abstract metaphysical pursuit, but a contemplation of this predicament in all its complexity; also, it was the endeavour of accumulating and systematising
the available stock of knowledge about man's natural and social environment with the objective of further improving that environment. This

is why the French *Encyclopédie* was the undertaking *par excellence* of the period, whose attitudes and goals constituted a kind of smallest common denominator for all of the conflicting trends of Enlightenment. The overall belief in progress and in the capacity of man to direct that progress – provided that man became the autonomous being Immanuel Kant hoped him to become by emancipating himself from his self-imposed moral and intellectual tutelage – was also the an inheritance from the Age of Enlightenment that survived even the crucible of the French Revolution, and remained influential into the nineteenth century.

The expulsion of the Turks did provide Hungary with a chance to partake in that recovery of confidence and in the dynamic processes upon which it was based, albeit the conditions in which this event found the country and the circumstances among which it took place made that chance difficult to grasp. First, the dismal effects of many decades of economic stagnation and decline combined with intermittent wars made the country the land of contradictions described in the accounts of early eighteenth-century western travellers: a land with proverbially fertile soil but vast areas of fallow and marshland (less than 2.4 per cent of its territory was cultivated in 1720), whose population was thin and miserably poor. For instance, by the time Buda was liberated, merely two survived of the approximately two hundred settlements Heves county once had; on an area of about 5,000 square kilometres south of the town of Vác in Pest county, there were also no more than two left out of sixty-four once thriving villages. Whereas Europe's population increased by about 60 per cent during the sixteenth and seventeenth centuries, that of Hungary in 1686 hardly exceeded the roughly 3.5 million it had around 1500, and the wars of liberation and the plague that raged towards the end of Rákóczi's War of Independence may have cost another few hundred thousand lives.

As commonly after demographic disasters, the regeneration thereafter was spectacular: by the mid-nineteenth century, the country had more than four times as many inhabitants as in the beginning. Besides natural growth, this was due to several waves of organised and spontaneous immigration, which accentuated the earlier tendency: from about fifty per cent around 1700, the proportion of Hungarians within the population further decreased to below forty per cent by the middle of the nineteenth century. Since manpower was essential to operate a relatively underdeveloped economic system, and since the contribution of the Serbs, Romanians and Germans (besides the Slovaks, Croats and Ruthenes whose internal migration also made a significant impact) to the cultural and ethnographic outlook of the regions they inhabited became especially valuable, the benefits of the resettlement are hard to overestimate. At the same time, not least because of the distortions of

7. Ethnic groups in Hungary
in the eighteenth century

Hungarians
Romanians
Ruthenian
Slovaks
Germans
Serbs
Croats
uninhabited area

Hungary's social structure during the Ottoman period which in the long run greatly prejudiced the rise of a modern civic mentality, these changes in the ethnic composition of the country generated tensions which, in the event, proved insoluble and led to the dismemberment of historic Hungary after the First World War.

I have already mentioned the embarrassing fact that because of the political developments of the preceding decades, as the anti-Ottoman liberation war started, Hungarian society and its elite was divided, and substantial segments of it found themselves on the 'wrong' side. The mass of individual efforts which contributed to the success of the war did not add up to being the concerted national political and military undertaking once envisaged by Zrínyi, and this was exploited by Habsburg propaganda, so as to represent and treat the Hungarians as an unreliable force to be suppressed and their country as a province conquered by force of arms. What is more, the Habsburgs were more powerful than ever. In the west, the hegemony of France, which had repeatedly challenged the emperors and caused them headaches by supporting Poland, the Ottomans or the Hungarian malcontents, was on the decline, while the success of the war in the southeast transformed Vienna from a beleaguered frontier city into the true centre of the new, 'Danubian' empire of the Habsburgs.

For Hungary, all this created a highly unfavourable situation, which Rákóczi's War of Independence to some extent redressed. Full separation, and the dynamic for social progress Rákóczi hoped to gain from it, was not achieved, and in view of the meagre external and internal resources the independence struggle was able to mobilise, it could not have been achieved. What was realistic was to challenge the existing internal structure of the Habsburg Monarchy and to endeavour to integrate Hungary as an autonomous unit within that broader political framework. That much was secured by the compromise of 1711, which, in turn, could not have been attained without the tremendous efforts made and risks taken by the participants of the independence struggle. With all the incompleteness and the negative features which from Rákóczi's standpoint could be legitimately attributed to the settlement worked out by Károlyi and Pálffy, Hungary undoubtedly obtained domestic peace and more favourable conditions for a gradual recovery of strength than what was available earlier. To be sure, the settlement favoured the ascendancy of the nobiliary estates, and thus its impact on the potential of socio-economic modernisation was ambivalent. However, as the case of Poland shows, among specifically East-Central European circumstances precisely the preponderance of corporate structures and the intertwining of the 'national' interest with the sectional interests of the nobility made full political independence a highly questionable guarantee not only of socio-economic progress, but ultimately also of sufficient weight to resist external conquest. In the Hungarian case, much depended on the ability and the willingness of the nobility to respond to stimuli in a world of accelerated change, sometimes from a place no other than Vienna, to employ improved methods of cultivation and administration, to absorb notions of the public good and social responsibility – in other words, to become imbued with the spirit of Enlightenment. Their failures bear supreme responsibility for the conservation of some ossified structures and relationships, and the difficulties of the country in coping with the challenges of modernity. Their successes, which on the whole seem to have been more numerous, prepared, and to a great extent constituted what was arguably the most vibrant chapter in the history of Hungary: the Age of Reform and its cathartic culmination, the Revolution and War of Independence of 1848–1849.

1. Monarchs and estates, and the limits of compromise

The administrative system established in Hungary after the Peace of Szatmár could still be described as absolutism, but it was of a milder, far more sober kind than the one introduced in Bohemia by Ferdinand II after 1620 or the one attempted in Hungary by Leopold I after 1670. Besides the difficulties in putting down the Hungarian estates as a result of the presence of the Ottomans and the existence of Transylvania, and the lessons of the struggles of Bocskai, Thököly and Rákóczi, the peculiar situation in which the new monarch found himself played a part in this difference. Charles III (as Emperor, Charles VI) had prepared to take over the Spanish inheritance of the Habsburgs, and was able to look at Hungarian affairs with some detachment and without personal emotions. Although the prospect of the unification of Spain and the eastern Habsburg possessions under the same ruler made his allies in the War of Spanish Succession withdraw their support and prepare for a separate peace, Austria's war against Louis XIV only came to an end with the Peace of Rastatt in March 1714, and Charles III wanted peace in the Hungarian hinterland. Soon after he had arrived from Spain – via Frankfurt, where he was elected and crowned emperor – in Vienna in early 1712, he summoned the Hungarian diet. On March 30 he approved of the Peace of Szatmár, and in his coronation charter of May 21 he promised to maintain the territorial integrity of Hungary and to govern it in conformity with its customs and statutes.

By and large, this was the tenor of the laws the diet (which had to be discontinued several times because of the repeated outbursts of plague) issued in 1714 and 1715. They codified the compromise of Szatmár: in other words, unlike in Austria and Bohemia, where the crown managed to shake off the control of the feudal estates in government and to some extent to curtail their privileges, including those related to taxation, in Hungary the balance between the crown and the corporate structures, that is, the political influence and social privileges mainly of the magnates, was preserved. The laws confirmed Hungary's autonomous status, and bound future monarchs to issue coronation charters securing the same and to summon diets at regular intervals. At the same time, the laws of the diets of Rákóczi were declared null and void, and the absent participants of the war of independence guilty of high treason. Principles were established to settle lawsuits relating to property recovered from the Ottomans. To put an end to the jurisdictional anarchy, a reorganisation of the system of courts was undertaken, despite some reluctance on the part of the Hungarian nobility. A permanent army was set up, to be directed by the Military Court Council, though the voting of recruitment and war subsidies were referred to the competence of the diet. All financial offices in Hungary were subordinated to the Hungarian Court Treasury whose permanent seat was in Pozsony. The Hungarian Court Chancellery was to be independent from all other court offices, though it was recruited from the closest circle of the ruler, and resided in Vienna, only moving to Pozsony while the diet was in session.

There was a promising reform initiative, too: a board of the estates was commissioned to work out a plan for the country's 'political, economic and military system'. Several of its proposals were elaborated by Count Károlyi, who tried to rely on his experience gained under the Rákóczi administration: besides the entrenchment of nobiliary interests, the projects also envisaged systematic resettlement policies, the curtailing of the guild system and the improvement of manufactures, the regulation of rivers with a view to navigation and increased trade, the building of canals etc. However, the board did not convene until the next diet was summoned in 1722, and most of its plans were abortive, mainly because there was no agreement on the distribution of contributions to the public fund to be established for these purposes. The task was finally entrusted to the organ whose establishment in 1723 rounded off the reorganisation of the administrative system of Hungary, the Viceregal Council (*Consilium Regium Locumtenentiale Hungaricum*) or Gubernium. All affairs other than jurisdiction and military and financial administration came within the competence of this body. It had twenty-two, later twenty-five members (aristocrats, prelates and nobles, with the preponderance of the first); it was presided over by the Palatine when the country had one, and by a lord lieutenant directly appointed by the ruler in the periods (like 1765 to 1790) when it had none. Though situated in Pozsony and, on the insistence of the estates, after 1784 in Buda, the Gubernium was directly subordinated to the ruler.

As regards the restoration of the unity of the lands of the Crown of Saint Stephen, as demanded by the Hungarian estates (but not those of Transylvania) in 1714–1715 and repeatedly later on, it was in effect denied. Obviously because of its role in the seventeenth-century independence struggles, Transylvania, together with the Partium, remained under separate administration (later even proclaimed a 'grand duchy' by Maria Theresa, thus emphasising its independent status). The southern zone of the military frontier region in Slavonia and Croatia became directly subordinated to the Imperial Military Council, whereas the Temes region, only re-conquered from the Ottomans in the war of 1716–1717 (concluded in 1718 with the Peace of Požarevac [Passarowitz]), was kept as the Banate of Temes under the administration of the Military Council and the Imperial Treasury until 1778, when in was reintegrated into the county system.

Another permanent source of tension was the religious settlement. Although Charles III, upon confirming the Peace of Szatmár, promised to maintain freedom of worship and the status quo that emerged as a result of the recovery of churches and educational establishments by the Protestants during Rákóczi's War of Independence, these were annulled in a decree of 1714, and the laws of the diet of 1715 secured Catholic ascendancy. Protestant worship was confined to places authorised back in 1681, and Protestant parishes came under the supervision of Catholic bishops. Direct persecution and forced conversions came to an end, but while Catholic proselytising was supported in all possible ways, Catholics could only convert to Protestantism with great difficulty. Religious tests, including an oath to the Virgin Mary, excluded Protestants from office-holding. With minor refinements, this settlement was later confirmed in the *Carolina Resolutio* of 1731, and became the background to the most successful period of the Counter-Reformation in the history of Hungary, one which lasted until Joseph II's Patent of Toleration in 1781.

The final stage in resettling Hungary's relations with Austria based on the compromise of Szatmár came in 1722–1723. The creation of the Gubernium has already been mentioned. However, the main objective of Charles III at the diet summoned in that year was to get the Hungarian estates to accept the succession arrangement known as the Pragmatic Sanction. This measure settled two issues, the indivisibility of the Habsburg domains and female succession in the House of Habsburg, and had rather complicated antecedents. Already in 1703, Joseph I and Charles had agreed in a secret family pact that should either of them die without a male heir, the offspring of the other would inherit his domains, and he who survived would be entitled to pass them down in the female line as well. Upon his succession in 1711, Charles III, heirless at the time, confirmed this arrangement in a decree which, however, remained unknown until 1713, when he discussed it with his closest advisors, including a few Hungarian aristocrats. In 1716, Charles's son was born, but he died as an infant before the end of the same year. During the following years, the Pragmatic Sanction was acknowledged by the daughters of Joseph I and by the Habsburg hereditary provinces, and by the 1730s the most important European powers as well.

Obtaining the assent of the Hungarian diet, however, seemed to be a problem. While Croatia and Transylvania, administered separately, accepted the Pragmatic Sanction in 1721 and 1722, respectively, the majority of the Hungarian nobility felt that the concessions of 1687 and 1711 were already excessive, and indeed, at the diet of 1715, Charles confirmed the right of the Hungarian estates to elect a king, should he have no male heir – still in the hope that he would have one. Thus, as the Hungarian diet was summoned in the spring of 1722, careful preparation was needed to have the Pragmatic Sanction acknowledged. The many informal discussions to ascertain the support of loyal aristocrats like Károlyi, the Pálffys or the Esterházys, the handing out of estates and other preferments, and frequent allusions to the still existing Ottoman menace, secured the desired result. Right after the deputies had convened, they recognised succession in the female line of the Habsburgs, though limited it to the daughters of Charles III, Joseph I and Leopold I, and retained the right of free election in case the progeny of these rulers died out entirely (a rather ineffective limitation, considering the fact that this progeny survives into our own days). Hungary and the hereditary provinces were declared to be linked 'indivisibly and inseparably', and to be obliged to mutual defence in case of aggression by foreign powers. Apart from a short intermezzo after the 1849 Declaration of Independence, these stipulations governed the constitutional relationship between Hungary and the Habsburgs until 1918, with frequent debates concerning the interpretation of the rather generalised and somewhat obscure phrasing of Laws I–III/1723. What made these laws a classic example of a compromise between the ruler and the estates, in particular the aristocracy, was that in return for the voluntary (though temporary) renouncement of further meddling with the issue of the relationship between Hungary and the Habsburgs by the latter, the former solemnly confirmed the country's corporate constitution and the privileges of its nobility.

Further, social aspects of that compromise were the naturalisation of a fair number of Austrian and imperial aristocrats in Hungary and the

building of closer ties between Hungarian magnates and the cosmopolitan aristocratic class gathering in Vienna. In the wake of the wars of
liberation, over two hundred members of the Austrian-Bohemian aristocracy became naturalised in Hungary and received huge estates in
reward for the services they rendered during those wars, as in the case
of the Harruckern, or in other ways, as the Althan, the Trautson or the
Schönborn families. Though many of these *indigenae* later either sold
their estates to native magnates because of unfamiliarity with local conditions, or became closely linked with them through intermarriage, the votes
they received at the diets made them objects of suspicion in the country.

True, Hungarian loyalists also greatly benefited from the distribution
of lands re-conquered from the Ottomans and confiscated from Rákóczi
and the other émigrés. There were approximately two-hundred aristocratic families in eighteenth-century Hungary, either of old stock, like
the Esterházy, the Batthyány, the Erdődy or the Pálffy, or new ones, who
arose with the successful augmentation of their estates, like the Gras-
salkovich, or service in the bureaucracy or the military, like the Orczy,
the Szapáry, the Dessewffy or the Festetich. Their weight within a nobiliary estate of about 400,000 was on the increase throughout the period. Their social and political ascendancy was conspicuous, while at
the same time the character of their leading role underwent a change
since the sixteenth and seventeenth centuries, when the seats – fortresses and fortified manor-houses – of the magnates were centres of
representation as well as those of military and political education for the
offspring of the lesser nobles of the surrounding area. By the eighteenth
century, they were either demolished or lost these courtly functions:
they were confined to being merely economic nuclei of the manors, the
only Court remaining the one residing in Vienna. During the reign of
Maria Theresa, when the relative tranquillity within the country and its
gradual reconstruction started to make an impact, about two hundred
new manor-houses were erected and became venues of polite and
fashionable intercourse among the higher echelons of the elite; and at
least one of them, that of Prince Miklós Esterházy at Fertőd, with its
splendid halls, parks, festivities, theatrical and musical performances
conducted by no other than Joseph Haydn, who was in the service of
the family for three decades after 1761, was quite successful by international standards in the great competition across Europe to emulate Versailles. But the chief centre where the future owners of these residences
acquired the taste for late baroque and rococo refinement was Vienna,
where some of them also owned palaces. While the role of Hungarian
aristocrats in the central administration of the Habsburg Monarchy
could not be compared to that of their Austrian and Bohemian counterparts, many of them held high offices in the Court Chancellery or the

Court Treasury, where they rubbed shoulders with the multi-national elite of the Habsburg capital.

The 'alienation' of this confident, cosmopolitan and refined elite from the 'fatherland' has often been exaggerated, at first by those contemporary middle and petty nobles who, after initial satisfaction with the consolidation, could not but recognise that Vienna did not equally and unconditionally need a modus vivendi with *all* of the nobiliary estates. Suspicious of the ambition and jealous of the success of those who rendered services to the court, even the roughly three-thousand families of *bene possessionati*, that is, well-to-do nobles (not to speak of the mass of 'sandalled' nobles of the provinces) were critical of the political conduct, the lifestyles and the interests of the aristocracy. High office in a foreign capital, lavish representation, fluency in modern western languages, secular and scientific studies and rich libraries reflecting these concerns might seem, for those 'within', a number of ways of raising the country's elite to the a level of its immediate western neighbours. But those 'within' were denounced as unpatriotic by those 'without', who felt that while the magnates were compensated in important ways for the loss of some of their traditional positions, the same process of growing centralisation and the decline of aristocratic courts blocked vital channels of upward mobility and the assertion of interests for the lower echelons of the nobility. As the earlier partnership ties dissolved, it started to matter far more than earlier that the life of a magnate was worlds apart from that of a county gentleman for whom infrequent diets and county assemblies made it difficult to show his talents, who remained boorish in his manners, administered his household as a patriarch, knew and cared little about European affairs, and whose boredom was offset by litigation, hunts and revelry. Their erudition mainly consisting of some Latin and 'the ancient laws' of the land, they had Werbőczy and the 'one and the same liberty' of the nobility on their lips. Indeed, identifying themselves with the nation and their own rights with national self-determination, their opposition policies largely consisted of presenting their grievances and entrenching their privileges (just as the residual opposition of the aristocracy was confined to securing their own positions).

This was to change significantly during the second half of the eighteenth century. But for the time being these attitudes were the causes of the first signs of the precariousness of the compromise between Hungary and the Habsburgs. At the diet of 1728–1729, Vienna, heavily in debt and finding Hungary's contribution to the budget unsatisfactory, wanted to raise the war subsidy. The estates protested, arguing that the tax burden on the peasantry was already too oppressive; and they rejected a proposal to assess the subsidy on the basis of *portae* on the grounds that this was a step towards taxing the nobility. However, the first real test of the strength of the compromise came in 1740, and the result was remarkable.

Charles III, the last male scion of the House of Habsburg died in October 1740, and the circumstances for carrying the Pragmatic Sanction into effect were rather inauspicious. The war fought against the Ottoman Empire in Russian alliance between 1737 and 1739 was remarkably unsuccessful: Eugene of Savoy died in 1736, and the poor commandership of those who replaced him resulted in defeats on the battlefield. In the Peace of Belgrade all of the acquisitions of 1718 except the Banate of Temes were lost. The failure, while it brought nothing into an almost empty treasury, added to the dissatisfaction in Hungary, where the quartering of troops caused many complaints and the territorial losses reawakened the sense of Ottoman menace. It was against this background atmosphere in Hungary that the title of Charles's daughter Maria Theresa, married since 1736 to Francis Stephen, Duke of Lorraine, was challenged. Frederick II (the Great), who had just succeeded to the throne of Prussia and was eager to test the strength of the formidable army raised by his predecessor, was the first to disavow the Pragmatic Sanction. He attacked Silesia, while the electors of Bavaria and Saxony, who were married to the daughters of Joseph I – and the latter even became King of Poland with the support of Charles III in 1735 – invaded Upper Austria, Bohemia and Moravia, where the estates quickly submitted to them. France, predictably, took sides with the enemies of Austria, while Russia was kept from entering the conflict by internal troubles after the death of Empress Anne, and Great Britain by its colonial war against Spain and France.

In this critical situation, virtually no-one in Europe doubted that the Hungarians would exploit the opportunity to attain their independence from the Habsburgs, but the contrary happened. At first, even though the diet summoned in May 1741 agreed to crown Maria Theresa on June 25, the relationship between the new ruler and the Hungarian estates remained strained, because the young queen recanted from her earlier promise to satisfy a long list of administrative and economic demands. However, as the military situation deteriorated even further in the summer of 1741, Maria Theresa decided to make a personal appeal to the diet, and on September 11 she recommended into the protection of Hungarian arms her domains, the Holy Crown, and her family (although the presence at the scene of the infant Joseph, who would succeed her, is a legend). The outburst of enthusiasm with which the estates offered their 'life and blood for our king [!]' (*vitam et sanguinem pro rege nostro* – an often used slogan now filled with content) puzzled most observers, though it is not at all surprising. It was less a chivalric gesture to an attractive young woman in plight (which was the romantic account of what happened) than an act of prudence: the estates had no suitable pretender, were warned anew of the Ottoman threat, and recognised that on the whole their situation was far more favourable than that of their counterparts elsewhere in the Habsburg Empire or in most of Europe.

The noble insurrection, the four million florins of subsidy and the thirty thousand recruits offered by the Hungarian diet were promises not entirely fulfilled: *vitam et sanguinem* the deputies might have been willing to sacrifice, *sed avenam non* – 'but not oats', that is, their fortunes. Even so, Hungary substantially contributed to the modicum of success achieved by the Habsburg Empire in the two dynastic wars of the mid-eighteenth century: the War of Austrian Succession (1740–1748) and the Seven Years War (1756–1763), fought to protect Maria Theresa's title and to regain territories lost early in the course of the former (in particular, Silesia, the most industrialised and economically powerful of all Habsburg possessions in Central Europe). The Hungarian troops and commanders fought with distinction throughout these wars, earning the respect of renowned adversaries, such as Frederick the Great, and preferential treatment from Maria Theresa, who introduced her future reforms with circumspection in Hungary (although the promises that the full independence of Hungarian administrative bodies would be observed, the country's territorial integrity would be restored and no-one but Hungarians would be consulted on Hungarian affairs were less than strictly kept). Ferenc Nádasdy and his hussars occupied Lorraine in 1743 and played a central role in inflicting the first great defeat on Frederick the Great in 1757 at Kolín; in the same year, the cavalry of András Hadik held Berlin to ransom.

But neither Hungarian arms, nor the intervention of Britain and the United Provinces on the side of Austria in 1743, nor the realignment known as the 'diplomatic revolution' that occurred before the outbreak of the Seven Years War (France allying itself with the Habsburgs and Britain with Prussia) did much to change the status quo which emerged by 1742. The interim Peace of Breslau concluded in that year between Maria Theresa and Frederick II confirmed the latter in his conquest of Silesia, which the Habsburgs never recovered. What they gained was that in the Peace of Dresden (1745), Frederick acknowledged Maria Theresa's husband Francis of Lorraine as Holy Roman Emperor, and in the Peace of Aachen (1748) he also recognised the validity of the Pragmatic Sanction and thus the title of Maria Theresa. The Peace of Hubertusburg in 1763 was concluded on the basis of the *status quo ante bellum*.

The lessons of the wars were of even greater consequence for Hungary than the military valour displayed in them by her commanders and common soldiers. First, Hungary was brought back into the focus of Vienna's interest: the contingencies awakened the court to the fact that its vast territory and natural resources destined Hungary for a central role among the bases of the Habsburg Monarchy's power. And resources, and their proper exploitation and allocation, were badly needed. For the wars and their outcome also demonstrated that in order to remain competitive against smaller but more efficient powers like Prussia, instead of, or at least besides, labyrinthine alliances, the Habsburg Monarchy's policies ought to be much more firmly based on her internal resources than earlier, which was hardly conceivable without far-reaching structural modernisation. This was the background of the governmental, administrative and economic reforms launched in the western lands of the monarchy in the 1740s. They soon reached Hungary as well. There, however, they inevitably clashed with the privileges of the estates, firmly entrenched in Hungary's corporate constitution.

The Theresan reforms began as early as in 1742, when an Austrian state chancellery (*Staatskanzlei*) was separated from the Court Chancellery. In 1746, a general directorate of commercial affairs was created, and in 1749, under the guidance of Count Friedrich Wilhelm Haugwitz, a comprehensive administrative reform aimed to suppress the power of the estates and to abolish the tax privileges of the nobility in the hereditary provinces. In the same year the Austrian and Bohemian chancelleries were replaced by a unitary body, the *Directorium in publicis et cameralibus*, while administration and jurisdiction was separated on the highest level by the creation of a supreme judicature (*Oberste Justizstelle*). Although in 1761 the Austrian and Bohemian chancellery was restored, now it was a unified organ, to avoid lobbying for sectional interests. Also in 1761, the famous Council of State (*Staatsrat*), whose deliberations were the major influence on Habsburg policies up to 1848, was created upon the initiative of Chancellor Count (later Prince) Anton Wenzel Kaunitz, who had masterminded the reversal of alliances in 1756.

Although its competence was nominally confined to the hereditary provinces, the *Staatsrat* effectively concerned itself with Hungarian affairs, too, and it was anyway the 'workshop' where all measures of Habsburg enlightened absolutism were engineered. But the attempts to extend the modernising endeavours to Hungary reach back to a decade before the *Staatsrat* was organised. They were embedded in a complex programme of remodelling the economy of the Habsburg Monarchy whose main thrust was aimed at invigorating all sectors of the economy, substituting for lost Silesia, and distributing the financial obligations of the subjects more equitably than before.

The attainment of the first and the second of these objectives was to be secured by the 1754 tariff regulations. Inspired by the principles of mercantilism and cameralism, the authors of the measure erected an internal customs barrier between Hungary and the rest of the Habsburg lands. West of the barrier, especially in Bohemia, existing manufactures and trade received substantial support from state funds, and while agriculture was to be modernised everywhere, Hungary was expected to become the major supplier of cheap food and raw material for the industrial regions and a market for manufactured products from the latter. All this was ensured by low duties on deliveries from the hereditary provinces and Bohemia into Hungary and very high ones imposed on articles from outside the Monarchy, and a high tariff on all Hungarian goods exported to non-Habsburg lands and on Hungarian manufactured products sold in the western Habsburg provinces. In 1775, protectionism was bolstered even further in favour of Austrian and Bohemian industries.

These regulations were clearly discriminative, to the extent that they even seem to justify the bitter complaint of late-eighteenth century enlightened noblemen-economists about the 'colonial' economic policy of the Habsburg court, referring to the parallel between the situation of Hungary and the North American colonists before the War of Independence. For the men of the diet of 1790, disaffected by Joseph II's absolutism but still inspired by his enlightenment, whose endeavour was economic and national emancipation, this was not only good propaganda but also a quite realistic interpretation of the current situation because in that endeavour their major adversary was the Viennese government. But on a broader temporal and spatial plane we might get a different perspective, which escaped those twentieth-century historians who have continued to interpret the economic policy of the Habsburg court as 'colonial'.

That policy certainly did not favour the growth of Hungarian manufactures, but it did not suffocate them either: there was very little to suffocate. The first important modern industrial plants in Hungary were founded by Francis of Lorraine in the 1740s. The economic inequality between Hungary and the western Habsburg lands did not emerge as a result of the new regulations, and did not increase as a result of them. While it is true that cattle exports to Venice, wine exports to Poland and Britain and grain exports elsewhere had been important before and were damaging losses now, even before 1754 Hungary had been an economic dependency of western regions. What now happened was that some of her main partners were changed. For the Hungarian purchaser it was probably inconvenient that better and cheaper products from Silesia and Germany were now replaced with somewhat inferior and more expensive articles from the neighbouring Habsburg lands. But for Hungarian craftsmen and the few industrialists, the competition of these products was less dangerous, and consequently more conducive to progress which, despite the confinements, did take place in the number of capitalist factories and the sophistication of their products as well (though out of altogether merely 125 such enterprises, there were only seven that had more than a hundred employees in 1790). Finally, the motives of the ruler ought to be contemplated: it is not surprising that imperial reason of state, the imperative of closing the gap between the Monarchy and her more advanced rivals, made Maria Theresa opt for developing the established branches of the economy in both halves of her empire. Hungary's backwardness was indeed exploited, modified, and adjusted to the needs of the Monarchy as a whole by eighteenth-century Habsburg economic policies, but it was owing to causes earlier and much more variegated than those policies. It is quite a different matter that the measure did not bring one of the expected results, namely, the increase of state revenues: the economic weakness of Hungary kept its market potential low, and thus the new regulation could not make up for the losses resulting from the tax exemption of the nobility, as it was initially hoped in Vienna.

The administration of Maria Theresa tried to raise more revenue from Hungary in other ways, too, gradually reaching the stage of challenging the tax privileges of the nobility. At the diet of 1751, the main point of debate was the war subsidy, which Charles III had attempted to increase in vain, and now Maria Theresa, referring to the financial strain the Monarchy was under as a result of the War of Austrian Succession, requested the estates to raise it from the annual 2.5 million florins approved in 1728 by an additional sum of 1.2 million. It was largely due to the mediation of loyal aristocrats that the reluctant nobles in the Lower Chamber, who even threatened with disrupting the diet, finally voted 700,000 florins. The middle nobility also violently protested against the issuing of royal charters to four towns because the chartered towns usually cast their votes in favour of the government, and thus the increase of their number seemed a 'dangerous weakening' of the power of the county nobility.

Maria Theresa made efforts to appease this nobility with a number of methods, such as enticing it, similarly to the aristocracy, to Vienna as a means of stimulating sympathy between them and the court, and to broaden their vision. The creation of a fund for Hungarian nobles to study in the Theresianum (an academy to train young nobles for state service in Vienna) in 1749, or the establishment of the Royal Hungarian Bodyguard in 1760 were such initiatives, and they did not entirely miss their target. Yet, as the diet of 1751 showed, there was a growing disaffection between the bulk of the nobility and the monarch, who grew increasingly impatient with the obstinate insistence of the Hungarian estates on their privileges, especially those concerning taxation, which their counterparts in the other Habsburg domains had already abandoned, however grudgingly.

There were a few voices in Hungary itself, too, which urged a change of attitudes. The Hungarian Chancellor Count Miklós Pálffy suggested in 1758 that since the general levy of the nobility, on which their privileges rested, was an obsolete fiction, it ought to be replaced with a standing army financed out of a 'noble subsidy', as the nobility's share in the general tax burden. Pálffy as well as the author of a pamphlet on the 'reformation' of the Kingdom of Hungary (probably Court Councillor Pál Festetich) also thought that improving the lot of the peasantry by lifting some of their obligations and standardising others would be crucial if the increasingly obvious backwardness of the country was to be surmounted. József Benczur, rector of the Lutheran high school of Pozsony, argued on historical grounds that the sovereignty and the scope of action of the Hungarian ruler could not be limited by the estates.

All these threads were woven together in a booklet on *The Origins and Perpetual Use of the Legislative Power by the Holy Apostolic King of Hungary*, published in 1764 by Ádám Kollár, a court librarian of Slovak origin and a protégé of Maria Theresa's advisor, Gerhard van Swieten. Though there is no evidence that it was commissioned by the court, the book in fact contained the main elements of the programme the Queen wanted to push through at the diet summoned in the same year. She demanded not only a further increase in the war subsidy, but also referred to the ineffectiveness of the noble insurrection and sought to convert it to cash payment by the nobility. Besides, she attempted to persuade the estates to establish the need for regulating peasant dues and services and lord-serf relations by law.

Kollár's book and its denunciations by the Hungarian nobility and clergy (which Kollár also proposed to tax) vitally influenced the atmosphere in which the diet convened. Now, even the majority of the aristocracy insisted on the division of authority between the crown and the estates; consequently, any insult of the latter passed for high treason, and the attempt to impose taxes on them for mere theft. Whereas the war subsidy was raised by another 700,000 florins (again, instead of the requested 1.2 million), the other initiatives were staunchly defied by the diet, whose assistance the monarch sought in vain in the realisation of the intended reforms. Even most of the hitherto loyal Hungarian leaders recoiled from the new programme of Vienna, and would have preferred to stick to the old form of compromise with the court. diets were relatively scarce under Charles III and Maria Theresa (both of them summoned three), and now she decided to dispense with them altogether. Instead of filling the vacant seat of the Palatine, she appointed his son-in-law, Duke Albert, as Lord Lieutenant of Hungary, and not until after the death of her son Joseph II in 1790 was the diet summoned again.

For nearly three decades, Hungary was governed by decrees worked out in consultation with a relatively small vanguard of inspired reformers and prudent practitioners of modern reason of state, and executed by a not too large group of dedicated officials imbued by the same ideals. As time went by, there were more and more Hungarian names on the list. For the time being, the moving spirits were based in Vienna. They included Chancellor Kaunitz, the shrewd diplomat with a vision of Austria's role on the European scene; van Swieten, the Dutch court physician and librarian who devoted much of his energy to matters concerning religious toleration and education; Joseph von Sonnenfels, the cameralist professor of political economy at the University of Vienna; or the aristocratic reformer Karl von Zinzendorf. Above all, there was the young Archduke Joseph, who succeeded his father Francis of Lorraine as Holy Roman Emperor in 1765 and was appointed co-regent by his mother in the same year. It was in the field marked out by these figures and the tension-ridden relationship between the more cautious and tradition-bound mother and the impatient son that Habsburg enlightened absolutism was inaugurated in Hungary in the middle of the 1760s.

2. Monarchs and estates, and the limits of the Enlightenment

The Enlightenment was not a merely intellectual pursuit of a few select geniuses aimed at masterpieces of abstract speculation, but a comprehensive movement to contemplate the unity of man and his physical and social environment in order to arrive at conclusions that could be turned to the improvement of that environment. Of necessity, therefore, it was not an indiscriminate declaration of war on the part of reason against tradition and authority, but an effort to assess that tradition in the light of reason, and to imbue authority with reason, in the hope that the order thus emerging would be a more stable one, capable of resisting the extremes of both superstition and enthusiasm, of arbitrary power and subversion. When d'Alembert listed Francis Bacon, René Descartes, Isaac Newton and John Locke as the precursors of the undertaking of the Encyclopedists in the Preface of that vast work, he did not refer to them as serene sages, but as very practical men who provided proper methods, frameworks and tools to understand the functioning of man and the universe.

Although the fact that the Turks were only expelled from Buda in the decade when the relevant texts of Newton and Locke were produced was not strictly propitious for the growth of an intellectual climate in which the Enlightenment could strike roots in Hungary, the tendencies that prepared the ground for it in the West, both within traditional modes of thinking and outside them, appeared here as well. We saw the rather unique case of Apáczai, the Puritan follower of Descartes. As the seventeenth century wore on and the eighteenth commenced, examples multiplied. Many of them were inspired by increasingly secular trends in religious thought, such as Protestant Pietism, which emphasised the need for the intimacy of the religious experience and its separation from worldly pursuits. The combination of social harmony and improvement, which Pietists held to be the goal of the latter, vitally depended on learning and education, preferably in the vernacular, as well as an efficient network of welfare institutions (health care, poor relief etc.). The leading German Pietist August Hermann Francke's important work on education was published in Hungarian as early as in 1711, and made a considerable impact. A similar combination of motives animated Ferenc Pápai Páriz, a late intellectual heir of Apáczai, who wrote influential textbooks on practical philosophy, education and a strikingly modern medical treatise, *Pax corporis* (1690), which continued to be used for several decades, but in 1708 he also revised Szenczi's century-old Hungarian-Latin dictionary, adjusting it to contemporary requirements. In the same period, Rákóczi's attempt to attain independence and create a national monarchy was explained by his propagandists in up-to-date versions of the idioms of interest, reason of state and natural law. Newtonianism came to Hungary in the 1740s thanks to the Catholic teaching order, the Piarists, who were increasingly preferred, on account of their flexibility, to the Jesuits. For the relatively early beginnings of the science of statistics – the collection and systematisation of data on geography, natural resources, history, legal and political institutions of the country: *Staatistik*, 'the science of the state' – we might turn back to the Pietists: the five volumes of the *Notitia Hungariae* (A Description of Hungary – in fact, ten of its counties) were published in 1735–1742 by Mátyás (Matej) Bél, the Slovak-Hungarian director of the Lutheran school at Pozsony, who also edited the first regular weekly newspaper, *Nova Posoniensa*, in Hungary in 1721–1722. The early appearance of advanced achievements in statistics also indicated the thrust of the Enlightenment which would be the most influential in Hungary, along with the rest of Central Europe: the one marked by, for instance, the Halle professor Christian Wolff, in which the emancipation of the individual was seen as part of a process whereby it was mainly order and efficiency that were to be increased in society, with a very serious role assigned to established authorities.

This account is certainly immensely more fragmented than reality was, but the tendencies described themselves were rather inchoate at the time when the project of enlightened absolutism was launched from Vienna in the mid-1760s. Still, they constituted a basis on which, first, a rank-and-file to carry out that project gradually arose in the country, and later it was also possible further to develop the commitment for the enlightened reform of the Monarchy into the programme of a national Enlightenment. Enlightened absolutism has often been described as the endeavour of the rulers and statesmen of peripheral states (in Scandinavia, in the Iberian and Italian peninsulas, in Central and Eastern Europe) to preserve their competitiveness *vis-à-vis* the powers of the 'centre' by increasing their administrative and economic efficiency. It must be added that the peripheries contained a great many islands, both in the material and in the virtual sense, whose level of development and sophistication was immensely higher than that of many internal 'peripheries' of the 'centre', and the real task of enlightened monarchs was to avoid that these islands sink into the surrounding bog. They needed tools to elicit the contrary effect, either by raising the bogs to the level of the islands, or by finding adequate supplementary roles for them. Backward regions, suppressed or neglected social groups were to be helped by processes of emancipation and improvement to contribute to the success of the realm in the international arena. An administrative system organised according to the precepts of political science would help statesmen and bureaucrats to work out and execute reasonable policies. Religious toleration would increase the pool from which those bureaucrats could be recruited. Better educated and better protected subjects would be more willing to obey those reasonable policies, and would be more accomplished and efficient in their trades. Since emancipation was not a goal for its own sake but a means to ends that were higher in the interpretation of enlightened rulers, the enlightened character of enlightened absolutism was limited. But these limits were nowhere so closely approached, maybe even transgressed, than in the Habsburg Monarchy under Joseph II.

Hungary being a predominantly agrarian country, approximately eighty percent of its population employed in that branch of the economy, the reform process started in that sphere. Even the tariff regulations of 1754 concerned that branch in the case of Hungary, however ambiguously, and now the government of Maria Theresa intended to approach the same issue from the angle of the producers, that is, the serfs. In the age of the western 'agricultural revolution', the agrarian sector in Hungary remained backward. While strenuous efforts were made to bring new lands under cultivation, nearly a quarter of the country's lowland areas, that is, potential arable lands, were marshland or inundated for most of the year. New crops, such as potato, corn or tobacco became increasingly popular and the stabling of animals started, but only restricted areas and a few select estates of magnates were raised to European standards, while elsewhere primitive methods like the two-field system and pastural stockbreeding dominated. Above all, no improvement could be expected from those most immediately linked to the land: the peasantry, afflicted by the growing war tax, the quartering of troops (there were no barracks in Hungary before the reign of Joseph II), the duty to provide transportation and free labour for the army, not to speak about the nobility's 'offensive' to expand their allodial possessions and increase the *corvée* of their serfs even beyond the already oppressive, though still legal three days per week in order to benefit from the high wartime agrarian prices. Several peasant riots and uprisings that had occurred since 1735 and gave rise to apprehension in 1766, humanitarian considerations, and the fact that the state could only count on the peasant as a taxpayer if it interfered with lord-serf relations, persuaded the Viennese government to push through the measure, whose very principle was rejected by the diet in 1764–1765, by decree in 1767.

Maria Theresa's Urbarial Patent, worked out by a committee set up on the day after the diet was dissolved, overthrew the fiction that feudal obligations were a private affair of the landlord and his tenants. The decree fixed the size of the peasant plot, with that of the arable and pasture belonging to it varying according to the productivity of the soil, and standardised the amount of dues that could be gathered from it as 'the ninth tenth' of the produce (that is, the ancient *nona*). The right of peasants to use forests for purposes other than hunting and to sell their wine was secured. Most importantly, the labour service was maximised to one day per week with, or two days per week without the use of animals.

The Urbarial Patent was especially welcome among the peasants of Transdanubia, whereas some of those in the Great Plain, who enjoyed relatively more freedom, were somewhat less enthusiastic; as a matter of fact, the nobility persevered, and it took a decade to enforce the decree by relying on royal commissars. Besides, population growth quite rapidly made the specifications of the tenant holding obsolete, no sufficient room being left for new generations. Nevertheless, slow, gradual and ambivalent improvement in the agrarian sector started, and profited from individual initiatives towards the end of the century inspired by German models and ones found in the work of the English agrarian specialist Arthur Young. Returning in 1767 from studies at German universities where he became familiar with modern farming methods and acquired a philanthropic approach to education, the Lutheran minister at the *oppidum* of Szarvas in the Great Plain, Sámuel Tessedik, established a model farm and, in 1780, a school where over the years about a thousand young peasants were trained in subjects like crop rotation, orchard management and the growing of forage plants. In 1784, he summarised his experience and theoretical findings in an influential treatise on *The Peasant in Hungary, What He is and What He might Become*. On a higher plane, the Georgicon, the first permanent agricultural academy on the European continent, was established by György Festetich at Keszthely in 1797.

But education at large was not left by the government to private initiative: indeed it was the second field of comprehensive reform in the first phase of Habsburg enlightened absolutism under Maria Theresa. 'Schooling is *politicum*, and will remain so', the Queen declared, but educational facilities in Hungary were ill suited to fulfil these expectations. The number of elementary school teachers, about 4,500, was roughly half the number of communities in the country, with most of them having a single schoolmaster; thus there was no elementary schooling in more than half of Hungary's villages, and the average number of children per school was nearly 300, with the result that a mere fraction of them actually attended school. The reform became especially urgent after the dissolution, in 1773, of the Jesuit order which operated Hungary's only university and the majority of its secondary schools. The university, which had not had a medical faculty until 1769, was now taken under state supervision and was moved from provincial Nagyszombat first into Buda in 1777, and then, in 1784, to Pest (with the first institute for engineering in Europe established at it by Joseph II in 1782).

As to the elementary level, the property of the order was converted into the Educational Fund, which made it possible to embark on the reform and the structural transformation of education in Hungary. The model for the reform was the one introduced in Austria in 1774 along the guidelines worked out by Johann Ignaz Felbiger, Abbot of Sagan. The Hungarian *Ratio Educationis* ('the system of education') of 1777 was prepared by a committee led by József Ürményi, a councillor of the Hungarian Chancellery. An independent Hungarian educational system was created, separated from the Church, and placed under the supreme direction of the Educational Commission set up within the Gubernium. The country was divided into nine school districts whose superintendents were to supervise the teachers in their execution of the centrally prescribed, uniform curriculum and the use of authorised textbooks. The complaints of Protestants against this uniformity, for they considered the state as 'Catholic' not only under the pious Maria Theresa but even under Joseph II, were to no avail. Elementary schooling between the ages of 7 and 13 became compulsory. Given the lack of proper means and facilities, this requirement remained unrealistic, as was the curriculum, which would have first form pupils learn the Hungarian as well as the German ('Gothic') alphabet, and those in the third form Latin as well. Much of the *Ratio Educationis* remained on paper. Yet, what was accomplished of it became one of the most lasting monuments of enlightened absolutism in Hungary.

But the momentum of the governmental system of enlightened absolutism culminated under Joseph II, who succeeded his mother in 1780. Joseph, who acquired a thoroughgoing education and was introduced into the *arcana imperii* well before he became co-regent in 1765, prepared for governing the Habsburg domains consciously and tirelessly. He spent about seven years of his life in search of experience by travel. He travelled abroad (in disguise, as 'Count Falkenstein'), as in France in 1777, where he studied the effects of the experiment in enlightened government by the great physiocrat scholar-minister Turgot; and he travelled in his own countries to assess their condition and their potential, as did the great rival of Habsburg enlightened monarchs, Frederick II, whom Joseph emulated with a peculiar mixture of admiration and hatred. Like Frederick, Joseph referred to himself as 'the first servant of the state', stressing that as such the monarch had absolute power to ensure that the interests of the community and the state took precedence over those of the individual and the estate, or the province and the locality. His empire was to be a *Gesamtstaat*, a unitary state not made up of heterogeneous parts, but established on the clear principles of reason and ruled by one ruler and a centralised bureaucracy and army. Inspired more by contemporary German natural law and cameralist science than French Enlightenment doctrines (cherished by the courtly aristocracy whose rococo frivolity he despised), Joseph recognised early on that the privileges of the nobility and the Church, regional rights and institutions were major obstacles in attaining these objectives. In the early summaries of his principles and aspirations, the 'Rêveries' (1763) and the 'Memorandum' (1765), he thought that the grandees should be humiliated, and dreamed of requesting his realm, upon his future accession, to grant him ten years' free hand 'to do all the good which one is prevented from doing by the rules, statutes and oaths'.

As a matter of fact, this was a mere *jeu d'esprit*. What he could and did do upon his accession in 1780 was to avoid being crowned King of Hungary, and thereby taking the coronation oath which would have obliged him to acknowledge Hungary's special status. In 1784, he even transferred the Holy Crown into the Habsburg treasury in Vienna, earning the nickname 'hatted king' and causing great consternation among the nobility. At the same time, he had a little flock of devoted followers who looked to him with confidence: the Hungarian Josephists, the first substantial stratum of a modern administrative and intellectual elite in the country. They understood and identified themselves with the ways in which care for the public good and imperial grandeur intertwined in Joseph's vision, partly because they seemed to them to overlap with the interests of the improvement of Hungary. They were ready to march a long way with him before becoming exhausted and disaffected. Trained in the citadels of contemporary learning, such as the University of Göttingen, they were versed in the most up-to-date literature on politics and economics, and travelled widely in the West. They formed a group closely knit through apprenticeship in law or university studies and intercourse in office, private socialising or membership in one of the country's roughly thirty Freemasonic lodges, where brethren forged and discussed ambitious projects without social prejudice. As district commissioners and officials they collected, systematised and interpreted data on the assets and conditions in the country, and thus left behind a legacy that proved invaluable for later reformers. Above all, whereas Joseph's magnetism and success imbued them with a susceptibility to modernity, his blunders and failures inspired in them a sense of patriotism, and this combination made them able not only to leave their imprint on the national movement immediately following the death of Joseph II, but even to form a bridge through their initiatives and followers with the 'great' reform generation of the 1820s and after. The Josephists included commoner intellectuals like the splendid lawyer József Hajnóczy, who might be described, if it were not anachronistic, as the first Hungarian liberal; nobles like the outstanding economic theorist Gergely Berzeviczy; and aristocratic politicians like Sámuel Teleki, Ferenc Széchényi or József Podmaniczky.

With the accession of Joseph II, the style of Habsburg enlightened absolutism markedly changed. Joseph did not care about the compromise which, despite the absence of the diet, was in the 1770s to some extent restored between Maria Theresa and the Hungarian nobility by preferments and distinctions as well as moves like the re-acquisition of the Saxon towns of Szepes county from Poland (in the course of the first dismemberment of Poland by Russia, Prussia and Austria in 1772), the reintegration of the Banate of Temes into the system of counties and the annexation of the port of Fiume on the Adriatic to Hungary. Always feeling that he was running out of time, Joseph threw himself restlessly into a torrent of reforms, all of them issued on the assumption that the king could legislate without consulting the estates.

The first group of measures concerned relations between the state and the Catholic Church, whose positions were already affected by some of the reforms of Maria Theresa, but in Joseph's opinion its privileges still made it a kind of state within the state. In addition, it was a source of tension and weakness from the point of view of the state that the Catholic Church was reluctant to practise tolerance *vis-à-vis* the other religions, although Catholics constituted no more than half of the population of Hungary, the rest being roughly equally divided between the Protestant (Calvinist, Lutheran and Unitarian) and Greek (Orthodox and Uniate) denominations (less than one per cent were Jewish and others). To begin with, Joseph confirmed and extended to Hungary the right Maria Theresa asserted in 1767 to proclaim papal bulls, brevets and other instructions only with the permission of the monarch (*placetum regium*). Joseph next removed censorship from ecclesiastical control in June 1781; in fact, he also started to control the correspondence of the Catholic clergy with the Vatican. The simultaneous liberalisation of censorship (the list of prohibited books shrank from over 4,000 to about 900 items) had remarkable results in the publication of all kinds of literary products, including ones critical of Josephian policies on corporate, patriotic or other grounds.

Then came the measure for which Joseph II is perhaps most remembered: the Patent of Toleration, promulgated in October 1781. The edict condemned religious persecution and removed most restrictions concerning worship, church building etc. that had afflicted the Lutherans, the Calvinists and the Uniates. They also received full rights as citizens (they could become guild masters, earn university diplomas etc.), and became eligible for service in government offices. Two years later, the right of free worship was extended to Jews, and though their civil disabilities were not removed, they were no longer subject to special legal regulations. To round off the Church-related reforms, in January 1782 Joseph dissolved all monastic orders not engaged in teaching, created a 'religion fund' out of their possessions and used it to establish a number of new parishes, to open new elementary schools and the General Seminary in Pozsony where future priests would be trained in the spirit of Josephism. With a view to cost effectiveness, the ruler even interfered with affairs like the number of processions and pilgrimages, the playing of music at services, the use of candles and ornaments in churches and (most absurdly) that of coffins at funerals, which evoked much hostility on the part of the Catholic clergy and laity alike. But even a personal visit of Pope Pius VI in Vienna in the spring of 1782 could not shake the determination of Joseph II.

As regards the administration, Joseph took care to address his officials directly at regular intervals in 'pastoral letters' consisting of instructions, declarations of principle and rules of conduct. Still in 1782, Joseph went on to reform the organs of central government, unifying the Austrian and Bohemian Chancellery with the Court Treasury, and the Hungarian Chancellery with that of Transylvania, while he attached the

Hungarian Treasury to the Gubernium and transferred the modern central magistrate that thus arose from Pozsony to Buda, the heart of the country, in 1784. In the same year, the ruler also issued the two decrees that caused perhaps the greatest furore among the Hungarian nobility. In May, he made German the language of all official communication and education in Hungary and Transylvania, arguing that Latin, which the nobility knew, was a dead language, while its use in Hungary demonstrated that the native tongue was imperfect and unsuited for civilised requirements (not to speak of the fact that it was not universally spoken in a country of populous ethnic minorities). Officials were to learn German within a deadline of three years.

The estates hardly had time to express their indignation before Joseph ordered a national census and land survey which extended to the whole of the population, including the nobility. One of the objectives of the census was to assess the number of potential recruits in the army. The German conscription forms that were used in the census gave rise to protest, and the initiative in general was denounced as violating the Hungarian constitution. As regards the land survey, the nobility suspected it to be a precursory measure to the lifting of its tax exemption. Virtually each of the counties remonstrated and demanded that a diet be summoned, and the military had to be dispatched on several occasions to carry out the census amidst the turbulence.

Yet it was carried out, and the results made public in 1787 surprised everyone: Hungary, with Transylvania and Croatia, turned out to have as many as 8.7 million inhabitants. The overwhelming majority were peasants, while the proportion of the nobility was an unusually high 5 per cent, about the same as that of the inhabitants of the free royal boroughs. With nearly 30,000 inhabitants, Pozsony and Debrecen were the largest urban centres, but the combined population of the twin cities of Buda and Pest was a respectable 50,000. Approximately 20,000 ecclesiastics lived in the country, while the number of officials and the secular intellectuals of commoner origin (*honoratior*), a group of crucial importance for the fortunes of Josephism, was a mere 5,000.

The completion of the census was an apparent success for Joseph II, but it created an irreparable breach between him and the counties, whereas the language decree was not only impossible to put into practice, but also gave impetus to the unfolding movement for the modernisation and the embellishment of the Hungarian language. This endeavour was not entirely new in the mid-1780s; its hotbed was, paradoxically, Habsburg enlightened absolutism, which broadened the vision of many young Hungarian nobles, training them in the Theresianum or the Royal Hungarian Bodyguard in Vienna, and employing them on missions into the western centres of social and intellectual ferment. The 'bodyguard-writers' became familiar, among other things, with the movement for the improvement of German, which developed into the language of Goethe by the 1770s. The publication of *The Tragedy of Agis* by one of these writers, György Bessenyei, in 1772, is usually considered to mark the starting point of a similar process in the case of Hungarian. Bessenyei went on to publish pamphlets on educational policy, endorsing the *Ratio Educationis*, but emphasising the need for the extensive use of Hungarian; and in order to make the language worthy of that task, in 1779 he proposed the establishment of a 'patriotic' learned society, arguing that 'every nation had become learned in its own language'.

The linguistic and literary revival thus began to overflow into a general cultivation of native traditions: Hungary arrived at the threshold of national awakening. And while the 'Hungarus' consciousness, that is, the simultaneous allegiance to one's ethnic background and the historic kingdom, continued to predominate among the literate in the country, the intelligentsia of the ethnic minorities started to display similar attitudes and endeavours. A Slavonian (that is, Croatian) grammar was published by Matija Reljković in 1767, although the Croat deputies at the diet of 1790, when protesting against adopting Hungarian as the official language, still preferred the keeping of Latin to the introduction of Croatian. Juraj Papanek wrote the first (Latin) history of the Slovaks (1780), and Anton Bernolák wrote a Slovak grammar and literary history (1787). The modern Serbian literary language started to emerge in the hands of Dositej Obradović. The Romanian revival was perhaps the most vigorous. It commenced in 1780 with the Romanian grammar of Samuil Micu-Klein, the most distinguished member of a group of authors that came from the renowned Uniate school of Balázsfalva (Blaj). A year later he published his *Historia Daco-Romanorum*, a powerful statement of the theory of continuity between the ancient Dacians and the modern Romanians in the territory of Transylvania. On the basis of the supposed historic rights derived from this theory, Josif Meheşi, secretary at the Transylvanian Chancellery, demanded the recognition of the Romanians as the fourth *natio* in the constitutional structure of Transylvania in *Supplex Libellus Valachorum*, a memorandum presented to the Viennese government in 1791.

Impatient with what he regarded as a narrow concern for privilege and infuriated by the occasional armed resistance against the census, Joseph embarked on what he had contemplated for some time, and hit at the hotbed of defiance: the county administration. In March 1785, he abolished that system along with its offices altogether, to be superseded with ten districts, each of them headed by reliable royal commissars endowed with broad administrative, jurisdictional and fiscal powers. The other functionaries were also nominated directly by the ruler, from among the devoted Josephists, among whom he still possessed sufficient residual loyalty, in spite of the fact that they also held some of his steps distinctly inconsiderate.

The third group of reforms launched by Joseph II, besides state-church relations and administration, concerned the peasantry, the rural economy and the revenues drawn from it. Early in his reign, he continued his mother's policy of interfering with lord-serf relations by issuing ordinances. Under the impression that the ruler was on their side, serfs in Transylvania, where the Urbarial Patent had still not taken effect, rebelled against their landlords in the autumn of 1784. The revolt of some 30,000, overwhelmingly Romanian peasants led by Vasile Horea (who had once petitioned Joseph II in person), Ion Cloşca and Gheorghe Crişan was the greatest in the century. While the revolt had an anti-Hungarian and anti-Catholic edge, its main demand was the abolition of serfdom. It was defeated by the end of the year, and two of the leaders were executed and quartered (the third, Crişan, committing suicide in captivity), but the other rebels captured were saved; and in August 1785 Joseph II abolished by decree the name 'serf' and conceded the right of free migration, of the free choice of profession and of the free disposition over property to the peasantry. The decree was of significant symbolic value, though it brought no material change in the lot of the peasantry. The plan for introducing taxation reform on physiocratic grounds failed entirely. The patent of February 1789 imposed a uniform tax on all landed property in the country: even nobles would have to pay 12.25 per cent of their income from the land into the treasury (the peasant owing a further 17.25 per cent, but no *corvée,* to the landlord).

Such an interference with the nobility's material and partly social status was unacceptable even for most of the enlightened minority, at a time when the Josephist agenda descended into an international crisis. Simultaneously with Hungary, resistance to Josephism also mounted in the Austrian Netherlands (now Belgium), where it took the shape of open revolt since 1787. That province, annexed to the eastern Habsburg possessions after the War of Spanish Succession in the beginning of the century, with its remoteness and strong corporate traditions only added to the heterogeneity of the Habsburg Monarchy and the difficulty of governing it according to Joseph's lucid principles; but his scheme to exchange it with neighbouring Bavaria was thwarted by the resistance of Frederick II. To aggravate difficulties, commitments undertaken in a treaty with Empress Catherine the Great in 1781 entangled Joseph in the war that broke out between Russia and the Ottoman Empire in 1788.

Joseph, though on the whole very cautious, had always been desirous of martial glory, and the military reforms initiated by him at the time when he was still co-regent created a modern mass army in the Habsburg Monarchy whose peacetime strength was nearly 200,000. But the new recruitment and the demand of supplies for the army in 1788 and 1789, especially in view of the poor harvests of those years, united the disparate elements of Hungarian society in opposition to Joseph II. Dissatisfied nobles entertained plans of an insurrection and the invitation of an English or Prussian pretender, or Charles August of Weimar, to replace the Habsburgs on the throne of Hungary. Ephemeral successes, like the conquest of Belgrade in October 1789, did not redress the poor military balance of the southern campaign, and could no longer appease the population. From the middle of 1789, the impact of the French Revolution added fuel to anti-absolutist, radical and pacifist sentiments in Hungary, which demanded the restoration of her rights and liberties and was on the brink of armed revolt. The Emperor's remaining Hungarian and Austrian adherents as well as his brother and future successor, Leopold, Grand Duke of Tuscany, suggested to him to make concessions. Joseph II, disillusioned and mortally ill, gave in: on January 26, 1790, four weeks before his death, he revoked all his decrees except the Patent of Toleration and the ones relating to parishes and the peasantry.

The death of Joseph II removed a major obstacle from the assertion of the potential inherent in the enlightened nobility, which drew its initial inspiration largely from his principles, but with whom their ways parted as his uncompromising insistence on his convictions lost touch with reality. To some extent, the situation became similar to that of Poland under the reign of Stanisław August Poniatowski, where educational and economic reforms similar in spirit to those of Habsburg enlightened absolutism were worked out by committees of the enlightened minority of the estates, and culminated in the constitution of 1791. This extended the foundations of the corporate state towards the burghers, and institutionalised the protection of the peasantry in a similar vein to Maria Theresa and Joseph II. Similarly to their Polish counterparts, the Hungarian nobles became increasingly imbued with the ideas of the French Enlightenment.

This was not an entirely new orientation. But earlier it was largely confined to interest in the libertinism associated with Voltaire, and in Montesquieu's flattering remarks about the indispensability of the nobility in a modern monarchy in general and the gallantry of the Hungarian nobility in particular. By 1790, as the crown was brought back to the country amidst general enthusiasm, and Hungary was preparing for a diet after a quarter of a century, Montesquieu started to figure as the oracle of modern constitutionalism based on the separation of powers, as well as the idea of confederacy; and Rousseau, with social contract and popular sovereignty, was also on many lips. To be sure, most readings of these authors remained somewhat selective. Yet, constitutional projects were drafted which argued that as Joseph II vindicated arbitrary power, sovereignty reverted to 'the people', and the government of Hungary should be based on a new contract. Péter Ócsai Balogh, formulating the programme of the radical nobility, still thought that the proper shape of this contract was the coronation diploma, which would ensure the dominance of the nobles (the *populus*) over the aristocracy in the senate, intended to counterbalance the ruler of an independent Hungary. Berzeviczy also argued that the Habsburgs had forfeited their claim to the Hungarian crown and that the time for the creation of national monarchy was ripe. Hajnóczy, who even earlier flirted with the idea of the violent overthrow of feudalism, went further and proposed to combine the 'new contract' with the full emancipation of the peasantry, the abolition of all tax privileges and the introduction of the right of non-nobles to hold office. Between these positions, there were a number of shades of opinion, and there were still many who thought that all change to the pre-Theresan order was dangerous.

The spring of 1790 was thus one of high hopes and heated debates; nor did the new monarch remain idle. Leopold II, who shared the fundamental principles but not the doctrinaire intransigence of Joseph, and was a shrewder politician than his brother, had tried and proved his talents in making Tuscany a model state of enlightened absolutism. Soon after his succession to the throne in March 1790, he organised a secret police and a network of informers, and his agents and propagandists worked persuasively on his behalf amongst the burghers and the peasants at the expense of the nobility. Censorship was also tightened. Leopold appeased many aristocrats, and summoned a congress of the Serbs who demanded autonomy and separate government organs. The former was denied, similarly to the *Supplex Libellum Valachorum* mentioned above, but an Illyrian (that is, Serbian) Court Chancellery was created. The new ruler certainly knew how to balance between conflicting ambitions. He also agreed with Frederick William II of Prussia that the latter would refrain from supporting the Hungarian 'malcontents', and concluded a rather unfavourable armistice with the Turks to secure himself internationally.

Among such circumstances, the diet that convened in June 1790 ended with a compromise based on the pre-Josephine status quo in the following March. Instead of the far-reaching programmes described above, the nobility tried to warrant Hungary's and its own special status within the Habsburg Monarchy. While in the laws of 1790 the Pragmatic Sanction was acknowledged, Hungary was described as a 'free and independent' kingdom, to be governed by its own laws only. Diets were to be summoned every three years and had the exclusive right to vote taxes and recruitment. The most progressive result of the diet of 1790–1791 was the creation of nine committees (*deputatio regnicolaris*) with the task of working out proposals for the comprehensive reform of the country's constitution, administrative, judicial and educational system, the institutions of health care, the economy (taxation, customs, communication, credit etc.). Many Josephists were active in the committees, as well as figures like Nikola Škrlec (Miklós Skerlecz), a leading representative of the Croatian Enlightenment and the author of profound economic treatises. In the same period, in a similar vein, Márton Schwartner completed the first 'systematic account of the main characteristics of the state': his *Statistics of the Kingdom of Hungary* (published in 1798 in German) was a comprehensive survey of Hungary's population, its division by religion, ethnicity, profession, income and housing conditions, its main crops and manufactures, weights and measurements, communications network, markets etc. Though the proposals elaborated by the committees were taken off the agenda for the following generation, the ninety-six volumes in which they were collected constituted a major source of inspiration for the next generation of reformists after the diet of 1825–1827 had them printed.

By the time the committees submitted their findings, Leopold had died unexpectedly, and was succeeded in March 1792 by his son Francis I (Francis II, as Holy Roman Emperor). Educated first in Florence under his father and then in Vienna under his uncle, from both of them he only acquired the taste for bureaucratic efficiency, but not for enlightenment; for four decades after the French Revolution, the Habsburg Monarchy and Hungary within it was ruled by an unimaginative and obstinate man whose main endeavour was to preserve what was already outdated. The changes that overflowed from a Europe replete with motion or were initiated within his own domains took place in spite of him. Though it was not his own choice, it is somewhat symbolic that the first major event of his reign was the outbreak of war between revolutionary France and the coalition of Austria and Prussia in April 1792.

From the beginning, the Hungarian enlightened nobility followed the events of the French Revolution with great interest. The Declaration of the Rights of Man and Citizen was translated into Latin by Hajnóczy and into Hungarian by János Laczkovics even before its final version was proclaimed by the French Constituent Assembly. Copies of the *Moniteur* were read in private company, reading societies and Freemasonic lodges; news from France constituted the main item in the Latin *Ephemerides Budenses* and the Hungarian *Magyar Kurir*. But as the French Revolution advanced into its more radical stage simultaneously with the unfolding of the war, opinions in Hungary, as elsewhere, became polarised. The captivity and then the execution of Louis XVI (and Marie Antoinette, who was the aunt of Francis I), not to speak of the Jacobin terror, gradually made most of the enlightened estates, however reluctantly and distrustfully, gravitate towards their traditional adversary, the Habsburg court. They voted through the recruitment and the war subsidies, and they protested less and less vigorously against the tightening of censorship. The 'umbrella' was thus removed from the more determined reformers like Hajnóczy, who earlier hoped to win over the nobles, but now became radicalised. In 1793, we already find Hajnóczy translating the Jacobin constitution, and assembling in the company of Berzeviczy, Laczkovics, Ferenc Szentmarjay, Ferenc Verseghy, Ferenc Kazinczy and several others in clubs and reading societies separate from the earlier organisations.

The growth of these initiatives into the national political movement of the Hungarian 'Jacobins' (a label assigned to them in condemnation by their enemies and used by posterity for want of any precise shorthand term) was owing to Ignác Martinovics, another disaffected admirer of Joseph II. Talented and erudite, but also conceited, limitlessly ambitious and mentally unstable, he had the character of an adventurer-intellectual. From Franciscan monk, he became a professor of natural history at the University of Lemberg; in 1791, he was enlisted in Leopold's secret police and tried to impress the ruler by reports on conspiracies by Jesuits, secret societies and patriots in Hungary, urging him to suppress its nobility and constitutional tradition. Dismissed by Francis I, his muddled ideas on social progress combined with wounded vanity to lead him into the company of the clubbists of Pest and Buda. The ex-spy now organised two secret societies, based on Hajnóczy's idea that before the more ambitious programme of the radicals could be realised, a moderate one acceptable for the enlightened nobility should be pushed through. The Society of Reformers aimed to establish, by noble insurrection, a republic dominated by nobles, with the estates of the Church and the dynasty nationalised, and the serf liberated, but only leasing land from the nobles instead of owning property. Until this plan would be accomplished, the members of the first society were to be kept in ignorance about the existence of the more radical Society of Liberty and Equality, which was dedicated to the complete abolition of noble ascendancy and the establishment of a popular republic. The misgivings of Hajnóczy and his associates were dispelled by Martinovics' allegation that he received orders and financial support from the French National Convent, and the Hungarian movement was part of a scheme for a general revolution in Central Europe. The outbreak of a national uprising in Poland against the second dismemberment of the country in

March 1794, led by Tadeusz Kosciuszko, gave some plausibility to this wholly unfounded claim.

The rather amateurish conspiracy involved some 200 to 300 individuals when, at the end of July 1794, nearly simultaneously with the fall of Robespierre in Paris, twenty 'Jacobins', including Martinovics, were arrested in Vienna. Mainly based on his testimony, in which the dimensions of the movement were greatly exaggerated, there were further arrests, and after lengthy preparations a relatively short trial of 53 persons accused of high treason. Seven leaders were executed in May and June 1795, while many others – 'the ornaments of the nation', as Berzeviczy wrote: leading literati like Ferenc Kazinczy, János Batsányi, Ferenc Verseghy – were sentenced to long terms of imprisonment in the notorious dungeons of Kufstein, Spielberg and Munkács. 'An example had to be set to make the country fear', Kazinczy commented, clearly recognising the nature of the trials.

After the formidable effort of enlightened absolutism collapsed, leaving behind an ambiguous legacy, and its offspring, the enlightened nobility, was deterred from the course it could have embarked on by historical contingencies, the third tendency generated by the Enlightenment in Hungarian politics and society, that of radical reform, ended in a desperate and abortive undertaking. It was now the turn of unenlightened absolutism.

3. Unenlightened absolutism and Hungary's Age of Reform

In the technical sense, the governance of Hungary was not absolutist under the reign of Francis I. Diets were summoned quite frequently, mainly because the constitution restored in 1791 required the consent of the estates to taxation and recruitment in the army, which the ruler badly needed in the wars against revolutionary and, after 1799, Napoleonic France. From the case of Louis XVI, he also concluded that the position of the monarch vitally depended on the maintenance of the whole network of privileges and institutions associated with the old regime. Therefore, while especially his first chief minister, Count Stadion, entertained plans of placing Hungary, in particular, 'on a new footing', Francis left these intact, as well as the organs of central government developed under his predecessors. However, he considered these authorities as a mere machinery for paper-work – hence the later observation of Chancellor Metternich, 'the Habsburg monarchy is not governed, but administered' –, and preferred to make crucial decisions in a secretive way, only consulting his innermost confidants, the 'camarilla', as it was referred to by contemporaries. Himself mediocre, he distrusted superior talents, including his own brother Archduke Joseph, the devoted, efficient and popular Governor and subsequently Palatine of Hungary from 1795 to 1847; Chancellor Prince Klemens Lothar von Metternich-Winneburg, who was at the head of Austrian foreign affairs from 1809 to 1848, was a remarkable exception which confirmed the rule. The other conspicuous feature of the system was the close government supervision of the public sphere. The spies of the secret police ruined many careers, but even more oppressive was censorship. In 1798 reading societies, and in 1799 lending libraries were banned. In the early 1790s, the Hungarian press consisted of nearly twenty regular periodicals which, besides the newspapers mentioned above, included the highly exciting literary and critical review *Magyar Museum* and the popular scientific journal *Mindenes Gyűjtemény* (Miscellany). By 1805, there were only five papers and journals, the only one in the Hungarian language being thoroughly uninteresting. Over 2,500 works published under Josephism were prohibited in 1803 by a new censorship committee; books were hunted down at the borders and within the country for fear of subversion.

Since the bulk of the Hungarian nobility now felt that in providing against the French contamination their interests coincided with those of the court, for nearly two decades the diet displayed a co-operative attitude to the Viennese government. Over this period it voted about a million recruits and thirty million florins for the purposes of the war against France, with almost the whole of this burden falling on the shoulders of the peasantry. There was one, rather inglorious exception: the last instance of the noble insurrection in the course of Napoleon's campaign of 1809, when the French forces advanced as far as Győr. Refusing Napoleon's appeal to rise against the Habsburgs, the diet called the nobility to a general levy, whose easy defeat and headlong flight became a powerful argument for later reformers against the privileges of the nobility. Somewhat more than a quarter of the imperial army, over 110,000 soldiers, were constituted by Hungarian units at any one time during the war, while Hungary contributed about one-third of the revenues of the treasury. The territory of the Kingdom of Hungary constituted more than fifty per cent of the Habsburg domains, which led the court often to complain about the disproportionately low share of the country in shouldering the overall financial burdens; an opinion which, however, failed to consider Hungary's relative poverty, in the light of which her contribution looks more than realistic.

The nobility's attitudes in taking a stand against the fashion of French principles were to a considerable extent coloured by the trappings of the national revival described in the previous chapter, without reaching the level of sophistication and intellectual distinction that characterised German political romanticism, which was provoked in the same period by the same challenge. The ancient virtues and glories of 'the nation' were extolled in poems, songs, orations and pamphlets; the wearing of national costume and the playing of *verbunkos* music – recruitment songs based on Hungarian folk motives – became fashionable. This 'nationalism of the estates' was occasionally displayed *vis-à-vis* Vienna, and each of the five diets between 1796 and 1811 resounded with grievances concerning unfair tariffs and requests for the use of Hungarian as official language. But as long as the wartime agrarian boom continued and the profits drawn from it were not put to hazard by administrative measures, differences could be bridged. Increased armies were a safe market for grain, whose price grew steadily, about thirteen-fold between the beginning of the revolutionary wars and 1811, in excess of the also considerable eight-fold inflation. All landowners, and even some of the peasantry, were able to benefit from this situation.

In 1811, however, the court, deeply in the red, embarked on a currency reform: the paper money it had issued in large quantity was devalued five-fold, which meant a proportionate increase in state taxation. The diet, which was not consulted, was outraged; but in May 1812 Francis dissolved it and introduced the patent of devaluation 'provisionally', that is, until a new diet was summoned, by decree. Though Metternich's memorandum in which he proposed the abolition of Hungary's separate constitutional status was rejected, the diet did not convene for thirteen years, and though the autonomy of the counties was maintained, royal commissioners and, when necessary, the military ensured that the will of Vienna was enforced. A case in question was 1821–1822, when the ruler ordered that the recruitment in arrears from the final campaigns against Napoleon in 1813 and 1815, be effected, and taxes voted ten years earlier in paper money be collected in silver coins (a *de facto* increase by about 150 per cent). Hungary without Transylvania and Croatia had 41 counties; only 17 of these executed both orders upon at least the second rescript without coercion, and the seven that persevered in refusing both of them to the very end had a quarter of the noble population of the country. Once again it became obvious that even if the adversaries of absolutism could be temporarily silenced and most of the nobility could be manipulated in a conservative direction, no broad basis could be developed for absolutism in Hungary, whose regional interests were, because of its sheer size, too important for Vienna to ignore. Prompted by Palatine Joseph, and now even by Metternich, Francis I reluctantly summoned the diet in 1825.

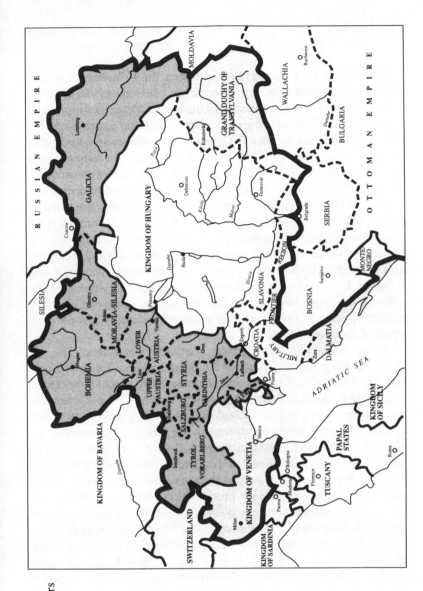

8. Hungary in the Habsburg Empire after the Napoleonic wars

Austrian Empire

boundary of the Habsburg Empire

boundaries of provinces

administrative centres in the Habsburg Empire

The fact that the Emperor (now of Austria, the Holy Roman Empire having been eliminated by Napoleon) needed the recruits and the taxes to fulfil Austria's role as a member of the Holy Alliance in suppressing revolutionary upheavals in the early 1820s in Italy and Spain should not mislead us into believing that the Hungarian estates resisted him out of swelling liberal sentiments. What most of them wanted was to return to the compromise of 1790–1791 and to entrench the ancient constitution. Their dominant mode of thinking was still in the *kuruc* independence tradition at best and legalistic 'Werbőczian' in its less attractive manifestations, with some admixture of light romantic touches. Nevertheless, the tradition of the Enlightenment did not lie entirely dormant. The experience of the three decades between the Jacobin trials and the beginning of a new contest between progressive and retrograde opinion in Hungary developed what remained of it, in terms of culture and attitudes, into a vigorous national romanticism, and in terms of sociopolitical ideas, into a programme of improvement imbued by the principles of liberalism.

As regards the major protagonists, continuity was indirect. The role of the surviving 'Jacobins' ought to be mentioned first. Two of the convicts of 1795, Ferenc Kazinczy and János Batsányi, started their careers as Josephists alienated from enlightened absolutism by its Germanisation policy. They were the co-founders of the literary and critical review *Magyar Museum*, mentioned above, in 1788. During imprisonment and after release, Batsányi continued the radical course he embarked on after the nobility's compromise with Leopold II. He not only wrote beautiful elegiac poetry, but also urged Hungary's independence from Austria, and translated Napoleon's proclamation of 1809 into Hungarian. Kazinczy pursued a less directly political agenda and became the somewhat charismatic leader of the movement for the reformation of the mother tongue. Since the prediction of Johann Gottfried Herder, the German philosopher of romantic folk nationalism, that the Hungarian nation would be diluted in the ocean of the surrounding Slav, German and Romanian peoples, became known in Hungary, language was an especially neuralgic issue. Hungarian was indeed the native tongue only of a minority of the population of the country. Kazinczy and the neologists wholly embraced the idea originally developed also by Herder that the nation, which is the only vehicle through which the potentials of the individual could be realised, vitally depended for its sustenance on the use of language.

Even in this early period, the championing of the Magyar tongue by the neologists involved a latent conflict with their counterparts among the non-Magyar peoples of the country, and the tendency to transform the more comprehensive 'Hungarus' patriotism into narrower Magyar nationalism, in rivalry with Romanian, Serbian, Croatian and Slovak nationalisms. This was a tendency further aggravated by the socially and culturally superior attitude of the Hungarian nobility, later transmitted to the intelligentsia and the middle class as well, towards the ethnic minorities, which, the Croats excepted, scarcely possessed a feudal elite. Still, the positive yield of the neologist movement would be hard to overestimate. Numerically, it comprised some ten thousand words (most of them used even today), which made the Hungarian language capable of playing a number of new functions. Above all, it created a kind of intellectual confidence by facilitating communication in the vernacular concerning all sorts of facts and relations in a changing world. Literature was foremost in importance among the relevant sorts of communication, for the new literary themes and style generated tastes, sensitivities and modes of conduct that were instrumental in the opening up of Hungarian society to modernity.

The debates in which the new literary language was born at first centred on the poetry of Mihály Csokonai Vitéz, a master of rococo lyricism as well as the more rustic style, who was also the first Hungarian poet to dream of living by his pen alone. But the age of neologism also bred Dániel Berzsenyi, 'the Hungarian Horace', who exhorted the nobility, fallen into moral decay, to regeneration in classic meters; and József Katona, the author of *Ban Bánk* (1820), a national drama whose hero became an emblem of resisting German domination in the court of the thirteenth-century King Andrew II, while also listening to the complaints of the peasants against oppression by their landlords. Katona's play was not put on the stage until several years later, although public theatrical performances at Pest in Hungarian go back to 1790.

The neologist and literary movements were reinforced by master printers who also held the ambition of improving the network of scientific and literary life in the country, such as the Trattner 'dynasty'. János Trattner was the publisher of *Tudományos Gyűjtemény* (Scientific Miscellany, launched in 1817) and *Aurora* (from 1821), a literary yearbook mainly devoted to the encouragement of young talents, as well as an intimate friend of leaders of the movement like Kazinczy, András Fáy, or Ferenc Kölcsey. Of rigorous aesthetic and ethical principles, Kölcsey later became one of the greatest orators and a leader of the liberal opposition in the reform diets of the 1830s. The most famous of his philosophical and political poems, the *Hymnus*, which is today Hungary's national anthem, was written in 1823, amidst the outcry against Francis I's unconstitutional impositions. By the time the 1825 diet was opened, the young poet Mihály Vörösmarty had published *Zalán's Flight* (1825), a romantic national epic on one of the feats of Árpád at the time of the Hungarian conquest.

Other one-time Josephists who continued to be influential into the nineteenth century included József Podmaniczky, until his death in 1823 the right hand of Palatine Joseph in the administration of Hungary. Gergely Berzeviczy, another survivor from the Josephian and 'Jacobin' era, leads us to the problem of Hungary's socio-economic condition and potential, and its contemporary assessment. In 1795, Berzeviczy withdrew to his estate in northern Hungary, and during the rest of his life he became directly involved politically only on one occasion: in 1809, writing a Hungarian draft constitution for Napoleon. He devoted his chief energies to two major economic treatises written in Latin (he rejected much of Kazinczy's programme in the name of broader Hungarian patriotism), *The Industry and Commerce of Hungary* (1797) and *The Condition of the Peasants* (1804) as well as a great many shorter pieces of analysis. While he demonstrated the harmful effect of Habsburg economic policies on Hungary and combated the prevailing western image (much encouraged from Vienna) of Hungary as barbarous and rebellious, he also disclosed the indigenous roots of backwardness. Like his fellow ex-Josephist, Ferenc Széchényi, he was deeply impressed by the consequences the dismantling of the feudal system had on the commerce and industry of England, and anticipated Széchényi's son, István, in identifying the economic, social and moral implications of serfdom as the primary cause of Hungary's dismal conditions. Inadequately protected against the landlord by the Urbarial Patent, the serf's income was shown by Berzeviczy's up-to-date statistical method to be insufficient to relieve him from misery, which meant that the life of the subsistence producer was one spent in lethargy and diffidence. Berzeviczy's pessimistic judgement on the contemporary Hungarian nobility made an *étatiste* solution his only hope.

Yet, for all the acuteness and the erudition of Berzeviczy and for all the relative backwardness of the country, his despondency soon turned out to be less than fully warranted. The reasons for this are the very ambiguities of Hungary's predicament. The islands Josephism once endeavoured to save from sinking into the bog almost imperceptibly expanded and proliferated. What made the paradoxically often dilettante bureaucratic absolutism of Francis I look so onerous was precisely the fact that it was ill-equipped to cope with the requirements of growth accelerated independently of it: that during (and in spite of) his reign the pace of material progress and the frequency of political and intellectual impulses, despite its modesty in absolute terms, was the greatest which Hungary and the whole region of Central Europe had ever experienced. For the affluent, enterprising segment, roughly one-fifth, of the over half-million strong Hungarian nobility, these developments might serve as incentives for the recognition of the merits of the liberal agenda, whereas for the rest, who supplemented the incomes of their modest estates or earned their full living as professionals, innkeepers, transporters, or even as cobblers or peasants, 'careers open to talent' and 'equality of opportunity' were not necessarily repulsive notions. To be sure, it was a formidable task to persuade the masses of petty nobility that they would in fact gain from losing the only thing that distinguished them from the peasantry: their privileges. Still, though their situation exposed them to manipulation by the government, it was at least possible to win a part of them for the rest of the liberal programme: equality before the law, civil liberties, representative and responsible government.

As regards the millions of the serf population, an enlightened young man with a fresh degree from a German university like Tessedik in 1767 could be astonished at the 'stupidity, diffidence, superstition, and prejudice' he encountered instead of pastoral idyll among the peasantry, whose living conditions only returned to the level before the decay begun in the seventeenth century by the end of the eighteenth. Yet, even though roughly sixty per cent of the peasants were cotters who did not have their own plot, the peasant *portae* in general started to display a greater level of comfort, even embellishment. About twenty per cent of the well-to-do peasantry seem to have been literate, not only because they were eager to read the religious, adventurous or even gothic horror histories available at every marketplace, but also because as small-scale entrepreneurs they needed basic skills in reading and the calculus. Criminality in the Hungarian countryside grew at the beginning of the nineteenth century not only because young men fled from press-gangs, but also because there was an increasingly plentiful booty to be looted. The tens of thousands who did not escape recruitment became exposed to hitherto unlikely experiences, with the result that their horizons were widened: they travelled in the army the breadth and length of Europe, and might even attain high rank, as the valiant '*óbester*' (*Oberst*, i.e., colonel) József Simonyi.

The wartime boom and the relative abundance of cash encouraged the enterprising nobles not only to renovate and decorate their manor houses and purchase 'luxury' items (like a new set of clothes, instead of the one passed down in the family through several generations), but also to make investments in the improvement of agriculture as well as in industry and communication. Though the first steam engine on the European continent was installed in a mine in northern Hungary in 1722, and there was a significant growth in the number of industrial plants under Joseph II, the mechanisation of Hungarian industries did not effectively start until the early 1800s, when a number of important initiatives commenced in textile, steel and leather industries, sometimes in co-operation between magnates and a nascent bourgeoisie. Hungary had one or two modern factories in each important branch of industry and a nascent industrial working class of about 30,000 by the 1840s, by which time its industrial output was four times as large as under Joseph II. Yet its value was a mere seven per cent of that of the whole of the Habsburg Monarchy (which, in turn, was far behind not only England or Belgium, but even France in terms of industrialisation).

Major industries still being the domain of the magnates, and the most lucrative trade, that of grain, in the hands of 'Greek' (Balkan) and later Jewish merchants, the weight of the burgher class was even more modest than its numerical strength. The population of the free cities grew by the 1840s to about 600,000, roughly the same as the size of the nobility, but only one-third of urban dwellers lived from trade or industry. Still, the growth exceeded the overall population increase since the census of Joseph II. There was a building boom, especially in Pest-Buda, as the twin cities came to be called by that time in order to emphasise that if not from the administrative point of view, in reality they began to constitute one common centre of the country, in spite of the fact that Pozsony was still the seat of several government offices and the diet. The combined population of 150,000 made Pest-Buda a worthy capital of the 1848 Revolution, and its cityscape started to display a keenness on refinement. By the 1840s, canalisation began, parks and fine villas appeared in the suburbs, and nearly half of the streets were paved and equipped with lighting.

The summoning, the convening and the work of the diet of 1825–1827 after an interval of no less than thirteen years did not mean that even these ambiguous potentials were immediately asserted, and the Age of Reform is no longer considered to have commenced until about 1830. The main items set on its agenda were, on the part of the court, taxation and the projects worked out by the commissions of the diet of 1790–1791, while on the part of the estates, the grievances suffered by them during the past thirteen years in terms of taxes levied unconstitutionally and violations of the constitution in general. The objective of the majority – or, since votes in the Hungarian diet were 'pondered' instead of being counted, the 'sounder', that is, the more influential part – in both houses was no more than the 'circumvallation' of the constitution by ensuring triennial diets, free communication between the counties and procedures against officials executing unlawful measures. The resulting compromise consisted of the confirmation of the relevant laws of the diet of 1790–1791 (that is, the abandonment by the court of the pretension to govern by decree) and the voting of taxes nearly to the amount requested by Vienna. The diet rejected a motion to decrease the burden of the serfs, while the court refused to discuss issues of commerce and customs as well as a bill on the simultaneous use of Hungarian and Latin in the corpus of laws. This very traditional outcome was only modified by two measures that were to have far reaching consequences. First, a committee was created to reconsider the projects of 1790–1791, especially the one on the most soaring urbarial questions, and to work out drafts for legislation to be discussed by the following diet. Second, the Hungarian Learned Society, the later Academy of Sciences, was founded, an initiative in which a crucial role was played by Count István Széchenyi. Following as a patron of the arts and sciences in the footsteps of his father Ferenc, who in 1802 had laid the foundations of the future Hungarian National Library and Museum by donating his own collection to the nation, Széchenyi offered one year's income from his estates to establish an institution for the promotion of national culture. Széchenyi was followed by a number of other donors. The Society started to operate, under the patronage of Palatine Archduke Joseph, in 1830, and soon became a central organisation not only of scientific discussion but of the public sphere and the Hungarian national movement in general.

The newly entrenched corporate constitution and the resumption of the reform projects of the 1790s at the committee sessions in 1828–1830 created a space in which the liberal nobility of the Age of Reform attempted a peaceful transition to modernity, and with Széchenyi the first of the dominant personalities of that age appeared on the stage. As a young scion of one of the richest aristocratic families of Hungary, Széchenyi took part in the final phases of the war against Napoleon as a cavalry officer; the combination of personal courage and charm earned him decorations as well as the grace of ladies at the Congress of Vienna. Talent, vision and responsibility prevailed over idleness as a result of extensive reading of modern classics of social and political thought from Rousseau through Adam Smith to Jeremy Bentham, and travels in Western Europe, Italy and the Balkans, which awoke him to the backwardness of his own country. As his father, he was particularly impressed by his experience of the laws, institutions, manners and social system of England. Already in the early 1820s, Széchenyi's frustration with the narrow-mindedness of the estates' opposition strategies in particular and Hungary's feudal system in general, became complete, and he was one of the founders of a liberal magnates' club at the diet. A well-informed and disdainful critic of the policies of the Holy Alliance against the liberal movements and freedom fights in Spain, Italy and Greece, Széchenyi also abhorred violence and revolution. But his proposal to mediate between the court and the nation in the process of inevitable transition from absolute to representative government and the concomitant socio-economic changes was rejected by Chancellor Metternich, who still preferred, if necessary, working with the old opposition to the 'new' reformers at the end of 1825.

In the following years Széchenyi emerged as a civiliser with a decisive impact on the shaping of attitudes favourable to changing the salient anachronisms of Hungarian society, especially its elite, which he expected to become the vehicle of transformation. He promoted schemes ranging from personal hygiene through fashion and leisure activities like skating and rowing to horse-breeding and horse-races which, he believed, were essential to the standards of refinement he encountered in England, though he suspected that most of his compatriots would be enraged to learn that in fact 'it was them, not their horses, whom he wanted to train'. In 1827 he founded, on the model of English clubs, the National Casino in Pest as a venue for 'the intercourse of minds', an initiative that was later imitated in many provincial centres and became a rallying point for young reformers. Later, he concentrated on more practical projects of improvement, mainly in the sphere of communications, which he found essential for surmounting economic backwardness. He became a moving spirit of the Danube Steamship Navigation Company, under whose auspices, after beginnings in the late 1810s, an efficient link was established between Vienna and the Lower Danube during the 1830s. This also depended on river regulation schemes, which also owed a great deal to Széchenyi. Upon his initiatives and supervised by him as a commissioner of the Gubernium, the regulation of the Danube started in the 1830s, and that of the Tisza in the 1840s, according to plans made by Pál Vásárhelyi. It was also Széchenyi who urged, partly as a means to stimulate the development of Budapest as a unitary capital, the creation of the first permanent bridge, the Chainbridge between Pest and Buda, constructed under the direction of British engineers between 1842 and 1849. Finally, in one way or another, Széchenyi was involved in the launching of banking and industrial enterprises that remained at the forefront of Hungary's economic development for several decades.

These commitments demonstrate that whereas Széchenyi was by no means indifferent to the cause of national independence, he considered the rhetoric of constitutional grievances employed by the country's elite against Vienna to be futile and wanted to direct his fellow nobles' attention to spheres in which they could more usefully and meaningfully exert any patriotic enthusiasm they might entertain. In other words, he championed an attitude that had its parallels amongst other subordinate partners in extended polities across Europe, such as in eighteenth-century Scotland: that neither modernisation, nor even a powerful civic consciousness inevitably depended on full political sovereignty, and the latter was only desirable when accompanied by the former. His verdict that while the policies of the court and Hungary's dependence on Austria had a fair share in the responsibility for the country's appalling condition, its main cause was the survival of the feudal system, was not only symbolically represented in the activities described above, but also argued in influential theoretical and polemical works.

The focal theme of his major book *Credit* (1830) was the paralysing effect of the lack of capital and credit on the country's economic potential, which in turn resulted from antiquated laws like that of *aviticitas* (the inalienability of noble land) and *fiscalitas* (the claim of the state treasury to noble land after the extinction of the family line). Because of such regulations dating back to the high Middle Ages, the Hungarian nobleman as owner of vast lands, the master of many unpaid hands and exempt from taxes, could nonetheless neither pay his debts nor modernise his estates because he could offer no security to the creditor. (Széchenyi himself felt the edge of these regulations, being denied a loan by his banker in 1828.) The polemic against these restrictions was supplemented in *Credit* and his subsequent works, *Light* (1831) and *Stages* (indicating a timetable for the necessary reforms, 1833), with a criticism of guilds, monopolies and other forms of bureaucratic interference with commerce and industry, and Széchenyi urged the abolition of these as well as internal tariffs, the serfs' forced labour service, the *nona* and manorial jurisdiction. Finally, besides exposing the economic inefficiency of the feudal system even from the point of view of its supposed beneficiaries, he also pointed out the moral injustice suffered by the unprivileged, whom he proposed to be elevated 'within the bulwark of the constitution'.

In the course of 1830–1831, two developments, one outside and one within Hungary, shaped an atmosphere in which the relevance of Széchenyi's activities and opinions loomed large. Unlike the freedom struggles of the early 1820s, which were confined to Southern Europe and, with the exception of Greece, collapsed in the face of the concert of the great powers of Europe, the wave of revolutionary upheaval in 1830 shook most of Western and Central Europe. Constitutional monarchy in France and some German states, the creation of an independent Belgium and electoral reform in Britain were the lasting results, but the revolts in the Habsburg possessions in Italy, the Papal States and especially the Polish attempt to shake off Russian rule also could not fail to make an impact on Hungarian minds. The barricades of Paris caused enthusiasm mainly among the young, especially students, but the nobility responded with apprehension, perceptible in the docility with which the short diet of the autumn of 1830 voted through taxation and recruitment requested by the court. However, the proclamation of Polish independence in January and the ruthless suppression of the uprising in September 1831 gave rise to demonstrations of sympathy and various forms of assistance to the Poles, such as collection of funds during and the sheltering of émigrés after the revolt, among the Hungarian nobility, which had close and multifaceted relations with its Polish counterpart. From early 1831 the Viennese government, which supported Tsarist Russia, became an object of mounting criticism in Hungary.

The other important event was the peasant revolt which broke out in the summer of 1831, the greatest since the one of 1784 in Transylvania. The immediate background of the revolt was the cholera epidemic whose death toll was a quarter of a million. The precautions taken by the authorities only served to enrage the destitute serfs of five counties in north-eastern Hungary. Vitally depending on seasonal work in the Great Plain, the cordon established to contain the spread of the epidemic cut them from their source of subsistence, while the primitive technologies of disinfection evoked allegations of well-poisoning. The revolt of over forty thousand indigent, predominantly Romanian, Slovak and Ruthene peasants was put down. While most of the frightened landlords blamed the spread of reformism and urged exemplary retaliation, there were also many who recognised that the tension involved in lord-serf relations and its aggravation by ethnic conflict was a permanent threat to social stability and made reform inevitable. The events of 1830–1831 on the international and the Hungarian scene contributed to the polarisation of political opinion in the country.

While more than one of Széchenyi's individual points were anticipated by men like Berzeviczy or another writer on economic matters, János Balásházy, the rank and the personality of the author as well as the coherence of his argument immediately made his programme for capitalism and emancipation an object of enthusiastic praise as well as bitter criticism. Some found *Credit* of seminal importance, whereas others considered it worthy of being burnt; the one public refutation by József Dessewffy, while going even beyond Széchenyi in a few particulars, was based essentially on the Enlightenment of the estates, whose goal was not the abolition but the renovation of corporate structures as a precondition to successful opposition to Vienna. Széchenyi, on the contrary, hoped to win the magnates and the court for his reform programme. Since both of these expectations proved to be, on the whole, unrealistic – the printing of *Stages* was prohibited in the spring of 1832, so it was published in Germany in the following year –, and Széchenyi distrusted the estates-based politics whose main force was the weighty middle nobility, his political scope of action became rather confined even amidst the general admiration for him.

Even within liberalism, political concepts started to diverge, which led to a gradual separation between Széchenyi and his close friend and political associate, his companion on his travels in the 1820s, the Transylvanian Baron Miklós Wesselényi. His *On Prejudices*, a political treatise that shared the fate of Széchenyi's *Stages*, contained in a less systematic form nearly all proposals found in the latter, and many more. Unlike Széchenyi, Wesselényi found not only that the redemption of the serfs' feudal obligations should take place under state supervision, but also that social change ought to be accompanied by the dismantling of absolutism, on which he laid the blame for backwardness, and the creation of constitutional monarchy with civil liberties. He also thought that corporate structures and the opposition of the estates were suitable to the propagation of reformist endeavours and susceptible to being transformed into the foundations of a modern state, while towards the estates his strategy was to emphasise not the novelty of the intended reforms but their tendency to the restoration of the ancient constitution of 'noble democracy'. Széchenyi disapproved of Wesselényi's more defiant policies. Based on his unparalleled knowledge of the government of the Habsburg Monarchy and international power relations, his fear that Vienna might retaliate before Hungary became sufficiently strengthened by economic, social and cultural modernisation, was not unfounded. It is for this reason that he laboured to avoid confrontation and to shift the reform initiative to the neutral areas described above.

In a way, both of these trends became vindicated in subsequent years. Széchenyi's groundwork was indeed essential to raise a vanguard and a rank-and-file that represented the cause of reform at the diets of the 1830s and 1840s with increasing determation and expertise. However, Wesselényi's appeal to the county nobility and his programme to invigorate it and transform it into a modern national opposition by internal reforms held out the promise of a more powerful political movement than Széchenyi's aristocratic preferences. And the leading force of this movement, imbued as they were with the ideas of Széchenyi and his own western models, became, contrary to his expectations, not the aristocracy, but the well-to-do gentry, who first demonstrated their commitment to reform and their moral authority at the forums of corporate politics so much distrusted by the father of Hungarian liberalism. As hoped by Wesselényi, it was during the discussion of the commercial, constitutional, jurisdictional and urbarial projects of the dietal committees by the county assemblies in 1831–1832 that they emerged as a recognisable political force. Together with the educated part of the nobility and the non-noble, *honoratior* intellectuals, they dominated the Hungarian political scene as a 'historic' middle class for a century to come. At the beginning of the 1830s, the reform-minded gentry were still in a minority. But the election of many of them, such as Ferenc Deák, Gábor Klauzál, István Bezerédj or Kölcsey, to the diet of 1832–1836, the records of the county debates of the projects, and to some extent even the instructions given by the counties to their deputies made it possible for them to appear at the diet with a programme of comprehensive reform.

The immediate objective of the opposition at the diet of 1832–1836 was, as Kölcsey put it, 'liberty and property': they wanted to promote the 'union of (national) interests' by liberating the serf from feudal bondage through 'optional redemption' (that is, on the basis of a compensation for the land and the manorial obligations freely negotiated between the peasant and the landlord). After protracted debates, the urbarial proposal was defeated, and the opposition had to be content with the possibility of redeeming forced labour and other feudal dues, but not the land. Similar was the fate of the attempt to abolish *aviticitas*, to introduce the right of the peasant to hold land, and to reunify Transylvania with Hungary, which Wesselényi urged at the Hungarian diet as well as at that of Transylvania in 1834–1835, partly as a means to offset the relative backwardness and the consequent weakness of the forces of reform in the principality.

As regards practical results, the first of the reform diets was largely a failure. At the same time, the basis of reform as well as the public sphere became broadened, and new strategies were developed for the mobilisation of political opinion in the country. In 1832–1836, the 'dietal youth' made its first appearance on the Hungarian public scene. Largely consisting of law students in their early twenties, this substantial group of young radicals represented absent magnates, or were commissioned by the counties to copy official documents, or merely took advantage of the freedom of attending the sessions of the diet. By their mere presence, but quite often by their boisterousness as well, they gave efficient support to liberal deputies. With Széchenyi's slogan 'nation and progress' on their lips, but also entertaining ideas of democracy based on popular representation, many of them came to play a major role in Hungarian politics during the liberal era. The first great service they rendered was as copyists of the *Dietal Reports*, edited from December 1832 on by Lajos Kossuth, himself a young jurist, the scion of a landless noble family and a representative of absent magnates from Zemplén county. As official minutes of the sessions of the diet were incomplete and published *ex post facto*, and censorship made the press an unreliable source of information on its proceedings, Kossuth's *Reports* made history in extending the public sphere. Taking the shape of private letters, they evaded censorship, but, produced in hundreds of hand-written copies, they reached several thousand readers and many more hearers, and became as important shapers of public opinion as the writings of Széchenyi. After the diet ended in Pozsony, Kossuth moved to Pest and went on to edit the *Municipal Reports*, not only giving an account of, but also influencing debates in the county assemblies and protesting against the measures taken by the court against leaders of the dietal opposition. Having consolidated its international situation through the treaties of mutual support against internal and external enemies signed with the other two authoritarian states of the region, Prussia and Russia, in 1833, the Habsburg government took concerted action to deactivate the Hungarian opposition from early 1835 on. In the same year, Francis I died and was succeeded by his feeble-minded son Ferdinand V, while Metternich shared ultimate authority in the newly created government body, the *Staatskonferenz*, with his rival Count Franz Anton Kollowrat, who became responsible for internal affairs. The newly appointed Hungarian Chancellor Count Fidél Pálffy was a dutiful instrument in orchestrating (after the dissolution of the Transylvanian diet in 1835) a trial accusing Wesselényi of treason and (after the end of the Hungarian diet in 1836) against László Lovassy and other leaders of the association of the dietal youth. The arrest of Kossuth, who was also an enthusiastic supporter of Wesselényi, followed in May 1837. Wesselényi could still exercise his legendary physical powers and bravery to save many lives in the disastrous inundation of the Danube in the spring of 1838 which killed over four hundred people and destroyed half the buildings of Pest, before being imprisoned and then released on the grounds of his rapidly deteriorating health. Blind and resigned, he spent the rest of his life as a recluse from politics. Lovassy, sentenced to ten years of imprisonment, lost his wits in solitary confinement. Kossuth, however, spent his three years' term reading classics of politics and economics and learning English, and emerged from his captivity with strengthened determination and great charisma.

This occurred by the political amnesty proclaimed in May 1840, as the court realised that the policy of repression had missed its target. Though ever fewer counties protested formally, they were also reluctant to solicit Vienna for pardon, which would have amounted to acknowledging the lawfulness of the conduct of the authorities; on the contrary, the increasingly influential opposition, now led by Ferenc Deák, insisted on putting and keeping the issue of freedom of expression on the agenda of the diet summoned in 1839. With clever manoeuvring Deák, with the assistance of a group of liberal magnates in the Upper House including, besides Széchenyi, Count Lajos Batthyány, Baron József Eötvös and others, managed to secure the refusal of the diet to discuss taxation and recruitment before the issue of freedom of expression was settled. The government, pressed by foreign policy complications and encouraged by a group of young Hungarian conservatives led by Count Aurél Dessewffy to launch a series of limited reforms instead of repression, agreed to a compromise. Pálffy was dismissed even earlier, and the diet of 1839–1840 not only achieved amnesty for the political prisoners, but also passed important reform legislation. In return for a fixed sum of manumission compensation, serfs could become free landowners. In other words, 'optional redemption' was fully secured, though it proved to be an insufficient solution: by 1848, a mere one per cent of peasant communities had been liberated in this way. The use of the Hungarian language in official communication was further extended. A half-century long process towards the full emancipation of Jews started by permitting them the (almost) free choice of their residence, trade or profession and the ownership of real estate. Laws relating to commerce, industry and banking passed in 1840 created a stimulating legal framework for the development of Hungarian capitalism for several decades.

With the court refraining from administrative retaliation, the situation was now favourable for the unfolding of reformist policies. In the 1840s, associations for charitable purposes, social service, self-help, economic or cultural improvement proliferated and contributed to the disintegration of the barriers between the estates. The combined membership of the approximately 600 associations in Hungary and Transylvania might have reached 100,000 by 1848. Some of the over two hundred casinos and reading societies, with tens of thousands of members, became thoroughly politicised, and were the hotbeds of the political parties that arose in 1846 and 1847. As a token of temporary reconciliation, Kossuth was not only released, but even permitted to launch a new liberal newspaper, *Pesti Hírlap* (Pest News), in January 1841. In fact, the government expected to kill two birds with one stone: first, it hoped that Kossuth's vehemence would split the liberal movement and, second, that through censorship he could still be kept under control. In fact, the traditional censorship was fully unequipped to cope with the difficulties posed by Kossuth's entirely new type of political journalism. Relying on a network of correspondents around the country dating back to the times of the *Municipal Reports*, Kossuth not only filled his journal with exciting and up-to-date news material, but, most importantly, used his own extraordinary talents as a publicist to address central issues of the contemporary public scene in over two hundred well-informed and challenging editorials, which amounted to his own programme for the transformation of Hungary. Within a few months, these merits earned *Pesti Hírlap* more than five thousand subscribers, which might mean as many as fifty thousand readers, or one-quarter of the public for newspapers at the time in the country. In due course, other papers followed Kossuth in revolutionising Hungarian journalism, and a press formerly consisting of the dry chronicling of events was transformed into one based on reporting and reasoning, opinion and persuasion and reflecting political cleavages.

Nor did Kossuth's editorial activity erode the co-operation of most shades of liberal opinion in Hungary, for although he was one of the few who were not averse to democratic ideas, he was disciplined enough to refrain from steps that might have cost him the support of the most influential liberals, led by Deák. During the first few months of the existence of *Pesti Hírlap*, the editorials exposed the most soaring cases of social injustice and the most salient phenomena of backwardness from the humiliating practice of flogging peasants at the order of overbearing lords to the miserable condition of roads, demonstrating that they were not merely contingent but resulted from the existing social and legal order. Kossuth's antidote was a true 'union of interests' through social and political emancipation, a more equitable distribution of burdens and economic modernisation, and cited examples from the experience of capitalism and political liberalism in Western Europe and America. Instead of the aristocracy, he considered the 'nobility of middling rank' as the vehicle of the reform process, which he found, or rather hoped, to be sufficiently imbued with an enlightened and liberal spirit to push through his programme. One of the cornerstones of the latter was the speedy manumission of serfs, which ought to be compulsory, landlords being compensated from state funds. This, in turn, required the abolition of tax privileges; but the violent resistance of the bulk of the county nobility to the inclusion of the demand for proportionate contribution to municipal taxes in the instruction to the deputies elected to the diet of 1843–1844 drove Kossuth one step further, to urge the extension of the constitution to non-nobles, and the reform of those already 'within', such as the oligarchical free cities.

Apart from the claim for the administrative reunion of Hungary with Transylvania, Kossuth did not raise the constitutional issue, but in several of his editorials he emphasised the importance of economic independence, which he considered a precondition of political independence. His reading of the German economist Friedrich List's criticism of *laissez-faire* and the alarming prospect of the incorporation of the Habsburg Monarchy into the German customs union (*Zollverein*) of 1839, which would have eliminated the internal customs barrier created in 1751 but would have exposed Hungary's modest factories to the competition of German industry, turned him from an advocate of free trade to a champion of economic protectionism. Kossuth's propaganda resulted in the rise of local 'Buy Hungarian!' movements, and he was elected director of the National Protectionist Association established by distinguished liberal aristocrats in 1844. While in the absence of a sound domestic industrial base the economic importance of the movement could be but limited, it contributed to nationalist and separatist sentiments. In general, too, Kossuth and the *Pesti Hírlap* encouraged the process of Magyarisation, even though he warned against the violent propagation of the Hungarian language.

Kossuth's programme was not only watched with increasing unease from Vienna, but had formidable critics within the country. One group of his adversaries was constituted by the aristocratic new conservatives (or cautious progressives, as they dubbed themselves) of Aurél Dessewffy, who advocated the strengthening of the government through aristocratic support, and the minimum of reform needed to make it more efficient and satisfy all the diverse corporate and national interests. To be sure, their own interests came first. They lent ambiguous support to reforms like the optional redemption of feudal obligations or equality before the law, but did not want to hear about the abolition of *aviticitas*, which they considered a 'nation sustaining force'; and while agreeing that the nobility should pay municipal taxes, they demanded the increase of their votes in proportion with their contribution. They urged a united front of the propertied against the propertiless, led by Kossuth, whom they saw as intoxicated by poorly digested liberal and radical maxims, and hoped to drive a wedge between him and figures like Széchenyi, Batthyány and Deák.

Széchenyi, for one, did not need stimuli to turn against the editor of *Pesti Hírlap*, whom he attacked in a book-length pamphlet, *The People of the Orient*, as early as June 1841. The conflict of the two dominant personalities of Hungary's transition to modernity is one of the themes that raises the process to a truly dramatic pitch, and naturally one of the most fruitful and often exploited topics of Hungarian historical discourse and political imagery ever since. For Széchenyi, Kossuth was the political heir of Wesselényi, whose superior talent also involved greater danger. Though avoiding explicit meddling with the constitutional issue, Kossuth played on national tunes, and the claim of self-determination was implicit in his programme; the dimensions of his success also risked a far graver retaliation from Vienna which Széchenyi had no doubt would come. To be sure, there was also an element of personal jealousy as well as a difference in political style involved. Széchenyi reproached Kossuth for his 'French manners' in seeking popularity through superficial criticism and ill-advised incitement against the existing order and authority, thereby preparing revolution and thus throwing the cause of reform into danger. He also criticised, in a famous speech at the Academy in 1842, the exaggerations of Hungarian nationalism (which he identified with Kossuth and his circle), adding that the nationalism of the ethnic minorities was merely self-defence in the face of that of the Magyars. These were opinions that could hardly have endeared Széchenyi to the bulk of contemporary liberals, whom he tried in vain to win in order to create a moderate liberal centre. The themes mentioned above dominated Széchenyi's polemic against Kossuth from *The People of the Orient* to the *Fragments of a Political Programme* (1847); and although he acknowledged Kossuth's credentials, and Kossuth repeatedly pointed out that his own policies were reconcilable with those of the count, whom he called 'the greatest of Hungarians', Széchenyi was moving, instead of the centre, into a political vacuum, while Kossuth became one of the most influential leaders of the opposition.

Széchenyi was the first to call attention to the problem of multiple nationalisms in the Carpathian Basin, which proved to be the great, ultimately insoluble dilemma of Hungarian liberalism. It was a liberalism based on the idea of the extension of noble rights to non-nobles, in the hope that in the course of a transition realised under the leadership of the nobility it might preserve its positions and political influence while acquiring capital as well as moral authority. This extension of rights would result in the replacement of the corporate *natio Hungarica* with a modern Hungarian nation of emancipated citizens. At the same time, language and ethnicity alone were not sufficient, in the view of the Hungarian liberals, to constitute a nation without a historical past and a historic state. Except for the Croats, they refused to acknowledge the claim of the ethnic minorities to nationhood. For the reformers whose roots were mainly in the Magyar-speaking nobility, it was only natural that the broader Hungarian nation, which would embrace Magyar as well as non-Magyar non-nobles invested with fully equal rights as individual citizens, ought to be defined in terms of Hungary's historic past and state, and its public sphere dominated by the Hungarian tongue. While explicitly all they wanted was the use of Magyar in public life, in economic and legal transactions and in higher education, they often supported the initiatives of individual counties or landlords to promote the assimilation of non-Magyars in their provinces through influencing the language of primary education, sermonising or in other ways. The obsession with Herder's prophecy, the chimera of Pan-Slavism (the idea of the brotherhood of Slav nations) and the belief that given the lack of a vigorous elite the ethnic minorities would easily abandon their identity, all played a part in these attitudes. Still, the organising principle behind the concept of the 'unitary Hungarian political nation' of Hungarian liberals was that the extension of individual rights would render collective rights superfluous even in the eyes of the ethnic minorities who, just as emancipated serfs would be reconciled with their former lords, would voluntarily assimilate into the Hungarian nation. On the whole, this was an illusion. Nevertheless, it constituted the positive side, the receptiveness of the Hungarian national movement which, especially in urban environments, proved highly successful, not only among the Jewish intellectuals or the German burghers of the capital, but among many Slovaks, Serbs, Greeks, Armenians and others as well. From the earliest times that charges of forced Magyarisation were levelled against the Hungarian political elite, there was always a fair amount of voluntary Magyarisation, too.

As regards the notion of the 'unitary political nation', nothing could have been farther from the views of the leading figures of the movements of national awakening among the ethnic minorities, who stressed the role of language and ethnicity in nationhood. Although it took some time for them to challenge the integrity of historic Hungary, and were content to defend themselves against Magyarisation and to demand linguistic and cultural rights, the mere fact that a language and its speakers define a territory (real or imaginary) implies the tendency to claim political sovereignty over that territory. In the light of the ethnic composition and the distribution of linguistic groups in the territory of Hungary until the end of the First World War, these conflicting perceptions could not but become a source of mounting tension. According to data collected by the famous statistician Elek Fényes, Hungary's population was nearly 13 million in 1842. Merely 38 per cent of this figure, 4.8 million, were Magyars; Romanians numbered 2.2 million (17 per cent), Slovaks 1.7 million (13 per cent), Germans 1.3 million (10 per cent), Serbs 1.2 million (9 per cent), Croats 900,000 (7 per cent), Ruthenes 450,000 (3.5 per cent), Jews 250,000 (2 per cent), and there were no less than ten further small groups as well. Only a part of each of them lived in contiguous blocks; the rest was inseparably intertwined with others in a patchwork-like structure, making 'national territory' impossible to demarcate with any precision. Against this background an otherwise quite innocent statement of enthusiasm for national language and identity, like that of the Romanian historian Kogalniceanu pronounced at the Academy of Iaşi in newly semi-independent Moldavia in 1843 – 'I regard as my fatherland all that territory where Romanian is spoken' –, might look somewhat ominous.

For all these reasons, the 1820s to the 1840s were an especially vibrant period for national cultures in the Carpathian Basin. Mihály Vörösmarty remained the dominant figure in Hungarian national romanticism with further historical epics and brooding, philosophical poetry that voiced the hopes and apprehensions of the reform movement; his *Appeal* (1837) became a second national anthem besides the *Hymnus* of Kölcsey. The popular manner, which lapsed into provincialism after Csokonai, was brought back into mainstream poetry by Sándor Petőfi and János Arany. Popular epics – *John the Brave* by the former and *Toldi* by the latter, extolling the virtues of the low-born hero –, fine lyricism and love songs, the cherishing of the beauties of the Hungarian landscape, and a poetry on the people and for the people in general made them the most popular Hungarian authors of all times among their contemporaries, especially Petőfi, who also became the quintessential revolutionary poet, owing to the powerful plebeian overtones and the explicit social criticism in many of his works. The historical novel also made its appearance in Hungarian literature with the works of the Transylvanian Baron Miklós Jósika and Zsigmond Kemény. The exploration of Hungarian folklore started with the collection of folk tales and the medieval literary heritage; and the work of eighteenth-century Jesuit historians was continued by the publication of official documents as well as narrative sources of Hungarian history. Historiography written in Hungarian for a wider public appeared early in the century, and while it largely remained focused on themes of national glory, in Mihály Horváth, who started to publish in the 1840s, Hungary had its first modern historian, with an interest in the history of social structures and conflicts.

Awakening to his Hungarian identity in the 1840s, Ferenc Liszt, the hitherto cosmopolitan hero of Parisian and Viennese concert halls and ballrooms, introduced *verbunkos* motifs, first popularised a generation earlier by János Bihari and his gypsy orchestra and superbly fitted to express romantic and national sentiments, into classical music. Hungarian national opera was born in the same period with *László Hunyadi* (1844) by Ferenc Erkel. Besides a great many touring companies, opera and drama was performed, from 1837 on, in the National Theatre of Pest, erected from donations. True, it was a rather poor edifice, especially compared to the great many splendid public buildings – county and town halls, court houses, assembly halls, or the National Museum in Pest (1847) – and palaces, town houses or manor houses erected in the classicist style according to the plans of accomplished architects like Mihály Pollack, József Hild and several others. Miklós Barabás emerged in this period as the first representative of Hungarian historical painting at a European standard.

Among the minorities, the standardisation of linguistic norms and the cultivation of the tongue and national literature were the main items on the agenda. It has been mentioned that the only ethnic group whose 'nationality' the Hungarian liberals were, on account of their being 'historic', ready to acknowledge, were the Croats. The Croat literary language emerged, after the abortive attempt artificially to amalgamate three dialects, under the banner of the political movement of Illyrianism (promoting South Slav unity) championed by Ljudevit Gaj, which selected the one richest in literary traditions and closest to Serbian (which had already been standardised in the grammar and vocabulary of Vuk Karadžić in the 1810s). In order to propagate the new norm, the *Hrvatske Narodne Novine* (Croat – later Illyrian – National Journal) was launched in 1835, and cultural associations were hosted at the Croat National House in the Zagreb palace of Janko Drašković. Whereas the Hungarian reformers acknowledged the claims to use Croat in the internal administration of Croatia, they emphatically refused the further claim (encouraged by Kollowrat, who was keen to use the Croats against 'adverse Magyarism') that the language of the Hungarian diet should be anything but Magyar, just so as to respect the sensibilities of Croat deputies.

The case of the Slovaks was somewhat different. The Lutheran intellectual elite continued for a while to insist on the predominantly Czech idiom promoted by Bernolák since the late eighteenth-century; it was in this that Ján Kollár wrote the apotheosis of Slavdom and the Bible of Pan-Slavism, the epic *Daughter of Slava* (1827). The worries caused by Pan-Slavism gave rise to anti-Slav agitation in *Pesti Hírlap*, which, in turn, prompted hundreds of Slovak clergymen to petition in Vienna. The result was the launching, in 1845, of the *Slovenskije Národnje Novini* (Slovak National Journal) by L'udovít Štúr, and various cultural and student associations. By promoting the popular middle-Slovak dialect and a Slovak national development independent of the tutelage of the Czech nobility on which Kollár and his associates had pitched their hopes, Štúr and his circle opened a new phase in the Slovak national movement.

The obsession with the Pan-Slav threat made the Hungarian liberals somewhat negligent of Romanian national aspirations, even though, as we have seen, they became quite pronounced by the end of the eighteenth century, and now manifested themselves through influential press media like the *Gazeta de Transilvaniae*, edited from 1838 by Gheorghe Bariţ. Besides the cultivation of the mother tongue (whose modernisation continued under the strong influence of French and Italian into the second half of the nineteenth century), the journal was increasingly devoted to protests against Magyarisation.

By the mid-1840s, the Hungarian liberal national movement seems to have emerged in full force, to some extent in competition with others in the historic Kingdom of Hungary. Opposition liberals were returned in fair numbers to the diet of 1843–1844, and yet the diet was largely a failure from their point of view. True, after heated debate, especially with the Croat deputies, the official status of the Hungarian language was passed, similarly to a law of symbolic rather than practical importance on the non-noble right to hold land. However, the more important bills on municipal reform and on customs regulations were rejected. The proceedings and the outcome of the diet gave occasion to a political realignment. In May 1844, the *Staatskonferenz* decided to entrust the government of the country to the new conservatives by appointing Count György Apponyi to direct the Hungarian and Baron Samu Jósika the Transylvanian Chancellery, and by replacing many of the *ispáns* of the counties and enhancing the role of their deputies, the 'administrators', who were in effect government officials often pursuing arbitrary policies. At the same time, Metternich took advantage of the differences within the liberal opposition. Frustrated with the meagre results of the diet, at the end of 1843 József Eötvös offered his support to the government in return for its commitment to reform.

Eötvös was probably the most politically erudite and intellectually sophisticated of the Hungarian reformers of the nineteenth century. The scion of an aristocratic family, he travelled widely in the West in his youth; having gone bankrupt in 1840, he became a professional politician and a freelance writer, and the leader of the 'centralist' group of liberal reformers. With the historian László Szalay, Ágoston Trefort, Antal Csengery and others, they idolised English whiggery, Benjamin Constant and Alexis de Tocqueville and advocated 'constitutional centralisation': rejecting 'municipalism', which in the Hungarian context meant the assertion of the retrograde potential of the conservative county nobility, they campaigned for a strong executive responsible to a representative parliament relieved from the instructions of their electors, and for a reorganised system of self-government to counterbalance the power of the central government. The criticism of the system of politics and public life based on the county, also manifest in Eötvös's social novel *The Village Notary* (1845), made the centralists seem a viable force for Metternich to work with, at least in pushing Kossuth aside. In mid-1844 the publisher of *Pesti Hírlap*, a confidant of the government, provoked the resignation of Kossuth, and his post was offered to Szalay. Kossuth, however, soon found a new outlet for his energy and a forum to assert his programme in the Protectionist Association; and although both the rather theoretical tone of the centralists and the difficulty of accepting their more forward-looking objectives for some of the spectrum mobilised by Kossuth cost many subscriptions to *Pesti Hírlap*, it remained the most important of all opposition papers.

However, the strong-handed management of the counties by the 'administrators' brought about a perceptible shift towards conservatism in the general political atmosphere, and despite several meetings and conferences in 1845 and 1846, it needed the challenges of 1846 to create the nation-wide political organisation of the opposition. First, the lessons from neighbouring Poland were again taken to heart. In February, an anti-Habsburg revolt of Galician nobles was put down largely on the backing of local Ukrainian peasants, who turned against their landlords and killed or surrendered to the authorities several hundred of them. Second, a national Conservative Party was founded in November, whose programme, formulated by Emil Dessewffy and Antal Szécsen, appropriated a number of reform proposals from the liberals, while avoiding the most crucial issues.

It was Kossuth again who took the initiative. In passionate articles published in the weekly journal of the Association of Industrialists, he urged a reluctant nobility to take action without delay. Pointing out the deficiencies of the conservative programme, and the possibility of the case of the Polish nobles being repeated in Hungary, he warned that reform was inevitable and would be realised 'with them [the nobles] and through them if they want it, without them and against them if necessary'. Széchenyi denounced Kossuth again as 'the ringleader of revolution' in his *Fragments of a Political Programme* published in early 1847. However, by that time an opposition committee chaired by Batthyány had prepared the national conference which, in March 1847, under the guidance of Kossuth, worked out the Opposition Manifesto, and approved it in June after final refinements by Deák.

This programme of the new Opposition Party, which advocated responsible and representative government and civil liberties in a defeudalised Hungary, also served as a basis for the instruction of Kossuth as deputy of the county of Pest at the diet: the rise of parties was in fact the prelude to elections into what turned out to be the last feudal diet in Hungary, opened in Pozsony on November 12, 1847. Retrospectively, the situation to a certain extent resembled that of France in 1788, when the last of the estates general convened, although at that time, unlike the Hungarian case, there was no blueprint for the transformation of the status quo as profound as ultimately effected. However, then as now, few would have predicted that a corporate assembly, while upholding the authority of the king and thereby observing political legitimacy, would bring about in a matter of weeks the dismantling of the feudal order of society and the economy, and erect a modern civil and bourgeois order in its place.

4. The Revolution and War of Independence of 1848–1849

At first it seemed that the court would be able to defy the liberal challenge. The royal propositions seemed to bear out the conservative allegation that the government was committed to reform: the proposals on *aviticitas*, on manumission compensation and prison reform divided the opposition, similarly to the activity of Széchenyi, who had himself elected into the Lower House to counter the influence of Kossuth, and advocated a comprehensive plan to expand railway communication (the first track of the projected Pozsony-Pest-Debrecen line was opened between Pest and Vác in 1846). Nor could the opposition extort the retreat of the government in the face of their attacks against the system of administrators. By February 1848, a stalemate developed at the diet, which was resolved under the impact of the wave of European revolutions.

The revolutions of 1848 were the outcome of a combination of factors, from the general tensions arising from the conservative international system created in 1815, through the economic and financial crisis prior to 1848, to the encouragement they mutually drew from each other in a chain-reaction of upheavals across the continent (even though these mutual effects were largely symbolic and superficial, and despite the roughly common ideology the outbreak, the goals, the events and the outcome of the revolutions reflected local circumstances). The Hungarian revolution fitted smoothly into this chain-reaction, preceded as it was by those in Palermo, Paris, central Italy, Piedmont and Vienna, and followed by those in Berlin, Milan, Venice, Prague and Bucharest. Though the first outbreak came in the Kingdom of Naples on January 12 and transformed it into a constitutional monarchy, the real catalyst were the events of February 22–25 in Paris, to which political innovators 'cast their eyes', in the words of Batsányi from 1789, ever since that time. The news of the overthrow of the rule of the 'bourgeois king' Louis-Philippe by a combination of *nouveaux riches* who wanted political influence, radicals who wanted to extend suffrage, and socialists who wanted social equality – goals obviously at variance with those of Central European liberals at the time – reached Pozsony on March 1 and caused great excitement, of which Kossuth immediately took advantage. In a fiery speech on March 3 he called his fellow deputies to 'elevate their policies to the level of the moment' and urged the immediate realisation of the full reform programme of the opposition. An address to the crown summarising the demands was drawn, while the circulation of the German translation of Kossuth's speech contributed to the atmosphere in which revolution broke out in Vienna, sweeping away Metternich and extorting the promise of a constitution and civil liberties, on March 13. Under the impact of the news of the Viennese revolution, Palatine Archduke Stephen swiftly got the Upper House to approve of Kossuth's address, and on March 15 a delegation of the diet set off to present the document to the ruler in the Habsburg capital, where the people received them with great enthusiasm.

On the same day, revolution broke out in Pest. Kossuth in fact had requested after 3 March the opposition circles of Hungary's effective capital to support his struggle at the diet with petitioning. The 'Twelve Points', drafted by József Irinyi, went even beyond Kossuth's address by also demanding (as the first item) freedom of the press and full equality before the law. Irinyi, the inventor of the safety match, was one of a group of radical intellectuals that became known as 'the young men of March' and included, besides Petőfi, the future great novelist Mór Jókai, the poet János Vajda, and a few dozen other members of a politically articulate young intelligentsia. Their regular meetings at Café Pilvax were also attended by students – there were about a thousand of them in Pest at the time –, burghers and even lower class people. They were now planning a mass meeting on March 19 to get further support for the petition. However, electrified by the news of the revolution in Vienna, which reached them on March 14, they decided to take immediate action. On the following morning, they mobilised the students, and marched first to Kossuth's one-time publisher to get the 'Twelve Points' and Petőfi's freshly written, spirited poem *National Song* printed without soliciting the permission of the censor, and then, already at the head of a crowd of twenty-thousand, to the city halls of Pest and Buda, and finally to the Gubernium, which all granted their consent to the 'Twelve Points'. The general enthusiasm was crowned by the release of Hungary's only political prisoner, the radical utopian writer Mihály Táncsics, and the staging of Katona's hitherto prohibited drama *Ban Bánk* at the National Theatre.

But even though the revolutionary events were not confined to Pest-Buda, and mass meetings at Győr, Székesfehérvár, Debrecen, Pécs, Temesvár and other centres in the provinces followed, revolutionary radicals never broke loose from their role of auxiliaries. Pest was not Paris: Kossuth welcomed its 'patriotic sentiments', but while he never missed an opportunity to refer to them in warnings addressed to reluctant Hungarian nobles or Vienna, he also made it quite clear that he would not suffer the capital to 'arrogate' the role of the 'master' of the country of which it was merely a part. The diet, dominated by Kossuth, remained the main vehicle of the transformation, especially after the news of the Pest revolution reached Vienna. The address of the diet was granted, and on March 18 the *Staatskonferenz* appointed Count Lajos Batthyány as Prime Minister of Hungary with the task of forming a cabinet. On the same day, revolution in Milan broke out, involving Austria in a war to keep its Italian provinces and, together with the complications at home, nearly completely paralysing it *vis-à-vis* the Hungarians. The only effective step the court was still able to make to counteract Hungarian pressure, one that proved to be of seminal importance a few months later, was the appointment of Josip Jelačić, a loyal officer of the Habsburg army and an ardent Croat patriot, as Ban of Croatia.

Elsewhere in Europe in 1848 it would have been the task of hastily summoned constituent or national assemblies to accomplish the goals of the revolution, but by the time they convened, the political climate had usually changed to the advantage of counter-revolution. By contrast, as the revolution broke out in Hungary, the last feudal diet was in session, and while it ostensibly merely reaffirmed the ancient liberties of the nation, in fact it codified, in the course of three weeks, the programme worked out by a generation of reformers in the struggles of the preceding two decades. The fact that fundamental rules of the *dietalis tractatus*, the procedural requirements of the old constitution, were violated in the process, makes the appellation 'lawful revolution', frequently used to describe the event ever sinse, somewhat apologetic, rather than accurate in the strict sence. Be it as it may, the Hungarian revolution not only triumphed, but its achievement also became consolidated by law in the spring of 1848.

The thirty-one April Laws, that is, a constitution modelled in several particulars after the one passed in Belgium in 1831, were sanctioned by Ferdinand V on April 11, 1848. Hungary became a hereditary constitutional monarchy while it preserved the unity of the crown and the link with the Habsburg Monarchy through the person of the king. The monarch retained the right to make war and peace (though the laws did not forbid Hungary to maintain her own foreign relations or to 'influence' those of the empire through a 'minister around the person of the king'), and of major appointments. The constitutional link between Hungary and Austria was further thinned by making the palatine a deputy of the king with full powers in the absence of the latter. But the decisions of neither of them were considered valid unless signed by one of the ministers in a government responsible to an annually convened legislature, which consisted of an upper house (of the titled nobility and high dignitaries), and a lower house elected every three years on the basis of a fairly liberal suffrage. The property qualifications were broad enough to extend the vote from a former 1,6 per cent to seven or even nine per cent of the population (more generous than, for instance, the English Reform Act of 1832 or the Prussian regulations of 1848). The reunion of Hungary and Transylvania was proclaimed. An independent Hungarian administration was to be created. The few restrictions on the freedom of the press angered Pest radicals, but did not prevent lively debate and vigorous criticism of the government in the flourishing periodical literature. Citizens became equal before independent law courts, and the security of the person and property under the law was guaranteed. The equality of received Christian denominations was declared. The full emancipation of Jews was withheld mainly for prudential reasons, lest it should provoke anti-Semitic violence; in fact, the revolutionary government treated the Jewish population most fairly, carning their unbending loyalty. Last but not least, the April Laws abolished tax privileges, *aviticitas* and all other restrictions on the free flow of land, commodities and labour; they suppressed the jurisdiction of the landlord over the peasant, liberated all serfs from personal bondage and manorial obligations; and while it was clear that many of the 900,000 cotters and domestic servants would remain propertiless agrarian labourers, the way was opened for over 600,000 urbarial peasants to become owners of the plots they had formerly held from the landlords, who received the promise of compensation by the state at an unspecified time in the future.

The Batthyány government, which moved to Pest on April 14, was a coalition. The 'minister around the person of the king' was Prince Pál Esterházy, an experienced conservative diplomat. Lázár Mészáros, a hussar general appointed as Minister of War, was politically unaffiliated, as was Széchenyi, who temporarily overcame his pessimism and acknowledged that the times justified Kossuth, and became Minister of Communication and Public Works. The moderate liberals were represented by Deák (Justice) and Gábor Klauzál (Agriculture and Industry), the left of the former opposition by Kossuth (Finance) and Bertalan Szemere (Interior), and the 'centralists' by Eötvös (Education and Ecclesiastical Affairs). The epithet of William Pitt's British administration in the early 1800s, 'the ministry of all talents', would befit Hungary's first modern government as well. Their broad vision, commitment, political expertise, the public trust and the relative lack of social tension in Hungary were all in their favour. Together with the circumstances of the transition, they helped them to remain in office longer than any of the revolutionary governments created in Europe in 1848.

However, there were two problems that proved to be intractable, and threw Hungary into a war against Austria, which swept the Batthyány ministry away in the autumn. One of them was the obscurity of the April Laws concerning foreign affairs and finances, and their silence about the military. It was not clear how revenues, or the state debt would be distributed (Hungarians flatly denied having to do anything with the latter), or even whether Hungary had the right to issue money. The unspecified nature of the competence of the 'minister around the person of the king' made the uncomfortable prospect of Hungary pursuing a different foreign policy from Austria quite conceivable; and the insufficient demarcation of authorities and responsibilities between the Austrian and Hungarian ministers of war, the vagueness of how troops were to be recruited and deployed caused hair-raising, even tragic complications.

Especially this last difficulty was further aggravated in light of a second fundamental problem: Hungary's relations with Croatia-Slavonia and the national minorities. The former, while subordinated to Hungary, was striving for the same status Hungary had just acquired within the Habsburg Monarchy. The national movement among some of the latter was passing from the phase of cultivating language and culture to the aspiration to secure collective rights, and drew encouragement and support from the rise, in 1829, of a practically independent Serbia and semi-independent Romanian principalities across the southern borders of Hungary within the Ottoman Empire. However, the Hungarian liberal constitution was silent about such rights; on the contrary, it established Magyar as the language of legislation and administration in the country, and denied any corporate rights, which were considered harmful vestiges of the feudal past.

Finding that only a handful of regular Habsburg troops were stationing within the country, only some of whom had been recruited in Hungary, the Batthyány government set to converting the best of the National Guards, the civilian militia originally set up to protect life and property, into an effective national defence force. The ten battalions of the 'defenders of the fatherland' (*honvéd*) raised in May, along with the regulars that remained loyal to the Hungarian government, were to be the core of the national army that was to fight in the war of independence. For the time being, they were needed elsewhere. A Croat national committee set up in Zagreb at the end of March demanded an independent responsible government, and Jelačić, encouraged by the Austrian Minister of War Latour (who was quite an anomaly in the liberal Pillersdorf cabinet), immediately started to organise an army. Though in early June Batthyány obtained at court the dismissal of the Ban of Croatia, the latter disobeyed. Soon enough, the Serbs were in turmoil as well: their congress, convened by their religious leader Metropolitan Josif Rajačić, declared the political autonomy of the Serbian Voevodeship within the Habsburg Monarchy on May 13. In the middle of June, armed fighting broke out in the south. Besides local Serbian rebels and freebooters from neighbouring Serbia, the imperial-royal border guards lined up on one side, oddly enough, against imperial-royal regulars and some *honvéd* sent by the Hungarian government under the same flag. The Slovak congress of May 10 also demanded a separate Slovak national assembly and territorial self-government, and at the meeting of the Romanians on May 15–17 a national committee, presided over by the Orthodox Bishop Andrei Şaguna, was created, which also voiced claims of autonomy.

It was against this background that elections were held in June and the Hungarian parliament convened on 5 July. Nearly one-quarter of the 415 members had been deputies in the last diet, and three-quarters of them were noblemen: the 'people' seemed to acknowledge the political expertise and the former services of the liberal nobility. Besides a handful of conservatives and about forty radicals, the overwhelming majority supported the government. The most urgent issue was to consolidate the army and to secure the necessary finances. Kossuth had been quite successful in creating something out of nothing in the preceding months, but was still compelled to begin issuing banknotes, thereby provoking Austrian resentment. Now, on July 11, he surveyed the international and domestic situation in a great speech, and concluded that Hungary was largely left to her own devices in the face of the upheaval, behind which he suspected the hand of counterrevolution. Roused by his address, the deputies voted over 40 million florins of credit and 200,000 recruits (40,000 of them immediately) by acclamation. At the same time, lest relations with the court and the dynasty further deteriorated, the parliament also voted the subsidy and recruitment requested by the ruler in the interest of concluding the war in northern Italy, but strictly on condition that the rights and liberties of the Italian people were fully guaranteed.

Kossuth's assessment of the situation was fundamentally correct. The Habsburg court took pleasure in the Hungarian government's embarrassment with regard to the national minorities, even though only Jelačić received direct encouragement from it. Britain stood aloof in splendid isolation, and France was occupied with internal problems, whereas Russia was a close and ever-present menace. It is true that the Hungarian delegates sent in May to the Frankfurt Parliament, whose task was to prepare the unification of Germany, were received with enthusiasm and could reasonably hope for a treaty of mutual assistance, but this prospect in July still seemed vague (and as the work of the assembly came to a stalemate by the autumn, nothing came out of it). Finally, Marshal Radetzky's triumph over the Piedmontese army in the Battle of Custozza on July 25 meant the consolidation of Austria's hold over northern Italy and the positions of conservatism in Vienna. The court returned to the capital after a temporary sojourn in Innsbruck, where it had fled from a second revolution in Vienna in May.

In such circumstances, the declaration of the Batthyány ministry on August 3 that in case of a war between Austria and the Frankfurt assembly it would not assist the ruler, was somewhat impolitic, besides being a flaw to the claims of legality and unbending loyalty. But even without it, Austria would have persevered, and Batthyány and Deák travelled to Vienna at the end of August in vain to clear differences. Instead, the Austrian Wessenberg government issued a memorandum on August 31, arguing that the April Laws were contrary to the Pragmatic Sanction in setting up separate Hungarian ministries of war and finance, and therefore declared them null and void. On Septembe r 4, Jelačić was restored to his office, and a week later he crossed the Hungarian border at the head of a fifty thousand strong army (largely of poorly equipped insurgents).

The Batthyány ministry stepped down on September 11. Széchenyi, under the impact of the Wessenberg ultimatum, suffered a nervous breakdown and had already been taken to a mental asylum near Vienna; Deák also became passive, and Eötvös was soon to emigrate to Munich. Though the Palatine appointed Batthyány to lead the administration as acting premier, which he did for another three weeks, on September 16, the parliament set up a six-member National Defence Committee, obviously fashioned after the famous French Committee of Public Safety of 1793 to cope with the emergency of war. To further complicate matters, the court appointed – without ministerial signature, that is, according to Hungarian interpretation, unconstitutionally – Count Ferenc Lamberg as Commander-in-Chief of Hungary in order to avoid Jelačić becoming the sole master of the situation. Prompted by Kossuth, who had just returned from a recruiting tour on the Great Plain, the parliament denounced Lamberg as a traitor; on September 28, as he was seeking to meet Batthyány, he was lynched by the Pest mob. It was after such antecedents that the advancing troops of Jelačić were halted and defeated in a skirmish of historic significance by the forces of General János Móga near Pákozd, forty kilometres south-west of Buda, on September 29.

The events between the Wessenberg memorandum and the Battle of Pákozd constitute the 'September turn', which transformed the Hungarian revolution into a war of self-defence and, ultimately, of independence, fought in order to save the achievement of the peaceful legislative process of the spring of 1848. The alternative would have been to sacrifice those achievements by submitting to the counter-revolution that started formally with the royal decrees of October 3, dissolving the Hungarian parliament and subjecting Hungary to military rule under Jelačić, now appointed royal commissar. The country was considered to be in a state of rebellion, and those who continued to resist as guilty of high treason. (According to this logic, Batthyány, who was forced to resign a day earlier and was executed after the suppression of the war of independence, counted as a victim of common murder!) The parliament, considering the decrees as unlawful, replied by ignoring them and by investing the National Defence Committee, headed by Kossuth, with executive power over the country on October 8.

The 'chain-reaction' of early March now seemed to repeat itself. The old supporter of Jelačić, Austrian Minister of War Latour, intended to dispatch Austrian troops to assist the Ban, whom the Hungarian forces chased as far as the Austrian border, but, understandably enough, the ex-Habsburg officers scrupled to pursue him beyond. The Viennese radicals, who idolised the Hungarian revolutionaries, now arose in a third revolution, which triumphed on October 6; Latour finished on the lamppost. The court left the capital again, this time for Olmütz (Olomouc) in Moravia, where, however, severe steps were taken. General Prince Windisch-Grätz, who had already proved his ability by suppressing the Prague revolt in mid-June, was appointed to the supreme command of all Habsburg armies, and in a week he blockaded Vienna with eighty thousand troops. This was a bite too large to swallow for the Hungarians, who finally (under the impact of Kossuth's personal visit to the camp) did march on to Austrian soil, but were easily put to flight in the Battle of Schwechat on October 30.

On the following day, the revolution in Vienna was put down; yet another day later the Hungarian high command resigned, and Kossuth appointed a thirty-year-old colonel, Artúr Görgey, to lead the army and to prepare it for the war that was to ensue between Hungary and Austria. It was an excellent decision, and yet one that was controversial nearly in the moment it was made, and has remained so until present times. Görgey's uncommon genius as a strategist and his authority among the soldiers was instrumental in saving a beaten army from being routed and reorganising it so as to defy one of the Great Powers of the age. At the same time, he resisted Kossuth's politically motivated instructions whenever his strong convictions (and detestation of things civilian) suggested that these were contrary to military reason, to the point of meddling with politics himself. His personality being diametrically opposed to that of Kossuth, the two men were bound to each other by an amalgam of admiration and hatred, and the animosity that evolved between them did not advance the cause they both pledged themselves to.

For the time being, the division of labour between them achieved spectacular results, even though Kossuth, who thought that any small victory extorted would greatly enhance the morale of the troops as well as civilians throughout the country, occasionally grew impatient with Görgey, who wanted to concentrate on keeping the army intact and teaching it discipline and the elements of warfare before engaging the enemy again. This, however, he did with great efficiency, while the indefatigable Kossuth, the National Defence Committee, the Ministry of War and the government commissioners sent out to the provinces organised recruitment and logistical support, created a war industry and erected military hospitals. By the spring of 1849, Hungary had a 170,000 strong army, les than one-third of whom were former regulars, the rest consisted of *honvéd* battalions, including sizeable units from the national minorities and many Polish émigré freedom fighters. It was one of the latter, General József Bem, who exercised his talents to prevent the Habsburg General Anton Puchner from invading Hungary from Transylvania, which might have put an end to the Hungarian war of independence before the end of 1848.

Puchner's offensive took place in the lull of fighting within Hungary, while the Austrian government was reorganising and preparing to strike back. First, on November 21, Windisch-Grätz arranged for his brother-in-law, Prince Felix Schwarzenberg, to form a new cabinet with a pro-gramme of centralism and absolutism extending to the whole of the empire, including Hungary. The second step was to remove the epilep-tic Ferdinand V, who had put these objectives to hazard by granting constitutions to Austria and Hungary. On December 2 he was replaced by his eighteen-year-old nephew Francis Joseph, under the fiction that he was not bound by the measures taken by his predecessor. Both this fiction and the succession of Francis Joseph was rejected by the Hun-garian parliament as violating the order of succession, which did not prevent Windisch-Grätz from launching his campaign 'to restore law and order' in Hungary on December 13. On December 30, a few days after General Bem had liberated Kolozsvár in Transylvania, a major Hungarian force was badly beaten just outside Pest-Buda, and on Janu-ary 1, 1849, the revolutionary government, along with the treasury, the mint, the arsenal and even the Holy Crown, evacuated the capital. Most offices set up their headquarters in Debrecen, while a parliamentary delegation led by Batthyány and Deák sent to negotiate the terms of peace with the Habsburg commander-in-chief learnt that he would only accept unconditional surrender. He was confident enough not to chase the enemy (although he did take Batthyány under arrest), but rather set to organising a counter-revolutionary government and reported to Ol-mütz that the rebellion had been suppressed.

Despite appearances, this was far from being the case. Though decimated by the number of those who defected to the Austrians or withdrew into a position of wait and see, the government offices and the parliament soon resumed normal functioning, and the war industry transplanted to the east of the country was working, too. Nor did par-liament lose control over the executive: although the National Defence Committee governed by decree, the legislature decided to sit until the struggle came to a conclusion, and the committee was frequently the object of severe criticism at its sessions as well as in the press. At any rate, the regime was far from being a revolutionary dictatorship, whose introduction in fact a radical minority led by László Madarász urged with increasing vigour. At the other end of the political spectrum was the so-called Peace Party, whom dynastic loyalty still led to seek unspecified ways of reconciliation with Vienna. Kossuth, while not completely un-assailable, firmly retained the initiative and his dominant position by balancing between the two extremes and relying on a numerous centre. However, all were aware that in the given circumstances decisive issues depended on the army, which was also the main concern of Kossuth.

As the civil authorities left Pest in early January, covered by a part of the army, Görgey sought to divert the attention of Windisch-Grätz by leading the other troops towards the north. His 'winter campaign', which involved little actual fight, was an act of outstanding strategic brilliance: with Habsburg forces on his heels and facing ones penetrating from Galicia, Görgey managed to save his army from annihilation for a second time, and in early February joined forces with the troops newly raised in the east. Simultaneously, Bem expelled the Habsburg forces and some Russian troops that arrived to assist them for a second time from Transylvania. At the beginning of his retreat, however, largely to prevent his officers suspicious of the radicalisation of the Hungarian leadership from deserting (but also expressing his own sentiments), Görgey issued a manifesto pledging the loyalty of the army to the April Laws and the king, which was indirectly to challenge the National Defence Committee.

Kossuth expressed his distrust by replacing Görgey with the Polish Count Henrik Dembiński as commander-in-chief. Soon enough it turned out to be a mistake. Dembiński's choleric temper failed to earn him popularity among the officers, and his incompetence in the battlefield helped Windisch-Grätz to victory in the Battle of Kápolna on February 26 and 27. Again, he triumphantly reported that the 'rebellious hordes had been smashed'. The court responded by dismissing the imperial parliament sitting at Kremsier (Kroměříž) and 'granting a constitution to His Majesty's peoples' on March 4. In this 'octroyed' constitution, which remained on paper, a centralised empire was envisaged, with a relatively liberal (though far from general) male franchise, a fair amount of civil rights and municipal self-government, but with no ministerial responsibility, and very narrow autonomy in provinces which, as regards Hungary, would have been completely rearranged. The project was unacceptable not only to the Hungarians, but also to the national minorities, who were not deceived by the pompous assertion of the equality of 'races' (*Volksstämme*).

Windisch-Grätz miscalculated things for a second time. The officer corps blamed Dembiński to a man for the defeat and clamoured for bringing Görgey back; Kossuth, surmising mutiny, arrived at the camp initially to punish the ringleaders, but then his reason prevailed. Dembiński was first replaced by Antal Vetter, an experienced strategist, and when he stepped down a few weeks later, with Görgey again. Perhaps the most glorious chapter in Hungarian military history opened. While Bem proceeded with capturing the Banate of Temes, and the Serbians were finally put down as well, the main army won a series of battles between the Tisza and the Danube in the early days of April. The offensive went on after Windisch-Grätz was punished for his failures by being replaced with General Ludwig Welden; further victories north of the Danube and the capture of Vác and Komárom followed, while Pest was also taken and Buda blockaded. Görgey did not pursue the imperial forces, which may have been an error, but the subsequent speculation that even Vienna might have been conquered, seems unfounded: the Habsburg army, on the retreat towards its own hinterland, was twice as strong as Görgey's. Instead, he returned to besiege Buda.

At the height of the successes of the spring campaign, Kossuth decided to carry out a plan which he had started to conceive as in the beginning of 1849 it became obvious that there was absolutely no hope of a reconciliation with the court, and which took the shape of a response to the Kremsier constitution that denied any sort of independence to Hungary. It was the deposition of the House of Habsburg and the declaration of Hungary's independence. While recognising that public opinion was in favour of such a measure, he hoped to take the wind out of the sails of the radicals and to prevent the increasingly popular army leaders from taking the initiative politically, while he also wanted to narrow the scope of action of the Peace Party. Finally, he expected that a Declaration of Independence would improve the chances of Hungary's international recognition. It was proclaimed, amidst great enthusiasm, in the Calvinist Great Church of Debrecen on April 14, 1849. The Habsburg dynasty was declared guilty of repeated breaches of the constitution and of making war against the nation, reasons found good enough to dethrone it. Kossuth became Governor-President of the state, whose form remained unspecified, and a new cabinet led by Bertalan Szemere was appointed.

The Declaration of Independence failed to bear the fruits Kossuth expected to reap from it. The constituent assembly he also wanted to convene in order to prepare the transition to a more democratic regime never materialised, and other domestic policy goals also remained unachieved. Nor did Kossuth's hope for international recognition come true. Curiously enough, it was the émigré Slavs, with whom the Hungarian envoy in Paris László Teleki came into contact through the vast network of informal diplomacy operated by the Polish Prince Adam Czartoryski from Hotel Lambert, who showed the most pronounced marks of solidarity. But the Frankfurt Assembly, on which high Hungarian hopes had been pitched, was no longer in session, and Prussia, Austria's main rival in the German-speaking world, did not yet want to challenge it. Of the two western powers, France was embroiled in domestic affairs, while the English foreign minister Palmerston himself told to the envoy of the Hungarian parliament that 'he did not know of Hungary except as a part of the Habsburg Empire', whose existence was a cornerstone of British balance of power policy. No-one even protested when Tsar Nicholas I proclaimed Russia's intervention in support of Austria in the Hungarian war of independence. 'Finish it as soon as possible', Palmerston reputedly told the Russian ambassador in London.

Russian aid was promised on May 9, in response to Francis Joseph's appeal to the Tsar a week earlier. The news started to reach Hungary before the recapture of Buda on May 21 and the re-entry of the revolutionary government in the capital could be celebrated. Defeat was now inevitable, even though few realised this in all seriousness, and spirits were generally high. After the final victory of Radetzky on the Italian front in March, the Habsburg army could be reinforced and reorganised. Under the new Commander-in-Chief General Julius Haynau, who had earned not only the nickname 'the hyena of Brescia' but also a reputation for military talent in the course of re-establishing Habsburg hegemony over northern Italy, it alone mustered a larger force than the _honvéd_ army, and from the middle of June it was supplemented with the 200,000 Russian troops of Marshal Prince Ivan Paskievich.

The operational plans were simple enough: Habsburg forces from the west, and Russians from the north and the east, would pocket the Hungarians and break their resistance. The counter-plan of concentrating most of the _honvéd_ army along the Danube and engaging the enemy one by one had a semblance of feasibility only until the real magnitude of the interventionist force became known. As the imminent disaster foreshadowed itself, the residual unanimity within the political and military leadership started to evaporate, and more and more of a disheartened population evaded conscription and submitted to a victorious enemy. Görgey was compelled to retreat before Haynau, who started the campaign in late June by inflicting a series of defeats on the Hungarian army west of the capital; it was meagre consolation that Görgey's fine manoeuvring again preserved the bulk of his forces even after the Russians arrived. He moved to the south, where, according to the modified Hungarian plans, he was supposed to unite his forces with those of Dembiński and Bem. Bem, however, arrived practically without troops from Transylvania, where most of them were annihilated or dispersed by the Russians; and the poor organisation of logistical support by Dembiński led to the devastating defeat of the southern army under his command in the Battle of Temesvár on August 9.

In early July, the revolutionary government had also moved to the south, first to Szeged and finally to Arad. Kossuth and his associates continued to display admirable determination, and initiated policies that remained a progressive, though continuously overmatched alternative in mainstream Hungarian politics for many decades. The idea of a reconciliation with the national minorities was not only suggested by Teleki, whom his contacts with the Czartoryski circle in Paris convinced that Hungarian independence would raise a number of issues in the region whose solution depended on the alleviation of ethnic tension. The experience of the worst instances of ethnic strife in the region, in the course of which Hungarians, Serbians and Romanians, instigated by their local leaders, massacred each other by the thousands in the villages of the south, also gave rise to ministerial drafts and armistice negotiations. Romanians started to realise that Russia was as great a menace to their integrity as the Hungarians, and the Slavs that while Austria keenly used them to suppress Hungarian claims, it was far less willing to honour theirs. Kossuth was only too happy to accept the offer of Nicolae Bălçescu, a leader of the Wallachian revolution suppressed in 1848, to mediate between the Hungarian government and the Romanians of Transylvania. The result was the 'Project of Pacification' of July 14, which gave all rights but territorial autonomy to the Romanian citizens of Hungary, and the same principles were extended to the other national minorities in a law voted by the parliament on July 28. On the same day, a law on the emancipation of Jews was passed, too. All this was not only a breakthrough in Hungarian political thinking, but also highly progressive in European perspective, and it is too simple, as has been often the case, to dismiss it as a desperate last attempt of a group of already fallen politicians.

To be sure, these measures came too late to have any influence on the course of events. After the disaster of Temesvár, Hungarian fighting force was reduced to Görgey's 30,000 exhausted soldiers whose ammunition consisted of one and a half bullets per shotgun. At a dramatic meeting on August 10–11, the members of the government resigned, bestowing with their last signature dictatorial powers on Görgey. As Kossuth, in the company of some troops and civilians, was heading towards the Ottoman border, Görgey did the inevitable. On August 13, he surrendered unconditionally at Világos – to the Russians instead of Haynau, still hoping that it might make a difference. The gesture, however, merely served to increase the sense of humiliation the Austrians felt because of earlier military setbacks and the need to rely on external help. Not that it was the cause of the astonishingly severe retaliation that followed. The fact of surrender was the only similarity between Nagymajtény in 1711 and Világos in 1849. Common sense and reason of state then prevailed at court and facilitated a compromise with the Hungarians, which had counted as a distinct possibility throughout Rákóczi's war of independence. On the contrary, there was not a single moment during the independence fight of 1848–1849 when Francis Joseph, Schwarzenberg or Haynau contemplated a compromise. Haynau said he wanted to deter Hungarians from revolutions for a hundred years, and set to organising a revenge whose brutality shocked contemporaries and subsequent generations across Europe.

CHAPTER VI

THE ADVENT OF MODERNITY AND THE PERSISTENCE OF THE OLD REGIME (1849–1918)

The history of the European continent in the 'long' nineteenth century followed a peculiar rhythm of international war and peace, domestic turmoil and tranquillity, and of the reciprocal relationship between these and economic and cultural developments. A quarter of a century's upheaval caused by the French Revolution, Napoleon, and the wars against them, was brought to a conclusion by the creation of the 'Congress system', a conservative international order designed to offset challenges to the status quo as defined by the peacemakers of 1814–1815 in Vienna. Notwithstanding the fact that the 'concert of Europe' (that is, of the great powers) started to show signs of strain quite soon, the following decades were marked by an absence of wars, the 'system' only being threatened by rather isolated domestic attempts of Spanish liberals and Italian *carbonari*, Greek and Polish freedom fighters, German student demonstrators and Hungarian reformers. However, in 1848 these movements coalesced into a revolutionary tide, and even though its results were at best ambivalent, and saw the last effective manifestation of the 1815 'concert' in the Russian assistance to Austria in suppressing the Hungarian revolution, it also showed that the Viennese settlement was no longer sustainable.

The international order established on the principles of legitimism and aristocratism was replaced by a network of regimes that did not necessarily contradict these principles, but represented new types of authoritarianism. The Second Empire of Napoleon III has often been described as the first of modern dictatorships; but similarly to France, authority in the Prussian polity constructed under Otto von Bismarck was also based on a novel combination of social exclusiveness, petty bourgeois sentiment and mass appeal; and even the guidelines of Schwarzenberg, along which the centralisation of Austria was carried out in the 1850s, were considerably different from those of earlier conservatives. At the same time, while determined to maintain domestic political stability, these regimes came into intense conflict with each other. The decades of domestic unrest and international peace before 1848 were followed by a series of wars which redrew the map of Europe between the 1850s and the 1870s, resulting in the emergence of a united

Italy and Germany and independent nation-states in the Balkans. In these wars, especially the Franco-Prussian war of 1870, the fighting parties already took advantage, in varying degrees, of the process of mechanisation that became known as the 'industrial revolution' in the first half of the nineteenth century. In turn, the long period of international peace which followed and lasted, apart from the Balkans, over four decades, was conducive to the further growth of a material civilisation based on modern industries and large scale consumerism over vast areas of the continent.

While these were developments from which relative benefits were reaped by all or most, labels reflecting tranquillity and prosperity, like the 'Victorian Age', '*la belle epoque*' and the 'happy times of peace' express in the first place the sentiments of a middle class taking satisfaction in the greater sophistication and accessibility of comfort, information and pleasures which were, to a considerable extent, of its own making. Nevertheless, the uneasiness of the European mind with the achievements of modernity found its most striking expression during the same period. The appearance of relativity in physics, the 'survival or the fittest' in biology, the discovery of the subconscious in psychology and the decadent overtones of the culture of modernism in general amounted to the dissolution of Enlightenment confidence based on the faith in reason and in harmony within both man and the universe, and between them. Harmony was certainly missing from the international scene marked, in the absence of a 'system' like the one in post–1815 Europe, by coalitions of powers competing for hegemony over markets and strategically important, though underdeveloped areas in Europe and, amidst the general global hegemony of the old continent, for possessions in the colonial world. After the sinuous movement of lengthy alternating periods of war and peace, Europe's long nineteenth century culminated in an armed conflict that surpassed all earlier ones in breadth and depth.

Hungary was affected by, and itself affected, these developments to a considerable extent, and 1848–1849 naturally occupies a pivotal place in these processes. In those two years Hungary held out longest in what was widely considered a fight for liberty and progress in defiance of a vicious alliance of Europe's worst autocratic powers, which earned greater interest in and acclaim for it in international public opinion than ever before or (with the possible exception of 1956) since. Nor did the 'April Laws' disappear without a trace: whereas the country's *de facto* sovereignty, modern parliamentary government and civil liberties were revoked, the social and economic reforms, including the emancipation of the serfs, were retained even amidst the abominable repression that followed. The bases of economic modernisation were expanded in the years of neo-absolutism after 1849, bringing about the general prosperity which reconfirmed Hungary's proximity to the West in civilisational terms after the political compromise between it and Austria in 1867. Indeed, the susceptibility of Hungarian society in this latter period to become imbued by the system of values developed in nineteenth-century Europe under the impact of industrialisation and urbanisation, is especially striking in the light of the long survival of attitudes and relations of subordination from the still recent feudal past.

It must be added that although Austria needed the failures on the international scene during the 1850s and 1860s to bow to necessity and make the *Ausgleich* of 1867 (which, in conformity with tradition, I shall render by the term Compromise, though a more value-free one, such as 'Settlement', might be more appropriate), it might not have taken the shape it did without the tribulations of 1848–1849. In 1867, Hungary became a constitutional monarchy (though certainly one not without anachronisms) and an equal partner of Austria within the Habsburg Monarchy, which, despite its recent setbacks, still reckoned as one of the great powers of the day on account of its strategic location. Most of the Hungarian political class as well as public opinion was thus lulled into a confidence concerning the resurrection of Hungary's real or imaginary 'greatness' in the glorious past. All of this made them conveniently forget about the fact that Francis Joseph's Hungary differed from that of Matthias I in a respect that became crucial in their age: its ethnic composition; and that 1848 showed not only the obsolete nature of controlling liberal aspirations by the police methods of the Habsburgs and the Romanovs, but also the mutual incompatibility of competing national movements. The problem that ultimately proved insoluble may well have been insoluble indeed: even the maximum of concessions that could reasonably be expected from the Hungarians (which was never offered until it was too late) would have been less than satisfactory for the national minorities, whose claims in the long run tended to challenge the integrity of the historic Hungarian state. It remains nonetheless true that whereas the Compromise of 1867, made by the ruler and political elites of two strongest national groups of the Habsburg Monarchy at the expense of the others, was a realistic one at that time, the system based upon it largely collapsed in the wake of the First World War because of the reasons foretold by most of its contemporary critics: the impossibility of finding, in the framework of dualism, a satisfactory solution to all constitutional issues, and the centrifugal forces unleashed by the nationality question.

1. Neo-absolutism and the Compromise

In the autumn and winter of 1849, Hungary was governed by a military dictatorship whose sole objective was, despite the recommendation of a 'well interpreted amnesty' by the Tsar to the Emperor, revenge and intimidation. Upon the firm insistence of the Russians, Görgey was saved from the firing squad and interned to Klagenfurt, from whence in 1867 he could return to Hungary for the last forty-odd years of a long and tormented life. Most other political and military leaders who remained in the country received harsh sentences. On October 6, 1849, Batthyány in Pest and thirteen generals of the war of independence (Germans, Austrians, Serbs, Croats as well as Hungarians by nationality) in Arad, were executed. There were altogether at least a hundred executions (a figure certainly augmented by the number of those court-martialled without record on official documents) and over 1,500 long term imprisonments. Between 20 and 30 per cent of the *honvéd* army were inducted into the imperial army for several years of service in remote provinces; Schwarzenberg even toyed with the truly innovative idea of establishing a concentration camp in Siberia where the ten thousand 'most dangerous' Hungarians would be interned. Kossuth and other leaders of a sizeable political emigration were executed *in effigie*, by having their names nailed on the gallows. It was largely under the impact of international indignation and protest that the torrent of violence came to an end by sending Haynau into retirement in July 1850.

The harshness of the reaction and the subsequent change in earlier Habsburg policies towards Hungary was frequently explained by diabolising those involved in the process, whereas it was fundamentally rooted in reason of state: Hungary's size, manpower, strategic and political significance, even amidst its relative backwardness, made it impossible for the Habsburgs to let it secede if Austria's great power status was to be preserved. The archaic, aristocratic imperial federalism, with which the maintenance of Hungary's special constitutional status was compatible, now championed by Windisch-Grätz and supported among a group of Hungarian conservative magnates, proved unsuitable for securing that objective, and was therefore swept aside. The *Verwirkungstheorie*, well-tried in the case of the Czechs after 1620, was now applied to Hungary: by rising up in armed revolt against their sovereign, the Hungarians were supposed to have 'forfeited' their ancient constitutional privileges laid down, among other fundamental laws, in the Pragmatic Sanction of 1723. They deserved to be absorbed into the empire and share the lot of the Austrian, Italian and Galician provinces in being governed by a strongly centralised bureaucratic and military machinery. Schwarzenberg, who conceived this programme of unrestrained absolutism and centralism, expected it to galvanise the latent strength of hitherto disjointed provinces and thereby to restore the crumbling great power status of the Habsburg Monarchy.

The Kremsier Constitution of March 1849 was formally retained, without actually exercising any of the precepts of modern constitutionalism, until it was annulled by the Sylvester Patent, issued by Francis Joseph on December 31, 1851. Based as it was on the bureaucracy and the military, the new regime was well suited to the personality of the ruler, who retained the management of affairs for himself. After the death of Schwarzenberg in early 1852, the young Emperor did not appoint a new premier, but governed by relying on a nine-member imperial council. Thoroughly unimaginative and, except for languages, rather confined as regards his education as well as his range of emotions, he had a powerful sense of responsibility, indeed of a mission to govern his peoples 'well' by the grace of God, while the strongly Catholic and soldierly character of his upbringing accentuated his natural bent to envision human and social relationships strictly in terms of super- and subordination. If Joseph II was the first servant of his peoples, Francis Joseph was the first bureaucrat of the realm.

The period of neo-absolutism in Hungary is remembered as the Bach period, after the Imperial Minister of the Interior Alexander Bach, a former revolutionary. The attempt to melt Hungary into the empire began already in the autumn of 1849 with the division of the territory of the historic state into districts equal in status with each other and the other provinces of the empire, in the hope that with the elimination of the old system of intra-regional features and inter-regional relations the roots of 'separatism' would be wiped out. Transylvania and Croatia-Slavonia as well as the southern border region were kept under separate administration, and a new Serbian Voevodeship was also created in the south as a new crown province. The rest of the country was divided, under the authority of the Gubernium (in effect, Archduke Albert, who became civil and military governor in 1852), into five districts, the boundaries between them drawn with an eye to ensuring the preponderance of non-Hungarian ethnic groups in each of them. Nevertheless, as Ferenc Pulszky, a leading figure among the 'centralist' Liberals of the Age of Reform, put it with irony, what the national minorities received for their anti-Hungarian stand in 1848–1849 as a reward did not differ from what was meted out to the Hungarians in punishment; or, in the opinion of one of Pulszky's close associates, Antal Csengery, all nationalities obtained the equal right to become Germanised. German became the official language of the whole of the country, including the Serbian Voevodeship and Croatia, whose self-government and separate diet was lost with the Hungarian constitution; autonomy was denied to Slovaks and Romanians, nor did the Saxon recover theirs. The administration rested on a large influx of German administrators, mockingly dubbed 'Bach hussars' after the Hungarian garment with imperial eagles on the buttons in which they were clad, while surveillance was ensured by an enhanced military presence (symbolised by the Citadel erected on Gellért Hill in Buda, its cannons overlooking Pest, the one-time hotbed of revolution), sixteen regiments of Austrian gendarms, a network of police informers whose main task was to detect the émigrés' domestic relations and sources of information, and strict censorship.

Censorship also meant that Hungarian culture was confined to 'neutral' areas, or compelled to develop methods of encoding politically delicate messages. True, sometimes the meaning of authors and artists – bereavement and defiance – was hardly concealed, as in the case of some of the historical novels of Mór Jókai or Zsigmond Kemény, or in the poetry of the old Vörösmarty, and János Arany, whose *Bards of Wales* is a lasting monument of the refusal to extol the glory of the conquering tyrant; or in historical paintings like *The Mourning of László Hunyadi* by Viktor Madarász, and others by his accomplished colleagues Bertalan Székely and Gyula Benczúr. Contempt for the Bach system was openly the *leitmotif* of *The Civiliser*, a satire by Imre Madách, who also wrote two great dramas: *The Tragedy of Man* and *Moses*, both of which touched the theme of humanity's search for freedom, harmony and happiness with the experience of the fallen revolution in the background. 'Official' cultural policies were confined to promoting, or at least not hindering, the development of the natural sciences. The Society for Natural History, the Society of Geology and the Association of Hungarian Physicians and Naturalists were the products of this period. These disciplines displayed a remarkable responsiveness to the most recent advances of western science: for instance, Darwin's *Origin of the Species* was favourably reviewed and interpreted in Hungary within a year of its original publication of 1859. Private initiatives for the promotion of scientific education, like the founding of the Pest Zoo by the renowned naturalist and globetrotter János Xantus (whose donations also enriched the Smithsonian Institute of New York), contributed to preserving something of the intellectual ferment that marked the Age of Reform. A happy side effect of police surveillance over printing houses was the more regular supply of copyright deposit copies to the National Széchényi Library. Above all, the Academy of Sciences managed to preserve, despite the appearance of ideological factionalism within its walls under the presidency of the conservative Count Emil Dessweffy, its role as a repository of Hungarian culture and its commemorations of the celebrities of national culture sometimes became occasions to protest against autocratic foreign rule.

Whereas the new regime made zealous efforts to win the support of the Catholic Church (it recalled the Jesuits, abandoned the *placetum regium*, and in the Concordat of 1855 gave up nearly all state control over schools, marriages and church discipline), civic and modernising devices were also relied on by the Bach system, largely as means to achieve the end of creating the Habsburg *Gesamtstaat*, a unitary state. The creation of a united customs area by abolishing the customs barrier separating Hungary from Austria, the introduction of uniform tariff regulations, taxation, weights and measurements, postal services, jurisdiction and of equality before the law were all found conducive to the attainment of this objective. The Austrian Civil Code, though it had major shortcomings when compared to the projects of Deák and his associates prior to and in 1848 with its curtailing of the right of association, or retaining corporal punishment, still promoted the free disposition of personal property.

One of the achievements of 1848 was the emancipation of the serfs, which liberated the peasantry both as economic actors, opening the way for them to becoming either free proprietors or potential wage labourers, and as members of the civil community. Because of the flux of events, many details were left unclear at the time, but the 'urbarial patent' and 'decree on compensation' issued by the Emperor on March 2, 1853, provided detailed regulations, which changed the settlement envisaged by the Batthyány government in some important particulars, but preserved its essence. Great difficulties arose from the variety in the legal status of land. Whereas manorial land was to remain in the possession of the landlord and land held as fiefs was to be transferred to the peasants with state compensation, there were also other types of land, like vineyards, whose fate was now left for the landlord to decide, or clearings, which the peasants were supposed to redeem themselves; and the matter was still further complicated by the vagueness or the complete absence of registers compiled under Maria Theresa, which were made the bases of determining the status of the land, in a great many localities. Endless litigation resulted from such circumstances.

About 40 per cent of the land suitable for cultivation in the country was transferred into the possession of former serfs, with about one-fifth of the compensation for such land paid by the peasants themselves, and very unequally distributed among the approximately one and half million peasant families who constituted three-quarters of the population. Only one-third of the former serfs had held fiefs, and only one in twenty among them had held ones large enough to qualify, after liberation, as 'well-to-do' farmers. On the other hand, nearly half of the peasantry, about 700,000 former cotters, received 'dwarfholdings' that kept them permanently on the verge of misery, whereas a further 300,000 were left entirely propertiless. Not surprisingly, among such circumstances, and with the preponderance of obsolete technology and methods of cultivation (the three-field system was still paramount), the transformation of agriculture was anything but automatic.

Another stratum grievously affected by the process was the overwhelming majority, about four-fifths, of the roughly 140,000 noble families, which did not possess sufficient manorial land to sustain their former status as 'genteel landholders'. They lost free labour while they did not gain credit. The payment of compensation was first delayed, and then took the shape of bonds, which those most in need of an instant injection of capital rushed to sell – with the result of losing about a third of the nominal value. Many of these nobles ended up in the ranks of the peasantry, the petty bourgeoisie or the 'genteel middle class' of officers, public servants and intellectuals, while preserving a great deal of their former attitudes of social superiority. On the other hand, the few hundred magnate families, who retained about 25 per cent of all land, were now able to convert their social prestige to an influence in the banking sector, and the investments they rapidly made helped them to start large-scale modernisation in their estates and to reap high profits from the agrarian boom of the 1850s and 1860s. While magnate, genteel landholder, peasant farmer, dwarfholder and agricultural labourer were in principle all free citizens equal before the law, the circumstances of the liberation of the peasantry favoured the conservation of the social hierarchy and relations of authority in Hungarian rural society until 1945.

Free trade brought great short term benefits, especially for those engaged in the production of corn, whose export increased sixfold during the period, but in the long run it contributed to the preservation of the dominance of the agrarian sector in the Hungarian economy. Still, the introduction of modern property laws and the capital accumulated in the trade of corn by a number of wealthy merchants, many of them Jewish, also gave a spur to industrial development, however lopsided it was. The most successful branch of Hungarian industry, the one financed almost exclusively from domestic investments and the single one in which mechanisation surpassed that in the Cisleithan parts of the Empire, was flour-milling. The first large flour mill was established in Pest in 1841; by 1867, the Hungarian capital had ten, and occupied a dominant position in the flour production of the Empire. Food processing in general was the leading industry in Hungary, although the development of distilleries was hampered by the survival of manorial rights, and that of the sugar industry based on home-grown sugar beet (rather than sugar cane) by shortages of capital and raw materials. Textile industry, which was elsewhere the first to become mechanised, was rudimentary in Hungary. Though more than twice as many hands were employed in it than in the rest of the Empire, the spinning machines were operated by a mere six steam engines, as against 480 on the other side of the River Leitha. Hungarian industry remained small-scale, the number of the industrial proletariat employed in factories and workshops only exceeding those of artisans in the 1860s. Nevertheless, there were a few European-sized factories based on mining and metallurgy, such as the iron works of Ábrahám Ganz in the capital, which supplied machinery for Hungary's rapidly expanding railway lines. In the period of neo-absolutism, over 2,000 kilometres were added to the previously existing 148, connecting the larger urban centres, the corn regions of the Great Plain and the livestock-breeding areas beyond the Tisza with the capital and European markets.

Political opinion in Hungary during the years of neo-absolutism was highly stratified, with a number of competing visions about the future of the country. There was certainly a minority willing to co-operate in the creation and operation of the institutions of the new regime. Besides moral identification, existential considerations played a part in this: after the liberation of serfs, taking office remained the sole means of subsistence for a broad segment of the impoverished nobility. However, the majority displayed such a resilience that martial law remained in force for five years after 1849. Even mere highwaymen were hailed as freedom fighters, irrespective of the true reason why they were hiding from the hated authorities. The 'old conservative' aristocrats led by Dessewffy and Apponyi, the dominant figures of the government party in the mid-1840s, certainly did not sympathise with the vision of the new leaders in Vienna, but their insistence on the platform of 1847 (that is, the restoration of Hungary's corporate constitution with some modifications) fell on deaf ears in the Habsburg capital for reasons outlined above. The 'centralist' Liberals, while deeply pessimistic about the possibility of resuscitating the fight for the full liberal programme of the Age of Reform, were also abhorred by the unmasked repression. Therefore, whereas Kemény, both in his pamphlet *After the Revolution* (1850) and as editor of the influential political weekly *Pesti Hírlap*, urged Hungarians to return to the programme of Széchenyi, Eötvös made efforts to point out to Vienna that the 'European necessity' of a large state in the middle of the continent could only be fulfilled by the Habsburg Monarchy if the existing historic rights were adjusted to the unity of the monarchy (through federation), and other ethnic and linguistic rights were also satisfied within that historic framework (through autonomies).

This was the tenor of Eötvös *On the Equality of Nationality Rights in Austria* (1850), and the more theoretical *The Dominant Ideas of the*

Nineteenth Century and their Influence on the State (1851–1854). In this seminal work, Eötvös, the Central European liberal, used his experience of competing nationalisms to enrich the views of contemporary western liberals like Lord Acton on the inevitable tension between the ideals of liberty and equality. The 'dominant ideas' of the nineteenth century, Eötvös suggested, caused so much suffering because they were but misinterpretations of the true notions of liberty, equality and nationality. They were all mistaken for the idea of sovereignty, which inevitably bred conflict, whereas rightly conceived they were merely devices to protect the integrity and ensure the self-fulfilment of the individual. Instead of popular sovereignty, based on the wrong 'dominant ideas', it was the civil liberties, primarily the right of association, that would effectively safeguard the individual and the group (including the ethnic group) against the modern state, which should be pretty powerful within its own province.

At the same time, there were trends in Hungarian politics that were unwilling to enter into any sort of dialogue whatsoever with the Bach regime, and the majority of politically articulate Hungarians belonged to them. Deák, the only leading politician of 1848 who survived the defeat unharassed despite not leaving Hungary, became the leader of one of these trends. In April 1850, Deák was invited to participate at a conference on private law in Vienna. He declined the invitation by explaining that 'after the woeful events of the recent past, and among circumstances that prevail even presently among us, it is impossible for me to participate actively in public affairs'. Though not intending to persuade anyone to follow him, the conduct of the erstwhile Minister of Justice set an example for many, and this letter became the programmatic statement of 'passive resistance', that is, non-cooperation with the authorities (refusing to take offices, evading the payment of taxes, feigning unfamiliarity with German and encumbering the life of the administrators in an environment foreign to them in all possible ways). Evidence on all sorts of collaboration uncovered by recent research suggests that the dimensions of passive resistance have been greatly exaggerated by national legend, but it still seems to have been the dominant type of political attitude in Hungary during neo-absolutism.

All this was far from being politically inactive. Deák ('the sage of the nation') himself attended meetings of the Academy, economic and cultural associations, making speeches hardly concealing his opinions; and his apartment at the Hotel Queen of England in Pest, where he moved after Széchenyi had bought his estate in 1854, became a sort of political casino, the most important venue of a 'second public sphere'. What Deák and this followers wanted was not to break Habsburg power, but to strengthen it in its proper functions. They were convinced that the

Habsburg Monarchy was not only considered indispensable by the Great Powers for the European balance of power, but it was also indispensable as a protective screen for Hungarians, wedged as they were between huge blocks of Germans and Slavs. The task for Hungarian politics was to accelerate the process whereby Vienna should recognise that Habsburg power was not viable without the co-operation of Hungary (or rather its political elite), and the way to regain it was to return to 1848, that is, granting it internal self-government within the empire.

If the conservative aristocrats chose 1847, and Deák 1848 as their basis of reference, 1849 played the same role for Kossuth, the émigrés and a not inconsiderable group within the country who looked to them for guidance and watched for signals of their return. They also thought that Hungary needed a 'screen' against Germanic and Pan-Slav pressure, but were sceptical concerning Austria's ability to play that role: their own struggle convinced them that it was only capable of sustaining itself in the face of centrifugal forces by relying on great power intervention. They acknowledged that independence would not be sufficient, but they increasingly saw the direction showed by the law on the national minorities passed in July 1849 as the way out. Deák and his followers thought that the minorities had stabbed liberal Hungary, which had attained freedom for all its citizens including them, in the back, and continued to reject the idea of collective rights. Kossuth, on the other hand, argued that although the 'camarilla' indeed intrigued the nationalities into rebelling against the Hungarian revolution in 1848, a reconciliation with them and the nascent states of the small nations along the Danube, which might with time be further developed into a democratic confederation, was a far superior alternative to insisting on the bankrupt Austrian relationship.

Kossuth dispelled all possible doubt as to the essence of his position as soon as he crossed the Turkish border in August 1849 by denouncing Görgey as a traitor to the national cause. Already in 1851, he summarised his ideas on the resettlement of the status quo in the Danube Basin in a draft constitution conceived in Kütahia, his temporary refuge in the Ottoman Empire. The political structure of the Hungary he envisaged was one based on a democratic suffrage, linguistic rights and broad local self-government (while he refused to go as far as László Teleki and György Klapka, who were also inclined to the internal federalisation of Hungary, with rights of territorial autonomy for the national minorities). Initially, also inspired by the views of Italian revolutionaries in the circle of Giuseppe Mazzini with whom he maintained contacts, Kossuth encouraged revolution-making in Hungary, but an abortive revolt in the Szekel region in 1851 and a failed attempt at the life of Francis Joseph in 1852 convinced him that times were inauspicious.

Kossuth still continued to believe that a 'great European upheaval' was imminent, and that it would provide an opportunity for the resuscitation of the independence struggle if the support of the Great Powers and the national minorities could be secured. Early on during his exile, he sent out letters to Hungarian émigrés everywhere, urging them to exploit and further stimulate the favourable atmosphere. His own tour of the United States and Britain in 1851–1852, with hundreds of widely acclaimed speeches, was a roaring success in moral terms with Washington congressmen as well as less prestigious audiences. Of course, no eloquence could attain the official recognition of the principle he campaigned for: 'intervention (by the western powers) for non-intervention (by others, Russia in particular)' in case a new Hungarian independence struggle broke out. But money and arms were raised, and the émigrés were ready for united action; and as Deák later confessed, he was not sure at the time whether it was his 'party' or Kossuth's that had the greater support within Hungary.

The 'European upheaval' Kossuth looked forward to came in the late 1850s. The propaganda of the émigrés undermined the passive support Austria received from the western powers in 1849, and it seemed equally unlikely that it would receive the active assistance rendered to it by Russia after the Tsar's favour had been returned by Francis Joseph with the ingratitude of remaining neutral in the Crimean War in 1854. Russia lost the war against Turkey, backed by Britain and France. Besides other decisions, the Paris peace conference of 1856 secured the *de facto* sovereignty of Serbia and the two Romanian principalities, and the latter were united under Prince Alexandru Ion Cuza in early 1859. The Hungarian émigrés soon discussed plans of reconciliation and cooperation with both Cuza and Prince Miloš Obrenović of Serbia. Shortly afterwards, Kossuth was received in Paris by Napoleon III, and was promised French troops to assist the émigré Hungarian Legion and a Hungarian uprising to attain the independence of Hungary. On the following day, May 6, 1859, the Hungarian National Directory, headed by Kossuth, was established as a government in exile. The Paris meeting of Kossuth and Napoleon III was mediated by Camillo Cavour, the Piedmontese Prime Minister. In the previous year Cavour, whose great ambition was the unification of Italy, had concluded a similar agreement with the French Emperor, who wanted martial glory and a sphere of influence. All of these endeavours could be satisfied by a war against Austria, which broke out at the end of April 1859 between Piedmont and the Habsburg Monarchy. Ironically, what went wrong from the point of view of the Italians as well as the Hungarians was that after France had entered the war, the Austrian forces collapsed dramatically. The decisive victory in the bloodiest battle of the century at Solferino on June 24 made Napoleon himself recoil and hasten to make peace, lest a too powerful Italy should emerge. Cavour, receiving only Lombardy, was frustrated, similarly to the Hungarians, their only consolation being that the terms of the agreement with Napoleon precluded a premature outbreak of the uprising in Hungary and thus saved them from the odium of precipitating another defeat and retaliation.

Yet, though the Hungarian cause did not win in the Italian war, the losses of Austria were even more severe, for the humiliating defeat clearly exposed the structural weaknesses of neo-absolutism, based as it was on the military which proved unsuitable for modern warfare and the bureaucracy which proved corrupt and unsuitable for securing a reliable hinterland. Already after the preliminary peace of Villafranca, Francis Joseph promised 'timely improvements' to his subjects. If there was initially little hurry in making good this promise, an increasingly hostile atmosphere would compel the government to speed up the process. Protest against the Protestant Patent, which was to curtail the autonomy of Protestant Churches, resulted in its revocation. As far as Hungary is concerned, a commemoration of Kazinczy in October 1859 developed into a mass demonstration, and an organised 'pilgrimage' to *honvéd* graves on 15 March 1860 in Pest ended in bloody clashes with the military; the successes of Giuseppe Garibaldi, whose revolutionary army included a fair number of Hungarian émigrés, in the struggle for a united Italy in the early summer were hailed all over the country. The country-wide mourning of the death of Széchenyi also coloured the atmosphere of 1860. The count, who recovered his intellectual powers by the middle of the 1850s, published a scathing satire on the Bach regime in 1859, and harassment by the authorities led him commit suicide on April 8, 1860. An Imperial Council greatly enlarged by German, Czech and Hungarian aristocrats, called into session in spring 1860, pressed the Emperor to transforming the centralist-bureaucratic system, and under the impact of further demonstrations he issued the so-called October Diploma as a 'permanent and irrevocable fundamental law' which he 'granted' to his peoples on October 20, 1860.

The Diploma claimed to have revived the 'historical individuality' of the lands and provinces of Habsburg Monarchy by restoring the pre–1848 institutions of government (in the case of Hungary, the Chancellery and the Gubernium, now headed by conservative aristocrats) and legislatures (the Hungarian diet and the *Landtage* of the hereditary provinces) while limiting their authority by leaving the most important budgetary issues in the hands of the Imperial Council, and foreign and military affairs entirely in those of the Emperor. The measure, in fact a mere cosmetic surgery that removed the ugliest excesses of the Bach regime, failed to satisfy either the 'constitutional centralists', that is, the liberal middle classes and intelligentsia of Austria, or the liberal nobility and intelligentsia of Hungary. Especially in the latter, mass unrest grew at the turn of 1860–1861 to the extent that it came to be referred to as a 'little revolution'. While finding the Diploma unacceptable and insisting on 'the basis of 1848', Deák and his followers wanted to utilise the political space opened by the restoration of the legislature and the counties, many of which now claimed that the taxes imposed autocratically were illegal and urged people not to pay them. Persuaded by his new minister of state, Anton von Schmerling, the leader of the group of Austrian polticians who endeavoured to reconcile the idea of a centralised, German-dominated Austria with their moderately liberal constitutional beliefs, Francis Joseph went one step further and issued the February Patent of 1861. The two chamber, 343 member *Reichsrat* which it created was a parliament indeed, in which each of the provinces of the empire were to send delegates. This central legislature obtained some control over the imperial government – and the right of endorsement on several budgetary issues, while foreign and military affairs still remained the ruler's preserve.

As the patent at the same time strengthened the hold of the imperial government over the provinces, Hungary's second representative parliament, which assembled in April 1861, was in an awkward position: what they had a chance to consider as a constitutional project was clearly contrary to all traditions in Hungarian constitutionalism. Their scope of action was further constrained by the fact that social consensus was missing on the two neuralgic issues of 1848–1849, the peasant and the nationality question. Despite serious peasant unrest early in 1861, the majority of the political class decided that the Urbarial Patent of 1853 ought to be retained in all its particulars and was unwilling to extend the range of state compensation beyond its specifications. Besides, even though there was some rapprochement between Magyars and non-Magyars, the slogan of '48 had the uncomfortable overtone of 'a unitary Hungarian political nation' for the nationalities, whereas the demand for autonomy by the Serbian and Slovak congresses convened in April and June 1861, respectively, raised fears among the Hungarians concerning the dismemberment of the historic state. Finally, with the proclamation of a united Italy in March 1861, Kossuth's 'European moment' was gone.

Among such circumstances, the championing of the '48 cause could not develop into genuine political struggle, but remained a declaration of principle. The Hungarian parliament instantly decided to refuse electing delegates to the imperial assembly (which was the main reason why the ruler summoned it), and the two main parties only differed as to the proper form of rejecting the constitution imposed on them. The radicals, led by Teleki who had been recently arrested in Saxony and brought back to Hungary but was then released, claimed that it was impossible to observe legal forms when dealing with an uncrowned ruler, and suggested that the position of the parliament be communicated to him as a mere resolution. Teleki committed suicide upon having realised that he remained a minority in his own party on the eve of the vote, which favoured the moderate Deák. Insisting on strict legality, Deák formulated an address to the crown, pointing out in a clearly argued interpretation of constitutional law and constitutional history that since the union between Hungary and Austria had never been 'real', merely 'personal', the basis of a reconciliation could not be anything short of the April Laws of 1848. 'The nation shall endure', he declared, were the ruler reluctant to respect its dedication to preserving its inherited constitutional liberties and passing them down to posterity.

The nation did need to endure: Francis Joseph dissolved the Hungarian legislature on August 22, and autocratic centralism was restored under Schmerling. It was intended to be a *provisorium*, to be abandoned as soon as the Hungarians would realise that they had no alternative but to join the imperial parliament. In a few years, it turned out to be provisional for quite different reasons.

The events of 1860–1861, the transformation of the international scene, the fate of Schmerling's experiment with constitutional centralism in Austria and the changing concerns of the domestic elite all put the policy alternatives that had congealed in the 1850s – compromise with the national minorities and neighbouring small nations, or compromise with Austria – in a new light. In May 1862, Kossuth's plan for a Danubian Confederation, at that time only intended to be used in diplomatic negotiations, was published in the journal *L'Alleanza* in Milan. The confederate state, envisaged in several particulars along the example of the United States, was to consist of Hungary (merely in personal union with Transylvania), Croatia, the Romanian principalities and Serbia. Besides economic union, there would be joint foreign and military affairs, under the authority of a two chamber assembly and a confederate council. Each member state would be sovereign in its domestic affairs, with full religious equality and language rights at the village and county level, as already suggested in the draft constitution of Kütahia.

The plan was noble but somewhat utopian, even though the talks of 1859 with the Romanian and Serbian princes provided grounds for some optimism. The harmonisation of the national and territorial demands of the small nations along the Danube, especially the ones living in minority status within Hungary, verged on the impossible, which made the plan of Kossuth, intended to preclude compromise with Austria, evoke the opposite effect. A publicist expressed the majority opinion by saying the 'the price of our reconciliation with Austria and its ruling house is smaller than the one demanded by the nationalities, which revolutionary blunderers would be willing to pay'. The probability that Kossuth's project risked a revolution was real indeed, as it implied the elimination of the Habsburg Monarchy. But however storm-beaten Austria seemed to be in the 1860s, Kossuth's vision of a 30 million strong confederate state taking its place in the European balance of power failed to convince the Great Powers of the need to re-arrange relations in Central Europe. Besides the nascent Hungarian-Romanian-South Slav co-operation, Klapka had recommended the restoration of Poland to the goodwill of the western powers in the 1850s. In 1863 the Poles rose up against Russia again; Britain and France watched in aloofness as the 'revolutionary blunderers' were smashed again by Tsarist troops. The mood was certainly no more revolutionary outside, than it was within the country. Unwilling to give up even more to the peasantry, suspicious of the national minorities and insisting on the fiction of the unitary political nation, tired of the puritanical policy of passive resistance, and desirous of the positions opening and the prestige accruing from them to the losers of the economic transition, the country's elite gradually drifted towards what Teleki once bitterly warned against: accepting 'the sparrow today, rather than waiting for the bustard to come tomorrow'.

Tastes in Austrian mouths also became more and more bitter as the 1860s advanced. The hopes created by Schmerling's 'constitutional centralism' were thwarted: not only did the Hungarians and the Croats continue to be absent from the imperial parliament, but the Czechs and the Poles also left it in 1863, to the great disappointment of the moderately liberal Austro-German middle classes, who started to accept that constitutionalism could not be imposed and imperial, but only national and based on consent. At first, at the turn of 1862–1863, the conservative Count György Apponyi was requested by the court to prepare a memorandum on the possible form of a compromise, but two years later Francis Joseph decided to negotiate, through confidants, secretly with Deák himself. The sum of these talks was published by Deák in his famous 'Easter article' of April 16, 1865, suggesting that it might be possible to abandon 'the basis of 1848': he still insisted on the maintenance of the fundamental laws of Hungary 'to the greatest possible extent', this extent, however, being defined by 'the fullest security' of the empire.

This security was increasingly fragile as Austria's position in the German world was challenged by the Prussia of Otto von Bismarck, who wanted to eliminate the 'dualism' of these two powers in the leadership of Germany and to exclude Austria from a Germany united under Prussian hegemony. As the Hungarian legislature convened in the autumn of 1865, the two German powers already quarrelled over the administration of Schleswig and Holstein they won in a war jointly fought against Denmark in the previous year. Concluding an alliance with Italy, Bismarck compelled Austria into a two-front war. As in 1859, Austrian military collapse was a matter of weeks. The humiliating defeat in the battle of Königgrätz (Hradec Králové) on July 3, 1866, meant that Austria became excluded from the German Confederation, which it had hoped to dominate. To Deák and his followers at first this seemed to be an undesirable outcome: they calculated that if Austia had become preoccupied with its 'western mission' again, Hungary would have acquired a better chance to recover its full autonomy within the Monarchy. As, on the other hand, they also did not intend to weaken Habsburg power from which they expected protection against Russia and Germany, they did not increase the price of compromise, which the bulk of Austro-Germans now also started to find more attractive. Without the German background, after Königgrätz they found themselves in a situation in the Habsburg Empire similar to those of the Hungarians in Hungary: the most numerous ethnic group, which nevertheless constituted less than half of the whole population. They came to accept the idea that the western half of the empire ought to be transformed into a state, like Hungary, under one nation's leadership, and the position of the leading nations in both halves of the empire ought to be consolidated by lending each other mutual support.

Gradually, Francis Joseph himself started to prefer constitutional dualism to the alternatives of retaining the centralised structure and the federal reorganisation of the empire, as suggested by Slav national leaders and Prime Minister Count Richard Belcredi, with whom he had replaced Schmerling already in June 1865. Besides Queen Elisabeth, whose pro-Hungarian sentiments have been subject to romantic exaggerations in Hungarian national legends, but were nevertheless real, it was Baron Ferdinand Beust, appointed Foreign Minister in October 1866 and Imperial Prime Minister in February 1867, who finally convinced the Emperor that the domestic precondition of all *revanche* in Germany was compromise with the Hungarians.

As a matter of fact, a partner to negotiate with was needed. Deák paved the way to the compromise and had a party in parliament to push it through, but was determined to remain an *eminence grise* at most in the new era. The Hungarian delegation that negotiated the Compromise in January and February 1867 was headed by Count Gyula Andrássy, who enjoyed the full confidence of Deák and Hungarian liberals as well as the royal couple, even though his name was on the list of the émigrés hanged *in effigie* in the aftermath of 1849. Having returned to Hungary in 1857, he was an experienced politician, with an instinctive skill for brilliant improvisations. Andrássy was appointed Prime Minister on

February 17, after the heated debates about the necessary adjustments of the often obscure specifications of the April Laws of 1848 came to an end. Besides him, the most important members of the delegation were Eötvös, who represented continuity with 1848 and, as at that time, became Minister of Education and Ecclesiastical Affairs, and the internationally renowned financial expert Menyhért Lónyay, who became Minister of Finance. Liberal commoners as well as aristocratic magnates were represented in Hungary's third responsible ministry.

The sixty-nine Articles of Compromise (Law XII of 1867) were passed by the Hungarian parliament on 20 March. The two halves of the empire were to be self-governing states as regards their internal affairs, and both of them were to have their representative and responsible ministries. They were bound together, in the spirit of the Pragmatic Sanction, by the rights of the ruler, the common affairs arising from this relationship – defence, foreign affairs and the finances covering these – being managed by joint ministries reponsible to the emperor-king and to delegations consisting of sixty members from both parliaments. The ruler remained supreme warlord, and also reserved for himself the right of 'presanctioning' laws, that is, government bills could only be presented in parliament by his prior approval.

Predictably, Kossuth was one of a minority who were unimpressed. In his famous 'Cassandra letter', the first in a series of open letters addressed by the 'hermit of Turin' to his countrymen, published on May 26 in a Pest journal, he argued that Deák's policy line culminated in abandoning Hungary's claim to be an independent state, at a time when the 1866 crisis created the most auspicious circumstances to obtain independence. Königgrätz demonstrated that Austria was a dilapidated structure bound together merely by the dynasty and doomed to collapse in the age of the nation-state. The Compromise, namely, the common affairs, involved a trap. Hungarian self-determination suffered irreparably by involvement in foreign policy schemes that might be contrary to the nation's interests, and might throw it into conflict both with the two Great Powers against which Deák sought for protection, and her neighbouring peoples whose friendship was essential for Hungary's well-being. Hungary lost the 'mastery over her future', and it would never be able to take advantage of the ever more frequently arising occasions to gain full independence.

Kossuth was right in a very profound sense, namely, that Hungary's twentieth-century history rather fatefully verified some of his predictions. At the same time, Deák was undoubtedly also right in pointing out that the 'expected event' (that is, the ultimate collapse of Austria) might not occur before it was too late 'for our harrowed nation' to take advantage of it. Deák never pretended that the Compromise was the best of all solutions, but he was convinced that it was the best of all possible ones: in fact a 'realistic 1848', which the peace delegation sent to Windisch-Grätz (including Deák) would have been only too happy to accept. It corresponded to the social and national relations of power in 1867, and it was quite exceptionally successful in laying the foundations of a political establishment that was to last for half a century.

On June 8, 1867, Francis Joseph I took the coronation oath on a mound erected for the purpose at the Pest side of the Chainbridge from pieces of earth from all over the country, and was crowned King of Hungary in Matthias Church. He sanctioned the Articles of Compromise four days later. A rebellious nation and an autocratic ruler seemed to have been reconciled.

2. The 'happy times of peace', or the mirage of greatness

In both halves of the Austro-Hungarian Monarchy, which became the official name of the new state in 1868, the Compromise could be interpreted with satisfaction as well as with dissatisfaction, and in individuals these attitudes were mixed in different proportions in both of them. Naturally enough, each side felt that it had lost more in the bargain than the other: Austria the idea of centralised monarchy, and Hungary a part of national self-determination. The device of 'common affairs', therefore, received much criticism, and the ways in which they were managed often became objects of acrimonious debate.

In Hungary, the existence of a united imperial army, under dynastic insignia and German as the language of command, evoked resentment, and was only suffered because a separate *honvéd* army (along with the Austrian *Landwehr*) was also set up. The other delicate issue between Austria and Hungary was the 'economic compromise': the customs union, commercial agreement, common currency, postal service and transport system, and the share of the two halves of the empire in the expenditure for common affairs (the 'quota', according to which Hungary's contribution increased from 30 per cent in 1867 to 36.4 per cent in 1907). To be renegotiated every ten years, the economic compromise was the only flexible element in the politically rigid settlement (in principle, even the break-up of the customs union remained possible), one which held out the promise of redressing the supposedly unfavourable aspects of 1867 for both partners. Besides innumerable occasional items, the language of command of the army and the quota were constant themes in Hungarian grumbling about the 'constitutional issue' (that is, the relationship between the monarch and Hungary), which supplied the terms in which the rather shallowed patriotism of the parliamentary opposition to the shape, though not the essence, of the Compromise was expressed through most of the fifty-one years of the Dual Monarchy.

At the same time, it was well understood in Austria that the Compromise was arguably the only way to preserve the great power status of the Habsburg Monarchy, and in Hungary that it not only increased, rather than decreased, the chances of national survival, but also offered a means to partake of that great power status. Though none of the defence ministers, and few in the high command of the armed forces of the Dual Monarchy were Hungarian, 30 per cent of the diplomatic corps and four out of its ten foreign ministers were subjects of the Hungarian crown. In the light of the role which the glorious medieval Hungarian 'empire' had played in the Hungarian national awakening, it is not surprising that in an age when nationalism imbued the attitudes and ambitions of powers great and small, Hungarian nationalists became dazzled by the prospect of governing a half-empire, whose economic and demographic dynamism might soon shift the intra-imperial balance of power in their favour, and even compel the dynasty to remove its residence from Vienna to Budapest (an idea first entertained, under different circumstances and for different reasons, by none other than Kossuth in 1848).

Another element of Hungary's past cherished among liberals was the supposed parallel between the constitutional development of Hungary and that of England (the Magna Carta preceding the Golden Bull of Andrew II by a mere seven years), popularly held from the end of the eighteenth century. On the domestic policy level, it was certainly a convincing argument in favour of the Compromise that for the two leading nations of the Habsburg Monarchy it did represent a shift from absolutist to liberal representative government, albeit with shortcomings; and for the bulk of Hungarian liberals some of these very shortcomings made it more attractive than potential alternatives. The strong personal power of the ruler, whose survival made it for the rest of Europe quite difficult to recognise the important changes, was certainly not one of these. The discretionary powers reserved for Francis Joseph, such as the right of approving government legislative drafts, maintained his influence in the domestic affairs of both states, whereas his Cabinet Bureau and Military Bureau had a role nearly equal to that of the joint ministries in common affairs. Relying on a broad network of unofficial advisors whose loyalties belonged primarily to the dynasty (an old tradition among the aristocracy, the bureaucracy and the officer corps), he exerted a broad influence, especially in view of the fact that the delegations, sitting only once a year, could not exercise efficient constitutional control. Second, there were the limitations deriving from the nature and basis of liberalism in Hungary. At its inception, it was a liberalism of noblemen, largely directed to offset, to moderate or to exploit the effects of capitalist development in a predominantly rural society – priorities reflected in the way in which, after the waning of the enthusiasm of the Age of Reform and the Revolution of 1848, the dismantling of feudalism took place. Relations of dependence and hierarchy and the traditional respect for authority were preserved in attitudes. A slap in the face would be the normal measure to discipline agricultural workers, and when a back-bencher asked a member of the Upper House the time, the latter would place his watch on the desk and step back while the former was looking at it, rather than answer him. Liberal equality remained a fiction even within the political elite. The Compromise, which was, after all, a conservative step, checked whatever emancipationist momentum Hungarian liberalism still had. It became increasingly confined to the espousal of free enterprise, the introduction of modern infrastructure and, with considerable delay, to the secularisation of the public sphere and the regulation of state-church relations. Political power remained in the hands of the traditional elite, with which newcomers were assimilated, with roughly 80 per cent of MPs permanently drawn from the landowning classes. The franchise, extending to c. 6 per cent of the population throughout the period, was acceptable at its beginning, but grossly anachronistic by its end in European comparison. Most districts being the patrimony of local potentates and political groups, elections were, as a rule, managed, and there was large-scale patronage at all levels in the administration. If Hungary's constitutional liberty resembled that of England during the time of Kálmán Tisza's premiership from 1875 to 1890, it mainly resembled the England of the 'whig oligarchy' under Robert Walpole a century and a half earlier. And yet, the Hungarian parliament being a largely independent agent in its dealings with the crown, Hungary's constitution was 'more free' in the Montesquieuan sense than any east of the Rhine.

Besides the many-sided tensions involved in the settlement of Austro-Hungarian relations, there were others arising from the fact that the limited blessings of constitutionalism did not satisfy those citizens of Austria and Hungary who did not belong to either of the two leading nations. In the Austrian half, dualism was unacceptable to the Czechs, who either demanded the federal reorganisation of the empire or hoped for 'trialism', and could not be placated by the mere transfer of the Czech coronation insignia from Vienna to Prague. The less ambitious claim of autonomy voiced by the Poles of Galicia was refused, lest it should provoke Russian resentment. Austro-German hegemony was thus preserved in Austria, just as Hungarian supremacy survived in Hungary.

There the case of the Croats was unique, somewhat similar to that of the Czechs beyond the Leitha on account of the 'historical legitimacy' of their claims of self-government. After the Compromise, their status was placed on a new footing in the Hungarian-Croat constitutional agreement (*Nagodba*) of 1868. Like the Austro-Hungarian Compromise, it was in effect a treaty of union, but unlike its counterpart, it was a union of unequal partners. Croatia was acknowledged as a 'political nation with a separate territory, and an independent legislature and government in its domestic affairs'. However, the latter were confined to internal administration, the judiciary and educational and ecclesiastical affairs. As regards the common affairs of the empire as a whole, Croats were represented (by six members) in the Hungarian delegation, and as for Croat-Hungarian common affairs, the forty-two deputies of the Croatian *sabor* to the Hungarian parliament constituted a minority that could be easily outvoted. Also, the fact that while the Ban of Croatia was responsible to the *sabor*, his appointment by the monarch also required the approval of the Hungarian government, was a restriction of Croatian autonomy. Although the agreement secured important elements of statehood and a broad range of opportunities to develop national cultural and political institutions, it is little wonder that the Croatian *sabor*, which in 1861 had declared a mere personal union to be the only acceptable tie between the two countries, had to be dissolved repeatedly before a pro-Hungarian majority could be secured to get the *Nagodba* voted.

This was still considerably more than the other nationalities felt they received in what was at that time, ironically, the only comprehensive piece of legislation in Europe apart from Switzerland that addressed the respective status of ethnic groups in the polity, and a remarkably liberal one. Although the endeavour to satisfy the 'reasonable' demands of the nationalities was a frequent theme in public discussion on the eve of the Compromise, the network of broad collective rights as suggested by the Kossuth emigration on the basis of the nationality law of 1849 was not seriously contemplated, and even the proposals of Eötvös, who drafted the bill in the spirit of his theoretical writings from the 1850s, were restricted after heated debate in the course of which some of the non-Magyar deputies walked out of the chamber. Law XLIV of 1868 became established along the idea that 'all Hungarian citizens constitute a nation in the political sense, the one and indivisible Hungarian nation', that is, on the fiction of a Magyar nation-state on the Western European model. It denied the political existence, and thus the claims to collective rights and political institutions, of the national minorities, for whom the assertion that 'every citizen of the fatherland ... enjoys equal rights, regardless of the national group to which he belongs', was meagre compensation. At the same time, in granting individual rights the law was thoroughly liberal, even surpassing in some particulars the demands of the nationalities themselves. It gave extensive opportunities for the use of the native tongue in the administration, at courts, in education and in religious life; the right of association made it possible to establish cultural, learned, artistic or economic societies and schools using any language; and the law even required the state to promote primary and secondary schooling in the mother tongue and the participation of the ethnic minorities in public service.

The opponents of the law at first criticised its shortcomings, but later they mainly complained because it was increasingly neglected by the Hungarian authorities. Indeed, its major drawback was that it contained no guarantees. Contrary to the spirit of Eötvös and Deák, their successors interpreted the concept of the equality of all Hungarian citizens as meaning that all non-Magyars who assimilated with Magyars would be considered as equal. From the 1880s on, Magyarisation was no longer merely 'encouraged with all legally permissible means', but also enforced with some that evaded or violated the law of 1868.

The relationship between the two halves of the empire, the narrowness and the archaisms of the political system, and the nationality question were time bombs which the Compromise placed in the structure of dualist Hungary. Nevertheless, it took a long time, and the contribution of international contingencies, for these bombs to explode. Dualism in Hungary is generally reckoned to have been in a crisis during the whole of the second half of the period. Yet, the stirrings on the 'constitutional issue' from the late 1880s were not sufficient to shake it, and the dynamism of economic and cultural progress did much to blunten the edge of the social and the nationality issues from the 1890s through to the 1910s. As a result, the *vis inertiae* of the peculiarly modernised Hungarian old regime lasted until military defeat in the First World War. For these reasons, the tension-ridden era was also one which had for contemporaries and posterity as well an atmosphere of stability and permanence.

As to political cleavages in post–1867 Hungary, two peculiar features of the emerging party system are worth mentioning. First, the political parties were in fact to a great extent gentlemanly associations, bound together by personal loyalties at least as much as convictions regarding policy issues, with relatively loose institutional ties drawn somewhat closer at times of elections. Second, if there were any matters of principle that united them, they related to the 'constitutional issue', that is, the attitude to the Compromise itself, rather than ideological or social questions. The government party of 1867, which retained power until 1875, was largely recruited from the 'Address Party' of 1861, and was called the Deák Party, out of deference to its dominant personality who did not take office but remained one of the most influential political voices in the country until his retirement in 1872. Andrássy, Eötvös, Lónyay, and Minister of Justice Boldizsár Horvát were the most prominent figures of the party, which commanded a two-thirds majority in the House of Representatives. Their main opponents were the heirs of the 1861 'Resolution Party', led by Kálmán Tisza and Kálmán Ghyczy, and adhering to the programme of the 'Bihar points', issued in April 1868. They demanded increased Hungarian independence within the Monarchy: the abolition of common ministries and delegations, separate Hungarian defence forces, commerce and finances. However, the hundred or so deputies (in a 409 member legislature) of the Left Centre Party, as it came to be called, defined its role as a loyal opposition, refraining from 'incitement' against the Compromise, merely intending to make it more favourable.

Besides these two major parties which shared the allegiance of most of the aristocracy and the gentry as well as the elite of the middle classes, there was a sizeable minority that repudiated the Compromise altogether. The social basis of the 'extreme Left' (later the '48er Independence Party) was some of the intelligentsia, the petty bourgeoisie and the peasantry. It drew great moral support from the fact that it undoubtedly had the sympathy of Kossuth, whose spirit dominated their attitudes to the relations with Austria (a mere personal union) as well as democracy (universal suffrage, the reform of the Upper House etc.) and the social and nationality issues. Former émigrés like Dániel Irányi, Ignác Helfy or József Madarász were the leading figures of the party whose popularity and political importance rose, in spite of the strong administrative measures against the peasant unrest and the democratic circles which it supported in 1868, until its decline in the late 1870s.

Andrássy's government made use of the legal and constitutional independence gained in Hungary' internal affairs by renewing some of the laws of 1848 and adding new ones that were still needed in order the satisfy the basic criteria of a modern, civic state, while making the general character of the new political settlement more conservative than that of 1848. Civil liberties were proclaimed, but whereas the new press law lowered the deposit needed to start a newspaper or journal, it also increased the ability of the government to intervene in libel suits. The rights of assembly and association were regulated merely by decrees, instead of laws, making it practically impossible to obtain legal remedy in case these rights were violated. The new rules of legal procedure (1868) proclaimed the equality of all citizens before the law, and were based on the independence of judges. A conspicuous case of the amalgam of liberal and conservative principles and motives was the regulation of county and municipal self-government (1870). The county and municipal assemblies were acknowledged as the only legitimate bodies of political discussion outside the parliament. They were entitled to address national political issues at their sessions, to make their resolutions on these issues public, to petition the government on these issues or to remonstrate against measures they deemed illegal or unsatisfactory. On the other hand, the Minister of the Interior obtained wide powers of supervision and discipline over the municipalities, and could decisively influence their deliberations through his confidential men, the *fóispáns* of the counties, whose authority was also extended. Villages were, as they had always been, subordinated to the county administration, depriving the bulk of Hungary's vast peasant population from most of the blessings of self-government and a political role. Finally, the fact that only a half of the municipal assemblies were actually elected (a process from which those 'under the authority of a superior', like domestic servants, agrarian workers or day labourers, were excluded), and that the other half was reserved for the greatest taxpayers (*virilists*) of the community, resulted in the emergence of a quasi-hereditary class of local legislators by legally guaranteeing the political power of the richest section of society. Most of the anti-democratic features of these measures placed the ethnic minorities, which were over-represented among the rural poor, at a peculiar disadvantage.

The most unequivocally liberal in spirit and letter was the 1868 law on elementary schooling, worked out by Eötvös. The appalling literacy statistics (in 1869, 59 per cent of the male and 79 per cent of the female population over the age of six were illiterate) made new legislation urgent. Elementary education between the ages of 6 and 12 were made compulsory, and was to be obtained in the mother tongue; the backward system of confessional schools was placed under state supervision, with a new network of school inspectors; schools were to be established in every locality with over 30 school age-children. The law also arranged for 'higher elementary' education, until the age of 15. Over the following two decades, more than 3,000 new schools were added to the nearly 14,000 existing. The proportion of school attendance increased from 50 to 81 per cent, and illiteracy dropped to 34 per cent among men and 53 per cent among women. The law was strongly resented by the Churches. Indeed, the liberal state in Hungary did not yet take any further steps towards the equality of denominations until the 1890s. Among such circumstances the re-proclamation of the civil and political equality of the Jews was less than full emancipation, for the Israelites continued to be excluded from the range of 'received religions'.

The limitations notwithstanding, Hungary was a civic state with constitutional government and the rule of law by the time Andrássy became

Common Minister of Foreign Affairs in 1871. The premiership went to Lónyay, whose prestige earned as a revolutionary, an émigré and a financial expert was soon dispelled by his aggressive pursuit of personal ambition and nepotism. Of the other outstanding figures in the government party, Eötvös died in 1871 and Deák, disgusted with the opportunism, corruption and conservatism he increasingly experienced around himself, soon retired from politics. The Deák Party started to fall into squabbling factions even before Lónyay was thrown out by parliament at the end of 1872 and was followed by three other ephemeral, faceless administrations under József Szlávy, István Bittó and Baron Béla Wenckheim. Under the disastrous effects of the 1873 economic crisis, during which national bankruptcy was only avoided thanks to a huge loan from the Rothschild consortium on extremely unfavourable terms, the position of the government party was further undermined.

On the other hand, the Left Centre was also compelled to revise its earlier strategy. The creation of the German Empire required, while the failure of the Czech endeavour, also supported in Croatia by Juraj Strossmayer's People's Party, to obtain a 'trialistic' settlement pointing towards the federation of the empire, and Andrássy's new appointment (all in 1871), demonstrated the political consolidation of dualism. At the same time, the economic crisis and the general failure of the rank-and-file of the Left Centre's supporters in capitalist entrepreneurialship made the conquest of administrative positions a vital matter for the party. As the Deák Party was facing disintegration and the Left Centre was abandoning the stance of opposition control over the Compromise, both of them gravitated towards the merger. This took place in March 1875, when Kálmán Tisza abandoned the 'Bihar points'. The bulk of both parties were united in the Liberal Party, while a minority of the former government party established the Conservative Party led by Baron Pál Sennyey. After elections, Tisza became Prime Minister in October 1875, retaining that office for fifteen years.

Tisza exercised his remarkable tactical skills at first to create a party in which he commanded the unbending loyalty of a host of 'Mameluks', as his yes-men were referred to, in parliament. They were bound together by a network of liberal-patriarchal compromises, and often with economic preferments. Once in office, Tisza embarked on a policy of 'improving', instead of criticising, dualism, but he encountered one of the dilemmas encoded in the system of dualism: the limited success that was feasible at all in this field was deemed less than satisfactory, especially from a one-time opponent of the Compromise, for the Hungarian public. Its national credentials thus questioned, the government took and gave compensation by shaking, mostly in rhetoric, an iron fist at the nationalities. The other, less spectacular, but more efficient and positive result of the failure to loosen the economic ties between Austria and Hungary was Tisza's concentration on systematic, piecemeal work of which he was a real master, to refine the governmental, administrative and judicial machinery through hundreds of laws and measures, none of which were of seminal importance, but rounded off the framework for economic and cultural progress. *Quieta non movere*, 'not to disturb tranquillity', was the slogan associated with the fifteen years of the Tisza era, the one which best deserves the epithet assigned to the whole period: 'the happy times of peace'.

The first task of the Tisza administration was to put public finances into order, which it did, exploiting the credit which it was able to raise in international banking spheres through contracting long term debts and by imposing new direct taxes as well as increasing the excise taxes. In the meantime, the government started negotiations with its Austrian counterpart on issues related to the economic aspects of the Compromise. Its main goals were the modification of the commercial and customs regulations, a more proportionate distribution of excise revenues, and the breaking of the monopoly of the Austrian National Bank in the issuing of currency. The larger issue was whether the only ostensibly flexible element in the Compromise of 1867 was capable of expressing changes in the relations of forces between Austria and Hungary, or of improving the positions of the latter. On each of the particular questions, the result was a compromise, which the Hungarian public, especially in the light of the pretentious promises, interpreted as a shameful retreat, and nearly cost Tisza his parliamentary majority. He even resigned, but was reappointed because he had no alternative within his party, and the opposition was unable to assume power. As the negotiations came to an end in 1878, the modified customs regulations strengthened the positions of Hungarian magnates and Austrian industry, whereas the Austrian National Bank became 'dualised' as the Austro-Hungarian Bank, with directorates in both capitals, issuing bilingual banknotes. Hungary shared both in the Austrian state debt and the bank revenues.

The debate on the economic issues took place against the international background of permanent unrest in the Balkans, and came to an end when the emergence of a new status quo south of Hungary made the compromise most timely. In 1873, urged by Bismarck who wanted to surmount the diplomatic isolation of Germany resulting from its previous wars, and contrary to the personal intentions of Andrássy who had hoped to use the Habsburg Monarchy to prevent the expansion of Russia, the Three Emperors' League was concluded. Not even after the outbreak of an anti-Ottoman uprising in Hercegovina and Bulgaria in 1875 brought the conflicting interests of Russia and Austria-Hungary to the surface, was an anti-Russian line feasible. After the defeat of the revolts and the intervention of Serbia and Montenegro in their favour by the Turks, the two powers defined and separated their interests in protracted negotiations, as a result of which Russia could also count on the neutrality of Austria-Hungary in the war it declared on the Ottoman Empire in 1877. However, Russian arms proved too successful: although deterred from marching as far as Constantinople by the appearance of the British fleet, in March 1878 they concluded the Peace of San Stefano, practically ending Ottoman rule in the Balkans and creating Greater Bulgaria, which was unacceptable to any of the Great Powers.

It was on the insistence of Andrássy that the Berlin Congress convened in July 1878 in order to revise the settlement in the Balkans. Russia was forced to concessions: Bulgaria's growth was checked, while the full independence of Romania, Serbia and Montenegro was acknowledged, and Austria-Hungary was entrusted with the occupation and administration of Bosnia-Hercegovina. The diplomatic gain could only be materialised at the expense of a three-month campaign and several thousand casualties, and gave rise to intensive political debate, some demanding annexation instead of mere occupation, and others being afraid of a further increase of the Slav element in the population of the Dual Monarchy. Although in 1881, Austria-Hungary, Germany and Russia signed a secret agreement guaranteeing the status quo in the Balkans, Russia no longer figured in the diplomatic schemes of the empire. The cornerstone of its foreign policy was the Dual Alliance with Germany in 1879 (Andrássy's last contribution, expanded into the Triple Alliance with the inclusion of Italy in 1882), and a network of agreements with the new Balkan states (with Serbia in 1881 and Romania in 1883) that ensured the Monarchy's hegemony in the peninsula. As for Bosnia-Hercegovina, it was relegated to the province of the Common Finance Minister. It became pacified in the early 1880s when that post was occupied by the Hungarian Béni Kállay, an expert on South Slav relations. Yet by expansion in the Balkans, the empire got entangled in a trap from which it was never to escape. The occupation being immensely unpopular in Hungary when it took place, Tisza's majority was shaken, and in the face of the uproar in parliament his cabinet resigned. However, as earlier, the ruler retained him.

On the domestic scene, the most noteworthy features of the Tisza era included the first instances of a policy to restrict the nationality law of 1868, legislation affecting servants and labourers, and the appearance of new political forces. As early as in 1875, the Matica Slovenská (the Slovak cultural association) was banned upon charges of Pan-Slav agitation under the pretext of literary pursuits, and henceforth the nationalities were to be allowed to maintain only cultural and literary associations. In the following year, a so-called 'law on servants' in principle laid down the contractual relationship of servants (including agricultural labourers) and 'masters', but retained the earlier patriarchal means of discipline, including corporal punishment. To restore order, the employer was entitled to call in the gendarmes, the rural police force established in 1881. The Tisza era also saw, after a series of spontaneous movements of the industrial working class, the rise of an organised labour movement, at first in the shape of associations, culminating in the establishment of the Non-Voters Party and the Hungarian Workers' Party in 1878. The two united in 1880 as the General Workers' Party; having joined the Second International and adopted a Marxist line, in 1890 it was officially renamed the Hungarian Social Democratic Workers' Party. In all these developments, a major role was played by Leó Frankel, a prominent figure of the Paris Commune of 1871 and later an associate of Marx and Engels on the High Council of the International.

For the time being, however, the significance of other anti-liberal trends that surfaced in the same period was greater, on account of their appearance on the immediate political scene, that is, in parliament. It is true that they did not constitute a menace either to Tisza or to the ascendancy of the Liberal Party. Nevertheless, the 'agrarian movement' of conservative magnates who criticised the one-sidedly 'mercantile' sympathies of the Tisza government and spoke out in the interest of capitalist latifundia, started to foreshadow their later importance while gaining positions in the Moderate Opposition dominated by Count Albert Apponyi. As for political anti-Semitism, it initially emerged as a rival of the Independence Party, which, on the one hand, toned down its former radicalism on the question of independence, while the general nationalist atmosphere also made it drop the accent on reconciliation with the nationalities. The nascent anti-Semitic movement had the potential to overtake the Independence Party on two accounts. First, it was more outspoken, indeed aggressive in its attempt to mobilise the instincts of national 'self-defence'. Second, the chief audience it targeted was also well represented among the voters of the Independence Party: the losers of capitalist development, a process which benefited the Jewish middle classes.

Largely through immigration from Galicia and Moravia, from a modest 83,000 or one per cent of the population under Joseph II, the Jewish population of Hungary rose to nearly one million or five per cent by the eve of the First World War. Immigrant Jews established family wealth in the trade of corn, wood or wool; their sons turned it to interest in credit institutions or industrial assets, and the grandsons of the most successful bought their way into the titular aristocracy. To be sure, they were a tiny minority in a mass of small-scale businessmen and professionals, and they represented no competition to the livelihood of the genteel class, which considered the civil service as the only respectable form of employment. Nevertheless, the foreignness and capitalist success of Jews made them viable scapegoats in the eyes of an ailing gentry, in spite of the fact that they assimilated and supported the idea of the Hungarian nation-state with great enthusiasm – which, however, also meant that the anti-Semitic card could earn a fair number of votes among the national minorities. The anti-Semitic movement, led by Győző Istóczy, tried to capitalise on the death of a servant girl at the village of Tiszaeszlár in eastern Hungary in 1882, by accusing the Jews of having murdered her for ritualistic reasons. At the height of the anti-Semitic agitation, in 1883, a National Anti-Semitic Party was also established, the stake being nothing less than bringing down Tisza, whom his liberal convictions and ties with the Jewish *haute bourgeoisie* led to take a firm stand against the movement. But the Independence Party resisted the temptation to join forces with the anti-Semites, who figured rather poorly at the 1884 elections, and, having become discredited by the outcome of the trial of the blood libel case, disappeared from the political scene by the end of the decade.

The fall of Tisza was finally precipitated by his inability to work out a compromise on the delicate issue of a reform of the defence forces that was acceptable both to the ruler and to the Hungarian parliament. The bill introduced by him on the issue in early 1889 evoked not only heated debates in parliament, but also violent demonstrations. Although it was ultimately passed, Tisza realised the changing mood even within his own party. When the Council of Ministers rejected another motion of his, he tendered his resignation, which was this time accepted by Francis Joseph. The period of consolidation was followed by one of ever more chronic political crisis. Tisza held the office of Prime Minister for fifteen years; in the following fifteen years, Hungary had seven prime ministers, struggling ever more helplessly to cope with the same problems.

The limited liberal thrust of Tisza's policies continued in the 1890s under the administrations of his former associates, Gyula Szapáry and Sándor Wekerle. Szapáry himself was a rather mediocre figure, but thanks to his talented ministers, some of them inherited from Tisza, important infrastructural, financial and welfare measures were taken under his premiership between 1890 and 1892. Gábor Baross completed the scheme of the nationalisation of railway lines, begun in the early 1880s, and although some private lines remained, the preponderance of national ones ensured lower fares and uniform standards. Baross also made remarkable efforts to develop Hungarian maritime navigation, centred on Fiume (Rijeka) on the Adriatic. Mainly Italian as regards its population and claimed also by the Croats, Fiume was nevertheless annexed directly to Hungary, connected with Budapest since 1873 by rail, and became the tenth largest port of Europe by 1914. The fiscal reforms of 1892, executed in Hungary by Wekerle as Finance Minister, introduced the crown, a new stable currency based on the gold standard (following the general European trend since the 1870s) to the whole of the Monarchy. In 1891, the parliament passed legislation on health insurance schemes for labourers, and Sunday became an obligatory day of rest. On the other hand, the authorities shook an iron fist at the rural proletariat of the 'Storm Corner' (the area between the Tisza, the Maros and the Körös Rivers in the Great Plain), where unrest was endemic from 1891 through the trial of the 'agrarian socialist' leader János Szántó Kovács in 1895 to the end of the decade.

It was also under the Szapáry government that the proposals for the reform of church-state relations, introduced by the Wekerle administration, were worked out. In Hungary, only a minority of the Catholic clergy, associated with the names of Ottokár Prohászka and Sándor Giesswein, was imbued with the spirit of critical adjustment to bourgeois modernity that was to be the foundation of the Christian Socialist movement, represented by Pope Leo XIII. However, even the reformist Pope opposed the contemplated separation of Church and state in an encyclical specifically devoted to Hungary. Also backed by the profoundly religious ruler, who considered the Church one of the strongest pillars of the monarchy, it successfully resisted innovations that had been introduced in most of the western countries a few decades earlier: civil marriages, state registration of births and deaths, the freedom of religious choice and of having no religious affiliation, the acceptance of the Israelite religion as a 'received' faith. Against a background of intensive public interest and heated debates in parliament, these reforms were finally introduced in 1894 and 1895, and became outstanding pieces of liberal legislation in Hungary.

Francis Joseph gave up his reluctance upon the church-state issue in the hope that the concessions, which answered widespread demand, would quell the swelling disquiet on 'national' issues, fuelled by the main opposition parties. The National Party, founded in 1892 by the increasingly popular and influential Apponyi, not only aimed to 'improve' the Compromise in order better to satisfy agrarian interests, but shared the demands of the Independence Party to enhance the Hungarian element in the Monarchy by the more frequent and extended presence of the court in Budapest, the more frequent display of the Hungarian coat-of-arms, the use of Hungarian in the training of officers etc. These were devices of appearance rather than substance, nevertheless they were suitable to the exertion of mass appeal, especially in the atmosphere created by the ruler's refusal to allow the public mourning and official funeral of Kossuth, who died in Turin in 1894.

Wekerle, discredited with the nation by his retreat on the issue of the Kossuth funeral, and with the ruler by his failure to quell the discontent merely through the reform of religious affairs, stepped down and was replaced by Dezső Bánffy, the 'Pasha of Doboka' (the *főispán* of that county), in January 1895. The nickname concealed a ruthless and impatient administrator who had a reputation as a 'devourer of Socialists' and an ardent defender of Magyar supremacy. He was expected to check social unrest and to ensure that the growing patriotic fervour was channelled in a direction acceptable from the point of view of the Compromise at a time when the imminent millenary celebrations of the Hungarian conquest of the Carpathian Basin gave ample opportunity to its expression.

The millenary year of 1896 was indeed marked by a temporary peace between the contending political forces in the country. Public events, ceremonially opened establishments mainly in the capital, the grandiose exhibition that took stock of the Hungarian achievement of ten centuries and especially contemporary times, were all supposed to disseminate the image of a stable and 'great' nation fulfilling a civilising mission in its historical habitat. The most comprehensive foundation of the political *treuga dei* of 1896 was Hungarian nationalism, whose outlook had undergone a considerable change since mid-century. The emphasis in it shifted from the pursuit of the most complete independence possible, combined with the most complete freedom for all, to the argument that Hungary's heritage and the responsibility towards posterity obliged it to grasp the opportunity presented by 1867 and recover the standing of power it once enjoyed through economic progress, Magyarisation and the obtaining of better positions in the common government, whose focus might once be transferred to Budapest.

On the whole, the treatment of the national minorities in Hungary before the First World War could still be described as relatively tolerable, especially compared with contemporary Eastern and South-Eastern Europe. The security of the law was provided to all who were prepared to observe the principle of the 'unitary Hungarian political nation'. Nevertheless, in the pursuit of grandeur, the impatience of Hungarian nationalism materialised into an ever greater number of Hungarian lessons in schools and the vigorous promotion of Hungarian in all areas of public life; into about 90 per cent of civil servants speaking Hungarian as their first language (while only a quarter of the country's non-Magyar inhabitants knew Hungarian); into legislation Magyarising the names of localities and into encouragement given to people to do the same with their names. Administrative and juridical action was taken against those leaders of the nationalities who not only protested against the violations of the 1868 nationality law, but also criticised that law on account of its ignoring the political individuality of non-Magyar peoples, and campaigned for national recognition and territorial autonomy.

From 1881, a united Hungarian and Transylvanian Romanian National Party demanded the separation of Transylvania, with its former autonomous status, from Hungary, and in 1892, enjoying the support of the Romanian King Charles I, addressed a Memorandum to Francis Joseph listing its grievances and claims. While the ruler forwarded the document, unread, to the Hungarian government, it was also made public by its authors, providing a pretext for the authorities to raise a lawsuit against them on account of subversive propaganda, resulting in harsh sentences. Libel suits and police harassment afflicted many activists of the national minorities after the Congress of the Nationalities in Budapest in 1895, which also rejected the idea of the Hungarian nation-state and demanded territorial autonomy.

Social and political conflict also grew more intense in the second half of the 1890s. The Declaration of Principle of the Social Democratic Party issued in 1890 was adjusted to the 'revisionist' standards prevailing in the contemporary western working-class movement: it proposed to take advantage of the 'general crisis' and 'irresolvable internal contradictions' of capitalism not through revolutionary action, but through the evolutionary democratisation of the state by universal suffrage, welfare legislation etc. Though the organisation of trade unions and strikes continued, for the sake of legality the party even abandoned agitation among the agricultural labourers in 1897. More serious were the agrarian disturbances that continued east of the Tisza with the guidance of István Várkonyi, a former Social Democrat who also harboured anarchist ideas. A general harvesters' strike, rioting and spontaneous land distribution in 1897 and 1898 ended in the intervention of the military, the expulsion of 'agitators' and a wave of arrests. The subsequently issued 'slave law' facilitated serious administrative interference in the contractual relationship of the employer and the employee, on behalf of the former, and introduced severe penalties for strikes, while it also regulated wages and redressed the most salient abuses.

Simultaneously with, and even more than the lower-class movements, the governing Liberal Party was concerned about the proliferation of opponents and the weakening of its own support in the political arena. The growing influence of the agrarian interest within the rank of the party threatened its coherence and position in general, especially as it was the main trend in the opposition National Party, was powerful in the Catholic People's Party established in 1895 by aristocratic opponents of the reform of religious affairs, and was also represented by a strong pressure group of conservative magnates and landowners who dominated the Hungarian Agriculturalist Association created in 1896. As neoconservatives elsewhere in Europe, the Hungarian agrarians demanded protectionism for agriculture, the control of 'foreign' and 'mobile' capital, and promoted the co-operative movement to obtain easy credit and secure markets. All this involved light touches of anti-Semitism and heavier ones of social demagogy. In addition, the Independence Party still commanded massive support, although it was increasingly refraining from championing democratic initiatives and its patriotism became ever more superficial and rhetorical. The government party still enjoyed a parliamentary majority, but the fact that in 1896 it was ensured by massively rigged elections only served to aggravate tensions.

The situation became untenable when the prolongation of the economic compromise, already agreed in 1896 but its parliamentary debate having been postponed because of protracted government crisis in Austria, came on the agenda in 1898. The draft contained concessions to Hungary, but it also proposed to raise Hungary's share in shouldering common expenses, and was severely opposed by the Independence Party. Finally the two governments agreed, and Francis Joseph declared, in the Clause of Ischl, that the customs union would remain in force even without legal regulation. The Hungarian parliament was ablaze in consternation upon the abandonment of the nation's right to make her own economic arrangements. Debate was acrimonious, personal assaults were exchanged and duels were fought; Bánffy and the younger Tisza, István, tried in vain to reform the standing orders of the House to suppress parliamentary obstruction by the opposition, which even won the support of some of the government party. An extra-legal situation arose: 1899 began without the budget having been passed. Bánffy was obliged to give up his seat.

It soon turned out that the turmoil was not about matters of high principle, and the obstructionists could be appeased by petty concessions, without solving the critical issues, and winning only a temporary lull. The new Prime Minister, Kálmán Széll, was Deák's son-in-law and a man whose personality was ideally suited to making the compromises necessary for constitutional government. With a skilful management of rival factions, he brought back a sizeable number of dissidents led by the younger Gyula Andrássy into the Liberal Party, and with some retreat on agrarian issues he also won Apponyi's National Party for the government camp. The rather empty formula that Hungary, in the absence of the prolongation of the customs union as required by the Compromise of 1867, became an autonomous customs area but prolonged the union voluntarily, sounded good enough for the opposition, too. But the parliamentary truce was deceptive. It lasted only until the changing international atmosphere made itself felt on the neuralgic point of the constitutional issue: the position of the common army. Around 1900, amidst an already escalating armaments race among the Great Powers, Austria-Hungary's international position was waning. A temporary rapprochement with her great Balkan rival, Russia, did not offset the fact that whereas the latter had secured her position through an alliance with France, the renewal of the Triple Alliance in 1902 hardly veiled Italian irredentism directed at South Tyrol and German misgivings concerning the monarchy's ambitions in the Balkans. Great Britain was also abandoning its traditional policy which favoured the Habsburg Empire. The Austro-Hungarian army was lagging far behind the other powers. Among such circumstances, the raising of the annual recruitment quota seemed imperative, and not even the Hungarian parliamentary opposition objected to the bill that suggested a 25 per cent increase. In return, however, they demanded the introduction of Hungarian as the language of command and Hungarian insignia for the units recruited in Hungary, and the reduction of the length of compulsory service. The latter claim made it possible to present the issue as a struggle against 'militarism' to the Hungarian public, which had anyway reasons good enough, dating back to 1849–1849, to resent the generally pro-Habsburg mentality of the army. Széll was unable to break obstruction, which broke him in June 1903, as well as his successor Count Khuen-Héderváry, the former Ban of Croatia and a confidant of the monarch, three months later. Francis Joseph's general army orders of Chlopy (Galicia), emphasising his insistence on the unity of his army and its benefit for all the 'races' of the empire, added fuel to the fire: Magyars did not fancy being considered merely as one of the 'races' of the empire. The ruler now turned to István Tisza, who had emerged as a dominant figure in the Liberal Party, and was convinced that the maintenance of dualism was the only chance for the survival of historic Hungary.

Regarded as stubborn, taciturn, even misanthropic, Tisza was a politician of a stature and integrity unknown in Hungary since the passing of the last representatives of the great reform generation. Among the traditional elite he might have been alone in recognising the full relevance not only of industrialisation and capitalism, but also to some extent of the social and nationality issues to the predicament of Hungary in the early twentieth century. Yet, he believed that he could have the one without the other: that the achievements could be retained through eliminating, instead of solving, the tensions they generated. His traditionalism, the paternalistic and aristocratic brand of liberalism he inherited from his father led him to turn his recognitions to 'disciplining' the historic classes and awakening them to an awareness of where their true interests lay: in the consolidation of dualism. He was adamant in breaking the obstruction of the opposition by a strictly rigorous application of the standing orders, in order to ensure the proper functioning of the legislature. At first he seemed successful, but when his draft to modify the rules was voted in November 1904 in a dubious manner by the liberal majority, a faction of the Liberal Party led by Andrássy the younger left the government party and joined forces with the coalition of all of the parliamentary opposition on the basis of a programme to 'improve' the dualist system. At the last session of the legislature on December 13, 1904, violence broke out and furniture was smashed in the House of Representatives. Parliament was dissolved, and at the ensuing elections of January 1905 the coalition, headed by the leader of the Independence Party, Kossuth's son Ferenc, gained a substantial majority.

The limitations of constitutionalism and national independence in the Hungary of dualism now became unmasked: protracted negotiations between the ruler, who was unwilling to make concessions on issues like the army which involved his reserved rights, and the coalition, which was similarly unwilling to compromise, led into a stalemate. At the same time, the instability as well as the news of the revolutionary events in Russia encouraged strikes in urban centres and rural areas around the country. Among such circumstances, in June 1905 Francis Joseph appointed the former head of his bodyguards Baron Géza Fejérváry as Prime Minister in a non-parliamentary caretaker government. It was expected to mediate between the crown and the new parliamentary majority, but nothing of the sort happened. The leaders of the coalition protested, and urged the counties to passive resistance; somewhat later, plans were drafted in Vienna for the military occupation of the country. By the autumn, the 'bodyguard government' also launched an attempt to become an independent political force. Minister of the Interior József Kristóffy, in particular, wanted to win the Social Democrats and the nationalities, and negotiated a pact with the social democrat leader Ernő Garami regarding the introduction of universal suffrage. On September 15 ('Red Friday'), there was a general strike, and about a hundred thousand pro-government demonstrators submitted a petition to parliament and abused the 'gentlemanly rebellion' of the counties. Faced with reform from above, Tisza and the Liberal Party, who initially gave prompts to Fejérváry to show strength to the coalition, also joined the 'national resitance'.

However, on February 19, 1906, the parliament was occupied by the military and dissolved by a royal commissar, and in the spring the resistance of the counties was also broken. The coalition retreated into the pact offered by the ruler in early April: it would be asked to form a government in return for forsaking its army programme, enacting the international trade agreements signed during the crisis, and introducing electoral reform. While Wekerle formed his second cabinet, which included Andrássy, Ferenc Kossuth, Apponyi and other respectable names, Tisza dissolved the Liberal Party, and opted for temporary retirement from politics. At the elections of May 1906, the coalition scored a great victory (the Independence Party alone winning 60 per cent of the seats), and was opposed in parliament only by two dozen representatives of the nationalities and a few unaffiliated members.

The evaporation of the government party of the past three decades was a landslide indeed, but whoever expected fundamental changes, was wrong. The pact of April 1906, the 'new compromise' was a complete abandonment of the programme of the coalition. The crisis ended with the system of dualism unchanged, and the drastic political realignment conceived by Kristóffy unaccomplished. What the 'national resistance' of 1905 and its aftermath revealed was the unbridgeable gap between the political elite and the masses, and the contradiction between great power pretensions and the democratic agenda. It certainly did not help that the main organised representative of the latter, the Social Democratic Party, openly declared its standing over petty national issues, but the democratic camp was anyway strong enough only to stimulate the dynasty and the Hungarian ruling classes to close their ranks. The Habsburgs and the Hungarian landed nobility had never been the best of friends, but their interests, sometimes after much bloodshed, had always coincided in defence of the Monarchy and its system of rule. The dynasty often played off the peasantry and the nationalities against the unruly Hungarian nobility, but never thought of governing through them; Francis Joseph had an intense dislike of opposition magnates and the pretentious gentry, but was aware that they were indispensable for the great power status of his empire. The social and political conservatism of both parties mutually reinforced each other, the ruler preferring a submissive coalition to Kristóffy's unpredictable social engineering, and vice versa.

At the outset, the coalition had a considerable capital of popularity stemming from the aura of its 'defending the constitution', and even some of its steps that seemed contrary to its slogans were accepted as necessary sacrifices. However, the concert of the parties united by hardly more than their earlier opposition status, started to crumble soon, and the consistently '67er and conservative policies of the coalition led to the defection of fledgling groups, a growing disaffection of the public, and a complete moral crisis by 1909. The first truly frustrating arrangement, both for the coalition that made it and the public that swallowed it, was the outcome of the 1907 negotiations of the renewal of the customs union: the victory scored by the Hungarian government consisted in renaming the 'customs union' a 'custom treaty' and the increase of agricultural tariffs, and was bought at the price of a two per cent increase of the Hungarian share in the quota. The continuing strikes and disturbances among the urban and rural workers were calmed, instead of any comprehensive programme, by a mixture of repression and legislation that combined restrictive measures and social reforms. The promise of electoral reform, for which a crowd of a hundred thousand demonstrated for a second time on 'Red Thursday', October 10, 1907, came to nothing. Instead of the universal suffrage demanded, Andrássy submitted a bill that would have expanded the suffrage but would have made it plural or partial according to property and education, and was not at all unhappy when even this was rejected by the parliament. His proposal to decentralise the administration and to extend county autonomy met a similar fate.

Whereas the coalition was quite impotent in representing the nationalist position in the face of Vienna, it fell with far greater vigour on the nationalities. The dimensions of 'forced Magyarisation' have been often exaggerated, even if the ratio of Magyars within the population of Hungary (without Croatia) climbed from 41 to 54 per cent between 1848 and 1910; and nationalism was as intense among the non-Magyars of the region as among the Hungarians. The difference was that the latter had the state machinery at their disposal to promote the realisation of the ideal of the Hungarian nation-state. The school law of 1907 known as the 'Lex Apponyi', while raising the salaries of teachers, obliged non-Hungarian schools to ensure that by the end of the fourth form their pupils knew Hungarian. In the same year, knowledge of Hungarian became a precondition for employment at the state railways, a measure which evoked the great 'Croat obstruction' in the Hungarian parliament. Still in 1907, gendarmes killed twelve Slovak protesters in a scuffle in the village of Csernova (Černová) in northern Hungary who wanted to prevent the new church from being consecrated by a priest other than their own (incidentally, the later Slovak nationalist leader Andrej Hlinka). News of the affair spread across the West, and did great damage to the reputation of Hungary, especially in the English-speaking world, where it was given publicity through the works of the historian Robert William Seton-Watson. Many of the survivors of the 'massacre of Černová' later received sentences of imprisonment, as did members of the Serbian Independent Party, charged with agitation against the Monarchy, in 1909.

Agitation indeed there was; what is more, it was encouraged from Serbia whose Prime Minister Noviković claimed in February 1909 that the Serbian nation included those seven million Serbs (a somewhat exaggerated figure) who lived 'against their will' in the Habsburg Monarchy. This was an angry response, shared by Russia and her western allies as well as the Ottoman Empire, to the Austro-Hungarian annexation of Bosnia-Hercegovina, occupied since 1878. Foreign Minister Alois Aerenthal, who wanted to catch up with the active power policy of the Monarchy's ally Germany in the only region suited for that purpose in the case of Austria-Hungary, the Balkans, actually cheated Russia. Having concluded a deal with his Russian counterpart Alexander Isvolskii regarding the annexation in return for supporting Russia's claim for free access to the Turkish Straits, he announced the annexation without waiting for Russia to prepare the ground for the latter with the other great powers. In spite of some Hungarian hopes that, because of the medieval precedents of overlordship, Bosnia-Hercegovina would be placed under Hungarian jurisdiction, it became an imperial province.

Although the re-arrangement of the Hungarian political scene as envisaged by Kristóffy during the 1905 crisis did not occur, new political forces emerged during the coalition years, especially as it was demonstrated that the former opposition, once in government, constituted no real alternative to its predecessors. The first independent political organisations of the well-to-do peasantry, suspicious of the agrarians of the coalition, appeared between 1906 and 1910 in the Independent Socialitst Peasant Party of András Áchim, a rich farmer of Slovak background, and the National Independence and 48er Farmers' Party led by András Nagyatádi Szabó. Both of them campaigned for universal suffrage. The former, which withered after the assassination of Áchim in 1911, added an eclectic programme including the improvement of the situation of the nationalities, progressive taxation and the distribution of all large estates among the peasantry. The latter demanded the state redemption of latifundia and mortmains. The Social Democratic Party also gained in influence, thanks not in the least to its talented leaders like Garami, mentioned above, or the excellent orator Dezső Bokányi, and intellectuals turned to socialism like Ervin Szabó, an original Marxist theorist of international stature.

Szabó also maintained close links with the most articulate of all the challengers of the regime, the radical democrats, who raised their standard in the social science journal *Huszadik Század* (Twentieth Century), launched in 1900, and the Society for Social Science, founded in the following year. The group, whose ranks contained a fair number of young assimilated Jews, argued on the basis of profound sociological analysis, inspired by social Darwinism and to some extent Marxism, in favour of universal suffrage, the elimination of 'feudal' remnants like the latifundia and the promotion of the co-operative movement among the peasantry, democratic local self-government combined with the enforcement and the extension of the nationalities law, educational reform, improved insurance schemes. They had a broad network of sympathisers from dissident Independentists through the Galilei Circle of university students and Freemasons to respected literary men like the prophetic poet Endre Ady. They did not emerge as a political party until 1914. Yet, their programme was already conceived by 1907, and published by their leader Oszkár Jászi in his article 'Towards a New Hungary', foreshadowing the ideas in his huge scholarly synthesis of 1912 on the nationality question: that there was a way to reconcile national independence and democratic progress, 'the Hungarian idea and free thinking', in the historic state transformed through pertinent reforms into a brotherhood of nations.

However, the dated and old-fashioned liberalism of the previous generations defied the democratic challenge, and the coalition collapsed of its own efforts. A part of the leaders and most of the supporters of the Independence Party, disillusioned by the failure of the government to achieve the 'national goals', had already been alienated from the government by the time a dispute over the Austro-Hungarian Bank broke out in 1909. Gyula Justh, who by that time bitterly regretted having ceded party leadership, for reasons of prestige, to Ferenc Kossuth, now seceded with about a half of the parliamentary deputies of the party. In January 1910, Wekerle had to step down and was replaced by the old liberal Khuen-Héderváry. This was the time for Tisza to re-emerge on the political scene at the head of a party largely recruited from the *haute bourgeois* and landowning supporters of the one-time Liberal Party. His new National Party of Work won a convincing victory at what turned out to be the last elections in the Hungary of the dualist period in June 1910.

The main item on the agenda of the new legislature, as many times before, was the bill from 1903 on army development, made timely by an escalating armaments race, in which Austria-Hungary lagged behind, and an increasingly tense international atmosphere, marked in 1911 by the Second Moroccan Crisis and the Italian-Ottoman war. In principle, the opposition did not object; but whereas the former coalition tied their agreement to the traditional national demands, the secessionists of Justh, who gravitated towards the Social Democrats and other democratic forces, established with them the Franchise Alliance and campaigned for universal suffrage. Obstruction in parliament started again, and Tisza came to the conclusion that the strengthening of dualism and of historic Hungary as he envisaged it was no longer compatible with observing the niceties of parliamentarism. His view prevailed in the party of one-time Liberals in the spring of 1912, when Khuen-Héderváry was replaced by László Lukács as Prime Minister and Tisza had himself elected speaker of the House of Representatives. A mass demonstration in the capital against his hardly concealed plans degenerated into street fighting between the police and protesters, with six people mortally wounded on 'Bloody Thursday', May 23, 1912. On June 4, the new speaker refused to let the opposition speak, and had its protesting members removed from the parliament by the police. Undisturbed by obstruction, the government party deputies passed the army bill. Similar methods were used in the debate of a rather lightweight and much criticised electoral reform bill, voted through in April 1913, and of measures taken as precautions in case the major war which Tisza had no doubt would some time break out between the Habsburg Monarchy and its adversaries in the region: laws that curtailed the freedom of association, assembly and the press, prohibited republican propaganda and made it possible for the government to wield emergency powers.

The expectations of Tisza, who took over the premiership from Lukács in June 1913, were warranted by the fact that the Balkans became a powder magazine simultaneously with the offensive of the National Party of Work in domestic politics. Encouraged by the success of Italy against the Ottoman Empire in the war fought for Mediterranean hegemony in 1911–1912, the alliance of Serbia, Montenegro, Bulgaria and Greece attacked their one-time suzerain in October 1912. The First Balkan War ended in defeat for the Turks, and a quarrel of the victors over the prey, namely, Macedonia. Greece and Serbia, also supported by Romania, defeated Bulgaria in the Second Balkan War of 1913.

The two Balkan wars were a serious embarrassment to the Habsburg Monarchy, on several accounts. They showed that it was no longer able to keep the new states of the Balkans, which in terms of nationalist greed were in no way inferior to the mightier powers of Europe, from pursuing their goals in a region it had long considered its own sphere of interest. Of its potential allies in the area, Bulgaria was exhausted, and Romania proved to be unreliable by being instrumental in regional destabilisation. Of the Great Powers, not even Germany supported Austro-Hungarian diplomacy during the crisis; and the confidence that Serbia, backed by Russia and potentially by the Triple Entente in her ambition to create a united South Slav state, drew from the outcome, bade ill for the future of the Monarchy and especially Hungary. Whereas the war party, centred especially around the general staff and its chief Franz Conrad von Hötzendorf in Vienna, urged a military showdown with Serbia already during the Second Balkan War, Tisza and the traditional political elite in Hungary, while in principle they were not against it, feared that such a step would stir up nationalist sentiments among Hungary's Serbs and produce a counter-effect. Tisza therefore experimented with concessions: whereas he considered an understanding with the South Slavs hopeless, he negotiated with the leaders of the Romanian National Party to offset the magnetic influence exerted on the Romanians of Transylvania by the Romanian nation-state across the border, and to secure the latter's loyalty as an ally. However, the gap between the maximum he was willing to offer and the minimum acceptable to the Romanians proved to be unbridgeable.

It was against this background that the fateful visit of the Emperor's nephew Archduke Francis Ferdinand, heir apparent to the throne of Austria-Hungary since the suicide of Archduke Rudolph in 1889, took place in Sarajevo. The visit and the concomitant army exercises in Bosnia were intended as a show of strength in the Balkans, and the timing of the parade in the capital was an implicit provocation to Serbian national sentiment: June 28 was the anniversary of the fall of the medieval Serbian state in the Battle of Kosovopolje in 1389. At the same time, the heir apparent was widely known to be a sworn enemy of Hungarian hegemony in the eastern half of the empire, flirting both with the ideas of trialism (raising Croatia to the status of Hungary) and plans of reorganising the monarchy into a centralised federation of 'Greater Austria', as put forward by the Romanian Aurel Popoviçi. His violent removal seemed desirable for a double reason to the military intelligence service in Belgrade, which was the counterpart of the Austrian general staff in paving the way to war: it would do justice to Serbian nationalist passions, and prevent a reform of the Habsburg Monarchy that might allay the enthusiasm among its South Slavs for union with Serbia. The strings pulled from the Serbian capital, Francis Ferdinand and his consort were shot to death in Sarajevo on June 28, 1914, by Gavrilo Princip, a Bosnian Serb studying in Belgrade. The times of peace had been less and less happy for a while, and the stage was now set for the time of war.

3. *Progress, prosperity, and the flowers of decay*

This section is about the growth of material civilisation, some peculiarities of the social structure and the different forms of popular as well as high culture in Hungary during the period of dualism, particularly in the years known as the *fin-de-siècle* or turn of the century, ranging rather freely among these diverse subjects. I chose to depart from my general rule of writing an 'integrated' history not only because the complexity of the age implies difficulties for weaving such themes coherently into the outline of political history presented in the previous section. I also wanted to stress a number of things. First, this period witnessed probably the greatest, and the relatively least ambivalent, of the very few success stories in Hungarian economic history. Next, a disproportionately large part of the most conspicuous constructions that dominate the man-made landscape of the country (mainly in the capital, but in other urban centres, too) is owing to the vigour of this *Gründerzeit*, an age of founders, which also bred some of the attitudes and habits, ways of living, forms of entertainment and pastimes that are still relevant a century later. Finally, the *fin-de-siècle* modernity also nurtured an exciting modernist culture and coincided with the formative years of many of the individuals with whose names the 'Hungarian genius' has become associated across five continents in the course of the twentieth century.

On the bases of post–1848 legislation and the political arrangements of the Compromise, Hungary was transformed by a somewhat belated industrial revolution from an underdeveloped agrarian country into a relatively rapidly developing agrarian-industrial one. While agriculture remained the dominant branch of the economy, industry, or, more properly, some industries and business areas became its most dynamic branches. The overall growth of GDP (between an annual 2.4 and 3.7 per cent, according to different calculations) corresponded to, or even slightly exceeded, the European average (falling behind other 'latecomers', such as the Scandinavian countries and Germany, and in the same category as both Russia and erstwhile pioneers of industrialisation like Britain or Belgium and the Netherlands, but leaving behind Southern Europe and the Balkans). The output of the Hungarian economy thus grew at least threefold, perhaps even fivefold, between 1867 and 1914. In industry, which in 1910 employed 18 per cent of the labour force and accounted for a quarter of the national income, the pace of growth was 4.5 to 6 per cent each year, while in agriculture, with 62 per cent of the labour force and 44 per cent of the national income, it was no more than 1.7 to 2.2 per cent. At the same time, in terms of per capita national income, the most general indicator of the level of economic development, Hungary was only at the top of the third tier of European countries, reaching a mere 40 to 50 per cent of British and Scandinavian and 80 per cent of Italian and Austrian figures, and exceeding only the most underdeveloped countries of Southern, Eastern and South-Eastern Europe. Despite truly momentous changes, the vision of a speedy catch-up with the vanguard of European economic development was a mirage, just as much as the hope of the resurrection of Hungary as a great power.

Agriculture was still the fundamental sector of the Hungarian economy, and the process of mechanisation that took place over the period gave it powerful incentives. The most spectacular of all changes was brought about by the increasing use of the threshing machine, operated at first by steam, then by internal combustion engines. Ploughing was also made easier, especially in the large and medium sized estates, by machinery. As result of these innovations, as well as state intervention in the technological modernisation of agriculture from the 1880s, cereal growing, which remained the most important branch within agriculture, preserved its competitiveness after the crises occasioned by the influx of cheap overseas grain in Europe from the 1870s. Other developments which favoured increasing outputs included the draining of marshlands, as a result of which the percentage of arable land left fallow in the country fell from 25 to 8 per cent during the period. Modern systems of crop rotation which replaced the three field system, the scientific improvement of seed quality and the introduction of chemical fertilisers were to the same effect: outputs were doubled or trebled (as in the case of wheat, corn and rye), or even multiplied (potato and sugar beet). Grain yields surpassed those in France, not to mention Hungary's immediate neighbours and elsewhere in Southern Europe, although they were a mere 50 to 70 per cent of those in Denmark or Belgium. Wine production survived the devastating phylloxera which, between the mid-1880s and the end of the century, destroyed over half of the vineyards; besides the 'historic' wine regions, like Tokaj or Villány, new stock was planted on the sandy soils between the Danube and the Tisza. This was also the period when products of Hungarian vegetable farming and orchardry, like the paprika of Szeged, the onion of Makó, or the apricot of Kecskemét, started to earn a reputation even beyond the borders of the country. Livestock breeding also underwent remarkable progress, its direction being from extensive to intensive methods. The stock of cattle and pigs not only increased steadily, but its composition changed, too: the grey longhorn Hungarian cattle, driven to the West on their feet by the hundred thousand in the early modern period, was largely replaced by the speckled Simmenthal breed valued for its milk, as were Hungarian breeds of pig by the more prolific lard pig of Balkan origin. Over four hundred privately owned and four big state stud-farms bred prize-winning horses, like the fabulous Kincsem, never defeated in the course of fifty-four races between 1876 and 1879, and later even sculpted.

The undoubted momentum of the changes in the rural economy contrasted markedly with the overwhelmingly static image of the rural hierarchy of social relations and attitudes, to the extent that sociologists and historians have claimed that in this period Hungary developed a 'dual social structure', stratified not only horizontally in terms of material status, prestige and influence, but also unusually sharply divided vertically into 'traditional' (largely rural) and 'modern' (largely urban) blocks. The greatest problem of the Hungarian economy, and the most salient anachronism of Hungarian society was constituted by the extremes of 'latifundia' and 'strip-holding', unknown elsewhere in Europe except in Romania: the fact that while slightly over two thousand magnates with over 1,500 acres (among them, less than two hundred possessing more than 15,000 acres and one, Prince Móric Esterházy, about

700,000) owned nearly a quarter of the land, hundreds of thousands of peasant families literally vegetated on plots of a few acres. These were utterly incapable of any sort of modernisation; and whereas most of the major landowners successfully participated in the capitalist economy, these successes contributed to the consolidation of the economic power and social prestige, and the preservation of much of the political influence and value system, of the traditional elite.

At the top of this scale stood the barons, counts and princes, whose numbers were boosted by parvenus to some 800. Four-fifths of the members of the Upper House of Parliament, some 15 per cent of MPs, ten out of sixteen premiers and one in three ministers came from their ranks during the half-century of dualism. With economic modernisation, their prestigious names also appeared in increasing number on the boards of banks and business companies. As a block, they seemed to constitute a separate caste, secluded in their palaces, surrounded by servants and private tutors, maintaining the National Casino as their preserve and leading a life marked by ceremonious occasions of conviviality, evening parties, hunts, horse races and tennis games. This is not to say that they were a homogeneous class: in terms of lifestyle, exclusivity and priorities the foreign and 'supra-national' families, like the Schönborn, the Pallavicini or the Odeschalchi differed markedly from the established houses of Transdanubia, venerated in national tradition, like the Széchenyi or the Károlyi, and even more from the relatively less affluent, but politically also very active Teleki, Bethlen or Bánffy of Transylvania. Cleavages were distinct between the latter two categories as well: the former shopped around in Paris and spent their vacation in Cannes or Nice, while 'fashion' for the latter meant that of Budapest or Vienna, and they went on a holiday on the Adriatic or at one of the spas of Upper Hungary. They were similar in outlook to the bulk of the magnate class, the well-to-do gentry, from whom they were not separated by an impenetrable barrier. On the other hand, the last group of major landowners, the enriched bourgeoisie who bought land and held about one-fifth of latifundia, largely remained outside the circles of the aristocracy.

At the other end of the rural hierarchy, and indeed outside both the old, noble and the new, bourgeois society, stood the landless agricultural labourers (seasonal workers, harvesters, farm servants), who comprised with their families about a quarter of Hungarian society, and the 'dwarfholders' whose tiny plots hardly provided them with a proper means of subsistence. The latter constituted one-third of the landed peasantry, the most substantial segment (38 per cent) of Hungarian society, of which a mere fraction owning over 50 acres of land was able to benefit from the agrarian booms of the period. While all of the dwarfholders and the rural proletariat lived in great poverty and backwardness, labouring fourteen or sixteen hours a day from spring to autumn and reduced to idleness during the winter, they were also far from being a monolithic bloc. The smallholder, though reduced to devices from co-leasing to undertaking occasional day labour, was 'a man of his own', possessing a horse or a cow and some of them living in a house built of bricks and tiles rather than dried mud and thatch. The agrarian labourer, by contrast, had a poor hut and one or two pigs at best, and the most down-trodden of them, the numerous group of farm servants, lived in miserable, stable-like quarters, with often more than one family sharing a room. What was a common experience for these social categories was the hopelessness of improving their condition.

Not even education, which underwent drastic changes and became a major vehicle of progress in the period, provided a channel of mobility for the 'people of the *puszta*' (to borrow the title of the acute and eloquent sociographical account of their life by the writer Gyula Illyés). I have already quoted figures illustrating the effects of the 1868 law on elementary education. Higher up the scale, the number of grammar schools almost trebled and exceeded 210 by 1914; a Technical University in Budapest, and new universities of sciences were opened in Kolozsvár, Pozsony and Debrecen, and the number of students in higher education grew from less than 1,000 to more than 17,000. The numerical increase was also accompanied by better standards. Academic liberty, the founding of specialised colleges and other reforms raised Hungarian higher education from its earlier provincialism, while the superb equipment and professional and pedagogical expertise of teachers in the secondary schools was the basis of striking individual achievements. It was in these educational establishments at the turn of the century that six out of altogether eight Hungarian Nobel Prize winners (including Albert Szent-Györgyi and Jenő Wigner), as well as the composers Béla Bartók and Zoltán Kodály, the social scientists Károly (Karl) Mannheim and Károly Polányi, the philosopher György (Georg) Lukács, the mathematician János Neumann, the physicist Leó Szilárd, or the film director Sándor (Alexander) Korda acquired their general education.

But none on this impressive list of luminaries, and very few others who received secondary and higher education came from a poor rural background. The 'people of the *puszta*' accounted for a mere 2 per cent of grammar school pupils, and 1 per cent of university students. There was a similar disproportion at the expense of the national minorities (the first language of 85 per cent of university students being Hungarian), which, for historic reasons outlined in previous chapters, were over-represented at the bottom of the rural social hierarchy. No wonder that they, especially the Slovaks and Ruthenians, were especially numerous among the two million citizens of Hungary who in the twenty-five years prior to the First World War chose the only escape open for the truly destitute: emigration, mainly to the United States and Canada. One and a half million émigrés (only one-third of them being ethnic Hungarian) never returned. They settled in clusters in or near large emerging industrial centres like Cleveland, Pittsburgh or Detroit and became miners or workers; they stubbornly maintained their identities, but never realised their original goal of returning to Hungary and buy some land as soon as they had raised enough money to do so.

Between the extremes of the wealthy, prestigious and powerful magnates and the indigent farm hands, there were middling strata, which were quite variegated even within the 'traditional' segment of the dual social structure. I have already mentioned the relatively well-to-do peasantry, some of whom were able to accumulate and many more merely to carve out a secure though laborious existence. Arguably, however, the special flavour of the Hungarian social landscape under dualism was owing, more than any of the strata mentioned so far, to the 'genteel' or 'historic' middle class or, in short, the gentry. It comprised the few thousand families of noble background who still retained estates sizeable enough to lead the life of landed entrepreneurs, and the hundred thousand strong crowd of other nobles who lost all or nearly all of their land and constituted a kind of administrative intelligentsia in the state, the Church or on the estates of magnates. Providing nearly a half of the MPs and over three-quarters of the key officials in the county administration, the gentry dominated the Hungarian public scene in the period, a circumstance which reflects their strong political interest and historical consciousness. Besides these qualities, they also displayed patriotic devotion, commitment to a peculiar 'code of honour' and gallantry. At the same time, the system of gentry attitudes involved, largely as corrupted versions of the features just mentioned, superiority and arrogance, nationalistic and anti-democratic sentiment, superficiality and self-destructive idleness – organising principles of a way of life marked, in somewhat exaggerated but nevertheless expressive legend, by card games for high stakes, unpaid debts, and reckless debauchery to the tunes of bitter-sweet gypsy music.

It should be clear from the aforementioned that the traditional elements of Hungarian society adapted, for different reasons, incompletely and with difficulty to capitalism, which nevertheless did arrive in Hungary in the period of dualism with a momentum sufficient to change its face beyond recognition. Given the circumstances, large-scale industrialisation was not an immediate possibility, and the areas of emphasis became the creation of a modern credit system, transport and communication infrastructure, industries directly erected upon agriculture, and the production of raw materials. The spectacular achievements in these fields were supplemented by a number of outstanding business ventures in other branches as well, and accompanied with the rise of a distinctive *haute bourgeoisie*, a respectable modern middle class, and an exciting urban culture.

As regards the chronic shortage of credit Széchenyi once complained about, it became definitively a matter of the past. What is more, even though the policies of Hungarian credit institutions were largely dictated by Austrian and French concerns, the share of foreign investment in them fell to 25 per cent by the end of the period. In 1867, the number of different credit institutions hardly exceeded one hundred. By 1913, there were nearly six thousand, and during the same period the amount of stocks and savings they held grew from 17 million crowns to 6.6 billion. The improvement of the transport and communications network was just as striking. Railway mileage, slightly over 2,200 kilometres in 1867, increased fivefold by 1890, and was again doubled by 1913, yielding 22,000 kilometres altogether. In terms of density, Hungary left Italy behind and fell into the same category as Austria; compared to the size of the population, it was only surpassed by France. The system also worked efficiently. Whereas it had taken about thirty hours for the coach service to cover the distance between Vienna and Buda, the Orient Express connected the two capitals in less than five hours. By 1900, over 92 per cent of goods in the country was carried by rail and a mere 1 per cent by carts (and the rest by steamships), while the absolute amount of freight also multiplied. The telegraph service was first established in Hungary in 1847, and the network grew to 17,000 kilometres in 1867 and 170,000 in 1914. The telephone exchange, a Hungarian invention of Tivadar Puskás, was installed in Budapest in 1881, and thirty years later there were twenty-thousand telephone appliances in the capital alone.

As mentioned above, and continuing the trend begun in the years of neo-absolutism, the structure of industry reflected that of the economy as a whole, and thus the leading branch was the production of foodstuffs. About 15 per cent of the industrial labour force was employed in it, and they supplied around 40 per cent of the production value of Hungarian industry, a share slightly declining after the turn of the century when heavy industry grew in importance. Grain production being central to Hungarian agriculture, milling continued to be the main sector of industry, with Budapest ranking as the first milling city in the world until overtaken, at the turn of the century, by Minneapolis. Its ascendancy was not only due to the fine wheat, mainly from the southern regions of Bačka and the Banate, but also to technological excellence arising from innovations by brilliant engineers like András Mechwart of the Ganz factory. Other branches in the production of foodstuffs that made rapid progress were sugar industry and brewing. The consumption of beer started to gain momentum in a nation of wine-drinkers. As regards other industries, Hungary had to offset the disadvantages of the common tariff zone, which favoured the traditionally far more advanced Austria and Bohemia. Especially from the 1880s, Hungarian governments embarked on a well-considered policy of supporting industrial development through interest-free loans, tax allowances and subsidies whose amount, by 1913, reached an annual 10 million crowns. As a result, whereas Hungarian industry consisted of 170 joint-stock companies and a few hundred private firms employing less than 100,000 workers at the time of the Compromise, by 1914 there were about 5,500 industrial plants with a labour force of well over half a million. The power of machinery they operated grew from 9,000 to 900,000 horse power, a hundredfold increase. The Hungarian textile industry, which was the main vehicle of industrialisation in the classic model of England and some other countries, remained quite insignificant in the shadow of its Czech and Austrian counterpart. On the other hand, mining and metallurgy developed robustly, and, remarkably enough, became the foundation of a sophisticated machine industry that was on a par at least with that of the other Habsburg lands, and was pioneering in technological innovation by European standards. The most prestigious of these plants, the Ganz machine works, served as the main workshop for these inventions. Mechwart's roll mill has already been referred to. Another young engineer of the factory, Kálmán Kandó, developed the electric locomotive (first used in Italy) between 1896 and 1898; the first Hungarian internal combustion engines were produced at the Ganz factory under the direction of Donát Bánki and János Csonka, who in 1891 also invented the carburator. By 1914, over a thousand automobiles were driven on Hungary's dusty roads. Finally, Hungary was at the forefront of the progress in the most modern branches of industry, the chemical and electricity industries. Again, it was electrical engineers of the Ganz works (Miksa Déri, Ottó Bláthy and Károly Zipernowsky) who invented and patented the transformer in 1885.

The industrial revolution in late nineteenth-century Hungary had its captains and its rank-and-file. The former included some 800 to 1,000 individuals belonging to an exquisite high bourgeoisie, but even within that class a group of about 150 families could be clearly distinguished who were closely knit through business and intermarriage, and displayed an exclusiveness as striking as that of the highest echelons of the aristocracy. The Dreher and the Haggenmacher laid the foundations of Hungarian brewing, and the Hatvany-Deutsch those of the sugar industry; the Goldberger family ran a huge textile complex; Zsigmond Kornfeld directed the Hungarian Credit Bank. The greatest of success stories was perhaps that of Ferenc Chorin, the scion of a family of poor rabbis who ended up at the helm of the Salgótarján mining company, or Manfréd Weiss, whose modest factory of tinned food grew into the largest arms works of the Habsburg Monarchy.

The names, of course, are expressive of the composition, not only of the top ranks, but also of the lower echelons of the Hungarian bourgeoisie. Their background was partly that of the old families of German patricians of the free royal boroughs; a part of them were recent immigrants from Austria, Germany or Switzerland; and many were Jews, numerous enough in the capital (nearly a quarter of the population) to earn it the disparaging name 'Judapest' among the followers of Vienna's anti-Semitic Christian Socialist mayor, Karl Lueger. Similar was the case with the free professions, which also counted as middle class and comprised about a hundred thousand individuals, and Jews constituted nearly fifty per cent in some occupations (among lawyers and doctors, for instance). At all levels, these foreign elements assimilated enthusiastically, and acquired many tokens of acceptance. The great bankers and industrialists wielded economic power comparable to that of the aristocracy, and they even received titles of baronetcy or nobility; their political influence also grew, similarly to that of the middle class whose presence in parliament and in government offices rose sharply after the turn of the century. Mild, but unmistakable forms of segregation continued to exist. Aristocrats and bourgeois attended different casinos, clubs and coffee houses. The former had their country houses on the northern, the latter villas on the southern shore of Lake Balaton. Christian and Jewish citizens took advantage of the same liberal atmosphere in the economy, in culture and in politics where their intercourse was that of polite equals, but to a great extent they lived side by side, rather than coexisted.

The increasing vigour of Hungarian industry also asserted itself in the volume and structure of foreign trade, which grew at a pace of 3 per cent annually and accounted for 45 per cent of the GDP (although only 25 percent if the western Habsburg lands, with which Hungary constituted a unified tariff zone, are discounted). By 1910, the contribution of industry to exports equalled that of agriculture, although half of the industrial exports came from foodstuff production; and 60 per cent of imports was still comprised by finished industrial products. Home trade still depended to a great extent on the well-tried weekly, seasonal and national fairs, but by the turn of the century more modern forms of the exchange of goods were also available. Budapest had five huge market halls, and in 1911 the Parisian Department Store also opened its gates to customers. Commerce as well as industry was geographically very unevenly distributed in the country. Twenty-eight per cent of the industrial labour force was concentrated in the working class districts of the capital where only five per cent of the country's population lived; and none even of the larger urban centres could match the elaborate network of specialised shops of Budapest, the characteristic venue of retail trade still being the general store.

The process of urbanisation which, in Hungary as elsewhere, accompanied industrialisation, was itself made somewhat lopsided by the dynamism of the capital whose pace of development was only eclipsed in this period by some American cities. Hungary's population (without Croatia) grew in the age of dualism by about one-third, from 13.5 million to more than 18 million. Within it, the population of settlements with more than 10,000 inhabitants doubled and reached 4.5 million, while that of Budapest rose from 270,000 to 880,000 (or over a million, if the urban agglomeration is taken into consideration), a threefold increase. Apart from the capital, only Szeged hit the 100,000 mark. Even in Budapest, as late as in 1914 half of the buildings consisted of only one storey (in Vienna the same ratio was one in ten, in Berlin, one in twenty). On the other hand, a great many of the regional administrative and transportation centres, which also started to become industrialised (Győr, Kassa, Nagyvárad, Temesvár, Kolozsvár, Szeged or Fiume), as well as some of the market towns (the one-time *oppida*, such as Debrecen, Kecskemét, Kiskunfélegyháza or Szabadka) displayed features associated with urbanisation. These included, in varying compositions, factory chimneys around the city and tenement houses within it; paved streets, at least in the central areas where new public buildings (town halls, courts of justice, banks, post offices, institutions of secondary or higher education) were erected in the eclectic or the secessionist style; a broad main street with fancy shops and, exceptionally, a tram line between the centre and the railway station; the development of a system of public utilities and electrification; flourishing local journalism, some of it produced by leading lights of Hungarian literature, and permanent theatre companies to satisfy the bourgeois tastes of the local middle class. Contradictions abounded: behind the polished facades, there were dusty thoroughfares, with peasant homes, carts, farm animals. Depending on the criteria chosen, one quarter to one third of the population of Hungary can be considered to have lived in urban settlements on the eve of the First World War. Most of these were dull and sleepy when judged by modern standards or viewed from the perspective of the capital. But they seemed to have been havens of civility seething with energy when compared to the primitive and motionless conditions of the villages and farmsteads of the countryside.

The case of Budapest was indeed exceptional. Nowhere in Hungary was it more true than there that it was the city which set the tone and pace of modern society. To a considerable extent, its unusually dynamic growth was fuelled by national consciousness: after the Compromise, the creation of a national capital worthy of the name and equal to Vienna was an important item on the patriotic agenda. Thanks to the efforts of municipal authorities, including a few outstanding mayors like István Bárczy, also supported by the national government, the economic affluence and the local pride of its citizens, Hungary's capital became a true metropolis. Massive public works created the most striking elements of the present cityscape during the decades after the city's unification (from Pest, Buda and Óbuda) in 1873. New bridges were built across the Danube and linked to a system of boulevards and avenues flanked with impressive blocks of flats, magnificent public buildings and sumptuous bourgeois homes (a process to which much of the charm of the old, largely classicist centre of Pest fell victim). By 1914, one-tenth of the Budapest proletariat, more than fifty thousand people lived in modern tenement houses rented to them at reasonable rates, built out of government or municipal effort (while many of the rest were crammed in miserable slums). Most streets were, from 1856, gaslit, but electric lighting also appeared from 1873 on; urban transport was revolutionised by the construction of over 120 kilometres of tram lines between 1887 and the First World War. Under the ground, a sewage and water supply system was created that bore comparison with that of any city west of Budapest, and the first electric underground railway of the European continent was opened in 1896, connecting the city centre with the site of the Millenary Exhibition and the complex at today's Heroes' Square, including the new Museum of Fine Arts and the millenary memorial. Indeed, much of the bustling construction, directed by outstanding architects, was centred on the symbolic year of 1896. The 1890s witnessed the renovation of Matthias Church and the Royal Castle, and the construction of the Fishermen's Bastion in Buda; on the Pest side, the new Parliament was completed by 1902, and Europe's largest building for a stock exchange by 1905. These buildings, indeed most of modern Budapest, was erected in the historicist-eclectic style by Miklós Ybl, Frigyes Schulek, Imre Steindl, Alajos Hauszmann, Ignác Alpár and other outstanding architects. However, several blocks of flats as well as buildings like the Hotel Gellért or the Gresham Palace represented Art Nouveau, which Ödön Lechner and others also experimented with to enrich with specifically Hungarian ornaments. These efforts resulted in buildings highly controversial in their time, such as the Museum of Applied Art, the Post Savings Bank, or the ones Károly Koós designed for the Budapest Zoo.

The city was, among many other things, a way of life, not only with its many paths to pursue business, or professional interests or merely to subsist, but also with the varied opportunities it offered for leisure, entertainment and culture. Characteristic urban venues of these were the coffee house, the club or association room, the theatre, the cinema, or the sports club. To proceed in a reverse order, sport started to break free from its former exclusivity and conquer the wider masses, with football playing a dominant role in this development from the moment it came to Hungary at an uncertain date in the 1890s, the first official match taking place in 1897. Hungary ranked high in competitive sports, winning a gold and several other medals at the very first modern Olympic Games in 1896. Motion picture was another form of popular entertainment that established itself with astonishing speed. The first films were brought into the country in 1896, and in the same year pictures were shot of the millenary visit of Francis Joseph in Budapest. Three years later the first permanent cinema was opened in the capital, followed before 1914 by nearly a hundred in Budapest and almost three-hundred country-wide, with a combined capacity of tens of thousands of spectators who attended with great enthusiasm the screening of burlesques, educational films or renderings of novels and stories by Hungarian writers. Korda and several other Hungarians who later rose to fame in Hollywood began their careers at the Hunnia Studio, launched in 1911. Many of the scripts of the films were written by outstanding literary figures, who also ensured a steady supply of plays of differing seriousness for the largely middle class audiences of theatres, which no city could afford to do without. The newest and most popular ones of the capital were the Comedy Theatre (the home of modern acting in Hungary, still existing on the Great Boulevard), the Hungarian Theatre, the People's Theatre and the King Theatre. Actors enjoyed tremendous popularity and had considerable influence of sorts: upon the request of the celebrated prima donna Lujza Blaha, sung after a heated performance, the Emperor pardoned a group of conscripts sentenced to death for killing a cruel officer.

But the quintessential 'second home' of the city dweller where he could expect to have polite company and spirited conversation, a game or two of billiard, chess or cards, or solitary immersion in the news of the wider or the closer world while refreshing himself with good coffee or just a glass of water, was the coffee house. Entire lives were spent talking politics, chatting and disputing over artistic, literary or everyday issues, or browsing newspapers and journals, even encyclopaedias in these peculiar institutions, which numbered more than 600 in Budapest and nearly 1,400 across the country in 1896. The whole selection of the Hungarian, and a fair range of foreign papers was permanently available at prestigious locations like the Central, the Lloyd, the Fiume, the Japanese, and above all, the magnificent New York, opened in 1894. But, quite uniquely, coffee houses were venues not merely of the consumption, but also of the production of the press: for instance, the whole editorial office of *A Hét* (The Week), the most important literary weekly before the launching of *Nyugat* (The West), operated from Café Central. The daily and periodical press underwent something like an explosion: by 1914, papers and journals numbered almost 2,000, with a combined print run of a quarter of a million. Besides the approximately one hundred more or less established political dailies, the yellow press appeared and conquered. its most successful organ, *Az Est* (The Evening), launched in 1910, soon had 200,000 readers at a time when *Pesti Hírlap* had only 40,000. Cultural weeklies of a popular cast, like *Tolnai Világlapja* (Tolnai's World Journal) commanded the interest of 100,000 readers, similarly to some of the dozens of satirical papers. By contrast, *Nyugat*, the epoch-making journal of progressive writers, sold a mere 3,000 copies, not considerably more than the high quality professional journals which all major disciplines enjoyed by that time. The publishing sector in general made vigorous progress: the number of publications brought out in 1899 was 5,665, twice as much as in the whole decade 1850–1859. To be sure, the most popular reading was still the annually published almanac of practical knowledge and entertaining stories. The regular reading public of literature might have consisted of about a hundred thousand people, even though cheap editions of Hungarian classics like Jókai or Arany sold in 200,000 copies, as many as pulp fiction or contemporary horror. The standard print run of contemporary classics like Dumas or Tolstoy was ten to thirty thousand; the latter figure was also the number of copies sold of the new multi-volume Pallas and Révai encyclopaedias – in other words, one in ten secondary school graduates bought one.

In art, music and literature, too, the era of dualism was one of transition. National romanticism continued to exercise the talents of painters, composers and authors into the 1890s, when it gradually faded into forms of expression that reflected the complex *fin-de-siècle* feeling of fascination as well as frustration with modernity, scorn and nostalgia for vanishing times, apprehension of the future, vain search for beauty and comfort in decadence. The powerful historical tableaux and portraits of Viktor Madarász, Bertalan Székely, Mór Than and Gyula Benczúr, with their appeal to patriotic sentiment, commanded authority even after the Compromise. But the most popular painter of the period was Mihály Munkácsy, some of whose works still contained an element of romantic theatricality, but many others – genre-paintings, paintings of religious and historical subjects – employed his brilliant skills to create a sense of realism that prefigured *fin-de-siècle* naturalism. At the same time, in the late 1860s and the 1870s, young Pál Szinyei Merse used techniques unusual anywhere outside the circles of the French Impressionists to convey images of light, air and colour. Disillusioned by a cool response to his early masterpieces, he withdrew to his estate until he could join, in the 1890s, a number of younger painters called the Nagybánya group after the artists' colony they created, and mainly hallmarked with the name of Károly Ferenczy. Their impressionism was not the only trend of emerging modernism.

Naturalists, such as László Mednyánszky, were active in Szolnok and Pre-Raphaelites at Gödöllő, just outside Budapest; Art Nouveau had several outstanding representatives, above all, József Rippl-Rónai, who moved home from Paris, where he was brought up, in the beginning of the twentieth century. Modernism started to become institutionalised by the early 1900s, when Szinyei was appointed Director of the College of Fine Art in Budapest (though the painters of the old school continued to sell incomparably better).A small avant-garde, led by Károly Kernstok, seceded even from these innovators. Finally, there were two artists of exceptional talent impossible to classify: Tivadar Csontváry Kosztka and Lajos Gulácsy, who recreated on their canvases their self-styled magical realities, the former even approaching surrealist forms of expression.

Unlike fine art exhibitions, whose audience was rather confined, music, at least some forms of it, had a broader appeal – if not Wagner, whom his father-in-law Ferenc Liszt nevertheless started to popularise in Hungary, to some extent Liszt himself, who was active until the mid-1880s. His works carried the tunes of the *csárdás* far and wide, and firmly established a place for folk motifs in formally composed music. The romantic tradition survived into the early twentieth century, and became modernised by Jenő Hubay and the outstanding Ernő Dohnányi. The Academy of Music, the Opera (whose superb conductors included Gustav Mahler for a short period) and the Philharmonic Society did much to refine the musical taste of the educated public, but the allegiance of truly sizeable audiences was commanded by other, lighter genres. One of these was operetta, tremendously popular especially across the middle classes. At first, their main favourites were Johann Strauss and other foreign composers, but by the beginning of the new century, their Hungarian counterparts also attracted full houses. By the time *The Merry Widow* started the triumphal march of the Hungarian-Viennese Ferenc Lehár in 1905, the pieces of Jenő Huszka had created operetta with a specifically Pest flavour. The 'prima donna/romantic hero/happy end/catchy, sentimental tune' recipe was ostensibly a rather simple one, but it could be employed with great sophistication, as by Imre Kálmán in the *Csárdás Princess*, arguably the most lasting success of all turn of the century operettas. The immensely popular 'musical' version of Petőfi's *John the Brave*, by Pongrác Kacsóh, leads us to a somewhat different genre, that of the song-and-dance popular play,

whose themes were largely drawn from an idealised and sentimental-
ised image of peasant life, and whose melodic design owed much to
'gypsy' music. Sometimes melancholic, sometimes lively, gypsy music
was suitable to evoking simple but intensive emotions of gaiety and
gloom, and to displaying enormous virtuosity in playing the violin. Its
great master Pista Dankó was honoured by his native Szeged with the
erecting of the only statue in the world dedicated to a gypsy.

It was disaffection with the old romantic school in which they were
brought up and with the fake folkishness so popular in their times, as
well as familiarity with the most up-to-date trends in western music and
sheer musical genius, that made two young men, Béla Bartók and
Zoltán Kodály, embark on a different path. Beginning in 1906, they
made a series of field trips to discover the authentic, pentatonic folk
song, with which what had passed for it had little to do: they recorded
thousands of tunes and dances mainly among the Magyars, the Slovaks
and the Romanians around the Carpathian Basin, also exploring their
ethnographic background. As composers, Kodály based his work, as
the string quartet of 1908 or the cello and piano sonata of 1911, specifically on the Szekel ballads, while Bartók's opera *Bluebeard's Castle*, his
Allegro Barbaro, and his music for the ballets *The Wooden Prince* and
The Miraculous Mandarin, were also strongly influenced by the avant-
garde revolution in music. Bartók and Kodály became members of the
Academy of Music, yet they encountered stiff resistance from the circles
of academic and political conservatism. Bartók's opera was refused to
be put on stage in Budapest, they failed in their effort to launch a new
musical society, and it was not until considerably later that their work
became the foundation of modern Hungarian musical culture.

Any brief review of Hungarian literature in the dualist period must
begin with a discussion of the man who wrote the lyrics of Strauss' operetta *The Gypsy Baron* – Mór Jókai, 'the great story-teller' and the last
survivor of the 'young men of March' from 1848. He was the best known
and most widely read Hungarian writer of his times within and outside the
country. The 100 volumes of his collected works (altogether 202 of them)
published in 1894–1898 guided the reader through all periods of Hungarian history from Ottoman times through the Rákóczi War of Independence, the efforts of Habsburg centralisation, the Age of Reform and
the Revolution of 1848 to the experience of modernisation in the second
half of the nineteenth century. Naturally enough, themes of heroism and
patriotic self-sacrifice dominated the oeuvre of this incomparable master of weaving a plot, though the recurrent triumphs of harmony and
humanity were somewhat self-deceptive in an age of radical change
with its disturbing overtones. Of the younger generation, Géza Gárdonyi wrote in a similar vein on historical subjects; Ferenc Herczeg fo-

cused on the contemporary gentry, described in his novels, short stories and dramas as a light-hearted, even irresponsible, but still loveable class essential for sustaining the nation and its fundamental character. Jókai's most outstanding successor, with a unique talent for a compelling plot interspersed with anecdotes, was Kálmán Mikszáth. Like Jókai and Herczeg, he was an MP for several decades, but his experience shaped his estimation of the bulk of the political class ever more critical: in his later works, the once powerful and respectable nobles (men of unquestioned integrity in Jókai and gentlemanlike bohemians in Herczeg) are corrupt politicians or dowry-hunters portrayed with increasingly bitter irony.

The tone of criticism also appeared in the representation of peasant life, which was one of purity and harmony according to the national-romantic tradition. The sociographically coloured novels and short stories of Ferenc Móra and others did not shrink from casting light on the profound cleavages and ubiquitous misery of the peasantry. It was Zsigmond Móricz whose realist and naturalist prose went farthest, and achieved the highest artistic standards, in revealing the reality of rural society – the hopelessness and the disastrous moral effects of the incessant struggle for land among the downtrodden, and the indifference among their social betters. Urban life, that of the middle class, also had its bards, sympathetic as well as critical. Sándor Bródy, a born rebel, wrote naturalistic prose in the fashion of Zola to jar the sensitivities of the 'Christian-Hungarian' or genteel, as well as the philistinism of the new middle class, while Jenő Heltai caused consternation among conservatives by light, frivolous representations of the everydays of music hall singers and dancers, journalists and other urban bohemians of cabarets, theatres and coffee houses. But the most successful representative of this trend of literature was the novelist and playwright Ferenc Molnár, whose portrayal of urban modernity was less iconoclastic and his irony more subtle, but his skill in character description and his wit and stage mastery were incomparable in his time, and earned him fame at Broadway, too. The writer who probably knew most about the world of both the big city and the small town, and represented them with unparalleled charm, was Gyula Krúdy.

The writers of the turn of the century were often propelled to fame by, and then contributed to the authority of, influential literary journals. The first one of great importance was the *Budapesti Szemle* (Budapest Review), launched in 1873 and hallmarked by the name of Pál Gyulai, the foremost critic of the period. Another forum of traditional taste was *Új Idők* (New Times, from 1895), edited by Herczeg, while Bródy, Krúdy and many others indebted to modernism acquired renown on the pages of *A Hét* (from 1890). The truly epoch-making *Nyugat* was established in 1908. It was a successor of *A Hét* in terms of continuity of contributors as well as in frequently incurring the charges of cosmopolitanism, decadence, 'un-Hungarianness' and aesthetic shallowness. In fact, it united the most outstanding talents keen on cultivating the Hungarian tradition while responsive to the challenges of modernity and western artistic and literary trends. The prose writers who rallied around *Nyugat* included Móricz and Krúdy, already mentioned above, as well as Frigyes Karinthy, a philosophically-minded satirist of the highest order. Dezső Kosztolányi wrote excellent, refined prose and poetry imbued with impressionist impacts, while Mihály Babits, a somewhat reclusive master of poetic form, carried on the lyrical legacy of Arany, adjusted to contemporary western standards. The *Nyugat* circle was at the forefront of progressive thought in Hungary: though the literary avant-garde, epitomised by Lajos Kassák, remained beyond its reach, it was close to other intellectual workshops, like Jászi's *Huszadik Század*, already mentioned above, or the Sunday Circle of young philosophers like Lukács and social scientists like Mannheim and Polányi.

But more than any of the literati mentioned so far, the quintessential voice of Hungarian modernism, one whom perhaps only linguistic isolation denied the place of a Bartók in twentieth-century culture, was Endre Ady, the poet of the disturbing predicament of modernity in general and in the Hungarian context in particular, and the prophet of a potentially ominous destiny awaiting the country. The scion of impoverished nobles from the one-time Partium became the heart and soul of *Nyugat*, and the icon of a radical democratic intelligentsia by employing his sophisticated and rousing symbolism not only to the representation of sensual love, but also to the relentless criticism of the 'Hungarian fallow' created by what he saw as centuries of stubborn selfishness on the part of his own, by now utterly anachronistic, class. His 'new songs of a new age', sung in the idiom of Baudelaire and Verlaine grafted on to that of rebellious Protestant preachers and the destitute 'outlaws' of Thököly and Rákóczi, declared war on the conservative provincialism of the genteel class and proclaimed a programme of national rejuvenation through the collaboration of progressive forces of any social or ethnic background.

There were few in Hungary who recognised the dilemmas, the tensions and the traps the country faced on the eve of the First World War in all of their depth. On one side of the ideological divide, Ady was the greatest of all of them, and he singled out with characteristic acuteness his counterpart on the other: István Tisza. In the troublesome summer of 1914, the 'deranged man of Geszt', as Ady called the Prime Minister after the seat of the Tisza estate, hesitated for two weeks, but in the end he gave his sanction to decisions that made inevitable the war which ultimately demolished historic Hungary in a way unwanted by any of its Hungarian critics.

4. Hungary in the Great War

In political and military circles in Vienna, the assassination of Francis Ferdinand was mostly seen as a golden opportunity to settle scores with Serbia and to re-establish the prestige of the Monarchy. William II of Germany and his generals thought that armed confrontation between the Central Powers and the Entente being inevitable, it was better to fight it before Germany's hard-won advantage in the armament race was completely diminished. They brought pressure on the common Council of Ministers, especially Tisza, who was worried both by the prospect of a Romanian attack and by the plan for annexations in the Balkans and elsewhere, urged by the bellicose Austrian Chief of Staff Conrad von Hötzendorf and several political leaders both in Vienna and Budapest. Considerable territorial expansion, according to him, would have tipped the ethnic balance again in favour of the minorities, and thus risk the triumph of federalism in the Austro-Hungarian Monarchy. He favoured a diplomatic solution, until reassured that Romania would not attack and no additional Slavs would be incorporated into the Monarchy. Without positive knowledge of Serbian complicity in the Sarajevo assassination, a harsh ultimatum demanding, among other things, an official denunciation of the movement for Greater Serbia and the free involvement of Austro-Hungarian agents in investigating the case on Serbian territory, was dispatched to Belgrade on July 23, 1914. It soon turned out that the great powers of the opposite camp were also not against war. Serbia rejected the ultimatum two days later not on grounds of innocence, but because it was prompted to do so by her Entente supporters, who also realised that the time for the general conflagration expected for several years by all with the slightest interest in and knowledge of public affairs, had indeed come. Within two weeks after the Austro-Hungarian declaration of war on Serbia on July 28, 1914, allied obligations, nationalist and imperialist dreams involved nearly the whole of the European continent in war.

In Hungary, as elsewhere, the initial response to the outbreak of war was an outburst of patriotic enthusiasm. In parliament, which was prorogued and reconvened in November, the opposition Independence Party leader Count Mihály Károlyi spoke of suspending political debate, hoping for democratic concessions in return for supporting the war effort. A similar motivation resulted in similar attitudes among the extraparliamentary Social Democrats; even the national minorities caused few headaches to the belligerent government in the early phases of the war, their leaders issuing declarations of loyalty or, a few of them, emigrating. Soldiers set out to the front amidst cheerful ceremonies, in the hope of returning victorious, as the German Emperor William said, 'by the time the leaves fall'.

However, the war plans of the Central Powers were thwarted. Germany failed to inflict decisive defeat on France in a lightning war, and could not lend sufficient support early enough to the Austro-Hungarian Monarchy for the containment of the Russian advance and the breaking of Serbia. Especially in view of the unexpectedly rapid Russian mobilisation, the forces of the Monarchy were not equal to coping with these tasks simultaneously. Although Belgrade was occupied in early December 1914, the Russian army posed a direct threat to Hungarian territory. Over half of the initial Austro-Hungarian fighting force of 1.8 million died, was wounded or fell into captivity during the first stages of the war on the fronts in Galicia and Serbia.

By 1915, the type of warfare so peculiar to the First World War, the war of position, centred on the foot soldier in the trenches armed with the machine gun and on heavy artillery bombardment, had developed, and with it a military deadlock which made diplomacy, initially considered insignificant, gain in importance. As regarded securing new allies, until the entry of the United States into the war in April 1917, the sides were roughly equal, and the military results were even slightly in favour of the Central Powers. Turkey, hoping to take revenge on Russia for the losses it suffered in the preceding century, and Bulgaria, ambitious to expand in the Balkans, joined the Central Powers in the autumn of 1914 and 1915, respectively, which finally helped the monarchy put down Serbia. By then, the Austro-Hungarian army somewhat recovered from the losses suffered early on in the war, and was capable, with some German assistance, of considerable achievement against earlier formal allies which now joined the war on the side of the Entente. One of these was Italy, which was promised territorial acquisitions in South Tyrol, the Adriatic and Africa in the secret treaty of London in April 1915, and declared war on the Central Powers in the following month. A powerful Russian advance in the summer of 1916 on the eastern front, as well as a similar agreement in August 1916 prompted Romania to invade Transylvania. In the bloody battles fought on the slopes of the Alps and along the River Isonzo, the forces of the Monarchy fought with great determination, and inflicted a decisive setback on the Italians at Caporetto in November 1917; the Romanian offensive collapsed within weeks, and in December 1916 even Bucharest was occupied by the Austro-Hungarian army.

At the same time, there was another field of diplomacy: besides propaganda directed at the hinterland of hostile countries, which naturally affected the ethnic minorities of Austria-Hungary, the western allies gave shelter to the national committees of émigré politicians and encouraged their campaign for the dismemberment of the Monarchy and the creation of 'national' states. The Yugoslav Committee, led by the Croatian Frano Supilo and Ante Trumbić, was established in London on May 1, 1915, with the programme of uniting Serbia and the South Slav inhabited territories of the monarchy in a single, federative state (while their Serbian counterparts envisaged the future of the same area as a centralised state governed from Belgrade); the leaders of the Czech emigration in Paris, Tomáš Masaryk and Eduard Beneš, urged the creation of a Czecho-Slovak state including the Carpatho-Ukraine, and linked with a corridor to the future South Slav state to separate the Germans and the Hungarians from each other. The Romanians, with claims raised not only to Transylvania but also other areas of Hungary east of the Tisza, emerged relatively late, founding the Council of Romanian National Unity in Paris only in the last weeks of the war.

Until relatively late in the course of the war, the support given by the Entente powers to these high-blown demands of the national committees was largely tactical, and until the spring of 1918 they contemplated various alternatives to the 'destruction of Austria-Hungary', as called for in a widely circulated pamphlet by Masaryk and Beneš in 1916. They preferred (as did the representatives of the Czechs, the Ukrainians and the South Slavs in the Austrian parliament convened in May 1917) a federal reorganisation of the monarchy with wide-ranging autonomy granted to the nationalities, until it became clear that German influence over Austro-Hungarian policies was too great to negotiate a separate peace with it, and they convinced themselves that it could not be expected to play the traditional role of a counterpoise in the European balance of power any longer. Only then did No. 10 of the American President Woodrow Wilson's famous Fourteen Points of January 8, 1918 ('the peoples of Austria-Hungary should be accorded the freest opportunity of autonomous development') start to acquire the meaning of the creation of new states. Besides, the Congress of Oppressed Nations in Rome in April 1918, with the recognition of the Czecho-Slovak and South Slav claims to sovereignty and, subsequently, their committees as belligerent governments, served as a means to weaken the cohesion of the Central Powers between Russia's falling out of the war, sealed in the Peace of Brest-Litovsk on March 3, 1918, and the arrival of American troops on the western front in the summer of 1918, a period when the military balance temporarily seemed to turn in favour of Germany and its allies.

In fact, the multinational empire, including Hungary, was on the brink of utter exhaustion by this time. Its economic and military resources had been under great strain since the first setbacks on the eastern front, which also started to undermine the morale of the civilian population. In four years, Hungary sent somewhat over one-third of the

9 million soldiers of the monarchy to the front, but among the casualties it was only the number of those wounded, 1.4 million, that roughly answered this proportion; half of the more than one million dead and nearly half of the two million captives came from the Hungarian half of the empire. Soldiers sent home increasingly exasperated letters, and by 1917 desertion, disobedience of orders, even mutiny started in the army.

From behind lines, they received reports on food shortages, inflation, requisitions, rationing, a thriving black market and general unrest. The shortage of labour caused by massive mobilisation to the front could hardly be offset by the employment of women and prisoners of war. Amidst a general decline of productivity, the output of bread cereals was halved by 1918. Placing about 900 major industrial plants under military supervision by the end of the war helped little to boost production, though it quite efficiently regulated distribution in favour of the war machine. The absence of breadwinners hit virtually every family. Especially grievous was the condition of those on fixed incomes or wages whose real value fell to between a half and two-thirds of their pre-war level. The ever more numerous war-widows, orphans and disabled servicemen lived at a subsistence level. Social tension was made only more intense by the fact that at the same time, while there were quite numerous humanitarian initiatives on their part, the rich were compelled to change little else than their vacationing and shopping habits. Hunger marches, assaults on public granaries and agrarian socialist agitation was on the agenda in the countryside, while the membership of trade unions increased sixfold, and the general strike of June 1918 involved about half a million people in all the major cities of Hungary. By this time, the traditional means of police, gendarmerie and censorship were increasingly ineffective in suppressing the growing pacifist sentiment and the demands for social and political reform.

As in public opinion, in politics, too, new winds started to blow by 1916, when the signs of exasperation at the fronts and in the country became unmistakable. The majority of the government party, with Tisza in the first instance, insisted on persevering in the war effort until final victory, not only because of the prime minister's legendary obstinacy and personal responsibility in the declaration of war, but also because they realised quite clearly what consequences Hungary was facing in the event of defeat, whatever policies were adopted before that time came. A moderate opposition led by the younger Andrássy and Apponyi agreed that the war aims and the alliance policy ought to be maintained, but thought that well-considered reforms, instead of repression, would best ensure the internal consolidation needed. Finally, a secessionist group of the Independence Party led by the increasingly influential Károlyi, from mid-1917 on closely co-operating with the extra-parliamentary radical democrats of Jászi, the Social Democratic Party, a group of Christian Socialists and the Bourgeois Democratic Party in the 'Suffrage Bloc', campaigned for universal suffrage and 'peace without annexations'. As long as the aged ruler lived, all of this was unrealistic. But Francis Joseph died, at the age of 86, on November 21, 1916, and Charles IV, who succeeded him, felt the need to calm the discontent through concessions and peace feelers. He gave his blessing to secret negotiations between Károlyi and the Entente, and initiated his own; he even dismissed Tisza in May 1917. However, his successors Móric Esterházy and, during his third term as prime minister, Wekerle, brought about only a modicum of electoral reform, while the land distribution also urged by the opposition was conveniently forgotten. As regards the diplomatic initiative, the main condition of a separate peace, a break with Germany, was not met, not only because Charles' personal indetermination, even weakness, but also because the French Prime Minister Clemenceau had the Habsburg proposal made public, creating a situation in which Charles was obliged to apologise in Berlin and strengthen ties with Germany.

In the face of mounting discontent, Wekerle offered his resignation several times in the course of 1918, but the ruler and his advisors refused to opt for the alternative, that is, calling the opposition led by Károlyi to office. Strikes and mutinies were on the agenda throughout the year, now also fuelled by new converts to Bolshevism who started to return from the Russian camps of prisoners of war. Even amidst all of this domestic turmoil, the military situation looked deceptively good until a few months before the end of the war: Austro-Hungarian armies were still deep in hostile lands, with the war aims apparently accomplished. It was only after the last great German offensive in the West collapsed in August 1918, and the Entente counter-offensive started there as well as in the Balkans, that the Monarchy's positions on the fronts became untenable. Commenting on the impending surrender of Bulgaria, Foreign Minister István Burián's evaluation of the situation before the Common Council of Ministers on September 28 was brief and unequivocal: 'That is the end of it.'

On October 2, the Monarchy solicited the Entente for an armistice and peace negotiations, based on Wilson's Fourteen Points, only to be disappointed to learn from the reply that, having recognised the Czecho-Slovak and the South Slav claims, Wilson was no longer in a position to negotiate on the basis of granting the ethnic minorities autonomy within an empire whose integrity would be maintained. The Monarchy was collapsing into chaos by this time. Charles' desperate attempt on October 16 to flee ahead by announcing the federalisation of Austria (which did not affect the Hungarian half of the empire) was to no avail. By the first half of October, all the nationalities had their national councils, which proclaimed their independence, a move which now enjoyed the official sanction of the Entente; on October 11, the Poles, between the 28th and the 31st the Czechs, the Slovaks, the Croats and the Ruthenes seceded, followed on November 20 by the Romanians. Now, the provisional assembly in Vienna also declared Austria an independent state. At the front, the Italians took bloody revenge on the disintegrating army of a state no longer existing in the offensive launched in the valley of the Piave on October 23, imprinting an indelible mark of horror on the memory of a generation of men. The armistice with Italy was finally signed on November 3 in Padua.

By this time the crumbling of the whole edifice of the old Monarchy changed the face of Hungary quite beyond recognition – a process whose details already belong to another chapter in Hungarian history. Paradoxically, the dissolution of the historic Kingdom of Hungary, one of the greatest shocks the country suffered and survived as regards the nation's economic resources, political influence and, most of all, self-appreciation, also created the opportunity for a new beginning. The situation held out the promise of overhauling those ossified social and political structures and institutions that bore some of the responsibility for the disaster of dissolution. History, largely that of international developments, would decide whether the potential of this democratic transformation would materialise.

CHAPTER VII

IN SEARCH OF AN IDENTITY (1918–1945)

The armed hostilities of the First World War formally came to an end with the armistice signed between the Entente and Germany at Compiègne on November 11, 1918. However, fighting did not cease everywhere, certainly not along the borders of Hungary, where the seceding nationalities were lending weight to their territorial claims through force of arms, creating the status quo sanctioned by the victors who assembled in Paris to reconstruct the order of Europe and the wider world on January 12, 1919. It was largely the inability, indeed the impossibility of tackling this situation that swept away the pacifist democracy that took over in Hungary at the end of the war, and altogether thwarted the first chance which the country obtained for a transition to democracy in the twentieth century. The democratic experiment was followed by red, then white terror, and the flaws and shortcomings of the peace treaty system dictated by the Allies confirmed, and lent credibility to, the inherent nationalism and revisionism of the conservative regime that became consolidated thereafter.

The war, and to some extent the peace settlement, undoubtedly advanced processes that started perhaps with the American and the French Revolutions, by dealing a mortal blow on the conservative institutions of the multi-national empires of Central, Eastern and South-Eastern Europe. Nationalism triumphed, in the belief that this was consistent with the cause of liberty and democracy, and very few lamented, with quite good reason, the fall of the Hohenzollern, Habsburg, Romanov and Ottoman emperors. To be sure, the western Allies, who won the war and made the peace, were motivated, besides the ideal of national self-determination, by power policy considerations in their decision to discard the Austro-Hungarian Monarchy: they not only believed that its ethnic minorities, once liberated from imperial oppression, would automatically emerge as liberal democracies, but also that the *cordon sanitaire* created out of the new states emerging in its place between Germany and Soviet Russia would be able to play the traditional Habsburg role of an equipoise in the European balance of power.

Both expectations proved to be fundamentally wrong. With the partial exception of Czechoslovakia, the democratic credentials of the new states were rather weak, not to speak of the fact that the settlement failed to solve ethnic tensions in the countries of the region and created new ones; and socio-economic backwardness fuelled nationalist sentiments, creating disunity between the potential partners and making them a poor match for the potentially formidable strength of the losers of the peace settlement. These included, besides Germany, Austria and Hungary, also Italy, which felt that its victory was 'mutilated' by several of its claims being unsatisfied, and Soviet Russia, which suffered significant territorial losses and was ignored altogether at the peace conference. What is more, there was objective reason to criticise the conduct of the peacemakers. Whereas Wilson's Fourteen Points were in principle accepted as guidelines by them, in fact they were concerned with meting out punishment to the losers, stigmatised by the famous clause on 'war guilt' in the treaties – a course of action whose bogusness evoked the contrary effect and strengthened the defiance of the accused. Also, the peace settlement could be justly charged with employing a double standard, deviating from its professed principles for the sake of power policy interests, dividing the peoples of Central Europe into friends and enemies of the final arbiters, and distributing satisfactions one-sidedly between them.

After a critical initial period of much bitterness on the part of the losers, and an apparent consolidation in the more favourable climate of the 1920s, the political and moral foundations of the Paris peace settlement proved to be too fragile to survive the effects of the economic crisis beginning in 1929. Economic isolationism bred xenophobia, nationalism and political extremism; the successor states of Austria-Hungary were torn even further apart, which created favourable conditions in the region for the penetration of Nazi Germany, whose ever more impudent violations of the Treaty of Versailles went unpunished. It not only became the most important economic partner of most countries in Central and South-Eastern Europe. Hitler was also cheered by crowds in Vienna as the *Anschluss* took place, and accepted as an ally in the revision of the Paris settlement in Hungarian political circles (with reservations in some and without reservations in others); he found forces to work with among the disgruntled minor partners in the Czecho-Slovak and South Slav agglomerates and in Romania; using the pretext of the bulky German minority in the Czech lands, he exploited the attitude of appeasement among the western powers at the expense of Czechoslovakia, the most cherished among the children of the one-time peacemakers of Paris. Central Europe as a symbolic and actual operational base was crucial for Hitler's plan to acquire *Lebensraum*, living space, for the Germans, as outlined in *Mein Kampf*; and he set out to pursue that end by means of formal war after having reached an agreement which amounted to dividing the lands between the Baltic and the Black Sea into spheres of interests with Soviet Russia, which represented the opposite ideological extreme of Nazi Germany only in ideological terms, but as regards the evaluation of the Paris peace settlement was on the same side. Various reasons have been assigned to the dissolution of historic Hungary. Whereas some continue to believe firmly that it was a viable unit dismembered by a combination of rival nationalisms in the region with the complicity of western great powers, others predicted its ruin even before the event, and explained it afterwards, as an inevitable product of centrifugal forces. Most historians today would agree with the latter view, while acknowledging that the precise way in which the process took place was fundamentally influenced by the contingencies of the war and the peace that concluded it. Indeed, the outcome shocked even those who had been the sharpest critics of the darker aspects of the pre-1914 socio-political scene in Hungary and the policy towards the nationalities.

It was all the more shocking for them since they came largely from the politically more progressive camp, who were well disposed towards the western liberal democracies, but whose future on the public scene was destroyed by the circumstances of peacemaking. The tragedy of the aftermath of the First World War and the Peace Treaty of Trianon consists, far more than merely putting the seal on the unavoidable, in the fact that it contributed to the survival of socio-political structures which had steered the country towards the war and its consequences. Hungarian national consciousness was tailored to the reality of a medium-sized state of twenty, in far-flung dreams even thirty million inhabitants in which Magyar primacy was based not on the vulgar principles of statistical majority and racial identity but on historical and political achievement; it was bewildered by being forced within the confines of a small country with a population of eight million. Given the fact that the flaws of the settlement gave some justified basis to the general spirit of outrage and revenge, compressed in the slogan 'No, no, never', no political force entertaining hopes of success in Hungary could afford neglecting the issue of revision on its agenda in the inter-war period. It was embraced both by the conservatives of the traditional political elite who dominated the political scene in Hungary during the consolidation of the 1920s, and the radical right, with which the former alternated in government in the 1930s and during the Second World War. Predictably enough, Hungary fought that war in alliance with Germany again, with devastating results. The post-feudal structures saved even amidst the collapse of historic Hungary in the First World War, whose dismantling was relegated into relative insignificance by the political priorities of the inter-war period, now finally fell with the regime; but, as before, factors largely beyond the control of Hungary and the Hungarians would decide what would replace them.

1. Revolutions and dismemberment: Hungary in the new order of Central Europe

October 1918 was a month of dramatic scenes in the Hungarian parliament; perhaps none so much so as when István Tisza, by then widely held in the country to bear supreme responsibility for all the suffering of the past four years, declared: 'I agree with what Count Károlyi said yesterday. We have lost this war.' He referred to a speech made on October 16, the same day Charles IV announced the federalisation of Austria, by the leader of the opposition, who also warned that Hungary might lose the peace as well, unless suitable policies were adopted. These ought to have included, in the first place, the appointment of an administration acceptable to the western Allies as well as to a people whose mood by then was revolutionary, in order to save, as far as it was possible at all, the territorial integrity of the country, and to prevent it from falling into anarchy.

The third cabinet of Wekerle indeed stepped down on October 23, and on the night of that day Károlyi organised the Hungarian National Council from members of his own Independence Party, the Bourgeois Radical Party, the Social Democratic Party and various groups of intellectuals from the capital. Its twelve-point proclamation called for the immediate conclusion of a separate peace treaty, the independence of Hungary, far-reaching democratic reforms and reconciliation with the nationalities, without harm to the territorial integrity of the state. The National Council functioned as a counter-government in the following week or so, for, contrary to expectations and political common sense, the ruler hesitated to call Károlyi to office. He preferred Count János Hadik, a follower of the younger Andrássy who was popular among the MPs hostile towards Károlyi, but had no party, and could only count on the demoralised military to maintain order. On October 28, as a mass of protesters was marching from Pest to Buda Castle to demand Károlyi's appointment from Archduke Joseph, the representative of the monarch, three of them were shot dead by the police. Strikes and further protests followed during the next two days, with occasional clashes between members of the newly organised Soldiers' Council and leftist Socialists on the one hand and government units on the other, while Károlyi and the National Council advised moderation and awaited the outcome, even though on October 30, troops were ordered against their headquarters at the Hotel Astoria. That was decided by the desertion of most of the soldiers, carried away by the enthusiasm of the civilians who swarmed on to the streets of Budapest cheering the National Council, and captured public buildings, railway stations and telephone exchanges. Asters, on sale for All Souls' Day, replaced the insignia torn off from uniforms and appeared in the button-holes of civilian suits – hence the name 'Aster Revolution', which triumphed on October 31, with the appointment of Károlyi as Premier. It claimed few lives, one of the victims being, symbolically, Tisza, murdered in his own home by a group of soldiers in the afternoon of the same day, just before the new government took its oath.

The government programme was virtually the same as the twelve points published a week earlier, and Károlyi's cabinet was also recruited from the same forces as the National Council, with members of his own party obtaining most of the seats. Whereas the collapse of the dualist system cleared important obstacles from the way to a democratic transition, the absences from the new government were symptomatic of the belatedness of this development, which very seriously limited its scope of action. Between them, the parties of the National Council represented a small minority of the aristocracy and the nobility, some of the bourgeoisie, different shades of the intelligentsia, the skilled workers and the trade unions. Missing were influential segments of society which, between the first signs of the crisis of dualism and the outbreak of the war, might have been more favourably disposed to the revolution than after it. The *haute bourgeoisie*, indeed most of the middle classes, whether 'Christian' or otherwise, might have welcomed the removal of the competition of Austrian capital and the curtailment of aristocratic influence, but the involvement of their highest strata in the war business tied them closer to the old regime, and the events in Russia made all of them loathe revolution, whatever the label. Similarly, the truly generous terms Jászi, who became Minister of Nationality Affairs in the new government, offered to the leaders of the Slav and Romanian national parties in an attempt to draw them into the Hungarian National Council, might have achieved the desired result before 1914, but not in 1918.

In spite of these discouraging antecedents, it was hoped that a proper and consistently pursued policy line towards the nationalities, combined with the good relations Károlyi had developed with the Entente politicians, would save Hungary from the consequences of the secret agreements the latter had concluded with the Slavs and the Romanians during the war. The first indications were rather disappointing: the western Allies seemed more ready to satisfy their partners in the region, even at the expense of departing from Wilson's principles, than to reward the political changes in Hungary, and not even full autonomy could keep the Slovaks and the Romanians within Hungary. (Croat claims were deemed justified by practically everyone in Hungary, while the Serbs did not even consider negotiating.) As the terms of the armistice of Padova were not accepted as valid by the commander of the French forces in the Balkans, General Felix Franchet d'Esperey, and his forces crossed the Sava into Hungarian territory, Károlyi, hoping that the measure would be but temporary and the final settlement would be more favourable, was forced to sign, on November 13 in Belgrade, a military convention requiring the withdrawal of the Hungarian army beyond the Drava-Maros line, its severe reduction, and also the right of free passage for Entente troops across Hungary.

The simultaneous negotiations of Jászi with Romanian leaders at Arad were also to no avail. On November 20 they proclaimed their seceding from Hungary; by the end of the month Romanian troops advanced to the demarcation line, and even beyond that, as far as Kolozsvár, after the Romanians of Transylvania proclaimed their union with the Kingdom of Romania at the meeting of Gyulafehérvár on December 1. Although the Slovak leader Milan Hodža was inclined to accept autonomy as a provisional solution until the peace treaty was signed, others, and particularly the Czechs, disavowed him and, while fighting broke out along the Slovak border, secured a memorandum from the Entente requiring the Hungarians to withdraw beyond a line which, by and large, became the later border of the country. The Ruthenians were the only nationality who, as the unification of all Ukrainian land was unlikely, accepted the autonomy offered to them. Hungary had lost more than half of its former territory and population by the time the Paris peace conference convened on January 12, 1919. Jászi's idea of a Danubian United States, outlined at book-length, remained in the realm of dreams. Not infrequently since then, the Károlyi government has been blamed for not showing more determination in resisting especially the Romanians. In fact, the armed forces at its disposal would have hardly been a match for those of the hostile camp. More importantly, its legitimacy was to a considerable extent pitched on its supposedly good relations with the Entente powers, and it felt it could not afford to discard 'Wilsonism' even when they did so.

What was held by many people for the failure of the Károlyi government in averting the greatest of Hungary's national tragedies since Ottoman times could not but prejudice its chances to cope with domestic difficulties. In the initial hope that the new government would be able to secure Hungary's old borders as well as law, order and property, the old elite accepted, after the abdication of Charles IV, the dissolution of parliament, the investing of the National Council with provisional legislative authority, and the proclamation of the republic on November 16. They were, for a short while, also impressed by the relatively little violence the revolution implied, at least in the urban centres. However, they soon became opposed to the regime as, simultaneously with the evaporation of the fair expectations regarding territorial integrity, Károlyi embarked on the social and political reforms announced in his programme. This was not only standing up to promises, but also badly needed, in view of the explosive atmosphere in the country. The economic blockade by the Allies being still in force, economic ties with Austria disrupted, and territories of crucial economic importance in the north, east and south of Hungary being occupied, shortages of raw material and fuel caused chaos in the productive sector, while the most fundamental means of subsistence were unavailable for millions in a country inundated by demobilised soldiers, returning prisoners of war and refugees from beyond the demarcation lines. City dwellers suspected landowners and well-to-do peasants of holding back deliveries; many of the latter were indeed leaving their land uncultivated because of the impending land reform, which the rural proletariat urged ever more impatiently.

There was probably no political force in Hungary at the time that would have been able to answer all of the conflicting interests and expectations in these turbulent times; Károlyi and the democrats around him, whose undoubtedly considerable talents were suited to peaceful and stable situations but not to emergencies, were certainly unable to achieve that. The land reform of February 15, 1919, was a step whose significance can hardly be overestimated, but satisfied nobody. Estates over 700 acres were to be reallocated among the peasantry – a limit found unacceptably high by the rural poor and unacceptably low by the magnates, while the Social Democrats campaigned for the abolition of all medium-sized and large estates but wanted to preserve them as cooperative farms, arguing that ownership would make the peasantry 'conservative'. There was anyway no time left for the measure to take effect; it was only a part of Károlyi's own estate that was, in a rather demonstrative manner, distributed a week after the decree had been issued. Similar was the fate of the broad electoral reform, increasing the proportion of those who had the vote to half (it was only higher in Scandinavia at the time): elections for the future constitutional assembly were scheduled to a date by which the Károlyi regime (headed by Károlyi as President since January 11, 1919, Dénes Berinkey serving as Prime Minister) had fallen. Nor could the effects of the progressive social legislation, including the introduction of unemployment benefit and the eight-hour working day, the abolition of child labour, or the extension of insurance schemes, be felt as yet. Amidst the frustration of national aims and a post-war depression hardly alleviated by reforms, which nevertheless annoyed the old upper class, the political scene became inevitably polarised, involving the appearance of radical tendencies both on the Right and the Left.

By the beginning of 1919, the traditional political elite started to recover from the shock of the collapse of the Dual Monarchy, not the least because they felt the need to counter the effects of what they saw as incompetence causing instability and national disaster on the part of the Károlyi government. The Party of National Union, established by magnates and experienced politicians in February 1919 and led by the Transylvanian Count István Bethlen, wanted to restore the pre–1914 relations of power. While they realised the need to improve the conditions not only of the 'historic middle class', but also the peasantry and the working class, they adamantly rejected the radical endeavours of the 'immigrant (an euphemism for Jewish) intelligentsia', and envisaged 'the union of the lower and the upper strata in the harmony of national sentiment' under the paternalistic dominance of the latter.

Besides other parties in which the traditional Right started to become organised, a more striking development was the appearance of political groups advocating radical changes, but not along the lines in which they were being carried out by the government. Rightist radicalism had its strongest basis among the many thousands of demobilised officers and dismissed public servants, many of them from the territories now lost to Hungary, whom the dissolution of the Monarchy affected not only in their national sentiments, but destroyed their whole existence. In their view, the military collapse and the break-up of historic Hungary was largely the fault of the enervated conservative liberalism of the dualist period, which they proposed to transcend not by democracy and land reform, but by authoritarian government in which they would have a greater say, and measures aimed at the redistribution of property in favour of the Christian middle class and at the expense of mobile, predominantly Jewish, capital. Unlike Károlyi, and even Bethlen, who also hoped to negotiate more favourable terms with the victors of the war, groups such as the Hungarian National Defence Association, led by Gyula Gömbös, or the Association of Awakening Hungarians impatiently urged the armed defence of the country from November 1918 on.

But the streets, for the time being, belonged to the political Left. Appeals of moderate Social Democrat ministers to order and patience evoked the contrary effect, and served to alienate the disaffected masses from them. Their new heroes were the Communists, organised as a party on November 24, 1918, by Béla Kun, a former journalist and trade union activist recently returned from captivity in Russia. Similarly to many others who shared his lot, Kun became convinced of the superiority of the system of Soviets on the Russian model to paliamentarism and democracy, and communist propaganda promised equality and an end to all exploitation through the nationalisation of property, as well as international stability arising from the fraternity of Soviet republics whose triumph the Communists prognosticated all over Europe. Within a few weeks, this attractive utopia, underpinned by well-designed social demagogy, earned the Communist Party a membership of about forty thousand, and several times as many supporters whom they could mobilise, mainly among the masses marginalised by the post-war depression and the young intelligentsia susceptible to revolutionary romanticism. By January 1919, a wave of strikes had swept across the country, in the course of which factories, transport and communication installations were occupied; in addition, land seizures and attempts to introduce collective cultivation marked the communist initiative, which also included the demand not only to eradicate all remnants of feudalism, but also the proclamation of a Hungarian Soviet Republic, and a foreign policy seeking the friendship of Soviet Russia instead of the Entente powers.

While the radicals of both the Right and the Left openly challenged the fundamental tenets of the new regime, Károlyi's own party evaporated. Unhappy with the reform projects which Károlyi embraced and which seemed too radical for them, most of the erstwhile Independentist leaders left the government, similarly to Jászi, disillusioned by the abortion of his scheme to keep the nationalities within Hungary. The main government party were now the moderate Social Democrats, struggling rather helplessly to tame the radical left of their own party, who constituted an internal opposition to the government, and gravitated towards the Communists.

The government, albeit rather belatedly, attempted to counter the forces threatening the regime from both sides: the Defence Association was suppressed and, after a Communist-organised demonstration culminated in shooting, thirty-two prominent Communists including Kun were arrested on February 21. At the same time, Károlyi decided to exert more vigorous policies to save what could still be saved of the country's territory. Hungarian diplomats established direct links with those of the western Allies in Vienna and Bern, the only two European capitals where they were officially accredited. They tried to convince them that besides the American financial aid programme directed by Herbert Hoover, from which Hungary hoped to benefit to put its economy in order, an acceptable settlement of the border question was also vital if a communist take-over was to be avoided. At home, Károlyi assured the public that he would not sign a peace treaty dismembering the country.

However, he did not have the chance to see the peace terms. On March 20, the Károlyi government received a memorandum from the French General Vix, which communicated the decision of February 26 made by the peace conference, authorising the Romanian troops to advance even further, and establishing a neutral zone including major Hungarian cities like Debrecen and Szeged. Whereas the main goal of the Allies was to secure a base of operation for intervention in Soviet Russia, the demarcation line proposed overlapped with the frontier promised to Romania in the treaty of Bucharest in 1916. Károlyi and the general public thus suspected this demand to form the basis of a final settlement and considered it unacceptable, while the president also felt that giving in to it would exacerbate the domestic crisis. He rejected the memorandum, and planned to proclaim national resistance, relying on the assistance of Soviet Russia that was defying the Entente just across the Carpathians. Wilsonism being compromised, proletarian internationalism now seemed to be the antidote of national disaster, and Károlyi appealed to the Social Democrats to lend greater weight to the decision by assuming sole government responsibility. On March 21, the latter accepted the call, only to accelerate and conclude the negotiations they had been conducting with the imprisoned Communist leaders about a united workers' party since early in the month. A new government, the Revolutionary Governing Council, presided by a Social Democrat but in effect led by Béla Kun, was formed on the same day, with the declared aim of establishing the dictatorship of the proletariat.

Even amidst the urgent tasks of national defence, which had a not inconsiderable role in propelling them to power, the Revolutionary Governing Council set to realising this goal with great application. They certainly needed to make up for lost time. The principles upon which the Aster Revolution was based were rather weakly embedded in Hungarian society, but at least they looked back to two decades of determined effort to cope with the crisis of the dualist Monarchy and to find a democratic solution to it. By contrast, the egalitarianism of the agrarian socialist movements was hazy and utopian in character, and the vision of classless society as put forward by the Social Democrats related to an indefinite future; they were not amalgamated in a single coherent programme for immediate political action before the end of 1918. Viewed from another angle, the transformation now proposed, and the discontinuity to be caused, was also far more profound: the changes brought about (or rather, envisaged) by the Károlyi government in terms of the composition of the political elite and the electorate as well as the balance of property were radical indeed, but they did not affect the system based on private property and political pluralism, as was the case with those of its successor.

Within two weeks of its accession to power, the Revolutionary Governing Council took measures that effectively eliminated the foundations of the bourgeois order. On March 26, factories and mines with more than twenty (shortly later cut back to ten) employees, transport companies, credit institutions and tenement houses were nationalised (the use of more than one room per person and more than three rooms per family was declared illegal). On April 4, all large and medium-sized estates, in other words, nearly sixty per cent of the arable land of the country, were decreed to have passed 'into the property of the proletarian state', to be farmed by the co-operatives of the agrarian proletariat (small- and dwarfholdings being left in the hands of their owners). Schools and educational institutions, a substantial part of which had been run by the churches, were also nationalised, and religious instruction in them was replaced by education in social relations. These initiatives went beyond anything attempted in Soviet Russia at the time in the belief that Hungary's more advanced conditions made intermediate steps such as land distribution redundant. Their counterpart in the administrative and political reorganisation of the country was the replacement of old local, municipal and county bureaucracies with the soviets of workers, peasants and soldiers. These were elected by an extended electorate – from which, ironically, former 'exploiters', that is, most pre–1918 voters, were excluded – on April 7 from a single list of candidates set up by the new Socialist Party. Especially important was the role of the Budapest Workers' Soviet in controlling and influencing government policies. The National Congress of Soviets, intended as a constituent assembly and elected by the soviets of the councils and the municipalities, sat between June 14 and 23 to vote through a socialist constitution. The infrastructure for maintaining law and order was radically remodelled, too: already on March 25, revolutionary tribunals were created in which the majority of 'judges' were laymen, and procedures were greatly simplified, largely at the expense of legality, to facilitate the attainment of their major goal: neutralising counter-revolutionary alarmism and subversion. However, capital sentences were largely beyond their scope. A Committee of Public Safety was organised to put pressure on the civilian population where it was needed in order to maintain the dictatorship of the proletariat, its head Tibor Szamuely travelling in his 'death train' to trouble spots to preside in summary courts. He was assisted by a number of commandos whose political loyalty was beyond doubt, such as the notorious 'Lenin Boys', created to supplement the Red Guard, which took over the ordinary functions of the police and the gendarmerie. Besides common murders of actual or alleged enemies by the 'elite' detachments, some 120 death sentences were meted out by the tribunals for political reasons.

The great momentum of the changes was partly intended to convince people that the realisation of the socialist utopia was imminent. Social policy measures, the expected alleviation of housing shortages through public ownership of accommodation in a country flooded by refugees, the nationalisation of large firms, improved educational opportunities, the more effective supply of food and consumer goods through rationing and supervised distribution indeed met with widespread approval, especially among the urban population. Many of the intellectual elite, who applauded the democratic reforms of the autumn of 1918, were initially also allured by the attractive goals of the Soviet Republic. They included not only Communists like Lukács, who became People's Commissar (in effect, a minister in the Revolutionary Governing Council) for Education, or Kassák, but also most members of the *Nyugat* circle who held positions in the Directorate for Literature, and Bartók and Kodály, who became members of the one for music. Newly appointed professors of the University of Budapest included Mannheim, Babits, the psychologist Sándor Ferenczi, the art historian Lajos Fülep and (although he did not occupy his chair) the historian Gyula Szekfű.

Gradually, however, most of these figures became disaffected, as did the middle classes and the intelligentsia, and the prominent leaders of the revolution of October 1918, of whom Jászi emigrated as early as the beginning of May 1919. (True, Károlyi stayed until the end of July, when he even offered to mediate between the Soviet Republic and the Entente.) At that time, Szekfű was already at work on his highly influential *Three Generations* (1920), hostile not only to the communist revolution, but also to democracy and liberalism which he blamed for paving the way for Kun; Móricz, enthusiastic at the outset, was complaining about the failure to satisfy the hunger of the peasantry for land; and Dezső Szabó, another early sympathiser, was soon to publish *The Sweptaway Village*, a fountain-head of populist intellectual trends with an anti-urban, anti-revolutionary and anti-Semitic content, which were in high currency in interwar Hungary.

The revolution and the village were indeed unable to come to terms with each other. Besides being economically unsound amidst the shortage of raw materials and fuel to supply the machinery supposedly more efficient in large-scale co-operatives than on small plots, the nationalisation scheme embittered not only the well-to-do peasants who actually lost land, but also the lower strata of the peasantry, the domestic servants and the agricultural labourers whose dreams of becoming independent farmers were thwarted by the same urban revolutionaries who had formerly encouraged land seizures. Decrees regarding the compulsory delivery of agricultural surplus and requisitioning further undermined whatever popularity the government still enjoyed in the countryside. The latter, in turn, blamed the food shortages on the peasantry, which exacerbated the already existing rift between town and country, and served as a pretext for the administrative centralisation of the economic life of the country under the Central Economic Council. The anticlerical measures taken by the government also annoyed the tradition-ally devout peasants, concerned about the security of the 'family hearth'. All of this made them all the more susceptible to counter-revolutionary propaganda, which did not fail to emphasise the 'foreign' (that is, Jewish) character of the revolution (over half of the commissars were indeed of Jewish origin). Organised counter-revolution consisted of two groups, both of them based outside the territory controlled by the Kun government but operating through sympathisers within it: the Hungarian National Committee (or 'Anti-Bolshevist Committee), cre-ated in Vienna in April by representatives of nearly all of the old parties and led by Count István Bethlen, and a counter-revolutionary govern-ment headed by Count Gyula Károlyi set up under French tutelage at Arad on 5 May, later moving to Szeged.

Paradoxically enough, the Soviet Republic was maintained in power for over four months, besides the increasingly dictatorial means it em-ployed, mainly by the temporary successes it scored on the national is-sue; and it collapsed not in the face of internal counter-revolution but when its military position against the allies of the Entente in the region became untenable. The communist take-over in Budapest at first brought to the surface the disagreements between the western Allies at the peace conference: the Americans and the British interpreted it as the outcome of a situation created by the violations of Hungarian interests, resulting from the extravagant claims of France on behalf of its protégés in the region. It was agreed that Kun's request for negotiations would be satisfied by sending General Ian Christian Smuts, the prime minister of South Africa, to Budapest, mainly to obtain reliable information about the situation there in early April 1919. Smuts seemed inclined to reduce the neutral zone in eastern Hungary, and in his report to Paris he even supported the Hungarian counter-proposal to call a meeting of all those concerned, including the losers of the war, to discuss border issues. As a matter of fact, this was unrealistic, especially as Smuts also concluded that Hungary truly had a government of Bolshevik character, which gave weight to the French Prime Minister Clemenceau's already mooted idea of suppressing German revanchist designs as well as the spread of the Russian disease into Western Europe by a *cordon sanitaire* estab-lished out of the new states in Central Europe.

Accordingly, a massive Romanian offensive was launched in mid-April in the east, soon reinforced by a Czechoslovak invasion from the north. By the beginning of May the areas of Hungary east of the River Tisza were under the administration of the Romanian military, resulting in the execution, internment or deportation of numerous local leaders, revolutionary or otherwise. Czech forces occupied the industrial region around Miskolc. It was not before the middle of May that the superiority of the hostile forces was to some extent offset by the recruitment campaign of the Revolutionary Governing Council, which inherited an army of a mere 40,000 from its predecessor. Then, however, 'the Communist met the Nationalist on the common ground of the defence of the fatherland', as one provincial journalist wrote. Not only Budapest workers and refugees from eastern Hungary, but also talented officers like Aurél Stromfeld, who became the Chief of the General Staff, flocked to the Red Army – ironically, about a dozen future generals of the Hungarian army in the Second World War fought under the flag of the Soviet Republic in 1919. As a result of this as well as the temporary embarrassment of the Romanians by the Ukrainian Red Army, not only the Miskolc area was relieved, but Stromfeld's northern campaign drove a wedge between the Czech and Romanian armies by penetrating into Slovakia, where even a short-lived Soviet Republic was proclaimed on June 16.

However, the world revolution that was expected to sweep away the corrupt bourgeois politicians of the peace conference and their allies failed to commence. The Bavarian Soviet Republic, proclaimed on April 7, 1919, hardly survived into May, the communist revolt planned by Kun's agents in Vienna on June 15 failed, and General Denikin's counter-revolutionary offensive in Russia thwarted hopes of help from across the Carpathians. Facing an ever more turbulent domestic situation marked by widespread peasant unrest and an uprising of the students of the military academy in Budapest, the government, after heated debates, decided to give in to the demand of he peace conference and withdrew Hungarian forces from Slovakia behind the demarcation line at the end of June. Stromfeld resigned in protest against the decision, and some of his fellow officers now started to join the National Army, organised as the military branch of the Szeged counter-revolutionary government under the command of Vice Admiral Miklós Horthy, formerly an adjutant of Francis Joseph and the last commander-in-chief of the Austro-Hungarian navy.

Kun, supported by some of the other people's commissars, now made a last desperate bid to regain an apathetic, even hostile hinterland through military success: arguing that whereas the Red Army had evacuated Slovakia, the Romanians refused to retreat behind the neutral zone as envisaged, a surprise offensive was launched along the Tisza. After initial advance, it proved to be abortive and ended in a disorderly flight of the Red Army. On August 1, as the Romanian forces were marching towards Budapest, the commissars gave in to the argument of trade unionist and Social Democrat leaders that the creation of a government acceptable to the Entente powers was the only way to avoid complete foreign occupation. Kun and the other communist commissars fled to Vienna, where they obtained political asylum, and on the next day the government of Gyula Peidl, a trade unionist leader who had been opposed to the unification of the workers' parties and played no role under the Soviet Republic, took office.

In an atmosphere burdened by the experience of a lost war and two fallen revolutions, with rearguard actions fought by the residual forces of the second one in the western half of what remained of the country while the east was under foreign occupation and the counter-government also continued to function in Szeged, it is no wonder that the plan of the unionist government to consolidate its position as well as the conditions of Hungary by rejecting the dictatorship of the proletariat on the one hand and defying a conservative restoration on the other, came to nothing. It was regarded as crypto-Bolshevik not only by the conservative circles, but also its intended coalition partners – Liberals, peasant democrats and Christian Socialists –, and failed to obtain recognition from the Entente. Assisted by the Romanian army, which in the meantime occupied Budapest, a coup forced the government to resign on 6 August 1919.

The new government, headed by István Friedrich, a small-scale industrialist and an erstwhile state secretary under Károlyi, immediately set not only to annulling the measures associated with the Soviet Republic (mostly, the nationalisation process), but also to dismantling the main achievements of the democratic revolution (for instance, the ones relating to civil liberties and social policy). At the same time, revolutionary tribunals were replaced by counter-revolutionary ones, which packed prisons with workers, poor peasants and intellectuals, and by the beginning of 1920 passed roughly as many death sentences as their counterparts (mainly on the lackeys of the 'red terror', such as the 'Lenin Boys'). The intellectual elite of the country suffered a serious blow. Bartók and Kodály were prosecuted, Móricz even imprisoned, while several dozens including, haphazardly, Lukács, Mannheim, Polányi, Korda, the art sociologist Arnold Hauser and the multi-talented artist László Moholy-Nagy, left the country.

Government retaliation was not the only, nor even the main concern of those who emigrated or withdrew to internal seclusion. Besides the Friedrich cabinet, the Romanian army, which even occupied the north of Transdanubia in August, also took part in the 'pacification' of the country, while systematically transporting cattle, machinery and the new crop to Romania as 'war reparation'. Thirdly, there was the National Army of Horthy, who transferred his now independent headquarters to Transdanubia and refused to surrender to the government. Without any title, the army controlled and gave orders to the local authorities, and its most notorious detachments were the instruments of naked terror. In three months, they may have killed as many as two thousand actual or suspected former Soviet members, Red Army soldiers, and sometimes individuals who were in no way associated with the proletarian dictatorship, but were Jews. Besides the executions and lynchings, about seventy thousand people were imprisoned or sent to internment camps during the same period.

Quite paradoxically, whereas the normalisation of the situation in Hungary was indispensable for the Allies in order to bring the work of the peace conference to a conclusion, they refused to recognise the Friedrich government, because it was appointed by Archduke Joseph, nominated by Charles IV to represent him a year before and now considering himself as Regent, which raised fears of a Habsburg restoration. Romanian withdrawal, another condition of consolidation, was difficult to obtain because of Romania's dissatisfaction with a planned peace treaty that fell short of the promises of 1916, and required it to guarantee minority rights, which it felt a limitation on its sovereignty. The first result of the mission sent by the peace conference to Budapest in October 1919 under Sir George Clerk was the commencement of the withdrawal of Romanian troops, whose place was taken, despite protest by the Social Democrats and other left-wing forces, by the National Army of Horthy, who ceremonially entered Budapest on November 16. His speech before the notables of the capital, stigmatising it as a 'sinful city' that had rejected its glorious past, Holy Crown and national colours for the sake of red rags, suited an atmosphere in which most remaining adherents of the two revolutions were neutralised in one way or another, and the people at large, disappointed in Wilsonism and Bolshevism, hoped to heal the wounds caused by the war and its loss by returning to order, authority and the so-called Christian-national system of values.

It was also due to the increasing influence of Horthy and the changes in the political balance that Clerk abandoned his initial insistence on securing an important role for the Social Democrats and the Liberals in the new coalition government whose creation the peace conference demanded. Commanding as he was the only troops capable of maintaining order, and ready to subordinate them to the new government, it had to be acceptable to Horthy personally and the military in general. As a result, the cabinet of Károly Huszár, formed on November 24, 1919, was one in which the members of the Christian National Unity Party and other conservative-agrarian groups prevailed over those of the Independent Smallholder Party, the Social Democrats and the Liberals. The Huszár government was soon recognised by the peace conference, and the long-awaited invitation to send a Hungarian delegation to Paris arrived on December 1.

However, before the peace treaty, a vital, even if painful condition of Hungary's integration in Europe's post-war order, could be set on the agenda, Hungary was facing national elections. Even though the great powers insisted that voting should take place by universal and secret ballot, the circumstances were unfavourable to fulfilling any illusion of a democratic outcome. The half-hearted commitment of the Huszár government to ensure the freedom of the elections could not offset the terrorist actions of the detachments of the National Army and the recovering extreme right wing organisations, such as the Association of Awakening Hungarians, designed to intimidate the candidates and voters of the Social Democrats, and to some extent also the Smallholders and the Liberals. In protest, the Social Democrats boycotted the elections of January 25-26, 1920, and withdrew from the political arena until mid-1922.

The Smallholders and the Christian National Unity Party emerged as the strongest parties at the elections, returning between them 150 members into a one-chamber, 218 member parliament whose first major task was to determine the form of the state and choose a head of state. Whereas there was near-universal agreement to drop republicanism, intertwined as it was with the revolutions, monarchists were sharply divided between legitimists and 'free electors'. For both of them, monarchism meant the historical continuity of the new regime and the legality of Hungary's claim to the lands of the Holy Crown of Saint Stephen. The former – aristocrats and other members of the traditional political class loyal to the dynasty, but also others, like the Jewish middle class, hostile to Horthy – expected Hungary's recovery with the restoration of the Habsburgs. The latter included not only those who simply reckoned with international realities, namely, the categorical rejection of a Habsburg restoration among the great powers as well as Hungary's neighbours, but also those imbued with old independentist sentiment, and those linked to Horthy by ties of personal loyalty or ambition. They insisted that the throne was vacant, and the only viable candidate for the regency, a medieval institution now resuscitated, was Horthy. To lend greater weight to their arguments, the army occupied the square in front of the Parliament, and a few officers even followed Horthy into the building on March 1, 1920, when he was elected Regent, with moderately strong presidential powers.

Three days later, a new coalition government of the Smallholders and the Christian National Unity Party was formed under Sándor Simonyi-Semadam, and the major task it faced was the signing of the peace treaty. The Hungarian delegation, led by Count Albert Apponyi who enjoyed great authority across the Hungarian political spectrum, reached Paris on January 6, 1920 and produced a great variety of historical, ethnic, economic and strategic arguments against the terms that had been essentially worked out by the spring of 1919 and presented to them shortly after their arrival at the peace conference. The Hungarian delegates demanded the alteration of some of the borders suggested, and proposed plebiscites in disputed areas. The earlier differences between the great powers were now temporarily reawakened. The Americans and the British had initially intended to leave most of the overwhelmingly Hungarian-inhabited pale immediately across the present borders in Hungarian hands, and now Prime Minister Lloyd George again warned that peace would be precarious in Central Europe with one-third of all ethnic Hungarians surrendered to the neighbouring states. Finally, however, lest the situation be destabilised through violating the interests of the successor states, the arbiters left the treaty unaltered, refusing only the most extreme demands (such as the 'Slav corridor' between Bratislava and Zagreb, the Czechoslovak claim to the Miskolc industrial region or the Romanian claim to the area around Debrecen).

The peace treaty, signed in the hall connecting the Petit and the Grand Trianon Palaces at Versailles on June 4, 1920, by two representatives of the Hungarian government who did not want to take part in public life in the future, deprived Hungary of two-thirds of its former territory (without Croatia) and nearly sixty per cent of its population, including thirty per cent of ethnic Hungarians. Besides its new neighbours (Czechoslovakia, Romania, the Serb-Croat-Slovene Kingdom – later Yugoslavia – and Austria), even Italy (Fiume) and Poland obtained some of its former territory, now reduced from 282,000 to 93,000 square kilometres, with only 7.6 million of the former 18.2 million inhabitants. Well over ninety per cent of the land that had to be ceded went to Romania, Czechoslovakia and Yugoslavia, the ratio of Hungarians in the territories each of these states gained exceeding thirty per cent. About half of the nearly 3.2 million Hungarians finding themselves in minority status lived in compact blocs contiguous with Hungary across the new borders. Compared to its new neighbours except Austria, Hungary became ethnically nearly homogeneous, ninety per cent of its population being Magyar (Germans, over six per cent, constituting the largest minority group). Even so, Yugoslav troops refused to evacuate the area around Pécs until August 1921. Tension also arose between Hungary and Austria over the Burgenland, the western border region, parts of which Hungarian paramilitary units occupied and left only when, simultaneously to an ultimatum of the Entente, representatives of the two countries agreed that in and around Sopron a plebiscite would be held in December 1921 (which, despite the slight German majority in the area, ultimately favoured Hungary). As a result of the territorial resettlement, the Hungarian economy was deemed hardly viable by most contemporary observers. The country retained none of its salt and precious metal mines, a mere ten per cent of its forests and iron resources, and only half of its once flourishing food processing industry, whose

9. Hungary and her neighbours after the
Peace Treaty of Trianon

——— borders before 1914

-■-■-■ borders after 1920

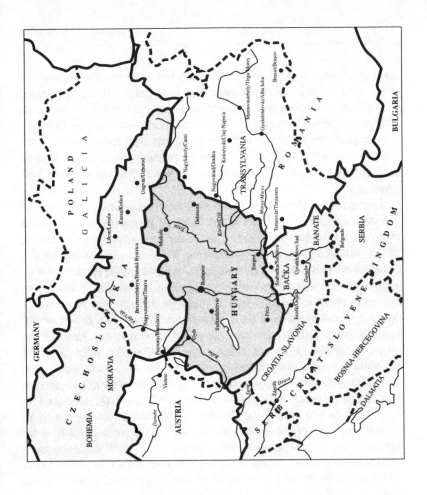

capacity, however, still by far exceeded what was now supplied by the contracted arable lands. Thus, more than ever before, Hungary became dependent on exports and imports, and was extremely vulnerable to changes in the world economy. Besides the territorial changes, Hungary was required by the treaty to pay reparations, and forbidden to relinquish its sovereignty (that is, become reunited with Austria) and to maintain an army other than an infantry consisting of up to 35,000 volunteers.

Ever since, on the day the Treaty of Trianon was signed, hundreds of thousands protested against it in the streets of Budapest, it has haunted Hungarian collective memory. The sheer magnitude of the losses, which cannot be compared to anything but those occasioned by the Ottoman conquest in the sixteenth century, combined with the dubious arguments that were supposed to justify them, are sufficient to explain the bitterness they engendered. In addition, the minority treaties that ought to have guaranteed the rights of the Hungarians in the neighbouring states largely remained on paper. The fact that, besides the plight of the Hungarian minorities in the neighbouring states, some of the country's social and economic problems could indeed be blamed on the peace settlement, was a convenient ideological pretext for a nationalist regime opposed to far-reaching reform to impute all hardships to a vicious treaty whose revision became the alpha and the omega of its policies for a quarter of a century. This was all the more possible as all parties in the otherwise variegated Hungarian political spectrum were united in slogans like 'Justice to Hungary!', even if they were divided as to the precise ways and extent in which they hoped to obtain it. Trianon has continued to plague the Hungarian public scene after its reissue in the wake of the Second World War, even when it seemed to lay dormant under the veil of socialist internationalism, and today, when the attitude to the Hungarian minorities and their circumstances is of necessity an important item of the domestic policy. On a broader horizon, if Hungarian policies in the dualist period poisoned ethnic relations in Central Europe, the post-war settlement did nothing to heal them, but served to keep, with tragic consequences, the nationalist agenda in its nineteenth-century form awake into the late twentieth, and quite possibly into the twenty-first century.

2. The consolidation and the trials of a conservative regime

Born out of unbridled terror, the Horthy regime owed its very existence perhaps less to internal support than to international contingencies, and in spite of its roots in the extreme right it bore the imprint of the priorities of the western peacemakers that assisted at its inception even in the 1930s, when the changing international atmosphere made it lean ever more heavily back towards those roots. The emblematic figure of the period embodied these contradictions appropriately enough. A rather unimaginative scion of a Calvinist gentry family from eastern Hungary, Admiral Miklós Horthy played no part in politics until, in the summer of 1919, over the age of fifty, he temporarily took the helm of the radical anti-parliamentarian aspirations of the Christian (that is, non-Jewish) middle class, whose other proponents largely belonged to a younger generation, but like them he was attracted to authoritarian courses of action. These engagements and inclinations made him a suitable partner of Hitler in the 1930s, although, throughout, he was also a hesitant one. For his cast of mind was fundamentally conservative and traditionalist. The western Allies were certainly over-optimistic and less than well-informed, maybe even cynical, when in the autumn of 1919 they merely saw in him the strong-handed soldier who would first restore order and then parliamentary government. Yet this is what happened, albeit under pressure and with serious limitations; and as it was happening, the old conservative-liberal landowning and capitalist elite gradually returned to the political scene and overshadowed the extreme right until the 1930s, when the influence of the victors of the First World War in the Danube Basin also shifted into the hands of Nazi Germany and fascist Italy.

To be sure, the restoration concerned only the elite of the old monarchy, but not its political system, which in the Horthy era reflected both the external and domestic pressures under which it was born: it was more democratic, with an extended suffrage and the presence of peasant and workers' parties in parliament, but at the same time less liberal, with harsher censorship, police surveillance and official anti-Semitism of varying intensity. Besides, and arguably even more than Horthy himself, the architects of this political outlook were Hungary's two prime ministers in the period between 1920 and 1931, Count Pál Teleki, and especially Count István Bethlen. Both of them came from old Transylvanian families, and were sincere admirers of the liberal achievements of the post–1867 era. At the same time, the post-war events led them to the conclusion that liberalism had to be controlled, and argued that Central and Eastern Europe, including Hungary, was as yet immature to

graft democracy on to the parliamentary system, which they nevertheless considered the only acceptable form of government. Teleki and
Bethlen therefore advocated a 'conservative democracy', guided by the
aristocracy and the landed nobility, as the proper response of the region
to the challenges of the democratic age. They opposed all endeavours
aimed either at the radical extension or the complete abolition of the
liberal rights enshrined in the parliamentarism of the dualist period. Liberal democracy seemed to them a mechanical application of the majority principle, undermining political responsibility and stability. They despised communism and were suspicious of social democracy because
of their campaign against private property. Finally, they opposed the
right wing radical and fascist trends epitomised by Gyula Gömbös and
the other 'protectors of the race' who thought that the parliamentary
system had outlived itself and ought to be replaced by authoritarian rule
which would facilitate a redistribution of economic functions at the expense of the Jewish bourgeoisie and in favour of the Hungarian Christian middle classes.

These priorities clearly influenced the process of political consolidation and return to the rule of law in Hungary after the Treaty of Trianon
had been signed. The appointment of the generally respected Teleki at
the head of a cabinet including other distinguished personalities on July
19, 1920, marked the end of the period of transitional governments, the
return of the traditional elite to politics after many months of biding their
time, and the beginning of conservative balancing-act policies whose
real master would be Bethlen. Whereas those serving prison sentences
of less than five years for involvement in the revolutions received amnesty, and those guilty of the atrocities during the 'white terror' were
pardoned, the government took action to push extremes both on the
right and on the left underground. It put an end to the depredations of
the officers' squads by banning some of their organisations and arresting several of their members, though they soon found employment in
state and administrative offices. On the other hand, the edge of the 1921
law 'for the more efficient protection of order in the state and society'
was mainly directed against the Communists, while it was occasionally
also used against radical rightists: Mátyás Rákosi in 1925 and Ferenc
Szálasi in the late 1930s, future dictators of Hungary in different political
colours, were both sentenced to prison terms under this law. The leaders of the Soviet Republic were unable to maintain a viable underground
movement from exile in Vienna, and later in Moscow. The scope of action for the organisations of the working class, about a quarter of the
population, was systematically narrowed, and confined to state-funded
parties which commanded little support. At the same time, Horthy established the 'Order of Heroes', that is, those who had proved their

commitment to Christian and national values (and their loyalty to the Regent) by distinguishing themselves in the fight against revolution.

To alleviate the tensions caused by the anomalies in the structure of landed estates, and to take the wind out of the sails of the Smallholder Party, the Teleki government introduced a land reform scheme in December 1920. About 425,000 families, mostly landless agricultural labourers, received a maximum of five acres each, three acres on the average. The measure, affecting merely 8.5 per cent of the arable land of the country, was a poor match compared to the one attempted by Károlyi or those effected in neighbouring states (which, of course, could afford to be more generous, relying on the estates formerly owned by Austrian or Hungarian magnates).

The reform indeed attained its main goal, namely, playing on the pride, or rather the illusion of ownership which fed into loyalty to the regime for a now widened segment of the population, even though the high repayment rates forced many of the beneficiaries to relinquish their newly acquired plots quite soon. However, it did not affect the structure of society: it added to the number of dwarfholdings, and still left nearly half of the peasantry (or over twenty per cent of the whole population) landless agricultural labourers. They fell largely outside the scope of the very slow process of modernisation that started to alter the life of the better-off people of the villages in the shape of electricity, improving access to medical facilities or changing habits of clothing. They continued to share houses between several families (and their animals); their children drank milk once in a month, and hardly knew what butter was; they did not benefit from compulsory insurance schemes. It was mainly among them that tuberculosis took its death toll, 10,000 per year on average during the interwar period. Nor did they find relief, as they did in the dualist era, in large public works schemes and overseas emigration, which the United States now seriously discouraged.

On the other hand, the land reform left about thirty per cent of the country's land in the hands of less than four hundred magnates who possessed more than 1,500 acres each. The lands distributed in 1921 roughly equalled those possessed by the Catholic Church – or about five Esterházy estates. This also meant that the economic weight, together with the manners and lifestyle of the aristocracy in Hungary remained as striking a feature of the Horthy era as it had been in the dualist period, even though there were many who, in consequence of Trianon, could no longer afford the ostentatious habits of the happy times of peace. The social exclusiveness of the aristocracy manifested itself not only in their young ladies leaving charity balls as soon as they had been opened, lest they should be asked for a dance by 'obscure strangers', and segregation in general, but also in their conservative contempt for the right radicalism of 'petty officers and housekeepers'. However, in addition to their sense of refinement and affectation, it was also a tradition of humanistic upbringing that made most of them repudiate, and some of them actively oppose, the fascist tide.

But even in 1920, besides pressure and administrative action against the right wing radical organisations, measures to placate the anti-Semitic Christian middle class (as well as the 'people of the *puszta*') were needed to create stability. The *numerus clausus* law answered this need by regulating university admissions so as to reduce the ratio of Jewish students, which indeed fell from 24 per cent of the overall intake (46 per cent in medicine and 33 per cent at the Technical University) in 1914 to between 8 and 12 per cent between 1920 and 1935 (though this still exceeded the proportion of Jews, 6 per cent, in Hungarian society).

The Teleki government was brought down in the spring of 1921 by the royalty issue. Teleki was a legitimist, but many of the Smallholders in the governing coalition being in favour of free elections, the coalition was split on the issue, and a political realignment began even before an abortive attempt by Charles IV to recover his throne. In the belief that he had the support of some French political circles as well as the Vatican, and that the ground had been prepared for his restoration in Hungary, he returned from his exile in Switzerland at the Easter of 1921. He immediately negotiated with Teleki and thereafter with Horthy, who, although he had been ostensibly supporting Charles' claim, now refused to relinquish his power. While the neighbouring states also mobilised their armies to prevent a Habsburg restoration, Charles, who seems to have contemplated far-reaching social reforms, could not but leave the country again. A week after his departure, Teleki had to resign, and his office was taken over by Bethlen on April 14, 1921. He was to retain it for just over ten years.

The new Prime Minister stood his first major test in October 1921, when the ex-monarch attempted a second coup. This time Charles did not intend to bargain with Horthy. His plane landed in the territory disputed between Hungary and Austria, occupied at the time by troops under legitimist officers, and a 'royal army' took the train towards the capital on October 22, 1921. On the following day, however, they were dispersed by Hungarian regulars mobilised by the government and commanded by Gömbös near Budaörs, west of Budapest; Charles and his consort Zita were detained, handed over to the commander of the British fleet on the Danube, and exiled to the island of Madeira, where the last king of Hungary died six months later. The incident once again gave occasion for Hungary's new neighbours to clamour for tough measures, but the great powers only insisted on the official dethronement of the House of Habsburg, which the Hungarian National Assembly enacted on November 6, 1921.

The royal coups were the last, rather pathetic tremors of the earthquake that shook Hungary in the aftermath of the First World War, and their outcome helped the consolidation of Hungary's international position and domestic conditions along the lines envisaged by Bethlen. After the dethronement of the Habsburgs and the final settlement of all border issues, there were no more obstacles to granting, in September 1922, Hungary's application for Hungary's membership in the League of Nations. The unsuccessful attempt of Charles eroded legitimism as a political force, and its political arm, the Christian National Unity Party, rapidly disintegrated. Bethlen, with the approval of Horthy, now embarked on his plan to create a powerful government party by strengthening the conservative agrarian wing of the Smallholder Party and to conquer it, as it were, from inside. With a number of his followers he joined the party in January 1922, and even though István Nagyatádi Szabó formally remained its president, his peasant democrat supporters were soon outmanoeuvred by those of Bethlen in the ensuing struggle for key posts. In the meantime an agreement, the so-called Bethlen-Peyer Pact, was also reached between the Prime Minister and the head of the Social Democratic Party, who agreed to refrain from organising public servants and agricultural labourers, strikes for political goals and republican propaganda. He also undertook to use the party's international relations to further Hungary's foreign policy aims, and to severe its ties with its émigré leaders. In return, the Social Democratic Party, whose presence in the National Assembly Bethlen considered important for the image of the country abroad and as a safety valve domestically, acquired greater freedom of action. As a final touch to the tailoring of Hungary's political scene to his conception of 'conservative democracy', in March 1922, Bethlen decreed a new electoral law which lowered the proportion of voters from about 40 to 28 per cent, which placed Hungary on a level with South-Eastern Europe, or the most conservative countries of Western Europe in this respect, like France or Belgium. Still worse, without parallel in contemporary Europe, apart from the capital and seven other urban centres, voting was made public, which meant that only one in five of the deputies was elected by secret ballot.

Largely as a result of this, the number of peasants and the representatives of the free professions declined, and that of landowners and bureaucrats increased among those returned at the elections of May and June 1922. Bethlen's new Party of Unity (the common shorthand for the Christian Smallholder, Agrarian and Bourgeois Party) gained a comfortable 60 per cent majority, with a mere fraction of its deputies being former Smallholders. The fundamental character which the political system of the country retained until the German occupation in March 1944 emerged by now as a result of Bethlenite consolidation. Hungary became a parliamentary state with strong elements of authoritarianism and a hegemonistic party structure, in which the institutions inherited from the liberal era were operated in an anti-democratic fashion. The government acknowledged a lawful political opposition, consisting on the left of Social Democrats, bourgeois liberals led by Vilmos Vázsonyi and later by Károly Rassay, and after 1930 a rejuvenated Independent Smallholder Party; and on the right, of different groups of Christian Socialists and right radicals, such as the Party of Racial Defence founded by Gömbös, who seceded from the government party in 1923. However, the adjustment of interests took place, not at the sessions of parliament, but rather at the conferences among the various factions within the government party; its decisions might have been criticised, but were rarely changed by the opposition, which the peculiarities of the system also deprived from a chance to implement alternative policies by assuming power. True, whereas the locks were more or less watertight towards the Left, they were more permeable towards the Right, and the ties forged between conservative and extremist counter-revolutionaries in 1919–1920 were never fully severed – a circumstance which, together with the 'Trianon syndrome', accentuated the infatuation with all things Hungarian, easily falling into chauvinism and racism, that characterised much of Hungarian public discourse in the whole of the Horthy era. Nevertheless, the Horthy regime was fundamentally distinguished from Nazi Germany or fascist Italy by the fact that it never even considered mobilising the masses for revolutionary action against what was to a great extent a post-feudal and aristocratic order. Despite restrictions of varying kinds and intensity on the freedom of expression, it did not attempt a systematic regimentation of the press and cultural life in general, nor did it require explicit ideological identification from the ordinary citizen.

The restoration of political stability, of course, also depended to a great extent on a credible policy of economic reconstruction; after all, the landslides between 1918 and 1920 occurred among circumstances in which the living standards of the different strata of the common people fell to between twenty and forty per cent of their pre-war level, which made them especially exposed to all kinds of political extremism and social demagogy. In the aftermath of the war, over thirty per cent of workers were unemployed, while the state bureaucracy, tailored to the needs of a country three times as large as Hungary now was, still employed over 200,000 public servants. As a combined effect of the war and the peace, in 1920 the output of agriculture was about fifty per cent, that of industry a mere thirty-five per cent of what it had been in 1914;

inflation was already soaring during the war, but the Hungarian crown fell to about ten per cent of its mid-1919 value by the end of 1920, and to 0.3 per cent by the end of 1923. Hyper-inflation did not reach German or Austrian dimensions; still, economic stabilisation was one of the top priorities of the Hungarian governments. Initial experiments to improve the situation by relying exclusively on internal resources like increasing taxation, reductions in the size of the bureaucracy and other austerity measures were doomed to failure; nor could the successive inflationist policies attain their goal of stimulating an exhausted economy. In May 1923 Bethlen decided to follow the example of Austria in applying for a loan from the League of Nations. This step led to domestic complications – Gömbös and his followers seceded from the government party in protest against what they interpreted as placing Hungary at the mercy of domestic and international Jewish capital – and several weeks of negotiations in London, Paris and Rome. In the face of the resistance of the French, also prompted by their lesser allies in Central Europe, British and Italian support earned Hungary about half of the sum requested, 250 million gold crowns, on rather unfavourable conditions. Hungary also had to undertake the payment of 180 million crowns of war reparations within twenty years, and to place its economy for two and a half years, the expected duration of the stabilisation, under the supervision of commissioners of the League of Nations. Thanks to further reductions in the size of the bureaucracy and increased taxes, which by the mid-1920s exceeded the level of 1912 by sixty per cent, from 1925 a substantial part of the loan could be turned, with the approval of the commissioners, into investments, mainly into the improvement of the infrastructure and cultural activities. The successful stabilisation, crowned by the introduction of the new currency, the pengő, on January 1, 1927, was based on the first international success of Hungary since the war, and earned the confidence of private creditors for the country.

Even so, and even though the growth rate of the Hungarian economy slightly exceeded the European average, the economic results of consolidation were contradictory. The Paris peace settlement tore apart not only the 'prison of peoples', as the Habsburg Monarchy was occasionally rhetorically referred to among its critics, but also what had been a well-functioning economic unit shaped by centuries of piecemeal adjustment of different needs and services to one another, in which people and commodities travelled unhindered between Trieste (now in Italy) and Lemberg (Lviv/Lvov, now in the Ukraine). After 1920, something like a permanent state of customs war developed among the states that inherited the various parts of that unit, each of them endeavouring to attain economic self-sufficiency, instead of maintaining intensive co-operation. For Hungary this meant high protective tariffs, which could be as high as 75 per cent, imposed on about forty thousand products, mainly of industry, especially in branches that had been underdeveloped before the war.

As a result, the modest economic prosperity of the second half of the 1920s was rather uneven: textile industry gained, while food processing lost about ten per cent in its share in the output of Hungarian industry. Machine industry also declined; characteristically, as earlier, the country's limited economic potential caused several seminal Hungarian inventions, such as Oszkár Asbóth's helicopter or György Jendrassik's turbine engine, to be tested and manufactured outside the country. The beginning of the exploration of bauxite sites around Veszprém in Transdanubia in 1925 was an important development for a country suffering acute shortages of industrial raw materials. Exceptionally, as in the case of the electrical industry, Hungary could retain the high standards and the competitiveness it achieved in the pre-war period, with striking results in developments that had a visible effect in everyday life, such as electrification (reaching nearly a third of the settlements of the country, in which two-thirds of the inhabitants lived, by 1933) or the spread of radio appliances (over 300,000 in the same year). Even though Hungary was one of the least developed countries of Europe in terms of motorisation, this also made advances, the number of automobiles exceeding 15,000 by the 1930s and regular bus-routes appearing in Budapest and twenty-two other towns. Yet, despite the steady growth of industry, its output only exceeded the pre-war level by twelve per cent in 1929, and agriculture, where the same figure was a mere two per cent, remained the dominant branch of the Hungarian economy. The reasons for stagnation included the proliferation of dwarfholdings where the introduction of intensive methods of cultivation was unthinkable, and the fact that technological improvement could not offset the neglect of other means of increasing yields. The productivity of Hungarian agriculture thus hardly exceeded that of the Balkan countries, and the gap between it and the top-ranking western countries like Belgium or Denmark, broadened. Cattle stocks, even as late as 1938, remained behind what they had been in 1911.

The economic recovery made only a marginal impact on the life of the lower classes. The situation of the rural poor has already been referred to. As to the industrial working class, over 10 per cent of them, at least 100,000 people, were continuously unemployed even during the relatively prosperous years after 1925, and the real wages of those who worked never reached the pre-war level before the economic crisis. With the exception of Budapest, running water and electricity hardly reached the suburbs where they lived, and even in the capital, these achievements added little to the comfort of their miserable, slum-like housing estates. Their dissatisfaction burst out in strikes and hunger marches, and hitherto underground Communists and leftist Social Democrats who defected their party responded to it by founding the Hungarian Socialist Workers' Party in April 1925. Although it refused to abide by the terms of the Bethlen-Peyer pact, and the government tolerated it for about a year, it failed to win any substantial support, and the attempt ended in tough police measures and show trials in the summer of 1926.

However, repression was not the only way the government tried to tackle the problem of working class disaffection. Besides the trade unions, which were highly efficient means of self-help in the 1920s, from 1927 on workers and other groups of employees, though not the peasantry and the rural proletariat, could benefit from considerably expanded state insurance schemes affecting sickness, old age, disability and widowhood. Other conservative reforms included a second *numerus clausus* law in 1928, which shifted the criteria of university admission from racial to social grounds (defining desirable proportions according to parents' occupations), and the restoration of the Upper House in the Hungarian legislation in November 1926. Consisting overwhelmingly of magnates, high state officials and ecclesiastical leaders, its task was to ensure 'permanence', in other words, to counterbalance even the limited changes that a highly controlled electoral system might cause in the composition of the Lower House. Needless to say, the measure originated from Bethlen, who nevertheless had little to fear from such changes: at the general elections of December 1926, the Party of Unity even increased its parliamentary majority, whereas all of its rivals lost seats.

Shortly before the elections, Bethlen had tendered his resignation, which Horthy refused to accept. The cause was an international banknote forgery scandal in which government circles, including the Prime Minister, were indirectly implicated, just at a time when a political scene earlier marked by acrimonious debates and extremist passions started to become more peaceful, and the economy began to function. In December 1925, a Hungarian diplomatic courier was arrested as he tried to exchange a false one thousand franc note at The Hague. His luggage contained a suitcase full of fakes, which turned out to have been printed at the National Cartographic Institute, headed by Teleki, who was also in charge of secret policies aimed at the revision of the Trianon peace settlement. The rather far-flung idea of throwing the French economy into chaos while drawing resources for the financing of revisionist goals originally came from right-wing army officers, and the threads seem to have reached the Chief of Staff and Gömbös. However, although in February 1926 the co-ordinator of the forgerers, Prince Lajos Windisch-

Grätz, police chief Imre Nádasdy and some small fry were tried and received jail sentences, these threads were not investigated – a fact which
showed that the split that occurred between the conservative and the
radical right in the years of the consolidation was less than complete and
irreversible. The opposition hoped in vain that the international consternation caused by the forged francs affair would sweep the Bethlen
government away: not only was the Regent's confidence in his Prime
Minister unswerving (which was what really mattered in the given political system), but Bethlen's person was also considered to be the guarantee of political stability in Hungary by the British and Italian governments, and he continued to enjoy their support.

Hungary's reputation suffered from the scandal, but it did not seriously affect its ambiguous and circuitous route out of international isolation in the 1920s. Hungarian foreign policy was initially bewildered by
the circumstances in which it found itself after the revolutions and
amidst the preparation of a disastrous peace treaty. As the unacceptabil-
ity of the latter was axiomatic, from the outset there were two, ultimately
irreconcilable, courses of action for it to take: integration in the new order of Europe and border modifications based on earning the goodwill
of the great powers and détente with the neighbouring states, or a forcible restoration, whether complete or partial, of the old status quo based
on armed co-operation with the other losers of the First World War.

A fundamentally hostile and suspicious environment was certainly
not appeased by the fact that interest in both of these alternatives created contradictory foreign policy lines in the first months of the Horthy
regime, and even less by the attempts of Charles IV to recover his
throne. As a result, in the course of 1920 and 1921 Czechoslovakia, Romania and Yugoslavia signed bilateral treaties of mutual defence which,
taken together, made up the 'Little Entente', an alliance system under
French tutelage whose aim was the protection of the Versailles status
quo in Central Europe. With the border dispute between Hungary and
Austria, relations with Germany confined to the links of the Hungarian
Right with the militants around General Erich von Ludendorff, and
hopes of co-operative ties with Poland thwarted when the latter chose
to sign an alliance treaty with Romania in March 1921, Bethlen could not
but temporarily give in to what Hungary's current predicament dictated.
In Germany, too, the dominant foreign policy line initiated by Gustav
Stresemann in 1923 became that of 'accommodation', and Bethlen,
while describing it as a 'self-denial' required by the spirit of the times in
spite of justice, opted for the same. Hungary's admission to the League
of Nations and the reconstruction loan were rewards for the new trend,
although they also implied further restrictions on Hungarian sover-

eignty by adding financial commissioners to those whose task was to control, since the ratification of the peace treaty, Hungarian armaments. Even so, with the neighbouring states the normalisation of relations was the maximum that was possible. In view of the unfounded assumption that pro-Hungarian sympathies among the Slovaks and Ruthenes of former Upper Hungary would soon facilitate the restoration of that province to Hungary, the improvement of ties with Prague was neglected, and the overtures of President Masaryk, who informally admitted that Hungary should struggle for a rightful revision of the Treaty of Trianon, were not taken up. Because of the significance of Transylvania in Hungarian history and national consciousness, its loss was especially painful, which made amicable relations with Romania out of the question. The rapprochement with Yugoslavia in 1925 and 1926, which held out the promise of a Hungarian free port on the Adriatic and mutual neutrality in conflict against a third party, came to nothing because of Horthy's reluctance and the objections of Italy and the Little Entente countries. Hungary's relations with the neighbouring states were also strained because of the situation of the Hungarian minorities. Even in Czechoslovakia, where the relatively democratic structures favoured the organised assertion of Hungarian interests in the public scene, assimilationist endeavours were hardly concealed; in Romania and Yugoslavia, the Hungarians suffered discrimination in the execution of land reform schemes, were exposed to resettlement policies aimed at changing the ethnic character of regions, increasingly deprived of educational facilities in their mother tongue, and their cultural associations, theatres, newspapers were suppressed.

During the first half of the 1920s, when the scope of action of Hungarian foreign policy was very limited, besides membership in the League of Nations its tangible results were, ironically enough, confined to an agreement regarding the exchange of political prisoners with the Soviet Union in 1921. The huge ideological and political differences precluded a more intensive co-operation between Hungary and perhaps the harshest and most outspoken contemporary critic of the Paris peace settlement. Throughout these years, the Hungarian government pinned its hopes of obtaining better terms from the victors on collaborating with them, especially (as France obviously threw all its weight in favour of the Little Entente countries) with Britain. However, by the middle of the decade the British government lost most of the interest it formerly had in the affairs of Central Europe. It was of little consolation that the Hungarian cause found at least one influential and steadfast British supporter in the person of the press magnate Harold Sidney Harmsworth, Lord Rothermere, who, partly under the impact of the charms of a Hungarian aristocratic lady, published his article 'Hungary's Place under the Sun' in the *Daily Mail* in June 1927.

Rothermere's proposal that, both in the interests of peace in Central Europe and the more effective containment of Bolshevism, the predominantly Hungarian inhabited borderland areas of the other successor states should be restored to Hungary, embarrassed the British government and evoked a mixed response in Hungary itself. On the one hand, the initiative to awaken 'the conscience of the world', which was being pursued much less effectively by Hungarian propaganda, was hailed, and inspired the foundation of the Hungarian Revisionist League of several hundred economic and social organisations and corporate bodies; on the other hand, an ethnically based revision of the Treaty of Trianon seemed less than satisfactory for many official circles and was fully acceptable only for the social democratic and liberal opposition. Rothermere's action coincided with two developments: growing and well-founded disillusionment with schemes for peaceful revision, and the recovery of some of Hungary's scope of action through the departure of both the foreign financial and the military commissioners by early 1927. As soon as surveillance was lifted, Hungary, similarly to the other losers of the First World War, started to evade the military stipulations of the peace treaty. At the same time, it responded to the initiative of Mussolini, searching for an ally in the back of Yugoslavia, against which Italy had territorial claims and whose sheer weight in the Adriatic region was one of its chief causes for resenting the peace system. The Italian-Hungarian treaty of friendship and co-operation signed on April 5, 1927 marked not only the end of Hungary's international isolation, but also that of the policy of accommodation. Bethlen and Mussolini agreed that the status quo created in Europe by the Paris settlement was temporary, and both of them expected Germany to play a major role in changing it – even though it was as yet too cautious to respond to their feelers. During 1927 and 1928, instead of 'self-denial' required by the circumstances, Bethlen emphasised the need for new borders with increasing frequency.

Besides foreign policy, cultural policies were conspicuously put into the service of revisionist aims through the resources and efforts devoted to the demonstration, assertion and increase of Hungary's alleged cultural superiority in the Carpathian Basin, one of the supposed bases for revisionist claims. The strategic importance attributed to culture is demonstrated by the high proportion of the budget allocated to its purposes (10 per cent, about twice as much as before the First World War), turned to good use by the outstanding Kunó Klebelsberg who served as Minister of Culture nearly throughout Bethlen's tenure as Prime Minister. Although his successor, Bálint Hóman, belonged to the Gömbös circle, the trend continued and the priorities remained the same during the 1930s, too. The first major reform of Klebelsberg was the re-establishment, by 1923, of the universities of Pozsony and Kolozsvár, lost after the First World War, at Pécs and Szeged, respectively. These as well as the University of Debrecen and the new Faculty of Economics in Budapest received generous funding, and earned a renown for high standards, especially in natural sciences and medicine, crowned in 1937 by the Nobel Prize awarded to Albert Szent-Györgyi (then at Szeged) for the discovery and medical use of Vitamin C. It must be added, however, that the predominant 'Christian course' forced some of the most innovative minds of their time, such as the mathematician János Neumann, or the nuclear physicists Tódor Kármán, Leó Szilárd, Ede Teller and Jenő Wigner, to seek their fortunes and make their names abroad. On the other hand, Klebelsberg himself advanced the cause of Hungarian learning by establishing scholarships for study abroad, and planned to create a network of Hungarian institutes to serve as outposts of Hungarian culture and bases for scholarship holders in the major European capitals, such as the Collegium Hungaricum in Berlin and Vienna, and the Accademia d'Ungheria in Rome.

However, as the population which remained in Hungary after the Treaty of Trianon was proportionately larger than the number of schools, one of the major tasks was the overhaul of elementary education, especially in the rural areas very inadequately served with educational facilities. As soon as the economic recovery made it possible, a major programme of building 3,500 new classrooms (including over 1,000 entirely new schools) and 1,750 homes for teachers was launched, and was completed by 1930. Although, as a result of the rise in school attendance, the teacher-pupil ratio did not change significantly and one-fifth of schoolchildren still attended undivided schools, illiteracy dropped to a near-Western European 7 per cent by the end of the 1930s. Secondary education also improved steadily, and continued to display the high professional standards acquired in the dualist period. At the same time, newly introduced curricula abandoned all semblance of value-free intellectualism and placed a great emphasis of the inculcation of Christian and national values. The school day started and ended by reciting the 'Hungarian Credo', which linked belief in God to belief in the resurrection of (historic) Hungary, whose integrity was the main lesson to be drawn from the history and geography curriculum. Leftist ideas, including bourgeois radicalism, were to be discouraged as leading to the 'internationalisation and Judaisation' of the Hungarian intelligentsia. Extra-curricular activities like the boy scout movement or the specifically Hungarian *levente* movement were favoured not only because of their Christian spirit and tendency to enhance group solidarity, but also because their organisation and their emphasis on physical training made them a kind of substitute for military education and conscription, forbidden in the Treaty of Trianon. The ideological character of education increased in the 1930s, similarly to the bias in the distribution of study awards, which were quite numerous, but did little to offset the social imbalance on the higher levels of education.

Among such circumstances, cultural life in general was Janus-faced in the inter-war era, which it would be difficult and rather useless to divide into sub-periods. The fundamental cleavage of pre-war times, between nationalist-conservative traditionalists and humanist-democratic reformers, remained, and with the survival of a thin radical avant-garde and the admixture of the 'populist' trend, provided an exciting scene. At the same time, the intellectual climate did not favour the modernist and progressive trends that emerged so strikingly in *fin-de-siècle* culture. The dominant tone of that climate was set by Gyula Szekfű in his *Three Generations*, already mentioned above, in which the author identified the causes of the post-war crisis in the erosive effects of liberalism on the moral and economic status of the Hungarian gentry, vulnerable to these effects because of such weaknesses of the 'Hungarian character' as vanity, ephemeral enthusiasm, jealousy and lack of public spirit. While some of Szekfű's historiography was also devoted to the exploration of these highly ideological themes, the multi-volume *Hungarian History* he co-authored with Bálint Hóman was a scholarly achievement of very high standards which remained the definitive treatment of the subject even when their authors fell into discredit after the Second World War. Hungarian historical scholarship in the period was also distinguished by Sándor Domanovszky's work in cultural history, and the thoroughly innovative efforts by István Hajnal to establish social history on a comprehensive basis, similarly to his French contemporaries in the *Annales* circle.

The ideas of the *Three Generations* imbued, rather than historiography, the novels of Ferenc Herczeg on romantic historical themes and the more decadent recent past. Herczeg now became the true representative of the literary establishment, boasting high honours, membership in the upper house, nomination for the literary Nobel Prize by the Hungarian Academy, and as many subscribers for his paper *Új Idők* as all other literary journals taken together. This was quite symptomatic of the tastes and interests of even the more refined segment of the general public, which coincided only marginally with the endeavours of the outstanding authors. On the whole, *Új Idők* and a few other conservative periodicals like the Klebelsberg-sponsored and significantly titled *Napkelet* (East) marshalled a host of rather mediocre talents, unlike *Nyugat*, which also survived and took advantage of the fact that all of the great authors who established its fame before the war, except Ady, were still alive; and besides Móricz, Babits, Kosztolányi and Karinthy, new generations also arose. These included, among many others, two poets worthy of being included in any 'world's classics' series: Miklós Radnóti, the sensitive humanist, and Attila József, who might be described as a lower class counterpart of Ady as regards his genius, rebellious nature, power of expression and charisma. Finding, with some justification, that *Nyugat*, while maintaining the artistic standards achieved earlier, had lost much of its critical radicalism, József and a few like-minded writers went on to launch *Szép Szó* (Beautiful Word) in 1936 to make up for that loss. Writers who were unconnected with either of these journals but expressed urban, bourgeois values and sentiments included Sándor Márai and Ferenc Molnár, who after a brief silence imposed on him in 1919–1920, remained Hungary's most successful stage author in the Horthy era as well – until he felt compelled to choose emigration.

However, perhaps the most important development in the literary life of the Horthy era was the movement of 'village explorers' or – for want of a better translation of the word *népi* – 'populist' writers. Drawing their inspiration partly from Móricz and partly from Dezső Szabó, these young intellectuals predominantly of peasant origin wrote sociographic, or sociographically based literary presentations to reveal the economic and intellectual poverty of life in rural Hungary and to awaken the upper classes to the inevitability of change. In ideological terms, some of them, most notably László Németh, advocated a 'third way' for Hungary, a middle course between East and West or the Soviet system and capitalist individualism; others, like Imre Kovács and István Bibó, maintained strong ties with the bourgeois democrats; still others, including Géza Féja, Gyula Illyés, Ferenc Erdei and Péter Veres, sympathised with socialism, and there were also some attached to the radical Right. Their top priority was the improvement of the lot of the poor peasantry (that is, distribution of land among them), and as a group they showed a willingness to co-operate for this end with the extreme Left as well as the extreme Right. This, as well as the emphasis on the Hungarian roots of the village and the village as the roots of 'Hungarianness', with its latent racist overtones, brought the 'populists' into polemical engagements with cosmopolitan democrat 'urbanist' intellectuals of largely Jewish background, represented most characteristically by Pál Ignotus, Béla Zsolt and Ferenc Fejtő. Such a dispute was symptomatic of a wider cleavage, occasioned among different shades of Hungarian progressives by the contradictions of the country's modernisation process resulting in distorted social and political structures, survived the efforts to homogenise the cultural scene in Hungary under communism, and has continued to divide the intelligentsia in the period of transition to democracy.

While thus it was literary life that penetrated the public scene most profoundly, the high standards achieved at the turn of the century were also maintained in music and the creative arts. Hubay and Dohnányi continued to earn most of the official esteem in musical life, but the reservations towards Bartók and Kodály also diminished (even though the former emigrated in 1940, as a protest against anti-Semitic legislation). Both of them were at the height of their creative power, rose to world fame and had a number of talented followers including Leó Weiner and Lajos Bárdos, though the differences in their outlook became more pronounced: Kodály's commitment to the Hungarian folk tradition increased (*Psalmus Hungaricus, Budavár Te Deum*), while Bartók was more interested in blending this with modern trends and primitive music (*Cantata Profana, Music for Strings, Percussions and Celesta*). By now their initiative to discover the 'pure fount' resulted in a fashion for learning and singing folk songs especially among the intellectuals of rural background, though it did little to offset the soaring popularity of 'gypsy' music. Of the classics of Budapest operetta, Lehár, Kálmán and Huszka continued to work, but the number of box-office hits was less striking than in the pre-war era. At the same time, thanks to the radio and the gramophone, jazz and other kinds of modern dance music also started to appear and become popular in the 1920s, much to the unconcealed annoyance of those with conservative tastes.

In the creative arts, too, there was a nearly unbridgeable gap between traditionalist trends, represented largely by neo-Baroque architecture, nationalist academism and a mass of heroic monuments and irredentist sculptures, and more progressive schools. These included post-impressionism in the Nagybánya tradition, maintained, besides Rippl-Rónai, by Béla Czóbel, István Szőnyi and József Egry; the so-called 'Great Plain school', whose endeavours were akin to those of the 'village writers'; and different individuals and groups of the avant-garde. Most of the latter were attached to the working class movement, and some of them emigrated in the aftermath of 1919, like László Moholy-Nagy, who worked first at the Bauhaus school and then became famous in the United States, or Béla Uitz, who settled in Moscow. The most important among those active in Hungary were Lajos Kassák, also significant as a poet and novelist, and the highly original painter influenced by cubism, Gyula Derkovits.

Entertainment, leisure and pastime activities became more variegated in the inter-war years, and a far greater number of people were involved in them than earlier. Budapest was renowned for its night-life, though it certainly did not attract masses – unlike cinema, which made a real breakthrough by the 1930s, when Hungarians spent as much on cinema tickets as on newspapers, periodicals and books, including the yellow press and pulp readin, taken together. Most of the more than two thousand films screened in the cinemas, which numbered about nine hundred by the end of the Second World War, were foreign (about half of them American). The Hungarian film industry even declined in the 1920s, when many of the best directors left the country and foreign competition was severe, but recovered thereafter and became far more important than anywhere else in the region, as a result of the advent of sound-pictures which evidently favoured Hungarian films, as did protectionist intervention by the state. The overwhelming majority of the Hungarian films of the period were Hollywood style comedies, dramatic or happy-ending love stories. Despite their general shallowness, many of them were realised at a high level of professionalism; besides, they reflected the social priorities, manners and ideals of the period. The protagonists, predominantly men and women from the genteel classes or the Christian middle class and sometimes from the *haute bourgeoisie*, were played by excellent actors, some of whom wholly devoted themselves to the film screen, but others earned their fame originally on the theatre stage, which also enjoyed a great boom.

It was also in the interwar years that sports, similarly to cinema, started to reach out to the masses, continuing the tendency begun at the turn of the century. The 'white sports' (tennis, fencing, sailing) remained the preserve of the elite, but swimming, athletics (field and track) or football were accessible to anyone, especially as the improvement of the number and the quality of sports facilities was spectacular. During the 1930s, over 100,000 Hungarians were involved in competitive sports, in which the country started to emerge as a frequent champion, partly assisted by the support of the Hungarian governments, which realised the significance of sport successes for national propaganda. Sport also assumed political relevance from another point of view. The rivalry between the two most prestigious Budapest clubs, Ferencváros Sports Club and the Hungarian Sports Club also assumed a political character on account of the conflict between the former's following among petty bourgeois and déclassé elements and the latter's predominantly Jewish middle class background. Also, sports teams might become substitutes for otherwise illegal working-class organisation, and hiking in remote countryside areas served as occasions for illicit political discussion.

Out of the asphalt jungle and into nature was, of course, in general a perfectly respectable middle class pursuit. Regular vacationing at spas and other resorts was formerly the luxury of a privileged 100,000 or maybe 150,000, including those travelling abroad as well as those seeking diversion within the country. Their number was about ten times as high by the 1930s, when vacation became part and parcel of the life of middle class families, many of which started to erect their own cottages at Lake Balaton or in the villages along the Danube near the capital.

The spread of new forms of recreation and entertainment, together with the other achievements of technological modernisation mentioned above like motorisation, electrification or the radio, show that the tendency towards mass welfare society begun at the turn of the century continued, even accelerated in the Horthy era. However, for the time being it also served to broaden the gap between urban and rural Hungary, which remained overwhelmingly a stranger to these blessings. At the end of 1929, came a watershed which accentuated from another point of view the great divide between the two poles of Hungary's 'dual social structure'. It was the great economic depression.

The effects of 'Black Friday', the New York stock exchange crash of October 24, 1929, first reached Hungary in the form of drastically diminished agrarian prices. Over three-quarters of Hungarian exports consisted of agrarian products throughout the interwar period, and thus the average 54 per cent (in the case of wheat, 75 per cent) price fall resulted in losing 60 per cent of exports-generated national income, especially as even at the lower prices it was difficult to retain the markets. This inevitably limited imports, and with them the domestic market as well. The first segment of society that was hard hit was the most vulnerable one: smallholders who had contracted debts to modernise or merely to sustain their tiny plots immediately became unable to repay them, and about 60,000 of them were forced to auction the land they had acquired a few years earlier. Half a million rural labourers lost their work, and about the same number were forced to accept starvation wages. Of course, the tide did not stop at city limits, though the dimensions of the crisis were less dramatic in industry; yet, production had to be cut by 28 per cent, one in seven factories was closed down, unemployment among the industrial proletariat rose to 30 per cent, with an acute shortage of provisions and no unemployment benefits available. The wages of those who retained their jobs were cut, as well as the salaries of those state employees and professionals who were not dismissed; and, as a matter of fact, fresh graduates had to share the lot of their unemployed colleagues, especially teachers and engineers. By 1932, small tradesmen and retailers also began closing down their businesses in increasing numbers. The government was unable to halt the process. Bethlen's effort to overcome the financial crisis by arranging further foreign loans came to nothing after the collapse of German banks and, on May 11, 1931, the Viennese Creditanstalt, when the loans were recalled. The country's foreign currency and bullion reserves were exhausted, and even the bankruptcy of the National Bank was only narrowly averted.

From early on in the crisis, there was mounting social unrest, first culminating in the mass strike and demonstration in Budapest on September 1, 1930, ending in police shooting, death and casualties. Underground Communists became active again, and radical rightist organisations, such as the Scythe-Cross movement, exerted considerable influence in the countryside. Rioting, demonstrations and hunger marches became endemic in towns and rural areas, and already in 1930 Horthy contemplated the introduction of summary jurisdictional procedures to control the situation. The blowing up of a train (as it turned out, by a maniac, but initially blamed on the Communists) in September 1931 provided the occasion for doing so, and two communist leaders were indeed arrested and court-martialled in July 1932. However, political stability was also undermined by the crumbling of the unity within the government party. The one-time representatives of the Smallholder Party in it allied themselves with other leaders of the well-to-do peasantry, and established the Independent Smallholder Party on October 13, 1930. The other major interest groups on whose reconciliation the Bethlenite consolidation rested, the magnates, the *haute bourgeoisie* and the state bureaucracy, also started to advocate differing ways out of the crisis, largely by changing the system at the expense of their former partners. Even though the government party preserved its majority at the elections of June 1931, Bethlen, sensing its disruption, finding the further unpopular measures rendered inevitable by the financial crisis to be political suicide, and hoping to re-emerge in his former role in better times, resigned from his office shortly after celebrating his decennial as Prime Minister, on August 19, 1931.

Horthy appointed as his successor Count Gyula Károlyi, who was the one-time head of the 1919 counter-revolutionary government and a close personal friend of the Regent. Amidst outbursts of popular discontent that surpassed anything hitherto experienced and were hardly contained by police terror, Károlyi was unable to re-accommodate the factions in the government party, which were only united in being increasingly unhappy to see that Károlyi was essentially experimenting with the same policies which had brought no success to Bethlen. Financial retrenchment not only supplied fuel to already critical levels of unrest, but also defied the demand of the agrarian lobby for subsidies for the farming sector and agricultural exports, and angered state employees because it implied further salary cuts. They were all the more embittered by the conviction that all of this hardly affected the positions of the *haute bourgeoisie*: the Chorin, the Weiss, the Fellner, the Hatvany-Deutsch, that is, the predominantly Jewish captains of finance and capitalism. The latter were increasingly considered as bearing supreme responsibility for the whole calamity afflicting the backbone of Hungarian society consisting of the genteel landed elite and the Christian middle class intelligentsia, which was also alleged to suffer from the competition of its Jewish counterpart. The other scapegoat, predictably, was the vicious peace treaty which in strained circumstances deprived Hungary of economic viability. When the Károlyi government decided to consider the plan of the French Prime Minister, André Tardieu, for the economic and financial recovery of the countries of Central Europe in February 1932, it was considered by many within and outside the government party as a disgraceful surrender to hostile forces that had once ruined Hungary. A fascist Hungarian National Socialist Peasant and Workers Party seceded from the Party of Unity in June 1932, and although it was upon Bethlen's proposal that Károlyi stepped down in the autumn of that year, his position was in fact made untenable by the nationalist pressure group susceptible to rightist extremism whose voice, strength and influence was reinforced not only by the hardships, but also by the tendency to economic nationalism generated by the crisis. On October 1, 1932, Horthy appointed the leader of this group, Gyula Gömbös, to replace Károlyi as Prime Minister.

3. Hungary on a fixed course: Hitler's reluctant satellite and the Second World War

In many ways, the economic crisis aggravated the adverse effects of the Paris peace settlement on the situation in Central Europe. By tearing the Danubian economies even further apart, it amplified the tendency to isolation on all levels of intercourse; mutual animosity among the countries of the region was fuelled by the fact that the suspicion against, and clamour for the eviction of supposedly parasitic minorities intensified everywhere, and besides Jews, the nature of the situation made Hungarians the sufferers of this in most places. In the 1930s, right wing radicalism became a force to reckon with in the region outside Hungary, too, especially in Romania and among the resentful minor partners in the Czecho-Slovak and Serbo-Croat unions. In Hungary, the crisis re-awakened social attitudes and brought to prominence those political endeavours rooted in them, which first entered the limelight in the troubled years after the First World War and were toned down during the years of consolidation in the 1920s. Although the nature of the Horthy regime did not fundamentally change in 1932, after a decade of dominance by the conservatives who grafted authoritarianism on to the parliamentary system, they alternated in government with the representatives of the radical Right until the end of the Second World War.

Ever since 1919, Gyula Gömbös was the main organiser of the extreme Right, well-known for his hostility to the old aristocracy and the predominantly Jewish bourgeoisie, and as a champion of breaking what he considered an anachronistic social structure by the redistribution of political and economic advantages in favour of the Christian middle classes. However, in 1928, compelled by lack of support, he dissolved his Party of Racial Defence and returned to the government party; even in 1932, he was accepted Prime Minister by Horthy and a parliament whose majority still vaguely followed Bethlen on the understanding that he would restore order without meddling with the existing system. Nevertheless, the new Prime Minister launched an attempt to rejuvenate the Hungarian public scene and, ultimately, to create a totalitarian state organised along fascist lines. His 'National Work Plan', a ninety-five point programme which Gömbös announced on the radio with a vigour and in a tone un-experienced in Hungarian politics, was a wish-list of demagogical promises (land and tax reform, boosted agricultural exports, new jobs, progressive social legislation and, of course, 'Greater Hungary') whose hardly concealed aim was to rally support for this end. He also stressed his commitment to the 'leader principle', while refusing that it meant dictatorship. After the repeated failure of the fragile bourgeois order restored from its ashes after the war and the revolutions, after a decade of frustration with revisionist dreams and afflicted by the economic crisis, broad segments of the population were indeed in the mood for revolutionary change. The ailing and splintered right-wing groups became galvanised during Gömbös' premiership by the impression that his programme in effect endorsed their vision of a Hungary cleansed of 'non-Turanic' elements in influential posts and of 'Jewish profiteers', restored to its ancient borders, and reshaped by thoroughgoing social and political reform. Besides the movements and parties mentioned above and launched before Gömbös' accession to office, the period saw the establishment of the United National Socialist Party by Count Fidél Pálffy in 1933, and the Party of National Will by Ferenc Szálasi, a cashiered officer, in 1935.

These groups were also pleased with the new Prime Minister's foreign policy goals. Italy, which had been the main proponent for the revision of the Paris settlement up to 1933, had a prominent place in the plans of Gömbös, whose first state visit was to Mussolini. At the same time, he was anxious to take advantage of the changes taking place in Germany since the end of the 1920s, sealed by Hitler's rise to power at the beginning of 1933. Even though Hungarian politicians were deeply worried by the very real prospect that a powerful Germany, once the chains of Versailles were shaken off, would annex Austria, and Hungary's sizeable German minority was also a source of tension between the two states, co-operation had much to promise. Germany now expected, instead of negotiating border modifications through accommodation to the peace settlement, to extort them through its subversion, and the countries of *Mitteleuropa* or the *Südostraum* played an important role in the new vision of German activity as suppliers of agricultural products and raw materials. Besides hoping to find markets for Hungarian exports, Gömbös also wanted to awaken the Führer's interest in a German-Italian-Hungarian-Austrian revisionist alliance when, as the first European leader, he visited Hitler in June 1933.

Both of Gömbös' hosts were interested in strengthening economic ties, and soon treaties were signed regarding increased Hungarian agricultural exports (and Germany soon followed Italy in assisting Hungarian rearmament). However, Hitler rejected the plan of the great revisionist alliance as well as closer co-operation with Hungary in the full revisionist programme on the recognition that it was only *vis-à-vis* Czechoslovakia that the interests of the two countries coincided, while Germany needed to maintain good relations with Romania and Yugoslavia in view of its imports from them. Nor did the Rome Protocols, signed by Italy, Austria and Hungary in March 1934, yield any tangible political result, even though they had prestige value, and not only annoyed the Germans, but also exercised some restraint on them in relation to Austria.

Gömbös's record on the domestic scene was equally ambivalent. He launched new government newspapers to make propaganda more efficient, and he vigorously set to reorganising the government party, renamed as the Party of National Unity, as a totalitarian mass party with 'vanguard fighters' placed at the head of its local units; he even took some steps to merge the party organisation with the state apparatus, which underwent a blood-transfusion, and wanted to create a powerful economic ministry. However, these attempts largely miscarried on the resistance of the old guard of the government party itself, who certainly did not welcome Gömbös' dictatorial ambitions, and even co-operated with the opposition in defeating the Prime Minister's initiative to abolish the rights of self-government that Budapest enjoyed in early 1934. Of the offensive to enlarge the scope of action of the cabinet and the executive in general at the expense of the legislature, only the proposal to extend the Regent's prerogative, to include the proroguing and the dissolving of parliament, was successful. Bethlen in particular, who continued to command great authority, sharply criticised the whole government programme, and even more the hardly disguised attempt to create a totalitarian state resting on party rule, economic planning and the corporate system, which he thought undermined the country's tranquillity, credibility and security. Indeed, by the beginning of 1935 Gömbös worked out a plan to transform Hungary into a corporate state largely based on the model of Italy. However, the idea of uniting employers as well as employees in 'corporations' while banning strikes was not only opposed by the Social Democrats and the trade unions, but was also unacceptable for the industrialists, because it implied government interference with private enterprise. Finally, although Bethlen, Teleki and their circle agreed that the friendship of Germany was vital for the realisation of Hungary's essential foreign policy aims (that is, the revision of Trianon), they feared, as it turned out with good reason, that exclusive commitment to the side of the fascist Axis would ruin Hungary in a war fought against the western democracies. Therefore, they wanted a government that would secure German assistance in regaining the lost territories, but retain the goodwill of Britain and France and avoid being embroiled in war as Hitler's ally – an attitude which the Führer, who had a rather low opinion of Hungarians, later described by saying that they wanted too much, and too cheaply. Bethlen also thought that a German-Italian foreign policy orientation by no means made the domestic growth of National Socialism imperative.

As a result of these disagreements, Bethlen left the government party shortly before the elections of April 1935, which the party nevertheless won, and the victory was mainly that of Gömbös: most of the new deputies belonged to his radical rightist followers. Besides the peculiarities of the electoral system and rigging that exceeded even the usual dimensions, this was due to modest economic successes and the beginning of a slow recovery from economic crisis, in which the trade agreements with Italy and Germany were certainly instrumental. Paradoxically enough, however, the same improvement made government intervention in private enterprise even more resented among the entrepreneurial class than before. Similarly, the land reform Gömbös initiated in 1934 came short of the expectations he raised, and there was no sequel to it. The Prime Minister, shortly after the election success, started to lose support among the National Socialist revolutionaries who felt he was not, or could not be radical enough, and thus emerged as a right wing opposition to the government. The Smallholders, who gravitated towards Gömbös as his conflict with Bethlen arose, now broke with him again because his side of a promise for mutual support at the elections remained unfulfilled.

The isolation of Gömbös became complete with the futility of his foreign policy dreams. Hungarian-German relations had been strained since the Nazi coup in Vienna in July 1934. Hungary's prestige suffered by little founded accusations of Hungarian complicity in training Croat nationalist Ustashas, one of whom assassinated the Yugoslav King Alexander II and the French foreign minister Barthou in October 1934. Italian-French rapprochement, and French-Russian and Czechoslovak-Russian treaties of mutual assistance in 1935 seemed to increase Hungary's isolation, which could not be offset by the fact that Hungary also established full diplomatic relations with the Soviet Union, and reached an inconclusive agreement of co-operation with Poland. Finally, whereas the second Berlin trip of Gömbös in September 1935 earned a huge German loan and arms consignments, his courtship again failed to win Hitler for his alliance plans, and when Horthy paid his first visit to the Führer in August 1936, he was also advised to show self-restraint *vis-à-vis* Romania and Yugoslavia. Finally, as in 1936 Mussolini in effect gave a green light to the *Anschluss* of Austria, Hungary's value for Germany as a partner to be seduced with concessions, became even further diminished.

It was the premature death of Gömbös in October 1936 that prevented his dismissal by Horthy, who had also lost confidence in him, especially under the influence of discussions with Bethlen and his political friends. The appointment of the pragmatic conservative Kálmán Darányi as Prime Minister marked an attempt to return to the order of the 1920s by bringing extremism under control, and by following a more balanced foreign policy line. In the given context, this meant the suppression of fascist groups both within and outside the government party, and a preference for the settlement of Hungary's revisionist claims through great power arbitration, even through some adjustment of interests with the neighbouring states, rather than through sharing Hitler's dubious methods and being involved in his bold but risky strokes which, the Bethlenites thought, a country of Hungary's weight could not afford. Neither of these objectives turned out to be feasible. The economic advantages of co-operation with Germany, with which the western powers could not compete in Central Europe, were too great; in light of the little interest shown by Britain and the Habsburg successor states to respond to half-hearted Hungarian feelers, even the prospect of the limited assistance Germany was willing to render in the revision of Trianon was too seductive; and these circumstances also seriously narrowed the domestic scope of action for Hungarian conservatives.

Darányi's move to purge the government party of the followers of his predecessor had rather ambiguous results: those who did secede now swelled the ranks of the fascist organisations that had been mushrooming since 1932, but started to converge by the time their chief Hungarian mentor died. Two main fascist rallying grounds were emerging: the Hungarian National Defence Association, revived from counter-revolutionary times when it was established as a para-military organisation of extreme rightist officers but now also admitted an increasing number of civilians, and the Party of National Will, whose leader Szálasi established close links in Germany during a visit made in the autumn of 1936. Through these links, German influence, and through other means, German political pressure increased in Hungary. These means included the country's growing economic dependence on Germany: by the end of the 1930s, over 50 per cent of Hungarian foreign trade, which yielded nearly a quarter of the national income, was with Germany, the safest market of Hungary's chief export products. Besides, the half million strong German minority and the fact that it had been exposed, largely through the anomalies of the education system, to assimilationist efforts under the Horthy regime, provided Hitler with a pretext for interference on their behalf. Flooded by Nazi propaganda and financial support from Germany, their ethnic organisations started to campaign for education not only in the tongue, but also in the spirit of the fatherland, a process crowned by the legalisation of the *Volksbund*, the National Socialist association of the Germans in Hungary at the end of 1938.

The government took measures to contain the trend towards Nazification. Szálasi was arrested in April 1937, and even his party was banned because of subversive agitation among the industrial workers; shortly before then, the weapons of the Defence Association were confiscated upon rumours of plans of a German-supported *coup d'état*. Even the further extension of the Regent's prerogative was meant to safeguard the country's integrity against a possible German intervention in the event of Horthy's death: besides increasing the time allowed him to 'consider' laws passed by parliament before sanctioning them, it also conferred on him the right of nominating his successor. At the same time, Darányi also employed the tactics of alternatively tightening and slackening the reins of power over the extreme right. The Defence Association could continue its activities, and Szálasi was not only soon released, but on October 23, 1937, was also able to establish the Hungarian National Socialist Party ('Arrowcross' Party, after its symbol) which unified most of the radical Right. Concessions were made to the German minority, too, without actually satisfying Nazi demands. Besides, the Prime Minister tried to take the edge of the fascist threat by stealing some of the items on their agenda. In a programmatic speech made a few days after Szálasi's arrest, while condemning dictatorship, Darányi proposed to alleviate rural unemployment by a reforestation and irrigation programme, and unemployment among professionals by 'solving the Jewish question' – that is, by reviving the policy embracing the *numerus clausus* law of the early 1920s and by extending its scope.

Non-governmental anti-fascism was on the whole more consistent, but no more successful in resisting the tide. In the second half of the 1930s, the struggle against National Socialism became one of the priorities on the agenda of the Social Democratic Party, whose new leaders included the sound theorist Illés Mónus and the pragmatic Árpád Szakasits. However, they scored little success in regaining the support of the masses which the party, similarly to the trade unions, lost in terms of votes as well as membership in the aftermath of the economic crisis when it was unable to present an alternative to the solutions preferred by the radical Right. While in principle the Social Democrats favoured a popular front strategy, that is, a broad co-operation among anti-fascist forces, they were reluctant to collaborate with the underground Communists, who also urged a joint struggle, but were making futile efforts to gain influence through infiltrating legal organisations. They also remained largely excluded from the March Front, created on March 15, 1937, by the 'populist' writers, disillusioned with the scope and the style of Gömbös' reforms, from whom they initially expected more. Recalling 1848, they issued a twelve-point programme, demanding bourgeois democracy, thoroughgoing land reform, precautions against the spread of Nazism, and emphasising the need to co-operate with the peoples of the Danube Basin. However, the front was ultimately unable to enlist the support of both the Social Democrats and the Smallholders, and disintegrated by early 1938, with some of its members gravitating towards the Right again, and others establishing the left-oriented National Peasant Party. At the other end of the political spectrum, the Catholic hierarchy in Hungary, in line with the views of Pope Pius XI, was also critical of the growing influence of National Socialism, but it emphatically linked the need to fight against it with the determination to defy Bolshevism, and used the 'Holy Year' of 1038 (the 900th anniversary of the death of Saint Stephen, when Hungary also hosted the Eucharistic World Congress) to emphasise the role of Hungary, wedged between 'two pagans', as – once again – a bulwark of Christendom.

Changes in the international scene between 1936 and 1938 also encouraged the fascist organisations in Hungary. Hitler's re-militarisation of the Rhineland only evoked consternation and protest, but no action on the part of the western powers; the German-Italian axis eventually came into existence and rounded off with Japan in the 'Anti-Comintern Pact'; General Franco's arms were gaining the upper hand in the Spanish Civil War. At the same time, Darányi's foreign minister, Kálmán Kánya, negotiated in vain with his opposite numbers from the Little Entente countries during the summer and autumn of 1937 in order to secure a non-aggression pact linked to the settlement of the minorities' problem and the acknowledgement of Hungarian military parity; and he also failed to re-awaken British interest in Hungary in order to counter Germany's growing influence. As a result, these moves only served to annoy Hitler, who, having decided on action against Austria and Czechoslovakia, nevertheless assured the Hungarian leaders that he considered their claims against the latter as valid and expected them to co-operate in the execution of his plans. The *Anschluss* on March 12–13, 1938, still took the Hungarian establishment by surprise, the more so since they were expecting Hitler to cede the Burgenland to his new neighbour, which he was unwilling to do. On the other hand, the German annexation of Austria was hailed among the followers of Szálasi who, in spite of a second arrest of their leader and the banning of the Arrowcross Party shortly earlier, were able to exert formidable propaganda and political agitation. This prompted Darányi to work out an agreement with the extremists, who, in return for moderating their programme, were legalised again under the name Arrowcross Party/Hungarist Movement.

This was too much for the conservatives as well as Horthy himself. Darányi's last important move was, on March 5, the announcement of a massive rearmament programme to equip a fighting force that was already more than twice as large as stipulated in the Treaty of Trianon. He was dismissed from his office by Horthy on May 13, 1938.

Darányi's replacement was Béla Imrédy, who had the reputation of an outstanding financial expert and a determined Anglophile. Ironically and tragically, it was under his premiership that Hungary's commitment to the German side became complete and irreversible. While 'Hungarism' was averse to his political taste, he not only arranged the speedy enactment by parliament of the new military budget (which resulted in a great boom: a 21 per cent increase of industrial output by 1939, nearly as much as the growth since 1920), but also the anti-Jewish legislation prepared under Darányi. The law on 'the more efficient assurance of equilibrium in social and economic life' established a 20 per cent ceiling on the employment of persons of the Israelite faith in business and the professions, depriving about 15,000 people of jobs to which they were qualified. Some of the government party as well as Liberals and Social Democrats in parliament, and prominent figures of cultural and intellectual life including Bartók, Kodály, Móricz, protested, while the radical Right found the measure too indulgent.

In foreign policy, Imrédy hoped to capitalise on his good personal contacts in Britain, while Kánya, who retained the post of foreign minister, embarked on another round of negotiations with the Little Entente to secure some of Hungary's revisionist aims by peaceful means. In return for Hungarian commitment to non-violence, at the conference of the Little Entente in Bled in August 1938 Hungary's military parity was indeed acknowledged, and promises were made to improve the condition of the Hungarian minorities in the neighbouring states. The agreement was never ratified, yet it was against this background and in view of Hungary's military unpreparedness that at the subsequent Kiel meeting with Hitler, who was determined to crush Czechoslovakia and offered the whole of one-time Upper Hungary if his guests were willing to launch an attack on Slovakia, that Horthy and Imrédy were reluctant to play the role of the *agent provocateur*. Instead, they suggested a settlement based on the ethnic principle in Slovakia as well as in the German-inhabited western fringe of Bohemia, the Sudetenland. Having been summoned to the Führer again on September 20, the Hungarian leaders gave in and mobilised an ill-prepared army, and were relieved to learn that the Czechoslovak crisis would be resolved at the conference of the great powers in Munich. While at Munich Hitler embarked, with British, French and Italian assistance, on accomplishing the second item on the agenda laid down in *Mein Kampf* – the unification of German-inhabited territories, after shaking off the constraints imposed by Versailles on German sovereignty and before acquiring the East European *Lebensraum* – by laying his hand on the Sudetenland, the conference stipulated Czechoslovak-Hungarian negotiations on the Hungarian claims. These having proved fruitless, and the western powers refraining from interfering with the issue, Germany and Italy acted as arbiters at the meeting on November 2, 1938, which awarded nearly 12,000 square kilometres of territory with over a million inhabitants to Hungary (between 57 and 84 per cent of them being Hungarian, according to Czechoslovak and Hungarian censuses, respectively). The first success of revisionism, whose fairness in ethnic terms was quite beyond doubt, was welcomed even by the Hungarian opposition, while in the establishment and especially right wing circles there was also some bitterness because of the failure to recover the other parts of Slovakia and Ruthenia. However, a planned operation to occupy Ruthenia at the end of November 1938 was called off because of Hitler's objections.

Nevertheless, the First Vienna Award made it clear that any further success in the revision of Trianon would depend on German support, and a political crisis quite paradoxically even helped Imrédy to demonstrate Hungary's pro-German commitments. The Premier's attempt to govern the recovered territories by decree resulted in a vote of non-confidence, hitherto unprecedented during the Horthy era, but as his alternatives refused to take office, Imrédy could form a new government, which he thought it was inevitable to pack with pro-German politicians. Kánya, in particular, was replaced by István Csáky, a firm believer in the need to tie Hungary's resurrection to the success of German arms, a fact beyond reasonable doubt according to him. It was during the subsequent months that the Nazi *Volksbund* became legalised, and that Hungary announced its decision to leave the League of Nations and to join the Anti-Comintern Pact. To a considerable extent against his own wishes and because Britain, after all, remained apathetic towards to Hungary, Imrédy became over-anxious to please the Germans, which led to his dismissal, in circumstances quite similar to that of his predecessor, in February 1939.

Like in 1920, Pál Teleki now took office with the goal of securing political consolidation by bridling extremism and putting it into the service of conservative nationalist policies. If the auspices had been ambiguous at that time, now they were distinctly unfavourable. In the last year of an increasingly fragile peace, National Socialism, with its cult of power, the dynamism it radiated, its promise to wipe out ossified social structures, political institutions and cultural habits, its ideas of racial superiority and *Lebensraum* (applied to the role of Magyardom in the Danube Basin), exerted an ever greater appeal to broad segments of the civil servants and the officer corps, of the petty bourgeoisie and even the working class, especially among the younger generation. The growth of fascism naturally worried not only many intellectuals, the Jewish professionals and middle classes and the political Left, but also the whole of the traditional elite, who feared its social revolutionary character, were unhappy about the tendency towards the limitation of the country's sovereignty by Hitler's intervention on behalf of the German minority and other means, and had misgivings concerning the superiority of German arms. For all these reasons, they, including Horthy, sought to maintain contacts with the western Allies. Nevertheless, especially as now they were intoxicated by the taste of the first success in revisionism (which, as we saw, was bitter-sweet), all Hungarian politicians, responding to the expectation of most of the general public, were willing to subordinate other considerations to the restoration of historic borders more than ever before. Teleki was no exception from this rule, and while he secretly hoped for the ultimate victory of the western democracies in the conflict he deemed inevitable between them and the fascist dictatorships, in the meantime he wanted to take advantage from the fact that the current domination of the Central European scene by the latter made it possible to redress Hungarian grievances suffered at the hands of the former. This policy has been rightly blamed as narrow and shortsighted, leading down a dangerous path, which eventually proved to be not only lethal to the regime Teleki served, but disastrous for the country itself. At the same time, consistently resisting Hitler's wishes in 1939 (which Hungarian governments certainly did not intend to do) was likely to throw Hungary into a situation similar to that of Poland.

Teleki scored a distinct success by achieving the long-coveted common border with Poland, thus breaking the circular grip of the Little Entente, a month after taking office. The occupation of Ruthenia or the Carpatho-Ukraine – acquiring a territory nearly as large as that recovered in terms of the First Vienna Award, but three-quarters of its population being Ukrainians, justified on strategic and historical, rather than ethnic grounds – took place as a move synchronised with Hitler's liquidation of Czechoslovakia on March 15, 1939. Teleki's initiative to supply the Carpatho-Ukraine with broad autonomy came to nothing in the following summer. Tensions almost immediately arose between Hungary and the Slovak satellite state created by Hitler under the leadership of Jozef Tiso; this, as well as the revisionist claims Hungary started to raise against Romania around the same time, only served to help Hitler play his small partners off against one another and act as an arbiter between in the region. Nevertheless, the second step in the 'augmentation of the country' earned a great many votes and secured a 70 per cent majority in parliament for the government party, renamed as the Party of Hungarian Life, at the elections of May 1939. Whereas the Smallholders and the Social Democrats suffered further setbacks, the other great winner of the elections, with almost 20 per cent of seats, was the radical Right. Strikingly enough, the Arrowcross Party was very successful in working class districts, taking advantage of the fact that elections were now secret, and also from the ambiguous policies Teleki pursued in its regard (while Szálasi was still imprisoned and its other representatives prosecuted, the party could participate at the elections).

Shortly before the elections, new legislation was passed for the further 'limitation of the encroachment of Jews in public life and in the economy'. Criteria were shifted from religion to race, the ceiling placed on the Jewish share of business ownership and participation in the professions lowered (in the state bureaucracy it became zero), and the pace proposed for the realisation of the new thresholds accelerated. The law directly affected about 200,000 Hungarian citizens, and indirectly all of the Jews of the country (numbering over 600,000 before and more than 800,000 after the re-annexations between 1938 and 1941). Their ostracisation became, from the demands of a small minority a few decades earlier, part of a dramatic atmosphere in which, for instance, the number of mixed marriages dropped sharply even before they were made illegal in a third anti-Jewish law in 1941.

During the sinister summer months of 1939, economic recovery based on increased trade with Germany and the boom generated by the armaments programme, and revisionist successes, lulled many in Hungary into believing that the country was safely on the way to 'resurrection', as urged ever since the debacle of 1918–1920. Some still hoped that further advance was possible without the general conflagration predicted by others. As far as the government was concerned, it was certainly aware of Hitler's preparations against Poland at least a month ahead of the invasion, but in a fit of sobriety it not only refrained from participating in the campaign, but also refused the passage of German troops and the use of the railway lines in northern Hungary by them, even rejecting Slovakia, which the Führer offered to Hungary. Besides being afraid of losing whatever goodwill Britain still might have retained towards Hungary, Teleki also had the long history of Polish-Hungarian friendship in mind when, after Hitler's onslaught against Poland on September 1, 1939, he declared Hungary a non-belligerent country and subsequently made arrangements for the sheltering of over 100,000 Polish refugees in Hungary. Some of them stayed there until the end of the war, but others, through Yugoslavia, moved on to the western powers and organised Polish Legions.

Although Britain's and France's fulfilment of their allied obligations to Poland by declaring war on Germany was, for the time being, largely of symbolic importance, the Second World War began, and its first major events included not only the German elimination of the western half of Poland, but also the incorporation of its eastern provinces into the Soviet Union by the terms of the notorious Nazi-Soviet pact of August 23, 1939. The launching of the Russian programme of revision of the Paris settlement of 1918, which involved the liquidation of the Baltic republics and the war against Finland in the winter of 1939–1940, caused anxiety in Budapest, where it was feared that the new common border would encourage the underground Communists, and that Stalin would demand Ruthenia, where the majority of the population were Ukrainian. Diplomatic relations between the two countries, which were broken in the beginning of 1939, were now re-established, though Hungary supported Finland with volunteers and by other means.

At the same time, the Hungarian leaders were sure that there was a community of interests between themselves and the Soviet Union *vis-à-vis* Romania: as Hungary wanted Transylvania, Stalin would demand Bessarabia and northern Bukovina, lost after 1918 (and in the pact of August 1939, Hitler indeed acknowledged the Soviet claim to these territories). The revisionist claims against Romania were at the top of the Hungarian government agenda during the first phase of the war, while divisions arose as to the proper means of making these claims good when Hitler, sensing that Stalin was again becoming a rival out of an ally, contemplated the pre-emptive occupation of the Romanian oil fields in the spring of 1940. Military circles and the rightists within and outside the government, who were at the same time enthusiastic of German triumphs in the western front, urged closer co-operation with

Germany including free passage for and military assistance to the German troops. However, Teleki, who had become discernibly more cautious since the outbreak of the war, wanted to avoid unreserved commitments, especially as he received warnings through secretly established links from Britain, which was still a guarantor of Romanian integrity. He even made steps to establish, if necessary, a Hungarian government in exile in the United States. It was rendered unnecessary by Hitler's decision to call off military action in Romania. However, after, and in the light of, Romania's yielding to Stalin's ultimatum to cede the territories demanded at the end of June, it was Teleki who explained to Berlin that Hungary would have to resort to force, should Romania be reluctant to do the same in relation to Transylvania. Hitler, who wanted to avoid any turbulence in the region that endangered the steady flow of supplies to the German war machine, forced the Romanians to bilateral talks with the Hungarian government, and when these failed and both countries mobilised, Hitler and Mussolini offered arbitration again. The Second Vienna Award of August 30, 1940 returned northern Transylvania, 43,000 square kilometres with two and a half million inhabitants (about 50 per cent of them being Hungarian), to Hungary.

Teleki was thus unable to avoid German tutelage in the newest advance in the policy of revision, which, while welcomed with ebullient joy in Hungary, was (unlike the First Vienna Award) disputed by the United States and Britain as a dictated measure, and cost the country a further reduction of its independent scope of action. The Nazi *Volksbund* became the single legitimate organisation of the German minority in Hungary; consignments of foodstuffs and raw materials to Germany were increased at the expense of internal needs; German troops marched across Hungary into Romania, now led by the right-wing dictator Marshal Ion Antonescu; the preparation of the third anti-Jewish law began. The latter was also a gesture to the extreme right, which took advantage of the circumstances. Szálasi was prematurely released from prison, and became the head of the Arrowcross Party, further strengthened through a merger with other fascist groups at the end of September 1940. In the following month, Imrédy, who by then had emerged as the leader of the right wing of the government party, seceded from it and established the Party of Hungarian Revival. Most importantly, it was also in acknowledgement of German support in the achievement of revisionist aims that Hungary abandoned its policy of neutrality by joining (along with its disaffected neighbours Slovakia and Romania), on November 20, 1940, the Tripartite Pact concluded by Germany, Italy and Japan two months earlier.

Three weeks later a treaty of 'eternal friendship' was signed between Hungary and Yugoslavia, its only neighbour still unaffected by the territorial changes of the past two years. In the calculations of Teleki, it mainly served to secure Yugoslav neutrality in case a conflict broke out between Hungary and Romania over the southern parts of Transylvania, which continued to figure prominently in his plans; at the same time, Hitler expected him to encourage the current pro-German Yugoslav government to follow Hungary into the Tripartite Pact. As soon as this had taken place, the overthrow of that government in the military coup of March 27, 1941 upset all of these calculations. As a compliant *Südostraum* was to be the basis of operation against Russia in the struggle for German *Lebensraum*, Hitler decided to eliminate Yugoslavia. Besides enlisting the participation of Italy and Bulgaria in the operation, he required the Hungarian government to secure passage for German troops and to send forces, too, offering at the same time the return of the southern provinces lost at Trianon.

The Hungarian leaders faced a vicious dilemma. They either accepted, at the cost of breaking a three month old treaty and incurring the wrath of the western powers, the return of the nearly half million Hungarians in those provinces, which they and the public opinion held rightful and right extremists vigorously demanded; or they defied their larger ally, retaining the sympathy of the Allies, but risking military occupation by Germany. Teleki collapsed under the weight of the moral and political responsibility. Leaving behind a desperate letter of dramatic self-accusation to Horthy and causing some international sensation, he shot himself dead on April 3, 1941, after German troops had already started to march against Yugoslavia and he as well as the Regent and his fellow ministers decided to comply with Hitler's demand. A week later, the new Premier, the former ambassador to Bucharest, László Bárdossy, instructed the Hungarian army to cross the border, too.

The move resulted in the acquisition of an additional 11,000 square kilometres of territory, with over 1.1 million people, thirty-odd per cent of whom were ethnic Hungarians. In two and a half years, German-supported Hungarian revisionism achieved the re-annexation of 80,000 square kilometres, nearly half of the territory lost at Trianon. Half of the five million old-new citizens of Hungary were Magyars. Hungary became a multi-national state again, only 79 per cent of its population belonging to the 'state-nation'; the miniorities included over a million Romanians, 700,000 Germans and half a million Ruthenians, besides Slovaks, Serbs and Croats. In spite of the fact that no political force in interwar Hungary questioned the rightfulness of the revision of Trianon, no plans were worked out for the re-integration and administration of the territories that were to be recovered. Marked differences thus arose in their treatment; what was uniform were the wrongs suffered by the minorities, mainly in the Bačka, where the Serbs who settled after 1918 were at once evicted, and where the most infamous of atrocities committed by the Hungarian military during the war, the massacre of over three thousand civilians at Újvidék (Novi Sad) in retaliation for guerrilla activity in the area, took place in January 1942. The initial euphoria of the 'liberated' Hungarians was also damped by the fact that all inhabitants of the re-annexed territories were treated with some suspicion, and most of the positions in the new administration were given, on considerations of loyalty, to the swollen Christian middle classes from the 'mother country'.

Internationally, as a result of the participation in Hitler's war against Yugoslavia, Hungary became more isolated and more compelled to seek German goodwill than ever before. Although the worst fears, that is, British and American declarations of war, were not realised, Churchill at once broke diplomatic relations with Hungary, and President Roosevelt called it an aggressor. With the creation of German satellites out of the remains of Serbia and Croatia, with Tiso's Slovakia and Antonescu's Romania, Hungary was encircled by a kind of Nazi Little Entente, surely even more embittered against it by the losses than the pro-French one had been by the gains. Besides the resulting dependence on Germany, it was the latter's impressive military performance, the influence of the extreme Right and widespread anti-Bolshevism that ultimately defeated the caution advised again by pro-western conservatives and opposition democrats when Hungary had to decide whether or not to join the German campaign against the Soviet Union in June 1941. Even so, unlike Italy and Romania, Hungary at first only broke diplomatic relations with Moscow; only after, on June 26, the city of Kassa had been bombed by unmarked planes which the first news alleged to have been Russian, did Horthy declare war on the Soviet Union – based on his prerogative, submitting his decision for approval to the government and the parliament after the event. At the outset, only the so-called Carpathian group of the rapid army corps (some forty thousand troops) were dispatched to the Russian front and, after having advanced to the Donets by November, they were recalled and replaced by occupation forces. This did not prevent Great Britain, after repeated urging by Moscow, from declaring war on Hungary on December 7, 1941. As for the United States, it did not consider Germany's 'vassals' as sovereign states and did not follow its ally; it was Bárdossy who, upon Hitler's insistence, declared war on Washington.

The news of the war against Russia, with which Hungary had no territorial disputes, but plenty of bad experience, was received unenthusiastically among the Hungarian population. Nevertheless, the country's resources were now completely placed into the service of the war machine, which in effect meant their surrendering to Germany. Ninety per cent of Hungary's bauxite and half her oil production, large quantities of all kinds of agricultural products went to Germany, as well as the main economic benefits drawn from the revisionist successes: the grain surplus of Bačka, or the output of the Transylvanian mines. The population did not profit from the impressive growth of iron and steel production or the prosperity of the armaments industry, and, from 1942 on, was afflicted by the inflation generated by the fact that Germany was a less and less reliable debtor (from 140 million marks in 1941, its debts to Hungary rose to 1.5 billion in 1944), and the Hungarian governments resorted to issuing banknotes without security. In spite of the compulsory delivery and central distribution of agricultural products, and the rationing of an increasing range of them, a thriving black market developed. However, while living standards declined substantially, the basic needs of most of the population were not affected until relatively late in the war, which was one of the reasons why opposition to and protest against government policies remained rather isolated and lacked mass support.

This is not to say that the anti-fascist movement did not receive an impetus from Hungary's entry in the war. On the contrary, important demonstrations took place on October 6, 1941, the anniversary of the execution of the *honvéd* generals in 1849, and on All Saints Day, with the participation of bourgeois democrats, Social Democrats as well as Communists; similarly, the contributors of the Christmas issue of the social democratic daily *Népszava* advocating an anti-fascist stand included, besides the above, the populist writer József Darvas, the erstwhile rightist Endre Bajcsy-Zsilinszky, and even the one-time ideological icon of the Horthy era, Gyula Szekfű. By February 1942, a co-ordinating organ of these endeavours, the Hungarian Historical Memorial Committee, was established, its first step being a mass rally on March 15 at the Petőfi monument in Budapest, demanding an independent and democratic Hungary.

While the deterioration of conditions was a phenomenon that affected all but a small privileged minority, for another minority the war years were times of increasingly savage ordeal. In the name of 'racial defence', the third anti-Jewish law of August 1941 made marriages between Jews and non-Jews illegal and qualified sexual relationship between them as 'defamation of race'. Conscripted Jews were not allowed to do armed military service, but were put to work in the hinterland and sent to the front in labour battalions unarmed and defenceless, which was, besides brutalisation by their officers, one of the reasons for the unusually high death rates among these units. However, even amidst harsh discrimination, the life of most Jews in Hungary was not in immediate danger until 1944, as a result of which about 100,000 Jews sought and found refuge in Hungary from neighbouring Slovakia, Romania and

Croatia, where they were exposed to pogroms and deportation to death camps from 1942 on.

By the end of 1941, when the Soviet Red Army halted the advance of the *Wehrmacht* near Moscow, the hopes of a *Blitzkrieg* were definitively thwarted, and Foreign Minister Ribbentrop and Chief of the High Command Keitel visited Budapest in January 1942 to demand more intensive military involvement from Hungary. German intervention acquired a most effective tool in Imrédy's party, which in the autumn of 1941 absorbed other National Socialist groups, too, and was more inclined to serve German interests than the Arrowcross Party, which pursued Szálasi's muddled ideas of a 'Hungarist' empire. But Bárdossy himself could be brought to compliance: he not only undertook to send an army of 200,000 to the Russian front in the first half of the year, but also agreed to the recruitment of up to 20,000 men into the *Waffen-SS* among the German minority in Hungary. However, the pattern known from the cases of Darányi and Imrédy was set into motion again. For those who, like the Regent himself, still wanted to preserve a minimum of an independent Hungarian policy line, which included western ties, Bárdossy seemed to have swung the pendulum too much to the German side. They were also alarmed by the Premier's failure to prevent the atrocities of the military in and around Újvidék, which did great harm to Hungary's name (even though the culprits were not prevented from escaping to Germany before they were to be tried in 1943). For these reasons Bárdossy was replaced, on March 9, 1942, with Miklós Kállay, an agricultural expert and a well-known conservative opponent of National Socialism.

Yet, during the first months of Kállay's premiership there was little change in the thrust of Hungarian policies. The army requested by the Germans was raised and sent to the Russian front, supplemented with Jewish labour battalions as well as 'penal battalions' consisting of Social Democrats and trade unionist functionaries, and activists of the illegal Communist Party, some of whose leaders were tortured to death in prison or executed. The Israelite faith ceased to be a 'received' religion, and Jewish landed property was nationalised and distributed – a deplorable substitute for the long overdue settlement of the pressing land issue. While Kállay at the same time also showed some determination to rein in the extreme right with an attempt to contain agitation by the *Volksbund*, it was not until late 1942, when the anti-fascist coalition started to launch counter-offensives on several fronts, that the policies of his government materially changed. From that time on, these policies were based on the long-term prospects of an Allied victory and the expectation that, as at the end of the First World War, the western powers would land in the Balkans and quickly make their way to the Hungarian frontier; they were aimed at keeping the Red Army off the country's borders and securing the occupation of Hungary by Anglo-American forces (which also meant that until this became realistic, breaking with Germany would be suicidal). Similarly to the émigré Smallholder leader Tibor Eckhardt, who in 1941 launched his 'Independent Hungary' movement in the United States and tried to convince the western leaders that current Hungarian policies were shaped under serious constraints, Kállay also established clandestine contacts with the Allied governments to explain them that Hungary was not a totalitarian state and would leave the German camp as soon as the western Allies reached the country's borders. On the domestic scene, in October 1942 Kállay refused the German demands to launch the 'final solution' of the Jewish question. However, the government also refrained from any cooperation with the anti-fascist opposition, though the latter was given more breathing space than earlier.

Kállay's double-edged policies accelerated after the demise of the Second Hungarian Army on the Russian front in the beginning of 1943. In terms of equipment and supply, the Hungarian forces were inferior not only to the Germans, but even to the Soviets, and this, combined with their numerical weakness, made the task of maintaining a 200 kilometre line of defence along the Don south of Voronezh illusory from the outset. Several thousand soldiers perished in a cold of 40 degrees below zero by the time the decisive Soviet offensive was launched on January 12, 1943. The fact that the army received, on Hitler's insistence, completely senseless orders from its commander Gusztáv Jány to persevere to the utmost, but no assistance from German comrades in a disorganised retreat, explains the loss of 40,000 dead, 35,000 wounded and 60,000 captives, two-thirds of the entire fighting force. Though the true dimensions of the disaster were played down by the authorities and became at first only known in Hungary to those who listened to the Hungarian broadcasts of the BBC (until August 1943, by the historian Carlile Aylmer Macartney) or the Moscow-based Radio Kossuth, the arrival of the remnants of the army at the end of April destroyed whatever enthusiasm there still was for the war among the general public.

The Kállay government, while refusing Hitler's demand to send another Hungarian army to the eastern front, stepped up its efforts to pull out of the war by negotiating an armistice with the western powers. The younger Miklós Horthy was placed at the head of a special bureau created for this purpose, and Kállay's envoys sought contacts with British and American diplomats in the neutral capitals: Madrid, Lisbon, Istanbul and Stockholm. They offered, in the event of Anglo-American forces reaching Hungary, surrender and a change of allegiances (which in their interpretation no longer implied a breach of allied obligations after the Tripartite Pact became defunct with the fall of Mussolini in July 1943). At the same time, while it was emphasised in the memoranda submitted to the Allies that Hungary expected at least to retain the territories re-annexed to it between 1938 and 1941, all other aspects of the inter-war regime were intended to remain unchanged by Horthy and Kállay, who not only repudiated any communication with the Soviets, but were also unwilling to co-operate with the representatives of the democratic alternative that started to take shape in Hungary by then.

The latter now even included an exclusive circle of aristocrats and *haute bourgeois* around Bethlen who established a National Casino, and then went on with the Liberals of Károly Rassay to create the Democratic Bourgeois Alliance with a programme of gradual reforms. In the summer of 1943, Endre Bajcsy-Zsilinszky and Zoltán Tildy of the Independent Smallholder Party not only submitted a memorandum to the government urging it to break away from Germany and to conclude a separate peace, but also worked out a common programme of democratisation with the Social Democrats. Further left on the political spectrum, the conference of mainly young intellectuals attached to the 'populist' writers at Balatonszárszó in August 1943 was divided between commitment to the 'third way' advocated by László Németh, and the more radical, communist-inspired alternative proposed by Darvas, Erdei and Veres. Despite the great wave of persecution in 1942, the Communists also reorganised themselves under the cover name Peace Party, which made it easier for them to collaborate with anti-fascists in the 'Independence Movement' who at the same time harboured anti-Bolshevik sentiments.

The western powers, while not averse to a reasonable redressing of Hungary's Trianon grievances based on the ethnic principle, were not only opposed to the restoration of 'historic borders' and the 'Hungarian ascendancy' in the Danube region which it implied, but also would have preferred to deal, after the war, with a thoroughly reformed Hungary governed by a 'popular front' of Liberals, Smallholders and Social Democrats (though certainly not the Communists). Nevertheless, they were willing to arrive at arrangements with anyone if they weakened the opposite side without undertaking commitments. As a result, they passed on, via Istanbul, a 'preliminary armistice agreement' to the Kállay government on September 9, 1943, requiring Hungary to diminish its contribution to the German war effort, to withdraw its troops from Soviet territory, and to surrender unconditionally as soon as the Allies reached the Hungarian frontier.

Kállay accepted these terms, but the failure of the realisation of the conditions on which the practical value of the agreement depended, soon annulled it. At the Teheran meeting of Churchill, Roosevelt and Stalin in late November 1943, it was decided that the Anglo-American landing would take place in France, and the struggle against the remnants of the Axis in Eastern and in the South-Eastern Europe were to become the task of the Red Army. Hitler also prevented the withdrawal of Hungarian occupation troops from the Russian front. At the same time, the German intelligence service acquired detailed and up-to-date information about Kállay's peace feelers, and as early as in April 1943 Hitler demanded at their meeting in Klessheim that Horthy dismiss his Prime Minister. Upon the Regent's refusal, the Germans prepared a parliamentary coup orchestrated by Imrédy's National Socialist Party Alliance, which was thwarted by the prorogation of the Hungarian parliament in the beginning of May. However, from September 1943 on, plans for 'operation Margarethe', that is, the military occupation of Hungary were worked out in Berlin. As the advance of Soviet troops enhanced Hungary's strategic importance, the operation was prepared in early March 1944, and Horthy was ordered by Hitler to Klessheim again to give a semblance of legality to the move. Though the Regent, deeply upset, refused to make an official appeal for German troops, under threats that Romanian and Slovak forces would be used instead and having been promised that the Germans would leave after the appointment of a 'loyal' government, he agreed. Upon orders from the Chief of the General Staff, the Hungarian army received the German occupying forces as 'friends' on the following day, March 19, 1944. After negotiations with Edmund Veesenmayer, the German ambassador and the plenipotentiary of the *Reich* in Hungary, the Regent replaced Kállay with former ambassador to Berlin, Döme Sztójay, at the head of a government now exclusively consisting of politicians of the extreme Right.

The Sztójay government was a conscientious partner of the Germans in executing all policies which had been long demanded by them as well as the Hungarian National Socialists, but to which its conservative predecessors had tried to resist. Opposition parties were outlawed, and the Gestapo, assisted by the Hungarian police and gendarmerie, arrested about 3,000 persons by the end of April on account of their political activities and sympathies; of prominent ex-premiers, Kállay sought refuge at the Turkish embassy, and Bethlen was hiding at friends in the countryside. Instead of the planned withdrawal of forces from the eastern front, the First Hungarian Army, augmented with new conscripts to about 300,000 soldiers, was dispatched there. In retaliation, and mainly to disrupt communication lines, the Allied bombing of Budapest and other Hungarian cities started in April 1944. The spoliation of the economic resources of the country by Germany continued and even increased, with no remuneration whatever for the raw material, foodstuffs and armaments shipped out of the country. Some of the largest industrial plants were placed directly at the disposal of the SS, with their predominantly Jewish owners allowed to emigrate to neutral Portugal.

For most of Hungary's other Jews, the German occupation brought about the horrible reality of the *Endlösung*. Officially, the Hungarian gendarmerie were to hand the Jews, obliged to wear the yellow star, over to the *Judenkommando* under the command of Adolf Eichmann in order to augment Germany's labour force. In fact, there was little doubt that Auschwitz, where the trains were heading, was an extermination camp. Amidst sporadic examples of courageous assistance to the Jews in evading their fate, about 440,000 of them from the Hungarian countryside were deported by the end of June; 320,000 never returned. Thirty to fifty thousand Roma shared their lot. Upon protests by the kings of England and Sweden, President Roosevelt, the Pope, Hungarian public figures including Bethlen and prominent ecclesiastical leaders, as well as under the impact of further German military defeats and the Allied landing in Normandy, Horthy stopped the deportations in early July, which, for the time being, saved the lives of the 200,000 Jews of Budapest.

In April 1944, the Hungarian Council in England was established by organisations of émigré Hungarian democrats under the leadership of Mihály Károlyi with the goal of working for an independent and democratic Hungary on friendly terms with its equally rejuvenated neighbours after the war, but it had virtually no contacts with and no impact on developments at home. In May 1944, the Independent Smallholder Party, the Social Democratic Party, the National Peasant Party, the Peace Party and the legitimist Apostolic Cross Alliance launched the Hungarian Front as an underground resistance movement, but the appeal it addressed to the people of Hungary to launch a popular uprising against the rule of the Germans and the Hungarian Nazis largely fell on deaf ears. Besides the general repression and the vague indebtedness which still many felt to Germany because of its assistance in redressing the injustices of Trianon, the lack of a resistance movement that could be compared to that in France, Poland or Yugoslavia was also due to the abhorrence of the Red Army and the Soviet system, which were associated with any movement involving Communists. In fact, communist groups, having become accustomed to conspiratorial techniques in the past quarter of a century, were the most successful in distributing pamphlets and carrying out acts of sabotage, even minor military operations, but their efficiency was greatly limited by the arrest of many potential leaders in March and April

The Hungarian Front was also in touch Horthy, who, however, preferred to rely on the habitual means of simply changing the guards when the moment seemed auspicious. That moment came when, on

August 23, Romania, on the threshold of being overrun by the Red Army, denounced Germany and declared war on it. While the German forces were embarrassed by the resulting opening of the front lines in Romania, together with the simultaneous anti-fascist revolt in Slovakia, this also meant that Hungary was on the way to becoming Hitler's last satellite, which promised little good at the future peace conference. Sztójay was replaced by General Géza Lakatos who, while he stood up to the Germans by releasing several political prisoners and winding up Eichmann's bureau, lost precious weeks by still expecting the impossible (the arrival of western forces) and failing to do the inevitable (negotiating with the Soviets). Only after Soviet troops had expelled the Hungarian forces sent to halt them from southern Transylvania and started to appear on the Great Plain, did Horthy decide to send a secret mission to Moscow.

The preliminary armistice signed on October 11, 1944, required Hungary to give up the territories re-annexed since 1938 and to declare war on Germany. After so much procrastination, that risky step was politically and militarily ill-prepared and poorly executed, with Horthy and the general staff bearing supreme responsibility: the former committed blunders and acted inconclusively, and the latter in effect behaved treacherously. The Regent informed the Hungarian Front about his plans, but was still unwilling to make political concessions as demanded by the parties united in it. The army and the population were taken by surprise by Horthy's radio proclamation on October 15, unlike the Germans, who acted upon ready-made plans for such an event, and already two weeks earlier had alerted Szálasi to prepare to grasp power. Men of the Arrowcross indeed occupied strategic points of the capital by the evening of October 15. In his proclamation, Horthy mentioned the armistice as a measure still pending, and only called the army to stop fighting the Soviets, but not to turn against the Germans; nor was the relevant order communicated to the troops by the general staff. Blackmailed by the kidnapping of his son, Horthy withdrew his proclamation on the following day, appointed Szálasi as premier, and resigned from the regentship. He was taken into 'protective custody' in Germany, and Szálasi occupied the position of head of state as 'Leader of the Nation'.

Still inspired with the obsession of ultimate German victory, the reign of terror inflicted by the Arrowcross Party caused immense suffering to the people of 'Hungaria United Ancient Lands', as the new masters chose to call the country, practically confined to the capital and Transdanubia. Bajcsy-Zsilinszky and other leaders of the Liberation Committee of the Hungarian National Uprising, which succeeded the Hungarian Front with the goal of organising armed resistance, were betrayed and executed. Eichmann returned, and the Jewish population massed in the ghetto of Budapest, were now exposed to being systematically exterminated; despite acts of international and Hungarian solidarity, nearly half of the 200,000 Jews of the capital fell victim to horrible mass murder, and few of the 50,000 driven westwards in labour battalions survived. Dismantled factory equipment, cattle, and anything moveable was also dragged away by the retreating German forces, now mainly interested in entrenching themselves along the western borders of Hungary, leaving it for Szálasi to win time for them. The Leader of the Nation announced total mobilisation (in principle extending to all men between the ages of 14 and 70), and rejected appeals from Hungarian ecclesiastical leaders to abandon Budapest after it had been surrounded by Soviet forces by Christmas 1944. The senseless persistence of the Arrowcross and the Germans resulted in a siege of over one and a half months, with heavy bombardment and bitter street warfare, a 'second Stalingrad', as recalled in several German war memoirs.

Budapest was taken by the Red Army on February 13, 1945. A last German counter-offensive collapsed in Transdanubia in the middle of March; armed hostilities ceased on Hungarian territory on April 12, 1945. The Second World War for Hungary was over, leaving it under a foreign occupying force with devastated resources, a broken conscience and an identity crisis arguably still worse than at the beginning of the period which it thus ended.

CHAPTER VIII

UTOPIAS AND THEIR FAILURES (1945–1989)

In a statement that became legendary in Hungary on account of its falla-ciousness, László Németh said at the Balatonszárszó conference in August 1943 that the end of the Second World War found Hungary in a far better condition than was the case at the end of the First. True, at that time it was not an inaccurate assessment of the situation. Despite the tragedy of Voronezh, Hungary's war casualties were still much fewer than a quarter of a century earlier, and while there was privation in the hinterland, it could not be compared to what the country suffered dur-ing the First World War. Not even the pessimists would have predicted that four years after the beginning of the war the end was still twenty months ahead, during which period the face of Hungary would be vio-lently transformed beyond recognition. The German occupation, with the economic plundering of the country and the Hungarian Holocaust; the Arrowcross' reign of terror; the bitter struggle in what became a theatre of war for eight months, with requisitioning and atrocities by So-viet troops – all these made Hungary one of the most seriously afflicted countries of the Second World War, its losses only surpassed by those of Poland, the Soviet Union, Germany and Yugoslavia. Forty per cent of its national wealth was destroyed, but this average figure conceals signifi-cant variations: an even greater proportion of key assets like factory equipment, cattle, railway lines and rolling stock was lost. The national income for 1945–1946 was less than half of that for 1938–1939. In addi-tion, Hungary could expect huge reparation bills to be presented by Czechoslovakia, Yugoslavia and the Soviet Union. The bridges over the Danube and the Tisza were blown up by the Germans in their retreat, a quarter of the housing stock (as a matter of fact, considerably more in the capital) were damaged by bombing and shelling. The human toll was no less dramatic. After the re-annexations of 1938–1941, the popu-lation of Hungary was 14.5 million. The war cost over one million lives, half of these being the victims of the Holocaust. Extra sets of hands were missed from the country in the period when reconstruction was on the agenda. Upon orders by the Arrowcross to evacuate the country, and from fear of the Soviets, one million Hungarians fled west in the winter of 1944–1945, 100,000 of whom never returned. Whereas the 300,000 who surrendered to the western Allies were released during 1946, half of the nearly 600,000 captives (over 100,000 of them civilians) deported mostly to forced labour camps in the Soviet Union only returned in 1947 and after.

Among different geo-political circumstances, the astonishing dilapidation, the near-*tabula rasa* that remained after the war, could have even proved advantageous for the future of the country. The failure in the war was largely that of the anachronistic, semi-feudal social and political order, which collapsed into ashes at the turn of 1944–1945. While the outcome of the First World War only threw it seriously into discredit, that of the Second uprooted it, which in principle ought to have created even more favourable conditions for the transition to liberal democracy based on the market economy. This was indeed how the history of Hungary, as well as that of the other countries of Central Europe, seemed to start anew: with free elections and an experiment with multi-party democracy in order to develop a form of government and policies suitable to their peoples, as proposed by the Yalta declaration of the Allies on February 11, 1945.

The one weakness of the Yalta declaration was also the most serious conceivable: its violations could be neither prevented nor redressed. The western powers did not officially agree with the Soviet Union in Yalta or elsewhere about dividing the liberated territories into spheres of interest. Nevertheless, what happened to the countries of Central and South-Eastern Europe in the aftermath of the war reflected the informal 'percentage deal' which Churchill outlined to Stalin about how to share influence over the region in October 1944, or Stalin's view of the peculiar nature of the current war as being an instrument for each power to impose its own socio-political system on the lands it occupied, rather than the earlier plans worked out in British and American circles on how to build a socially and ethnically equitable order through democratic coalitions, federations and border revisions. Churchill and Roosevelt may not have deliberately surrendered the region to Stalin, but it was virtually abandoned by the decision to open the second front in Normandy instead of the Balkans, which enabled the Soviets to realise an expansive strategy of directly incorporating the lands acknowledged as their sphere of interest in the 1939 pact with Germany, and creating a belt of impotent vassal states west of them.

Hungary belonged to the outer zone of that belt, where a transitory period was contemplated by the new conquerors before complete Sovietisation could be achieved, though this latter was undoubtedly their goal from the very beginning. Horthy's failure to pull out of the war, which immensely increased the reconstruction tasks and fully eliminated any remaining legitimacy, meant that the period of transition could be considerably shortened. The power vacuum and the economic chaos favoured the Communists, whose confident activism, ready-made and simple solutions, and undoubted organisational skills exerted magnetic attraction in an atmosphere in which masses leaving the shelters, returning from the fronts – whether military or labour battalions – or POW camps, were thirsty for convincing programmes of building society anew. Nothing better suited this desire than the attitude expressed in the rallying song which ended in the confident prediction: 'We shall have turned the world around by tomorrow'. Largely because of the appeal of this dynamism that so deceptively seemed to represent the spirit of the times, in several countries west of Hungary, the Communist Parties did not need the presence of the Red Army to score highly at elections in the post-war years. That presence was the distinctive force that led to the elimination of political pluralism, the introduction of economic planning, a total change of the elite and excessive egalitarianism, and the hegemony of the Marxist-Leninist ideology in the countries that shared the lot of Hungary.

As a matter of fact, there were many in Hungary who willingly and knowingly, and many more who unwillingly or naively collaborated with the Soviets in transforming it into a totalitarian regime dependent on Moscow. The times of Sovietisation were a painful test of social and political morality for Hungarians, which added to the confusion they inherited in that respect from the already trying interwar decades, and which they stood with varying success – if not better, certainly not worse than was the case elsewhere. The point, however, is that among the given circumstances less collaboration of either sort would have made very little or no difference. On the other hand, both sorts and all levels of collaboration were, in the first place, occasioned by the limited sovereignty of Hungary, and it must be considered highly likely that without those limits the democratic beginnings of the period between 1944 and 1948 – which, although representing a distinct break with the conservative and nationalist authoritarianism of the inter-war period, were still organic in Hungarian society, unlike Bolshevik totalitarianism – would have yielded a very different outcome. Not for the first time in Hungarian history, limitations on the country's sovereignty arising either from foreign military occupation or from an adverse international situation or from a combination of both (1849 and 1918 are cases in point) prevented it from unfolding the potentials inherent in the domestic social and political scene. Sometimes it is alleged that the rapidity of Hungary's Sovietisation is a testimony of its essentially East European character, with all that implies for the vigour of structures connected with civil society, individual initiative and the pluralism of values, ideas and endeavours, versus the omnipresence of the state and the homogeneity of a mass of subjects. The promising democratic initiatives of the post-war years even amidst the conditions of limited sovereignty, and the fact that in 1956 Hungary fought the only anti-totalitarian revolution in history – all of this, significantly, without a serious possibility of the recovery of the pre-war conservative authoritarianism – seems to indicate the contrary.

1956 repeated the pattern of 1849, 1918–1920 and 1944–1948 in that international contingencies once again, and perhaps even more shockingly than ever before, deprived Hungary of the opportunity of lifting the limitations on its sovereignty and going the way it wanted. After 1956, a pattern also well known from post-1849 (or post-1867) and post-1920 domestic history repeated itself, too: a regime born out of naked terror consolidated itself by means that were acceptable to a broad segment of Hungarians made pragmatic by having tried the strength of their backbones. Viewed from another angle, and also similarly to 1848–1849, the revolution of 1956 did not fail in the sense that it created the basis of a compromise by compelling the Hungarians to a realistic assessment of their predicament, and Moscow to recognise that there were limits to their subjection. The latter circumstance opened a space of varying breadth for Hungary's new leaders in which they could win the acceptance of most, though the devotion of relatively few, Hungarians by benefits that were not available for the citizens of other countries in the Soviet bloc. Cautiously measured freedom of expression and access to cultural goods, carefully steered processes of upward mobility for broad sections of a society formerly marked by exclusiveness, and especially consumerism, with which equally broad sections of the society had been formerly unacquainted, reconciled people to the rule of the party bureaucracy, the communist 'nomenclature' under Soviet tutelage, and to certain taboos like the one-party system or the qualification of 1956 as a 'counter-revolution'. However, neither the liberalisation, whose actual limits at all times responded sensitively to the twists in the relations of power within the Hungarian party as well as to the winds that blew from Moscow, nor the increasing foreign loans contracted to supplement it, were sufficient to maintain, let alone surpass, the standards reached by the 1980s; which, to all intents and purposes, meant that the regime was unable to keep its part of the tacit deal. Even so, few Hungarians – with diffidence having become their second nature, and lulled into political laziness by the little compromises required in return for modest comforts – were prepared to be presented by international developments with a fourth chance in the twentieth century, after 1918, 1945 and 1956, to establish democracy, this time as unlimited masters of their fate and succeeding or failing entirely on their own account.

1. Reconstruction, democracy and 'people's democracy'

The Red Army, whose conduct in the occupied territories justified the pessimists and quickly disillusioned those who received them as liberators, had not yet started the blockade of Budapest, when in the eastern parts of Hungary 'national committees' started to reorganise local administration, and the former opposition parties set to creating their country-wide networks. Four old parties (the Smallholders, the Communists, the Social Democrats and the National Peasant Party), the newly organised Bourgeois Democratic Party and the representatives of the trade unions founded in Szeged on December 2, 1944, the Hungarian National Independence Front, which appealed to the allied powers for assistance in establishing a democratic political system based on land reform and private enterprise (with the nationalisation of a few large companies), and promised to abandon revisionism *vis-à-vis* neighbouring countries, to dissolve fascist organisations, and to call those responsible for Hungarian policies during the war to account.

The Allies acknowledged the Independence Front as the body representing the political efforts to consolidate the situation in the country, and allowed it to make arrangements for convening a Provisional National Assembly. The members of this non-elected body were nominated by the parties and chosen by improvised rallies, and sat on December 21-22, 1944, to appoint the Provisional National Government (designated earlier in Moscow). The cabinet headed by Béla Dálnoki Miklós, one of the few generals of Horthy who went over to the Soviets on October 15, had the character of a coalition, in which positions were apparently evenly distributed among the above-mentioned parties. In reality, the officially non-party Erik Molnár, and Ferenc Erdei of the Peasant Party, who was appointed to the crucially important Ministry of the Interior, ensured a communist ascendancy in the government.

This reflected the relations of power at that time in a peculiar way. The Independent Smallholder Party was only rivalled by the Social Democrats in terms of pedigree and prestige, and by far outdid them in terms of social embeddedness and membership, which rose to a truly impressive 900,000 in the summer of 1945. This highly stratified party stood for the defence of private property in a peasant-bourgeois democracy in general, and for land reform in particular, one which created more equitable property relations and was economically sound at the same time. Its respected leaders, the party chairman and Calvinist pastor Zoltán Tildy and the party secretary of peasant origin, the popular Ferenc Nagy, hoped to rely on the support of the western powers, but were open to co-operating with any political force for the above ends, and realised that in Hungary's current situation the friendship of the Soviet Union was in its interest. What they realised only when it was too late was that it was not friendship that interested the Soviet Union. Indeed, it is plausible that Stalin only decided temporarily to spare the setting of parliamentary democracy at the end of the war in Hungary and Czechoslovakia in order to make the western powers reconciled to his already planned move to destroy it soon in Poland, Bulgaria and Romania. But he insisted on a sharing of power between the government, the Soviet occupying forces, and the newly created State Security Department (ÁVO) or political police, whose head became the Communist Gábor Péter.

Despite their initially small number (about 3,000 party members at the end of 1944), the Communists started to dominate the scene with the self-assurance drawn from these advantages. Deriving from the long years of being outlawed and the sense of their initial isolation within the population, they developed a strong *esprit de corps*, in spite of the many instances of personal animosity within the party leadership, and its falling between 'Muscovites' sheltered in the Soviet Union, 'home grown' Communists who operated in illegality before and during the war, and western émigrés (veterans of the Spanish Civil War among them). The former were of course the main transmitters of Soviet intentions. They included the man whom Stalin chose to lead the Hungarian party: Mátyás Rákosi, the commander of the Red Guard of the Hungarian Soviet Republic in 1919, sentenced to life imprisonment upon returning from his first exile and only released to Moscow in 1940 in exchange for the *honvéd* flags captured by the Russians in 1849; Ernő Gerő, who spent a longer period in the Soviet Union, but also worked in Western Europe for the Communist International until its dissolution in 1943; the party ideologue József Révai; the agricultural expert Imre Nagy; and many others. Among others who quickly rose to prominence we find László Rajk, a former teacher who fought in Spain in the International Brigades, and later became one of the organisers of anti-fascist resistance, similarly to János Kádár, a worker who served the communist cause in Hungary ever since he became involved in the movement.

By the time of the elections of November 1945, the communist vanguard managed to create a mass party of half a million members as a result of a quite unscrupulous recruiting campaign. With a rhetoric carefully avoiding the slightest hint to their long-term goal (unlike the Social Democrats, they did not mention socialism as being even their strategic goal) and centred on the most pressing tasks of reconstruction combined with reform, their avowed programme was essentially the same as that of the Independence Front; however, they did not refrain from occasionally playing nationalist tunes. Workers and small peasants out of conviction, intellectuals out of idealism, civil servants out of fear and opportunism, lumpen elements out of fortune-seeking augmented the party ranks; the decimated Jewry joined out of gratitude for the liberators and searching for a new experience of community, while Arrowcross men were rewarded with impunity if they exchanged their green party membership card for a red one. Besides boasting an ever growing influence on its own, the Communist Party was also able to manipulate the other parties of the Left. The Social Democratic Party, whose 350,000 strong membership possessed a powerful working class consciousness, and whose leader Árpád Szakasits soon proved very manageable for the Communists, found it increasingly difficult to resist the call of the Communists for working class unity. As for the National Peasant Party, chaired by Péter Veres, led by intellectuals inspired by 'populist' writers like him and considering itself the spokesman of the rural poor, its main commitment was radical land reform, and both within the party leadership and the 150,000 strong membership it contained a fair number of communist sympathisers. It is no wonder that the party resisted the attempts of the Smallholders to draw closer ties of co-operation with them, but chose instead, together with the Social Democrats, to join the Communists in the Left Wing Bloc on March 5, 1946.

In the beginning of 1945, in a coalition of parties with conflicting outlooks and endeavours, consensus still prevailed as to the most immediate tasks. The first of these was to sign an armistice with the Allies, which took place on January 20, 1945, and required Hungary to withdraw to within its 1938 borders, to send troops against Germany, to pay 300 million dollars of reparations to the Soviet Union, Czechoslovakia and Yugoslavia, to liquidate all pro-German and fascist organisations, and to accept the supervision of the Allied Control Commission as to the execution of these stipulations. As the latter body was under the direction of Soviet Marshal Kliment Voroshilov, the last clause in effect legalised Soviet influence, especially as it was in the authority of the Commission to ban parties, to arrest people and to exercise censorship.

The changing of the guards also started at the different levels of the administration, special committees being charged with ascertaining whether the post-1939 conduct of officials 'violated Hungarian interests or not'. The gendarmerie was dissolved and its tasks transferred to a reorganised and enlarged police. As both of these operations took place under the auspices of the Communist-dominated Ministry of the Interior, the results were quite predictable. Simultaneously to the banning of twenty-five parties and associations qualified as extreme rightist, the ÁVO started to arrest, and 'people's courts', each consisting of lay members and a trained judge, to prosecute those charged with war crimes. To a certain extent similarly to 1919–1920, among the 60,000 who were charged and the 10,000 who were sentenced by summary procedures, there were many victims of a political showdown, and it is also true that others who could not be brought to court but were considered as *personae non gratae* were interned by the police without further ado. Nevertheless, the majority of those who received sentences were indeed guilty of crimes against humanity. Of the wartime political leaders of Hungary, Horthy was spared because of his intervention on behalf of the Budapest Jews and his abortive attempt to pull out of the war (he died in exile in Portugal), and Kállay and Lakatos because of their anti-German stand. But Bárdossy, Imrédy, Sztójay, Szálasi and the latter's ministers were among the 189 who were executed.

The third great measure taken by the Provisional Government was the land reform. All of the coalition parties agreed that the system of latifundia ought be liquidated, and that Hungary ought to be transformed from a country of 'three million beggars' (landless agricultural labourers or peasants with 7 acres or less) into one whose agrarian sector was dominated by prosperous peasant farms but also included collectively or state managed large holdings. Of the two rival schemes presented, that of the Peasant Party (also adopted by the two workers' parties) was found too radical by the Smallholders, but upon the intervention of Voroshilov who wanted to avoid further delay, and in view of the growing impatience of the masses of the rural poor, it was decreed effectively without debate on March 17, 1945. The measure affected eight million acres of land, 35 per cent of the country's arable. Extreme rightists and war criminals, as well as the owners of estates bigger than 1,500 acres, were to be fully dispossessed; smaller 'genteel' landowners could keep a maximum of 150, peasants 300 acres. Compensation was symbolic. Forty per cent of the land thus obtained became state and collective property, while the rest was re-allocated among 640,000 families.

The land reform had far reaching social, economic and political consequences. The aristocracy and the gentry, which had dominated the Hungarian public scene for several centuries, lost their traditional means of subsisting as distinct classes, and disappeared as such. The 'centuries old dream of the Hungarian peasant' came true. While all of the coalition forces as well as the overwhelming majority of the general public conceived of this outcome as meting out historical justice, the Smallholders were rightly concerned about its economic soundness. The average size of the plots allocated to the recipients was 7 acres, as a result of which the proportion of 'classic' dwarfholdings diminished, but that of the farms generally considered as viable and competitive in the Europe of the time, ones between at least 50 and 100 acres, diminished, too. The rationale behind the measure was quite obviously the ruthless destruction of an influential elite group, to establish the principle of egalitarianism even at the expense of economic efficiency, and to use the glory of satisfying the hunger for land for winning support for the Communist Party whose Minister for Agriculture, Imre Nagy, became remembered from then on as 'the land distributor'.

The land reform, together with the drastic reduction of draught-stock, machinery and implements whose redistribution was also problematic, added to the economic disarray and the difficulties of supply that the country faced. Rations, especially in the cities, were at starvation level: that of the hard physical worker, which considerably exceeded the urban average, was a mere 1,000 calories per day. The hardships and shortages were in several ways aggravated by the Soviet presence in Hungary. Besides the war reparation, whose payment was immediately started, the country was exposed to harassment by an occupation force of 1.5 million (half a million even in 1946) whose needs it was supposed to supply by food, fuel, free transportation and other services. After the Germans, the Soviet troops removed industrial installations, art treasures, and all sorts of movables. In addition, Hungary's debts to Germany (30 million dollars) were now due to the Soviet Union, which also collected the nearly 300 million dollars Germany owed to Hungary. The process of inflation which already started during the war, could not but spiral among such circumstances: at the black market the dollar was worth 1,320 pengős in July 1945, 290,000 at the end of the year (and 4,600,000 quadrillion by the end of July 1946, the greatest hyperinflation in history). The Hungarian currency was increasingly replaced by gold, foreign currency and barter as the basis of exchange relations. The government tried to suppress a thriving black market by severing the compulsory delivery of an increasing range of products by the peasantry. Yet, even amidst all the privation and against the odds, the people set to the most pressing reconstruction tasks with astonishing vigour. Thanks to government initiative and international relief organisations, health care and educational facilities operated surprisingly well, and transport services were also gradually re-launched.

It was thus an indigent, but overwhelmingly still optimistic Hungarian society that was preparing for general elections in the autumn of 1945. The announcement of elections was not only required by the Yalta agreement, but also called for by the fact that the truly revolutionary transformations of 1945 in the social and political status quo in Hungary bore only the stamp of a government and a legislative assembly whose composition itself meant a radical break with the past. Obvious doubts concerning the strict legality of many aspects of the changes, later confirmed by the fact that well before the peace settlement, in September 1945, special ties were developing between Moscow and Budapest in the shape of an agreement on close economic co-operation and even the resumption of full diplomatic relations, led the western powers to urge free elections in Hungary and to refrain from acknowledging the Provisional Government until the Soviets agreed to hold them.

The elections, by secret ballot and without census, of November 4, 1945, were the most democratic and the freest in Hungary until 1990. Only the leaders of the dissolved rightist parties, volunteers into the SS, and those interned or being prosecuted by the people's courts, were barred from voting. The liberal electoral law was also supported by the Communists, who were not even bothered by the failure of their proposal to field a single list of candidates on the part of the coalition parties, which would have ensured a majority of the parties of the Left: intoxicated by their recruitment successes and misjudging the effect of the land reform on their appeal, they expected an 'enthralling victory' (Révai predicted to score as much as 70 per cent). To their bitter disappointment, the result was nearly the opposite: the Smallholders, winning the contest in all of the sixteen districts, collected 57 per cent of the votes, the Social Democrats scoring slightly above and the Communists slightly below 17 per cent, and the National Peasant Party a mere 7 per cent (the rest of the votes going to the Bourgeois Democratic Party and the new Hungarian Radical Party of Jászi's followers).

Of the many reasons for the success of the Smallholders and the failure of the Communists at the elections, one was surely the fact that Cardinal József Mindszenty, the head of the Hungarian Catholic hierarchy, infuriated at the loss of the overwhelming majority of its landed property without compensation and at the clergy's being excluded from the elections upon Communist initiative, condemned the 'Marxist evil' in a pastoral letter and called the faithful to support the Smallholders. Nevertheless, the verdict of nearly 4.8 million voters, over 90 per cent of the enfranchised, clearly showed their preferences in general when confronted with parliamentary democracy based on private property and the market economy on the one hand, and socialism with state management and planning in the economic sphere on the other. They hoped that these preferences would prevail in spite of the presence of the Soviet occupying forces, who were expected to leave once the peace treaty was signed. However, guided by the same expectation and wishing to avoid confrontation until then, the Smallholders yielded to Voroshilov, who made it plain that a 'grand coalition' in which the Communists preserved the gains already secured (that is, the Ministry of the Interior and control over the police), was the only kind of government acceptable to the Soviets.

The cabinet was formed after the debate on the form of the post-war Hungarian state decided, in spite of a vigorous monarchist campaign led by Primate Mindszenty and some uncertainty on the issue among the Smallholders, in favour of a republic. Zoltán Tildy was elected its president on February 1, 1946, while Ferenc Nagy became Prime Minister of a government in which the Smallholders retained half of the portfolios. Besides the Minister of the Interior (Rajk), the Communists supplied the Deputy Premier (Rákosi) and the transport and social welfare ministers. Enlisting also the support of Social Democrat and Peasant Party ministers, they exploited these positions with tactical skill and ruthlessness against a Smallholder majority, which hesitated to take a tough line against the Soviet supported left wing grouping, especially as the latter became formally consolidated by a step that emphasised the exacerbation of class warfare and the need to proceed with social revolution: the creation of the Left Wing Bloc on March 5, 1946.

On the same day, Winston Churchill made his famous speech referring to the 'iron curtain' separating the Soviet occupied regions of Europe from the rest, and although it was a full year later that the 'Truman doctrine' was announced regarding America's assistance to all states fighting against communism, and the Marshall Plan was launched to put this into effect, the Cold War was imminent in 1946 and induced Stalin to accelerate the process of Sovietising the occupied territories in order better to prepare for the hot one. This was the background against which, in 1947, the Communists in Hungary also accelerated the elimination of their rivals little by little – slicing them up by the 'salami tactics', as Rákosi called it –, which was nevertheless begun as soon as the Nagy government took office.

Besides taking advantage of Soviet support, the Communists also exploited the fact that the leaders of the other parties were not always entirely unhappy with the removal of rival groups or individuals among their ranks. The Premier was perplexed to find that each of his initiatives served as occasions for his coalition partners to sharpen cleavages and test the lengths to which he was willing to go in pursuing his policies. His effort to make the proportions of political affiliation among state officials, which had shifted in favour of the Left during 1945, more conformable to the outcome of the election results, was countered by the further purges in the administration by Rajk through the compilation of ever newer lists of 'right-wing' elements, and often through carefully orchestrated 'public meetings' (ostensibly the features of 'primitive democracy') which denounced the accused and forced them to resign. Over 60,000 officials were thus removed between May and October 1946. Nagy also wanted to investigate the abuses and the violations of the land reform decree in the course of its execution (because of the number of applicants, in many places the limits set to expropriation were unobserved), to which the parties of the Left replied by inciting or supporting demonstrations with the slogan 'No lands back!', and charged the Smallholders with wanting to turn the clock back. They soon started to clamour, as people chanted at the mass demonstration organised in Budapest by the Left Wing Bloc on March 7, 1946, for 'the eviction of reactionaries from the coalition', and threatened that 'the worker's iron fist will strike where it must'. Sensing the Soviet dominated allied Control Commission in the background, the Smallholders recoiled, and expelled twenty 'reactionary' parliamentary deputies who, led by Dezső Sulyok, later established the Hungarian Liberty Party. The last operation in the communist political offensive in the course of 1946 was the dissolution, upon the pretext of security reasons after the murder of a Soviet officer, of 'reactionary associations', such as the Catholic Youth Association as well as about 1,500 others in July 1946. A new leadership took over the Boy Scout movement, until it was also abolished in 1948

Many people were worried by these developments. Cardinal Mindszenty spoke of one kind of dictatorship being replaced with another; István Bibó, who was on the way to becoming a major theorist of democracy and ethnic relations in Central Europe, wrote of the crisis of Hungarian democracy; and Szekfű, while accepting the difficult post of ambassador in Moscow, confidently warned of the possibility of a new 'age of occupation' (drawing a parallel with Ottoman times). Indeed, the slicing up of the Smallholder salami continued in early 1947, the target now being Béla Kovács, the dynamic Party Secretary with well-known anti-Communist opinions, and a close friend of the Prime Minister. The pretext was the prosecution of the so-called Hungarian Brotherhood Community, a group of conservatives whose dreaming about a political turnabout after the departure of the Soviet troops was magnified as a 'conspiracy against the republic' by the ÁVO, which did not hesitate to extort confessions that were bound to point towards the Smallholders. When the legislative refused to suspend Kovács' parliamentary immunity, on February 25, 1947 the Soviet military authorities simply arrested and abducted him to the Soviet Union upon charges of spying for western intelligence services. Another fifty member group of deputies now left the Smallholder Party (partly out of protest, and partly forced to do so). A few months later they established, with the leadership of Zoltán Pfeiffer, the Hungarian Independence Party, intended, like Sulyok's party, as a rallying ground for the conservative-bourgeois opposition. Their secession meant that the Smallholders lost their absolute majority in parliament, not to speak of the blow the whole affair dealt to the backbone of the party.

The turmoil of the first months of 1947, which concluded in the show trial and death sentences on the leaders of the Hungarian Brotherhood Community, launched a wave of emigration among the current political elite. After leftovers from the Horthy regime and besides Smallholder leaders, prominent democrats like the Social Democrat Károly Peyer, or the Peasant Party secretary Imre Kovács now augmented the ranks of Hungarian political exiles. Most importantly, Ferenc Nagy was affected, too: while on a rest cure in Switzerland, he received a telephone call on May 30, 1947, from his deputy Rákosi, informing the premier that the Soviet authorities had detected evidence of his own complicity in the 'conspiracy'. Rákosi added that the family of Nagy would be allowed to follow him into exile if he resigned from the premiership, which Nagy did. Amidst lukewarm protest by the western powers, concerned at that time with solving a critical situation in Greece which was far more important for them than Hungary, Nagy was replaced with Lajos Dinnyés, a Smallholder leader inclined to work with the Communists.

The immediate antecedents of Nagy's removal included not only a memorandum he submitted to the Soviet government, requesting the release of Kovács (which did not take place until eight years later), but also his speaking out, before his departure to Switzerland, against the abolition of private property in general, and the planned nationalisation of the great banks and industrial companies in particular. There had been state-managed companies in Hungary before the war, and there was a rough consensus among the coalition parties that coal mines and perhaps a few industrial mammoths should be added. However, this was not the same as the Communists' idea of economic management. The institutional background to the implementation of the Communists' views on the economy arose in January 1946 with the creation of the Supreme Economic Council, which was able to circumvent the economic ministry (not in communist hands) by its being empowered to grant loans, distribute raw materials and intervene in the decision-making processes of large companies. The workers' committees in the large factories were increasingly infiltrated by the Communists, and had a growing influence on determining wages and prices. Arresting the inflation, of course, was another occasion to demand and justify greater state intervention in economic affairs. The replacement of the pengő with the forint (reviving the medieval florin) on August 1, 1946, was followed by a programme of austerity aimed at stabilising prices and creating confidence in the new currency, with the agrarian sector suffering discrimination in the course of establishing the new prices. The forint became stable, although it was not accepted as convertible in the international money market; the government was also able to achieve the minimal goal of raising the workers' real wages to about 50 per cent of their pre-war value. The nationalisation of coal mines, on July 26, 1946, also met with little objection. This was followed by taking five large industrial companies (the Ganz Electricity and Machine Works, the Weiss Metal Works, the Rimamurány Iron Works and the Győr Wagon and Metal Works) into state ownership on December 1, 1946. As a result, the proportion of state-employed industrial workers increased to 43 per cent, which was already more than what most Smallholders found acceptable. Nevertheless, more was to come, as predicted by the resolution of the third congress of the Hungarian Communist Party in October 1946, demanding the preparation and the implementation of a three-year plan.

That only happened after the removal of Nagy. The last important act of the government while he was still in office was the signing of the Paris Peace Treaty on February 10, 1947. The outcome of the war made it obvious that there was little Hungary could hope from the peace conference as regarded the border question. Whereas the Smallholders and the Peasant Party thought that some modification of the terms of Trianon on ethnic lines could be possible, the two workers' parties considered even this unrealistic. On the other hand, all of the coalition parties agreed that maintaining cultural and economic ties with the Hungarian minorities in the neighbouring countries, securing their rights and even, as the Smallholders urged, territorial autonomy for the Hungarian 'enclaves', was a major task of Hungarian foreign policy.

During the final stages and shortly after the war, these minorities were exposed to maltreatment that vied with those suffered by the Slovaks, Romanians and Serbs in the territories re-annexed by Hungary a few years earlier. In the autumn of 1944, the Serbs paid back in kind for the massacre of Újvidék, and the Hungarians of the Szekel area in Transylvania did not fare better in the face of the returning Romanian forces. Over 200,000 Hungarians escaped to Hungary from these two countries before their nationalities policy was for a short while consolidated in Romania under the administration of Petru Groza, and in Yugoslavia more lastingly under Josip Broz Tito. Hungarian educational facilities (including the Bolyai University in Kolozsvár/Cluj) and theatres were opened, journals and cultural associations were (re-)launched, although later several of them were gradually dissolved in Romania, where the Hungarians were also discriminated against in executing the land reform. The closing down of their schools and cultural institutions was also the major complaint of the nearly 40,000 Hungarians who left Czechoslovakia even before President Beneš submitted the plan of inflicting collective punishment on the Hungarians, as was the case everywhere in Central and Eastern Europe with the Germans on account of their serving as a 'fifth column' for Hitler. As the great powers objected to the forced resettlement of the whole Hungarian minority, a population exchange agreement was signed between the Czechoslovak and the Hungarian governments in February 1946, which eventually concerned 70,000 Hungarians evicted in return for about as many Slovak volunteers from Hungary. Many of the Hungarian refugees occupied the places of those 185,000 Germans who had to leave Hungary in accordance with the terms of the same policy dictated by the Allied Control Commission. The large scale migration of peoples in Central Europe after the Second World War thus greatly affected Hungary in one way or another, making it vulnerable to inter-national acrimony in a region now increasingly dominated by an ideology of internationalism.

As regards the territorial issue, a Hungarian peace delegation visited the allied capitals during 1946 with proposals of modest readjustments of the Trianon borders, and requesting autonomy for the Szekel area in Transylvania. None of these were granted in the peace treaty. In relation to Czechoslovakia, the western powers were not in a position, after Munich, to insist even on the ethnic principle; whereas the Soviets, who did not intend to cede Bessarabia, found it important to appease Romania with the whole of Transylvania. Hungary was confined within the Trianon borders again, even with a few additional villages surrendered to Czechoslovakia. This outcome, which showed that not only the historic frontiers, but also an equitable settlement was unattainable, caused much bitterness, but one of a resigned, sobering kind, nothing like the hysterical repudiation a quarter of a century earlier. Besides other clauses of the treaty, which limited the Hungarian army and concerned the reparations and the dissolution of fascist organisations, there was one which apparently favoured Hungary by stipulating the withdrawal of allied armed forces from Hungary within three months of the ratification of the treaty. However, the addition that the Soviet Union was entitled to maintain forces needed to secure the communication with its occupation zone in Austria, effectively annulled this promise.

It was in the shadow of Soviet arms that the country was preparing for general elections again in the summer of 1947, when the Communists intended to exploit the situation that arose as a result of the disarray of their main rival for gaining a majority in the legislature. During these preparations, two events clearly indicated the politicisation of economic issues and the economic significance of political decisions. Upon pressure from Moscow, on July 10 the Hungarian government announced its abstention from the conference that was discussing the Marshall Plan for the post-war reconstruction of Europe, which, as Stalin realised, was an attempt of the United States to counter the Soviet military and political dominance over Central and South-Eastern Europe by economic machinations. Slightly earlier, a State Planning Office was created, the three-year plan as urged by the Communists in the previous year was enacted, and on August 1 its implementation began. After these further steps away from the western democracies and towards a Soviet type system, the elections were held on August 31, on the basis of a new electoral law pushed through by the Communists, which excluded about half a million people from the vote on grounds of political unreliability. In order further to guarantee success, the elections were severely rigged by the Communists, who nevertheless managed to increase their share in the votes to a mere 22 per cent, and even with the other parties of the Left Wing Bloc it did not attain absolute majority. Though the demoralised Smallholders only scored 15 per cent, the groups that had seceded from them did well: the Democratic People's Party of István Barankovics came second at the elections, and Pfeiffer's Independence Party did not lag far behind the Social Democrats. However, the left wing of the Smallholders thwarted a coalition initiative from the two main opposition parties, and the old coalition remained, with the manageable Dinnyés kept by the Communists at the head and dutiful communist sympathisers from the other parties at ministerial posts of the government for the sake of preserving the parliamentary facade.

That facade turned out to be completely redundant very soon thereafter. With the announcement of the Marshall Plan and Moscow's decision to keep the countries in its sphere of interest away from implementing and benefiting from it, the Cold War was in full swing, and Stalin abandoned the gradual approach to the communist seizure of power in the region. He explained the new directives to the representatives of the Communist parties concerned at the statutory meeting of the Information Bureau of Communist Parties (Cominform) at the end of September 1947, a few days after the Dinnyés government had been formed. Events in Hungary, as well as in the neighbouring countries, gained momentum: within a year and a half only the memory of the coalition remained and the Communists wielded exclusive power, rendering the period 1944 –1947 a short democratic interlude.

The 'salami tactics' now continued at accelerated pace. No more show trials were needed, intimidation was at this stage always sufficient to realise communist goals. Of the opposition parties, in view of the demise of the Smallholder Party and the communist charges against its leader Dezső Sulyok who went into exile, the Hungarian Liberty Party dissolved itself even before the elections. The pattern repeated itself in October 1947, when, oddly enough in the given circumstances, the Hungarian Independence Party was accused of electoral rigging, and its deputies were deprived of their mandates; to avoid arrest, its leader Zoltán Pfeiffer also emigrated, and the party was banned on November 20. The Democratic People's Party grew increasingly passive. As regards the Smallholders, after the departure of Nagy they ceased in effect to operate as a party and were easy to keep under control, especially after even Dinnyés was replaced by the radical István Dobi at the end of 1948. By that time Tildy had also been shelved: the President was made to resign and taken into custody after charges of corruption and espionage against his son-in-law (later executed) had been revealed in July 1948.

Tildy's replacement as nominal head of state was Árpád Szakasits, who had already proved his compliance with Communist strategies by agreeing to the merger of the two workers' parties, or rather the absorption of the left wing of the Social Democratic Party into the Communist Party. This took place – after some leading opponents of the move, like Károly Peyer, had been forced to emigrate, and others, like Anna Kéthly and tens of thousands of common members, expelled from the party – on June 12, 1948, and was immediately followed by the first congress of the now 1.1 million strong Hungarian Workers' Party. Szakasits was rewarded for his services by being raised to the completely meaningless post of party president; real authority was in the hand of Rákosi as General Secretary, with another Muscovite, Mihály Farkas, the left-wing Social Democrat György Marosán and Kádár serving as his deputies. In its programme, the party pledged itself to the Marxist-Leninist ideology and to the building of socialism through a continuing struggle for the removal of 'reactionaries' from the public scene, friendship and cooperation with the Soviet Union and the other people's democracies, further nationalisations and comprehensive economic planning. 1948 became remembered as 'the year of the turning point'.

By this time, major battles had been won by the Communists in the war for minds, that is, the struggle for dominance over the network of education and cultural life in general, by transforming their structure and content. As in the political and economic spheres, here, too, the destruction caused by the war, the desire to create something out of nothing and the vacuum which could be penetrated, favoured the most tightly organised force on the scene: the damage caused in school buildings, on educational and research equipment, library holdings and public collections by the warfare or by German and Soviet pillage was matched by the number of casualties of war among teachers and intellectuals, especially writers, who fell victim to the Holocaust by the dozens. However, as the circumstances bred a defiant optimism, and the initial Communist strategy of gradual take-over asserted itself here, too, the cultural scene was at the outset also characterised by a 'coalition' of forces committed apparently without exception to the values of liberty, democracy and to abolishing old cultural and educational monopolies without creating new ones. The first National Council for Public Education, created in April 1945 and chaired by Albert Szent-Györgyi, included members as diverse in their orientations as Gyula Szekfű, Zoltán Kodály, Péter Veres and Béni Ferenczy. Its main initiative was the transition to the eight-year elementary school system (already proposed in 1940) which, besides skills in literacy and arithmetic, also made the acquisition of fundamental knowledge in the social and natural sciences possible. In the new curricula of the former, material reflecting conservative and nationalist predilections was replaced by the so-called 'progressive tradition', sometimes arbitrarily chopping up the *oeuvre* of figures associated with it. The transition to the new system was completed by the end of the 1940s, although true improvement in the quality of education was as yet hindered by the fact that over half of the schools were still undivided and that, despite intensive re-training, 70 per cent of the teachers did not have the qualification to teach special subjects. At higher levels of education, the first and liberating experience was the opening of the gates, especially at the university level, where admission became free and the number of students suddenly doubled, to the advantage of the strata hitherto excluded. As a matter of fact, this could not but adversely affect the standards of education, similarly to the adult education schemes launched to re-train workers and peasants as loyal cadres of the regime of people's democracy. Another vehicle of rapid change in the professional elite was the Alliance of People's Colleges, which helped several thousand of young people of humble origin to gain access to education, including major figures of the Hungarian cultural and intellectual scene of subsequent decades (at least one of them, the film director Miklós Jancsó rising to international renown).

In this very short initial period, when the exhilaration, excitement and hope of the end of the war had not yet turned to apathy and despair, the cultural scene was still vibrant with a vigorous and colourful press in which all of the trends that survived the war-time crucible represented themselves with excellent periodicals; with applauded theatrical and musical performances and a host of films representing the highest standards of the international cinema industry. However, the debates over aesthetic and ideological issues related to literature and culture, invariably initiated by the circle of Lukács, the Communist supreme judge on such matters, among the particular political circumstances increasingly took the shape of a witch hunt against the 'apolitical' or 'decadent' representatives of the tradition of *Nyugat*, or the 'populist' writers who were charged with rightist inclinations and not standing close enough to the people. The Hungarian Academy of Sciences was also denounced by Lukács, as early as at the party congress of October 1946, as the 'stronghold of reaction', and the removal and destruction of several thousand volumes of 'fascist, anti-Soviet and chauvinist literature' from its library by the political police a few months later bade ill for the future. As in politics, 1948 became the 'year of the turning point' in the cultural status quo, when the winding up of the non-communist press started, and the Communists scored perhaps their most important success in the *Kulturkampf* against its most formidable rival, the Catholic Church, with the establishment of state control over ecclesiastical schools. The introduction of the eight-year elementary school and the nationalisation of textbook publishing had already evoked violent protests especially among the largest and most hierarchically organised clergy. Pastoral letters, sermons and demonstrations denouncing the planned nationalisation of schools were all in vain: parliament enacted the measure on June 16, 1948. It concerned about 6,500 schools, about half of them being in Catholic hands.

In a similar manner to the 'nationalisation' of education and culture, state ownership indeed became near-complete in the industrial sector by the end of this 'year of the turning point', as 1948 became remembered, quite rightly, thereafter. The nationalisation of the large banks and the companies controlled by them, which was the ultimate test of the Smallholder Party, was enacted on September 29, 1947. The bauxite and aluminium industry followed two months later; on March 25, 1948, all industrial firms employing more than 100 workers were taken into state property by a decree prepared in great secrecy and taking even the newly appointed 'worker directors' by surprise. In the case of some joint ventures, most notably the Hungarian-American Oil Company and the British Standard Electricity Company, show trials upon charges of espionage and sabotage against managers and engineers gave more weight to the measure. By the time of the complete Communist takeover, over 80 per cent of the industrial sector was in state management in Hungary.

As regards agriculture, the earlier, gradualist approach was also abandoned by the Communists in the summer of 1948. Although the organisation of co-operative farms was their long term goal from the outset, they realised, especially in the light of their own experience in 1919, that the sympathy of the peasantry depended on land reform, and therefore they supported it, in the most radical form possible. Even in early 1948, a long and gradual transition to co-operative farming was foreseen, but in view of the June resolution of the Cominform, which censured the Yugoslav party because of its 'indulgent' attitude to the peasant issue, Rákosi also urged the speeding up of the process, setting aside a few years to its accomplishment.

Finally, not surprisingly, Hungary's foreign economic relations underwent a profound transformation during the post-war years. The Soviet Union took over Germany's place as its foremost foreign trade partner, accounting for a quarter of exports and imports by 1949, a process sealed by the signing of a treaty of friendship and mutual aid between Hungary and the Soviet Union on February 18, 1948, and the upgrading of similar, rather exploitative bilateral treaties between the latter and other countries of the region into an entire network of exchange through the creation of the Council of Mutual Economic Aid (COME-CON) on January 20, 1949. Besides, after the initial depredation, and as their grip on Hungary became ever firmer, the Soviets realised that they could save the expenses of dismantling, transporting and reinstalling equipment, and, in addition, use Hungarian labour while exerting greater control over the country's domestic economy, by creating or re-organising companies of key importance (shipping and air transport, bauxite exploitation and aluminium production, oil extraction and re-finement) as mixed concerns.

The three-year economic plan, whose task was bringing reconstruc-tion to completion (meaning the restoration of pre-war production lev-els), was accomplished, ahead of schedule, by the end of 1949. One of the priorities was the overhaul of the transport infrastructure. The num-ber of railway engines and rolling stock rose slightly above 1938 levels, and motorised traffic grew threefold; the building of Ferihegy Airport outside Budapest, begun during the war, was also completed. Huge in-vestments, in view of the rapid escalation of the Cold War, were pumped into enhancing industrial output, especially in heavy industry which was of the main strategic importance. Plan targets in that branch were considerably exceeded, at the expense of agriculture, which suf-fered from low investment, in spite of the fact that its share in the na-tional income was the same as that of industry. The entirely unreason-able project of transforming Hungary, whose mineral resources are in-significant, into 'a country of iron and steel', began during the three-year plan. One of the corollary effects of this imbalance was that, while the population in general was satisfied with the modest increase of living standards when compared to the appalling conditions of 1945, the plan target of surpassing pre-war consumption levels was unrealistic.

Another cherished plan of the Communists, that of the systematic remoulding of the fabric of society, was also under way, as a result of the combined effect of political offensive and economic initiative. While the mobility between the main sectors of the economy was as yet insignifi-cant, the project of social levelling advanced into an intermediate stage between the extreme polarisation that characterised the pre-war status quo and the ultimate communist ideal of classless society with no pri-vate property – a stage which was not against the wishes of very broad segments of the population. As a result of the land reform, the nationali-sations and the politically motivated mass removal of officials from their posts, 'genteel' Hungary, that peculiar amalgam of post-feudal, capitalist and bureaucratic structures of social dominance and systems of values, sank into oblivion (or, as Rákosi claimed triumphantly, 'was thrown into the dustbin of history'). The magnates, the capitalists and the Christian middle classes, on whose increasingly conflict-ridden alliance that world had rested, either emigrated and carved out a new existence for themselves in Western Europe or overseas, or attempted to do the same among far more adverse circumstances in Hungary, holding jobs in the service industries, becoming engineers, mechanics, even factory workers or shepherds. These strata not only lost their political influence, but ceased to exist as social classes, also shown by the fact that their share in the national income, formerly over 40 per cent, dropped to around 10 per cent, roughly the proportion they represented in the population. On the other extreme, the mass of rural paupers became elevated to the status of small proprietors, who determined, for a brief period, the face of Hungarian society. After the 'year of the turning point', however, in vain did they hope that this status quo would be consolidated in the face of the Communist offensive to 'intensify class struggle' – the Newspeak term for the strategy of creating a Soviet-type totalitarian state.

2. The Fifties: Stalinism, the 'new course' and the 1956 Revolution

Similarly to its national socialist and fascist counterparts, communist totalitarianism was more than mere dictatorship: it served as a comprehensive idea and practice of social and political organisation. Unlike Nazism and fascism, while also repudiating much that it considered as decadent in modern western civilisation, it claimed to be the ultimate fulfilment of all that was 'progressive', if not properly understood, within it. 'Democracy' is a case in point: the adjective 'socialist' was added to it, to distinguish it from the liberal version – leading to the ironic saying that was in high currency in the Hungarian 'secondary public sphere' from the 1970s on, which suggested that 'socialist' was in effect a privative suffix. Nevertheless, the pivotal idea in communist totalitarianism, quite similarly to nationalism, was that the individual is *only* capable of self-realisation as a member of the community, with the emphasis shifted from nation to class as the community in question, and with the amplification of the consciousness that the relationship of individuals to the community and each other is interpreted and determined by a self-styled vanguard of superior illumination: the Party possesses the most profound knowledge of one's merits and shortcomings, desires, even instincts. As a result, it was claimed that spontaneous social relations were to be thwarted, citizens isolated from each other and tied directly to an institutional framework created by the supposed depositories of ultimate wisdom, ostensibly expressing and answering the needs of the whole. To attain this goal, explicit identification with the established order and full conformity with an official ideology was required, and any criticism of partial aspects of the Brave New World was stigmatised and punished as complete subversion. Therefore, a network for the comprehensive surveillance to detect, and of coercion to provide against 'deviance' from the standards in all areas of life considered by the current notions of the despised 'West' as private (morals, economic, professional and intellectual pursuits). It was a messianic system which drew strength from vigorous proselytisation and occasionally purged itself from heterodox elements through rituals of self-criticism and excommunication, even inquisition and *auto-da-fés*. Failures in the system (which, deriving from its nature, were many) were blamed on the invisible evil, the internal or external 'enemy', and the need to struggle against it supplied a further pretext for vigilance and repression.

It is generally known how, and with what consequences, this vision was put in the Soviet Russia of the 1920s and 1930s into the service of preserving international competitiveness through the consolidation of the state under party rule and investing it with the task of marshalling a modernisation process that was lagging far behind its main rivals, thus jeopardising the great power status of the empire. That effort was successful, inasmuch as in the final stages and the aftermath of the Second World War Stalin managed to exploit the resources accumulated with unprecedented ruthlessness for extending the boundaries of the empire and for putting even the belt of states that was, in the interwar period, meant to contain Bolshevik contamination, to subjection. The recipe of étatism-*cum*-party rule was exported to them, too, notwithstanding the fact that these societies had in the past centuries developed strategies for closing the perceived gap between the advanced countries and themselves that were markedly different from the one now foisted on them. Besides the establishment of monolithic party rule in the state and the whole social organism, the circumstances of the post-war changes in Hungary and elsewhere in the region also made the uncritical adulation, indeed the profession of the principles serving as the basis of, and distilled from, Soviet experience as dogma, inevitable. National peculiarities were represented as irrelevant and the national interest was sacrificed by local leaders whose loyalty arising from past indebtedness, present status and fears from a future always unpredictable in despotic systems, led them to display unhesitating subservience to the Soviet Communist Party in general and to Stalin in particular.

After the 'year of the turning point', it only remained for the Hungarian Communists to execute some cosmetic surgery on the face of the system to invest their *de facto* rule with the paraphernalia of constitutionality. As a means of completely eliminating the remnants of the multi-party system, the Independence Front of 1944 was revived under the name Hungarian Independence-Popular Front on February 1, 1949. The rumps of the remaining parties, largely consisting by now of Communist fellow travellers, merged in it with the Hungarian Workers' Party and undertook to submit to the decisions of its national board led by Rákosi as President, Dobi and Erdei as deputies and Rajk as General Secretary. They also pledged themselves to the construction of socialism, acknowledging the leading role of the HWP in that process. Those who espoused other programmes were denounced as enemies of the Hungarian people, rather than any sort of 'loyal opposition'. The member organisations of the Popular Front agreed to put forward a common list for the general elections, which were held after its local organisations had been created, on May 15, 1949. Predictably, 96 per cent of the electors voted for the candidates of the Popular Front, of whom 71 per cent belonged to the HWP. Roughly the same was the proportion of workers and peasants among the deputies of the new legislature, further illustrating the triumph of the dictatorship of the proletariat.

Shortly after the creation of the Popular Front, organised opponents of monolithic communist rule either evaporated or were forced into compliance through repression. Within a week, Barankovics emigrated, the Democratic People's Party dissolved itself, and Cardinal Mindszenty was brought to court upon fabricated charges of espionage and subversion. Having struck at the two foundations of the influence of the Church, landed property and the education of youth, the Communists had early on evoked the wrath of the militant prelate who, with his stubborn defence of both the religious liberty and many anachronistic privileges of the Church, in turn became the target of a coarse campaign as the head of 'clerical reaction' from 1947 on. His sentencing to life imprisonment on the basis of an extorted confession and in spite of all evidence did not abruptly break the influence of the Church among is adherents, but its resisting power considerably decreased, especially as on September 5, 1949 obligatory religious instruction was abolished, and the circumstances did not encourage parents to send their children to optional classes: by 1952, only a quarter of elementary school pupils took them.

The collection of all sorts of data in order to fabricate evidence against a growing number of individuals on account of their actual, potential or alleged hostility to democracy (in fact, Sovietisation) and extorting confessions from them, had been the standard practice of the political police (the ÁVO, from September 1948 renamed as the State Security Authority, ÁVH) since its inception, but the victims of show trials were opponents outside the Communist Party. After the elimination of the extra-party opposition, they became, as in the Soviet model, a de-

vice to combine the removal of rivals within the party with the maintenance of an atmosphere in which vigilance and terror seemed justified.
As, after a decade-long interval, a large-scale showdown took place in
the Soviet Communist Party at the end of 1948, Rákosi, true to his by-
name 'Stalin's best Hungarian disciple', faithfully followed the master.
The bitter conflict between the Yugoslavia of Marshall Tito and the Soviet Union, largely because the latter rightly perceived the former's independent policies *vis-à-vis* its neighbours in the Balkans as a threat to
Soviet hegemony, provided an occasion for a show of loyalty to Moscow while getting rid of a supposed rival. The person concerned, László
Rajk, was an ideal candidate for the role of the accused: his former ardent ruthlessness as Minister of Interior amplified the 'astonishment effect' of the case, which was to convince people of the need for an iron
fist, and the fact that Rajk had worked in the western communist movement before the war lent some plausibility to the fantastic allegations
that he was an imperialist agent now collaborating with the excommunicated Yugoslavs. True to the role in which he was cast, and convinced
by Kádár and Farkas that the class enemy must be intimidated and after
all he would not be harmed, Rajk made the confession expected from
him. The charges against Rajk were made public in June 1949. In October, he was executed along with two 'accomplices'; many others accused in the case were put to death, jailed or interned later, opening a
series of purges in the party (afflicting mainly the non-Muscovites) and
institutionalised terror against citizens outside the party that would last
until 1953.

By that time, the country had a new constitution, modelled after the
one Stalin gave the peoples of the Soviet Union in 1936. Hungary became a 'people's republic' established on the idea of popular sovereignty, the sovereign rights being exercised by the parliament, to which
the executive was responsible, while justice was administered by independent courts. While the separation of powers was thus apparently
maintained, the nature of the institutional framework and its operational
procedures effectively annulled it; even more importantly, the role of
the state organs was at all levels confined to the practical management
of affairs, while general guidance and control remained in the hands of
the party elite. General elections were to be held on the basis of universal suffrage every four years, but their significance was merely propaganda in favour of the regime: the few token non-party members could
only be returned to parliament on the goodwill of the Hungarian Workers' Party and its successor, and even when multiple candidacy was introduced after 1966, all candidates were put forward by the Popular
Front to whose programme they had to subscribe. Hence the marvel-
lously satisfactory electoral statistics, which for four decades tended to

repeat the outcome of May 1949. Next, by stipulating merely two short sessions of parliament per year, the constitution minimised its legislative role and made it a rubber-stamp body authorising the statutes issued by the twenty-one member Presidium. The latter was a collective head of state exercising extensive legislative functions. The independence of courts of justice and the rights of the citizen were mentioned in the constitution, without being very specific about them and without guarantees. Municipal administration was reorganised into a network of soviets on the village, district, town and county level, with the remnants of local autonomy raised from the level of villages to that of districts, whose supervision was less problematic. The key office holders of the soviets were not elected by their members, but appointed from above on the basis of strict political reliability. Municipal elections being based on similar procedures to the national ones, the results were invariably similar, too.

The majority of the over 200,000 members of the soviets elected in 1950 were new to their posts and thus lacked any experience, similarly to other officials in a new civilian bureaucracy and a military also augmented to a strength of 200,000 (300,000 when the air force and the ÁVH is added), in which the expertise of the increasingly neglected old officer corps was supplemented by Soviet advisors. In the civilian sphere, the same role of providing 'comradely advice' belonged to the functionaries of the party apparatus, whose structure replicated that of the state administration. About 40,000 people worked in the factory, village, district and county party committees, headed by secretaries receiving directives from the central party organs and communicating them to the corresponding officials of the administrative apparatus.

Formally, true to the principle of 'socialist democracy', the chief policy-making forum of the party was the congress, held triennially. In fact, the meetings of its thousand-or-so deputies were highly ceremonial occasions for approving the reports and the directives put forward by the party leadership, with carefully orchestrated demonstrations of loyalty to the party line, the saving of appearances by sporadic 'constructive criticism', and storms of applause, especially upon the mentioning of the names of Stalin and Rákosi. As regards the actual shaping of policies, even the seventy-one member Central Committee of the party was dwarfed in significance by the Political Committee, which met every week; even within this body, the 'Muscovites' formed an inner circle; even within that inner circle, the 'triumvirate' of Rákosi, Gerő and Farkas (sometimes supplemented by Révai into a 'quartet') emerged, thanks to their most immediate ties with Moscow and their consequent knowledge of the current strategy of the Soviet leadership, which was the ultimate source of decisions affecting Hungary; and even within the triumvirate, Rákosi, the General Secretary of the party and later also the Chairman of the Popular Front, stood above all others in the hierarchy and was surrounded by a personality cult of astonishing dimensions, unparalleled even in the Communist bloc of the time except in the Soviet Union.

The elite of the state-party thus had a firm grip on the organs of the party-state. As a precaution to maintain this status quo the mechanism of terror and indoctrination, whose foundations had been laid down during the post-war coalition years and was meant to ensure the infiltration of the cells of society by party influence, was further refined and set into full motion after 1949. The dimensions and the cruelty of the terror are hardly comprehensible, though it can be explained to some extent by a number of factors whose coincidence amplified the effect of each of them. Especially against the background of the policy of seclusion initiated by the Soviet Union as a Cold War strategy, there was an inevitable drive to cast the blame for the failures and shortcomings of the regime on enemies and traitors; and the vigilance psychosis was an instrument of heightening an atmosphere of insecurity in which everyone felt dependent on the goodwill of unpredictable superiors. Due to their subordination to the Kremlin, those at the top of the hierarchy were no exception to the rule, and in many cases their anxiousness to prove their loyalty to the communist cause made them *anticipate*, in a rather exaggerated fashion, what Moscow expected them to do.

The main organ of repression, the ÁVH, was in 1950 separated from the Ministry of the Interior and put directly under the authority, first, of the council of ministers, and then of the Defence Committee – the body in which the 'triumvirate' institutionalised its special status after the outbreak of the Korean War. Its permanent staff originally consisted of 28,000 officers, striking at individuals or refractory groups or rivals of the leaders upon direct orders from the latter, and based on 'evidence' collected by about 40,000 informers also employed by the political police. Records were kept on about one million citizens, that is, over 10 per cent of the population including the infants and the old.

There were two main thrusts of the terror: it was intended to eliminate enemies in class warfare, alleged to be ever more intensive, and to purge the party itself from impure elements who had supposedly infiltrated its ranks. Even apart from the terror, after the merger of the two workers' parties a large scale screening – resulting in a massive exercise of the communist ritual of penitence, voluntary self-criticism in the presence of a full meeting of the local party organisation – diminished the membership of the party by about 350,000, expelling mainly former Social Democrats, who were still resented because of their 1921 pact with the Horthy regime, and 'petty bourgeois elements'. After the showdown with the 'nationalist deviants' or 'the hirelings of Tito' in the Rajk case, the Social Democrats (including leaders like Szakasits and Marosán) were the suffering party in the next wave of show trials in 1950, followed by 'home-grown Communists' like Kádár in the course of 1951 and 1952. The completely unfounded charges included collaboration with the police of Horthy in inter-war times, and espionage for Britain and the United States thereafter. By 1953, the tide even reached such experts of the operation of the very system of repression like Gábor Péter, the first chief of the political police. About eighty leading party members were executed, tortured to death or committed suicide in consequence of these prosecutions, and the number of other zealous Communists who served prison terms was in the thousands.

However, the case was far more than just the revolution devouring its own children. Of the one million citizens on the files of the authorities, around 650,000 were prosecuted and nearly 400,000 received sentences to be served in prisons, internment or labour camps, mostly quarries and mines. There were about one hundred of these, with an aggregate capacity of over 40,000, exploited to the full. In addition, without any legal procedure 13,000 'class enemies' (aristocrats, former officers and officials, factory owners etc.) from Budapest and an additional 3,000 from provincial towns were evicted from their homes with a minimum of posessions and resettled to rural areas where they were compelled to do agricultural labour under strict supervision. The official justification was, of course, their unreliability at a time of 'imperialist incitement' and the 'sharpening of class struggle on the international scene'; in reality, their removal was a means of satisfying the demand for suitable housing for the new bureaucratic class.

These shocking figures not only demonstrate the supreme inhumanity of the regime, but also serve to represent what was behind it: its dehumanising effect, poisoning private relationships, breaking consciences and eroding public commitments. In an atmosphere marked by such figures, it is easy to imagine how varying degrees of mistrust pervaded the relations of individuals, if not necessarily in their families and with intimate friends, surely with colleagues, neighbours, fellow members of a sport club or choir and virtually everyone in everyday intercourse. Sudden disappearances from one's immediate environment bred doubts and fears concerning the regime; the resulting uneasiness fuelled a repressed hatred of it, while the same fear prompted the public display of conformity, even solidarity with it; the consequent crisis of self-respect only increasing the bitterness. The fact that the people's democracy, acting on behalf of the people, committed the most horrendous crimes against the people, with none of the people daring to ask any questions, also deepened that bitterness, which was in salient contradiction with the officially disseminated image of the new order as the fulfilment of what was noblest in humanity. Finally, the gap between the official proclamation of the highest form of democracy and the reality of helplessness against the obvious violations of its principles made people apolitical in a highly politicised age, and turned them away from civic commitments amidst pretentious public assertions of the primacy of values associated with the community.

A complete remoulding of the public self was also the main mission of educational and cultural policies. The most important steps towards doctrinal monopoly had been taken by the Communists through the nationalisation of denominational schools and the abolition of obligatory religious instruction. Nevertheless, further measures aimed at minimising church influence, which as they correctly reckoned was still considerable, and compelling the clergy to fall into line. First, they were required to take an oath of allegiance to the new constitution, and upon refusal to do so by the Catholic higher clergy a new offensive was launched against the 'fifth column of imperialism' (an alternative shorthand amounting the same as 'clerical reaction'). With the mediation of compliant churchmen who spoke out against the 'Cold War policies' of the Papacy and became known on that account as 'peace priests', József Grősz, Archbishop of Kalocsa and next in rank to Mindszenty, was persuaded to sign an agreement in August 1950, acknowledging the political order of the Hungarian People's Republic, and undertaking to refrain from exploiting religious sentiments for the purposes of subversion. Monastic orders were dissolved, except the remnants of one female and three male orders teaching in the few secondary schools exempted from the nationalisation. Most of the bishops still being reluctant to take the oath, Grősz and a few further victims of yet another show trial were jailed in June 1951, and the newly created State Office of Ecclesiastical Affairs acquired the right to supervise investitures and removals from office and church life in general through ministerial commissioners. What remained thereafter was passive resistance on the part of some of the clergy to the governance of the 'peace priests' invested.

Even before the elimination of the autonomy of the Churches, that of another key institution of intellectual life, the Hungarian Academy of Sciences, was also destroyed. After the earlier harassment and infringements, a small minority of the members passed new statutes in October 1949, changing the number and composition of departments, and halving the membership. The goal was clearly to create a docile body purged of politically difficult elements: three-quarters of those removed were pre–1945 members, and the representation of the social sciences, considered as more intractable, was lowered to one-third both in terms of members and departments. Subscription to the tenets of Marxism-

Leninism became the fundamental criterion to decide whether established academics could retain their titles, and others could obtain ones, in the newly introduced Soviet model of ranking.

To ensure the hegemony of the Marxist-Leninist ideology in society at large was the all-pervasive endeavour of educational and cultural policies of the new regime, while the considerable investment in indoctrination, though lagging far behind, for instance, military expenditure, brought about significant quantitative changes in these areas. In 1954, apart from the participants of night courses, the number of secondary school pupils (130,000) was nearly double that of the highest pre-war figures, and three times as many students (33,000) went to universities, including several newly established ones. Through militantly pursued affirmative action, generating new tensions even in adolescent society, the proportion of young people of peasant and working class origin, formerly barred from higher education, swiftly rose to above 50 per cent. Besides the adverse effect which the numerical growth exerted on the student-professor ratio, other factors also combined to undermine earlier standards, as a result of which masses of half-educated intellectuals were trained in the period. Adult education, aiming to replace the old middle class with a new one consisting of 'vanguard workers' retrained as managers, foremen or executives, confirmed this tendency; what is more, the subjects of this effort themselves often collapsed under the pressure of their new tasks and identities.

The universal goal of educating the youth in a spirit that would qualify it for success in the building of socialism by inculcating the values of Marxism-Leninism and safeguarding it against the influence of reactionary, idealist and clerical views, was emphasised at all levels in the new curricula. To satisfy this requirement, the whole gamut of textbooks was changed, new ones being commissioned and completed under careful supervision by the relevant party organs and, especially in higher education, supplemented with brochures translated from Russian (meant to make up for the expulsion of proper specialised literature from reading lists). The teaching of foreign languages was confined to Russian, which, however, became compulsory from the fifth form of the primary school in spite of the lack of such a tradition and the scarcity of qualified teachers. Departments of Marxism-Leninism were created at universities and colleges to bring the gospel to students of all subjects, while a host of professors who were likely to deviate from it were removed. The ultimate sanctuary of branches of sciences like dialectical and historical materialism, or the history of the Soviet and Hungarian Communist Parties, was, of course, the party high school, where the elect few were prepared for careers as highly placed and reliable cadres.

The party reached out for the young in the shape of opportunities for extra-curricular activity which carefully steered them along the desired path while providing enjoyable recreational activities: camping, hiking, sports tournaments, or fun on the 'Railway of Pioneers'. The Pioneer Movement was launched in 1946 upon the Soviet model to provide an alternative, and later the replacement, to the Boy Scout Movement for the generation under 14, while for the over–14s the same role was played by the Alliance of Working Youth, founded in 1950. The mission of both organisations was to raise a healthy and optimistic youth capable of coping with the difficulties involved in the building of socialism. For similar reasons, mass sport was greatly encouraged, with half a million participants each year at the national tournaments of the 'Ready for Work and Fight' movement. As regards competitive sports, the meaning of the resounding Hungarian successes in several branches at the 1948 and 1952 Olympic Games, and the triumphal march of the 'Golden Team' of footballers in the stadiums of Europe, was quite different for the authorities and the people. From the perspective of the former, they had a huge propaganda value as testimonies of the superiority of the socialist system, and were greatly subsidised and extolled. For the people, they were some compensation for the humiliations of the recent past and some consolation for the abominable present, and occasions to express otherwise repressed national pride.

Other areas of the broad cultural sphere were highly politicised, too: it was not only through the '*Szabad Nép* sessions', the collective reading and interpretation of the articles relevant to the party line from the central HWP daily at the workplace each morning, that the ordinary citizen was daily exposed to official ideology. Public holidays, including religious ones, were nationalised and 'filled with a progressive content'. The plebeian undercurrent was emphasised in the 1848 tradition, and March 15 became the occasion to confer the Kossuth Award, the newly established highest official distinction; August 20, formerly associated with Saint Stephen, was renamed Constitution Day and marked the 'new foundation of the state'; Santa Claus transubstantiated as Father Winter, and Christmas as Pine Holiday. Cinemas and the screening halls of the rapidly proliferating 'homes of culture' played predominantly Soviet films with predictable lessons and their replicas made in the other 'friendly countries', to which the Hungarian film industry, after the promising neo-realist experiments of the post-war years and despite the availability of first class actors deserving a better lot, became assimilated. The disciples of Kodály wrote rallying and marching songs, sonatas and cantatas in praise of the new order. 'Bourgeois' classics and other 'retrograde' literature was purged from libraries and expelled from the book market, and the huge increase in the output of educational literature was largely thanks to the appearance of original texts and interpretations of the oracles of Marxism and other agitation and propaganda material in the supply. The press was homogenised; the coffee house was denounced as the vestige of a decadent bourgeois lifestyle. So were many authors for whom they once provided a second home and who were now condemned to silence – Németh, with his advocacy of the 'third way', superb lyricists of the *Nyugat* tradition like Milán Füst or Sándor Weöres, and many others. After his withdrawal from politics in contempt of the show trials, even Lukács became an object of criticism, as well as the socialist novelist Tibor Déry, whose prose was found too subtle to answer the requirements of 'socialist realism' as demanded by Révai, the new dictator of taste. Some writers conformed to the expectation of producing schematic works whose task was to extol the struggle of the masses for the triumph of socialism and inspire enthusiasm and optimism in them, and even the best of those who were allowed to publish did so occasionally or more generally; while many readers were desperately trying to decipher the clandestine meaning between the lines which they were sure was there. The same authors did produce masterpieces, which, however, remained in their drawers, just as some canvases by first class painters were hidden in studios, while other works of the same artists decorated the walls of monumental public buildings planned by equally more deserving architects.

Art and culture was supposed to reflect the heroic efforts and the successes of the working class in constructing a better world, and to inspire them to aim at ever greater heights – 'there is no limit but the stars in the sky' was a favourite slogan of Rákosi's. After the year of the turning point, the Communists had even less difficulty in bringing the nationalisation of industry and services to completion with taking the companies with more than ten employees into state property on December 28, 1949, and making the remnants of the private sector untenable, so that it became effectively confined to some repair services. The three-year plan just having been accomplished, the measure formed part of the strategy to ensure the success of the First Five-Year Plan, launched in January 1950, whose goal was to start 'laying the foundations of socialism' by accelerating socialist industrialisation and the transition to co-operative farming in the agriculture. Both projects were based on a servile imitation of the Soviet experience of the 1930s, when the (partly self-imposed) economic isolation of the Soviet Union fuelled Stalin's obsession with creating a solid heavy industrial background to modernisation, and the difficulties in reducing the countryside to obedience generated a similarly obsessive pursuit of breaking the backbone of the tightly knit village communities by a relentless transformation of property relations. The Cold War, especially in the light of the establishment of NATO in 1949 and the Korean War in 1950–1951, seemed to justify both the efforts towards economic self-sufficiency in the interest of the increase of military potential, and 'the transfer of class war to the countryside' and turning its shield against the class enemy there: the *kulak*, that is, in principle the well-to-do farmer with anything more than 40 acres, but in practice anybody whom it pleased the party to stigmatise as such on account of his being politically undesirable.

In order to transform Hungary, as the confident economic minister Gerő was fond of prognosticating, into 'a land of iron and steel' in five years, an unprecedentedly high one-quarter, possibly even one-third of the national income was re-invested, nearly half of it into heavy industry (mining, energy production, metallurgy and machine industry). As a result, its growth rate, 20 per cent annually, exceeded that of the interwar years, by 1954 its output was three times as much as in 1938, and its share in the GDP rose from over a third to over a half. To be sure, this impressive figure was considerably short of the 200 per cent aggregate growth originally targeted by the party (which, enchanted as it was by fantastic numbers, nevertheless raised it to an even more unrealistic 380 per cent in 1951). But the real shortcoming of this severely one-sided strategy of development consisted in the long-term distortions, felt even during the post-1989 transition, it caused to the economy of a country lacking the raw materials necessary to supply the branches that now devoured resources and energies. A side-effect of the same strategy was to place Hungary even more at the mercy of the Soviet Union in a period when its economic ties with the West had been completely severed, and those within the COMECON had not yet developed. At the same time, the production of light industry, which depended on raw materials that were available, stagnated and later even dropped, while the development of modern industries (electronics, precision engineering, telecommunication etc.), which needed more expertise than raw materials, had respectable traditions in the country and were undergoing great progress elsewhere, were neglected. However, Socialist Man was claimed to be capable of overcoming petty technical obstacles, and he was regimented by tens of thousands into the 'battle for coal' and the 'battle for iron' into industrial monsters like the Rákosi Metallurgical Works (earlier the Manfréd Weiss Works), or the metallurgical complex of Sztálinváros (Stalin City) and about a dozen of its likes erected within a matter of a few years together with the horrible domiciles called modern cities around them.

Regimented they were in the literal sense: the economic plan not only prescribed production levels broken down into production units (in very remote relationship with reality), but it also regulated the movement of the labour force between them to cope with the shortage of it that arose in spite of the fact that unemployment was fully eradicated during the period of the First Five Year Plan. Therefore, changing jobs without authorisation could be prosecuted as 'endangering the interests of the economic plan' (resulting in 15,000 lawsuits in 1951–1952). The artificially swollen industrial sector swallowed 120,000 formerly unemployed men and 160,000 formerly unworking women, not to speak of the large-scale constructions, which mainly attracted the roughly 350,000 who fled from the forced collectivisation of the agriculture. Yet, as the efficiency rates of industry were very low, it demanded even more hands. This was partly due to the fact that, besides the obsession with spectacular new projects, repair and renovation were neglected, which, together with the exclusive preoccupation of the planners with quantitative growth, led to an incredible amount of substandard products issuing from the hands of the Hungarian would-be model workers emulating the legendary Stakhanov in the course of Soviet-style 'labour competition'.

By the summer of 1948, when Rákosi, to use the combative language of the period, declared war on the propertied peasantry, a mere 100,000 acres had been turned in on a voluntary basis by 13,000 farmers, mainly small- and dwarfholders hoping for a more secure subsistence, into less than 500 collective farms. To improve this record, rather pathetic from the Communists' point of view, a massive campaign was launched in order to separate the peasants from their newly acquired lands in the autumn of 1949, employing a great variety of methods. Taxation, commassation and compulsory delivery were the most important ones, besides administrative and police coercion against the recalcitrant. The land tax trebled between 1949 and 1953, even apart from the extras imposed on about 70,000 peasants put on the '*kulak* list', who were also exposed to ceaseless vilification and were discriminated against in their access to public office and educational opportunities. In addition, one quarter of the arable lands of the country were subjected to commassation, that is, forcibly exchanged between the peasants and the co-operatives, ostensibly for the sake of more economical farming on the emerging contiguous large holdings of the former, invariably depriving the latter of the more fertile lands. The resulting sense of the insecurity of property led many peasants to join the co-operatives, or give up farming, but in many cases simply not investing in the cultivation of a plot which might soon belong to someone else – with adverse effects on agricultural outputs. Finally, and most importantly, peasants were obliged to deliver their produce for central distribution at prices considerably below not only the free market price, but nearly as much below the production cost as well. Failure to do so brought about a visit by the authorities and prosecution for 'endangering public supply', as occurred in about 400,000 cases when the suspect was found to be 'hoarding' stocks. The 'sweeping of the lofts' under the supervision of ÁVH officers became an everyday reality in the life of rural Hungary, especially in 1951 and 1952, when poor harvests brought tensions to a climax.

Years of bullying and repression helped the number of co-operatives increase above 5,000 with a membership of 380,000 by 1953. However, even counting the masses who left the agricultural scene, most of the peasantry still remained private cultivators, owning two-thirds of the land, the rest divided between co-operatives and state farms; the tragedy of the peasantry was also less than the success expected by the party. Most of all, the trials of the Hungarian countryside wreaked a disastrous effect on the conditions of Hungarian agriculture. The cultivated area shrank year by year; productivity rates sank as a result of the uneconomical use of machinery concentrated in special stations, inadequate fertilisation and the mass replacement of qualified agricultural experts with uneducated (or hastily trained) peasants in key positions. After a short interval, the rationing of a wide range of foodstuffs was reintroduced in Hungary in 1951.

As agricultural output was at best stagnating, the considerable increase in the per capita national income during the first five year plan thus mainly resulted from the growth of industry; and in view of the high rate of re-investment, it is not surprising that consumption and living standards were falling. The egalitarianism of the regime thus in the first place inevitably meant levelling down: the income of the new elite, such as company managers, was only twice as much as that of secondary school teachers and three to four times as much as the lowest paid simple workers – who, however, lived slightly above or below the avowed subsistence level. The latter category may have amounted to as much as 50 per cent of the population.

Similarly to other spheres, the development of social welfare policies and institutions (which were no exception from the rules of a command economy and had their own plan targets) was measured in strictly quantitative terms: an increasing number of citizens were involved in social security schemes, obtained pension, or free medical care, at lower standards. While health statistics indicated a slight general improvement, housing conditions could not keep pace with the influx of people to the new industrial centres. Rents in the housing sector, nationalised in 1952, were symbolic, but the maintenance of the buildings received as little attention as that of the industrial equipment.

To be sure, the party operated, among other things, as an immense machinery of patronage through which non-measurable benefits (mainly job promotion and its likes) could be earned; and for the members of the party bureaucracy various perquisites were available according to rank. At the top echelons, these included, among other things, living in a sumptuous villa in the Buda Hills, being driven around in one of the legendary curtained black limousines, special schools for the children, free luxury commodities from specialised shops, vacationing at exclsive holiday resorts – in salient contradiction with the professed ideal of equality and the frequent calls to ever tighter austerity in the interest of a glorious future. It was truly a society in which all were equal, except a few who were more equal than others.

Aversion of the personality cult and the ideological terror, the hatred of police repression, bewilderment at the stupidities of economic planning and anger at the anomalies it caused, and utter exasperation and disillusionment with the regime in general were sentiments occasionally expressed in strikes and perceptible across the Hungarian social spectrum by the time Stalin died on March 5, 1953. Besides sparing Hungary and the other countries of the region from the grim consequences of having to 'import' another wave of terror started in the Soviet Union in the preceding months, the ensuing power struggle and its outcome favoured important changes in the tone and methods, if not the content and substance, of the communist regimes. Of the main contenders for Stalin's inheritance, the formerly dreaded Interior Minister Lavrentii Beria and Prime Minister Georgii Malenkov urged these changes; and after the former had been shot in 1953 and the latter demoted in 1955, their rival Party Secretary Nikita Khrushchev, seconded by Anastas Mikoyan, also held up the anti-Stalinist line against Foreign Minister Molotov. The power struggle in the 'imperial centre' resulted in circuitous policies, inevitably causing immediate repercussions, mainly in the form of personnel changes, in the 'provinces', including Hungary. Nevertheless, with the permission, and indeed upon the insistence of Moscow, 'de-Stalinisation' could be started throughout the Soviet bloc.

The new rulers in the Kremlin were mainly motivated by the recognition that the armaments race required the East to make incomparably greater efforts and sacrifices than the West, which threatened domestic stability; however, the communist parties, themselves weakened by the senseless purges, would be unable to hold out in the face of growing dissatisfaction caused by terror and Soviet exploitation, unless their recognition and morale was strengthened by economic concessions aiming to raise living standards, and more autonomy. This was inconceivable without serious cutbacks on the military expenditure, which led to a modification of foreign policy doctrine: it was acknowledged that the confrontation between the 'imperialist warmongers' and the 'peace camp' was not inevitable, and 'peaceful coexistence' between them was possible. As the first intimations of the 'new course' to Rákosi, who was also Premier since 1952 and thought that things would return to 'normal' once the power struggle in the Kremlin was over, brought no change in Hungary, he was summoned to Moscow again in the middle of June 1953. In the presence of a party and state delegation, he was reprimanded in a humiliating fashion by the Soviet leaders for policies implemented in imitation of their own earlier practice and upon their own demand: the personality cult, the terror, the senseless industrialisation and the forcible collectivisation of agriculture, and the appalling living standards.

It was now the turn of Rákosi and the 'quartet' to perform the ritual of self-criticism, which they did at the session of the Central Committee of the party on June 27-28, 1953. The subsequent party resolution emphasised the damages caused by the personality cult, the violations of the principle of collective leadership and democracy within the party, and called for the redressing of the policies criticised from Moscow. As required by the Kremlin, Rákosi stepped down as Prime Minister, and was replaced by Imre Nagy, who, because of his divergent opinions on the collectivisation issue, had fallen into disfavour in 1949, and although from the following year he gradually returned into the party leadership, managed to remain untainted by the subsequent terror. The announcement of the new government programme and the demotion of Rákosi caused exhilaration except in some party circles; as regards the whole of the turn of events, there was much celebration in the countryside, while most others were torn between hope and disbelief (felt in differing proportions according to one's position); and there was great perplexity among the 'new middle class' of cadres, unable to predict whether the future changes in Moscow would favour Nagy or Rákosi, who retained the party secretaryship, in the power sharing that emerged. In any case, the government programme promised, and during its twenty-one month tenure the Nagy government implemented corrections of a significance that more than justifies the description of this period as a 'new course' or 'thaw'.

The first large set of these corrections concerned the modification of investment policies at the expense of heavy industry in the interest of restoring a healthier economic structure more suitable to Hungary's peculiarities, and especially of the production of consumer goods. Several large investment projects were cancelled altogether; dozens of measures (mainly price reductions up to 40 per cent and wage increases of an average 15 per cent) were taken in the second half of 1953 and in early 1954 to increase purchasing power. Most importantly, gestures were made towards the peasantry: delivery quotas of the different kinds of produce were lowered by 15 to 40 per cent, their sum was fixed for three years, and not only was forced collectivisation abandoned, but peasants became also free to leave the co-operatives, whose membership and landholding thus decreased by about one-third within a year. The 'thaw' was particularly perceptible in the ideological and the intellectual sphere. The atmosphere of rallies and meetings, which still continued to be the order of the day, became de-formalised: there being no longer the compulsion to chant the names of Stalin and Rákosi and pledge loyalty in various ways at regular intervals, the impression was created that real issues could be at stake. This was certainly the way the new situation was reflected in the press and literary life. In the editorial board of the party daily *Szabad Nép*, in particular, the followers of Nagy set a fresh, critical tone. Silenced writers and poets (László Németh, Sándor Weöres, Lőrinc Szabó, János Pilinszky, Miklós Mészöly, Géza Ottlik and Áron Tamási among others) could enter the literary scene again, and joined their now penitent fellows who were subservient to the regime (like Zoltán Zelk) and younger authors (László Nagy, Ferenc Juhász, Sándor Csoóri, Ferenc Sánta, István Csurka, Endre Fejes) in establishing truthfulness as the main standard. The Writers' Association and its journal *Irodalmi Újság* (Literary Journal) became important rallying points of the intelligentsia anxious further to broaden the new breathing space in which they did much to reveal the true situation of the country, and from early 1956 a debating society, the Petőfi Circle of young intellectuals, also spoke out against the abuses of the previous years and urged the renewal of socialism. For the majority of those involved in the post-1953 'revolt of the mind' were party members, faithful to the ideals to which they were genuinely converted after 1945 – ideals whose betrayal by their idolised leaders they were unable or unwilling to admit before the circumstances changed, and the disillusionment and self-censure made them all the more furious and uncompromising critics of the crimes of Stalinism. At the same time, they were convinced that these could be avoided in a communist system based on the same principles as the initiatives of Nagy.

The reign of terror was indeed mitigated as soon as Nagy took office: internment camps were wound up, the deported could return to their domiciles (though not their earlier homes) and the scope of action of the ÁVH became strictly limited. At the same time, the amnesty decrees were not general and only concerned specific groups of the victims of repression. The reconsideration of the cases of the Communist comrades defamed by the show trials started, but was an agonisingly slow process: Kádár was only released in June 1954, Rajk was not rehabilitated until November 1955, the ex-Social Democrat leaders left prison by the spring of 1956, and about two hundred out of the more than seven hundred persons concerned were only rehabilitated in 1962. They were still privileged in comparison with the non-party political convicts, who were in effect not cleared of their alleged crimes until after 1989.

Of course, there were formidable forces that were interested in this procrastination, and it is also no wonder that they became aligned behind Rákosi, whose personal responsibility (only known at that time to a narrow circle of party leaders) would have been clearly revealed by the least consistent review of the show trials. While to some extent he acknowledged this responsibility, he laid most of the blame, first, on the former ÁVH chief Gábor Péter and then, in 1956, on Farkas, while he and his clique did everything in their power to block the process of rehabilitations in particular and the implementation of the 'new course' in general. Unlike Nagy, who undertook the corrections ordained from Moscow out of genuine conviction as to their urgency and wanted to make them the pillars of a comprehensive system of reformed and humanised communism, Rákosi grudgingly chose to abide by the orders and conformed to them until he felt the situation was ripe to strike back.

The profound division of the party along these lines became quite obvious by 1954. Undeterred by the facts that Nagy was encouraged to pursue the line he had taken at a visit to Moscow in January 1954, and that his own policies were repeatedly rejected by the Kremlin, Rákosi consistently undermined Nagy by criticising mainly the modifications of economic policy. Indeed, the effects of the reforms included the shrinking of job opportunities as a result of the shift in economic priorities, and also the decline of productivity: during the previous years, discipline in the factory was based on compulsion, with a very unfavourable impact on work morale upon its removal. Rákosi managed to increase his support within the Central Committee and packed the Political Committee with his own followers, which Nagy tried to counter by reorganising the Popular Front through the involvement of a variety of social bodies as a meeting ground of 'reform communist' endeavours. Now called the Patriotic Popular Front, it was launched at the end of October 1954.

Shortly thereafter, however, the positions of Nagy were shaken by the weakening of those of his protector, Malenkov, in Moscow, and after the latter's dismissal the rules of the game made his own status untenable. In January 1955, he was censured by Khrushchev and his colleagues for the 'radicalism' of the reforms and ordered to correct the 'mistakes'; his subsequent illness was exploited by Rákosi to prepare charges of 'right-wing deviation' and 'nationalist tendencies' against him and arrange for his dismissal on April 18, 1955. His replacement was András Hegedűs, a young man considered tractable by Rákosi and Gerő.

Another wave of the forcible collectivisation of agriculture and a sharp growth following the earlier decline in the number of political prisoners were among the most readily visible marks of re-Stalinisation, besides expulsions form the party which, by the end of 1955, affected Nagy himself. Unwilling to repent through self-criticism, he withdrew from the public scene and started to commit his ideas of reform communism into writing. However, a complete return to the pre–1953 domestic status quo depended on the further escalation of the Cold War and the consequent tough stance on the part of the Soviets, which Rákosi expected, but did not happen. Although in reply to the accession of West-Germany to NATO and in order to create legitimacy for the continuing presence of Soviet troops in Romania and Hungary after the impending signature of the Austrian State Treaty, the Warsaw Pact of friendship and mutual support among the 'people's democracies' was created on May 14, 1955, it was more of a political means to ensure the loyalty of the signatories than a step towards military confrontation with the West, which Khrushchev wanted to avoid. His repentance visit to Belgrade (and his insistence that the Hungarian leaders do the same) later in the same month, the Geneva talks with the western leaders in June 1955, and especially the resolutions of the Twentieth Congress of the Soviet Communist Party in February 1956 indicated that the Kremlin now deemed the amount of terror that would be needed to maintain the pace of the armaments race unaffordable. Although after his return from the congress, Rákosi claimed it had confirmed that there was no need for further steps to restore 'socialist legality', the illicit listeners of the Munich based Radio Free Europe knew that the 'secret' speech of Khrushchev put the seal on the policy of de-Stalinisation, the toleration of different 'national paths' to Communism, and the peaceful co-existence of the two 'world-systems'.

Whereas the reform Communists who rallied around the expelled Nagy and consolidated their ranks as a 'party opposition', drew encouragement from these developments, perplexity started to grow among the orthodox, especially as the party leadership itself seemed to be unable to adopt a clear policy line. It did not dare to defy Moscow, but it was reluctant to follow it; outspoken articles in a press that started to come to life again, contributions to debates that were deemed provocative, evoked rebukes, warnings and threats, but no arrests. Debates there were a-plenty, the ones organised before audiences of several thousands by the Petőfi Circle in the spring and early summer of 1956 being especially important. Originally intended to address professional issues of, among other things, historiography, philosophy or the liberty of the press, they caused real storms by the participants' stringent criticism of the policies of the past few years and the demand to establish the responsibility for them. A return to the programme of Imre Nagy, together with his rehabilitation and Rákosi's dismissal, were also called for. A limited resumption of the 'new course' indeed took place, with material concessions, promises to observe legality, and the release of more prisoners; Rákosi sacrificed Farkas, and even admitted his own partial responsibility for the show trials. As this failed to quell the discontent, he resorted to a well-tried method: he arranged for a Central Committee resolution condemning the Petőfi Circle as subversive on June 30, and went on to call for a liquidation of the 'conspiracy' of Nagy and his followers.

But without support from Moscow he did not dare to move; and when Moscow moved, it was in the contrary direction, finally realising that Rákosi was a handicap. Rákosi's swashbuckling seemed extremely untimely just a few days after a less explosive situation in Poland ended in rioting among the workers of Poznań and was put down at the expense of considerable bloodshed by army units on June 28. Mikoyan was quickly dispatched to Budapest with instructions to procure the dismissal of Rákosi. Relieved of his office on July 21, 1956, 'because of ill health', he was taken 'for medical treatment' to the Soviet Union (where he died in 1971). Gerő succeeded him at the head of the party, with freshly rehabilitated victims of the purges like Kádár and Marosán in the Political Committee; but Nagy would only have been re-adopted at the price of exercising self-criticism, which he was unwilling to do.

It was obviously, but quite mistakenly believed in the Kremlin that by dropping Rákosi things would return to normal. His replacement by another veteran Stalinist did nothing to satisfy either the Hungarian party opposition, or the Yugoslav Communists whose voice started to matter since the reconciliation between Moscow and Belgrade. Discredited party functionaries were exposed in the press, the Petőfi Circle continued its sessions with debates on burning issues like economic policy or the condition of agriculture and education, and their demands boiled down to what was also urged by the Yugoslavs: bringing Imre Nagy back to the political scene. He was finally re-adopted in the party a week after the public re-burial of the remains of Rajk and his associates on October 6, undertaken by the party leadership as a result of considerable pressure from the opposition and the general public, turned into a 100,000 strong silent demonstration – not of sympathy with the ruthless communist minister, but against the crimes of Stalinism in which he shared. The re-burial also did justice to Tito, who now graciously received a *mea culpa* visit by the Hungarian leaders.

By the time the delegation returned from Belgrade, matters had reached a boiling point in Budapest: what was initially a struggle of reformers and orthodox Stalinists within the party, set off by and adjusting to changes in Moscow, and in the meantime triggered off a growing ferment among the intelligentsia, now became a national anti-Soviet revolution. From October 20 on, meetings were held at the universities in Budapest and in the provinces and drafted lists of demands. These included the reconsideration of Hungarian-Soviet relations and the withdrawal of Soviet troops from Hungary; a new government headed by Nagy and free, multi-party elections; freedom of expression and the calling of Rákosi, Farkas and others to account before the people's court; the adjustment of economic planning to Hungary's specific conditions and putting an end to the discrimination against the private sector in agriculture; a return to the old national symbols. Upon receiving the news of the stabilisation of the situation in Poland through the raising of Władysław Gomułka, the recently rehabilitated leader of de-Stalinisation to the head of the party there on October 20, it was decided that a peaceful demonstration of solidarity with Poland would be held on October 23 to lend weight to these demands. Caught in confusion, the party leadership at first banned the demonstration, but then gave the green light; marching from the statue of the revolutionary poet Petőfi to that of the Polish general of 1848–1849, József Bem, and then to the Parliament, the crowd grew to nearly 200,000 and chanted 'Nagy into the government, Rákosi into the Danube!', 'Hungarians march with us!', and 'Russians go home!'. Some stayed near Parliament to hear a fairly flat speech by Nagy on the need to resume the 'new course' and to rejuvenate the party; others pulled down the gigantic statue of Stalin near the City Park; still others went to the headquarters of the Radio to have their demands broadcasted. Meeting with refusal and hearing, instead, Gerő's speech denouncing the demonstration as 'nationalist' and threatening retaliations, the first shots were exchanged.

With the successful siege of the Radio by the crowd, the revolution began, and Gerő did not waste time requesting Soviet military assistance. At the same time, Nagy was co-opted into the Political Committee and was appointed Prime Minister, but for a while he was no exception to the rule of general confusion in the leadership. Fighting started between Soviet tanks and largely young (often teenage) working class urban guerrillas armed with Molotov cocktails and weapons taken from barracks, factories and police stations with the support of the people in general; at this stage even Nagy called them 'counter-revolutionaries', albeit all they agreed about was the desire to restore national sovereignty and to put an end to dictatorial rule, and no list of demands included a revision of nationalisations, let alone a return to the pre–1945 order. The Prime Minister imposed martial law and a curfew, but hesitated to send the ÁVH, as urged by the freshly formed Military Committee at the party headquarters, against the violators of the latter.

On October 25, even larger crowds than two days earlier marched to demonstrate at the square in front of Parliament, where shooting, most probably by ÁVH units hidden on nearby rooftops, killed almost a hundred of them. The massacre released new passions, especially as news of similar events were arriving from some of the provincial towns (while the countryside remained relatively silent); a hunt after members of the ÁVH started, resulting in lynchings and tortures. Among such circumstances, a step which might have quelled the discontent a few months earlier, the replacement of Gerő with Kádár at the head of the party (an initiative of the Soviet advisors, Mikoyan and Suslov, who arrived on October 24), went almost unnoticed. Fighting continued, while the party organisation and the local administration subordinated to it started to collapse, their role being taken over by spontaneously emerging local revolutionary committees and councils; workers' councils were created in factories. Nagy had to decide between crushing the uprising by resorting to Soviet arms, and trying to solve the crisis in co-operation with the revolutionaries.

By October 27, he had chosen the second alternative. He reshuffled his cabinet to include some relatively creditable Communists like Lukács, and two former Smallholder leaders, Tildy and Béla Kovács. On October 28, he dropped the label 'counter-revolution' and started to talk about a 'national democratic movement', also announcing a cease-fire and even the withdrawal of Soviet troops from Budapest. He acknowledged the revolutionary bodies created during the previous days, and promised amnesty, the disbanding of the ÁVH, and reformed agrarian policies. On October 30, the Soviet military units were indeed beginning to leave the capital and, from groups of insurgents, the National Guard was created; while further negotiations of Nagy with the Soviet emissaries already concerned the establishment of a pluralist political system, reflecting the fact that in the meantime not only the Hungarian Workers' Party became re-formed as the Hungarian Socialist Workers' Party (led by Nagy, Kádár, Lukács, and prominent reform-minded Communists like Ferenc Donáth and Géza Losonczy), but also the old coalition parties became active again. After the initial uncertainty, the Prime Minister kept pace with developments in the streets, closing the gap between himself and the revolutionaries step by step. The policies he adopted from October 27 on culminated in the formation of yet a new cabinet on a fully multi-party basis (including Communist, Social Democrat, Smallholder and Peasant Party ministers) on November 2, 1956, and played a part in the fact that normal conditions started to return slightly more than a week after the outbreak of the revolution. The workers' councils decided to resume production, shops opened, public order was relatively stable. In an atmosphere marked both by jubilation and anxiety, the popular uprising became consolidated by political means.

However, this manner of consolidation, which involved the collapse of the whole system of institutions of the party-state upon which the cohesion of the Soviet empire rested, was in the end unacceptable for the Moscow leadership, which thought it could not afford losing a country of Hungary's geographical location, with its freshly explored uranium resources, from its belt of satellites. At first, the 'Finlandisation' of Hungary, that is, the acquisition of full sovereignty in domestic affairs and the maintenance of close co-operation with the Soviet Union internationally, seemed a possibility in the last days of October, indicated by the withdrawal of troops from Budapest and the apparent willingness of the Kremlin to re-negotiate Soviet military presence in the country. The radicalisation of the revolution, however, eliminated this possibility, and the international scene turned favourable for a military showdown. The British-French-Israeli intervention in Egypt to prevent the nationalisation of the Suez Canal by the Soviet supported Nasser government on October 29, made the outcome of the Hungarian revolution dependent on superpower bargaining. Neither of the latter were interested in military confrontation, but both of them were concerned to defend their strategic interests; the Soviets were willing to remain passive in the Near East if they received assurances that Hungary was not ot be interfered with by the West. This was done on October 30.

An express promise widely disseminated from western radio stations, which played no small role in the optimism of the Hungarian insurgents, was thus broken, while the Soviet leaders sought and obtained the agreement of Tito to the planned intervention. Informed about the resumption of Soviet troop movements, Nagy urged the United Nations to put the 'Hungarian issue' on its agenda (with no immediate result) and announced Hungary's neutral status on November 1 while going to great length to stress the desire for harmonious relations with the Soviet Union. These resulted in sham negotiations at the headquarters of the Soviet Supreme Command outside Budapest, ending in the arrest of Nagy's new Minister of Defence, General Pál Maléter.

The Hungarian military thus did not resist when the offensive against the capital started in the dawn of November 4, 1956. Defiant resistance by insurgents continued for about a week in Budapest and some provincial centres, with fierce street fighting of grossly unequal forces costing some 2,500 lives in the capital and around 3,000 country-wide. Despite the desperate belief and true heroism of the insurgents, the revolution in effect came to an end with two radio announcements in the morning of November 4. One of them was an appeal by Nagy on behalf of the 'lawful and democratic government of Hungary', before he and leading members of the one-time party opposition sought asylum at the Yugoslav embassy. The other broadcast came from a Soviet-controlled station at Szolnok, and proclaimed the struggle against the 'counter-revolution' on behalf of a newly formed 'Revolutionary Workers' and Peasants' Government', with the assistance of the Soviet army. The second speaker was János Kádár, who, after announcing the formation of the HSWP and declaring himself to be in favour of neutrality, left the government headquarters on November 1, as it turned out later, for the Soviet embassy. From there he quickly found himself in Moscow. Like his predecessors, he was now selected by the Soviet leaders to assist them in steering Hungary on a course acceptable for them. Having undertaken the role assigned to him, Kádár entered Budapest with his cabinet in Soviet tanks on November 7, 1956.

3. *'The longest path from capitalism to capitalism', or the limitations of Realsozialismus*

The parallel between Kádár and Francis Joseph has become a staple in the general perception of Hungarians about their history, on account of the salient contradiction between the circumstances of their accession to power and their subsequent acceptance by the populace, albeit never without reservations, because of their achievement in terms of social and political stability and the limited material well-being associated with them. With some qualification, the company could be extended to include Horthy, and not only because the above features are also perceptible in his political career in Hungary. Of the last 150 years of Hungarian history, 126 are associated with these three men, the respective 'eras' bearing their names not the least because their personality so adequately expressed the 'spirit' of the age. If out of a sanguinary tyrant Francis Joseph became the first bureaucrat of his realm, imperial and royal in descent, but rather bourgeois in manners and lifestyle, and Horthy the conservative Christian middle class gentleman *par excellence*, Kádár (the son of a rural labourer, born in the Adriatic port of Fiume, and a mechanician by training) came to represent the puritanical, publicity-shy and apolitical 'little man'.

'Apolitical' might seem a strange description of an expert political tactician; yet, his own conduct *vis-à-vis* Moscow, retaining some freedom of movement at the expense of refraining from meddling with fundamental dogmas, was in perfect harmony with his frequently emphasised creed that the 'little man' was interested simply in a decent living, instead of the great political issues of the day. After the tribulations of the Rákosi dictatorship and the shock of 1956, it is not surprising that Hungarian society was in the mood to take such a message, and somewhat grudgingly started to wink back in the eye of its newly imposed leader. Kádár used the scope created by the very revolt on whose ruins he built his power to buy this complicity of Hungarians by methods rather heterodox in communism. These were the foundations of the 'Hungarian model' of 'existing socialism' in the 1970s, admittedly a far cry from the ideal one. With characteristic persistence, he managed to earn legitimacy, and retained it until it was realised, in the increasingly ironic 1980s, that 'existing socialism does not function, and a functioning socialism does not exist', and in reality it was merely 'the longest path from capitalism to capitalism'.

To be sure, at the outset Kádár was the most hated man in Hungary. His betrayal might well have been grounded upon a realistic appraisal of the international situation and the options they held open for Hungary, deciding to intervene in order to spare it from still worse to come. If so, no-one thought of him like that at the time, and it would have gone unappreciated anyway. The new government was completely isolated in a hostile country conquered by foreign arms. Although the pockets of armed resistance had been mopped up by November 10–11, the most peculiar formations of the revolution, the workers' councils, started to exert their true impact after November 4, with an attempt to organise a nationwide network. Initially set up as strike committees, their basic idea was self-management in the factory, owned in principle by the workers. Upon the initiative of the workers' councils, a massive wave of strikes lasted into January 1957. The intellectuals, rallying mainly in the Writers' Association, the students' committees and the Journalists' Association, founded the Revolutionary Council of the Hungarian Intelligentsia, chaired by Zoltán Kodály, and demanded the restoration of the country's sovereignty and representative government. István Bibó, who held a ministerial post in Nagy's last cabinet, drafted a proposal for a compromise solution to the 'Hungarian issue'. Since November 4, that issue had been on the agenda of the United Nations, which echoed the demands of the Hungarian protesters, while the Pope (upon the initiative of Mindszenty, who was released during the revolution and then found refuge at the American embassy) forbade the clergy all political co-operation with the puppet government.

Kádár initially did not have a clear policy to cope with this situation. The government programme (drafted at the beginning of November while he was in Moscow) included promises of welfare measures, amnesty, worker's self-management, indulgent policies towards the peasantry and small-scale private enterprise in general, and vaguely even a transition to the multi-party system and a re-negotiation of the presence of Soviet troops (once order was restored). But this was clearly not the reason why his Moscow patrons needed him. While the uncertainty as to his real goals remained, he was busy in organising special police squads for the purposes of retaliation and maintaining order. In February 1957, these were replaced by the more permanent Workers' Guard, a 60,000 strong para-military force directly under the command of the party's Central Committee. Whereas the ÁVH was officially dissolved on December 3, 1956, there was nothing to prevent its members from joining the armed forces.

By this time, the policy line of the regime started to crystallise, at least as far as the short term was concerned: extorting submission by intimidation. While constantly being watched, advised or ordered by Soviet leaders visiting Budapest or from Moscow, Kádár surely knew himself what his job was, and needed to demonstrate his loyalty. Although he negotiated with the leaders of the Budapest Worker's Council on November 22, on the previous day the special squads prevented the creation of a National Workers' Council and in early December, two-hundred leaders of the movement were arrested. November 22 also saw the abduction of Nagy and his associates, who left the Yugoslav embassy upon assurances by Kádár, but were taken by Soviet forces to Romania. The revolutionary committees were now also dissolved; police rounds killed nearly 100 demonstrators in Salgótarján, Miskolc and Eger. Simultaneously, the ideological justification for the impending campaign of retaliation was created at a party conference, which identified the causes of the October events as (1) the mistakes of the Rákosi-Gerő faction, evoking (2) the boundless and unconstructive criticism of the Imre Nagy circle which undermined the party and paved the way to (3) a capitalist-feudal counter-revolution of the forces of Horthyite fascism also supported by (4) international imperialism.

Absurd as this diagnosis was, it was vintage Kádár with the emphasis on the 'two-front struggle' of a virtuous centre against both Stalinist orthodoxy and revisionist deviance (besides the class enemy within and without the country), and served as the basis of the bans, arrests and prosecutions that started while summary justice was introduced, as in 1919–1920, in January 1957. True to principle, the offensive also struck on both sides, but the standards were very unequal. While some of those guilty of pre-1956 violations of legality received prison sentences, most of the main culprits (like Rákosi, Gerő or Révai) were never called to account; on the other hand, involvement in the October revolution was deemed a capital offence in many cases. All of the intellectual associations mentioned above were banned or suspended, and the people's courts were busy until 1959. 35,000 prosecutions yielded 22,000 imprisonments and 229 death sentences, but the number of those actually executed was around 350; besides this figure, 13,000 people were sent to the re-opened internment camps without any legal procedure. Over

200,000 people emigrated again, the contemporary and potential intellectual elite and other icons being over-represented among them. The poet György Faludy, the pianist György Cziffra left the country in 1956, but so did Sándor Puskás, the fabulous striker of the 'Golden Team' of footballers. Of the well-known figures who stayed and received sentences, the names of Bibó, Déry and Zelk were mentioned above; others included the writer Gyula Háy, the writer, translator and post-1989 Head of State Árpád Göncz and the historian Domokos Kosáry, and many more.

As a matter of fact, the case of the greatest significance was that of Imre Nagy and his associates, who were secretly tried in the spring of 1958, after József Szilágyi had already been executed and Géza Losonczy had died in prison during artificial feeding. Not surprisingly, the accused were found guilty of the preconceived charge, that is, 'conspiracy for the overthrow of the order of people's democracy'; Nagy, his advisor Miklós Gimes and Defence Minister Maléter were executed on June 16, while others were jailed. The other death sentences meted out because of involvement in the revolution afflicted almost invariably armed insurgents; in the case of those spontaneously raised to positions of authority in factories or localities on account of their personal esteem (a quality that made them potentially dangerous in the eyes of the regime), imprisonment or internment was the rule. Finally, it is hardly possible to assess the number of those who were removed from their jobs as punishment or in order to narrow their sphere of intercourse and thus their influence.

With all its horror, Kádár's post-1956 terror was not the Stalinist kind in which Rákosi indulged. While it was an act of arbitrary power, its victims were not selected in an arbitrary fashion and it did not collectively afflict whole social groups in the name of some general political strategy, but aimed, on the basis of very specific political calculation and selectively, at individuals who proved (or were thought to have proved) to be dangerous. The isolation of this active minority through administrative and police measures from the largely passive majority of citizens, and the simultaneous satisfaction of a gradually broadening range of needs of the latter group, were policies which Kádár, true to principle, pursued with varying emphases, but with great consistency from nearly the beginning to the end. There were ups and downs, dependent on a combination of external and domestic developments. The consolidation of the personal authority of Kádár and its coincidence with the ultimate decision of Khrushchev, with whom he had an almost friendly, and even closer political relationship, to break definitively with Stalinism, inaugurated a period in which the 'new course' of Nagy and the programme of the pre–1956 party opposition were effectively resumed – without, of course, saying so.

In 1962, the 'Rákosi doctrine' ('he who is not with us is against us') was replaced by a New Testament paraphrase which Kádár chose as his own 'doctrine': 'he who is not against us is with us'. That fluid and indefinite amalgam of the absence of liberty in general but access to some liberties; of the mitigation of repression and a limited autonomy of the economic and cultural spheres; of lip service paid to strong political consciousness and a de-politicisation of everyday life (relieving and annoying at the same time); above all, of the trimming of the wilder branches of the command economy and the endeavour to satisfy the desire for consumerism – 'Kádárism', as this amalgam came to be known, was born in that period, culminating in the 'new economic mechanism' introduced in 1968. Re-Stalinisation became impossible, and even though the reservation of the new Soviet leadership under Leonid Brezhnev regarding the reforms, confirmed by the 1968 Czechoslovak crisis, led to some reversal after 1972, the Kádár regime continued to capitalise on the favourable image it created internationally, and the economic crisis of the late 1970s steered it back to the path of reforms, with steps towards a mixed economy and a cautious opening up of the political system.

No sooner had the people's courts begun to pass their death sentences than, in early 1957, Kádár also embarked on policies designed to obtain the confidence of those deemed to belong to the 'passive majority'. Direct aid in the value of about 100 million dollars (from East and West alike), and huge Russian and Chinese loans were instrumental in the reconstruction of the damages as well as in gestures towards virtually all of the important strata. The wages of industrial workers, miners and teachers, as well as pensions were increased; profit-sharing schemes and productivity-based differential wages were introduced in factories; the freedom of the labour market was decreed. The discriminatory tax rates of private artisans were substantially lowered, and shops and units in the catering trade could be rented at favourable terms and promised high incomes. The compulsory delivery of agricultural produce was abolished, better and fixed exchange terms were offered to peasants, who could also benefit from social security and pension schemes. The dissolution of about 3,000 co-operatives (leaving only 2,000) was accepted, even though Kádár did not abandon the ultimate goal of collectivisation and, seeing the inefficiency of simple persuasion, in 1958 launched a massive campaign to speed up the process.

Kádár's complex strategy started to take effect fairly soon. By May Day 1957, after extensive precautions had been taken, the regime was able to muster 400,000 people who took part in the march at Heroes

Square and the subsequent festivities – a demonstration of force on the part of the new political masters, but also a demonstration of acquiescence, if not sympathy, by the people of a capital which, after the shocks of invasion and destitution, could not but want to believe in the message of tranquillity and safety that the concessions transmitted. Party membership rose from a mere 40,000 in December 1956 to 400,000 a year later. Despite the efforts of Révai, who returned from Moscow in January 1957 and tried to arrange a reversal to orthodoxy, Kádár received reassurances from Khrushchev and was confirmed in his position by the party conference of June 1957 through the election of a 'centralist' leadership, including Marosán and others not implicated in the pre–1956 illegalities like Ferenc Münnich, Gyula Kállai, Jenő Fock, Dezső Nemes and others. At the same time, the reorganised Patriotic Popular Front, whose new task became the transmission and popularisation of party priorities to society at large, was chaired by the hard-liner Antal Apró. After the disintegration of the Alliance of Working Youth, the Communist Youth League was set up on March 21, 1957, to take care of the ideological orientation of young people and ensure a supply of future cadres. Purges and voluntary resignations among the officer corps, the confirmation of Kádár in his premiership (later passed on to Münnich) and the approval of his policies by parliament in May 1957 and general elections along pre–1956 lines in November 1958 rounded off the restoration of the system of the party-state. The external guarantee was an agreement, signed on May 27, 1957, as to the 'temporary residence' in Hungary of Soviet troops, whose number became stabilised around 80,000 once the Hungarian army was deemed politically reliable in consequence of the purges.

Its *de facto* stability notwithstanding, significant passive resistance and the lack of international recognition still denied full legitimacy to the regime. As a result of the concessions of 1957, the outright hostility of the peasantry abated, but it was only as a result of the persistent campaign after 1958 that it abandoned its defiant clinging to private ownership. A mixed message of promises and threats was brought by a crowd of agitators swarming to the countryside, but the earlier brutality was abandoned, and instead of denigrating the well-to-do '*kulaks*', it was attempted to seduce them first, knowing that they commanded respect and would be followed by others. Seventy-five per cent of the peasantry had indeed become members of the co-operatives by the end of 1961, a mere 6 per cent of them remaining private farmers (the rest being agricultural labourers on state farms). They did so wearied of the decade-long resistance to collectivisation, which now seemed unavoidable, and also on the offer, after all, of better conditions. Of these, the most important was that about 15 per cent of collectivised land remained 'household farms', cultivated individually by intensive methods, which soon yielded about 40 per cent of the total produce of co-operatives (especially meat, poultry, milk and fruit).

Besides the peasantry, another group whose long-standing animosity towards the regime was only embittered by the events of 1956, was the Church. The movement of 'peace priests' virtually collapsed during the revolution, and their remaining leaders were removed by the Vatican thereafter. Gestures to get out of the impasse included the broadcasting of religious services on the radio and, more importantly, a party resolution in July 1958 differentiating between 'ideological struggle' and 'political opposition' on the part of the Church, and confining the rightfulness of coercive means to the latter. The episcopacy returned this with a pastoral letter emphasising that the mission of the clergy was the care of souls, and the temporal well-being of people belonged to the province of the state. The subsequent normalisation was based on the regulation of religious instruction and of the oaths of allegiance, the reorganisation of the State Office of Ecclesiastical Affairs in 1959, and the 1964 agreement with the Vatican, whose right of investiture was acknowledged by the Hungarian government.

The third group whose non-compliance was embarrassing, was the intellectuals. Those writers who were neither in prison nor in exile, were unappeased by Kossuth Awards given to hitherto neglected authors like László Németh and Lőrinc Szabó, and other figures of high integrity like Kodály or the sculptor Miklós Borsos, and were reluctant to have their voice heard in the newly launched literary journals. Only after the cultural policy principles of the party, which acknowledged the merits of the 'populist' movement and the humanist trends of 'bourgeois' and religious inspiration, were published in the summer of 1958, did most of them start to take advantage of the fact that they were allowed to do so (provided that they observed the taboos) without the need to pass self-criticism. Their acquiescence was also confirmed by the partial amnesties of April 1959 and April 1960, the dissolution of internment camps, and the release of Déry and Háy as well as two convicts of the Imre Nagy trial: Nagy's advisor Ferenc Donáth, and Zoltán Tildy, the former president who also held a ministerial post in the 1956 cabinet.

With Khrushchev firmly behind him, and having secured at least the passive acceptance of the majority of the population, including the bitterest of earlier opponents, Kádár embarked on making de-Stalinisation formal and irrevocable by a resolution of the Central Committee of the party in August 1962 condemning the personality cult and the show trials, and expelling Rákosi, Gerő and several others from the party on account of their responsibility for the abuses. All of the communist victims of the terror (but not others) were rehabilitated. At the subsequent congress of the HSWP (numbered eighth, which suggested the continuity with its predecessor) in November in the same year, Kádár triumphantly and somewhat pompously announced that the foundations of socialism in Hungary had been laid, but the really important part of the message was the suggestion that the construction of socialism was an all-national task, dependent on the co-operation of Communists and non-party members, irrespective of personal convictions. There was no class war. The 'Kádár doctrine' started to take effect.

Finally, the amnesty was also the basis upon which Kádár could start improving his international reputation. Hungary's mandate in the United Nations Organisation, of which it had been a member since 1955, was suspended in 1957, especially in view of the Kádár government's refusal to allow a committee of the UNO to carry out investigations on the 'Hungarian issue' in the country. The ice began to melt after the 1960 amnesty, when Kádár spoke at the General Assembly of the UNO; the 'Hungarian issue' was removed from the organisation's agenda and Hungary's full membership was restored in 1963 upon the promise of a more general amnesty, which was also promulgated in March 1963. It also affected those guilty of violations of legality before 1956, but not those convicted upon charges of murder, as were the armed freedom fighters of 1956. Nevertheless, by 1963 Hungary had become the subject of an unlikely consensus: Khrushchev as well as American government circles praised it as a model communist country which had been the most successful in dismantling Stalinism.

The amnesty, the showdown with the rearguard of the Stalinists and cosmetic changes to the political institutions after 1966 (the replacement of the party list with individual constituency voting, the possibility of multiple candidacy at elections, the 1972 constitutional amendment) were achievements which Kádár could afford because there were other, more fundamental ones, which were attained in the deeper structures or 'subsystems' of society, and affected the quality of life in the broadest sense. Ironically, if we disregard the pathetic condition of the civic sphere, besides the *fin-de-siècle*, the Kádár era was the greatest period of *embourgeoisement* in Hungary: year by year, a slightly greater range of material and cultural satisfactions was made available for a slightly wider range of people. This was based, in the first place, on a thorough reconsideration of the priorities of economic policy and the mechanism of economic management. As it was obvious that the main source of the tensions of the 1950s was the senselessly high reinvestment rate, especially in industry, after 1957 the proportion of the national income that was reinvested fell from a third to one-fifth, and the share of industry in it from nearly one half to slightly over one-third. The preponderance of heavy industry remained, but the weight of agriculture increased, which was more suitable to the economic character of Hungary and could be better turned to the purpose of boosting consumption which, together with the improvement of the living standard, became the central target of the government. Simultaneously, a rather radical plan to reform the system of the command economy was called off, yet it was made more flexible through limited initiatives like the abandonment of the obsession with quantitative indices and of the centralisation of the labour market, and the introduction of self-interested incentives and opportunities for personal gain. In 1959, a more realistic pricing system was also adopted. In the early 1960s, the hierarchy of management was simplified by liquidating the industrial directorates wedged between the companies and the ministries, and by uniting companies in one or two large firms per each branch of industry.

In agriculture, the combination of higher investment with 'household farming' and share cropping, which accounted for about a third of the whole agricultural output, brought about a remarkable regeneration – which in the given context did not mean more that, as regards its level of mechanisation and productivity rates, Hungarian agriculture in the 1960s climbed back into the European middle echelons where it was in the interwar period. One of the important changes was, at last, the spread of labour-intensive cultures, which, together with animal husbandry, constituted the basis of 'household farming': viticulture and the growing of fruits and vegetables now yielded over 20 per cent of the overall income from farming, while the proportion of stock-raising within agriculture as a whole rose to nearly a half. Besides the self-exploitation of the peasants in the semi-private sphere, the introduction of hothouse planting, the considerable growth of the use of artificial fertilisers, the massive expansion of soil amelioration and irrigation schemes (together with the final touches on the regulation of the Tisza with the erection of two river barrages) all played a part in bringing about a steady growth of 2.5 per cent annually in agriculture. Considering the fact that the proportion of the population employed in the agrarian sphere, after having dropped during the 1950s from over 50 per cent to 30 per cent in 1960, continued to diminish and was 25 per cent in 1970, the growth was undoubtedly the result of the improvement of efficiency.

The case was very different in industry, where growth rates, about 7 per cent per year on average, exceeded anything earlier experienced in Hungary (except of course the 1950s) and what was normal at the time in the developed countries, but were based on the expansion of productive capacity and the consequent influx of labour force, rather than the increase of productivity. Yet, production structures changed quite conspicuously. In the 1950s, machine industry meant turn-benches, tractors, motor vehicles; in the 1960s, refrigerators, vacuum-cleaners, motorcycles and washing machines figured just as prominently – reflecting the shift of priorities from forced industrialisation to consumption.

One of the main problems of Hungarian industry was still the unstable quality and narrow range of products, especially conspicuous in more directly consumption-oriented industries, like the textile or the food industry, despite the respectable tradition of the latter in Hungary. The other was the shortage of industrial raw materials and sources of energy. The only mineral resource of which Hungary possesses large quantities, bauxite, was mostly processed as aluminium in the Soviet Union, from whence a part of the finished product returned as payment for the raw material. It was largely in a similar fashion that Hungary obtained much of the other raw materials and energy supply needed by its industries. Ninety-five per cent of Hungary's imported raw iron and over 50 per cent of the steel came from the Soviet Union. A number of coalmines were closed down on the highly belated recognition that they operated very uneconomically, whereas the extraction of oil and natural gas from the newly explored fields on the Great Plain increased at a galloping pace in the 1960s. However, in 1970 Hungary needed over 80 per cent more energy than in 1960; by 1970, energy import was 110 per cent higher than a decade earlier, with the share of the Soviet Union in this import increased from one-quarter to a half. Hungary paid in Ikarus buses, telecommunication appliances, products of agriculture and the chemical industry, especially the pharmaceutical industry, in which Hungary revived respectable traditions and emerged as an important factor in the world market by the 1970s. The same items constituted a substantial part of Hungary's exports in the framework of the comprehensive barter agreements within the COMECON, reflecting the policy of specialisation in specific products by the individual member states. In the 1960s, the COMECON, which accounted for over two-thirds of Hungary's foreign trade relations (the Soviet Union representing over 35 per cent), operated as a closed economic sphere not unfavourable from the Hungarian point of view. Although the Soviet-inspired industrial growth, whose momentum still continued, made the country even more dependent on external resources, these were available, for the time being, fairly inexpensively, while the 'friendly' countries provided a safe market for products, not all of which would have been competitive elsewhere.

This Janus-faced development, which was the result of the post-1957 decision to adopt more flexible economic policies and took place largely by realising the targets set for the 1961–1965 Second Five Year Plan (after a three year plan had overcome the problems that arose in the wake of 1956), only accentuated the dilemma that already exercised the minds of those whose more radical reform projects were rejected in

1957: the existing system was still not conducive enough to productivity, and the limitations in the scale of labour force that could be mobilised made the transition from extensive to intensive growth imperative. The plans of a more comprehensive economic reform were worked out, uniquely in the Soviet Bloc, after the political consolidation of the regime in 1962–1963. Not even Khrushchev's replacement with the conservative Leonid Brezhnev in 1964, and upon the latter's behest, Kádár's withdrawal from the premiership in favour of Gyula Kállai whilst remaining content with the post of Party Secretary in 1965, halted its preparation. The main engineer of the reform was Rezső Nyers, a former master printer whose route led to the Communists through the Social Democratic Party, as Secretary of the economic policy department of the Central Committee from 1962 on.

There were several fundamental principles of the reform, resolved by the Central Committee in November 1965 and launched in January 1968 as the 'New Economic Mechanism'. First, whereas annual and five-year plans were preserved as a regulation on the macro-economical level, they were not broken down to the company level by 'commanding' production volumes, but strove to influence production through various incentives (subsidies, taxes, loans etc.), while the autonomous decision-making authority of companies increased. Second, a mixed pricing system was introduced, with 60 per cent of agricultural products and over 70 per cent of domestically produced raw materials and half-finished products still being sold at fixed prices, but the prices of finished products were liberalised. Third, while unemployment was not to be apprehended, for it would have been politically unsustainable for the regime, a far more marked differentiation in wages and other benefits than earlier was introduced.

As a result of this grafting of some of the mechanisms of the market economy on to the command economy, considerable progress took place. Again, this was especially the case in agriculture where the annual growth rate doubled, and in the 1970s the country climbed close to the top on international lists regarding productivity: Hungarian grain yields exceeded the average in the EEC countries, per capita meat, fruit and vegetable production came second only to the most advanced economies of the world, and in terms of the general standards of agriculture Hungary was esteemed to rank closely behind the eight most developed countries of Western Europe. The growth was not only due to the fact that the reform accentuated the earlier tendency towards motorisation (which became complete in some operations in the cultivation process) and the use of fertilisers. It also stimulated the intensive cultivation characteristic of small-scale and 'household' farming by lifting the limitations placed on them, while in the large-scale sphere it encouraged initiatives like the introduction of industry-like methods of stock raising (pioneered at the internationally renowned state farm of Bábolna) and the coalescence of co-operatives (whose number, besides a slight increase of the area they cultivated, fell to just over 1,300 by the end of the 1970s, a mere third of the 1961 figure).

Industry could boast more modest results, though what was achieved indeed reflected the principles at first advanced in 1957 and matured during the preparation of the 'New Economic Mechanism': greater emphasis on branches dependent on higher technological expertise and less raw material. Of the products that were deemed to answer the highest international standards (still a rather meagre one-fifth of the whole range), the best known were some medicines and products of the pharmaceutical industry, Videoton television sets from Székesfehérvár and Lehel refrigerators from Jászberény, Ikarus buses (also Székesfehérvár) and Rába trucks (Győr). In the building and construction industry, as well as the light industries (furniture and clothing in particular), the main achievement of the reform years was the alleviation of the shortages so soaring in earlier years, besides an improvement in quality which was considerable by Hungarian and relative by international standards. The gap between European fashion and the Hungarian ready-to-wear industry was narrowed to six to eight years. Items of emblematic significance of the '60s ('hurricane' raincoats or nylon stockings) remained cherished contents of packages from relatives in the West, and 'original' blue jeans were only available through foreign travel and at the secondhand or the black market until the opening of a Levi Strauss branch in Hungary in 1978. A half of the 3.5 million flats registered in Hungary in 1980 were built after 1960, with 1.6 million people, 15 per cent of the population living in the 500,000 (characteristically two-room, full comfort) flats of the new housing estates. For the masses of Hungarians formerly living in domiciles with no conveniences these homes, whose average size was one-third of contemporary western standards, were a cause for relief and exhilaration, before they rightly started to feel confined and alienated in the 'concrete jungle'.

The post-1968 years at last brought significant, albeit unequal, development within the 'third sector', that is, the infrastructure. On the one hand, the telecommunication network, in conspicuous contrast to Hungary's erstwhile pioneering role in the field, not only lagged far behind western countries, but was also inferior to most COMECON partners. On the other hand, the electrification of Hungary's settlements was brought to a conclusion in 1962, regional centres of primary and secondary importance underwent marked development to offset the preponderance of the capital (often at the expense of preserving their historical character), steam locomotives were replaced by electric ones (though not completely until 1984), the road transport network improved steadily. In 1963 and 1965, respectively, comprehensive projects for the improvement of the area of Lake Balaton and the Danube-bend, north of Budapest, were also launched, partly to answer the leisure and vacation needs of the population (at this stage mainly through the erection of company holiday resorts), but also in view of the vigorous development of a fundamentally new source of national income: a rising tourist industry. Already in 1965, Hungary received over a million foreign visitors, a quarter of them adventurers from beyond the Iron Curtain; by 1978, the number of tourists was 12.5 million.

The growth of tourism in Hungary aptly illustrates the combination of political opening and economic considerations, just as its reciprocal side, the fact that the number of foreign travel permits given out to Hungarian citizens rose from 300,000 in 1960 to over 5 million in the 1980s (in both cases, between 10 and 15 per cent of them to the West), was based on the coincidence of the indulgent attitude of the regime and growing affluence. Applications for travel permits were sometimes rejected on absurd bases, for instance, to under–10s to visit an aunt in West Germany; but in general, if one was prepared to stand the day-long queues for visas (no longer needed to the Eastern Bloc countries, except the Soviet Union, and to Yugoslavia from the 1960s) and economise on the 'hard currency allowance' one could buy triennially, one did not even need an invitation from a relative or a friend to travel beyond the Iron Curtain.

Liberalism was cautious and meant imprecisely codified, but more or less predictable and permanent norms; and both a significant reduction in the parades of arbitrary power on the part of the authorities, and their shift towards catering for a sense of comfort, rather than the subsistence of the citizen. Whoever refrained from openly defying or criticising the party line had a decent measure of liberty in his or her private pursuits and relationships, and was not required to participate in activities intended as shows of ideological identification with the regime (though he was encouraged and sometimes expected to do so by subtle but unmistakable messages). Harassment and police measures were confined to activities considered by the authorities as explicitly subversive: in the 1960s, practically the only cases in question concerned some priests doing clandestine pastoral and instruction work outside the 'constitutional' clerical framework. Membership in the party (or for the younger generation, in the Communist Youth League) was, except for a quite clearly definable range of positions, not an unconditional requirement and even less a sure guarantee of social climbing or simple goal-attainment, though for the vast majority of members it was a part of career-building strategy, rather than a matter of conviction. The competitions between 'Socialist brigades' were increasingly a formality, a far cry indeed from the Stakhanovite movement of the 1950s; habits like churchgoing or listening to 'hostile' radio stations were often pilloried in the press and party discourse, but were tolerated except among party members and to some extent teachers.

'Soft dictatorship' created and reflected circumstances under which 'goulash communism' or 'refrigerator socialism' could flourish – epithets in which the overtones of recognition and disparagement so eloquently mingle to express the character of the system. Foreign travel appeared in family budgets as a result of the radical changes in the structure of expenditures in Hungary in the 1960s and 1970s. Real incomes doubled during that period, reaching an all-time maximum in 1978. While official working hours decreased steadily, the five-day week being introduced by the 1980s, considering the rapidly increasing workload people were willing to undertake in the 'second economy' (extra work in the main job or elsewhere, legalised under the 'New Economic Mechanism'), the rise in living standards was actually achieved at the expense of greater sacrifices; nevertheless, people considered them worth making. The fact that the share of foodstuffs in the spending of the population dropped from over 40 per cent to less than 30 per cent, meant that not only that, for the first time in history, with few exceptions Hungarians could meet their primary needs, but also that they turned the surplus income to the acquisition of durable consumer goods. The ten- or twenty-fold or ever more impressive growth in the number of television sets, refrigerators, vacuum-cleaners, washing machines, record players and tape recorders propelled Hungary ahead of most Eastern bloc contries and Southern Europe in terms of the mechanisation of households. The number of privately owned cars rose from 18,500 in 1960 to over 220,000 in 1970, nearly hitting the one million mark and reaching the international average figure per thousand inhabitants by 1980 – most characteristically, specimens of the Soviet-made Fiat (that is, Lada), or the Trabant, the East-German equivalent of the 'people's car', that pathetic, two-stroke plastic pride of hundreds of thousands of new Hungarian 'petty bourgeois'. Finally, by 1980 the savings also allowed over 116,000 Hungarian citizens to maintain private 'weekend-houses' near Lake Balaton, at resorts along the Danube, or somewhere in the hills; besides many miserable hovels, even decommissioned buses, set up on tiny plots for the same purpose: to serve as a base for inexpensive recreation in privacy.

Besides earnings, savings and the tokens of material well-being these could purchase, living standards also owed a great deal to social welfare policies like the state subvention of housing, the expansion of social security schemes, free education and medical care. In 1972, compulsory

social insurance was made universal by being extended to private farmers, tradesmen and artisans. Pension regulations also became uniform.
The patient-doctor ratio was outstanding on international comparison
(still concealing vast, though diminishing differences between the
capital and the provinces, and in terms of hospital beds Hungary was far
worse off). Hungary pioneered the three year child care benefit in 1967;
in addition, by 1980 twice as many families took advantage from support schemes that were to avert (in vain) the decrease of the Hungarian
population. There was a great breakthrough in nursery education, comprising by the 1980s 90 per cent of the 3 to 6 age group, with high professional standards. Elsewhere, one of the important changes was that
while the curricula still emphasised the 'stimulation of the development
of the communist personality' as the main task of education, in practice
more attention was paid to questions of substance, and gradually ever
more latitude in the teaching material was allowed through measures
like its division into a mandatory 'core' and a wide range of optional
supplements, and the re-introduction of the teaching of western languages. The latter also figured prominently in extra-curricular and adult
education, with English conquering the formerly dominant role of German in the 1970s (and, by the number of holders of a state certificate,
soon surpassing also Russian as regards actual proficiency, despite the fact
that learning the latter was still compulsory from the age of 10 upwards).

After an unwarranted increase in the number of secondary schools
during the early 1960s was cut back, the material conditions and the
qualifications of the teaching staff steadily improved. As a result, the
high standards of the *fin-de-siècle* and the inter-war period were ap-
proximated again, and although the gap between, for instance, some
highly reputed Budapest gymnasia and their new small-town counterparts was enormous, the average knowledge of the 200,000 or so Hungarian secondary school pupils stood any international comparison. On
the university and college level, which involved about 65,000 students
by the mid-1970s, affirmative action in admission procedures on behalf
of the children of 'physical workers' ceased (although they were still
preferred when scores were equal), and the preference given to the offspring of the nomenclature did not seriously distort the principle of
merit as regarded the student body. The main hazard to standards was
counter-selection, which lost momentum since the 1950s, but was still
quite evident among the teaching staff, especially at social science fac-
ulties, with the result that multi-lingual professors of international
reputation taught side by side (and often subordinated to) ones whose
main merit consisted in political reliability.

Spending on social security amounted to 12 to 16, and that on education between 4 to 6 per cent of the national income in the period (both

figures only equalled or exceeded in Scandinavia and a few, but not all Western European countries at the time). With its cultural policies in general, the regime made even further efforts to influence the mental well-being of the citizens. These policies took stock of the appetites naturally awakened by growing material affluence, some more breathing space and a somewhat limited access to the wider world, and not only satisfied but also generated demand for cultural goods, while finding usually subtle ways to exercise control over their enjoyment. This was achieved in terms of a strategy described in Hungarian with reference to the 'three Ts' (*tilt, tűr, támogat*), a division of the cultural sphere into products that were, for the sake of preserving the alliteration, prohibited, permitted and promoted. Ones that were not subjected to the widely exercised practice of self-censorship and violated one of the relatively few, but firmly established taboos (the one-party system and the 'leading role of the party' in achieving national goals; Hungary's relations with the Soviet Union and its membership in the Warsaw Pact; naturally, 1956), or had a clearly and explicitly anti-Marxist character, were simply denied access to the audience by the authorities supervising publishers, film studios etc. as politically hostile to the regime or undermining public morality. This was not a very difficult thing to do, since the infrastructure of culture, too, was highly centralised and state managed. Next, there was a category of tolerated works of art and intellectual achievements, which were deemed neither likely to have a subversive affect, nor to be particularly conducive to the attainment of the professed social and political goals of the regime. These were allowed publicity, and even some share in the subventions the cultural sphere in general depended on, but far from the degree those supported on account of their actual or supposed representation of the 'socialist value system'.

This policy line was the application of the 'He who is not against us is with us' maxim to the cultural sphere, quasi-officially proclaimed at the Ninth Party Congress in 1966 and mainly associated with the name of György Aczél, Deputy Minister of Culture at the time and later Secretary of the Central Committee for cultural affairs. The system was not rigid, and the categories not very clearly defined; from the nature of things, the boundaries between 'prohibited' and 'permitted' very especially blurred, resulting in a great many comic blunders on the part of the censors – like in the case of a highly effective satirical film on the fifties, allowed to be made and then put aside for several years, or that of a somewhat heterodox biography of the 1919 Bolshevik leader Béla Kun, printed in many thousand copies and then destroyed. Nevertheless, on the whole it operated highly efficiently. If it did not bar the population from 'prohibited' works, it largely immunised people against them by the manipulation of the other two categories. More importantly for the general cultural condition of Hungary, it not only allowed, but encouraged a diversity in literary, artistic and scholarly trends, styles, tastes and moods, while it kept them under state tutelage and prevented them from becoming independent agents; and in return for suppressing the thirst for the forbidden fruits, it habituated Hungarian society to a steady supply of high (and less high) quality cultural goods at very inexpensive prices.

By the 1970s, the first generation of 'populist' writers, ill at ease with the regimes ever since they made their appearance in the 1930s, became acknowledged as national classics, with full editions of the *oeuvres* of Illyés, Veres, Németh, Kodolányi and Erdei. Of the younger members of the same tradition, Sándor Csoóri wrote influential essays on social and historical subjects, and László Nagy and Ferenc Juhász poetry remarkable on account of its original combination of the populist tradition with surrealistic and avant-garde elements. The latter also edited the important literary journal *Új Írás* (New Writing). Others within the same tradition revived the sociographic mode of writing, their attention beginning to shift from the peasantry to the problems of Hungarian minorities abroad and various types of social delinquency as constituting central Hungarian 'problems of fate'. The bourgeois-humanistic tradition associated with the heritage of *Nyugat* survived, too. The sometimes playful, sometimes philosophical master of poetic form, Sándor Weöres, the Christian-existentialist János Pilinszky and the often highly abstract Dezső Tandori belong here, as well as already mentioned prose writers like Géza Ottlik, Miklós Mészöly, or Iván Mándy, whose lyrical and nostalgic novels and short stories recall the *fin-de-siècle* art of Krúdy. Tibor Déry turned from the realist representation of social conflict to parables on order and liberty. The 'one-minute' stories and dramas of István Örkény represent Central European grotesque at its best; irony was also a dominant element in the highly experimental prose of writers who grew to intellectual maturity during the Kádár era, like Péter Esterházy and Péter Nádas. Besides the latter two, György Konrád is generally considered as a standard bearer of the 'urbanist' tradition. After the forcible silencing of two pre–1945 camps of Hungarian literary and intellectual life between the late 1940s and 1956, during the first two decades of the Kádár era they lived in peaceful coexistence and dialogue, of which the main forums were journals like *Új Írás*, *Élet és Irodalom* (Life and Literature), *Kortárs* (Contemporary) and *Valóság* (Reality). The cleavages started to re-open during the unfolding of the crisis of the regime in the 1980s. Amidst circumstances made doubly difficult by repressive regimes and minority status, Hungarian literature managed to maintain high standards in Slovakia, Transylvania, and the considerably better-off Vojvodina, too, with emblematic figures like Zoltán Fábry, András Sütő, and a host of younger authors. Besides the more sophisticated literature represented by these figures, the period also abounded in high quality literature of the more popular kind, but the print runs of Déry or Örkény also hit and surpassed the 100,000 mark (while books of the other category might sell in 500,000 to even one million copies, in a country of ten million inhabitants).

Besides the often merely symbolic prices of books, which now included, with few exceptions, the whole range of western classics of literature (less so of the social sciences), the general prestige of reading obviously played a part in this. Over one-third of Hungarians were regular readers of books as well as newspaper and journals; one in five of them were members of about 9,000 lending libraries whose aggregate holdings rose sevenfold, to 50 million volumes in the period.

They were also unusually frequent theatre- and concert-goers, not the least because they received very good value for the price of the ticket (not the least because they actually paid less that half of it, the other part consisting of a state subsidy). The cinema became somewhat less popular than earlier, no doubt because the television was a powerful rival from the time the first broadcast in 1957 started to change leisure preferences. At the same time, Hungarian film-making entered a new golden age, first, with spectacular and very popular historical films (often renderings of novels by Jókai or Gárdonyi), whose master was Zoltán Várkonyi; second, with art films on eternal human themes often subtly related to sensitive issues in Hungary's past and present by directors like Zoltán Fábry, Károly Makk, Miklós Jancsó, István Szabó, András Kovács, Zoltán Huszárik (the peak of the many international successes being the Oscar for Szabó's *Mephisto* in 1982); and with *cinema vérité*-style half-documentaries on tension-ridden social and historical topics by Sándor Sára, Gyula Gazdag, Pál Schiffer and others.

The creative arts were also greatly relieved by the removal of the straitjacket of social realism, the most original artists being the constructivist Jenő Barcsay and the unclassifiable painters Ignác Kokas and Béla Kondor. Exhibitions of the oeuvre of major twentieth-century western artists, including Pablo Picasso, Henry Moore, Marc Chagall, or the Hungarian originated Amerigo Tot, reached Hungary for the first time in these years. In music, Bartók was at last assigned his proper place, and a new generation inspired by him and Kodály, consisting of Emil Petrovics, Sándor Szokolay, Zsolt Durkó, György Kurtág and others, produced outstanding musical pieces. Individual virtuosi (Zoltán Kocsis), orchestras and opera singers (Szilvia Sass) who later became favourites of international audiences started their careers in the 1970s.

Music was also a sphere in which quite revolutionary changes that affected popular and youth culture in general were taking place. The survival of the popularity of traditional genres like operetta and 'gypsy' music only accentuated the explosive effect of beat in the 1960s (although the interwar advent and later survival of jazz, and the twist-craze of home parties in the late 1950s to some extent prepared the ground). After beginnings at club-level in the early 1960s, the Hungarian Lennons and Jaggers were somewhat unwittingly helped into the limelight and to the hair-rising of fans of Hungarian Sinatras by the high publicity pop-song festival broadcasted by Hungarian Television in 1966. Their actual and supposed nonconformity initially evoked harassment by the authorities, a pattern that repeated itself in the 1970s and 1980 in the case of most of the new arrivals on the rock scene, which closely followed the international development of the genre. Nevertheless, it became integrated in the Hungarian cultural landscape, interestingly reflecting its cleavages in the distinction between more cosmopolitan (underground and new wave) trends and ones closer to the national musical tradition. At the same time, the modern devotion to the national tradition has found its most appropriate expression today in the dance house movement: the revival of authentic peasant music and the customs clustered around it, which has also attracted sizeable crowds of young people. On account of its alleged nationalist overtones, the attitude of the authorities was initially ambivalent in this case, too; however, by now Márta Sebestyén and several groups have already made the initiative familiar to international audiences.

The 'three Ts' were, as a matter of fact, also the signposts that were to steer academic life in the direction held desirable by the authorities. The main co-ordinator of research and the training of researchers was the Hungarian Academy of Sciences, whose network of specialised institutes was greatly expanded (some of the new institutes, like those for history and philosophy, created with the hardly concealed purpose of giving an 'asylum' and a research opportunity for scholars who had proved 'unreliable' in 1956, while isolating them from university students). While its intertwining with the political hierarchy and its representation of the official ideological priorities was quite clear, research was more or less free even in the social sciences (publication, of course, being a separate issue), and many gestures showed that the regime was keen on maintaining an image of academic liberty. In 1977, the outstanding, non-party-affiliated anatomist János Szentágothai was allowed to be elected to the quasi-ministerial post of President of the Academy. Early on in the period, the Hungarian Academy in Rome and the Collegium Hungaricum in Vienna were re-opened, and were soon accompanied by Hungarian cultural institutes elsewhere (the ones in the West occasionally serving the purposes of intelligence, besides the maintenance of cultural ties).

Political viewpoints, of course, did not seriously affect the natural sciences, where theoretical mathematics yielded the greatest results in the work of Lipót Fejér, Frigyes Riesz, Pál Erdős and their disciples (although the Hungarian Nobel Prize winners of the period – Jenő Wigner, György Hevesy, György Békésy and Dénes Gábor – all worked outside Hungary). The achievement of Károly Novobáczky in quantum physics is also worth mentioning, and Hungarian pharmacologists, zoologists and computer scientists have also been held in international esteem. In the social sciences, the recovery of sociology and psychology, effectively banned in the 1950s as vestiges of 'bourgeois' science, and the subsequent growth of political science (to rival 'scientific socialism') were important developments, but the internationally best known and most challenging achievement was probably the analysis of the characteristics and the limitations of the command economy by the economist János Kornai. Monumental multi-volume syntheses, the results of collective effort in which high academic standards often shine through the glaze of Marxist jargon, marked the era in literary science, history, ethnography and art history.

There were interesting cases of counter-productive policies here, too. The debate officially stimulated in the 1960s in historiography regarding nationalism, in order to emphasise class war as the vehicle of history, the relative insignificance of national independence movements and the importance of supra-national commitments, evoked the opposite effect by encouraging inquiries into the history of nationhood and national consciousness. These inquiries later served as a background to the widely known thesis of Jenő Szűcs concerning the historical regions of Europe. The same debate also spurred a revival of interest in and a realistic assessment of Hungary's place in the Habsburg Monarchy, especially after 1867 – hardly reconcilable with the simultaneous cult of the 'revolutionary' or 'progressive' tradition (the absurd continuity between 1848, 1919 and 1945, emphasised in official ideology). In philosophy, the work of György Lukács in the 1960s made a great impact within as well as outside the country, not only because of the writing of great syntheses of aesthetics, moral philosophy and ontology by the master, but also on account of the growth of the 'Budapest School' of critical Marxism around him.

The fate of the 'Budapest School' (Ferenc Fehér, Ágnes Heller, György Márkus and Mihály Vajda representing a first, and György Bence and János Kis a second generation) was one of the symptoms of a changing climate in Hungary in the early 1970s. Its members advocated a reconsideration of the necessary link between Marxist philosophy and the political goals of the working class movement, they called for pluralism within the tradition, and criticised theoretical dogmatism as well as practical steps associated with it, such as the 1968 suppression of the Czechoslovak effort to create 'socialism with a human face' by the invasion of the Warsaw Pact countries. In 1973, they were expelled from the party and their jobs, and barred from publication; a few years later some of them emigrated, while others became marginalised and suppressed into clandestine (*samizdat*, literally self-published) literature until 1989. In the same year, the prosecution of Miklós Haraszti, the author of a heterodox sociographical description of 'piece-work' (the title of the account), indicated that the case of the philosophers was not an isolated phenomenon. In 1974, the arrest of Konrád and Iván Szelényi, whose manuscript on 'The Path of the Intelligentsia to Class Power' was deemed a subversive interpretation of the roots and prospects of the socialist system, continued the story. It was also in 1973 that the police arrested 'nationalist demonstrators' who dared to commemorate March 15 (the anniversary of the 1848 Revolution) independently of and with slogans different from those of the 'Revolutionary Youth Days', officially organised under the sign of the supposed continuity of the 'progressive' tradition of 1848–1919–1945, mentioned above.

The resumption of ideological warfare after what was (despite sporadic action, mainly against religious nonconformists and New Left 'deviants') a decade of relative peace, took place against a general background of the blockage of the Hungarian reform process. Even before the reforms of 1968 were introduced, the endeavour of opening the system had been criticised by various voices in the political and intellectual elite as diluting the commitment to the socialist system of values and jeopardising egalitarianism and the prospects of the rise of the 'socialist type of man' (without ever actually defining what it was) by the revival of 'petty bourgeois' love of gain and individualism. These critics drew reinforcement from the conservative trend in the Soviet leadership, which already started after the accession of Brezhnev in 1964, but became especially pronounced precisely after 1968, the year of the 'Prague Spring'. Besides, at first the reform process indeed rather adversely affected the positions of workers of the uncompetitive industrial giants, who felt that they were handicapped by the reforms which seemed (quite rightly) to favour more flexible companies and professional expertise and managerial work; and a powerful pressure group consisting of the managers of large trusts found spokesmen in influential members in the Political Committee of the party like Béla Biszku and Zoltán Komócsin.

Already at the conference of the Budapest Party Committee in February 1972, the reform process was sharply criticised by the 'workers' opposition' on account of its abandoning the monopoly of state property, neglecting the working class in the redistribution network, and tolerating the revival of 'petty bourgeois' values. The same reproaches were made to Kádár shortly thereafter on a Moscow visit by an even more commanding source. Later, but still in the same year, Brezhnev turned up on a lightning visit in Hungary, and although the story that upon being presented a list of reformers to be removed from the leadership, Kádár simply replied: 'one name is missing – mine', may be apocryphal, it is not a far cry from what actually happened subsequently. The concerted attack on the reforms at first resulted in re-centralisation through a number of measures. Household plots of the peasantry, ancillary industrial plants of agricultural co-operatives, secondary jobs, especially of professionals, were subjected to more severe regulations. The fifty largest industrial companies were again relegated under direct state management, and their deficit was balanced out with incomes drawn from profitable enterprises. The 'hand management' of companies, that is, their subjection to direct ministerial order, was revived; among the criteria of cadre selection, political reliability gained weight again, and holders of managerial posts were sent to courses in Marxism-Leninism (most of them run by the party high school, which had risen to the status of university in 1968). To top the changes, in March 1974 Nyers and Aczél were demoted, and in 1975 the reform-minded Prime Minister Jenő Fock was replaced with the conservative György Lázár.

The effects of this reorientation for an economy ridden with contradictions in spite of the reform of 1968 were only aggravated by the simultaneously emerging world economic crisis. The fivefold increase of oil prices, and an almost similar growth in that of raw materials in general within a few years after 1973 constituted a serious challenge to the Hungarian economy (dependent as it was on these very commodities) precisely at a time when it was most ill-equipped to cope with it. The rise in prices of finished products, which were mostly inferior and uncompetitive anyway, lagged 30 per cent or more behind that of fuels and raw materials; Hungary, which earned about half of its national income from foreign trade, lost over 20 per cent of its trade within a few years. In 1980, eight times as many buses were transported to the Soviet Union in return for the same amount of oil as in 1970. While the fiction that the oil resources of the Soviet Union were inexhaustible and would continue to form the solid basis of Hungarian industry maintained itself and encouraged further unreasonable investments in oil refineries and the chemical industry, efforts were made to develop independent sources of energy. Of these, however, only the Paks nuclear power plant (launched in 1983) became a success; on the other hand, the plan to build a gigantic network of water dams to serve as an electric power station in co-operation with Czechoslovakia remained unaccomplished until it became, on account of its predictably disastrous ecological consequences, an object of intensive political debate in the late 1980s and was finally abandoned.

The Kádár regime, whose legitimacy was based on growing living standards and full employment, could not afford to respond to the crisis by dismantling energy-dependent companies, by reductions, dismissals, austerity measures and technological innovation, as was the case in the more developed market economies of the world. Also, motivated by the expectation that the crisis would not last long, it was decided to maintain the rapid growth rate. The fact that foreign trade dramatically declined, instead of the 10 per cent annual growth it ought to have yielded to answer these requirements, resulted in a deficit that in ten years equalled a full year's national income, or nearly the amount lost during the Second World War. There was only one way to offset these effects: the incurring of loans in western financial markets, in order to finance investments, to counterbalance deficits and to raise (and later merely to maintain) living standards.

The fact that western creditors welcomed Hungarian approaches was at least to some extent a reward for the favourable image the Kádár regime was able to build up internationally during the decade after the consolidation of 1962–1963. By way of an interesting dialectic, in the post-1974 years when 'reform' became increasingly confined to rhetoric but was less evident in a perceptible growth of actual well-being, foreign recognition also rose to prominence among the factors that comprised the domestic legitimacy of the regime. Viewed from yet another angle, while 1956 confined Hungary to some extent to a diplomatic ghetto, and even during the period after consolidation the conditions of domestic liberalisation were bought at the price of subservience to Soviet interests on the international scene, the fruits of liberalisation ripened and brought applause in western circles and, consequently, slightly more freedom of movement, albeit with a somewhat ironic delay of phase: more precisely, by the time the brakes were put on the momentum of the economic reforms within the country.

Hungary's foreign policy in the 1960s was marked by sometimes covertly grudging, but apparently unconditional loyalty to Big Brother on all accounts. These included the strengthening of the *Pax Sovietica* (the imperially imposed suppression of conflicts between the small nations of the region) by acquiescing to measures adversely affecting the condition of the Hungarian minorities in Czechoslovakia and Romania at the turn of the 1950s and 1960s; imitating Soviet policies in the opening-up towards third world and non-aligned countries, whose significance was mere propaganda at the time; zealously echoing the Soviet position concerning the diverging trends within the communist camp, for example, the break with China and Albania after 1963; consistently voting in line with the Soviet representative in the United Nations; and, in spite of Kádár's desperate effort to mediate between the Kremlin and the Czechoslovak leadership of Alexander Dubček, whose experiment of 'socialism with a human face' was not very different from what was happening in Hungary at the time, it also implied taking part in the Warsaw Pact invasion of Czechoslovakia 'to avert a counter-revolutionary take-over' in August 1968.

Yet, at the same time 'real' diplomacy began to supplement the ritual exchanges of visits between the leaders of Hungary and other Eastern Bloc countries. The first instances of this change were the Budapest talks of the Austrian Chancellor Josef Klaus in 1967 and the Finnish President Urho Kekkonen in 1969, with the message that the path of peaceful coexistence between the two 'world systems' led through co-operation with the neutral countries which nevertheless lived in a different social order. More decisive was the rapprochement with West Germany, greatly facilitated, in the face of opposition by Brezhnev and Hungarian dogmatists, by the conciliatory *Ostpolitik* championed since 1966 by Willy Brandt as Foreign Minister, and later Chancellor. As a result of the swift development of ties between the two countries after the assumption of full diplomatic relations in 1973, by the 1980s West Germany came only second to the Soviet Union as a partner of Hungary in economic and cultural exchanges. It was also in 1973 that, after the restoration of diplomatic relations on the ambassadorial level in 1966, an agreement on compensation for American property nationalised in Hungary after 1945 was signed with the United States. Against the background of steadily improving relations thereafter, the Holy Crown of Saint Stephen (smuggled out of the country by Szálasi in 1945 and captured by the Americans as war booty) was restored to Hungary by the Carter administration in 1978, and an Institute of Hungarian Studies was established at Indiana University (Bloomington) in 1979. The United States also played a part in the normalisation of relations between Budapest and the Vatican by way of a compromise concerning Mindszenty's embarrassing presence at the United States embassy in the Hungarian capital. The Cardinal was pardoned and allowed to leave the country, while Pope Paul VI removed the somewhat disgruntled prelate from his office. As a result, the restoration of the full hierarchy of the Roman Catholic Chruch in Hungary could take place, with the appointment of László Lékai as Archbishop of Esztergom in 1976.

From the mid-1970s on, mutual visits between Kádár and the top-ranking leaders of the western world demonstrated not only that Hungary was seen by them as a model child of the Eastern Bloc, but also that the formerly despised puppet of the Kremlin emerged in their eyes as a wise political pragmatist who established unparalleled economic and cultural liberty beyond the Iron Curtain and was a consistent partner in endeavours to peaceful coexistence – at a time when Romania's defiance of Soviet policies was counterbalanced by its appalling human rights record, and the other countries of the Eastern Bloc (except Poland, but only until the introduction of martial law in 1981) were ruled by ossified Brezhnevite regimes. Hungary earned this recognition by, and used it for, cautiously expanding its sphere of movement and asserting some independence in foreign policy. One of the cases in question was Kádár's repeated declaration of his acknowledgement of the 'Eurocommunism' of the Western European communist parties, which accepted the market economy and political pluralism, and were therefore sharply criticised by the Soviets. In a more sophisticated fashion, and also with serious limitations, Hungary started to test the flexibility of the *Pax Sovietica.*

Among the neighbouring countries, the condition of the half million (by 1980, only 430,000) strong Hungarian minority in Yugoslavia was relatively the most favourable. Although the one-party system prevented them, as well as others, from politically representing their interests, they drew advantages from the federal structure of the republic. Hungarian was one of the five official languages of the autonomous area of Vojvodina; they were well supplied with schools, maintained an independent publishing house and extremely high quality dailies and cultural journals, and in 1969 the first Institute of Hungarian Studies in Central Europe was opened in Novi Sad (Újvidék). After the abandonment of the visa requirement between the two countries in 1966, the development of a vigorous border-traffic seemed to warrant the statement of Kádár and Tito upon the latter's Budapest visit in 1964 that the minorities played the role of a bridge between the two countries. It was in the late 1980s, along with the tightening of the Yugoslav regime under Slobodan Milošević on other fronts as well, that mass harassment of the Hungarians in the Vojvodina started, culminating in the lifting of the autonomy of the area in 1991.

As regards the other neighbouring countries, whereas under Stalinism Moscow strongly discouraged the competing state nationalisms, ethnic self-government was also no more desirable than other kinds of autonomy. Yet, for the Hungarians in Romania (1.5 million in 1960 and 1,670,000 in 1980), after the promising signs under the post-war Groza administration and their thwarting thereafter, things seemed to take a turn for the better again with the creation of the Hungarian Autonomous Territory in the ethnically nearly fully Magyar-inhabited Szekel area. After 1956, a series of anti-Hungarian measures included restrictions of the use of Hungarian outside that territory, the prosecution of several leaders of the Hungarian National League who protested against the measure, the unification of many Hungarian educational institutions with Romanian ones (including the Bolyai University of Cluj/Kolozsvár in 1959), and the transformation of the ethnic composition of the autonomous territory in favour of Romanians by changing administrative boundaries in the country. An even worse phase started with the accession of Nicolae Ceauşescu at the head of the Romanian Communist Party, with his thinly veiled nationalist programme. The Autonomous Territory was abolished in 1968; a 'national homogenisation programme' drastically restricted education in the mother tongue; and various administrative measures aimed at minimising the contacts of the Hungarian minority with the mother country. Finally, in Czechoslovakia, after the collective punishment in the post-war years, the Hungarian minority (530,000 in 1960 and 580,000 in 1980) regained their rights of citizenship and were allowed to launch a the Cultural Association of Hungarian Workers in Czechoslovakia and a daily newspaper in 1949. After a relative standstill, the situation definitely worsened in the 1960s, when the administrative units were shaped with a view to eliminating earlier Hungarian majorities in the districts, and access to educational facilities in the mother tongue (and at university level even in Slovak) became limited for Hungarians. The 1968 law on the national minorities made no allowance for cultural autonomy.

By the end of the 1970s, Kádár occasionally openly referred to the fact that (after the earlier expectation that the minorities would automatically assimilate under socialism had been abandoned) from the 1960s on the minorities in Hungary enjoyed expanding educational and cultural facilities, and their rights as collective entities were acknowledged in the constitutional amendment of 1972; and expressed his hope that the Hungarians across the borders would enjoy the same benefits. But in the 1960s, when the Hungarian minorities in Romania and Czechoslovakia were exposed to a progressive deterioration of their lot, most of the references to their situation on the part of Kádár himself, or the long-serving Foreign Minister János Péter or other Hungarian leaders, were made with a tone of satisfaction. The sporadic criticism at the end of the decade of the assimilationist tendencies in 'certain countries', clearly referring to Romania, was mainly instigated from Moscow, where it was thought that Ceauşescu deserved occasional scoldings and admonitions because of his independently minded endeavours.

This rather cynical and selective approach changed in the 1970s, when Kádár and his colleagues thought that more serious attention to the problem of the Hungarian minorities was an attitude they could now both afford to display because of the freedom of movement already attained, and one they could exploit further by gaining support from

Hungarian intellectuals sensitive to the issue within the country and sympathy outside it. A case in question was the 1975 Helsinki Conference on European Safety and Co-operation, where Kádár very strongly endorsed both the inviolability of current European borders and the clause on human rights and the free movement of ideas, a combination which greatly strengthened the Hungarian position in any potential dispute over the condition of the minorities. Hungarian delegates at subsequent conferences always showed considerable interest in human rights issues. On this basis, Kádár even intervened with Ceauşescu at two meetings in 1977, unsuccessfully. On account of the Hungarians of Transylvania, relations with Romania became tense in the 1980s; Kádár's belated and half-hearted effort also failed to boost his support at home (in fact, the contrary happened).

Even if, on the whole, the recognition of the West did much to sustain the regime long after it started to show symptoms of dysfunctioning, the dimensions of the economic crisis called for structural solutions. In 1978, Hungarian exports already yielded less than the interests of the debts contracted, as a result of which even the interest payment became dependent on new loans. By that year, Hungary's foreign debts amounted to 8 billion dollars, ten times as much as in the beginning of the decade. In October 1977, the Central Committee decided not only to return to the reforms abandoned between 1972 and 1974, but to steer them more radically towards the market economy, to abandon import-substituting industrialisation and to stimulate export capable sectors to production for a world market. To lend weight to the decision, the chief opponents of reform, Biszku and Apró, were removed from the leadership in 1978. One cluster of measures concerned the system of large industrial companies, some of which possessed a monopoly over entire sectors; to enhance competitiveness, these were decentralised, not only in industry, but also in services. A single Ministry of Industry, whose role was confined to industrial policy-making, replaced the different branch ministries which directly interfered with the management of firms. Foreign trade was liberalised, companies could obtain independent foreign trade permits, and the establishment of joint ventures with western firms was encouraged. The labour market became fully liberalised, too. A radical reform of the pricing system aimed to keep, through continuing heavy subsidies, only the prices of basic commodities (30 per cent of fundamental consumption goods) and some services like public transport, and cultural goods, from following real values. The introduction of long-term land leases was intended to give further incentives to small-scale intensive farming. But the most characteristic and far-reaching part of the wave of economic reforms beginning in 1978 was the abandonment of earlier reservations relating to small-scale enterprise in general, and the lifting of earlier restrictions that concerned it in industry. After the Central Committee acknowledged, in February 1980, that the 'secondary economy' performed useful functions in each of the economic sectors, new 'economic communities' started to proliferate within and outside company gates to provide for the eagerness to supplement incomes from work done beyond the forty hour week.

The reforms begun in 1978 – which were unopposed either by the mortally ill Brezhnev or his successors – brought about profound changes in the structure of the economy and life patterns in Hungary. Four hundred new state managed companies were launched, a quarter of them authorised to pursue foreign trade on their own. Even more significantly, by 1985 there were (besides 140,000 private small-scale artisans, nearly the same figure as prior to the last nationalisations in 1948) about 30,000 new 'economic communities' in industry and services providing a source of extra income for practitioners of a wide range of occupations from bakers and designers through masons and barbers to electricians and language teachers. Approximately two-thirds of the population became involved in the secondary (or, in the cases of many of them, the tertiary) economy consisting of small companies with little administration, flexible enough to take advantage of, but also vulnerable to, the frequent changes and inconsistencies in the relevant regulations – the unpredictability of the system, with the result that a mentality of predatory capitalism, a 'take what you can as soon as you can' attitude, characterised much of this preliminary stage of the return to the market economy in Hungary. Nevertheless, or precisely for this reason, the secondary economy may have provided as much as one-third of the whole output of agriculture and the services in this period, with industry rapidly closing the gap; and as much as 40 per cent or more of incomes may have been earned in it.

However, the reform process failed to produce the expected result. After a short initial period of growth, in the second half of the 1980s it tended towards zero. Inflation, practically unknown in Hungary since 1946, now started to climb, at official annual rates (which might mean considerably more in reality) of 8 to 10 per cent and over 15 per cent in the second half of the decade; nevertheless, true to the principles of Kádárism, real incomes had to be at least maintained or slightly increased, which could only happen through the incurring of further debts. By the end of the decade and the era, these amounted to 20 billion dollars, or the largest per capita debt in the world. In 1982, state bankruptcy was avoided by an extremely narrow margin, thanks to a short-term loan from the International Monetary Fund, of which Hungary became a member in the same year. Again, the fact that state guidance still required a considerable but practically idle bureaucracy meant a low cost-efficiency, while the regime could not afford dismissing it because unemployment was unacceptable for ideological reasons. The intractability of the debt crisis by traditional methods and within a framework which included even the slightest remnants of communism, demonstrated the unsustainability of the regime for 'reform economists' and segments of intellectuals who were familiar with the details or knew from hearsay what was carefully concealed from the public. However, the public was able to assess the situation from experience. The one-third who were unable or unwilling to become involved in the secondary economy, were embittered because their living standard was deteriorating in absolute as well as in comparative terms. According to data of the Central Statistical Office, in 1987 1.9 million people, nearly 20 per cent of the population, lived on or below the 'social minimum' level.

Although not specifically related to these circumstances, some types of social delinquency became aggravated in Hungary: in the mid-1980s, the country ranked first in international suicide statistics, and second in those relating to the consumption of spirits and liquors. Though the system discouraged the articulation of social tensions, they perceptibly imbued everyday life. While the long-standing cleavage between Jews and non-Jews was, to all intents and purposes, confined to the intelligentsia in the capital, resentment against party members, generally regarded as social climbers, was ubiquitous among those outside the party. Anti-Roma sentiments were also widespread. The incompleteness of the integration of the Roma population in the ordinary structures of Hungarian society was made more conspicuous by their dynamic demographic growth, as they became overrepresented among groups that were objects of suspicion, despised or envied: criminals, paupers or successful new businessmen.

During the second half of the 1980s, many of the two-thirds of Hungarian society who did supplementary work soon began to feel that the sacrifices they were making were grossly disproportionate with the rewards that accrued to them. The fact that growing self-exploitation was hardly sufficient even to maintain the standards already achieved, let alone raising them, gradually undermined the terms of the legitimacy of the Kádár regime: the comforts they could earn now seemed more limited than warranted by their renouncements. Instead of the earlier self-congratulation, they now became annoyed when reminded that they were still comparatively well-off, referring to the greater repression, poverty, cultural boredom and external isolation of other Eastern bloc countries. There was, in the sixties, a turn of phrase recurring in the performances of a Soviet cabaret actor, very popular in Hungary, that passed for an adage: 'We've got something – but not the real thing ...' – a bitter-sweet piece of self-irony, poignantly expressing the slight *mal-*

aise the citizen under Kádárism felt upon contemplating that, after all, he was just happy with the 'something'. By the second half of the eighties, the sweetness had gone. Without knowing precisely what it was, people started to desire the real thing. The disaffection of the general public was creeping, rather than bursting, into the atmosphere of the 1980s in Hungary. True, it was first aggravated by the sham optimism of official statements during party conferences or at the Thirteenth Congress in March 1985, and two years later by the open acknowledgement of the failure of the reforms to produce any improvement. Yet, it did not fuel active resistance or mass disobedience as in virtually all of the other Eastern bloc countries in 1989–1990 (or, in Poland, earlier); it would have hardly led to the changes of 1989, and the circumstances of the fall of Kádár in the previous year might have at least been very different, without several other factors that emerged simultaneously with the economic crisis of the regime. The international climate also changed markedly; this, together with the economic crisis, precipitated also a moral and political crisis resulting in strife within the party elite; and all of these circumstances made it possible for the small and hitherto isolated opposition groups to emerge as an alternative political elite willing and able to replace its predecessor by way of a 'negotiated revolution'.

After the détente of the 1970s, Soviet-American rivalisation entered into a new phase of ideological warfare and armaments race, whose pressure the Soviet Union was unable to withstand, and had a leader who was capable of acting upon such a recognition, but did not realise (as no-one realised at the time) that the path he chose to do so would lead to the disintegration of the Soviet empire. A considerable amount of money was spent already under the Carter administration for the support of human rights movements and agencies, with the goal of undermining the Soviet bloc through the financing and advising its internal critics; but ultimately it was the 'Star War' programme launched under Ronald Reagan in 1985 that constituted a challenge with which the Soviet economy could not cope. Mikhail Gorbachev, who succeeded to the head of the Soviet Communist Party in the same year, not only hoped to galvanise the empire through comprehensive economic and political reform, but also inclined to avoid confrontation. In order not to be distracted from the soaring internal problems of the empire, by the end of 1988 he clearly seemed to have abandoned the 'Brezhnev doctrine' in terms of which the Soviet Union undertook to resort to military force in critical situations in the eastern bloc countries. In other words, he intimated that the events of 1956 in Hungary and 1968 in Czechoslovakia (and one could add 1981 in Poland, where invasion was only prevented by the announcement of martial law) would not be repeated.

Kádár, the one-time pioneer of reforms in the Soviet bloc, was deeply disturbed by the aspirations of Gorbachev, for they now made virtually any depth of reform possible, whereas the ones effected up to 1985 were the maximum he was willing to concede. Perceiving this, it was rumoured among the broad segment of reformers in the party rank-and-file, whose expectations were heightened by the 'Gorbachev-phenomenon', that the Soviet party leader's statements were censored in Hungary as well as in the more rigid socialist countries. At the final stage, multiple candidacy was introduced in 1983 at general elections with a chance for 'independent', that is, non-party candidates to qualify – with the result that 10 per cent of seats in the new parliament went to such deputies in 1985. Any step further, for instance, in the opening-up of the public sphere, would have inevitably challenged the taboos upon which Kádár's own status rested. This is the reason why, supported by a faceless crowd of yes-men of his own age in the party leadership, he stubbornly denied any allegation that Hungary was in crisis. As in July 1987, the falsity of the hitherto official representation of Hungary's situation had to be acknowledged, Kádár decided to drop the long-serving Prime Minister György Lázár, and replaced him with one of the several vigorous, relatively younger figures who were biding their time in the lower echelons of the hierarchy: Károly Grósz, the most characteristic representative of the new, technocratic type of cadres who was in favour of going on with the economic reforms without changing the political system.

The policy of transition to a market economy based on mixed forms of property (state, co-operative and private) was thus carried forward with the codification of the equality of private enterprise with the state managed sector, the elimination of subsidised prices, the return, after forty years, to a two-level banking system and the introduction of a new tax system, including a progressive personal income tax. Grósz continued the 'openness' policy towards the West by abolishing all travel restrictions, while winning Gorbachev's confidence as well. By this time, the latter had clearly no objections to getting rid of Kádár, who was aged, sick and tired in every sense of the word. He outlived his days; the stage was set for a succession struggle.

Besides Grósz, the main contenders included Nyers, the father of the 1968 economic reform, and Imre Pozsgay, whose commitment to reform, unlike the Prime Minister, extended to democratisation as well. He was not only supported by a sizeable reform-wing within the party and a group of social scientists who prepared, to some extent under his protection, a scenario of transition to pluralism in 1986 ('Turning-Point and Reform'), but also communicated with a segment of the opposition led by the 'populist' intellectuals. A party investigation against him, and the expulsion of four prominent reformist intellectuals from the party in the spring of 1988 were intended by Kádár and the 'old guard' to deter the party opposition. However, the measure missed its target and only reinforced the murmurers. On May 22, 1988, Kádár's political career came to an end: the party conference elevated him to the newly established and entirely impotent post of Party Chairman, and elected Grósz as Party Secretary while nearly completely reshuffling the Political Committee.

With this plurality of offices, Grósz concentrated considerable power in his hands, and under different circumstances he might have consolidated his own position as well as the bulwarks of the party-state for some time to come. However, the complicated problems of a rotten economic structure impossible to patch up, the increasingly unpredictable (or, much too predictable) horizons Gorbachev's initiatives were opening, the deep generational and political divisions occasioned within the party and the obvious loss of confidence among the population were many factors whose permanent flux undermined the self-confidence of the party itself, and it ceased to be a force that could be mobilised to defend those bulwarks. As more and more people put it at the time, it was on the way to decomposition, and while the Premier/First Secretary could and did exert occasional shows of power, his rank-and-file became diffident and impotent. On the other hand, by this time the different opposition groups that had been germinating for a considerable while in the 'secondary public sphere' (which, unlike the 'secondary economy', did not gain recognition) stepped forward into the primary one, and started to arise as political parties, presenting the public with analyses of the past and present of communism, diagnoses of Hungary's predicament, and antidotes to it, which proved to be more credible than the versions represented by officialdom.

From its inception in the late 1970s, the opposition that arose as a viable political alternative a decade later was distinguishable from the post-1968 dissidents both by their ideological-political orientation and their strategy. Instead of grafting pluralism and democracy on to Marxism, which experience showed to be futile, they drew on the liberal-democratic and Christian-national traditions; and instead of the similarly futile effort to represent these endeavours in the 'primary' public sphere, whose organs and institutions were dominated by the party, they created and maintained autonomous organisations. At the outset, these initiatives were confined to a few dozen individuals, maintaining contacts with a few hundred others among the intellectuals of research institutes, university departments, editorial offices and student circles; through these, their views started to infiltrate the pages of literary and social science journals of the 'primary' sphere that were testing the limits of utterability under circumstances still defined by the policy of the 'three Ts'. From the mid-1980s on, some of them also developed contacts with reformers within the party. At all times, the authorities possessed detailed and up-to-date information about the activities of the opposition and the groups linked with them. However, as one of the main constituents of its capital (in the most literal sense, considering the source of the loans) was its image in the West, the regime could not afford to show an iron fist. Whenever the opposition made itself visible to the general public by coming out on the streets (for alternative commemorations on March 15, or demonstrations on October 23, the anniversary of the 1956 Revolution), up to 1988 arrests, detentions and beatings invariably followed. Otherwise, the regime remained content with occasional harassment: sporadic searches, the confiscation of illegal publications, the rejection of travel permits, silences imposed on writers and the replacement of editorial boards in the 'primary' sphere when they were deemed to have gone too far in cultivating forbidden fruit.

Far from being homogeneous, from the outset the cleavages within the opposition reflected the old urbanist-populist divide, although they maintained a dialogue about ways to co-operate until the eve of the transition process. The so-called 'democratic opposition' laid the emphasis on human rights issues and an autonomous civic sphere. Their beginnings in 1977–1978 included a collection of manuscripts critical of Marxism (already from outside the tradition) by authors including Bence and Kis; protest against the suppression of the Czechoslovak opposition (the similarly human rights oriented Charter '77 movement); and 'flying university' lectures on sensitive issues in private apartments. In 1979, the first independent charity, the Poor Relief Fund, was launched by Ottilia Solt to challenge the regime on account of its concealing and neglecting pauperism. In 1980, Gábor Demszky began as a publisher of *samizdat* literature, the most renowned being the periodical *Beszélő* (Speaker, from 1981), available from the clandestine 'shop' run by László Rajk (son of the executed Communist minister).

As regards the 'populists', they identified national 'questions of fate' as their main commitment, such as the condition of Hungarian minorities in neighbouring countries, types of social delinquency, demographic problems, the condition of the Churches, the loosening of communal ties and the effects of communism on national consciousness in general. The neglect of especially the first of these issues by the government led to the beginnings of this trend, also at the end of the 1970s, with the suppression of the critical writings of Illyés on the subject and the subsequent first meeting of the group at the home of the poet and teacher Sándor Lezsák in 1979. From 1983 (the year Illyés died), Sándor Csoóri became the dominant figure among the 'populists', with polemical writings combining the above-mentioned themes with a criticism of the morally detrimental effects of socialism.

Among the legal organisations and bodies that were in various ways linked with either or both of the trends of the opposition, we find, predictably, the Writer's Association and a few social science institutes of the Academy; specialised colleges of university students (especially those of law and economics); groups of young artists; the Danube Circle of environmentalists; and different half-formal debating societies. Literary magazines like *Tiszatáj* (Tisza Region) and *Forrás* (Fount) sheltered contributions by the 'populists', as did the journal *Mozgó Világ* (World in Motion), while the new social science periodicals *Medvetánc* (Bear Dance, from 1981) and *Századvég* (Fin-de-Siècle, from 1985) largely succeeded in outmanoeuvring censorship and discussing in an objective manner an extensive range of sensitive themes, sometimes indeed taboos, like Stalinism in Hungary and the Soviet bloc, 1956, anti-Semitism and the condition of the Roma minority, pauperism, the fate of the economic reform, anomalies of the social security system etc. Finally, both shades of the opposition and the clustering around them established links with the leaders of the Hungarian minorities abroad and drew encouragement and support from the Hungarian emigration in the West (for instance, in the shape of scholarships from the New York-based Open Society Foundation launched by the Hungarian-American businessman George Soros in 1982, which also opened a legal office in Budapest in 1987).

Religious sentiment (according to polls, in the 1980s about 50 per cent of the population described themselves as religious, though only 20 per cent attended church services regularly) was part of the background on which the opposition, especially the Christian-national group, established its challenges of Marxist party rule. However, despite the latent conflict between the regime and the Churches, on account of the hampering by the former of religious instruction, the building of new churches or the readmission of banned orders, the latter failed to become particularly active in criticising the government. Both the Protestant Churches and the Catholics expected the preservation of their status as alternative focuses of allegiance for believers mainly from co-operating with the regime. The latter, especially, even obtained the support of the Vatican in denouncing the work of 'fundamental congregations' that grew under the leadership of priests who were committed on social and political issues (for instance, they spoke out against general conscription) and demanded genuine independence for the Church.

In the first half of the 1980s, the endeavour of anti-communist co-operation dominated the relationship of the two camps of the opposition, so different in outlook. The first of such instances, in 1980, was the

joint authorship and edition of a *samizdat* volume of essays commemorating the recently deceased István Bibó, who became an emblematic
figure of both sides on account of his personal integrity as well as democratic and patriotic credentials. The last one was a conference at Monor
in June 1985, whose speakers addressed and analysed the most soaring
issues of the then generalised crisis. As, however, with the further rapid
aggravation of that crisis the transformation of the system responsible
for it came on to the agenda, and programmes started to be worked out,
the ways of 'urbanists' and 'populists' parted. In June 1987, Kis, Solt, and
Ferenc Kőszeg published the programme of the democratic opposition
entitled 'Social Contract' in *Beszélő*. While the political pluralism they
called for, in view of geopolitical circumstances, was accompanied by
the preservation of some prerogatives on the part of the Communists
and due allowance for Soviet imperial interests, they were uncompromising in claiming that the current leadership was unsuitable to guide
the process. 'Kádár must go', the document therefore concluded.

This sounded too radical for the 'populists', who (without submitting
a comprehensive programme) envisaged a more gradual transition,
with an active role of reform-Communists in it. As a result, the democratic opposition did not receive an invitation to the meeting of the
'populist' camp, again at Lakitelek, where the creation of the Hungarian
Democratic Forum (MDF), a legalised movement with the obvious goal
of developing into a political party, was resolved in the presence of
Pozsgay and a few other reform-Communists, on September 27, 1987.
Its 'urbanist' counterpart, the Network of Free Initiatives was launched
on May 1, 1988, only after a third nascent party had been founded by
one-time members of the college of law students. The Alliance of Young
Democrats (FIDESZ), established on March 30, 1988, originally as an
alternative of the Communist Youth League, endeavoured to some extent to supersede the urbanist-populist divide and submitted a programme in which a mixed economy, human rights, political pluralism
and national values were equally emphasised, although it also identified
itself as a radical liberal initiative and during the transition process and
for some time thereafter it remained the closest political ally of the erstwhile democratic opposition. The latter developed the Network of Free
Initiatives into the Alliance of Free Democrats (SZDSZ) on November
13, 1988, after their hope of integrating all or most of the opposition became ultimately thwarted by the mushroom-like proliferation of quasi-
political and other organisations (professional associations, independent trade unions etc.) during 1988. Shortly afterwards, the 'historical
parties' reorganised themselves, too: the Independent Smallholder
Party re-emerged on November 18, 1988, followed by the Social Democrats in January and the Christian Democrats in April 1989.

Even though by mid-1987 it was by the thousands, rather than by the dozens that the number of those familiar with opposition activities in Hungary could be measured, it was in the period between the appearance of the first opposition programmes and organisations and the *de facto* restoration of a multi-party scene, the autumn of 1987 and the spring of 1989, that truly broad sections of the general public became conscious of the existence of these pretenders to the role of a political elite. This was thanks to a true watershed of openness in the press, partly as a result of the legalisation of *samizdat* organs and the appearance of new ones in the hands of the opposition, but also of the expanding space given to heterodox views in older dailies and journals. It was not merely that the membership, for example, of the MDF soon climbed to 10,000; neither of the new parties intended to, and neither of them did become mass parties. Nor were the people at large permanently activised by them. However, a sufficient number of Hungarians were sufficiently well-informed about their goals and sufficiently sympathised with them, in order for them to be able to show on a few well-chosen occasions and issues that Grósz was wrong in suggesting once at the end of 1988 that 'the streets belong to us'.

There were few mass demonstrations, but all of them were organised under the auspices of the opposition, and exerted a great effect with the clear messages they conveyed. In June 1988, a demonstration on behalf of the Hungarian minority in Transylvania, which of late had also been exposed to the threat of Ceauşescu's megalomaniac plan of destroying the historic network of villages and towns and amassing the population in 'industrial-agrarian centres', reminded the Communists that they had neglected the national interest. A protest march, in October 1988, against the construction of the hydro-electric system planned on the Danube called attention to the economic spoliation of communism and the disastrous ecological effects of its project 'to transform physical nature'. March 15, 1989, was clearly a competition for dominating the sequence of commemorative events; the opposition scored a sweeping triumph, the main message being that the 150 year old programme of civil liberty and representative government was, sadly enough, still on the agenda. Finally, the most dramatic of all events was the official reburial of the remains of Imre Nagy and his associates on the anniversary of their execution, June 16, 1956, amounting to the extortion of a public confession that its later (and by then highly questionable) achievement notwithstanding, in its origins the regime was built on terror and *justizmord*.

The fact that exactly a year before government representatives paid their tributes (besides over 300,000 citizens) to the martyrs of 1956, police had still used force to disperse a group of a few hundred demonstrators commemorating the Prime Minister of the revolution, illustrates the rapid erosion of the political resources of the authorities and the simultaneous expansion of space for the opposition by mid-1989. On the one hand, the government made further steps towards economic transition by the devaluation of the currency, the liberalisation of imports, the official abandonment of the dogma of full employment, and by legalising the transformation of state firms into different kinds of share-holding companies, thus taking the first steps towards creating the legal framework for the beginning of privatisation. In the short run, it also facilitated the extensive practice of the retention of state property in the hands of the managers of companies through the purchase of plants at symbolic prices with no prior advertisement – a way for the communist nomenclature to preserve its positions as a part of the new capitalist entrepreneurial elite. At the same time, Grósz was rapidly losing credibility, partly on account of his militancy on behalf of a pluralism strictly within the framework of the one-party system, and even more so because of his complete failure to extort any improvement from Ceauşescu for the Hungarians of Transylvania (who had been escaping by the tens of thousands across the border in the second half of the 1980s) from at a meeting in August 1988.

In November 1988 Grósz gave the premiership over to young Miklós Németh, who, contrary to his expectations, instead of a docile tool turned out to be one of the engineers of transition. He might have drawn reinforcement from the successful manoeuvring of Pozsgay, who arose as an emblematic figure of reform-Communist policies by sharpening the cleavages within the party through a number of publicly made statements from late 1988 on. Most notably, these included the breaking of the taboo of 1956: the recognition of the 'counter-revolution' as a 'popular uprising', and the urging of the introduction of a multi-party system. This was ratified by the legislature on January 11, and acknowledged by the party on February 11, 1989. Through a cabinet reshuffle in May 1989, the followers of Grósz were replaced in most posts by pragmatic reformers like Németh himself, whose main endeavour was to ensure that before the complete dismantling of the old system of institutions, the outlines of a new and workable framework was created. For a few months of gap between party dictatorship and the rise of the new power structure determined by the plurality of parties, this group was able to become a decisive political force. By the end of June, the First Secretary had to remain content being only a member of a quartet including himself, Németh, Pozsgay and Nyers at the head of the party – a step that, at this stage, did little to regain popular support, but much to undermine hard-liner positions in the party and to push it towards disintegration. The founder of the party did not live to see it. In early May

1989, Kádár was relieved of his offices, and died on July 6 – the day Imre Nagy was officially rehabilitated.

The summer of the *annus mirabilis* continued with its internationally most immediately conspicuous achievement: the dismantling the 'Iron Curtain', that is, the sealed frontier between Hungary and Austria, a process begun in May. As it was accompanied by allowing about 20,000 East German citizens seeking refuge at the Budapest West German embassy to cross the border into Austria, Hungary played the role of a catalyst in the disintegration of the whole of the Soviet bloc. Simultaneously, the scenario worked out by the opposition and Németh's pragmatists to facilitate an orderly transition was launched. Between June and September 1989, representatives of the Hungarian Socialist Workers' Party, the Opposition Round Table (established in March by eight organisations in order to reconcile their positions *vis-à-vis* the party) and the 'third side' (the Patriotic Popular Front, trade unions etc.) discussed the central issues of the process at the meetings of the National Round Table. The agreement they signed on September 18, 1989, emphasised their commitment to the creation of the legal and political conditions of the transition to multi-party democracy and the rule of law, along with the surmounting of the ongoing socio-economic crisis. In the interest of these, it required the amendment of the constitution of 1949, the establishment of a constitutional court, the re-regulation of the order of national elections, legislation on the operation and the finances of parties (the HSWP was to put resources at the disposal of the other parties until the first elections), and the amendment of the penal code. The two liberal parties, the SZDSZ and the FIDESZ, ultimately refrained from signing the document (which nevertheless became valid) because it also stipulated the election of a head of state before the elections, which they thought would favour the currently best known aspirant and probably the most popular reform-politician in the country: Pozsgay. They also hoped to drive a wedge between the MDF and the reform Communists by initiating a referendum on the issue in November, whose result was in their favour.

Before the measures required by the agreement were taken, one of the essential bulwarks of the old system collapsed. The Fourteenth Congress of the party in early October 1989 also proved to be the last one. Upon the initiative of the reform Communists and the pragmatists, on October 7 the vast majority of the deputies voted in favour of creating a new Hungarian Socialist Party, chaired by Rezső Nyers, defining its aims as akin to the Western European socialist parties. Membership was not carried through, and out of 700,000 members of the old party, only 50,000 went over to the new one until the elections March 1990. Shortly thereafter, the party's para-military organisation, the Workers' Guard, was also disbanded.

In the meantime, the Németh government codified, and got the legislature to pass the measures stipulated in the agreement of the National Round Table. Most importantly, the constitutional amendment was enacted, or, more properly, an interim constitution replaced that of 1949, 80 per cent of which was now changed. It defined the peaceful transition to market economy and the rule of law as the goal of the state, whose form became a republic (replacing the 'people's republic'), and civil democracy and democratic socialism its fundamental principles. It guaranteed civil and human rights, declared the establishment of the multi-party system and not only eliminated the clause referring to the 'leading role of the Marxist-Leninist party of the working class', but explicitly ruled out the exercise of public authority by a single party. Representative and responsible government, along with the separation of powers was enacted; the institution of the Presidium was abolished and replaced with the office of president with fairly weak powers, to be elected by the legislature.

The constitutional amendment was promulgated on October 23, 1989, and on the same day the republic was proclaimed by the speaker of the parliament, Mátyás Szűrös, who thereby also became interim President. The system of state socialism was eliminated both in fact and in principle. Shortly afterwards, the red star was removed from the top of the building of parliament.

EPILOGUE: INTO ANOTHER MILLENNIUM

At this stage, it must be admitted that the autumn of 1989 is an arbitrarily chosen landmark in the history of Hungary. Several other dates, equally arbitrarily, could have been selected as well: the effective removal of Kádár in May 1988 (symbolising the supposedly irreversible disintegration of the old regime and the beginning of transition), or the first free elections in March 1990 (the creation of responsible government), or the departure of the last Soviet soldier in June 1991 (the restoration of Hungarian sovereignty) could perhaps be just as plausibly selected as the ultimate watershed. It could also be argued that the principal events of October 1989 were largely symbolic, less decisive in importance than others. My choice is based on the following reasons.

Kádár's demotion (a kind of fall upwards) started something whose outcome was rather unclear at the time, whatever claims might be raised to the contrary now, in a retrospect of over a decade. In the autumn of 1990, a very well attended discussion of leading intellectuals, many of them active participants of the transition process, was held at Eötvös Lóránd University of Budapest to answer the question 'Did We See It Coming?' ('It', of course, referring to the events of 1989 in the way they happened). The consensus of participants and the audience was a unanimous negative answer: 'It' was unforeseeable almost until it was actually happening. The instability resulting from the fact that Gorbachev did not disclose his plans to start troop withdrawals until the very end of 1988 underlines this. As regards the elections of 1990, themselves based upon the decisions taken in the autumn of 1989, they put into operation one, but just one, of the essential institutions of multi-party democracy. On the other hand, the complete Soviet troop withdrawal took place *some* time after the likelihood of what it is supposed to have eliminated had become virtually zero (though precisely *how much* time might well remain impossible to tell: the Bush–Gorbachev agreement, with the latter's acceptance of the principle of non-interference on December 2, 1989, is a strong candidate).

By contrast, autumn 1989 marked a true end and thus a true beginning. The dissolution of the Hungarian Socialist Workers' Party and the constitutional amendment of October 1989 did something irreversible: they destroyed the legal and political foundations of the party state, the most durable of all the essentials of Communist totalitarianism, which from that time on could only have been restored by another revolution (or counterrevolution). True, the Hungarian 'revolution' of 1989 differed profoundly from the cases of Czechoslovakia, East Germany or Romania where change was abrupt and the 'break with the past', at least superficially, more dramatically visible. But nor was there a period of power sharing as in Poland, where the 'constructive' segment of the opposition was offered four seats in the cabinet of Mieczysław Rakowski already in September 1988, *before* the Polish roundtable discussions began. The last chance for a kind of power sharing in Hungary was thwarted by the failure of Pozsgay to become president of the new republic as a result of the referendum of November 1989, which decided to postpone choosing the head of state until after the general elections.

It might also be argued that the activity of the last parliament elected under communism, and that of the Németh government in the winter of 1989–1990, still qualifies for the *ancien régime*. A few 'time bombs', such as the unclear status of the national media, which caused intense political debate in the years to come, were indeed left behind by the Németh cabinet. Revelations of continued spying by the security service of the Ministry of the Interior on several opposition politicians also raised many eyebrows. It is also true that the circumstances of the peaceful and, therefore, somewhat procrastinated transition made it possible, as has been already hinted at, for parts of the old elite, itself responsible for the difficult predicament of Hungary, to exchange their political–administrative for economic power.

However, on the whole this period was neither the rearguard fight of communism, nor was it the agony of a defunct body. The institutional foundations of state socialism had been shaken by the end of 1989 and the measures which the cabinet, already liberated from party control, took thereafter – the creation of a National Property Agency to supervise the process of privatisation; the complete equality of religious denominations (the State Office of Ecclesiastical Affairs was already abolished in June 1989); the agreement on the withdrawal of Soviet troops; the application for membership in the Council of Europe – already belong to a new era. The main cleavages in the simultaneous campaign for the national elections only confirm this impression. The contest between the new Hungarian Socialist Party (MSZP) and the opposition as a whole was overshadowed by the increasingly acrimonious struggle between the opposition parties, especially the two most influential ones: the MDF and the SZDSZ (the former styling itself a Christian–conservative, cautiously reformist 'calm force' firmly rooted in the national tradition and the latter emphasizing its radically anti-Communist, modern, liberal and westernised credentials).

Viewed from yet another angle, my choice, as well as any of its alternatives, is avowedly a matter of convenience; and concentrating on other criteria – the complete transition to the market economy in practice as well as in the mind, the acquisition of civic attitudes characteristic of societies under political pluralism and the rule of law, Hungary's full integration with European organisations, and so on – would surely yield other landmarks, some of them still ahead of us, in the twenty-first century. If it is doubtful whether we already possess the necessary distance from the developments of at least the last stages of the Kádár era to assess them by the means of historiography, we undoubtedly do not yet have it in relation to the post-1989 period. This epilogue will not presume to evaluate the main events that took place and tendencies that asserted themselves in the course of the experiment of turning from collectivism and one-party rule to a market economy and political pluralism – formerly never tried, challenging beyond imagination. Nevertheless, it is necessary at least to provide a short catalogue of them.

Throughout the decade, there has been much, occasionally quite astonishing movement in the political spectrum, both between and within the parties, and in the domination of the institutions of the new democracy. The subjects of sometimes bitter debate between the politicians did not always reflect the priorities of the people. It took some time before many in the new political class, a disproportionately broad segment of which was initially recruited from the intellectuals of the social sciences and the humanities, realized that their fascination with issues of ideology was not universally shared, and once they had demonstrated their commitment to freedom and patriotism which suffered under Kádár, people became more interested in the solutions offered for those aspects of their lives which were tolerably well served under the old regime, at least for a while. This was all the more critical since for many of the latter it equally took some time to realize that the short-term effects of the transition would harm rather than favour the general conditions of their well-being, and since the unavoidable consequences of the dismantling of a paternalistic state and the creation of a competitive socio-economic sphere were accompanied by adverse developments that were all too avoidable. Bitterness bred nostalgia: in 1995, more than half of the population thought that the previous system had been 'better' than the current one.

They did have reasons for holding that belief. In the beginning of the 1990s, as a result of the twenty billion dollar strong inheritance of the past (that is, in terms of foreign debts, which continued to rise to thirty-three billion by 1995) and the difficulties of putting the economy on a different track, Hungary underwent a profound economic crisis. After a fall which greatly exceeded that at the time of the great crisis of the 1930s, the GDP was only climbing back to its 1989 value a decade later.

This should by no means be surprising: even though there was a rough consensus across the entire political spectrum with regards to the most immediate tasks of the systemic change, those tasks were formidable and offered different alternatives. The most important item on the agenda was the privatisation of state property. While some of it took the shape of re-privatisation or compensation (restoring once nationalised property, in the form of vouchers, to those – individuals or corporate bodies, the churches in the first place – who could raise a plausible claim), it was realized that a market based privatisation process was to be preferred, both because it might alleviate the debt crisis, and because it was deemed much more likely to create 'real' proprietors. However, the situation in which privatisation started, did not favour this option: the aggregate estimated value of state property in the last years of socialism exceeded about twenty times the means at the disposal of the population. As a result, the process was a staggering one, especially under the national conservative government of 1990–1994, which strongly preferred home-grown investors in order to foster the rise of a new Hungarian entrepreneurial class. The picture markedly changed after 1994, when the new socialist–liberal coalition threw the gates much more open to foreign capital.

It is indeed somewhat reassuring that Hungary has attracted the largest per capita foreign investment (chiefly in industry, banking, the energy sector, wholesale trade and telecommunications) among the new democracies of Central Europe, a development that played a part in increasing the share of the private sector in the economy to over 80 per cent; that the radical financial stabilisation programme of 1995 (inflicting an austerity regime that has become notorious, after the name of the finance minister, as the 'Bokros package') brought about spectacular improvement in macro-economic indices; or that the initial inflation rate of 35 per cent has by now diminished to slightly under 10 per cent. Also, there have been important infrastructural improvements: for instance, the earlier telecommunications misery has been virtually eliminated, and modern petrol stations have sprouted like mushrooms to supply a dynamically increasing (although still rather ancient) stock of cars. The computerisation of workplaces has advanced spectacularly in both the public and the private sector, and a national programme launched in 1996 has made massive steps in supplying schools with an Internet link. Much more controversial, distinguishing features of modern consumerism such as shopping malls have started their conquest of Hungary, and now have imprinted themselves on the cityscapes and daily life of a few urban centres.

However, all of this is far from sufficient to offset, and some of it even fuels, the disillusionment of those who consider themselves the 'losers' of a transition process as a result of which the income ratio between the highest and lowest earning 10 per cent of the population, formerly 5 to 1, has increased to 10 to 1. While this is not unusual elsewhere, the shock caused by the rapidity of the changes was aggravated in Hungary by the fact that the real value of wages, salaries and pensions dropped by 25 per cent between 1989 and 1996, until a slow growth started. As a result, the distance has greatly increased between a thin upper segment and the middle strata, who are struggling to avoid falling back into the 35–40 per cent of the population who live on or below poverty level. The groups most severely afflicted are nearly the same as in the previous era: unskilled workers, peasants and agricultural labourers, and pensioners, now supplemented by a crowd of unemployed whose proportion in the active part of the population had climbed to a peak of over 13 per cent by 1994 and was still between 8 and 10 per cent in the last years of the decade. People with large families and the Roma are significantly overrepresented in the bottom segments of the social hierarchy.

The gap has also been broadening between geographical regions that have evidently benefited from the transition and ones that have not. Foremost among the former are Budapest (or, to be precise, some neighbourhoods in it, while on the whole the capital also arguably reproduces the growing inequalities on the national level), and the urban centres of western Hungary with their surrounding areas. Among the latter, there are a few success stories. One of the truly instructive cases is Székesfehérvár, Hungary's first royal seat, which was a centre of the communications industry and for the production of audiovisual equipment before 1989. The collapse of large socialist companies first resulted in soaring unemployment rates in the town, but capital soon found the highly skilled labour force that had been trained to serve those companies, and the agglomeration of Székesfehérvár was among the ten fastest developing enterprise zones worldwide in the second half of the 1990s. For a counter-example one might turn especially to the north-east, for instance a region of heavy industry mammoths around Miskolc created in socialist times, and traditionally poor agrarian areas. In fact, the rural economy as a whole, afflicted by droughts and floods as well as mismanagement, has been in a permanent state of deep crisis throughout the period. An increasing rate of criminality, including the appearance of organised crime and new forms of delinquency such as drug abuse – from being a transit country on the clandestine routes, Hungary has become a target area for the drug trade – are also phenomena that have appeared simultaneously with the transition process.

At the other extreme there is a new elite of top and middle ranking managers, successful private entrepreneurs, technocrats and segments of the intelligentsia who in their work habits, standards of values, aspirations and lifestyles are increasingly difficult to differentiate from their Western European counterparts. In an environment still conditioned by a several decades' long tradition of bogus egalitarianism, this new elite has often been resented merely on account of its rise (made conspicuous partly by the ostentation of some of the *nouveaux riches*, and partly by the difficulties experienced by others), and a target of criticism on account of 'gentlemanly mischief': actual or suspected instances of corruption and various kinds of abuses in the privatisation process and other dubious ways in which large fortunes have been made. Under each of the three post-1990 administrations (and one should also include the last one prior to that date), there have been greater or lesser scandals in which privatisation issues were linked with the building of political clientele. Nevertheless, while some of the few post-1989 protest movements of any significance were inspired by unhappiness with some aspect of the spread of market relations – including the need to bring the legal framework of the Hungarian economy to conform with the requirements of the European Union), the several hundred-thousands who have suffered real deprivation have largely remained a silent mass; or in the few cases when their voice was heard, it was to no avail. Notice was mainly taken of, and at least a partial success went to those relatively small groups that were able to act as pressure groups: taxi drivers who paralysed the entire road system of the country by blockades erected in protest against a sudden and substantial rise of fuel prices in 1990, or farmers who employed a similar strategy to express their dissatisfaction with the government's agrarian policies in 1993 and in 1997.

These were in fact the only conspicuous instances of spontaneous popular engagement with affairs of politics during the whole decade. A third rather stormy, and also protracted conflict, the struggle for control of the state-owned electronic media (the 'media war') throughout the first half of the 1990s was overwhelmingly an internal affair of the political and intellectual elite, but precisely for this reason it received the greatest amount of publicity. (The strife in which especially the radical Right charged that the national television and radio services were under 'liberal–bolshevist' dominance, and Left-Liberals campaigned for the freedom of expression and against government interference with broadcasting, was supposed to come to an end with a law of 1996. This measure reconstituted this media as independent companies with presidents appointed by a board whose membership reflects the relative strength of parties in parliament – a solution that still seems far from ideal.) Not that there have been no soaring issues that have exercised the minds of people. But partly by tradition, and partly because of the developments and phenomena mentioned above, politics itself is widely regarded as 'gentlemanly mischief', and signs of a generalised anomie was occasionally experienced in the atmosphere of the country – as if the 'negotiated revolution' had turned into a 'transition with a spleen'. Even though this spleen has been relatively far from spilling over into an explicit questioning of the transition to political pluralism and the market economy, it is clearly and regularly expressed in opinion polls.

The satisfaction with and the trust in political institutions, not very high to begin with, was steadily falling during the 1990s in Hungary, in proportion with the diminishing belief in the value of political participation. It is not only the level of involvement in demonstrations, public gatherings or strikes that falls behind that found in most West European countries as well as the neighbouring new democracies such as Poland or the Czech Republic. Participation at the three parliamentary elections in Hungary since 1989 has not been very impressive (between 56 and 68 per cent), though it shows at least a satisfactory recognition of civic stakes by the people. The social mood has had its ups and downs; and although Hungary still has the reputation of an 'accommodating' country, intolerance towards otherness (Jews, homosexuals, refugees etc.) has sometimes been clearly visible on the public scene. Labels intended as condemnation like 'liberal–bolshevik', 'plutocratic', 'alien-hearted' and their likes, which are so frequent in the effusions of the nationalist radical Right, have the connotation of 'Jewish' in Hungarian parlance; and a full documentary volume from the printed and electronic press on 'anti-Semitic discourse in Hungary' could be collected just for the year 2000. Yet none of this has endangered the minimum of political stability (undoubtedly at least in part precisely because of the lack of a strong 'culture of participation'). Six months before the elections of 2002 it is beyond reasonable doubt that the current administration will follow its predecessors in staying in place until its mandate is over.

Despite many circuitous processes, the political scene has been marked by the emergence of the institutional framework of a parliamentary republic. No constituent assembly was convened to implement the change of regime: the basic principles of parliamentary government, the rule of law, the separation of powers and so on have been enshrined in a series of constitutional amendments. Hungary's governmental system has been characterised as one of limited parliamentarism in which (no doubt because of the endeavour of the legislators of 1989–1990 after the years of state socialism to avoid an all-powerful executive – the government's scope of action is limited by several factors: a Constitutional Court with unusually broad powers; a relatively frequent resort to the requirement of a two-thirds majority (not only for the election of major office-holders but also in legislation); a strong and extensive system of parliamentary committees; a system of local self-government that is also rather strong when it is considered that Hungary's constitution is not federal but unitary; the considerable independence of the Hungarian National Bank and so on. Successive prime ministers have been trying to break through or evade these limitations with different strategies, Viktor Orbán being by far the most successful in these efforts by increasing the powers of the Office of the Prime Minister, by reducing the frequency of parliamentary sessions and other devices. Although the institution of referendum (which can be initiated upon the collection of 200,000 signatures according to the current regulation) preserves traces of direct democracy, Hungarian democracy is dominated by the representative principle. The unicameral legislature is elected every four years by a system which combines the majoritarian and the proportional ones; the head of state is elected by parliament every five years (re-election is only possible once). Municipal elections are also held at four-year intervals.

After more than a decade of intensive movement across the political–ideological spectrum in the party system it seems that the tendency is a rather West European-like scramble towards the centre from left and right, a minority persisting on both extremes and the undercurrent of the old populist–urbanist divide sometimes surfacing in the form of 'patriotic' versus 'cosmopolitan' tensions. Of the sixty-five parties formed in 1988–1989, only twelve could run a national list at the elections of March 25, 1990, and the 4 per cent threshold (raised to 5 per cent by the 1998 elections) required to make it into parliament eliminated one half of them. Of the six parties that surpassed this minimum, the highest-scoring MDF invited the Smallholders and the Christian Democrats to form a centre-right coalition, pledging itself to Christian and national values besides democracy and the market economy, which enjoyed a 60 per cent majority. The opposition consisted of the two liberal parties, the SZDSZ (running second at the elections) and the FIDESZ, besides the Socialists, who struggled hard for a while to ascend from the political isolation the past had thrown them in to. Based on a 'pact' between József Antall, a historian and museum director who had become President of the MDF in the previous year and Hungary's first prime minister in the new democratic era, and the leaders of the SZDSZ, a prominent member of the latter party, writer and translator Árpád Göncz, was elected by parliament as President of the Hungarian Republic. In 1995, Göncz was re-elected. Especially under the centre-right coalition of 1990–1994 he made fairly extensive use of his prerogative to form a real counterweight to government power. Ferenc Mádl, a legal scholar who succeeded Göncz in 2000, has shown himself a far more willing partner of the current national–conservative government.

As a result of the first free elections after the fall of state socialism, there was a near-complete change in the highest echelons of the political elite: 95 per cent of the members of the legislature were new in that position. Nearly as dramatic was the change in the social and cultural background and political convictions of the new elite. Under the difficult conditions of regime change and economic transition it was only natural that the general disaffection with the political class as a whole, especially coupled with the still all too unstable party preferences, affected the government parties more than the opposition. With the death of Antall (replaced by his Minister of the Interior Péter Boross) following a protracted illness in late 1993, the MDF also lost a politician whose stature was unparalleled among its ranks. But the first setback for the MDF government came already in the autumn of 1990, with the municipal elections. The overwhelming majority of those returned in rural constituencies were 'independent' candidates, and on the local level the pre-1989 leaders were much less severely 'punished' than at the helm of the national government. In larger settlements the picture was different, but here the two liberal parties scored much better than the adherents of the government. The office of the Mayor of Budapest – crucial on account of the risks, the challenges as well as the influence and opportunities involved – went to Gábor Demszky, who had grown to prominence in the SZDSZ as the number one samizdat publisher of the erstwhile 'democratic opposition'. Having repeated his electoral victory in 1994 and 1998, in that respect at least Demszky may be regarded as the most successful politician in post-1989 Hungary.

But it was not only a shift in the political sympathies by a considerable bulk of the voters that started well before the parliamentary elections of 1994, whose outcome astonished many people from more than one point of view. A recasting of roles and ideological commitments, as well as a realignment of partnerships also started to take place among the parties roughly mid-way in the first parliamentary cycle. Even before, the MDF which had emerged as a movement for grassroots democracy and a 'third way' between capitalism and communism (also open towards a 'democratic socialism'), adjusted itself to the character of Antall, a *par excellence* conservative liberal – who then had to work hard to purge the party from its radical nationalist right wing, seceding in 1993 as the Party of Hungarian Justice and Life (MIÉP). After the electoral victory the MDF itself indulged in militantly anti-communist propaganda, which, given its previous history, found many of its supporters unprepared. This could be contrasted to the trajectory of the SZDSZ. A party that attempted to undermine the credibility of the MDF by the charge of collaboration with the Communists in the 1990 election campaign, during the 'media war' the SZDSZ felt that while any opening towards the right was dangerous to its core values (human rights, civil liberties, multiculturalism), its policies towards the left ought to be re-evaluated. This shift offered an opportunity for the MSZP to emerge from the political ghetto into which it was temporarily thrown after 1989, and indeed the way was paved for the later *rapprochement* between the two parties by the Democratic Charter, an initiative by intellectuals from the circles of both of them to counter the tide of national radicalism (at that time still harboured within the MDF). Among such circumstances the earlier close collaboration between the SZDSZ and the FIDESZ began to evaporate and the inherent differences between them became ever more visible. Of the latter party's three initial distinguishing features – anti-communism, an activism rooted in youth subculture and political liberalism – only the first was entirely preserved, while the second was quickly abandoned and the third gradually qualified by an increasing emphasis on a commitment to Christian values and tradition, and a belief in strong government. By 1994, FIDESZ redefined itself as a centre-right party, with an enormous (and it seems ultimately successful) ambition to become the integrative force of that segment of the political spectrum; a process intended to be symbolised by the change of the party's official name ('FIDESZ' now supplemented by 'MPP' which stands for 'Hungarian Civic Party') in 1994, and its resignation from the Liberal International for the sake of the European People's Party in 1999.

By the time of the parliamentary elections of 1994 – in what was a general tendency in the region and will remain a fruitful topic for historians and political scientists – the Socialists had recovered. The MSZP's pledges to the values of social democracy looked credible enough to earn it international respectability and admission in the Socialist International; its ideology-free pragmatism and its emphasis on modernisation and technocratic expertise won it a landslide electoral victory in a country where many were tired of the ideological struggles so visible in the early 1990s and dissatisfied with the achievements of the economic transition. Although the Socialists won over 50 per cent of the seats in the legislature, the SZDSZ accepted the coalition offer of Gyula Horn, chairman of the MSZP, the other four parties of the previous parliament constituting the opposition. As both new government parties emphasized, in spite of the vast differences in their fundamental values, similar attitudes to a number of pressing practical tasks, such as Hungary's Euro-Atlantic integration or monetarist reform, provided a wide scope for collaboration between them. In both of these priority areas they could legitimately boast of achievements, but none of these did much to alleviate the resentments many voters had harboured already under the previous administration. In addition, many among those of the SZDSZ were puzzled by the party's reconciliation with the Socialists and later also felt that its performance in the coalition cost much of its earlier character.

In light of this, it is no wonder that at the 1998 elections the SZDSZ followed the other great party of the 1990 regime change, the MDF, in falling into relative insignificance. The steadily growing support of the FIDESZ during the last phase of the second parliamentary cycle, besides the mistakes of the Socialists and their own skill, was not in the least owing to the desertion of voters from these two parties. While the Socialists preserved much of their popularity, the FIDESZ–MPP won by a relatively narrow margin (in fact, receiving fewer votes on the party list than the MSZP) and at the end of a campaign it pursued for 'less than regime change, but more than government change': the vision of a 'civic Hungary' in which the post-communist heritage is fully buried, while the state undertakes greater responsibility than before and supports the growth of a broad middle class indebted to national and Christian traditions. For the sake of a safe government majority, the then FIDESZ chairman and new prime minister Viktor Orbán launched this programme in coalition not only with the MDF, but also the Independent Smallholder Party (FKGP). While the historic FKGP had a respectable place in the tradition of democratic endeavours in twentieth-century Hungary, its present-day heir is an anti-elitist force with a populist understanding of democracy, notorious throughout the 1990s (and now beyond) for its stormy internal relations and the political style of its leaders. Besides the left-wing opposition of the Socialists and the SZDSZ, there is now a non-governmental rightist party in parliament which nevertheless frequently lends the government external support: the radical nationalist MIÉP, an advocate of 'real' regime change – anti-communism, anti-capitalism, anti-liberalism and anti-globalism, all of which are in its language quite indistinguishable from anti-Semitism. On the other extreme of the political palette, the radical leftist Workers' Party, which openly cherishes the heritage of the Kádár era, remained an extra-parliamentary opposition after each of the three elections.

This concise story of the development of the political scene probably illustrates the pirouetting that has taken place by virtually all participants until they have found their present, not necessarily ultimate, place in it. The tendency is nevertheless more or less clear. Whereas a fairly constant number of the electorate has supported a conservative–liberal line with national and Christian commitments (in whatever party colour it appeared at any given time), after their initial isolation, the preferences, the values and endeavours communicated by the Socialists have climbed roughly to the level of the former trend, while those associated with the Liberals almost fell to a level equal to the radical Right – a picture not very different from some Western European countries.

Despite the often acrimonious political debate, some major targets have been objects of a rough consensus. Foreign relations is a field in which a meeting of minds regarding priorities has perhaps been the most frequent (though the paths recommended for the attainment of goals have differed considerably). The changes after 1989 also redefined Hungary's place and possibilities in the international arena. The end of the Cold War and the dismantling of the Iron Curtain removed the political obstacles from taking steps towards Hungary's integration in Euro-Atlantic organisations. This was further underlined by the fact that with the disintegration of the Soviet Union, Europe's centre of gravity has shifted westwards (even though Russia naturally remains a dominant force, especially on the Central and Eastern European horizon). At the same time, the collapse of the bipolar world order and its replacement with the global dominance of the United States has not necessarily enhanced the prospects of international security – as has been dramatically shown by the events of September 11, 2001. And whereas the antagonisms and suspicions artificially created by the postwar division of Europe have been greatly attenuated after 1989, historical tensions related to the Hungarian minorities in the neighbouring countries and hitherto covered by a thin veil of internationalist brotherhood have resurfaced; all of this in a period when two cornerstones of the Versailles system were falling apart, Czechoslovakia in a negotiated process and Yugoslavia in several bloody wars.

Accordingly, the quest for security and prosperity through joining existing Euro-Atlantic organisations and a leading role in regional cooperation, and the protection of the interests of the Hungarian minorities abroad, became the focal points of Hungarian foreign policy after 1990. Nationalist sentiment has not been uncommon among some segments of the populace, and at least initially hopes of a revision of the Trianon borders were harboured by a sizeable minority, though of political forces only MIÉP has considered this a viable policy (and has never ceased to urge appropriate steps). It is true that in his very first interview as Prime Minister, Antall made the statement that 'in spirit, he felt to be the Premier of fifteen million Hungarians'. But this was a piece of unfortunate, because it is easily misunderstood, rhetoric aimed to emphasize the personal responsibility which he felt, and in his opinion all Hungarian politicians ought to feel, towards the Hungarian minorities abroad; it met much disapproval in Hungary itself (though considerably more irritation across the borders). In fact the ambition of no Hungarian cabinet since 1990 has been either more or less than to assist the legal organisations of the Hungarian minorities in their efforts to secure cultural rights and self-government. Between 1993 and 1996, treaties were signed between Hungary on the one hand and Ukraine, Romania and Slovakia on the other hand to ensure the inviolability of the borders and the rights of minorities. The Orbán government regarded these treaties as lacking proper guarantees, and also somewhat opportunistic, arising mainly from an over-zealous endeavour to conform to the requirements of the European Union in view of Hungary's planned accession. Therefore it has also started implementing a policy to supply the Hungarians of neighbouring countries with a 'Hungarian identity card' investing them with a special status (in labour relations, education and so on) in Hungary, which resulted in considerable strain, especially in relations with Romania and Slovakia.

Simultaneously, with the dissolution of the military and economic organisations of the Soviet bloc and the withdrawal of the Soviet troops (the final stages of these processes almost coincided, in June–July 1991), Hungary started to take steps towards intensive involvement in regional co-operation and Euro-Atlantic integration. The already existing Alps–Adriatic community of the border regions of Austria, Italy, Yugoslavia and Hungary developed into the Pentagonale (with the admission of Czechoslovakia), the Hexagonale (including also Poland) and finally the Central European Initiative (extending to the Yugoslav successor states). Apart from this, Poland, Czechoslovakia and Hungary launched the Visegrád initiative in 1991. All of these endeavours of economic and cultural co-operation lost momentum, or proved futile by the middle of the decade because of the lack of a sufficient level of economic complementarity, the growing dismissiveness of the Czech Republic, or Slovak distrust towards Hungary.

With regard to European integration, all significant political forces except MIÉP have been in favour of it. Although the Council of Europe responded positively to the Hungarian application already in November 1990, and Hungary became an associated member of the European Union in December 1991, the process will be considerably longer than was optimistically hoped for. Nevertheless, the Amsterdam and Luxemburg recommendations of the EU during 1997 provided for concrete negotiations on Hungary's full membership (alongside with the Czech Republic, Estonia, Poland and Slovenia), which indeed began in March 1998. Although by this time public opinion in the West was already remarkably sceptical about the expansion of the European Union, and governments (even that of Germany, still its most fervent advocate) started to show reluctance in undertaking the costs, Hungary continues to be regarded as a 'first round' accession country. The Hungarian government reports 'readiness' by the end of 2002, but at present assigning any date before 2004 for the accession seems to be overly optimistic.

NATO accession also required the meeting of severe conditions: a thorough-going overhaul of the whole structure of the military as well as technological modernisation. Besides, the protests of Russia against the admittance of Hungary (together with Poland and the Czech Republic) into NATO as a threat against her security, also delayed the process. However, already in 1994 the creation of NATO air force bases was authorised by the Hungarian government in South-Transdanubia, and Hungarian engineering corps took part in the postwar reconstruction work of the IFOR/SFOR in Bosnia. The agreement on the membership of Hungary and her two Central European neighbours in NATO was finally signed on March 12, 1999. Less than two weeks later NATO embarked on its first-ever war, against the criminal regime of Slobodan Milošević in Yugoslavia, using Hungarian air bases. At the time of writing, NATO is at war again, this time against global terrorism and it is as yet impossible to assess the consequences for Hungary. Time will only tell, for instance, whether Hungary's involvement – whatever its nature and profundity – will accelerate the process of her accession to EU; or on the contrary, whether in an atmosphere of growing anxiety for global safety, new requirements concerning border protection, policing or extradition will not cause further postponements.

Amid the gloom of the developments mentioned last, and perhaps not without ambivalence, Hungary's desire to assert an Occidental quality nevertheless stepped on the path of being realized at the threshold of the third millennium. Not for the first time, one might add. It is to be hoped that no more beginnings will be necessary.

LIST OF MAPS

NOTE ON PRONUNCIATION

The following rudimentary guidelines might soothe the agony of the foreign reader in trying to cope with the task of pronouncing the plethora of Hungarian names found in the text.

In Hungarian, word stress invariably falls on the first syllable.

Spelling is 'phonetic', that is, specific letters are always pronounced in the same way. Unfortunately, the few exceptions to this rule occur in surnames (e.g., Széchenyi, which should be pronounced as if it were spelt 'Szécsényi'.)

1. Vowels. Of each of these, there are short and long versions, the latter marked by long accents: *a* roughly corresponds to a short, open *o* in English ('hot'); *á* – pronounced as in 'hard'; *e* – as in 'get'; *é* – as in 'gate'; *i* – as in 'in'; *í* – as in 'green'; *o* – as in 'top'; *ó* – as in 'toe'; *u* – as in 'to'; *ú* – as in 'too'.

Besides *a*, foreigners sometimes have difficulties with the vowels with *Umlauts*. Of these, *ö* and *ü* are pronounced as in the German language; or, *ö* as in the French deux, and *ü* as in the French duc; *ő* and *ű* are their long counterparts.

2. Consonants. These are relatively more straightforward. The following might be problematic: *c* – pronounced as ts; *cs* – as (t)ch; *gy* – as dy; *j* – as y; *ly* – also as y; *ny* – as ng in French (e.g., 'cognac'); *s* – as sh; *sz* – as s; *ty* – as the 't' in 'Tudor'; zs – as j in French (e.g., 'jour').

In names, *cz* and *y* occur quite frequently. The former is pronounced as a Hungarian *c*, and the latter as a Hungarian *i*. Also in names, the *h* in the compound *th* is silent.

BIBLIOGRAPHY

The purpose of this Bibliography is to give the reader some indications of further reading (in English, and to some extent in French and German) on specific themes or periods in Hungarian history. In other words, I have not attempted to do full justice to those Hungarian historians past and present whose major works are unfortunately not (yet) available in the main western languages, even though it is mainly from such texts that I have primarily benefited while writing this book. For the sake of academic fairness, I still wish to record at least the names of those scholars whose more synthetic studies published only in Hungarian have been indispensable (some of them represented by other works below, while others not). They include, for Hungarian prehistory and the medieval period, Pál Engel, Erik Fügedi, György Györffy, Gyula Kristó, András Kubinyi, Gyula László, Elemér Mályusz, András Róna-Tas and Jenő Szűcs; for the early modern period and the Age of Enlightenment, Éva H. Balázs, Kálmán Benda, Domokos Kosáry, László Makkai, Ferenc Szakály, Katalin Péter, Ágnes Várkonyi and Vera Zimányi; for the nineteenth century, András Gergely, András Gerő, Péter Hanák, László Katus, Gábor Pajkossy, Éva Somogyi, György Szabad and Károly Vörös; for the twentieth century, T. Iván Berend, Gábor Gyáni, Tibor Hajdu, Zsuzsa L. Nagy, Mária Ormos, György Ránki and Ignác Romsics. Finally, although many general works on Central or Eastern Europe devote excellent chapters or sections to Hungary, I have generally avoided them in order to keep the Bibliography within manageable limits.

General works

Bogyay, Thomas von, *Grundzüge der Geschichte Ungarns* (Darmstadt, 1990)
Czigány, Lóránt, *The Oxford History of Hungarian Literature* (Oxford, 1984)
Eckhart, Ferenc, *A Short History of the Hungarian People* (London, 1931)
Engel, Pál, *The Realm of Saint Stephen: A History of Medieval Hungary 895–1526* (London, 2001)
Gál, István (ed.), *Ungarn ud die Nachbarnvölker* (Budapest, 1943)
Gerő, András and János Poór (eds), *Budapest. A History from Its Beginnings to 1996* (Boulder, 1997)
Glatz, Ferenc and Ervin Pamlényi (eds), *Etudes historiques hongroises 1985*, 3 vols (Budapest, 1985)
Halász, Zoltán, *Kurze Geschichte Ungarns* (Budapest, 1974)
Hanák, Péter (ed.), *One Thousand Years. A Concise History of Hungary* (Budapest, 1988)
Ignotus, Paul, *Hungary* (New York, 1972)
Kósa, László (ed.), *A Cultural History of Hungary* (Budapest, 1999)
Kosáry, Dominic, *A History of Hungary* (Cleveland, 1941)
—— and S.B. Vardy, *History of the Hungarian Nation* (Astor Park, Fla., 1969)
Lázár, István, *Hungary. A Brief History* (Budapest, 1989)
——, *Transylvania. A Short History* (Budapest, 1997)
Macartney, Carlile A., *Hungary* (London, 1934)
Makkai, László, *Histoire de la Transylvanie* (Budapest, 1946)
Molnár, Miklós, *The Concise History of Hungary* (Cambridge, 2001)
Pamlényi, Ervin (ed.), *A History of Hungary* (London, 1975)
Pascu, Štefan, *A History of Transylvania* (Detroit, 1982)
Radvánszky, Anton, *Grundzüge der Verfassungs- und Staatsgeschichte Ungarns* (München, 1990)
Ránki, György (ed.), *Hungarian History-World History* (Budapest, 1984)

——, and Attila Pók (eds), *Hungary and European Civilization* (Budapest, 1989)
Romsics, Ignác, *A History of Hungary in the Twentieth Century* (Budapest, 1999)
Sinor, Denis, *History of Hungary* (New York, 1959)
Sugar, Peter F. (ed.), *A History of Hungary* (Bloomington-Indianapolis, 1990)
Szűcs, Jenő, *Nation und Geschichte* (Budapest, 1981)
——, 'The Three Historical Regions of Europe: An Outline', in John Keane (ed.), *Civil Society and the State* (London, 1988), 291–332; full text in *Acta Historica Academiae Scientiarum Hungaricae* (1983)

Prehistoric to early medieval times

Bartha, Antal, *Hungarian Society in the 9th and 10th centuries* (Budapest, 1975)
Berend, Nóra, *At the gates of Christendom: Jews, Muslims and 'pagans' in medieval Hungary*, c. *1000–1301* (Cambridge, 2001)
Bogyay, Thomas von, *Stephanus rex. Versuch einer Biographie* (Munich and Vienna, 1976)
Dobó, Árpád, *Die Verwaltung der römischen Provinz Pannonien von Asugustus bis Diocletianus* (Budapest and Amsterdam, 1968)
Fodor, István, *In Search of a New Homeland: The Prehistory of the Hungarian People and the Conquest* (Budapest, 1982)
Györffy, György, *Wirtschaft und Gesellschaft der Ungarn um die Jahrtausendwende* (Vienna, Cologne and Graz, 1983)
——, *King Saint Stephen of Hungary* (Boulder, 1994)
Hóman, Bálint, *Geschichte des ungarischen Mittelalters*, 2 vols (Berlin, 1940–43)
Klaniczay, Gábor, *Holy Rulers and Blessed Princesses. Dynastic Cults in Medieval Central Europe* (Cambridge, 2001)
Kosztolnyik, Z.J., *Five Eleventh Century Hungarian Kings: Their Policies and their Relations with Rome* (New York, 1981)
——, *From Coloman the Learned to Béla III (1095–1196). Hungarian Domestic Policies and Their Impact on Foreign Affairs* (New York, 1987)
——, *Hungary in the Thirteenth Century* (New York, 1996)
Macartney, Carlile A., *The Magyars in the Ninth Century* (Cambridge, 1930)
Mályusz, Elemér, *Geschichte des ungarischen Volkstums von der Landnahme bis zum Ausgang des Mittelalters* (Budapest, 1940)
Moravcsik, Gyula, *Die byzantinische Kultur und das mittelalterliche Ungarn* (Berlin, 1956)
Róna-Tas, András, *Hungarians and Europe in the early Middle Ages: an introduction into early Hungarian history* (Budapest, 1999)
Vajay, Szabolcs, *Der Eintritt des ungarischen Stämmebundes in die europäische Geschichte* (Mainz, 1968)

The late medieval period

Bak, János, *Königtum und Stände in Ungarn im 14.–16. Jahrhundert* (Wiesbaden, 1973)
Bak, János and Béla Király (eds), *From Hunyadi to Rákóczi: War and Society in Medieval and Early Modern Hungary* (Brooklyn, 1982)
Baum, Wilhelm, *Kaiser Sigismund. Hus, Konstanz und die Türkenkriege* (Graz, 1993)
Birnbaum, Marianna, *The Orb and the Pen. Janus Pannonius, Matthias Corvinus and the Buda Court* (Budapest, 1996)
Domonkos, Leslie S., *The Political and Cultural History of Hungary in the Age of Matthias Corvinus* (New York, 1966)
Fügedi, Erik, *Kings, Bishops, Nobles and Burghers in Medieval Hungary* (London, 1986)
——, *The Elefánthy. The Hungarian Nobleman and His Kindred* (Budapest, 1998)
Gerevich, László, *The Art of Buda and Pest in the Middle Ages* (Budapest, 1971)

Held, Joseph, *Hunyadi. Legend and Reality* (Boulder, 1985)
Mályusz, Elemér, *Kaiser Sigismund in Ungarn 1387–1437* (Budapest, 1990)
Nehring, Karl, *Matthias Corvinus, Kaiser Friedrich III. und das Reich* (München, 1989)
Vardy, S.B., Géza Grosschmid and Leslie S. Domonkos, (eds), *Louis the Great, King of Hungary and Poland* (Boulder, 1986)

Early modern times

Balázs, Éva H. and Béla Köpeczi (eds), *Noblesse française, noblesse hongroise. XVe–XIXe siècles* (Budapest and Paris, 1981)
Daniel, David P., 'The Fifteen Years War and the Protestant Response to Habsburg Absolutism', *East Central Europe/L'Europe du Centre–Est I–II* (1981), pp. 38–51.
Dávid, Géza and Pál Fodor (eds), *Ottomans, Hungarians and Habsburgs in Central Europe: the military confines in the era of Ottoman conquest* (Leiden, 2000)
Depner, Michael, *Das Fürstentum Siebenbürgen im Kampf gegen Habsburgen* (München, 1938)
Fekete, Lajos, *Buda and Pest under Turkish Rule* (Budapest, 1976)
Földes, Éva and István Mészáros (eds), *Comenius and Hungary* (Budapest, 1973)
Kosáry, Dominic, 'Gabriel Bethlen. Transylvania in the 17th Century', *The Slavonic and East European Review*, XVII (1938), pp. 162–74.
Molnár, Andrea, *Fürst Stephan Bocskay als Staatsmann und Persönlichkeit* (Munich, 1983)
Perjés, Géza, *The Fall of the Medieval Kingdom of Hungary: Mohács 1526–Buda 1541* (Boulder, 1989)
Péter, Katalin (ed.), *Beloved Children. Aristocratic Childhood in Hungary in the Early Modern Age* (Budapest, 2000)
Slottman, William B., *Ferenc Rákóczi II and the Great Powers* (Boulder, 1997)
Sugar, Peter F., *Southeastern Europe under Ottoman Rule, 1354–1804* (Seattle and London, 1977)
Székely, György and Erik Fügedi (eds), *La Renaissance et la Réformation en Pologne et en Hongrie* (Budapest, 1963)
Tóth, István György, *Literacy and Written Culture in Early Modern Central Europe* (Budapest, 2000)

Enlightenment to revolution

Balázs, Éva H., *Hungary and the Habsburgs 1765–1800. An Experiment in Enlightened Absolutism* (Budapest, 1997)
——, R. Hammermayer and H. Wagner (eds), *Beförderer der Aufklärung in Mittel- und Osteuropa* (Berlin, 1979)
Barany, George, *Stephen Széchenyi and the Awakening of Hungarian Nationalism, 1791–1841* (Princeton, 1968)
——, 'Hoping against Hope: The Enlightened Age in Hungary', *American Historical Review* LXXIX (1971), pp. 319–57.
Benda, Kálmán, 'Probleme des Josephinismus und des Jakobinertums in der Habsburgermonarchie', *Südost-Forschungen* (1966), 38–72.
Blanning, T.C.W., *Joseph II* (Cambridge, 1994)
Böody, Paul, *Joseph Eötvös and the Modernization of Hungary, 1840–1870* (Boulder, 1985)
Bona, Gábor (ed.), *The Hungarian Revolution and War for Independence, 1848–1849. A Military History* (Boulder, 1997)
Csáky, Moritz, *Von der Aufklärung zum Liberalismus. Studien zum Frühliberalismus in Ungarn* (Vienna, 1981)
——, 'Joseph II's Hungarian Land Survey', *English Historical Review* (1991), 611–34.

Deák, Ernő, *Das Städtewesen der Länder der Ungarischen Krone (1780–1918)*, vol. 1 (Vienna, 1979)

Deák, István, *The Lawful Revolution. Louis Kossuth and the Hungarians, 1848–1849* (New York, 1979)

Dickson, P.G.M., *Government and Finance under Maria Theresia 1740–1780*, 2 vols (Oxford, 1987)

Drabek, A.M., R.G. Plaschka and A. Wandruszka (eds), *Ungarn und Österreich unter Maria Theresia und Joseph II* (Vienna, 1982)

Evans, R.J.W., 'Maria Theresa and Hungary', in H.M. Scott (ed.), *Enlightened Absolutism: Reform and Reformers in Later Eighteenth-Century Europe* (London, 1990)

Haselsteiner, Horst, *Joseph II und die Komitate Ungarns* (Vienna, Cologne and Graz, 1983)

Kecskeméti, Charles, *La Hongrie et la réformisme libéral. Problemes politiques et sociaux* (1790–1848) (Rome, 1989)

Király, Béla K., *Hungary in the Late Eighteenth Century. The Decline of Enlightened Despotism* (New York and London, 1969)

Kosáry, Domokos, *Culture and Society in Eighteenth-Century Hungary* (Budapest, 1987)

Köpeczi, Béla, *Hongrois et Français. De Louis XIV a la révolution française* (Budapest, 1983)

Macartney, Carlile A., 'Hungary', in A. Godwin (ed.) *The European Nobility in the Eighteenth Century*, (London, 1953)

Marczali, Henrik, *Hungary in the Eighteenth Century* (Cambridge, 1910)

Roider, Karl A., *Maria Theresa* (Englewood, 1973)

Silagi, Denis, *Der grösste Ungar. Graf Stephan Széchenyi* (Vienna-Munich, 1960)

——, *Ungarn und die geheime Mitarbeiterkreis Kaiser Leopolds II* (Munich, 1961)

Sugar, Peter F., 'The Influence of the Enlightenment and the French Revolution in Eighteenth-Century Hungary', *Journal of Central European Affairs*, XVII (1958), 331–55.

Sziklay, László (ed.), *Aufklärung und Nationen im Osten Europas* (Budapest, 1983)

The age of neo-absolutism and dualism

Barany, George, 'Ungarns Verwaltung, 1848-1918', in Adam Wandruszka and Peter Urbanitsch (eds), *Die Habsburgermonarchie*, vol. VI (Vienna, 1987), 304–468.

Berend, T. Iván and György Ránki, *Hungary: A Century of Economic Development* (New York, 1974)

Csáky, Moritz, *Der Kulturkampf in Ungarn. Die kirchenpolitische Gesetzgebung der Jahre 1894/95* (Graz, 1967)

Fischer, Rolf, *Entwicklungsstufen des Antisemitismus in Ungarn 1867–1939* (München, 1988)

Frank, Tibor, *The British Image of Hungary 1865–1870* (Budapest, 1976)

Frigyesi, Judit, *Béla Bartók and turn-of-the-century Budapest* (Berkeley, 1998)

Gerő, András, *Modern Hungarian Society in the Making. The Unfinished Experience* (Budapest, London and New York, 1993)

——, *The Hungarian Parliament (1867–1918). A Mirage of Power* (Boulder, 1997)

——, *Emperor Francis Joseph, King of the Hungarians* (New York, 2001)

——, Katalin Jalsovszky and Emőke Tomsics, *Once Upon a Time in Hungary* (Budapest, 1996)

Gluck, Mary, *Georg Lukacs and His Generation, 1910–1918* (Cambridge, Mass., 1985)

Glatz, Ferenc (ed.), *Hungarians and their Neighbours in Modern Times, 1867–1950* (Boulder, 1995)

Hanák, Péter, *Ungarn in der Donaumonarchie* (Vienna and Budapest, 1984)

——, *The Garden and the Workshop. Essays on the Cultural History of Vienna and Budapest* (Princeton, 1998)

—— (ed.), *Die nationale Frage in der Österreich-Ungarischen Monarchie, 1900–1918* (Budapest, 1966)

Hoensch, Jörg K., *Geschichte Ungarns 1867–1983* (Stuttgart, Berlin, Cologne and Mainz, 1984), published in English as *A History of Modern Hungary 1867–1986* (London and New York, 1988)

Jalsovszky, Katalin and Emőke Tomsics, *Kaiserliches Wien, königliches Budapest. Photographien um die Jahrhundertwende* (Budapest and Vienna, 1996)

Janos, Andrew C., *The Politics of Backwardness in Hungary, 1825–1945* (Princeton, 1982)

Jászi, Oszkár, *The Dissolution of the Habsburg Monarchy* (Chicago, 1929)

Király, Béla K., *Ferenc Deák* (Boston, 1976)

Lukacs, John, *Budapest 1900. A Historical Portrait of a City* (New York, 1988)

Macartney, Carlile A., *The Habsburg Empire, 1790–1918* (London, 1968)

Mazsu, János, *The Social History of the Hungarian Intelligentsia in the 'Long Nineteenth Century', 1825–1914* (Boulder, 1996)

McCagg, William O., *Jewish Nobles and Geniuses in Modern Hungary* (Boulder, 1972)

Péter, László, 'Die Verfassungsentwicklung in Ungarn', in Helmut Rumpler and Peter Urbanitsch (eds), *Die Habsburgermonarchie 1848–1918*, vol. VII, 1 (Vienna, 2000), 239–540

Puskás, Julianna, *From Hungary to the United States (1880–1914)* (Budapest, 1982)

Szabad, György, *Hungarian Political Trends Between the Revolution and the Compromise (1849-1867)* (London, 1975)

Vermes, Gábor, *István Tisza. The Liberal Vision and Conservative Statecraft of a Magyar Nationalist* (New York, 1985)

Walter, Friedrich, *Die Nationalitätenfrage im alten Ungarn* (Munich, 1959)

The interwar era and World War II

Baross, Gábor, *Hungary and Hitler* (Astor, Fla., 1970)

Berend, T. Iván, *Decades of crisis: Central and Eastern Europe before World War II* (Berkeley, 1998)

Borbándi, Gyula, *Der ungarische Populismus* (Mainz, 1976)

Borsányi, György, *The Life of a Communist Revolutionary, Béla Kun* (Boulder, 1993)

Braham, Randolph L., *The Politics of Genocide: The Holocaust in Hungary*, 2 vols (New York, 1981, revised edn, 1994)

Deák, Francis, *Hungary at the Paris Peace Conference: The Diplomatic History of the Treaty of Trianon* (New York, 1942)

Dreisziger, Nándor, *Hungary's Way to World War II* (Astor Park, Fla., 1968)

—— (ed.), *Hungary in the Age of Total War (1938–1948)* (New York, 1998)

Eby, Cecil B., *Hungary at War. Civilians and Soldiers in World War II* (University Park, PA, 1998)

Fenyő, Marion D., *Hitler, Horthy and Hungary. German-Hungarian Relations 1941–1944* (New Haven, Conn., 1972)

Hoensch, Jörg K., *Die ungarische Revisionismus und die Zerschlagung der Tschechoslowakei* (Tübingen, 1967)

Katzburg, Nathaniel, *Hungary and the Jews. Policy and Legislation 1920–1943* (Jerusalem, 1981)

Kertész, Stephen D., *Diplomacy in a Whirlpool: Hungary between Nazi Germany and Soviet Russia* (Notre Dame, 1953)

Kovács, Mária, *Liberal Professions – Illiberal Politics* (Washington DC and New York, 1994)

Lackó, Miklós, *Arrow-Cross Men, National Socialists, 1934–1944* (Budapest, 1969)

Macartney, Carlile A., *October Fifteenth. A History of Modern Hungary 1929–1945*, 2 vols (Edinburgh, 1956)

Mócsy, István, *The Effects of World War I. The Uprooted: Hungarian Refugees and Their Impact on Hungary's Domestic Politics* (Boulder, 1983)

Nagy, Zsuzsa L., *The Liberal Opposition in Hungary 1919–1945* (Budapest, 1983)

Ormos, Mária, *From Padua to the Trianon, 1918–1920* (Budapest-Boulder, 1990)

Péteri, György, *The Effects of World War I. Communism in Hungary, 1919* (Boulder, 1984)
Ránki, György, *Economy and Foreign Policy. The Struggle of the Great Powers for
     Hegemony in the Danube Valley 1919–1939* (Budapest, 1982)
Romsics, Ignác, *István Bethlen: A Great Conservative Statesman of Hungary, 1874–1946*
     (Boulder, 1995)
Sakmyster, Thomas, *Hungary, the Great Powers and the Danubian Crisis, 1936–1939*
     (Athens, Ga., 1981)
——, *Hungary's Admiral on Horseback. Miklós Horthy, 1918–1944* (New York, 1994)
Tőkés, Rudolf L., *Béla Kun and the Hungarian Soviet Republic. The Origins and Role of
     the Communist Party of Hungary in the Revolutions of 1918–1919* (Stanford, 1967)

Hungary under socialism

Aczél, Tamás and Tibor Méray, *The Revolt of the Mind. A Case History of Intellectual
     Resistance behind the Iron Curtain* (New York, 1960)
Berend, T. Iván, *The Hungarian Economic Reform, 1953-1988* (Cambridge, 1990)
——, *Central and Eastern Europe 1944–1993: detour from the periphery to the
     periphery* (Cambridge, 1996)
Felkay, Andrew, *Hungary and the USSR, 1956–1988* (New York, 1989)
Gati, Charles, *Hungary and the Soviet Bloc* (Durham, 1986)
Gerő, András and Iván Pető (eds), *Unfinished Socialism. Pictures from the Kádár Era*
     (Budapest, 1999)
Grothusen, Klaus-Detlev (ed.), *Ungarn. Südosteuropa-Handbuch*, vol. 5 (Göttingen,
     1987)
Hainbuch, Friedrich, *Kirche und Staat in Ungarn nach dem Zweiten Weltkrieg* (Munich,
     1982)
Hefty, Georg P., *Schwerpunkte der Aussenpolitik Ungarns 1945–1973* (München, 1980)
Kertész, Stephen D., *Between Russia and the West: Hungary and the Illusion of
     Peacemaking, 1945–1947* (Notre Dame and London, 1984)
Király, Béla K., Barbara Lotze and Nándor Dreisziger (eds), *The First War between Socialist
     States: The Hungarian Revolution of 1956* (Boulder, 1984)
Kis, János, *Politics in Hungary: For a Democratic Alternative* (Boulder, 1990)
Kovrig, Bennett, *Communism in Hungary. From Kun to Kádár* (Stanford, 1979)
Litván, György (ed.), *The Hungarian Revolution of 1956. Reform, Revolt and Repression
     1953–1963* (London and New York, 1996)
Lomax, Bill, *Hungary 1956* (London, 1976)
Marer, Paul, *East–West Technology Transfer: A Study of Hungary 1968–1984* (Paris, 1986)
Molnár, Miklós, *Victoire d'une défaite* (Paris, 1968), published in English as *Budapest
     1956. A History of the Hungarian Revolution* (London, 1971)
Péteri, György, *Academia and State Socialism: Essays on the Political History of
     Academic Life in Post-1945 Hungary and East Central Europe* (Boulder, 1997)
Swain, Nigel, *Hungary. The Rise and Fall of Feasible Socialism* (London and New York,
     1992)
Szelényi, Iván et al., *Socialist Entrepreneurs. Embourgeoisement in Hungary* (Madison,
     1988)
Toma, Peter A. and Ivan Volgyes, *Politics in Hungary* (San Francisco, 1977)
Vago, Raphael, *The Grandchildren of Trianon. Hungary and the Hungarian Minority in
     the Communist States* (New York, 1989)

Contemporary Hungary and the transition to democracy

Bodnár, Judit, *Fin de Millénaire Budapest: Metamorphoses of Urban Life* (Minneapolis
     and London, 2001)
Bozóki, András, András Körösényi and George Schöpflin (eds), *Post-Communist*

Transition. Emerging Pluralism in Hungary (London and New York, 1992)
Felkay, Andrew, *Out of the Russian Orbit: Hungary Gravitates to the West* (Westport and London, 1997)
Garton Ash, Timothy, *The Magic Lantern: The Revolution of '89 Witnessed in Warsaw, Budapest, Berlin and Prague* (New York, 1990)
Gombár, Csaba *et al.* (eds), *Balance: The Hungarian Govenment, 1990–1994* (Budapest, 1994)
Horváth, Ágnes and Árpád Szakolczai, *The dissolution of communist power. The case of Hungary* (London and New York, 1992)
Király, Béla and András Bozóki (eds), *Lawful Revolution in Hungary 1989–1994* (Boulder, 1995)
Körösényi, András, *Government and Politics in Hungary* (Budapest, 1999)
Róna-Tas, Ákos, *The great surprise of the small transformation: the demise of Communism and the rise of the private sector in Hungary* (New York, 1997)
Tőkés, Rudolf L., *Hungary's negotiated revolution. Economic reform, social change, and political succession, 1957–1990* (Cambridge, 1996)

INDEX

Throughout the book, localities that once belonged to Hungary are referred to by their Hungarian names (the alternatives being mentioned when they first occur in the text). In the Index, such localities can also be identified by their foreign names. Information on persons is rudimentary.